How do you engage students in academic reading?

- ✔ By organizing chapters around discipline themes rather than skills.
- ✔ By providing an abundance of readings from a variety of everyday sources.
- ✔ By giving students extensive vocabulary development and support.
- ✔ By providing access to Pearson's MyReadingLab for additional instruction, practice, and reading opportunities.

Students who are engaged in their learning are more likely to succeed in their academic endeavors, and beyond. With this in mind, David Rothman and Jilani Warsi, the authors of *Read to Succeed*, arranged the chapters around ten academic disciplines (more specifically a particular issue within the discipline), enabling students to build background knowledge of the major academic disciplines–particularly important for non-native speakers–while honing their reading skills. To further increase student engagement, the authors provide an unmatched variety of readings from sources ranging from textbooks to short stories to periodicals to blogs. Add extensive coverage of vocabulary to the academic themes and variety of genres, and you have a text that best meets the needs of future academic readers.

How do you engage students in academic reading?

By organizing chapters around discipline themes rather than skills.

"I like the way that the chapters center on a particular academic content. This helps the students with their comprehending. Practice reading selections from different academic areas may aid with the transference of skills to other subject areas."

ESSIE CHILDERS, BLINN COLLEGE, BRYAN CAMPUS

By organizing *Read to Succeed* by academic disciplines – specifically, a particular issue related to the discipline – rather than the discrete reading skills, David Rothman and Jilani Warsi establish an inviting setting for reading skill development and disciplinary introductions.

- Not only is each chapter centered on an academic discipline, but the authors focus on a certain issue within the discipline to foster student interest.
- Each chapter begins with an "Introduction to the Discipline" and "Discipline-Terminology Bank" to build students' background knowledge.
- The "Skills Focus" section of each chapter provides in-depth instruction for a particular reading skill, which is reinforced in the context of authentic reading practice within each discipline.
- Students are connected to career applications within each field, via the "Biographical Profile" and "Interview with a Professional" features.

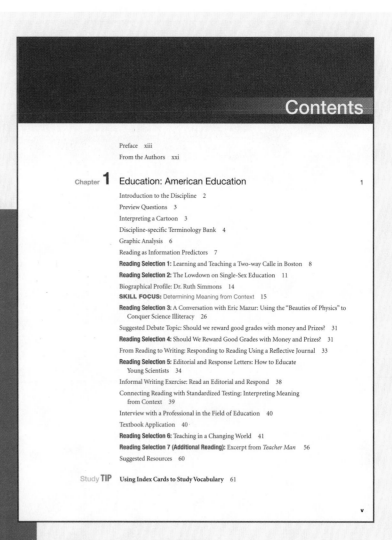

Contents

How do you engage students in academic reading?

By providing an abundance of readings from a variety of everyday sources.

"With 10 chapters, each containing a wealth of debates, interviews, skills development and practice, and supplementary materials, instructors have a treasure chest to choose from."

SHARYN NEUWIRTH, MONTGOMERY COLLEGE

198 | Chapter 4 E-Commerce

READING

Reading Selection 1

Newspaper Article

4.2 Flesch-Kincaid Grade Level 9.9

Collaboration

www.FriesWithThat?.com

Pre-Reading Questions

Before you read the following reading selection, get into small groups of three or four and discuss these questions.

1. Have you ever ordered your lunch or dinner online? If not, explain why. If you have, share what prompted you to place your food order online instead of ordering your food by phone and driving to a restaurant to pick it up.

2. Do you think more and more people will eventually be ordering food on-line? Discuss the factors that will change the ways in which people purchase commercial food.

3. In your opinion, as online food businesses gain popularity, what role should government regulatory agencies play to ensure that the food items sold on-line are safe for consumption?

Read the following article and answer the multiple-choice questions that follow it. Try to be an "information predictor" for the first part of the reading.

www.FriesWithThat?.com

By Stephanie Rosenbloom, the New York Times

August 5, 2007

ESL Annotation

4.3 ESL In many countries ordering food on-line is not a reality, so the topic may not be considered worthy of discussion.

Curb service: Kwany Spinks checks out the order he placed with Outback Steakhouse on West 23rd Street in Manhattan.

Stephanie Rosenbloom, "www.FriesWithThat?.com." From *The New York Times*, August 5, 2007. © 2007 The New York Times. All rights reserved. Used by permission and protected by the Copyright Laws of the United States. The printing, copying, redistribution, or retransmission of the Material without express written permission is prohibited. www.nytimes.com

David Rothman and Jilani Warsi feel that there is no substitute for high-interest, cohesive content that engages students and taps into their natural curiosity. Native and non-native English speakers will benefit from this large quantity of readings in order to improve their reading skills, background knowledge, and to gain more exposure to the English language.

- The authors provide a variety of genres to prepare students for future academic success, including textbooks, newspaper articles, short stories, interviews, biographies, magazine articles, and blogs.

- A Textbook Application reading in every chapter features an authentic, full-length textbook chapter for students to apply their skills and learn more about the specific discipline.

- Each chapter contains between six and eight readings so that students gain multiple perspectives of ideas within the disciplines.

How do you engage students in academic reading?

By giving students extensive vocabulary development and support.

"The emphasis on vocabulary development is pedagogically sound as most of the students do not have a firm grasp of academic vocabulary, which greatly affects their reading comprehension."

ZHEN HUANG, SUFFOLK COUNTY COMMUNITY COLLEGE

Vocabulary-building plays a large role in *Read to Succeed*; whether students are native, near-native, or non-native English speakers, vocabulary is the common denominator to reading success and enjoyment. Vocabulary coverage and exercises help students master readings that they encounter in college and beyond.

- Each chapter contains a Discipline-Specific Terminology Bank, which provides students with words that they will encounter in their readings within the chapter and help build reading fluency across academic disciplines.

- Academic Word Lists, presented in each chapter in the context of each reading selection, as well as in an Appendix, present high-frequency words found in college textbooks.

- Challenging words and idioms are defined in the margins of the reading selections to allow students to tackle challenging readings with minimal interruption.

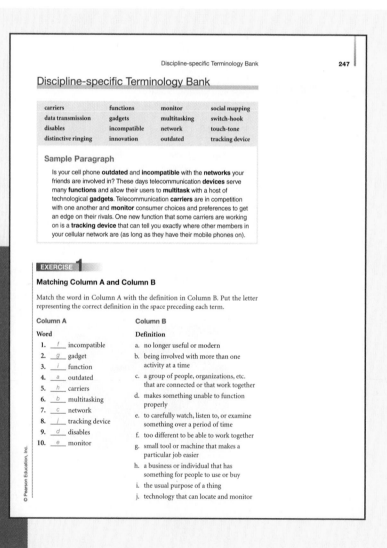

How do you engage students in academic reading?

By providing access to Pearson's MyReadingLab for additional instruction, practice, and reading opportunities.

. . . because there is practice and then there is BETTER practice.

Powered by two reading practice engines, MyReadingLab provides diagnostics, practice, tests, and reporting on reading skills and on student reading levels with the Lexile Framework for Reading developed by MetaMetrics™, an educational measurement expert.

What are the components of MyReadingLab?

- **Reading skill practice and assessment.** MyReadingLab includes a comprehensive skills tutorial with exercises, a new mastery-based format, open-ended questions, and the instructor's ability to reorganize the arrangement of topics.

- **Reading level practice and assessment.** A Lexile system (modified Cloze-tests and scoring algorithms) developed by MetaMetrics permits instructors to assess students' reading levels, and offers quantifiable data to measure reading level advancement.

- **Personalized Student study plans.** Based on results of the diagnostic pre-test and organization of topics established by the instructor, a study plan guides students to better reading.

- **Comprehensive Assessment.** Gradebook reports are available for students and instructors. Students can monitor their progress via their personal gradebook; instructors monitor progress at the individual level or class level.

- **E-book.** With select Pearson titles, students and instructors have access to an electronic version of their textbook. This allows students to refer back to their textbook as they go through MyReadingLab.

Read on or visit **www.myreadinglab.com/success.html** to see how MyReadingLab has been successful in improving results at hundreds of institutions.

myreadinglab™
Where better reading is   within reach!

SUCCESS STORIES
Student Survey Results

Recently, Pearson Education surveyed over 400 students who use MyReadingLab to improve their Reading skills. The results were overwhelmingly positive for MyReadingLab.

The overall student-user satisfaction of MyReadingLab was 90%

When asked if they agreed with the following statements, here is how students responded:

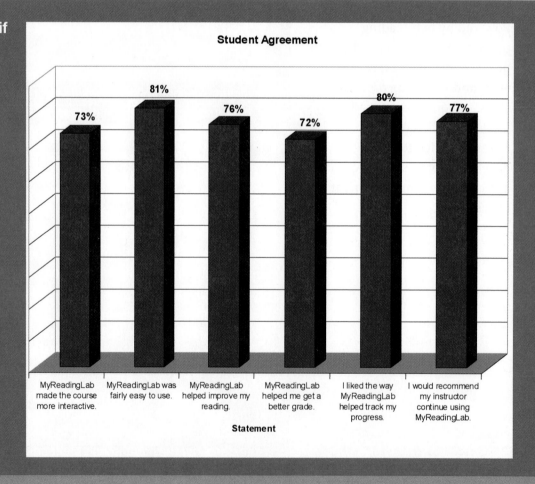

Student Agreement

- 73% — MyReadingLab made the course more interactive.
- 81% — MyReadingLab was fairly easy to use.
- 76% — MyReadingLab helped improve my reading.
- 72% — MyReadingLab helped me get a better grade.
- 80% — I liked the way MyReadingLab helped track my progress.
- 77% — I would recommend my instructor continue using MyReadingLab.

Statement

See more successes at www.myreadinglab.com/success.html

LONGMAN / PRENTICE HALL

myreadinglab
Where better reading is within reach!

Specifically created for developmental reading students, MyReadingLab is the first online application that combines diagnostics, personalized practice and tests, and powerful assessment tools to help improve student reading skills and reading level.

ASSESSMENT

MyReadingLab offers multiple opportunities for instructors to assess their students mastery of key reading skills.

PERSONALIZED STUDY PLAN

Each student's study plan is generated by the results of their diagnostic pre-tests and the topic organization established by the instructor. The study plan is organized by key reading skills and appears in an easy-to-reference "To Do" list that helps students stay on track while working in MyReadingLab.

PRACTICE

The extensive and effective practice opportunities in MyReadingLab come in two basic types:

- practice with the discrete skills to improve students' reading skills.

- practice combining multiple skills in a single reading passage to improve students' reading level.

IMPROVING READING SKILLS

Students practice reading skills through a mastery-based format in which they get an overview of the skill, see models of the skill at work, go through an abundance of practice exercises to apply what they've learned, then take a mastery test. Exercises include objective questions, open-ended questions, short answer questions, and combined skills exercises.

IMPROVING READING LEVEL

MyReadingLab assesses reading level using the Lexile Framework which measures both reader ability and text difficulty on the same scale. First, a student completes a carefully developed diagnostic and then the system assesses it to assign an initial Lexile level or number. Next, the student works through MyReadingLab and completes two types of exercises: combined skills and "cloze" with a goal is for a student to increase his or her Lexile reading level and overall reading skills..

ADVANCE PRAISE FOR

Read to Succeed: A Thematic Approach to Academic Reading

"This book does in one volume what now takes me three separate texts to accomplish in my course. [*Read to Succeed*] combines all three approaches (vocabulary development, skills development, and application practice) in a thematically united volume. Bravo!"

MARIE ECKSTROM, RIO HONDO COLLEGE

"[*Read to Succeed*] gives a clear, systematic presentation of skills, yet does not sacrifice interest level."

ELIZABETH EARLE, VALENCIA COMMUNITY COLLEGE

"I like the variety of the text. I think that using the text would help students come away with a tremendous amount of background knowledge that will help them in all of their courses."

LOIS HASSAN, HENRY FORD COMMUNITY COLLEGE

"It is a refreshing and logical change from the skill (and drill) approach presented in most other developmental reading textbooks."

ALISON KUEHNER, OHLONE COLLEGE

"I feel that [MyReadingLab] greatly reinforces every skill we focus on. That is exactly what my students needed."

TRUDY KEMP, BROOKDALE COMMUNITY COLLEGE

"This text truly integrates reading, listening, speaking, and to some extent, writing. Every example and exercise is either drawn from, or relates to, the topic of the chapter."

SHARYN NEUWIRTH, MONTGOMERY COLLEGE

"*Read to Succeed* gives students an opportunity to engage in readings that are fresh and of high interest."

ESSIE CHILDERS, BLINN COLLEGE – BRYAN CAMPUS

"I use [MyReadingLab] for my College Reading Internet course and have had good retention so far and improvement in reading skills."

RICH EDWARDS, KIRKWOOD COMMUNITY COLLEGE

Read *to* Succeed

A THEMATIC APPROACH TO ACADEMIC READING

David Rothman
Queensborough Community College

Jilani Warsi
Queensborough Community College

Longman

Boston Columbus Indianapolis New York San Francisco Upper Saddle River
Amsterdam Cape Town Dubai London Madrid Milan Munich Paris Montreal Toronto
Delhi Mexico City São Paulo Sydney Hong Kong Seoul Singapore Taipei Tokyo

Acquisitions Editor: Kate Edwards
Development Editor: Melanie Craig
Senior Supplements Editor: Donna Campion
Senior Media Producer: Stefanie Liebman
Marketing Manager: Thomas DeMarco
Production Manager: Bob Ginsberg
Project Coordination, Text Design, and Electronic Page Makeup: Pre-Press PMG
Senior Cover Design Manager/Cover Designer: Nancy Danahy
Cover Image: © NatUlrich/Shutterstock Images
Photo Researcher: Jody Potter
Senior Manufacturing Buyer: Dennis J. Para
Printer and Binder: Courier Corporation/Kendallville
Cover Printer: Lehigh Phoenix

Copyright © 2010 by Pearson Education, Inc.

All rights reserved. No part of this publication may be reproduced, stored in a retrieval system, or transmitted, in any form or by any means, electronic, mechanical, photocopying, recording, or otherwise, without the prior written permission of the publisher. Printed in the United States.

For permission to use copyrighted material, grateful acknowledgment is made to the copyright holders on pp. 606-608, which are hereby made part of this copyright page.

Photo Credits p. 1, p. 2: Ariel Skelley/Corbis p. 3: Randy Glasbergen p. 11: Masterfile p. 14: Courtesy of Brown University p. 27: Jodi Hilton/The New York Times/Redux Pictures p. 35: Thinkstock/Corbis p. 40: Courtesy Richard Vacca p. 42: Elizabeth Crews/The Image Works p. 47: Laura Dwight Photography p. 48: Jim Cummins/Corbis p. 49: James Leynse/Corbis p. 50: Bill Aron/PhotoEdit Inc. p. 63, p. 64: Jean Michel Foujols/Corbis p. 65: © Fran/CartoonStock p. 83: Mario Ruiz/Time & Life Pictures/Getty Images p. 90: John Powell Photography/Alamy p. 95: Rick Gomez/Corbis p. 103: Courtesy of Janice Thompson p. 105: Lew Robertson/Corbis p. 106: Lester V. Bergman/Corbis p. 110: Tom Stewart/Corbis p. 115: Wendell Webber/Jupiter Images p. 126, top to bottom: iStockphoto; DLILLC/Corbis p. 127: iStockphoto p. 128: Toles © 2002 The Washington Post. Reprinted with permission of UNIVERSAL PRESS SYNDICATE. All right reserved. p. 133: Johnny Johnson/Getty Images p. 137: Sara Remington/The New York Times/Redux Pictures p. 141: Courtesy University of Michigan Photo Services p. 150: Courtesy Arlington County, VA p. 157: Ludovic Maisant/Corbis p. 167: Courtesy of Marcus Zobrist p. 171: Tom Walker/Stock Boston p. 172: William E. Ferguson p. 173: Will McIntyre/Photo Researchers p. 177 (2): National Snow and Ice Date Center/World Data Center for Glaciology p. 178: Katharine Cherwyk p. 192, p. 193: Veer p. 194: Matt Buck p. 198: Hiroko Masulka/The New York Times/Redux Pictures p. 208: Ben Margot/AP Images p. 218: © 2006, USA TODAY. Reprinted with permission. p. 236: Courtesy of Daniel Wagaman p. 237: Diego Azubel/epa/Corbis p. 244, p. 245: Boris Lyubner/Corbis p. 246: Mark Parisi p. 256, top to bottom: Herbert Knosowski/AP Images; Lucas Lenci Photo/Getty Images p. 264: Suzanne DeChillo/The New York Times/Redux Pictures p. 272: Courtesy of Joseph Dennis DeStefano p. 282: Jeffrey Barbee/The New York Times/Redux Pictures p. 292, p. 293: Brandon Laufenberg/iStockphoto p. 294: © David Conney/Cartoon Stock p. 300: Veer p. 303: James Estrin/The New York Times/Redux Pictures p. 312: Ted Soqui/Corbis p. 319: CNN/Getty Images p. 330: Courtesy of Dr. Lawrence Kobilinksy p. 334: AP Images p. 347, p. 348: Adam Smith/Getty Images p. 349: © Richard Sly/CartoonStock p. 355: ERproductions Ltd/Getty Images p. 363: Library of Congress p. 393: Jose Luis Pelaez/Getty Images p. 409: Courtesy of Gloria Tovar p. 415: Bettmann/Corbis p. 416, top to bottom: Bettmann/Corbis; University of Iowa, College of Nursing, Iowa City, IA p. 417, top to bottom: Courtesy Millbank Memorial Library, Teacher's College, Columbia University. Reprinted with Permission; Michael Newman/PhotoEdit Inc. p. 433, p. 434: Neil Leslie/Getty Images p. 435: © Nick Kim/CartoonStock p. 443: Robert Caplin/The New York Times/Redux Pictures p. 449: CBS/Landov p. 466: Courtesy of Dr. Charlene Bang p. 468, clockwise from top left: Myrleen Fergusson Cate/PhotoEdit Inc.; Tony Savino/The Image Works; Michael Schwarz/The Image Works; David Young-Wolff/PhotoEdit Inc. p. 469: National Gallery, London/Art Resource, NY p. 470: Jeff Greenberg/PhotoEdit Inc. p. 475: Quavondo Nguyen/iStock Photo p. 481, p. 482: Big Stock Photo p. 484: Randy Glasbergen p. 489: Joerg Koch/AFP/Getty Images p. 493: Coke Whitworth/Aurora p. 496: Robert Pitts/Landov p. 507: Courtesy of Anya Ponorovskya p. 516: Courtesy of Mary Anne Poatsy p. 517: Reuters/Corbis p. 519: © The New Yorker Collection 1990 Joseph Mirachi from cartoonbank.com. All Rights Reserved. p. 522, top to bottom: Ritz Sino/The New York Times/Redux Pictures; Namas Bhojani p. 536, p. 537: Ken Davies/Masterfile p. 538: © Marty Bucella/CartoonStock p. 558: White House Photo by Pete Souza p. 576: Courtesy of Brian Pu-Folkes p. 583: Library of Congress

1 2 3 4 5 6 7 8 9 10—CRK—12 11 10 09

Longman
is an imprint of

www.pearsonhighered.com

Student Edition ISBN-13: 978-0-205-57805-4
Student Edition ISBN-10: 0-205-57805-5
Annotated Instructor's Edition ISBN-13: 978-0-205-73119-0
Annotated Instructor's Edition ISBN-10: 0-205-73119-8

Contents

Chapter **4** E-Commerce: Internet Marketing   192

Chapter **5**   ## Telecommunications: The Cell Phone Revolution   244

Chapter **6**   ## Criminal Justice: Criminal Investigation   292

Chapter **7**   Life Science: Nursing   347

Chapter **8**   Psychology: Human Nature   432

Appendixes

Preface: The Goals and Philosophy of *Read to Succeed*

Read to Succeed engages students in academic reading through its thematic organization around academic disciplines, an abundance of readings drawn from a variety of sources, and a sustained focus on vocabulary building.

David Rothman and Jilani Warsi's goals with *Read to Succeed* are to spur developmental readers to become active readers and engage them in academic reading by fostering intellectual inquiry through an exploration of contemporary themes related to popular academic disciplines. When a subject matter piques the student's interest—when the readings are provocative and engaging, when the vocabulary is made accessible through a focus on discipline-specific terminology, and when students have the opportunity to become active readers through expressing their opinions on controversial topics within a discipline—then the sparks will fly.

It is the philosophy of the authors that students more successfully master key reading skills when taught in the context of engaging readings. With this in mind, *Read to Succeed* is organized around ten academic disciplines, enabling students to build background knowledge of the major academic disciplines, while honing their reading skills. To further increase student engagement, the authors provide an unmatched variety of readings from sources ranging from textbooks to short stories to blogs. With an extensive coverage of vocabulary to the academic themes and variety of genres, *Read to Succeed* meets the needs of future academic readers.

Content Overview

Read to Succeed is organized into ten chapters, each focusing on a different academic discipline. A critical reading skill focus is integrated into each chapter, so that students can master reading skills in the context of engaging readings.

	Academic Discipline	Reading Skill in Focus
Chapter 1	EDUCATION	VOCABULARY IN CONTEXT
Chapter 2	NUTRITION	MAIN IDEA AND TOPIC
Chapter 3	ENVIRONMENTAL SCIENCE	SUPPORTING DETAILS
Chapter 4	INTERNET MARKETING	INFERENCES
Chapter 5	TELECOMMUNICATIONS	AUTHOR'S PURPOSE AND TONE
Chapter 6	CRIMINAL JUSTICE	FACT AND OPINION
Chapter 7	NURSING	PATTERNS OF ORGANIZATION
Chapter 8	PSYCHOLOGY	ARGUMENTS
Chapter 9	BUSINESS	AUTHOR'S BIAS
Chapter 10	POLITICAL SCIENCE	COMBINED SKILLS

Each chapter in *Read to Succeed* contains a "Skill Focus" section that highlights key reading skills, such as main idea, patterns of organization, or argument. The authors provide instruction, practice, and application opportunities to ensure that students have mastered each reading skill before moving on.

Throughout each chapter, the principle features are supported in a variety of ways. The culmination of the variety of features offered in *Read to Succeed* equips students for the reading and thinking expectations within and beyond their reading courses.

Special Features of *Read to Succeed*

Each chapter within *Read to Succeed* contains a variety of apparatus designed to engage students and support the principle features: themes of academic disciplines, a variety of genres, extensive vocabulary support—in addition to overall reading improvement.

How *Read to Succeed* augments each chapter's academic theme

- **Biographical Profiles** highlight well-known figures in each academic area. For example, Oprah Winfrey is featured in Chapter 9 on Business. Students will have the opportunity to learn about a famous figure, and complete Internet research on another prominent person in the field.

BIOGRAPHICAL PROFILE

Oprah Winfrey

Oprah Gail Winfrey, more popularly known as Oprah, is a famous American television host, business tycoon and philanthropist. She has received many honorary awards for her much-acclaimed internationally syndicated talk show, *The Oprah Winfrey Show*. In addition to being a popular talk show host, Winfrey is also a book critic, an Academy Award–nominated actress, and a magazine publisher. She has been ranked the richest African American of the twenty-first century, the only black billionaire for three consecutive years, and the most philanthropic African American who ever lived. Some people believe that she is the most influential woman in the world.

Winfrey was born on January 29, 1954, in rural Mississippi. A child born out of wedlock and raised in a Milwaukee neighborhood, she was raped at the age of 9 and gave birth to a son at the age of 14. The son died in his infancy, and she went to live with her father in Tennessee. It was there that she landed a job in radio at the age of 19. She never looked back since then, and after working as a talk show host in Chicago for a while, she finally founded her own production company and became syndicated globally.

Winfrey's meteoric rise to stardom did not happen overnight. She moved to Chicago in 1983 to host a morning talk-show *AM Chicago*. After she took over the talk show, it went from last place to the highest-rated talk show in Chicago. Such was her popularity as the talk show host that the show was renamed *The Oprah Winfrey Show*. On her twentieth anniversary show, Winfrey told her audience that the famous movie critic Roger Ebert had encouraged her to sign a contract with King World. Ebert had rightly predicted that Winfrey's show would generate 40 times as much revenue as his show. According to *Time* magazine, "Few people would have bet on Oprah Winfrey's swift rise to host of the most popular talk show on TV. In a field dominated by white males, she is a black female of ample bulk. As interviewers go, she is no match for, say, Phil Donahue. . . . What she lacks in journalistic toughness, she makes up for in plainspoken curiosity, robust humor and above all, empathy. Guests with sad stories to tell are apt to rouse a tear in Oprah's eye. . . . They, in turn, often find themselves revealing things they would not imagine telling anyone, much less a national TV audience. It is the talk show as a group therapy session."

Oprah's Angel Network, founded in 1998, encourages people around the world to help the poor. The Network provides grants to nonprofit organizations and undertakes projects all over the world to alleviate poverty and improve the lives of the underprivileged. Her network has raised $51 million for the cause so far. She personally covers all costs associated with the charitable projects. She has been listed by *Business Week* as one of America's 50 most generous philanthropists. Throughout her illustrious career, she has donated an estimated $303 million. She donated $10 million to support the Hurricane Katrina victims in New Orleans. Winfrey has helped 250 African American men get a college education. She received the first Bob Hope Humanitarian Award at the 2002 Emmy Awards for her services to television and film.

Some Questions for Group Discussion

1. Oprah Winfrey had an extremely difficult childhood and grew up in abject poverty. Still she persevered in her professional goals and became a talk show host at the age of 19. Discuss what inspired her to become a businesswoman and philanthropist.
2. As an African American woman, Winfrey had to work hard to climb up the ladder of success. Nevertheless, she overcame all the barriers with diligence and persistence and became extremely rich. Discuss the reasons for her phenomenal success.
3. There are more than 200 billionaires in the United States of America. Yet, not all of them are philanthropists. Winfrey is one of few billionaires who donate generously. Discuss why most of the billionaires keep their enormous wealth to themselves and do not share it with the poor and hungry.

Biographical Internet Research

Do research on the Internet and select a successful entrepreneur from the list below of individuals who have amassed wealth and have donated substantial amounts of money to a noble cause. Be prepared to share their biographical profiles with your classmates.

- Bill Gates
- Chris Gardner
- John D. Rockefeller
- George Soros
- Warren Buffet

- **Interview with a Professional** allows students to hear from professionals who majored in various academic fields and who are now successful in their careers. Content-based reading is critical to gaining a deeper knowledge of the issues related to academic major areas. Students will read interviews from such professionals and learn about how they managed their successful journey from college to the working world.

Dr. Charlene Bang

Interview with a Professional in the Field of Psychology

Profession: Psychologist, James J. Peters VA Medical Center (Bronx, New York)

How did you choose your current profession?

I emigrated from Seoul, Korea, to the United States when I was 9 years old. I only knew a few words of English, "Hi," "Hello," and "Thank you." I was placed in the fourth grade in an all-white school in a small town in Pennsylvania. It was a tremendous struggle for me to adjust to this new and foreign environment due to both cultural differences and limited English proficiency. It took me at least six months for me to feel somewhat comfortable to socialize with my classmates and neighborhood kids with whom I began to play after school. In retrospect, I did the best I could to adjust and respond to the immigration and the new environment. Even at a young age, I was curious about how others responded to various new situations as I witnessed my older siblings' different and somewhat rebellious responses to the immigration. In high school, I had an opportunity to take a psychology course, during which I began to learn about human and animal responses to various environment and situations. I knew then I wanted to continue to pursue psychology to satisfy my forever increasing curiosity of human behavior.

How did you prepare to reach your goal of becoming a psychologist?

In addition to majoring in psychology and taking all required courses, I needed to overcome my fears of speaking and writing English as I quickly learned there were many presentations and writing required as a psychology major. Initially, I had many doubts about my oral presentation and writing abilities. However, I took advantage of resources (e.g., tutors, writing workshops) that were available in college. As time passed with perseverance, hard work, and improved self-confidence, I believed I would be able to overcome my fears of writing and presenting and also believed I would be able to accomplish my goal of becoming a psychologist.

What did you struggle with most when preparing to become a psychologist?

There were several challenges I needed to overcome, including low self-confidence, learning English, and completing and presenting an independent research. Completing my doctoral dissertation and oral presentation of the study were struggles. However, I knew in my mind that if I could have the strength to adjust to a new culture and learn a new language, that I could overcome challenges of completing my dissertation and oral presentation of the study.

How did you overcome/get through this struggle?

In addition to perseverance, hard work, and believing in myself, I had a great mentor who guided me each step of the way and who gave me confidence that my dissertation was possible. And of course, he encouraged me to present over and over again until I felt comfortable. I have to say having someone to guide me through the tough times was a tremendous help. In addition, I practiced, practiced, and practiced . . . oh and I practiced . . . presenting the research until I got tired of hearing my own voice.

What do you enjoy most about your work?

I currently work with veterans from various wars, many who are young, who fought and were wounded in Iraq and Afghanistan. I enjoy learning about each one of my patients' life stories as each person brings unique and special background, personality, strengths, and weaknesses. Many suffered physical and emotional traumas and teaching the veterans better coping skills and providing services that may help them to reintegrate into civilian life are extremely gratifying. Even if I can help just one veteran, I am grateful I had the opportunity to do so and all my hard work was all worthwhile.

What advice do you have for a student considering a career in psychology?

Learn to be curious about each person's life story as each person comes with different and interesting background. Learn to be nonjudgmental of each patient whom you meet and treat. Appreciate different cultural, religious, philosophical backgrounds with different beliefs and values. Think flexibly with an open mind as novel and creative approaches can serve as wonderful treatments. Have passion for the field of psychology and passion for working with special and unique individuals, as an opportunity to help each individual is a privilege every time.

In your opinion what were the three most interesting points made by the interviewee? Discuss your choices with the class.

_____

_____

_____

_____

_____

- **Debate Topics** provide instructors an option of organizing lively class debates around provocative debate questions and readings within *Read to Succeed* to stimulate student interest in each academic subject area. From our teaching experience, we know that students enjoy exploring controversial topics, and class debates are the perfect forum for the free expression of diverse options.

Recommended debate topic: Should juvenile offenders receive the same prison sentences as adults?

    Brainstorm other debate topics related to Criminal Justice with your peers, and present your ideas to your instructor for approval. See the next reading to help you find and develop topics.

Your suggested debate topics:

   a. _____

   b. _____

   c. _____

    The following reading will help prepare you for the debate activity by providing background information on the topic of Juvenile Crime.

DEBATABLE TOPIC

- **Textbook Applications** are available in every chapter and contain an extended authentic textbook reading from an introductory text. The textbook content reflects the academic discipline focus of the chapter. Students can learn how to navigate a textbook chapter and are given ample practice to check their comprehension and reading skills with questions following each textbook chapter.

How *Read to Succeed* engages students with a variety of genres

- **A multitude of readings** — with a minimum of seven (7) per chapter— provide opportunities for students to master key reading skills. These selections are from a variety of genres, including magazines, newspapers, textbooks, literature, and blogs.

- **Suggested Resources** are offered at the end of each chapter, with a list of books, movies and websites, to inspire further student exploration of each academic area.

How *Read to Succeed* develops students' vocabulary

- **Discipline-Specific Terminology** is introduced at the beginning of every chapter – in addition to vocabulary-building activities – so that students can become familiar with key terms in the chapter's discipline.

- **The Academic Word List** (AWL) contains high frequency academic terms with which most proficient readers are familiar with and can readily incorporate them in speech and writing without having to look them up in the dictionary. The AWL is offered as an Appendix so that students can study this list. Furthermore, *Read to Succeed* has highlighted the AWL terms in the reading selections in each chapter. Students can determine the highlighted word's meaning through context, or look it up in a dictionary. Students ultimate goal is not

Appendix 1

Most Frequent Words of the Academic Word List by Sublist

Sublist 1 of the Academic Word List—Most Frequent Words in Families

This sublist contains the most frequent words of the Academic Word List in the Academic Corpus.

analysis	major	consequences
approach	method	construction
area	occur	consumer
assessment	percent	credit
assume	period	cultural
authority	policy	design
available	principle	distinction
benefit	procedure	elements
concept	process	equation
consistent	required	evaluation
constitutional	research	features
context	response	final
contract	role	focus
create	section	impact
data	sector	injury
definition	significant	institute
derived	similar	investment
distribution	source	items
economic	specific	journal
environment	structure	maintenance
established	theory	normal
estimate	variables	obtained
evidence		participation
export		perceived
factors	**Sublist 2 of Academic Word List—Most Frequent Words in Families**	positive
financial		potential
formula		previous
function	This sublist contains the second most frequent words in the Academic Word List from the Academic Corpus.	primary
identified		purchase
income		range
indicate	achieve	region
individual	acquisition	regulations
	administration	relevant
	affect	resident
	appropriate	resources
	aspects	restricted
	assistance	security
	categories	sought
	chapter	select
		site

to just memorize the words and make themselves familiar with them, but to use the high-frequency words in speech and writing.

- **Marginal Definitions** define particularly challenging words or idioms in the reading selections, in order to allow students to tackle reading with minimal interruption.

How *Read to Succeed* helps students' overall academic improvement

- **Reading Skills in Focus**, available in every chapter, provides in-depth instruction for a particular reading skill. Students work with examples and exercises to master these skills, and then work to apply them in the context of authentic reading passages within each discipline focus.

SKILL FOCUS
Identifying the Main Idea and Topic

When you are asked to find the *main idea* of a sentence or a paragraph, you are really being asked to identify the most important point the author wants to convey to the reader.

Movie Analogy: Understanding the Concept of *Main Idea*

Imagine a friend calls you and says she is in a hurry on the way to the movies and would like you to recommend a film. You tell your friend the name of the film you think she should see and she asks you to tell her in a sentence (there is no time to lose!) what the film is about.

- **From Reading to Writing** underscores the connections between reading and writing. Students are prompted to transfer their academic reading skills to the task of academic and professional writing.

- **Connecting Reading Skills with Standardized Testing** helps prepare students to pass a standardized Reading exam. While all of the major reading skills will be given an in-depth focus in *Read to Succeed*, it is important to make the connection between these skills and how they translate as question forms on standardized tests.

Connecting Reading Skills with Standardized Testing

Recognizing the Author's Purpose and Tone

Questions focusing on author's purpose and tone typically concern the whole reading passage, not one particular section of the text. Remember that the two question types are interrelated, as an understanding of the purpose can clue you in to the tone and vice versa. If the author's purpose is to inform, then his or her tone will most likely be objective (or neutral, unbiased). If the author's purpose, however, is to persuade, then the tone might be convincing, pessimistic, or emotional. Finally, if the author's purpose is basically to entertain the reader, his or her tone will match the purpose and might be humorous, ironic, or lighthearted.

You are being asked the author's purpose if the questions are worded in any of the following ways:

- The reason the author wrote this passage is to . . .
- The primary purpose of this passage is . . .
- The author wrote this passage in order to . . .
- The main purpose of the above passage is . . .

The focus of a test question is author's tone if it is worded in one of these ways:

- The tone of this passage can be described as . . .
- What is the overall tone of the passage?
- What is the author's tone?
- The author's use of irony indicates . . .

- **Study Tips** are available after every chapter to help students improve their overall academic performance and become active learners. Topics include time management, skimming and scanning, and annotation and highlighting.

Using Index Cards to Study Vocabulary

Study**TIP**

Overview

As you know, one of the most challenging parts of succeeding in college is to learn new vocabulary and jargon typical of a subject. There are many techniques to build vocabulary, but here we offer you an effective technique that will help you improve your active vocabulary. For this activity, you will need index cards that are blank on one side and lined on the other.

ESL Annotation

1.18 ESL This exercise is of particular importance to ESL students who need to build a solid vocabulary to succeed in mainstream courses.

Activity

As you come across an unfamiliar word while doing a reading assignment, write it on the blank side of the index card. On the lined side, write information related to the new word as follows. Keep in mind that you will need a good dictionary to do this exercise.

1. Look up the word in a dictionary and write how it is pronounced. Most dictionaries phonetically transcribe words, so it should not be difficult for you to write the sounds.
2. Find out what part of speech the word is and write it below. For example, write if the word is a noun, a verb, or an adjective.
3. Write the meaning of the word.
4. Make an example sentence using the new word in context.
5. Using a dictionary, write the words that are derived from the same root. For example, the words *marine*, *maritime*, *marina*, *submarine*, and *mariner* are all derived from the same Latin root *mar* which means "sea." This way you will learn that some words are associated with each other.
6. Write at least two or three synonyms of the unfamiliar word here.
7. Finally, write at least two or three antonyms of the new word here.

Let's take a look at an index card so that you can fully understand how to **create** your own index cards for vocabulary building. We will use the word *create* for this index card exercise.

From the Authors

We wish to acknowledge the contributions of our reviewers, who provided valuable critiques and suggestions, thus making *Read to Succeed* a much stronger book:

Holly Schaefer Hearne
Wor-Wic Community College

Nancy Olsen
Sacramento City College

Essie Childers
Blinn College- Bryan Campus

Deborah Spradlin
Tyler Jr. College

Sharyn Neuwirth
Montgomery College

Eva A. O'Brian
Midlands Technical College

Lynn Campbell
Fresno City College

Marie G. Eckstrom
Rio Hondo College

Elizabeth Earle
Valencia Community College

James Gray
St. Petersburg College

Michael Vensel
Miami Dade College- Kendall Campus

Sandra Peck
El Paso Community College

Merlene Purkiss
Miami Dade College

Penny Speidel
John Tyler Community College

Ursula Sohns
North Harris College

Allison Kuehner
Ohlone College

Susie Khirallah-Johnston
Tyler Junior College

Jesus Adame
El Paso Community College

Inna Newbury
El Camino College

Leslie Rice
San Jose City College

Polly Green
Arkansas State University

Lois Hassan
Henry Ford Community College

Donna Willingham
Lone Star College-Tomball

Zhen Huang
Suffolk Community College

We also give thanks to the wonderful professionals who contributed their time and their personal stories to the "Interview with a Professional" feature:

Richard T. Vacca
Professor Emeritus, Kent State University

Janice Thompson
University of Bristol

Marcus Zobrist & Kathy Hurld
The U.S. Environmental Protection Agency's Office of Water

Daniel Wagaman
Audiofy Corporation

Joseph Dennis DeStefano
Presidio Networked Solutions

Lawrence Kobilinsky
John Jay College of Criminal Justice

Gloria Tovar
Elhurst Hospital Center

Charlene Bang
James J. Peters VA Medical Center

Mary Anne Poatsy
Professor in Business & Computer Science; Author

Bryan Pu-Folkes
Immigration Attorney/Community Activist

We are absolutely indebted to Kate Edwards, our acquisitions editor, for her professional expertise and valuable suggestions. We are also very grateful to Melanie Craig, our developmental editor. We would like to thank Tom DeMarco, our seasoned Marketing Manager, for all of his creative ideas and his dedication to *Read to Succeed* from inception to birth. We have to thank Lindsey Allen, our editorial assistant, for putting up with and fulfilling our many requests. We cannot forget Peter Kang for his hard work with the book's many marginal definitions. Finally, David Rothman would like to thank Zlati, his wife, for her insightful comments and her unflagging support of this project, and Jilani Warsi would like to express his gratitude to Saloni, his life partner, for her patience, understanding and encouragement.

Sincerely,
David Rothman & Jilani Warsi
Authors, *Read to Succeed*

EDUCATION
American Education

*"Educating the mind
without educating the heart
is no education at all."*
ARISTOTLE

Objectives

IN THIS CHAPTER YOU WILL LEARN . . .

- About some contemporary issues in American education
- How to analyze graphic aids
- How to determine meaning from context
- Hints to improve your vocabulary
- How to keep a reflection journal

© Pearson Education, Inc.

Making Predictions

Consider this chapter's theme, Education. What subtopics relate to this field? (See Fig. 1.1.)

■ **Figure 1.1**

Teaching Tip:
This feature gives students a chance to brainstorm and categorize.

ESL Annotation

1.1 ESL In some cultures (Latin cultures in particular) the word "education" connotes the concept of "upbringing". It may be helpful to clear up this distinction between "child rearing" and "school learning".

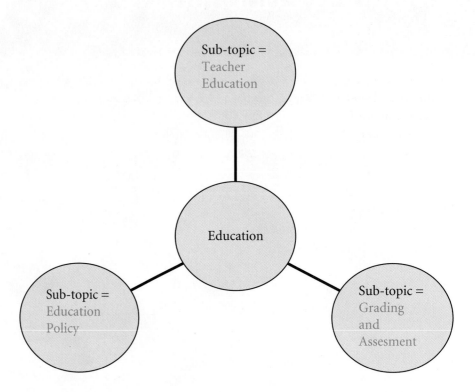

Introduction to the Discipline of Education

Teaching is one of the most challenging, demanding, and rewarding of professions. Teachers are not only expected to educate our children and provide them with an academically enriching environment; they also play a role in students' social development. Teachers have the huge task of preparing young minds for the world ahead of them. They model collaborative learning and critical thinking, and they introduce students to the technological tools that they will need to navigate the twenty-first-century classroom and beyond. The system of American education faces many challenges in the twenty-first century. In this chapter you will read about some of the issues that educators today must consider. Should new immigrant students be offered a bilingual curriculum? Are same-sex schools beneficial to public school students' academic achievement? What kinds of innovative teaching methods can help improve American students' low performance in the sciences and inspire more interest in scientific inquiry? Finally, how can we motivate underperforming students to work harder in their classes?

Preview Questions

The following questions are all related to the chapter focus area of Education. Share your views in small group discussion.

Collaboration

1. Do you believe that you received a quality education at your high school? Describe some of the positive aspects and shortcomings of your high school experience.

2. Many people argue that American public education is in crisis. If you agree, then who is to blame? In other words, who is most responsible for students' academic progress—students, teachers, parents, or the state educational system? Please give specific reasons for your answer.

3. When you hear that someone is "educated," what image comes to your mind about this person? In your opinion, what are some of the characteristics of an "educated" person?

4. In your many years of schooling, which of your teachers left the most lasting impression on you? What made this teacher so special?

5. Do you feel that you learn more when the teacher is lecturing to the class or when the teacher assigns small-group problem-solving tasks?

6. Are you in favor of bilingual education, or do you prefer an English-only classroom? Please explain your preference.

Teaching Tip:
Each chapters preview questions are designed to both give students an opportunity to share their background knowledge and to stir their curiosity on the chapter themes.

Interpreting a Cartoon

■ **Figure 1.2**

"There aren't any icons to click. It's a chalk board."

Copyright 1997 by Randy Glasbergen.

© Pearson Education, Inc.

Collaboration

Discuss the cartoon shown on p. 3 in small groups and answer the following questions.

1. What educational issue does this cartoon address?
2. In your opinion, what message is the cartoonist trying to convey to the reader?

ESL Annotation

1.2 ESL Students find these kinds of thematically focused vocabulary lists particularly useful.

Discipline-specific Terminology Bank

approach	context	enrollment	innovative
coeducational	curricula	facilitate	mentoring
concept	desegregation	feedback	reflecting
consensus	drilling	gender	strive
content	engage	incentive	uniformity

Sample Paragraph

There are many **innovative** pedagogical **approaches** being tested in classrooms across the country with the goal of **engaging** students more in their own learning. **Curricula** are being designed around the **concept** that today's educators need to provide various forms of **feedback** to **facilitate content**-based learning. Another approach focuses on advanced students **mentoring** other students within the **context** of specific classroom-based projects.

EXERCISE 1

Matching Column A and Column B

Match the word in Column A with the definition in Column B. Put the letter representing the correct definition in the space preceding each term.

Column A	Column B
Word	**Definition**
1. ___e___ feedback	a. male and female students studying together
2. ___f___ curricula	b. new ways of doing things
3. ___g___ concept	c. try hard to attain something
4. ___b___ innovative	d. the subject matter of a course
5. ___h___ facilitate	e. suggestions or criticism about someone's work
6. ___i___ mentoring	f. subjects taught in school or college
7. ___j___ context	g. an idea or principle
8. ___d___ content	h. to make a process easier
9. ___a___ coeducational	i. advising people with less experience
10. ___c___ strive	j. a situation that helps us understand its meaning

EXERCISE 2

Fill in the Blanks

In the following sentences, fill in the blank with a word from the terminology bank below that makes the sentence meaningful.

coeducational	concept	content	context	curricula
facilitate	feedback	innovative	mentoring	strive

1. Many researchers believe that learning can be optimized in a *coeducational* setting, as opposed to a single-sex school environment.

2. Students can benefit immensely from receiving constructive *feedback* on their work from both instructors and peers.

3. The Japanese educational system demands that students *strive* for perfection in their studies. Mistakes are usually not tolerated, and students are penalized if they do not succeed in meeting their academic goals.

4. Language teachers discourage their students from overly relying on the dictionary to learn unfamiliar words and recommend determining meaning from *context*.

5. Noam Chomsky, the father of modern linguistics, proposed that humans have an innate ability to learn language. This revolutionary *concept* startled many linguists and educators who had believed that languages were primarily learned through imitation.

6. Public speaking experts suggest that the speaker's body language is as important as the *content* of the lecture.

7. The president of the local college has instituted a *mentoring* program whereby less experienced instructors receive feedback on their teaching from their more experienced peers.

8. George Cutler, Director of the Department of Education at a prestigious university, recently taught a professional workshop focusing on *innovative* teaching techniques to make learning a more intellectually stimulating experience for students.

9. Research in education has begun to show that teacher-fronted classes are not conducive to learning. Instead, results of several studies support the view that teachers should *facilitate* learning by acting as a guide, speeding up the process without actively participating in it.

10. Nowadays most public universities in the United States are offering "Learning Community" courses pairing content and language *curricula*, enabling college students to improve their reading and writing skills while they take courses in hard sciences such as biology, physics, math, and chemistry.

© Pearson Education, Inc.

Collaboration

EXERCISE **3**

Pair Activity

Working with a partner, choose five words you have just learned, and create complete sentences with them.

1. _____

2. _____

3. _____

4. _____

5. _____

Graphic Analysis

Collaboration

Teaching Tip:
Developmental readers can gain from analyzing graphic information, an invaluable skill.

Whether you are studying Nursing, Computer Science, Business, Education, Biology, or another subject, most content-area textbooks contain graphic aids. The ability to analyze graphic material, in the form of bar graphs, pie charts, time lines, diagrams, maps, etc., is an essential college reading skill. In each chapter of this book, you will be asked to take a close look at a graphic aid and analyze the information it contains. It is only through practice that you will begin to interpret graphic information smoothly and accurately.

The graph shown here focuses on how the public and teachers hold different perspectives on the changes necessary to improve our nation's schools.

Examine the graph with a partner and answer the questions that follow.

■ **Figure 1.3**

	Public (percent)	*Teachers (percent)*
Discipline/more control/stricter rules	12	6
More teachers/smaller class size	10	12
Funding	5	8
Better/more qualified teachers	7	*
Higher pay for teachers	3	5
More parent involvement	3	18
Prayer/God back in schools	4	*
Security	4	*
Academic standards/better education	3	2
Dress code/uniforms	3	*
More/updated equipment/books/computers	2	3
Curriculum/more offered	2	*
* = Less than 1 percent.		

Source: Adapted from Carol A. Langdon and Nick Vesper, "The Sixth Phi Delta Kappa Poll of Teachers' Attitudes toward the Public Schools," *Phi Delta Kappan, 81*(8) (April 2000), pp. 607–611. Reprinted by permission of Phi Delta Kappan.

1. What, according to the public, is the first priority for change in schools?

   discipline/more control/stricter rules

2. What, according to teachers, is the first priority for change in schools?

   more parent involvement

3. What are two concerns that seem to matter to the public, but do not matter very much to teachers?

   better/more qualified teachers/prayer in school/security

4. What is the only concern listed that received over 10 percent for both the public and for teacher?

   more teachers/smaller classrooms

Reading as Information Predictors—Asking Questions as a Way of Understanding

When we begin reading an article, a section of a textbook, or a new chapter in a novel, we look at the first sentence and are naturally curious about what is coming next. We are given a little taste of information and wonder what information follows. As we continue reading, questions pop up in our heads, and this keeps us engaged in the text and guides us toward a better understanding of what we are reading.

Look at the example below. If you read this first sentence of an article, what else would you want to know?

Teaching Tip:
This feature encourages active reading and inquisitiveness.

Example
An angry student threw his textbook through the window during class.

List some questions that you have after reading this first sentence.

Answers will vary.

Answers will vary.

Answers will vary.

Answers will vary.

Answers will vary.

Answers will vary.

Answers will vary.

As you work with Reading Selection 1 in this chapter, and with all the first readings in subsequent chapters, you will be asked to predict what lies ahead by writing predictive questions for the first few paragraphs of each selection in the margin.

© Pearson Education, Inc.

READING

Reading Selection **1**

Newspaper Article

1.3 Flesch-Kincaid Grade Level 10.3

ESL Annotation

1.4 ESL Bilingual Education is an ESL high-interest topic.

Collaboration

Teaching Tip:
Ask students what "calle" means (calle means street in Spanish).

Learning and Teaching a Two-way Calle in Boston

Pre-Reading Questions

Before reading the following article, answer these questions in pairs or small groups. Discussing the questions will help prepare you to analyze the text with relative ease.

1. What kinds of challenges do recently arrived immigrant children face in American public schools?
2. How do you think the school system can help these students to overcome the challenges that they experience?
3. Do you think children whose first language is not English benefit more from bilingual instruction than they do from English-only instruction? Explain.

Read the selection below and practice your reading comprehension with the set of ten multiple-choice questions that follow. Write predictive questions in the margin each time you see the ? symbol.

Learning and Teaching a Two-way Calle in Boston

By Michelle Lefort, Special for *USA TODAY*

December 20, 2005

? Why is there a sign on the door?

1 BOSTON—It's Friday at the Rafael Hernandez Two-Way Bilingual School in Roxbury and a sign on the door of the four kindergarten and first-**grade** classrooms tells students they will speak English today.

2   When they return their homework Monday, everyone will learn songs, math and science in Spanish.

? Why is this particular
neighborhood so poor?

3   In one of Boston's poorest neighborhoods and named for a Puerto Rican poet who addressed the isolation of **migration**, Rafael Hernandez School was **founded** in the early 1970s to serve the children of Boston's growing Puerto Rican immigrant **community**. After Boston's 1974 desegregation order, Hernandez became a two-way language school.

4   Today, the school is highly **sought** after, with 250 applicants for 50 kindergarten slots. Although three-quarters of the students get free or reduced-priced lunches and many start school with little language in either English or Spanish, the kindergarten/first-**grade team** of Martine Lebret, Naomi Mulvihill, Brenda Rosario and Jessie Auger gets them off to a successful start.

? Why are there so few
neighborhood so poor?

5   Of last year's 50 first-graders, 45 were reading at or above **grade** level; 88% were meeting or exceeding math standards.

6   But state standards are only one measure of success for the teachers, who work long hours to build an **environment** of respect, pride, **community** and continual learning.

7   Lebret and Mulvihill teach kindergarten, and Rosario and Auger teach first **grade**. In each classroom, about half of the students are **dominant** in

Michelle Lefort, "Learning and Teaching a Two-Way Calle in Boston," *USA Today,* December 20, 2005. Reprinted with permission.

English and half **dominant** in Spanish. During the 90-minute morning literacy blocks, students change classrooms to work in their **dominant** language. Within each **grade**, the teachers **design parallel** curricula in each language.

8   The teachers, who average 13½ years teaching experience and have numerous **individual accolades**, each have distinct **styles** that are both loving and demanding.

9   But it's their teamwork that makes them click. They write almost all of their materials, coordinate plans and help one another improve.

10   "We sneak into each other's classrooms as often as we can" to watch each other teach to learn from each other and give honest **feedback**, Mulvihill says.

11   Peer critiquing can be intimidating, but the confidence they have in each other and their drive to improve helps them use criticism constructively. Their ability to learn from each other is the key, says **principal** Margarita Muniz. "They can listen to each other, critique each other without hard feelings."

12   "We are all different people, but we all have a desire to learn, a desire to share," Auger explains. "We're very proud of each other."

13   They also work together to help each child meet their own **goals**.

14   Carlos Piedad, now 8, wanted to move from the English-**dominant** group to the Spanish-**dominant** group. Over his two years with the team, the teachers developed **individual** assignments, gave ideas to his parents to work with him at home and nurtured his writing skills. He made the move midway through last year, ending the year fluent in both languages.

15   Parents Javier Piedad and Patti Lautner say Carlos wasn't particularly driven. "They motivated him," Lautner says. The **team** didn't spend any more time working with Carlos than they did with the other students, Lautner adds. It's not unusual for any of the teachers to work 12-hour days.

16   Even though they each teach classes of 24 or 25 students, each teacher sends regular progress reports home, or makes daily calls home if the parent requests. They also host small dinner parties for families where students write and illustrate their own books.

17   In keeping with the school's "**expeditionary** learning" **approach**, the **team** uses class projects to teach responsibility while meeting **academic** standards. Former eighth-**grade** classes transformed an abandoned lot into a **community** garden. Now, kindergarteners plant the garden each spring. The following September, both the first-graders and the new kindergarteners harvest plants for use in crafts such as swan gourd maracas or in making vegetable soup.

18   Learning and teaching in two languages may be doubly difficult, but also doubly rewarding.

19   Says Auger: "Learning two languages is incredibly intellectually stimulating."

accolades
praise and approval or even a prize given to someone for his or her work

feedback
advice, criticism, etc. about how successful or useful something is, given so that something can be improved

expeditionary
refers to a long and carefully organized trip, especially to a dangerous place

---

Reading Comprehension Check

In what follows and in multiple-choice questions throughout this textbook, circle the letter of the best answer.

1. What kind of school is the Rafael Hernandez School?
    a. a high school   c. an elementary school
    b. a middle school   d. a university

© Pearson Education, Inc.

2. The term *two-way* in the 3rd paragraph could be replaced with
   a. round-trip.
   b. bilingual.
   c. English–only.
   d. none of the above

3. In the 4th paragraph we read, "Today, the school is highly sought after. . . ." A synonym for *sought after* is
   a. desirable.
   b. troubled.
   c. attained.
   d. discarded.

4. What becomes clear about the school profile from the information in the 3rd and 4th paragraphs?
   a. Many of the students speak English only.
   b. Most of the students do not live in Boston.
   c. The vast majority of the students are poor.
   d. All of the students share the same first language.

5. The word *exceeding*, in the 5th paragraph, could be replaced with
   a. equal to.
   b. less than.
   c. successful.
   d. greater than.

6. It can be inferred from the 6th paragraph that
   a. students learn completely different material in each language.
   b. students cover the same material regardless of the language in which the content is given.
   c. This issue is not discussed in this paragraph.
   d. bilingual students are slower to learn.

7. In paragraph 9 we read, "They write almost all of their materials, co-ordinate plans and help one another improve." A synonym for the word *coordinate* is
   a. discriminate.
   b. synchronize.
   c. derive.
   d. deliver.

8. The term *peer critiquing,* as used in paragraph 10, refers to a collaboration between
   a. students and teachers.
   b. a group of students.
   c. two teachers.
   d. both teachers and their bilingual students.

9. What is Carlos's mother's main point about his teachers?
   a. They can teach in both English and Spanish.
   b. They work hard for the students.
   c. The teachers are not strict enough in America.
   d. Carlos is progressing.

10. In the final sentence of the article, one of the bilingual teachers says, "Learning two languages is incredibly intellectually stimulating." The word *stimulating* could be replaced with the word
    a. electric.
    b. contrived.
    c. exciting.
    d. enabling.

READING

Reading Selection **2**

Online Article

1.5 Flesch-Kincaid Grade Level 10.3

Collaboration

The Lowdown on Single-Sex Education

Pre-Reading Questions

Discuss these questions in groups.

1. Have you ever studied in a single-sex school? If yes, was your experience a positive one? If no, do you wish you had?

2. Is working together with members of the opposite sex a distraction or an advantage in a high school classroom? Explain.

ESL Annotation

1.5 **ESL** Students are more likely to have experienced a single-sex school environment.

The Lowdown on Single-Sex Education

By Hannah Boyd, Education.com (2008)

1   Not long ago single-**sex** schools were viewed as relics from another age, a time when boys took woodshop and girls studied home economics. Now the pendulum is swinging the other way. Legislators are considering funding single-sex public schools, and single-**sex** private schools are back in **vogue**. Why?

2   Call it Mars and Venus in the classroom. Experts say that boys and girls simply learn differently, and that ignoring inborn differences shortchanges both sexes. According to these experts, girls tend to **mature** faster both

vogue
popular acceptance or favor

Hannah Boyd, "The Lowdown on Single-Sex Education." Article reprinted with permission from Education.com, a website with thousands of articles for parents of preschool through grade 12 children, www.education.com

© Pearson Education, Inc.

socially and physically, and to develop language fluency, fine motor skills, and understanding of **abstract** concepts before boys do. Boys gain large motor control sooner, tend to be more literal than girls, and excel at spatial relationships. Perhaps more important, boys and girls behave differently.

3   "The behavior expected (and rewarded) in the classroom—quiet, patient, orderly acceptance of facts—favors how girls **approach** their classes," says Michael Obel-Omia, head of Upper School at University School in Hunting Valley, Ohio, which is all male. Like many, Obel-Omia believes boys enter coed schools at a disadvantage to girls, and may be shortchanged by a one-size-fits-all program.

4   Conversely, proponents of all-girls' schools say that deep-rooted sexism cheats girls in coed programs. Studies have shown that teachers call on girls less often than boys, and girls report feeling inhibited about speaking up in class. By removing the social pressure to impress the opposite **sex**, the reasoning goes, girls feel free to take more risks.

5   Although long-term **research** is lacking, **anecdotal evidence** seems to bear this out. Girls in single-sex schools are more likely to take math, computer science, and physics classes, as well as play sports, than their peers in coed schools; boys are more likely to study art, music, drama, and foreign languages. Some **evidence** suggests that boys in all-boys' schools are less competitive and more **cooperative**, which has led some to push for single-**sex** public schools in low-**income** areas.

6   Of course, we live in a coed world, and **eventually** everyone has to learn to work together. "With an all-girls' school you really need to take the initiative in finding male friends," notes Katharine Krotinger, a senior at the all-female Dana Hall School in Massachusetts. Otherwise, students of both sexes can feel like a fish out of water when they reach a coed college or the workplace.

7   Only you and your child can predict whether a single-**sex** school will be an educational haven or a social desert. As for Krotinger, she's looking forward to starting college in the fall—on a coed campus.

anecdotal evidence
an informal account, sometimes as a story or hearsay, to prove something

Reading Comprehension Check

1. As used in the first sentence of the article, "Not long ago single-sex schools were viewed as relics from another age," the word *relics* could be replaced by
a. plans.   c. strategies.
b. leftovers.   d. disasters.

2. The phrase "the pendulum is swinging the other way" in the first paragraph refers to
a. the fact that single-sex schools are now on the decline.
b. all boy's schools.
c. the fact that single-sex schools are coming back into fashion.
d. schools are moving.

3. As used in paragraph 2, in the phrase "ignoring inborn differences short-changes both sexes," the term *shortchanges* means
   a. destroys.
   b. considers.
   c. appreciates.
   d. does a disservice to.

4. Which advantage that young female students have over boys is NOT mentioned in the article?
   a. Girls mature faster.
   b. Girls develop fine motor skills earlier.
   c. Girls excel at spatial relationships.
   d. Girls develop language fluency faster.

5. What is Michael Obel-Omia's main point in the 3rd paragraph?
   a. Boys are discriminated against.
   b. Girls tend to exhibit behavior that is more suitable to classroom learning.
   c. All schools should be coed.
   d. Girls are more mature.

6. What evidence is cited about boys' performance in all boys' schools?
   a. They don't take art classes.
   b. They are less cooperative.
   c. They are more competitive.
   d. They are less competitive and more cooperative.

7. In paragraph 6, in the sentence "With an all-girls' school you really need to take the initiative," the phrase *take the initiative* could be replaced by
   a. invite someone.
   b. make an effort.
   c. be shy.
   d. consider all the issues.

8. The expression *fish out of water* in the second to last paragraph refers to
   a. how boys and girls coming from a single-sex school environment might feel when suddenly confronted with the opposite sex .
   b. how boys feel in all boys' schools.
   c. awkward girls.
   d. students in coed schools.

9. In the sentence "Only you and your child can predict whether a single-sex school will be an educational haven or a social desert," the term *haven* means
   a. nightmare.
   b. safe place.
   c. prison.
   d. heaven.

10. The author of the article believes that
    a. coed schools are a better choice.
    b. single-sex schools are of higher quality.
    c. both kinds of schools are nice.
    d. We do not know the author's viewpoint.

© Pearson Education, Inc.

Ruth Simmons

Dr. Ruth J. Simmons is the first African American educator ever to be president of an Ivy League institution and the first female president of Brown University. A poll conducted by the *Brown Daily Herald* in January 2007 showed her approval rating among the undergraduates at Brown University to be more than 80 percent. Ruth J. Simmons was born in 1945 in Grapeland, Texas. She grew up on a farm in East Texas and had a life of deprivation and hardship. Yet she recounts her life in Texas fondly. "My journey has not been all that arduous, contrary to the way that my life is often presented. I had this wonderful grounding by my parents, and then an extraordinary streak of luck."

Despite her meteoric rise to prominence in the field of education, she remains humble and grateful to her mentors who challenged, supported, and encouraged her to pursue her dreams. One of the most influential mentors was her mother, whom Ruth Simmons watched as a child pressing fabric for hours. She recalls, "I remember thinking what a horrible, horrible thing to have to do. And yet she would see a crease invisible to everyone else, and she would work on it until it disappeared." Her mother passed away when Simmons was 15 but not before teaching her the value of perseverance, a precious lesson that has stayed with her since then. Simmons studied at Dillard University and later at Wellesley College where she was inspired by President Margaret Clapp to view traditional gender roles in a different perspective. "That was defining for me, the notion that women didn't have to play restricted roles, that you didn't have to hold back at all," recounts Simmons. "The faculty demanded that you work up to your potential." She went on to earn a PhD at Harvard University in Romance Languages.

Simmons admits that shaking the traditional notion of gender was not easy for her. She recalled that her mother "believed herself to be subservient to the interests of men. I expected that in my relationship with men. I should pretend not to be smart. I never wanted to be valedictorian because I thought it was very important for a boy to be valedictorian."

She got married at the age of 22, had two children, and is now divorced. She was the director of studies at Princeton University and completed one of her most challenging assignments, a report on race relations that seemed to have divided the campus in the late 1980s. She rejuvenated black culture on campus and hired prominent black scholars such as Cornel West, Henry Louis Gates, and Toni Morrison to teach in the Department of African American Studies.

Simmons became president of Brown University in 2001 and gained popularity among students because of her successful fundraising, introduction of need-blind admissions, and personal charisma. She even recruited students to the campus. "It's probably the most important thing I can do on a national basis," she says. "[The best thing] any parent can do for a child is to give your child a sense of love and support to be open to the idea that they need to learn." Ruth Simmons is known to be a pioneer. She started the engineering program at Smith College. As president of Brown University, she has taken an ambitious $1.4 billion initiative known as the Campaign for Academic Enrichment to boost Brown University's academic programs. She remains dedicated to the cause of education and encourages students to succeed in their academic endeavors.

Some Questions for Group Discussion

1. Simmons was inspired by her mother to persevere in her goals. Do you believe that parents influence their children to succeed in their professional careers? Explain how. Do you have a mentor or a series of mentors who have inspired you to pursue your academic goals?
2. Simmons's road to success was replete with hurdles. In what way did she have to struggle to get to a high position as an educator?
3. Simmons believes that "[The best thing] any parent can do for a child is to give your child a sense of love and support to be open to the idea that they need to learn." What do you understand about Simmons's philosophy of education from this quote? Do you share her views? Explain.

Biographical Internet Research

Research another great figure in Education from the list below and share a biographical profile with your fellow students:

■ Paolo Freire
■ Socrates
■ Jonathan Kozol
■ Maria Montessori
■ John Locke

Teaching Tip:
Reading about inspirational figures across academic disciplines encourages students to aim high. Students will enjoy doing the Biographical Internet Research.

SKILL FOCUS
Determining Meaning from Context

Teaching Tip:
Reading skills are given focus, but are not taught in isolation. All reading skill activities are embedded into the chapter's academic content.

Regardless of the academic career you are pursuing in college, you are likely to encounter discipline-specific terminology—unfamiliar words and expressions in text and lectures given by professors. It is, therefore, essential that you build a strong vocabulary to comprehend the text and to do well on standardized reading tests administered by most U.S. state colleges. You may not have a dictionary at your disposal all the time, so you will need to rely on the context to figure out the meaning of the unfamiliar word, especially when answering multiple-choice questions. Although there is no single technique that will always work, the following strategies will help you determine meaning from context without turning to a dictionary.

Parts of Speech

When you come across an unfamiliar word in a sentence, try to find out what part of speech the word is. As you know, *nouns* are names of people, objects, phenomena, and places. *Verbs*, on the other hand, are usually actions carried out by people or nature. Some examples of verbs are *admire, love,* and *destroy*. Furthermore, *adjectives* modify the nouns describing their characteristics. *Beautiful, intelligent,* and *constructive* are all examples of adjectives. Finally, *adverbs* show the manner in which an action (the verb) is conducted. These are examples of adverbs: *skillfully, abruptly,* and *viciously*. Knowing the part of speech of the word will help you determine its meaning (see also the Parts of Speech section in Chapter 2).

EXERCISE 4

Read the following sentences and label nouns as N, verbs as V, adjectives as Adj, and adverbs as Adv. Be sure to write these labels right beneath the word. The first one is done for you.

1. The frustrated educator quit his job.
   Adj   N   V   N
2. Professor Smith's students flunked the standardized reading exam.
            N   N   V   Adj   N   N
3. New technologies have changed America's classrooms significantly.
   Adj   N   V   N   N   Adv
5. The history professor grudgingly allowed the student to turn the paper in late.
       Adj   N   Adv   V   N   V   N   Adj

Word Forms

Sometimes the roots, prefixes, and suffixes will help you arrive at the correct meaning of the word. For example, some nouns end with suffixes such as *ity, ian, ist, tion, ary,* etc., verbs have suffixes of a word such as *ate, ify, ize, en,* etc., and adjectives are formed by adding suffixes such as *ous, ish, less, y, ive, ful,* etc. Let's see how this works by looking at the verb *create*.

ESL Annotation

1.6 ESL Word forms are a trouble-spot for ESL learners.

Verb	Noun	Adjective	Adverb
create	creation	creative	creatively
	creator	uncreative	
	creature		

© Pearson Education, Inc.

EXERCISE 5

Complete the table below by writing in the different forms of the provided word.

Noun	Verb	Adjective	Adverb
product	produce	productive	productively
study	study	studious	studiously
success	succeed	successful	successfully
critique	criticize	critical	critically

For more complete coverage of prefixes, roots, and suffixes, see pages 23–26 in this chapter.

Connotation

ESL Annotation

1.7 ESL Students appreciate a strong focus on this area of connotation and word choice.

Most words have either a positive or negative connotation. Even if you do not know the meaning of the new word you have just encountered, most of the time you can tell whether it has a negative or positive feel to it. Examine the examples, below, of words with positive and negative connotation.

Word	Connotation
uplifting	positive
critical	negative
downtrend	negative
enlightening	positive
optimistic	positive

EXERCISE 6

In the table below, read the words in the left column and decide whether they have a positive or negative connotation. Put a check in the appropriate box.

Word	Connotation	
	Positive	Negative
consistent	✓	☐
disruptive	☐	✓
conducive	✓	☐
commend	✓	☐
distract	☐	✓

Contextual Clues

The context in which the word occurs can also lead you to its correct meaning. Read the sentence carefully and look at the words that precede and follow the unfamiliar word. If you are reading an entire passage, read the sentences that come immediately before and after the sentence that has the word in question. These adjacent sentences will provide the context that will help you zero in on the correct meaning of the new word. Let's look at an example in a multiple-choice question to see how this works.

Example

John runs his business like a dictator, but none of his employees have the **temerity** to defy his order.

In the sentence, the word *temerity* could be replaced by

    a. integrity.

    b. sincerity.

    c. audacity.

    d. brevity.

The following strategies will help you figure out the meaning of the word *temerity*.

Strategy #1: Identify Part of Speech

When you come across an unfamiliar word, first identify what part of speech it is. For example, is it a noun, a verb, an adjective, or an adverb? However, determining the part of speech of the word *temerity* is not going to help you in this case, because all of the four choices are nouns. This means that you will need to use another strategy to answer the question correctly.

Strategy #2: Determine the Connotation

As you learned above, most words have either a positive or negative connotation. Understanding the connotation of a word will clue you in to its meaning. If you look at the context, it tells us that John is a dictator, someone who likes to order his employees and probably does not care much about how they feel. To disobey John, an employee would have to have courage, strength, and boldness, which all have positive connotations. Therefore, you can deduce that *temerity* also has a positive connotation and determine that it means (c) audacity.

    Now that you have learned different strategies to determine meaning from context, let's do an exercise and apply these strategies.

EXERCISE 7

Read the short passage below and try to determine the meaning of the highlighted words from the context.

> Students with limited proficiency are required to take **remedial** reading and writing courses. Some students are **indignant** that these courses are given a noncredit status. However, until they pass these courses, they are not **entitled** to take most classes in their major.

Word	Part of Speech	Connotation	Your Definition
remedial	*Adj*	*Negative*	*Answers will vary*
indignant	*Adj*	*Negative*	*Answers will vary*
entitled	*Adj*	*Posititive/Negative*	*Answers will vary*

© Pearson Education, Inc.

PRACTICING THE SKILL
Practice 1

Applying the Skill to Readings

Let's practice "vocabulary in context" questions with a few short readings from *Foundations of American Education.*

Collaboration

Read the following paragraph with a partner and try to define the highlighted words using the clue strategy. Write your definitions for the bolded words first. Then look them up in a dictionary and compare your definitions. Do the same for the rest of the readings.

Passage 1

Assimilation is a process by which an immigrant group is **incorporated** into the **dominant** culture. The group either adopts the culture of the dominant group as its own or interacts with it in a way that **forges** a new or different culture that is shared by both groups. Members of a group experience a number of stages in this process. (p. 49)

	Your Definition	*Dictionary Definition*
1. incorporated	*Answers will vary*	*Answers will vary*
2. dominant	*Answers will vary*	*Answers will vary*
3. forges	*Answers will vary*	*Answers will vary*

Passage 2

All people have preferred learning and teaching styles that are **embedded** in their cultural backgrounds and experiences. Until teachers learn to recognize these differences and develop a **repertoire** of different strategies for teaching subject matter, some students will be **deprived** of appropriate support in the learning process. However, making generalizations about culturally diverse learners can be dangerous. (p. 120)

	Your Definition	*Dictionary Definition*
1. embedded	*Answers will vary*	*Answers will vary*
2. repertoire	*Answers will vary*	*Answers will vary*
3. deprived	*Answers will vary*	*Answers will vary*

Passage 3

The physical arrangement of a school into classrooms has organizational as well as instructional **implications**. For example, it is easy for teachers to be isolated in their classrooms. This geographic **isolation** contributes to their not knowing about or becoming **engaged** with issues that affect the whole school. Geographic isolation can affect the school as a whole too. The school staff might not be aware of community concerns or of what is going on in other schools across the district. Teachers and administrators must make **deliberate** efforts to learn about other parts of the education system. (p. 143)

	Your Definition	*Dictionary Definition*
1. implications	Answers will vary	Answers will vary
2. isolation	Answers will vary	Answers will vary
3. engaged	Answers will vary	Answers will vary
4. deliberate	Answers will vary	Answers will vary

Passage 4

In the past, an important and **unique** feature of education in the United States was local control, the belief that educational decisions should be made at the local level rather than at the state or national level. The **rationale** has been that people at the local level, including teachers and parents, know what is best for the students in their community. As has been described in this chapter, the **trend** over the last sixty years has been toward more federalism. The No Child Left Behind Act is the latest and heaviest centralization **initiative** by the federal government and includes many **mandates** to states, school districts, schools, and teachers. (p. 164)

	Your Definition	*Dictionary Definition*
1. unique	Answers will vary	Answers will vary
2. rationale	Answers will vary	Answers will vary
3. trend	Answers will vary	Answers will vary
4. initiative	Answers will vary	Answers will vary
5. mandates	Answers will vary	Answers will vary

© Pearson Education, Inc.

Practice 2

More Vocabulary in Context Practice

Read the following passages and answer the multiple-choice questions that follow. Remember to use the four strategies you learned earlier to determine meaning from context.

Passage 1

A sampling of large New York City high schools showed that the schools failed to notify the state of a significant number of violent or **disruptive** episodes in the 2004–5 school year, the city comptroller announced yesterday.

The comptroller, William C. Thompson Jr., said an audit showed that the city had not ensured that all principals accurately report violence in their schools, making it difficult for the public to **assess** their safety. The audit examined an array of records in 10 schools, comparing them with computerized data sent to the state. It found, for example, that officials at Brooklyn's Boys and Girls High School informed the state of 14 cases of violence or misbehavior through a special computer system, which the state uses to **comply** with reporting obligations under the federal No Child Left Behind law.

From Elissa Gootman, "Undercount of Violence in Schools." From *The New York Times*, September 20, 2007. © 2007 The New York Times. All rights reserved. Used by permission and protected by the Copyright Laws of the United States. The printing, copying, redistribution, or retransmission of the Material without express written permission is prohibited. www.nytimes.com

1. The word *disruptive* in the first paragraph means
   a. peaceful.
   b. obedient.
   c. unruly.
   d. quiet.

2. The word *assess* in the second paragraph means the same as
   a. ignore.
   b. disqualify.
   c. criticize.
   d. evaluate.

3. As used in the last sentence of the second paragraph, the word *comply* means
   a. disobey.
   b. act in accordance with.
   c. allow.
   d. violate.

Passage 2

A shy high school freshman, Harpal Singh Vacher, ended the school year last spring as the latest collateral damage in a citywide political tussle. What began as a childish argument with fellow students on May 24 ended with Harpal crouched on a bathroom floor at Newtown High School in Elmhurst, Queens, his previously unshorn hair littered on the ground around him.

In keeping with his Sikh faith, Harpal had kept his unshorn hair tucked inside a dastaar, a religious turban. The police say that his attacker, a high school senior named Umair Ahmed, had removed Harpal's turban and cut his hair to punish him for making **derogatory** comments about Mr. Ahmed's mother—comments for which Harpal had apologized. The Queens district attorney has charged Mr. Ahmed with a hate crime. The case is one of the few in which anyone has acted to stem bias-based

harassment in city schools, though only after the damage has been done. The City Council recognized and addressed the systemic gaps in countering prejudice and intimidation in public schools years ago, when it passed the Dignity for All Students Act in 2004.

From Neha Singh and Khin Mai Aung, "A Free Ride for Bullies." From *The New York Times*, September 23, 2007. © 2007 The New York Times. All rights reserved. Used by permission and protected by the Copyright Laws of the United States. The printing, copying, redistribution, or retransmission of the Material without express written permission is prohibited. www.nytimes.com

1. As used in the first sentence, the word *tussle* means
  a. gathering.   (c.) clash.
  b. convention.   d. organization.

2. The word *derogatory* in the second sentence of the second paragraph is *opposite* in meaning to
  a. insulting.   c. deprecating.
  b. offensive.   (d.) complimentary.

3. As used in the sentence "The case is one of the few in which anyone has acted to stem bias-based harassment in city schools, though only after the damage has been done," the word *harassment* means
  a. persuasion.   c. argumentation.
  (b.) aggravation.   d. celebration.

Passage 3

Military recruiters are frequently given free **rein** in New York City public schools and allowed into classes in violation of the school system's regulations, according to a report released yesterday by the Manhattan borough president and the New York Civil Liberties Union.

The report, based on surveys of nearly 1,000 students at 45 high schools citywide last spring, said the city's Department of Education exercised almost no **oversight** over how much access recruiters had to students at high schools.

"There were recruiters who were in the classroom not to talk to students about reading, writing and arithmetic, but to talk to them about how to get a one-way ticket to Iraq and all the benefits you will **accrue** by that process," Scott M. Stringer, the Manhattan borough president, said at a news conference. "This is something that must be stopped. It's outrageous, and it gives recruiters a captive audience."

ESL Annotation

1.8 ESL In many countries military service is compulsory. Thus, some students may not understand the concept of voluntary military service.

From Jennifer Medina, "Recruitment by Military in Schools Is Criticized." From *The New York Times*, September 7, 2007. © 2007 The New York Times. All rights reserved. Used by permission and protected by the Copyright Laws of the United States. The printing, copying, redistribution, or retransmission of the Material without express written permission is prohibited. www.nytimes.com

1. As used in the first sentence of the first paragraph, the word *rein* means
  a. coupons.   c. tickets.
  (b.) control.   d. vouchers.

2. The word *oversight* in the second paragraph means
  (a.) supervision.   c. modification.
  b. error.   d. overpaid.

3. The word *accrue* in the third paragraph means
   a. decrease.   c. decline.
   b. accumulate.   d. forsake.

Vocabulary Development with Common Prefixes, Suffixes, and Roots

Collaboration

In English we can often determine the meaning of a word by looking at the sum of its parts—that is, if we have good knowledge of common prefixes, suffixes, and roots, this gives us a great advantage in figuring out the meaning of unfamiliar words.

The following are a group of tables with common prefixes, suffixes, and roots (word bases). With a partner try to give two examples of words that are derived from these forms. Once you get started, you will realize how many words you already have in your active vocabulary!

1. Prefixes

Prefixes are words that attach to the front (*pre* = before) of a root. Give two examples of words with the listed prefixes.

Prefixes	Meaning	Example 1	Example 2
a- (an-)	not, without		
anti-	against, opposite		
dis-	not, away, remove		
il-	not		
im-	not		
in-	not		
ir-	not		
mal-	poor, bad, evil		
mis-	wrong, bad		
non-	not		
ob- (op)	against, stopping, in the way		
un-	not		
ante-	before in time/place in front of		
pre-	before in time or place		
post-	after in time or place		
inter-	between time or place		
sub-	below, under, lower		
under-	below, under, lower		
super-	higher, greater, larger, above		
sur-	higher, greater, larger, above		
over-	higher, greater, larger, too much		
out-	higher, greater, better		

2. Suffixes

The following suffixes are added to a root to change the form of the word. Identify the part of speech and give two examples of each suffix.

Suffix	Meaning	Part of Speech	Example 1	Example 2
-ion	act of doing			
-ish	like, similar to			
-ence	act of doing			
-ate	make or become			
-y	full of or covered w/			
-ment	state of being			
-en	to make			
-ent	like, similar			
-ness	state of being			
-ly	in a way that is			
-al	related to			
-ous	full or covered w/			
-ship	state of being			
-ity	state of being			
-ile (-ine)	like, similar			
-ify	make or become			
-ive	causing, having power			
-ic	like, similar			
-ize	make or become			

3. Roots

Roots are the base of a word that can accept prefixes or suffixes. Please add the meaning of the roots below and provide examples of words containing them.

Roots	Meaning	Example 1	Example 2
mar-			
ped-			
sol-			
mort-			
vis-			
terr-			
path-			
dict-			
prim-			
centr-			
medi-			
equi-			
circul-			
fin-			
-meter			
-graph			

© Pearson Education, Inc.

Once you have finished, check the tables that you and your partner have filled in against the completed tables below. Some of the words you came up with may be the same, some may be different.

1. Prefixes

Prefixes	Meaning	Example 1	Example 2
a- (an-)	not, without	atheist, amnesia	amnesty, anonymous
anti-	against, opposite	antonym, antiwar	antisocial
dis-	not, away, remove	disagree, dishonest	disconnect
il-	not	illegal, illogical	illiterate, illusion
im-	not	immature, impolite	imperfect, immortal
in-	not	invisible, insomnia	infinite, incomplete
ir-	not	irregular, irreligious	irresponsible, irregular
mal-	poor, bad, evil	malfunction	malpractice
mis-	wrong, bad	miscommunicate	misspell, misplace
non-	not	nonsmoker, nonstop	nonprofit, nonsense
ob- (op)	against, stopping, in the way	oppose, obstruct	obstacle
un-	not	unequal, uncover	unhealthy, uncommon
ante-	before in time/ place in front of	ancient, antique	anticipate
pre-	before in time or place	prefix, preseason	pretest, preview
post-	after in time or place	postpone, postwar	postindustrial, posttest
inter-	between time or place	interactive	interview international
sub-	below, under, lower	subway, subtitle	submarine, substandard
under-	below, under, lower	underground, undersea	underdeveloped, undernourished
super-	higher, greater, larger, above	superman, superstar	supermarket superlative
sur-	higher, greater, larger, above	surpass, survive	surcharge
over-	higher, greater, larger, too much	override, overpaid	overwork, overconfident
out-	higher, greater, better	outdo, outrace, outlive	outsmart, outnumber,

2. Suffixes

Suffix	Meaning	Part of Speech	Example 1	Example 2
-ion	act of doing	Noun	education	discussion
-ish	like, similar to	Adjective	sluggish	childish
-ence	act of doing	Noun	conference	audience
-ate	make or become	Verb	moderate	graduate
-y	full of or covered w/	Adjective	windy	funny
-ment	state of being	Noun	encouragement	agreement
-en	to make	Verb	darken	lighten
-ent	like, similar	Adjective	fragrant	pleasant
-ness	state of being	Noun	seriousness	kindness
-ly	in a way that is	Adverb	clearly	similarly
-al	related to	Adjective	dental	verbal
-ous	full or covered w/	Adjective	humorous	nervous
-ship	state of being	Noun	friendship	scholarship
-ity	state of being	Noun	clarity	complexity
-ile (-ine)	like, similar	Adjective	fragile	juvenile
-ify	make or become	Verb	verify	magnify
-ive	causing, having power	Adjective	festive	talkative
-ic	like, similar	Adjective	Arabic	athletic
-ize	make or become	Verb	publicize	memorize

3. Roots

Roots	Meaning	Example 1	Example 2
mar-	of the sea	marine	maritime
ped-	foot	pedestrian	pedicure
sol-	alone	solidarity	solitude
mort-	death	mortician	mortal
vis-	to see	visual	vision
terr-	land	terrestrial	terrain
chrono-	time	synchronize	chronology
dict-	word	predict	dictionary
Prim-	first, original	primordial	primitive
Centr-	a point in the middle	centralize	centrifuge

© Pearson Education, Inc.

Medi-	enclosed	Mediterranean	medicinal
equi-	equal	equivalent	equivocate
circul-	around	circulatory	circular
fin-	last	finality	finale
-meter	measuring device	centimeter	perimeter
-graph	something written or drawn	monograph	polygraph

The next Reading Selection allows you to apply the skill of determining meaning from context.

READING

Reading Selection **3**

Interview

1.9 Flesch-Kincaid Grade Level 7.4

Collaboration

ESL Annotation

1.10 ESL Many students from cultures where science education is widely respected may not be aware of the "low-standing" of the sciences in the American Public School System.

A Conversation with Eric Mazur

Using the "Beauties of Physics" to Conquer Science Illiteracy

Pre-Reading Questions

Discuss the following questions in small groups as an introduction to the topic of the reading.

1. Many high school students believe that science classes are taught in a "boring way." How was your experience with science courses in high school? Did you enjoy them? Did you like your teachers' methodology?

2. America's graduate programs in the hard sciences are filled with international students. Why do you think it is that, in general, Americans show little interest in pursuing careers in science?

3. In the interview Professor Mazur argues that students prefer an interactive classroom environment, and that the old way of students passively listening to a lecture does not work anymore. Do you agree with Professor Mazur? Why or why not?

A Conversation with Eric Mazur

By Claudia Dreifus, the *New York Times*

July 17, 2007

1   CAMBRIDGE, Mass.—In the halls of academia, it is the rare senior professor who volunteers to teach basic science courses to undergraduates.

Claudia Dreifus, "A Conversation with Eric Mazur: Using the 'Beauties of Physics' to Conquer Science Illiteracy." From *The New York Times*, July 17, 2007. © 2007 The New York Times. All rights reserved. Used by permission and protected by the Copyright Laws of the United States. The printing, copying, redistribution, or retransmission of the Material without express written permission is prohibited. www.nytimes.com

2   But Eric Mazur, the Gordon McKay Professor of Applied Physics at Harvard, is driven by a passion. He wants to end science illiteracy among the nation's college students; specifically, he strives to open them to the "great beauties of physics."

3   Mazur's own Harvard course, Physics 1b, is the kind of science class that even a literature student might love—playful, engaging, something like a trip to a science museum. Indeed, Dr. Mazur, 52, is as experimental in his classroom as he is in his **research** laboratory.

4   "It's important to mentally engage students in what you're teaching," he explains. "We're way too focused on facts and rote memorization and not on learning the **process** of doing science."

5   **Q.** *Why do you willingly teach an introductory physics course?*

6   **A.** First, it's part of my **job** description. Professors are supposed to teach. The problem is how we teach, particularly how we teach science to undergraduates.

7   From what I've seen, students in science classrooms throughout the country depend on the rote memorization of facts. I want to change this. The students who score high do so because they've learned how to regurgitate information on tests. On the whole, they haven't understood the basic concepts behind the facts, which means they can't apply them in the laboratory. Or in life.

8   On a physics exam, the student will see a diagram and they'll classify it. Then, it's simply a matter of putting the right numbers in the right slots and, sort of, turning a crank. But this is algebra. It is not physics. When you test the students later on the **concept**, they can't explain what they've just done.

9   This saddens me. In my laboratory, we've made some important discoveries. Several were accidental—serendipitous. If we'd only functioned on the standard knowledge, we wouldn't have recognized what was before us.

© Pearson Education, Inc.

10 **Q.** *What were these findings?*

11 **A.** Here's the biggest one: Just for the fun of it, we once put a silicon wafer into some gas we had lying around the lab. We then irradiated it with ultra-short laser pulses. What came out was a wafer as black as the blackest velvet. Until that moment, the conventional wisdom was that silicon was never black. So it certainly was possible to think of this thing as a mistake and to have tossed it away. Instead, we put it under an electron microscope where we saw that we had found a new material: 98 **percent** silicon, 2 **percent** embedded gas.

12   And today, we have a patent for this black silicon, which has important applications in communications and sensor technology.

13 **Q.** *Where were you educated?*

14 **A.** In Holland. At the University of Leiden. In my first year, we started out as 72 physics majors. By the second year, we were winnowed down to 11. Only those who could maintain themselves in rote memorization were able to continue.

15   I was one. But throughout my college years, I often thought of quitting, becoming an artist or a photographer instead. The lectures were deadening, frustrating. Only later, in graduate school, when I got into a laboratory did I see the creative part of science. It's beautiful to **design** an experiment.

16 **Q.** *Do you think you're better than the instructors you experienced as a student?*

17 **A.** When I first started teaching here in the 1980s, I didn't ask myself such questions. I did what everyone else did: lectures. And the feedback was **positive**. The students did well on what I considered difficult exams.

18   Around 1990, I learned of the work of David Hestenes, an Arizona State physicist studying how abysmally students in his **region** did in science. He'd given hundreds of undergraduates a test in **concept** comprehension before and after they'd taken their physics classes. The tests showed that even with a term of instruction, their understanding hadn't improved very much.

19   I felt challenged by this. I then tested my own Harvard students similarly. We had discussed Newtonian mechanics earlier in the semester, and the students had already solved some difficult problems. Yet, when I gave them a new "**concept**-based" exam, about half had no clue as to what Newtonian mechanics were about.

20 **Q.** *Perhaps this **concept**-based test was flawed?*

21 **A.** No. But it was different. It measured their knowledge of physics forces in daily life. If they'd really understood Newtonian mechanics, they would have aced it. One student asked me: "How should I answer these questions? According to what you taught me? Or according to the way I usually think about these things?"

22   That was the moment I fell out of my ivory tower. It was then that I began to consider new ways of teaching.

23 **Q.** *Doesn't good pedagogy have a performance element to it?*

24 **A.** It does, though that doesn't necessarily translate into better learning. I used to get in front of my students and do all the science for them. I should have been showing them how to do it themselves. If they were studying the piano, I wouldn't have gone, "sit down, I'll play the piano for you."

25 **Q.** *How do you teach undergraduate physics today?*

26 **A.** I have the students read the **text** before the **lecture**. This is standard practice in the humanities, but a **heresy** in science. I don't know why. I think perhaps science professors like to "present" material.

27   In my class, we talk about the applications of physics in everyday life. The lectures are broken up with these "**concept** tests," where the students move into groups to work on a physics problem together. They talk, argue—they teach each other. After some discussion, they enter their answers into a **computer** that tabulates their collective **response**. From that, I can see if they've understood the **topic** before we move on.

28   We don't **grade** on a curve. Modern science is a **cooperative endeavor**.

29 **Q.** *You permit students to take their textbooks into the **final** exam. Why?*

30 **A.** Life, you know, is an open book. They can bring any book they want to class. My **objective** is to see if they can solve a problem.

31 **Q.** *When a **task** force on teaching at Harvard gave its report this past January, its chairwoman, Theda Skocpol, **cited** you as one of Harvard's most innovative teachers. Have many of your **colleagues** since asked to observe your classes?*

30 **A.** A few. At Harvard, teaching is left to the **individual** professor. There isn't a lot of cross-pollination. The upside is that this "every tub on its own bottom" credo has made it possible to experiment with my own classes and not get much interference.

31   Now, I've walked into science classrooms here to see what the others do. Some of it makes me burn. You know, these great, fantastic performances by energetic professors where attendance is miserable and half the students seem asleep. Toward the front of the room, you see a handful of kids furiously taking notes, while others fiddle with their laptops. "Any questions?" the professor asks. There are none.

32 **Q.** *When you teach Physics 1b, do you give "fantastic performances"?*

33 **A.** You know, I've come to think of professorial charisma as dangerous. I used to get fantastic evaluations because of charisma, not understanding. I'd have students give me high marks, but then say, "physics sucks." Today, by having the students work out the physics problems with each other, the learning gets done. I've moved from being "the sage on the stage" to "the guide on the side."

---

heresy
beliefs or behaviors that are considered to be wrong by a particular religious, political, or social group

endeavor
an attempt or effort to do something new or difficult

Reading Comprehension Check

Read the following sentences carefully and determine the meaning of the bolded words from the context.

1. In the sentence "He wants to end science illiteracy among the nation's college students; specifically, he **strives** to open them to the 'great beauties of physics'," the word *strive* means

© Pearson Education, Inc.

    a. to impede learning.   (c.) to try hard to achieve something.

    b. to simplify the subject matter.   d. to complicate the content.

2. In the sentence "It's important to mentally **engage** students in what you're teaching," the word *engage* is similar to

    a. confuse.   c. exclude.

    (b.) involve.   d. explain.

3. As used in the sentence "The students who score high do so because they've learned how to **regurgitate** information on tests. On the whole, they haven't understood the basic concepts behind the facts, which means they can't apply them in the laboratory," the word *regurgitate* means

    a. to think deeply.   (c.) to repeat without thinking.

    b. to guess meaning from context.   d. to analyze carefully.

4. Professor Mazur says, "Until that moment, the **conventional wisdom** was that silicon was never black. So it certainly was possible to think of this thing as a mistake and to have tossed it away." *Conventional wisdom* in this sentence means

    a. new ways of thinking.   c. nonconforming views.

    (b.) a widely held belief.   d. unique concepts and ideas.

5. In the sentence "And today, we have a **patent** for this black silicon, which has important applications in communications and sensor technology," the word *patent* means

    a. illegal use.   c. counterfeit.

    b. contraband.   (d.) official license.

6. As used in the following, "I did what everyone else did: lectures. And the **feedback** was positive. The students did well on what I considered difficult exams," the word *feedback* means

    a. rejection of someone's work.

    (b.) suggestion or criticism about someone's work.

    c. dismissal of a lecture.

    d. assistance with difficult exams.

7. Professor Mazur recalls, "Around 1990, I learned of the work of David Hestenes, an Arizona State physicist studying how **abysmally** students in his region did in science." By *abysmally,* he means

    a. performing well.   (c.) performing poorly.

    b. passing an exam easily.   d. performing successfully.

8. In the question "Perhaps this concept-based test was **flawed**," the word *flawed* means

    a. impeccable.   (c.) erroneous.

    b. perfect.   d. accurate.

9. Answering a question about the concept-based test, Professor Mazur says, "It measured their knowledge of physics forces in daily life. If they'd really understood Newtonian mechanics, they would have **aced** it." The word *aced* in this sentence is *opposite* in meaning to

    a. excelled.   c. breeze through the test.

    b. get a high score.   (d.) flunked.

10. The interviewer asks, "Doesn't good **pedagogy** have a performance element to it?" The word *pedagogy* in the question is similar in meaning to
    a. the psychology of learning.
    c. the review of textbooks.
    (b.) the study of teaching methods.
    d. the evaluation of student work.

11. Read the following paragraph: "I have the students read the text before the lecture. This is standard practice in the humanities, but a **heresy** in science. I don't know why. I think perhaps science professors like to 'present' material." The word *heresy* means
    (a.) an opinion disagreeing with a common belief.
    b. an opinion agreeing with a common belief.
    c. a belief conforming to conventional wisdom.
    d. a belief adhering to a common practice.

12. Commenting on the grading system, Professor Mazur says, "We don't grade on a curve. Modern science is a cooperative **endeavor**." In this sentence, the word *endeavor* means
    a. failure.
    (c.) effort.
    b. resistance.
    d. assistance.

Recommended Debate Topic: Should we reward good grades with money and prizes?

Your suggested debate topics:

a. _____

b. _____

c. _____

DEBATABLE TOPIC

Teaching Tip:
See instruction manual for in-depth instruction on how to work with class debates.

Should We Reward Good Grades with Money and Prizes?

1.11 Flesch-Kincaid Grade Level 9.2

Pre-Reading Questions

Discuss the questions below with a partner. If your instructor has assigned a debate activity, read the opposing viewpoints offered in the reading and consider how you can integrate some of the information into your debate preparation.

Collaboration

1. Can you think of some examples from life where good performance is rewarded?

2. In your opinion what motivates a good student to do well in school?

3. Would giving money to the better students be fair to the weaker-performing ones?

© Pearson Education, Inc.

Should We Reward Good Grades with Money and Prizes?

NEA Today

May 2004

1   There is a wide **range** of perspectives about rewarding students for good grades. There also are differences in views about what is **appropriate** for teachers to do versus what parents should do.

Margo Ungricht, seventh-grade **English teacher, Lehi, Utah**

2   I believe we can offer prizes, food, money, or field trips to students for good grades. I don't see the difference between offering students prizes and money for good grades and having a "3.0 dance" or special **assembly**. A reward is a reward.

3   Most students who work hard for good grades would do it without the prizes and dances, so the prizes and money are simply an added bonus that they can choose to accept or **decline**.

4   Students who cheat, beg, badger, and whine for a good **grade** in order to earn money or prizes generally do not maintain a good **grade** for long. **Intrinsic values** usually have the upper hand in the end.

intrinsic values
those that are basic, essential, enduring

Tennille Jones-Lewis, high school guidance counselor, Alliance, Ohio

5   Students should be rewarded for good grades. I view school for students **similar** to the way I view a **job** for an adult, and I believe it's **appropriate** for parents to provide monetary rewards for good work and penalties for poor performance. If you are late for school, money is deducted. If you miss a day for illness, money is deducted. If your performance suffers, so will your pay. It gives students a chance to relate real-world experiences to school-related tasks.

6   This may not work for every family or for every child, but it's one of many things a parent can do.

7   My husband and I reward our eight nieces and nephews for earning good grades on their report cards. We give them $5 for each A and $3 for each B. Money is deducted for each C, D, and F. When their report cards come out, they call us immediately. They all do well in school and we want to show them we value their achievements, the same way a future employer will when they perform well in their jobs.

8   However, I don't think it is **appropriate** for teachers to use money as a reward. There's a fine line—a teacher giving the whole class a pizza party for a **job** well done could be **appropriate**, but a teacher giving money as a reward would cross the line.

Karen Barksdale, ninth-grade **English teacher, Memphis, Tennessee**

9   The only money and prizes a student should be given for good grades are the better money they will earn as **adults** and the prizes of self-esteem, pride, and **commitment** to attaining the highest level of their educational and intellectual development.

"Should We Reward Good Grades with Money and Prizes?" *NEA Today*, May 2004, p. 39. Reprinted by permission of the National Education Association.

10   Instead of the student asking, "What will you give me for trying?" we should be asking students, "What will you be giving yourself for your future if you apply yourself?" The ultimate reward for a good education is a secure and rewarding future.

Brenda Nelson, social worker, Barrington, Illinois

11 External rewards undermine students' natural eagerness to learn. When we offer kids money and prizes, we cheapen the value of learning. We have all seen kids who become so accustomed to **external** rewards that the presents, candy, or money are what they want, rather than the **academic** achievement itself. I recently overheard a teenage girl and her father arguing about how high her grades needed to be in order to get a car, and what kind of car it would be. The conversation had everything to do with the prize and nothing to do with learning.

12   Our ultimate goal is to **create** citizens who make decisions for the right reasons—not because someone is **dangling** a prize in front of them.

dangling
hanging or swinging loosely

Mary Bungert, special education teacher, Topeka, Kansas

13 When students receive good grades, it is because of a **team** effort. The parents in most cases have worked diligently in the evenings with homework, the paraprofessionals have put in time and effort, the teachers do the same. How do we determine who made that achievement possible?

14   We had a second-**grade** student who knew seven sight words when he came to our school. He was on **target** by the end of third grade. That happened because of his parents, classroom teacher, paraprofessionals, and the special education teacher who kept him focused, as well as the student's own **motivation** to learn. Who deserved a prize?

From Reading to Writing: Responding to Reading Using a Reflective Journal

Overview

Occasionally your instructor will ask you to reflect on what you have read by responding to the articles in writing. This type of informal writing assignment will enable you to comment on the author's main idea in a reflective way. Simply put, this assignment is about your own opinion of the topic, analysis of a controversial issue or claim, and pertinent questions you would like to formulate/raise about the main idea. This is a great opportunity for you to express your thoughts and ideas in an informal way.

ESL Annotation

1.12 ESL For some ESL students, the idea of keeping a free journal that will not be graded for the correctness of its content may come as a novel idea. Be sure to introduce this idea clearly.

Purpose

Responding to reading in informal writing serves many purposes. It improves your critical thinking skills, develops your fluency in the language, allows you to express emotional reactions to the original text, enables you to paraphrase and summarize the main ideas, and helps you explore your thoughts in writing. This type of assignment gets you to generate ideas in the language with less attention paid to mechanical aspects of writing. It goes without saying that the more you practice informal writing, the more you will learn to communicate clearly. Last but not least, keep in mind that reading and writing are active processes, and that you are actively participating in the process by responding to the articles you have discussed in class with your peers and instructor.

© Pearson Education, Inc.

What You Should Write About

Your instructor may assign one of the following informal writing tasks to you:

1. Give a thoughtful response to a pertinent question raised by you or your peers.
2. Raise questions about a difficult concept or a dubious claim made by the author.
3. Present your disagreement with the author's main idea.
4. Communicate with your instructor your own ideas about the topic that was discussed in class. Remember that the burden of clarity is on the writer, so be sure to express your ideas as precisely and clearly as possible.

Length

When doing this informal writing assignment, it is important that you focus more on quality than quantity. Your instructor can easily discern between a student who has made an honest effort to produce original thoughts and someone who has copied from various sources simply to fill the space. It is important to note that your instructor will be asking you to respond to the reading selections quite frequently, and he or she will become familiar with your writing style. Your instructor will be able to recognize when you have produced quality work and when you have put more effort into quantity. Sometimes your instructor may indicate a length, but generally speaking a paragraph or two is the minimum length of your response.

Writing Informally: Implications for Your Learning

The main purpose of this type of informal writing assignment is to help you improve your ability to communicate in writing. Since there is no restriction on your thoughts or the length of your response, you can consider this exercise as a casual conversation with your instructor who will provide you with constructive feedback on content and organization. Instead of worrying about grammar mistakes, focus on generating interesting and relevant ideas. This assignment gives you an opportunity to explore your thoughts in writing and gain from the invaluable experience. What follows are an editorial from the *New York Times* and several response letters written by newspaper readers. Read the editorial and the response letters carefully. For your first informal writing exercise, you will be asked to respond to an editorial from a leading newspaper.

READING

Reading Selection **5A**

Editorial

1.13 Flesch-Kincaid Grade Level 11.9

How to Educate Young Scientists

the *New York Times* **Editorial Board**

July 3, 2006

1   The United States could easily fall from its privileged perch in the **global** economy unless it does something about the horrendous state of science education at both the public school and university levels. That means finding ways to

Editorial, "How to Educate Young Scientists." From *The New York Times*, July 3, 2006. © 2006 The New York Times. All rights reserved. Used by permission and protected by the Copyright Laws of the United States. The printing, copying, redistribution, or retransmission of the Material without express written permission is prohibited. www.nytimes.com

enliven a dry and dispiriting style of science instruction that leads as many as half of the country's aspiring scientists to quit the field before they leave college.

2   The emerging **consensus** among educators is that students need early, engaging experiences in the lab and much more **mentoring** than most of them receive now to maintain their interest and inspire them to take up careers in the sciences.

3   Some universities have already realized the need for better ways of teaching. But this means revising an **incentive** system that has historically rewarded scientists for making discoveries and publishing **academic** papers, not for nurturing the next **generation** of great minds.

4   The Howard Hughes Medical Institute, the country's largest private supporter of science education, is well ahead of the curve, and has been pushing universities in this direction for several years under the leadership of Thomas Cech, a Nobel laureate. The **institute** recently announced its latest batch of 20 "million dollar professors," who will use their grant money to explore and expand **innovative** approaches to teaching science.

5   The **institute** has also awarded grants to 50 universities aimed at providing richer undergraduate science education as well as mentoring and early **research** experiences with working scientists. Many of the grants will be used partly to advertise the virtues of scientific study not just at universities but also in high schools and middle schools.

6   These programs send a powerful message at a time when the country needs to be paying attention to remaking science education. Congress, which has been casting for ways to address this problem, would do well to emulate them.

consensus
an opinion that everyone in a group agrees with or accepts

mentoring
a system of using people who have a lot of experience and knowledge to advise other people

incentive
something that encourages you to work harder, start new activities, etc.

innovative
using new ideas, methods, or inventions

READING

Reading Selection **5B**

Response Letters

Teaching the Joys of Science: Seven Letters in Response to "How to Educate Young Scientists"

The New York Times

July 9, 2006

1.14 Flesch-Kincaid Grade Level 10.8

Read the following seven responses to the editorial carefully, paying special attention to the various writing **styles** of each of the authors.

© Pearson Education, Inc.

LETTER 1

To the Editor:

1   I am fortunate that as a scientist I work with bright people from around the world. The problem with science in the United States is not a failure to educate and inspire, but a failure to retain. I have seen many young scientists come to this country for training and stay because of the opportunities, while many of my young American **colleagues** have left science to **pursue** more lucrative careers.

2   Science requires hard work, dedication, passion, persistence and perseverance. In a society where you can make tens of thousands of dollars flipping houses, we have to ask why would smart young people choose a career where success depends on working long hours for low wages, on the promise that one day, maybe, there will be **financial** rewards?

3   As long as jobs are plentiful, or until the system changes to make it financially beneficial for young people to stay in science, it will continue to be difficult to keep bright young Americans in this field.

CAITLIN E. HILL
Miami, July 3, 2006

The writer is a postdoctoral fellow in neuroscience.

LETTER 2

To the Editor:

4   As an English teacher for 30 years, I profess to be totally lacking in knowledge when it comes to science. But during high school, one science teacher, a nun in my private girls' school, did pique my interest for biology. Without any teacher-education courses or the help of "million-dollar professors," the nun taught the hands-on **method**: microscopes, beakers and all the **paraphernalia** whose names I have long forgotten.

5   At one point, studying herbs, I had a window box filled with basil, dill and thyme. Even today, whenever I pinch some basil for a dish, I think of Sister Anthilia and thank her for the science I know. It wasn't book learning that did it, it was digging my hands in the dirt.

PEG FISK
Port Chester, N.Y., July 3, 2006

LETTER 3

To the Editor:

6   While my second-**grade** students learn English and before they take their first science test, they learn to love science. They also learn two facts: science

paraphernalia
equipment necessary for a particular activity

is going to get much harder in the years ahead, and it is one of the few professions where you can make mistakes and still get paid.

7   Stronger science education efforts belong in the **primary** grades. College is too late.

VIRGINIA NELSON
Tigard, Ore., July 3, 2006

LETTER 4

To the Editor:

8   While I cannot **deny** that my college freshman physics course was dry, what really made people quit was the 30 **percent** failure rate in the class. While making the class easier would have improved retention, it clearly would not have provided a "richer undergraduate science education," as your editorial stated.

GABRIEL DESJARDINS
San Francisco, July 3, 2006

LETTER 5

To the Editor:

9   We would like to join *The New York Times* in its call to support and encourage innovative approaches to teaching science, a near obsession for many leaders in academia today. Slowing the steady **decline** in engineering enrollment is a **focus** for those of us in that field, too. But numbers are not the only **issues**.

10   We also need to do what we always have done best: produce more creative engineers. Infusing "**design** think" into undergraduate and graduate curriculums, for example, is an exciting **approach** by top engineering schools, and deserves wide **emulation**.

emulation
to imitate with an effort to equal

11   Our students start working with clients to develop solutions to real-world problems in their first year.

12   These include projects like planning methods for treating wastewater in developing countries; inventing devices to help people recover from strokes; and working with middle-school instructors to teach nanotechnology concepts.

13   Given opportunities to think beyond algorithms and equations, students **create**, rather than absorb, knowledge, which is **crucial** to success in our **global environment**.

JULIO M. OTTINO
Evanston, Ill., July 3, 2006

The writer is dean, Robert R. McCormick School of Engineering and Applied Science, Northwestern U.

© Pearson Education, Inc.

LETTER 6

To the Editor:

14   Science education may **benefit** from creative and engaging teaching, but a more profound problem stands in the way. Parents, teachers and educational administrators at all levels push a pervasive culture of building self-esteem, in which students are praised for thinking well of themselves instead of doing well.

15   As a result, many students are uncomfortable if they are told that their answer is wrong, whether it's a spelling, recitation of historical facts or **complex** science problem.

16   Studying science requires working through many problem-solving tasks with right and wrong answers. So until students stop being afraid of getting wrong answers, they will drop out of science disproportionately.

17   To overcome this problem, we must revamp teaching practices from elementary school through the university level, and support those who provide clear feedback on right and wrong answers, give timed tests that **promote** quick thinking about **complex issues** and **grade** students who master **academic** skills better than students who master the art of feeling good about themselves.

REBECCA A. STATES
Bayside, Queens, July 4, 2006

The writer is an associate professor in the **physical** therapy department at Long Island University.

LETTER 7

To the Editor:

18   Your **comments** about the small number of scientists coming from our educational system **focus** only on teaching **strategies**. As a science educator for the last 30 years, I appreciate the interest in exploring the most engaging, **dynamic** and effective methods to present science.

19   What you do not mention is the American **cultural** attitude toward science. "American Idol" is a **cultural phenomenon**. The average salary for a **major** league baseball player is greater than $2 million. The latest celebrity baby or **tryst** is news. Nobel Prize winners often get an article only in larger newspapers like yours. In Asia they are celebrities. Without such **cultural** change, I see little hope that large numbers of students will do the hard work that is necessary to be a successful scientist.

JOHN-MICHAEL CALDARO
Ballston Spa, N.Y., July 3, 2006

tryst
love affair

Informal Writing Exercise: Read an Editorial and Respond

Read an editorial from a leading American newspaper on an educational issue and write a brief response to the editor. When you have finished writing your response paper, submit it to your instructor for feedback on content and organization. Begin your letter with:

> ***To the Editor:***

> _____

> _____

> _____

> _____

Connecting Reading Skills with Standardized Testing

Interpreting Meaning from Context

In most U.S. states college students are often mandated to take standardized reading tests. Typically, a standardized reading test includes a series of reading passages, each of which is followed by a set of multiple choice questions designed to assess your reading skill ability. It is essential that you learn to recognize and easily distinguish between the different types of questions that are offered on standardized reading exams. In each chapter of the book we will examine the various ways questions related to a particular reading skill are worded. Below we can see some sample questions that focus on *determining the meaning of words used in the passage.*

- As used in line # . . .
- The author uses the phrase to describe . . .
- In the passage, the word/phrase means . . .
- In the fifth paragraph the word _____ could be replaced with _____
- A synonym for the word _____ in line 15 is . . .
- An antonym for the word _____ in the fifth paragraph is . . .
- The term _____ in line 17 refers to . . .
- In the sentence " . . . ", the word *X* means:

Most words have multiple meanings, so be sure to refer to the sentence in which the word appears. Don't simply assume, "Oh, I already know that word." You want to be extra sure to choose the definition of the word used in the context of the reading passage.

To successfully zero in on the meaning in context, focus not only on the sentence in which the word in focus lies, but the sentences that come immediately before and after it. These nearby sentences can provide the context, which can lead you to the meaning of the term in question. Review the helpful hints in the Skill Focus: Determining Meaning from Context section of this chapter (pages 14–27) to guide you toward mastering vocabulary questions on standardized exams.

Teaching Tip:
Students benefit greatly from familiarizing themselves with the wording of standardized test questions.

© Pearson Education, Inc.

Richard T. Vacca

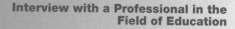

Profession: Professor Emeritus, Kent State University

How did you choose your current profession?

As a child who was a struggling reader and learner in the elementary grades, becoming a high school teacher and, later, a college professor was the last thing I ever dreamed would happen to me. I was the quintessential late bloomer. I had two or three teachers who believed in me. My basketball coach was one of them. He taught me never to give up, even though that was often my inclination in high school when the going got tough. By the time I was a senior in high school, I knew I wanted to be a basketball coach. To become one in the 1960s I knew I had to become a teacher. That was my initial motivation. In college, I was an average student. But I never gave up on my dream. Once I became a teacher, I knew this profession was my calling. I wanted to help other students who struggled with reading and learning as I did. Ironically, I never did become a basketball coach.

How did you prepare to reach your goal of becoming a professor?

I don't think I ever consciously prepared myself. I just began to believe in myself and my abilities. I became a reader by reading. I became a writer by writing. When I went to college, I chose English as my major, because I knew I could succeed at that academic discipline. As I developed confidence in myself, I began to identify myself as a "student" in the truest sense of the word. Confidence and competence go hand in hand.

What did you struggle with most when preparing to become a professor?

I struggled most with "sticking with it" when the going got tough. I wanted to bail out on a number of occasions. When I was having trouble with my doctoral studies, especially with statistics, I wanted to give up, but I stuck with it.

How did you get through this struggle?

My wife bought me a poster to hang in my study area of a seagull flying effortlessly over water. The caption on the poster read, "They can because they think they can." I joined a stats study group, which helped enormously. I spent hours reading and rereading 5 or 6 pages of statistics text until I understood the underlying concepts in the course. I asked questions. I hung in there and I thought a lot about my basketball coach and his belief in me; my wife's belief in me. I began to believe in myself as a doctoral student. The rest is history.

What do you enjoy most about your work?

I enjoy interacting with students and teachers: teaching by example; modeling the strategies I want teachers to use with students. I enjoy reaching thousands of teachers through my writings and textbooks.

What advice do you have for a student considering a career in teaching?

Those who enter teaching, and stick with it, view their profession as a calling, much as I did more than 40 years ago when I entered the profession. Teaching is one of the most demanding yet underappreciated professions in this country. My advice to students is the same as the advice my basketball coach gave me: Never give up on your dream.

In your opinion what were the three most interesting points made by the interviewee? Discuss your choices with the class.

- _____
  _____

- _____
  _____

- _____
  _____

Textbook Application

Teaching Tip:
Students will be working with subject-based textbooks throughout their academic career. Navigating text content is a very useful developmental skill and will help prepare students for academic coursework.

In each chapter of this book, you will have the opportunity to read extensively from an introductory chapter of a 100-level college course textbook. The ability to comprehend content-area texts is a critical ingredient in overall success in college courses. Read the following section from Chapter 1 of *Foundations of American Education* and try to accurately answer the multiple-choice questions, which are labeled by the topic you have studied. You will notice that the key points in the reading are highlighted to help you navigate the passage easily.

READING

Reading Selection **6**

Textbook Reading

1.15 Flesch-Kincaid Grade Level 1

Teaching in a Changing World

Chapter 1 of *Foundations of American Education*

As you read this book you will find many different perspectives on education as well as much information about our changing world, especially those **aspects** that **affect** the lives of educators and their schools. As an aspiring teacher, you are now hopefully in the **process** of developing your own tentative perspectives on what the **job** of teaching entails and what you need to know and be able to do to become an excellent and successful teacher. This **chapter** also will help you learn more about successfully completing your teacher education program and **eventually** finding a position as an educator and about the salary and benefits that you may receive. Answering these and related important questions about the profession of teaching are the topics of **Chapter** 1.

Although people hold many different perspectives on education, most agree that teaching is a profession that is critical to the well-being of youth and of society. Many students **indicate** that they have chosen teaching as a career because they care about children and youth. Teaching requires caring, but it also requires competence in the subject being taught and in the teaching of that subject. Teachers' knowledge and skills should lead to the ultimate goal of successful student learning.

Educators must **undergo stringent** assessments and meet high standards to **ensure** high quality in the teaching profession. The teaching profession includes at least three stages of quality **assurance**, beginning, most commonly, with college-level teacher preparation programs, such as the one in which you are likely now enrolled. Next, state teacher licensing systems give the public **assurance** that teachers are qualified and competent to do their work as educators. The third stage of continuing **professional** development is tied to retaining the state license and seeking national certification. Each of these stages is **accompanied** by performance assessments to determine whether individuals are qualified for the important **job** of teaching.

stringent
very strict

Reflection is one of the important characteristics of successful teachers. Professionals who reflect on and analyze their own teaching are **involved** in a **process** that is critical to improving as an educator. Individuals who are making a **commitment** to teaching, whether lifelong or short-term, should consider the responsibilities and expectations of a teaching career. In this **chapter**, you will begin exploring the realities of what it means to be a teacher.

In addition to these concepts, **Chapter** 1 presents a number of big ideas about teaching. These include the facts that education is extremely important in our society, that educators are members of an **established** profession, that educators are generally well respected and valued by the public, and that the future **job** market for educators is **complex** but promising.

© Pearson Education, Inc.

From James A. Johnson, et al., *Foundations of American Education*, 14th ed., pp. 4–15. Published by Allyn and Bacon/Merrill Education, Boston, MA. Copyright © 2008 by Pearson Education. Reprinted by permission of the publisher.

Today's Teachers

More than three million teachers provide the instructional leadership for public and private schools in the United States. Today's new teachers must meet rigorous national and state standards for entering the profession that did not exist a decade ago. Requirements for entering teacher education programs in colleges and universities are now more stringent than admission requirements for most other professions. **Grade** point averages of 3.0 and higher are becoming more common requirements for admission; tests and other assessments must be passed before admission, at the completion of a program, and for state licensure. Clearly, not everyone can teach. Teaching is becoming a profession that attracts the best and brightest college students into its ranks.

Teacher candidates today are diverse in age and work experience. Some of you are eighteen to twenty-two years old, the **traditional** age of college students, but still more of you are nontraditional students who are older and have worked for a number of years in other jobs or professions. Some of your classmates may have worked as teachers' aides in classrooms for years. Others may be switching careers from the armed forces, engineering, retail management, or public relations. Welcome to a profession in which new teachers represent such wonderfully diverse work experiences, as well as varying educational, **cultural**, and **economic** backgrounds.

The Importance of Teachers to Society

Society has great expectations for its teachers. "Nine out of ten Americans believe the best way to lift student achievement is to **ensure** a qualified teacher in every classroom," according to a national **survey**.[1] In addition to guiding students' **academic** achievement, teachers have some responsibility

*Teaching is a challenging, **complex**, and demanding profession that draws from many diverse groups in the United States.*

for students' social and **physical** development. They are expected to prepare an educated citizenry that is informed about the many **issues** critical to maintaining a democracy. They help students learn to work together and try to instill the values that are critical to a just and caring society. Teachers are also asked to prepare children and youth with the knowledge and skills necessary to work in an **information age**.

Given these challenging responsibilities, teaching is one of the most important careers in a democratic society. Although critics of our education system sometimes give the impression that there is a lack of public support for schools and teachers, the public now ranks teaching as the profession that provides the most important **benefit** to society. Public perceptions of the importance of teaching have improved over the past years.[2] In fact, respondents to a **survey** ranked teachers first by more than a three-to-one margin over physicians, nurses, businesspeople, lawyers, journalists, politicians, and accountants, as shown in Figure 1.1.

Teachers were also given a vote of confidence in a July 2002 Gallup Poll that asked people to **indicate** if most of the people in certain groups could be trusted or if you can't be too careful in dealing with them. Their responses are shown in Figure 1.2. This public trust should be both encouraging and perhaps a bit frightening to you as a future educator—encouraging because you will be entering a highly regarded and trusted **professional** group and frightening because you will be responsible for helping to uphold this public trust.

information age

The current age in which information and its management are critical to education and societal advancement.

FIGURE 1.1

Professions That Provide the Most Benefit to Society According to **Survey** Respondents

Source: Based on data from Recruiting New Teachers, Inc., *The Essential Profession: A National Survey of Public Attitudes toward Teaching, Educational Opportunity and School Reform.* Belmont, MA: Author, 1998.

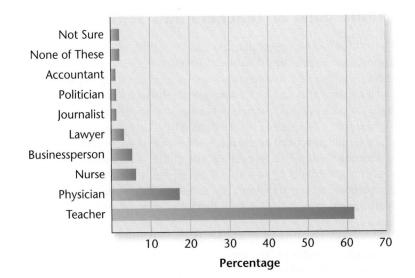

© Pearson Education, Inc.

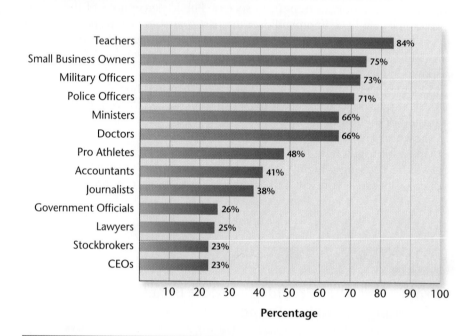

FIGURE 1.2

Teachers Get America's Vote of Confidence
You may not make as much as a CEO or a pro baseball player, but your stock has a lot more currency than theirs in the eyes of the American public.

In a July 2002 Gallup Poll, Americans were asked if most of the people in certain groups could be trusted or if you can't be too careful in dealing with them. Their responses showed teachers on top.

Source: Gallup Poll, July 2002, as reported in *NEA Today,* October 2002, p. 9.

Group	Percentage
Teachers	84%
Small Business Owners	75%
Military Officers	73%
Police Officers	71%
Ministers	66%
Doctors	66%
Pro Athletes	48%
Accountants	41%
Journalists	38%
Government Officials	26%
Lawyers	25%
Stockbrokers	23%
CEOs	23%

The Public View of Teachers and Schools

Teachers and the public agree that the quality of the teaching staff is of **primary** importance in selecting a school.[3] Parents, guardians, families, and students know who the effective teachers are in a school and will do everything possible to **ensure** that their children are in those teachers' classes. At the same time, they know the teachers who are not as effective, and they steer their children into other classes if possible. They know the value of an effective teacher to the **potential academic** success of their children.

The **annual** Gallup Poll **survey** on the public's **attitudes** toward public schools asks respondents to grade schools in both their local **area** and the nation as a whole. Figure 1.3 shows the results of this recent survey, which indicates that parents generally give high grades to schools, especially so for their local schools.

This same **annual** Gallup Poll asks citizens to **indicate** the most serious problems facing our schools. The results of the survey are shown in Figure 1.4. Parents in their combined opinions view discipline, getting good teachers, and overcrowding as **major** school problems.

No nation can remain free which does not recognize the importance of our education. Our public schools are the backbone of American life and character.

Samuel M. Lindsay

FIGURE 1.3

The Public's Opinion of Public Schools

Source: Lowell C. Rose and Alec M. Gallup, "The 37th Annual Phi Delta Kappa/Gallup Poll of the Public's Attitudes toward the Public Schools," *Phi Delta Kappan* (September 2005), p. 45. Reprinted by permission of Phi Delta Kappan.

Students are often given the grades of A, B, C, D, and FAIL to denote the quality of their work. Suppose the public schools themselves, in your community, were graded in the same way. What grade would you give the public schools here—A, B, C, D, or FAIL?

	National Totals '05 %	National Totals '04 %	No Children in School '05 %	No Children in School '04 %	Public School Parents '05 %	Public School Parents '04 %
A & B	48	47	45	42	57	61
A	12	13	9	11	20	17
B	36	34	36	31	37	44
C	29	33	29	37	29	24
D	9	10	9	9	8	10
FAIL	5	4	4	3	5	5
Don't know	9	6	13	9	1	*

*Less than one-half of 1%.

Curiously, the public and teachers do not agree on all of the changes necessary to improve schools, as shown in Table 1.1. Teachers would like to see more parental involvement, **whereas** the public sees discipline and stricter rules as most important. Both groups agree on the importance of having more teachers and/or reducing class size. Over half of the respondents in

FIGURE 1.4

The Public's View of Problems in Schools

Source: Lowell C. Rose and Alec M. Gallup, "The 37th Annual Phi Delta Kappa/Gallup Poll of the Public's Attitudes toward the Public Schools," *Phi Delta Kappan* (September 2005), p. 44. Reprinted by permission of Phi Delta Kappan.

What do you think are the biggest problems the public schools of your community must deal with?

	National Totals '05 %	'04 %	'03 %	No Children in School '05 %	'04 %	'03 %	Public School Parents '05 %	'04 %	'03 %
Lack of financial support/ funding/money	20	21	25	19	22	26	21	20	24
Overcrowded schools	11	10	14	9	9	12	15	13	16
Lack of discipline, more control	10	10	16	12	10	17	8	8	13
Use of drugs/dope	9	7	9	9	7	10	8	7	7

© Pearson Education, Inc.

TABLE 1.1	What Would You Change to Improve the Public Schools in Your Community?		
		Public (percent)	**Teachers (percent)**
Discipline/more control/stricter rules		12	6
More teachers/smaller class size		10	12
Funding		5	8
Better/more qualified teachers		7	*
Higher pay for teachers		3	5
More parent involvement		3	18
Prayer/God back in schools		4	*
Security		4	*
Academic standards/better education		3	2
Dress code/uniforms		3	*
More/updated equipment/books/computers		2	3
Curriculum/more offered		2	*

* = Less than 1 percent.

Source: Adapted from Carol A. Langdon and Nick Vesper, "The Sixth Phi Delta Kappa Poll of Teachers' Attitudes toward the Public Schools," *Phi Delta Kappan, 81*(8) (April 2000), pp. 607–611. Reprinted by permission of Phi Delta Kappan.

another **survey** were concerned about student drug use, school violence, student drinking, lack of parental involvement, teenage pregnancy, and students' lack of basic skills. They were less concerned about large classes and poor-quality teachers. Latino and African American respondents were more likely than others to find the lack of teacher quality a serious and **widespread** problem. Respondents also affirmed the desire to "keep the **guarantee** of a free public education for every child."[4] These differences between teacher and parent opinions on school problems again show that different groups hold differing perspectives on education.

Who Teaches?

Teachers should represent the **diversity** of the nation. However, white females are overrepresented in the teaching force, particularly in early childhood and elementary schools. Teachers come from varied backgrounds and

The common teacher is not common at all. He (or she) is bulging with talent, with **energy**, and with understanding. What we human teachers have to give, **ultimately**, is ourselves—our own love for life, and for our subjects, and our ability to respond to the **personal** concerns of our students.

Terry Borton, **Reach, Touch, Teach**

*In addition to being passionate about helping learners, teachers are good managers and take time to collaborate with their **colleagues**.*

hold a wide variety of views. Some are Democrats, some Republicans, and some members of the Reform and other parties. Some belong to unions, but others don't. They hold a variety of religious views. Because of these many differences, it is difficult to generalize about educators in the United States. However, some of the similarities and differences among teachers may help you to understand the current teaching profession.

PROFILE OF U.S. TEACHERS

Although demographic **data** are **elusive** and constantly changing, the following snapshot of educators in the United States should help you get an idea of the profile of U.S. teachers. The United States has about 2.7 million public school teachers, about 400,000 private school teachers, and about 932,000 college and university faculty members. Over 60 **percent** of the teachers work at the elementary school level. In addition to teachers, our schools have about 411,000 administrative and education professionals. Approximately 1.25 million teachers' aides, clerks and secretaries, and service workers staff the nation's public schools. There are another roughly one million education-related jobs, including education specialists in industry, instructional technologists in the **military**, museum educators, and training consultants in the business world. Altogether, there are approximately five million educators in the United States, making education one of the largest professions in the country.

REMAINING IN THE PROFESSION

A relatively high percentage of classroom teachers **eventually** decide that teaching is not the profession they wish to **pursue**. It is estimated that approximately 20 **percent** of the new teachers hired annually are not teaching three years later. Teachers leave the classroom for a number of reasons. Some decide to return to school full time for an advanced degree. Others decide to **pursue** another career that might be more satisfying or pays a higher salary. Other reasons for leaving teaching are related to poor working conditions in schools, including lack of administrative support, **perceived** student problems, and little chance for upward mobility.

Parental involvement ranks right up there with smaller class size and improved student discipline at the top of the list of (NEA) members' professional wish list.

Reg Weaver, NEA President

Instead of asking why women lag behind men in mathematics, we might ask the following: Why do men lag behind women in elementary school teaching, early childhood education, nursing, full-time parenting, and like activities? Is there something wrong with men or with schools that this state of affairs persists?

Nel Noddings

elusive
hard to define

© Pearson Education, Inc.

Most teachers enter and remain in their profession because of a desire to work with young people.

Like all other professionals, teachers become accomplished through experience. Most states do not grant a **professional** license to teachers until they have worked for at least three years. Teachers cannot seek national certification from the National Board for **Professional** Teaching Standards (NBPTS) until they have taught for three years. When teachers leave the profession in their first few years of practice, schools are losing an important developing resource. Induction and mentoring programs for new teachers increase the numbers of teachers who remain in the classroom. Good **professional** development programs for teachers such as **induction** programs also help to retain new teachers. When you search for your first teaching **job**, find out whether the

induction

The first one to three years of full-time teaching.

mentoring

An experienced professional helping a less experienced colleague.

school district provides induction, mentors, and **professional** development, especially for beginning teachers. These are services that help teachers improve their skills as well as their chances of being successful teachers who remain teachers over a longer **period** of time.

Many schools now have a system that provides **mentoring** among teachers. This peer mentoring system is designed to **facilitate** teachers helping one another. As part of a new teacher induction program, many of these schools assign an experienced master teacher to mentor beginning teachers.

Teachers Needed

Many **factors** influence the number of teachers that a school district needs each year. The number of students in schools, the **ratio** of teachers to students in classrooms, **immigration** patterns, and **migration** from one school district to another influence the demand for teachers. The supply of teachers depends on the numbers of new teachers licensed, teachers who retired or left the **previous** year, and teachers returning to the workforce.

Sometimes the supply is greater than the demand, but various estimates for the next decade **indicate** a demand for new teachers beyond the number being prepared in colleges and universities. The United States does not have a general teacher shortage. The problem is the **distribution** of teachers. School districts with good teaching conditions and high salaries do not face teacher shortages. However, inner cities and rural areas too often do not have **adequate** numbers of qualified and licensed teachers. There also are greater shortages of teachers in parts of the country with increasing populations, such as states in the Southwest.

TEACHER SUPPLY

The supply of new teachers in a given year consists primarily of two groups: new teacher graduates and former teacher graduates who were not employed as teachers during the **previous** year. Not all college graduates who prepared to teach actually teach. Generally, only about half the college graduates who have completed teacher education programs actually take teaching positions in the first few years after graduation.

It is estimated that nearly half the teachers hired by the typical school district are first-time teachers. A third are experienced teachers who have moved from other school districts or from other jobs within the district. Experienced teachers reentering the field make up the remainder of the new hires. Unfortunately, not all teachers who are hired have been even minimally prepared to teach before they take charge of a classroom. Over a fourth of newly hired teachers are not qualified for the beginning license to teach. Some new hires do not have a license; others have a **temporary**, provisional, or emergency license.

NEW TEACHERS   A number of new teachers are not recent college graduates. They are people who are changing careers or retirees from the **military** or business. These older new teachers with years of work experience often have completed **alternative** pathways into teaching through school-based graduate programs that build on their **prior** experiences. These teachers bring a different **perspective** on education to their teaching positions.

Still other new teachers have no preparation to teach; some do not even have a college degree. More often they have a degree in an academic **area** such as chemistry or history but have not studied teaching and learning or participated in clinical practices in schools. A number of states and school districts allow these individuals to teach with only a few weeks of training in the summer. Participants in these programs are more likely to be dissatisfied with their preparation than are teachers who have completed either regular or nontraditional programs for teacher preparation. They often have difficulty planning the curriculum, managing the classroom, and diagnosing students' learning needs, especially in their first years of teaching. Individuals who enter the profession through this path leave teaching at a higher rate than other teachers.

More than 200,000 new teachers graduate from colleges each year. Of them, about one-third never teach; about one-third teach for only a few years; and only the remaining one-third make teaching a career.

© Pearson Education, Inc.

The number of school-age children in the United States is expected to increase to 54.2 million by 2009.

RETURNING TEACHERS   A number of licensed teachers drop out of the profession for a time but return later in life. These teachers constitute about 20 **percent** of the new hires each year. Therefore, when you finish your teacher education program, you will be competing for teaching positions not only with other new graduates but also with experienced teachers who are returning to the classroom or moving from one school district to another.

TEACHER DEMAND

The demand for teachers in the United States varies considerably from time to time, from place to place, from subject to subject, and from **grade** level to **grade** level. One of the **major factors** related to the demand for teachers is the number of school-age children, which can be projected into the future on the basis of birthrates.

The projected demand for K–12 teachers is shown in Figure 1.5. Many teachers will be retiring over the next decade, raising even further the number of new and reentering teachers needed to staff the nation's schools. As you plan your teaching career, you will want to consider a number of **factors** such as salary, benefits, cost of living, workload, and so forth, that influence the demand for teachers. They may influence decisions you make about the subjects you will teach and the **area** of the country where you will teach.

STUDENT-TO-TEACHER RATIOS   Obviously, one measure of a teacher's workload is class size. The number of students taught by a teacher varies considerably from school to school and from state to state. Elementary teachers generally have more students in a class than secondary teachers, but secondary teachers have five to seven classes each day. Figure 1.6 shows average student-to-teacher ratios in public and private schools in the United States.

The demand for teachers has increased, in part, because some states and school districts are limiting the student-to-teacher **ratio**, especially in the **primary** grades. In large school districts, lowering the student-to-teacher **ratio** by even

FIGURE 1.5

Relative Demand by Field

Source: "Relative Demand by Field," *2006 AAEE Job Search Handbook.* Columbus, OH: American Association for Employment in Education, Inc., 2006, p. 15. Reprinted with permission.

Fields with Considerable Shortage (5.00–4.21)

Emotional/Behavior Disorders	4.39
Severe/Profound Disabilities	4.37
Visually Impaired	4.33
Multicategorical	4.33
Mild/Moderate Disabilities	4.33
Learning Disability	4.29
Hearing Impaired	4.25
Mathematics Education	4.22

Fields with Some Shortage (4.20–3.41)

Mental Retardation	4.18
Dual Certificate (Gen./Spec.)	4.17
Physics	4.16
Early Childhood Special Education	4.13
Chemistry	4.06
Bilingual Education	3.98
Languages—Spanish	3.95
Speech Pathologist	3.89
English as a Second Language	3.88
Earth/Physical	3.80
Physical Therapist	3.78
Biology	3.76
General Science	3.74
Audiologist	3.65
School Nurse	3.60
Technology Education	3.55
High School Principal	3.53
Middle School Principal	3.51
School Psychologist	3.45
Superintendent	3.44
Elementary Principal	3.43

Fields with Balanced Supply and Demand (3.40–2.61)

Home Economics/Consumer Science	3.38
Agriculture	3.34
Reading	3.32
Computer Science Education	3.25
Library Science/Media Technology	3.24
Languages—French	3.20
Counselor	3.19
Music—Instrumental	3.16
Gifted/Talented Education	3.16
Occupational Therapist	3.13
Music—Vocal	3.13
Elementary—Middle	3.13
Languages—Classics	3.11
Speech Education	3.10
Business Manager	3.10
School Social Worker	3.09
Music—General	3.06
Languages—German	3.02
Driver Education/Traffic Safety	3.00
Languages—Japanese	3.00
Curriculum Director	3.00
English/Language Arts	2.97
Business Education	2.96
Human Resources Director	2.96
Elementary—Intermediate	2.84
Dance Education	2.80
Theatre/Drama	2.78
Journalism Education	2.76
Elementary—Pre-Kindergarten	2.74
Art/Visual Education	2.70
Elementary—Kindergarten	2.67

Fields with Some Surplus (2.60–1.81)

Elementary—Primary	2.58
Health Education	2.46
Social Studies Education	2.43
Physical Education	2.42

Fields with Considerable Surplus (1.80–1.00)

None	

From preliminary data supplied by survey respondents. In some instances, the averages are based on limited input and total reliability is not assured.

Demand codes: 5.00–4.21 = Considerable shortage; 4.20–3.41 = Some Shortage; 3.40–2.61 = Balanced; 2.60–1.81 = Some Surplus; 1.80–1.00 = Considerable Surplus

one student creates a demand for many more teachers. Statewide **initiatives** to reduce the **ratio** have an even greater **impact** on the number of teachers needed.

LOCATION OF THE SCHOOL DISTRICT   Even within a given metropolitan **area**, population shifts may be causing one school district to grow rapidly, build new schools, and hire new teachers because of new housing developments,

© Pearson Education, Inc.

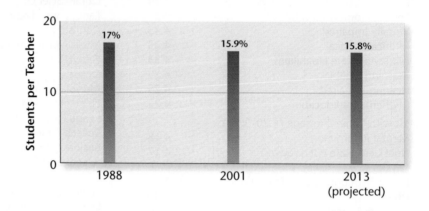

FIGURE 1.6

Pupil/Teacher Ratio in Elementary and Secondary Schools, with Middle Alternative Projections: Selected Years

Source: U.S. Department of Education, National Center for Education Statistics (NCES): Common Core of Data surveys, various years.

attrition rates

the rate of which teachers leave the field

while a neighboring school district is closing schools and reducing its number of teachers. Nevertheless, the greatest shortages are usually in urban schools with large proportions of low-**income** and culturally and linguistically diverse populations. Some teachers do not want to teach in large urban school districts because of poor working conditions in many schools and relatively low salaries as compared to schools in the wealthier suburbs. Many other teachers believe that teaching in a large city is challenging and fulfilling, with many advantages.

Urban schools are more likely than others to be staffed by unprepared teachers who have not met the qualifications for a state license. New, inexperienced teachers are disproportionately represented in the schools that need the best teachers. **Attrition rates** for new teachers in these districts are high in the first five years of teaching, leading to the **constant** need for replacements. To address this problem, some states have scholarships and loan-forgiveness programs to encourage teacher candidates to work in these high-demand areas.

Student enrollment also varies depending on the part of the country. By 2009, increases of more than 15 **percent** are expected in Arizona, Idaho, Nevada, and New Mexico; decreases are expected in most midwestern and northeastern states. Student enrollment in the District of Columbia, Maine, North Dakota, and West Virginia is projected to decrease by 7 to 12 **percent**.[5]

Almost all teachers can find a teaching position if they are willing to move to a place where jobs are **available**. One of the problems is that new teachers often want to remain close to home, which is more likely to be in small towns and suburban areas. To attract teachers to areas with teaching shortages, some school districts are offering signing bonuses and paying moving expenses. Others are exploring **strategies** to offer teachers housing and favorable mortgages.

TEACHING FIELD SHORTAGES   Teacher shortages are more severe in some fields than others. For **instance**, the number of students diagnosed with various disabilities has increased considerably over the last decade and now totals more than five million throughout the country. As a percentage of the total public school enrollment, the number of students requiring special education has risen considerably in recent years. Consequently, most school districts report the need for more special education teachers.

There is also a critical shortage of bilingual teachers. The need for bilingual teachers is no longer limited to large urban areas and the southwestern states. Immigrant families with children have now settled in cities and rural areas across the Midwest and Southeast. The projected demographics for the country **indicate** a growing number of students with limited-English skills, requiring more bilingual and English as a second language (ESL) teachers than are **available** today.

Licensed mathematics and science teachers are **prime** candidates for **job** openings in many school districts. One of the problems in secondary schools especially is that teachers may have a state license but too often not in the **academic area** they are **assigned** to teach. The National Commission on Teaching and America's Future reported that nearly one-fourth of all secondary teachers do not have even a college minor in their main teaching field. This is especially true for mathematics teachers. Among teachers who teach a second subject, about one-third are unlicensed in that field and about one-half lack a minor.

Teachers receive these out-of-field assignments when teachers with the **appropriate academic** credentials are not **available**. Sometimes the assignments are made to retain teachers whose jobs have been eliminated as enrollments **shift** and schools are closed. The tragedy is that students suffer as a result. It is difficult to teach what you do not know. The **federal legislation** commonly referred to as the No Child Left Behind Act (NCLB) is designed to significantly reduce this out-of-field teacher assignment problem in the near future.

Reading Comprehension Check

Supporting Details

1. In the introduction to the chapter, what skills are mentioned as required for teaching?
   a. caring and strictness
   b. caring and competence in the subject being taught
   c. competence in the subject being taught and strictness
   d. only caring

Supporting Details

2. Reflection is considered an important characteristic of successful teachers because
   a. reflection helps you relax in the classroom.
   b. reflection is a requirement.
   c. through reflection one can improve their teaching over time.
   d. teaching can get boring.

Vocabulary

3. In the first paragraph of the section entitled Today's Teachers we read: "Today's new teachers must meet rigorous national and state standards

© Pearson Education, Inc.

for entering the profession . . ." The word *rigorous* could be replaced by the word

a. healthy.   c. consistent.
b. demanding.   d. declining.

Statistical Analysis

4. Read the section The Importance of Teachers to Society. What percentage of Americans believe that the best way to lift student achievement is to have quality teachers in every classroom?

   a. 100 percent   c. half
   b. 75 percent   d. 90 percent

Graphic Analaysis

5. Figure 1.1 illustrates that

   a. accountants make very low salaries.
   b. teachers receive more benefits than do physicians.
   c. public perception of the importance of teaching is very high.
   d. none of the above

Graphic Analysis

6. Figure 1.2 shows that

   a. most Americans put their trust in lawyers.
   b. teachers are rarely trusted.
   c. teachers have the trust of the American people.
   d. journalists make less money than teachers.

Vocabulary

7. Read the quote by Samuel M. Lindsay in the sidebar. In the sentence "Our public schools are the backbone of American life and character," a synonym for the word *backbone* is

   a. behind.   c. vertebrae.
   b. moral fiber.   d. outline.

Negative Question

8. Figure 1.4 does not indicate that

   a. public school parents are more concerned than those without children in school about school overcrowding.
   b. those without children in school placed lack of discipline higher on their list of concerns.
   c. lack of financial support was considered the greatest concern.
   d. use of drugs is the most common concern for both groups.

Supporting Details

9. Read the section Who Teaches. According to the text, there is an overrepresentation of which group among teachers?

   a. black males   c. white females
   b. Asians   d. women

Negative Question

10. Read the section Remaining in the Profession. Which is not listed as a reason some teachers leave the profession?

a. to pursue other careers

b. poor working conditions in schools

c. to return to school for an advanced degree

(d.) to get more involved in their family life

Vocabulary

11. In the second paragraph of the section Remaining in the Profession, we read "Most states do not grant a professional license to teachers until . . ." In this context, the word *grant* means

a. delay.   c. scholarship.

(b.) allow.   d. deny.

Supporting Details

12. According to the text, what role does mentoring among teachers play?

a. It helps teachers climb up the pay scale.

b. It facilitates teachers helping one another.

c. It gives new teachers a chance to learn from more experienced ones.

(d.) both b and c

Supporting Details

13. Read the section New Teachers. What kinds of problems do teachers with only a summer of teacher training often experience?

(a.) They may have difficulty with curriculum planning and classroom management.

b. They may not know how to use a textbook.

c. They may not know how to work within the rules of the system.

d. none of the above

Supporting Details

14. Read the section Location of the School District. What is one strategy schools use to attract new teachers who do not live in the area?

a. They give new teachers a neighborhood orientation.

b. They give new teachers their choice of classroom.

(c.) They offer signing bonuses and pay moving expenses.

d. Most new teachers prefer to remain close to home.

Inference

15. Read the section Teaching Field Shortages. It is implied that there is a shortage of bilingual teachers due to

a. a lack of financial support.

b. a lack of bilingual speakers in the United States.

c. a lack of interest among educators to teach in this area.

(d.) an increase in the number of immigrant students with limited English language proficiency in certain regions of the country.

© Pearson Education, Inc.

READING

Reading Selection **7**

Additional Reading

Memoir

1.16 Flesch-Kincaid Grade Level 10.6

Excerpt from Teacher Man

Pre-Reading Questions

Frank McCourt, a former public school teacher, writes about an all-American tradition, the "Excuse Note." Before reading the memoir piece, discuss the questions below, which relate to the theme of the passage.

Collaboration

1. Have you ever made up an excuse to your teacher for not turning in an assignment on time? What types of excuses have you used?

2. Some teachers are unhappy about parents who knowingly defend their child's noncompliance with the rules of the classroom. They may write excuse notes for their child's lateness or incomplete assignments. What is the role of the parent in cases where a child is delinquent?

3. How much control does one teacher really have over a class over 20-plus students? In your opinion, who has the ultimate power over students' classroom behavior—teachers, parents or the students themselves?

From *Teacher Man,* Frank McCourt

(New York Scribner, 2005), pp. 83–87.

hostile
feeling or showing ill will

1   I said to one boy, Did your mother really write this note, Danny? He was defensive, **hostile**. Yeah, my mother wrote it. It's a nice note, Danny. She writes well. McKee students were proud of their mothers and only a lout would let that compliment pass without thanks. He said thanks, and returned to his seat. I could have asked him if the note was his but I knew better. I liked him and didn't want him sullen in the third row. He'd tell classmates I suspected him and that might make them sullen, too, because they'd been forging excuse notes since they learned to write and years later they don't want to be bothered by teachers suddenly getting moral.

2   An excuse note is just a part of school life. Everyone knows they're fiction, so what's the big deal? Parents getting kids out of the house in the morning have little time for writing notes that they know will wind up in the school garbage anyway. They're so harried they'll say, Oh, you need an excuse note for yesterday, honey? Write it yourself and I'll sign it. They sign it without even looking at it and the sad part is they don't know what they're missing. If they could read those notes they'd discover their kids are **capable** of the finest American prose: fluent, imaginative, clear, **dramatic**, fantastic, focused, persuasive, useful. I threw Mikey's note into a desk drawer along with dozens of others: notes written on every size and color of paper,

Reprinted with the permission of Scribner, a Division of Simon & Schuster, Inc., from Teacher Man: A Memoir by Frank McCourt. Copyright © 2005 by Green Peril Corp. All rights reserved.

scrawled, scratched, stained. While my classes took a test that day I began to read notes I had only glanced at before. I made two piles, one for the genuine notes written by mothers, the other for forgeries. The second was the larger pile, with writing that ranged from imaginative to lunatic. I was having an epiphany. I always wondered what an epiphany would be like and now I knew. I wondered also why I'd never had this particular epiphany before. Isn't it remarkable, I thought, how they resist any kind of writing assignment in class or at home. They whine and say they're busy and it's hard putting two hundred words together on any subject. But when they forge these excuse notes they're brilliant. Why? I have a drawer full of excuse notes that could be turned into an anthology of Great American Excuses or Great American Lies. The drawer was filled with samples of American talent never mentioned in song, story or scholarly study. How could I have ignored this treasure **trove**, these gems of fiction, fantasy, creativity, crawthumping, self-pity, family problems, boilers exploding, ceilings collapsing, fires sweeping whole blocks, babies and pets pissing on homework, unexpected births, heart attacks, strokes, miscarriages, robberies?

trove
a collection of objects

3   Here was American high school writing at its best—raw, real, urgent, lucid, brief, lying: The stove caught fire and the wallpaper went up and the fire department kept us out of the house all night. The toilet was blocked and we had to go down the street to the Kilkenny Bar where my cousin works to use their toilet but that was blocked too from the night before and you can imagine how hard it was for my Ronnie to get ready for school. I hope you'll excuse him this one time and it won't happen again. The man at the Kilkenny Bar was very nice on account of how he knows your brother, Mr. McCord. Arnold doesn't have his work today because he was getting off the train yesterday and the door closed on his school bag and the train took it away. He yelled to the conductor who said very vulgar things as the train drove away. Something should be done. His sister's dog ate his homework and I hope it chokes him. Her baby brother peed on her story when she was in the bathroom this morning. A man died in the bathtub upstairs and it overflowed and messed up all Roberta's homework on the table. Her big brother got mad at her and threw her essay out the window and it flew away all over Staten Island which is not a good thing because people will read it and get the wrong impression unless they read the ending which explains everything. He had the composition you told him to write but he was going over it on the ferry and a big wind came and blew it away. We were evicted from our apartment and the mean sheriff said if my son kept yelling for his notebook he'd have us all arrested.

4   I imagined the writers of excuse notes on buses, trains, ferries, in coffee shops, on park benches, trying to discover new and logical excuses, trying to write as they thought their parents would. They didn't know that honest excuse notes from parents were usually dull. "Peter was late because the alarm clock did not go off." A note like that didn't even merit a place in the trash can. Toward the end of the term I typed a dozen excuse notes on a stencil and distributed them to my two senior classes. They read, silently and intently. Yo, Mr. McCourt, what's this? Excuse notes. Whaddya mean, excuse notes? Who

© Pearson Education, Inc.

wrote them? You did, or some of you did. I omitted the names to protect the guilty. They're supposed to be written by parents, but you and I know the real authors. Yes, Mikey? So, what are we supposed to do with these excuse notes? We'll read them aloud. I want you to realize this is the first class in the world ever to study the art of the excuse note, the first class, ever, to practice writing them. You are so lucky to have a teacher like me who has taken your best writing, the excuse note, and turned it into a subject worthy of study. They're smiling. They know. We're in this together. Sinners. Some of the notes on that sheet were written by people in this class. You know who you are. You used your imagination and didn't settle for the old alarm-clock story. You'll be making excuses the rest of your life and you'll want them to be believable and original. You might even wind up writing excuses for your own children when they're late or absent or up to some devilment.

5   Try it now. Imagine you have a fifteen-year-old son or daughter who needs an excuse for falling behind in English. Let it rip. They didn't look around. They didn't chew on their pens. They didn't **dawdle**. They were eager, desperate to make up excuses for their fifteen-year-old sons and daughters. It was an act of loyalty and love and, you never know, some day they might need these notes. They produced a rhapsody of excuses, ranging from a family epidemic of diarrhea to a sixteen-wheeler truck crashing into a house, to a severe case of food poisoning blamed on the McKee High School cafeteria. They said, More, more. Could we do more? I was taken aback. How do I handle this enthusiasm? There was another epiphany or a flash of inspiration or illumination or something. I went to the board and wrote: "For Homework Tonight." That was a mistake. The word homework carries negative connotations. I erased it and they said, Yeah, yeah. I told them, You can start it here in class and continue at home or on the other side of the moon. What I'd like you to write is . . . I wrote it on the board: "An Excuse Note from Adam to God" or "An Excuse Note from Eve to God." The heads went down. Pens raced across paper. They could do this with one hand tied behind their backs. With their eyes closed. Secret smiles around the room. Oh, this is a good one, baby, and we know what's coming, don't we? Adam blames Eve. Eve blames Adam. They both blame God or Lucifer. Blame all around except for God, who has the upper hand and kicks them out of Eden so that their descendants wind up in McKee Vocational and Technical High School writing excuse notes for the first man and woman, and maybe God Himself needs an excuse note for some of His big mistakes. The bell rang, and for the first time in my three and a half years of teaching, I saw high school students so immersed they had to be urged out of the room by friends hungry for lunch.

dawdle
to take a long time to do something or go somewhere

Reading Comprehension Check

1. In the first paragraph, McCourt writes, "I liked him and didn't want him sullen in the third row." The word *sullen* means

    a. bright.

    b. anticipating.

    c. gloomy.

    d. considerate.

2. What does the author say about Danny's classmates?
  a. that they too had been forging excuse notes
  b. that teachers always bother them
  c. that they are more moral
  d. none of the above

3. In the second paragraph, McCourt describes students' parents as harried. The word *harried* means
  a. strict.   c. relaxed.
  b. in a rush.   d. stressed.

4. The author divided the excuse notes into what two categories?
  a. notes written by girls and notes written by boys
  b. forged notes and copied ones
  c. the ones written by the students and the ones written by their parents
  d. genuine notes and real notes

5. In the middle of the second paragraph, McCourt writes, "I was having an epiphany. I always wondered what an epiphany would be like and now I knew. I wondered also why I'd never had this particular epiphany before." The word *epiphany* could be replaced with
  a. a miraculous loss.   c. a fever.
  b. a meaningful realization. d. a guess.

6. In the second paragraph, "boilers exploding, ceilings collapsing, fires sweeping whole blocks" are mentioned as examples of
  a. genuine excuses.
  b. forged copies.
  c. excuses students use for not coming to school.
  d. destructive incidents.

7. In paragraph 3, McCourt writes, "We were evicted from our apartment . . ." A synonym for the word *evicted* is
  a. thrown out.   c. temporarily pushed out.
  b. delayed by.   d. invaded.

8. McCourt sells the idea of writing excuse notes in class by telling the students that
  a. one day they could write excuse notes for their kids.
  b. they will be writing excuse notes all their lives and should make them believable.
  c. excuse notes should be well-imagined.
  d. all of the above

9. In the last paragraph, in describing the students' reaction to this new kind of assignment, McCourt writes, "They didn't dawdle." The word *dawdle* could be replaced with
  a. rush.   c. waste time.
  b. laugh.   d. lie.

10. Why did McCourt's students not want to leave when the class ended?
  a. They were angry about the teacher's strange assignment.
  b. They were sleepy after a long class.
  c. They were wondering what the homework was.
  d. They were immersed in the art of writing excuse notes.

© Pearson Education, Inc.

Suggested Resources

Books

1. *Learning in Small Moments: Life in an Urban Classroom* by Daniel Meier. Practioners Inquiry Series, 1997. This book offers an introduction to urban elementary school teaching from the experience of a veteran teacher.

2. *Teaching and Learning in a Diverse World* by Patricia Ramsey. Teachers College Press, 2004. This text provides a framework for teaching in a multicultural context.

Movies

1. *Freedom Writers* (2007). Directed by Richard LaGravenese. This is an inspiring movie about a female high school teacher who inspires her underprivileged students to become creative writers.

2. *Stand and Deliver* (1988). Directed by Ramón Menéndez. Based on a true story, Edward Olmos plays a math teacher in East Los Angeles who defends his students against an unjust educational system.

3. *Mr. Holland's Opus* (1995). Directed by Stephen Herek. In this movie, an exceptional teacher goes the extra mile to share his passion for music with his students.

Internet Sites

1. www.ablongman.com/johnson14e

   This is the companion website for "Foundations of American Education," the education textbook chapter sampled in this chapter reading selection 6.

2. www.rnt.org

   If you are considering pursuing teaching as a career, this Web site offers practical information about this profession.

Using Index Cards
to Study Vocabulary

Overview

As you know, one of the most challenging parts of succeeding in college is to learn new vocabulary and jargon typical of a subject. There are many techniques to build vocabulary, but here we offer you an effective technique that will help you improve your active vocabulary. For this activity, you will need index cards that are blank on one side and lined on the other.

ESL Annotation

1.17 ESL This exercise is of particular importance to ESL students who need to build a solid vocabulary to succeed in mainstream courses.

Activity

As you come across an unfamiliar word while doing a reading assignment, write it on the blank side of the index card. On the lined side, write information related to the new word as follows. Keep in mind that you will need a good dictionary to do this exercise.

1. Look up the word in a dictionary and write how it is pronounced. Most dictionaries phonetically transcribe words, so it should not be difficult for you to write the sounds.

2. Find out what part of speech the word is and write it below. For example, write if the word is a noun, a verb, or an adjective.

3. Write the meaning of the word.

4. Make an example sentence using the new word in context.

5. Using a dictionary, write the words that are derived from the same root. For example, the words *marine, maritime, marina, submarine,* and *mariner* are all derived from the same Latin root *mar* which means "sea." This way you will learn that some words are associated with each other.

6. Write at least two or three synonyms of the unfamiliar word here.

7. Finally, write at least two or three antonyms of the new word here.

Let's take a look at an index card so that you can fully understand how to **create** your own index cards for vocabulary building. We will use the word *create* for this index card exercise.

© Pearson Education, Inc.

CREATE		
1. Pronunciation: /kri'jeit/		
2. Part of speech: verb		
3. Meaning: to make something new		
4. Example: The art students *created* a wonderfully colorful mural from cereal boxes.		
5. Family: creator – noun	creation – noun	creationist – noun
creationism – noun	creative – adjective	creatively – adverb
creativity – noun	creature – noun	
6. Synonyms – design, invent, devise, construct		
7. Antonyms – demolish, ruin, destroy, destruct		

Learning Implications

In order to succeed in college and later in your professional career, it is essential that you improve and continue to build your active vocabulary. Words that are part of your active vocabulary are readily available for speech and writing. In other words, you do not need to stop in the middle of speaking or writing and look up new words in a dictionary if your active vocabulary is expansive. At first, this exercise may seem challenging and somewhat repetitive to you, but soon you will realize that using index cards is an integral part of your active vocabulary development.

HEALTH
Nutrition

Chapter 2

"You are what you eat."
VICTOR LINDLAHR

Objectives

IN THIS CHAPTER YOU WILL LEARN...

- ✓ Fundamentals of Health and Nutrition
- ✓ How to distinguish between parts of speech
- ✓ How to collect data using a survey
- ✓ How to identify main idea and topic
- ✓ Outlining as a reading skill
- ✓ How to give a formal presentation

© Pearson Education, Inc.

Making Predictions

Consider this chapter's theme of Health. What subtopics relate to this field? (See Fig. 2.1.)

■ Figure 2.1

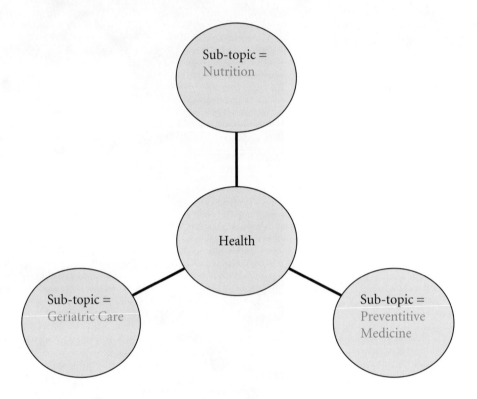

Introduction to the Discipline of Health

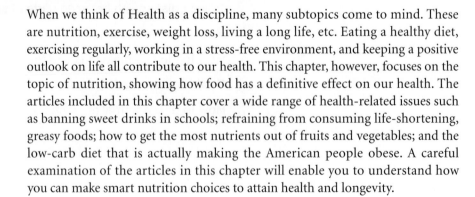

When we think of Health as a discipline, many subtopics come to mind. These are nutrition, exercise, weight loss, living a long life, etc. Eating a healthy diet, exercising regularly, working in a stress-free environment, and keeping a positive outlook on life all contribute to our health. This chapter, however, focuses on the topic of nutrition, showing how food has a definitive effect on our health. The articles included in this chapter cover a wide range of health-related issues such as banning sweet drinks in schools; refraining from consuming life-shortening, greasy foods; how to get the most nutrients out of fruits and vegetables; and the low-carb diet that is actually making the American people obese. A careful examination of the articles in this chapter will enable you to understand how you can make smart nutrition choices to attain health and longevity.

Preview Questions

Working in small groups, answer the following questions. Notice that they all focus on the topic of Health.

1. How would you define a "health nut" or a "health not"? What are some of the characteristics of these groups of people?

2. Do you know of someone who is an absolute health nut or an absolute health not? Describe this person's health and nutrition habits.

3. Do you consider yourself a health nut, a health not, or someone in between?

4. Some health advocates believe that unhealthy foods should not be available in certain places. Do you think that our eating habits should be regulated by the government? For example, should vending machines containing soda and candy be banned from public schools?

Interpreting a Cartoon

■ Figure 2.2

http://www.cartoonstock.com/director/N/Nutrition.asp

Examine the cartoon shown here and in pairs answer the following questions.

1. What is amusing about this cartoon?

2. In your opinion, what message is the cartoonist trying to convey to the reader?

© Pearson Education, Inc.

Discipline-specific Terminology Bank

advocacy	diagnosis	inherently	obese
ban	environmental	lifestyle	regulate
cholesterol	fiber	lobbying	saturated
clog	genes	longevity	sedentary
consumption	harm	nutrient	trend

Sample Paragraph

Read the following paragraph, which contains some of the discipline-specific terminology you will come across in the reading selections in this chapter. Pay attention to the highlighted words, and try to decipher meaning from context, a skill you learned in the previous chapter.

> Do some people live to 100 because they have superior genes, or does their **longevity** have more to do with **environmental** factors? Are those who live a **sedentary** life more prone to certain illnesses than are more active types of people? Clearly in the past 20 years there has been more government involvement in our eating habits. There is **lobbying** to **regulate** or **ban** our **consumption** of certain products. This is partly due to a recent **trend** toward healthier **lifestyles**. As a result of this trend, such terms as ***nutrient, fiber,*** and ***saturated*** fats have entered the mainstream.

EXERCISE 1

Matching Column A and Column B

Match the word in Column A with the definition in Column B. Put the letter representing the correct definition in the space preceding each term.

Column A

Word

1. _d_ sedentary
2. _e_ ban
3. _h_ consumption
4. _j_ longevity
5. _i_ trend
6. _c_ saturated
7. _a_ clog
8. _g_ inherently
9. _f_ lifestyle
10. _b_ nutrient

Column B

Definition

a. to block something
b. a substance needed to be alive
c. containing the highest amount of substance
d. sitting down and not moving
e. not allow
f. the way people live and work
g. in a way that is a permanent part of something
h. using food for energy
i. a developing change or situation
j. long life

EXERCISE 2

Fill in the Blanks

In the following sentences, fill in the blank with a word from the terminology bank that makes the sentence meaningful.

ban	consumption	lifestyle	nutrient	sedentary
clog	inherently	longevity	saturated	trend

1. Many ancient societies around the world that practice internal medicine have attempted to find various ways to attain health and _longevity_.

2. In many underdeveloped African countries, children suffer from a severe _nutrient_ deficiency because of a lack of agricultural produce.

3. Obesity is on the rise in the United States due to a combination of _sedentary_ jobs, lack of exercise, and poor food habits.

4. Christina's physician warned her that if she did not make some serious dietary changes, she could not lead a healthy _lifestyle_ and would most likely die prematurely.

5. Many geneticists believe that children acquire _inherently_ weak metabolisms from their parents.

6. The cardiologist examined Peter thoroughly and announced that his arteries were almost completely _clogged_ as a result of years of consuming unhealthy foods.

7. In New York City, the District Attorney has _banned_ restaurants from using Trans Fat in foods they serve their clients.

8. As a result of health magazines reporting findings of research conducted by nutrition scientists in the United States, the American people are gradually becoming aware of the consequences of eating foods containing large amounts of _saturated_ fat.

9. After the wild spread of the mad cow disease in England and other European countries, the U.S. government declared imported meat products unfit for human _consumption_.

10. In some health-conscious states in the United States, such as California and Oregon, it has become a _trend_ to produce and market organically grown food items.

EXERCISE 3

Pair Activity

Working with a partner, choose five words you have just learned, and create complete sentences with them.

1. _____

   _____

Collaboration

© Pearson Education, Inc.

2. _____

_____

3. _____

_____

4. _____

_____

5. _____

_____

ESL Annotation

2.1 ESL Word form focus is critical to the progress of ESL students' vocabulary development.

Vocabulary Development: Parts of Speech

Word Formation

For every new word you learn, there are associated forms that can strengthen your vocabulary further. Academic reading demands that you have the ability to identify different forms in different contexts. Suffixes in English have two primary functions: (1) to change the meaning of the root they are attached to, and (2) to change the part of speech of the root. The following rules show how certain words are formed in English. Keep in mind that word formation is not always entirely predictable, but that these rules apply in most cases.

Rule 1: Noun ⟶ Noun

-hood	brotherhood	parenthood
-ship	friendship	membership
-ist	novelist	guitarist
-ism	capitalism	socialism

Rule 2: Verb ⟶ Noun

-ment	enhancement	parchment
-er	trainer	mixer
-ation	purification	justification

Rule 3: Adjective ⟶ Noun

-dom	freedom	boredom
-ness	madness	sadness
-ity	equality	purity

Rule 4: Adjective/Noun ⟶ Verb

-ify	liquefy	solidify
-ize	legalize	prioritize

Rule 5: Noun ⟶ Adjective

-y	sunny	windy
-ous	religious	famous
-ful	beautiful	faithful
-ial	office	official

Rule 6: Verb ⟶ Adjective

-ive	relative	regressive
-able	believable	commendable
-ful	regretful	wishful
-ent/ant	competent	hesitant

Rule 7: Adjective ⟶ Adjective

-ish	smallish	greenish
-ly	sickly	lonely

Rule 8: Adjective ⟶ Adverb

-ly	politely	equally

EXERCISE 4

Word Formation

The following words are taken from "Fat Chance" by Emily Bazelon, an article you will read later (it starts on page 74). Practice word formation by using the above rules. Your task is to identify what part of speech the word is, write the rule that can change the meaning of the root, and write the derived form next to it. The first example is done for you. (The number in parentheses represents the reading selection paragraph in which the word appears.)

1. Obese (paragraph 1)

   Rule: (3) Adjective→Noun

   Derived Form: obese + ity→ obesity

2. Study (paragraph 3)

   Rule: _Noun→Adjective_

   Derived Form: _studious_

3. Sympathy (paragraph 3)

   Rule: _Noun→Verb_

   Derived Form: _sympathize_

4. Journal (paragraph 4)

   Rule: _Noun→Noun_

   Derived Form: _journalism_

© Pearson Education, Inc.

5. Benefit (paragraph 5)

   Rule: _Noun→Adjective_

   Derived Form: _beneficial_

6. Explain (paragraph 6)

   Rule: _Verb→Noun_

   Derived Form: _explanation_

7. Insist (paragraph 7)

   Rule: _Verb→Adjective_

   Derived Form: _insistent_

8. Biological (paragraph 8)

   Rule: _Adjective→Noun_

   Derived Form: _Biologist_

9. Anxiety (paragraph 10)

   Rule: _Noun→Adjective_

   Derived Form: _Anxious_

EXERCISE 5

Parts of Speech

The table below shows the different parts of speech for words from the terminology bank. The first two examples are done for you. Using a monolingual dictionary, find the derivations of the highlighted words and complete the table below. Keep in mind that some words may not have multiple forms, in which case simply put an X in the appropriate box.

ESL Annotation

2.2 ESL See Instructor's Manual for Activity Using Index Cards to Build Vocabulary.

Noun	*Adjective*	*Verb*	*Adverb*
nutrition	nutritious	X	nutritiously
diagnosis	diagnostic	diagnose	diagnostically
genes	genetic	X	genetically
obesity	obese	X	X
harm	harmful	harm	harmfully
environment	environmental	X	environmentally
ban	banned	ban	X
regulation	regulatory	regulate	X
saturation	saturated	saturate	X

In-class Health Survey

Refer to the following questions to interview at least two classmates. Please take notes as they respond to your questions, and orally report your findings.

Question	Respondent 1	Respondent 2
1. How often do you eat fast food?		
2. Do you ever cook at home, or do you usually eat out?		
3. When you are choosing what to eat, how much do you take into consideration the health value of what you are going to consume?		
4. In your opinion, what food items are the most hazardous to your health?		

Collaboration

Teaching Tip:
Students build collaboration skills with in-class surveys and enjoy the classroom interaction.

Fieldwork Health Survey

Please give the survey on the next page to the people in your neighborhood, at work, or school. (You can photocopy the form as many times as needed.) Tell the respondents that the survey is conducted solely for academic purposes, that their participation in the survey is totally voluntary, that their names will be kept confidential, that they will not be contacted in the future for further interviews, and that the survey should not take more than five minutes to complete. You can ask them to write brief answers to the survey questions if they prefer to do so themselves, or you can write down their answers as to your questions orally. Be prepared to report the results of the survey to your class later. The survey will help you learn more about health in general.

© Pearson Education, Inc.

ESL Annotation

2.3 ESL In some cultures, public surveying is considered threatening to both interviewers and interviewees. Make sure to discuss the central role surveys and questionnaires play in American life. Encourage students to practice this skill.

Health Survey

1. How many glasses of water do you drink every day?

   _____

2. How often do you exercise every week? What types of exercise do you do? Do you lift weights, or do cardiovascular exercise, or practice Yoga/Tai Chi?

   _____

3. Do you cook at home? If yes, then how often, and what kinds of food do you cook?

   _____

4. How many servings of fruits and vegetables do you eat every day?

   _____

5. How many times do you eat fast food? When you eat out, what do you usually eat?

   _____

6. How often do you eat processed foods such as donuts, cheese balls, chips, crackers, etc.?

   _____

7. What percentage of your daily intake consists of natural foods such as fruits, vegetables, and salads?

   _____

8. Do you weigh yourself regularly?

   _____

9. What time of day do you find yourself to be most energized? When and how often do you feel physically exhausted during the day?

   _____

10. What kinds of food did you eat growing up with your family members? How has your diet changed since your childhood?

   _____

ESL Annotation

2.4 ESL students and native English-speaking students are required to pass a proficiency exam in college, which includes graphic analysis. Make sure you explain the importance of mastering this skill to your students.

Collaboration

Graphic Analysis

In this section, you are asked to interpret a graph. The graph shown here is the Food Pyramid, which is recommended by the National Institutes for Health (NIH). Examine the content-focused graph and with a partner answer the questions that follow.

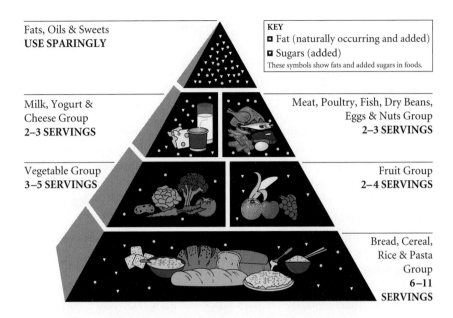

1. According to the food pyramid, what type of food should you eat the most of each day? _bread, cereal, rice, and pasta group_

2. Why are sweets at the top of the pyramid? _because they should be consumed sparingly_

3. What do all the food items in the second tier from the top of the pyramid have in common? _They are all protein sources (students must rely on prior knowledge to answer questions 3 and 4)._

4. Which food groups have the least fat content? _fruit group and/or vegetable_

Fat Chance

Pre-Reading Questions

Before reading the following article, answer these questions in pairs or small groups. Discussing the questions will help prepare you to analyze the text with relative ease.

1. What is more important to you, your ability to see or being slim? Explain.

2. What factors result in a person being "overweight"? In other words, is obesity genetically determined, or is it influenced by environmental factors?

3. Do you believe that American society is prejudiced against overweight people? If yes, how? Do the media play a role in reinforcing negative stereotypes toward these people?

Read the article below and practice your reading comprehension with the set of ten multiple-choice questions that follow. For the first few paragraphs remember, be an information predictor by writing questions about the text.

© Pearson Education, Inc.

READING

Reading Selection **1**

Newspaper Article

2.5 Flesch-Kincaid Grade Level 11.3

Collaboration

Teaching Tip:
Remind students to write questions next to the ? at the beginning of the article

The Food Pyramid

Fat Chance

Emily Bazelon is a senior editor at "Slate."

By Emily Bazelon, the *New York Times*

May 6, 2007

?_____

_____

_____

_____

ESL Annotation

2.6 ESL In some cultures being heavy is seen as a sign of wealth and having enough to eat.

exhortation
utterance conveying urgent advice

?_____

_____

_____

_____

marshal
to arrange in proper order

1   If you had to choose, would you rather be fat or blind? When a researcher asked that question of a group of formerly obese people, 89 **percent** said they would prefer to lose their sight than their hard-won slimness. "When you're blind, people want to help you. No one wants to help you when you're fat," one explained. Ninety-one **percent** of the group also chose having a leg amputated over a return to obesity.

2   This is shocking. But it seems less so by the end of "Rethinking Thin," a new book about obesity by Gina Kolata, a science reporter for the *New York Times*. Kolata argues that being fat is not something people have much control over. Most people who are overweight struggle to change their shape throughout their lives, but remain stuck within a relatively narrow weight **range** set by their genes. For those determined to foil biology, strict dieting is a life sentence. "I am a fat man in a thin man's body," an MIT obesity researcher who shed his unwanted pounds years ago tells Kolata.

3   He's one of the lucky and single-minded few. Study after study, Kolata notes, has shown that for most fat people the long-term rewards of dieting are modest at best. Yet as obesity rates have skyrocketed, **exhortations** to eat right, exercise and shed pounds have gone from loud to shrill. Kolata's understandable sympathy for those caught between the ever intensifying pressure to be thin and the stubborn size of their bodies, however, leads her to flirt with an unlikely **conclusion**: Maybe the outcry over obesity is itself supersized, and being fat isn't really unhealthy after all.

4   Kolata follows a two-year clinical trial at the University of Pennsylvania designed to test the low-carbohydrate, high-fat Atkins diet against a **traditional** low-calorie, low-fat one. Kolata wrote her book before she had the results for the trial, though a different study, **published** in March in the *Journal of the American Medical Association*, found that Atkins beats the low-cal diet for keeping off weight. The diet-versus-diet contest, however, isn't her real story.

5   Instead, she focuses on how little weight those who follow any diet usually manage to keep off. (The average participant on the Atkins diet reported in JAMA lost only 10 pounds over the course of a year.) Kolata tells the stories of four dieters in the Penn trial who are smart and likable. They had the **benefit** of a professionally led support group and the **status** of taking part in a well-financed study. They started exercising; they stopped eating mindlessly. After two years, they're a bit lighter. But none achieved the 50- to 100-pound weight loss they strove for (though one lost more than 30 pounds, 15 **percent** of his body weight).

6   Kolata **marshals** scientific **evidence** to explain why keeping weight off is so difficult. (The discovery last month of a garden-variety "fat gene" further backs her up.) Fat people have more fat cells than other people. Their metabolisms are

Marian Burros and Melanie Warner, "Bottlers Agree to a School Ban on Sweet Drinks." From *The New York Times*, May 4, 2006. © 2006 The New York Times. All rights reserved. Used by permission and protected by the Copyright Laws of the United States. The printing, copying, redistribution, or retransmission of the Material without express written permission is prohibited.
www.nytimes.com

normal but their appetites are larger—after they lose a **significant** amount of weight, one researcher explains, they often feel "a primal hunger" as strong as the urge a thirsty person feels to drink. Studies of twins and of adopted children show that inheritance may account for as much as 70 percent of weight variance. In one study of adopted children, 80 **percent** of those with two obese birth parents became obese, compared with 14 **percent** of those with birth parents of **normal** weight—and it didn't much matter what the adoptive parents fed the kids.

7   Given such proof of the power of genetics, Kolata asks, why do we continue to insist that fat people can become thin people if they only put their minds to it?

8   She's surely right to push back against bafflement and intolerance, and her argument that we've tilted too far toward blaming fat people's bad habits for their weight is convincing. But Kolata goes so far in arguing for biological predestination that she sometimes seems to completely dismiss the other part of the fat **equation**—what we eat. In all likelihood, the obesity rate has doubled in the United States since 1980 for all the familiar reasons: fattening food has never been so cheap, convenient and **cunningly** marketed. "The genes that make people fat need an **environment** in which food is cheap and plentiful," she writes. It's in a world of giant muffins and bowls of office candy that Americans need wider movie seats and larger coffins.

cunning
crafty, done in a shrewd or sly manner

9   Kolata knows this. She touches on reasons that poor people are more likely than rich people to be overweight, all of them environmental. But she treats childhood obesity as **virtually** inevitable. In addition to the twin and adoption studies, she cites **research** showing that teaching kids to eat right in school, and serving them leaner lunches, has no effect on their weights. The researchers concluded that the **intervention** was too limited—the children's diets needed to change at home as well as at school. But Kolata scoffs at the "popular solution," which is "not to question the premise but rather to increase the intensity of the intervention."

10   Given the rise in obesity, however, is it really credible to put all the blame on our genes—and ignore the gazillion-dollar food industry? And while it's useful to point out that obese people don't have higher rates of anxiety, **depression** or mood disorders, that doesn't mean these conditions are never a factor in causing obesity in those who are genetically susceptible to it. As some of the testimony of Kolata's own dieters attests, we eat not just because our appetites drive us to but because our psyches do, in search of both pleasure and relief from pain or **stress.** Rather than go where many authors have gone before, Kolata questions whether the current alarm over obesity is **overblown**—and whether the culture of dieting isn't itself harmful. The fat wars are less a legitimate public health campaign than a "moral panic," she suggests. In fact, she argues, some recent epidemiological studies show lower death rates for **somewhat** overweight people than for "so-called **normal**-weight people" or very thin ones.

overblown
exaggerated; done to excess

11   The **data** are certainly intriguing. But living longer doesn't mean that fat people are in good health along the way. In fact, they suffer from higher rates of diabetes, stroke, certain cancers and heart trouble. Kolata skirts this, because her argument is that thinness in and of itself is not a goal many people can **achieve**—or even an important one. She also quotes one **expert** who claims that "national **data**" do not show that Americans are in fact more sedentary than in the past. It's a surprising assertion that begs for development. Kolata ends on a quixotic note, by wondering if perhaps

© Pearson Education, Inc.

Americans weigh more for the same reason that we're taller on average than we were a century ago—because we're in better health. Maybe the extra pounds even help contribute to this well-being. No one has found the **smoking gun** in the mysterious fattening of America, but Kolata, following the obesity researchers Jules Hirsch and Jeff Friedman, briefly speculates whether, say, better early nutrition, vaccines or antibiotics somehow "precipitated changes in the brain's controls over weight." It's a twist on the usual evolutionary argument. The problem isn't that we evolved to store fat in times of famine and now can't handle our 24-hour, all-you-can-eat buffet of abundance. We're fat because we're changing in **response** to the **medical strides** we've taken.

12   A nice idea, maybe, but one as yet unsupported by **evidence**. What's more persuasive is Kolata's contention that we should replace the elusive goal of thinness with the goal of better health and greater happiness. Here her argument is eminently sensible: Sure, shape up your body. But mostly, make your peace with it.

smoking gun
definite proof of who is responsible for something bad or how something really happened

strides
advancements or progress

Reading Comprehension Check

1. What group of people was interviewed by the researcher?
   a. obese
   b. overweight
   c. emaciated
   d. thin

2. Gina Kolata, a *New York Times* science reporter, argues that most people who are overweight:
   a. find a way to lose weight and get slimmer.
   b. never lose any weight.
   c. usually stay around the same weight.
   d. die of an obesity-related illness.

3. What does the MIT professor who was once obese and found a way to lose weight mean when he says, "I am a fat man in a thin man's body"?
   a. His natural condition is to be fat.
   b. He is still overweight regardless of his diet.
   c. His body was never thin.
   d. He has been taking diet pills.

4. Why does Kolata follow a two-year clinical study of popular weight-loss diets?
   a. to learn more about obesity and genetics
   b. to see if these diets really have an effect on reducing obesity
   c. to see if one particular diet is more cost-effective than another
   d. to lose weight herself

5. What did a study of adopted children show?
   a. If their birth parents were obese, they would not be obese.
   b. There was no relationship between their birth parents' obesity and their own weight.
   c. In most cases, if the birth parents of the adopted children were obese, they too would likely be obese.
   d. The most important factor was the weight of their adoptive parents.

6. The author's mention that "fattening food has never been so cheap, convenient and cunningly marketed" is an example of a/an _____ factor in explaining the rise in obesity.

    a. genetic   (c.) environmental

    b. auxiliary   d. obsequious

7. In paragraph 9, "But she treats childhood obesity as virtually inevitable . . . ," the word *inevitable* could be replaced with

    a. preventable.   (c.) predictable.

    b. consistent.   d. curable.

8. Kolata makes the connection between Americans being much taller than a century ago with Americans also being much heavier to show

    a. he dangers of obesity.   (c.) that perhaps being bigger is a sign of

    b. how everything changes   a more affluent, healthier society.

       over time.   d. the politics of eating.

9. In the final paragraph, the author criticizes some of Kolata's assumptions, arguing that they are not

    a. believable.   (c.) supported by evidence.

    b. logical and convincing.   d. based on truth.

10. The author concludes by agreeing with Kolata's contention that

    a. losing weight is more important than the pursuit of happiness.

    b. weight loss is an economic issue.

    (c.) better health and happiness should take precedence over slimness.

    d. only affluent people can be both content and thin.

READING

Reading Selection **2**

Magazine Article

2.7 Flesch-Kincaid Grade Level 11.0

Collaboration

Over the Limit?

Pre-Reading Questions

Discuss these questions in pairs or small groups before reading the article.

1. Have you ever consumed a high-energy drink? If yes, how often do you drink them? Does it work in helping to keep you awake?

2. Do you think drinks with high levels of caffeine are healthy? Explain.

3. In your opinion, why do so many teenagers and young adults not get the amount of sleep they need each night?

Over the Limit?

By Nancy Shute, *US News and World Report*

April 4, 2007

1   Linleigh Hawk starts the day at 5:30 a.m. by downing her first cup of coffee. She then stops at Starbucks for a grande vanilla skim latte on the way to Winston

From Nancy Shute, "Over the Limit? Americans young and old crave high-octane fuel, and doctors are jittery," *U.S. News & World Report*, April 15, 2007. Copyright 2007 U.S. News & World Report, L.P. Reprinted with permission.

© Pearson Education, Inc.

Churchill High School in Potomac, Md., where she's a senior. At 3 p.m., it's time for a jumbo iced tea to power her through hip-hop dance rehearsals and yearbook meetings. Homework, which often keeps her up past 1 a.m., requires more coffee. "I've got so much to do," she says. "I've got to have the caffeine." The java-fired **schedule** has paid off, says Hawk: She's been accepted by 15 of her 16 college choices, including first pick Wake Forest.

sleep-deprived
not getting enough sleep

crave
to want something very much

buzz
a state of stimulation as from alcohol or caffeine

2   Hawk may sound like an anomaly, but she isn't. Overworked and **sleep-deprived** Americans young and old so **crave** a **buzz** these days that even alcoholic drinks come loaded with caffeine, and doctors are getting worried. In the past three years alone, the number of 18-to-24-year-olds who drink coffee daily has doubled, from 16 **percent** to 31 **percent**—and some of them go on to pop prescription stimulants such as Adderall or Ritalin for late-night study sessions. Energy drinks like Red Bull and Cocaine, with several times the buzz of a can of Coke, have mushroomed into a $3.5 billion-a-year industry.

3   "I can't go out and keep up with these 20-year-olds without it," says Jeremy Freer, a 29-year-old music teacher from Virginia Beach, Va., of his Saturday-night beverage of choice: vodka with Red Bull. (Partyers can opt instead for the new double espresso-double caffeinated Van Gogh vodka or a Bud Extra, a caffeinated beer.)

wired
very stimulated or excited

4   Health experts understand all too well why Americans gotta get **wired**. People of all ages are chronically sleep deprived, from teens who catch the bus before sunrise to working mothers who report they spend less than six hours a night in bed, according to a poll released in March by the National Sleep Foundation. But we may be pushing the limits of self-medication. Poison control centers and emergency room doctors report increasing numbers of people suffering from the rapid heartbeat and nausea of a caffeine overdose—like the 14-year-old boy who earlier this year showed up at a Minneapolis emergency room in respiratory distress after washing down caffeine pills with **energy** drinks so he could play video games all night. Instead, he spent the night in the pediatric intensive care unit, intubated, until the caffeine exited his system. They're also seeing more teens and young **adults** in distress after having bought or "borrowed" stimulant drugs from friends.

5   And, in the extreme, there are tragedies like that of James Stone, a 19-year-old from Wallingford, Conn., who died last November of cardiac arrest after taking nearly two dozen caffeine pills. His parents say he had been putting in long hours on a **job** search. Doctors are particularly troubled to see youngsters forming the caffeine habit, even as toddlers. Children's consumption of soft drinks has doubled in the past 35 years, with sodas supplanting milk. A 2003 study of Columbus, Ohio, middle schoolers found some taking in 800 milligrams of caffeine a day—more than twice the recommended **maximum** for adults of 300 milligrams. "Their body weight is low," says Wahida Karmally, director of nutrition for the Irving Center for Clinical Research at Columbia University Medical Center. "They can't tolerate as much caffeine as **adults**."

guzzling
drinking a lot of something eagerly and quickly

6   Since scientists have never studied how caffeine affects growing bodies and brains, children who go through the day **guzzling** soda after iced tea after energy drink are serving as tiny guinea pigs. "This is something that nobody is looking at carefully," says Nora Volkow, a psychiatrist who directs the National Institute on Drug Abuse. "We really have no idea how it affects development long term."

7　　The appeal to kids of high-octane **energy** drinks has some officials concerned enough to act. Just last week, the Food and Drug Administration announced it had sent a warning letter to the manufacturer of Cocaine Energy Drink, Redux Beverages LLC of Las Vegas, for marketing the beverage "as an **alternative** to an illicit street drug."

8　　Until last week, the manufacturer's website boasted "Cocaine-instant rush." Hyping the performance enhancements caffeine offers at the time you're introducing the drug to children "is a terrible message. It has **implications** for drug use in the future," says Roland Griffiths, a professor of behavioral biology at Johns Hopkins University Medical Center who has studied caffeine's effects for more than 30 years.

implications
something suggested as naturally to be understood

9　　And last month, Doherty High School in Colorado Springs, Colo., banned a drink called Spike Shooter. Two students were taken to the hospital complaining of nausea, vomiting, and heart palpitations after drinking an 8-ounce can, which packs 300 mg of caffeine—the same as almost four Red Bulls.

10　　For **adults,** and in reasonable doses—the **equivalent** of three 8-ounce cups of coffee, six Excedrin Migraine, or a half-dozen 12-ounce colas a day—caffeine has much to recommend it. As the world's most popular habit-forming drug, it fights fatigue, brightens mood, and eases pain while it's forestalling sleep. Test subjects dosed with the amount found in a cup of coffee come out ahead on problem-solving tasks. And by triggering the **release** of adrenaline to help muscles work harder and longer, caffeine so clearly enhances athletic performance that until 2004 it was considered a controlled substance by the International Olympic Committee. Supercaffeinated **energy** drinks like Redline RTD are marketed to bodybuilders.

Elixir of Life

11　The latest findings on coffee suggest that it even **staves off** disease. Caffeine reduces the risk of Parkinson's disease, for example, by blocking receptors for adenosine, a neurotransmitter that plays a **role** in motor **function**. It is now being tested as a Parkinson's treatment. Caffeine also heads off migraines by contracting blood vessels in the brain.

stave off
to prevent in time, forestall

12　　And probably because coffee, like blueberries and broccoli, contains potent antioxidants, it appears to reduce the risk of colon cancer, gallstones, and liver cancer, among other illnesses. In 2005, Harvard researchers found that drinking six cups of coffee or more daily cut the risk of getting type 2 diabetes by half in men and 30 **percent** in women. One study of 80,000 women showed that those who drank more than two or three cups of coffee daily reduced their risk of suicide over 10 years by a third.

13　　Alas, that glorious rush of **energy** isn't entirely benign. Numerous studies have found no **link** between caffeine and cardiovascular disease. But it can cause anxiety, jitters, and heart palpitations, particularly in people who are sensitive to it. It also can cause stomach pain and gastrointestinal reflux, may make it harder for a woman to get pregnant, and may increase the risk of miscarriage or a low-birth-weight baby. Doctors advise pregnant women to give up caffeine, or keep consumption down to a cup or two of coffee daily. Sleeplessness, not surprisingly, is a notorious side effect of caffeine. In recent years, as the number of people taking prescription sleeping pills has soared, more

© Pearson Education, Inc.

than a few doctors have wondered if people should reconsider their use of caffeine before downing an Ambien or Lunesta. According to Medco Health Solutions of Franklin Lakes, N.J., use of such medications by **adults** ages 20 to 44 increased 114 **percent** from 2000 to 2005. In kids, lack of sleep is both a worrisome cause and effect of the caffeine craze. Wilkie Wilson, a professor of pharmacology at Duke University Medical Center and coauthor of *Buzzed,* a guide to commonly used drugs, says he's stunned by how little sleep kids get these days. Teenagers, he says, need at least nine hours of sleep a night; **grade** schoolers, 10 to 12 hours. Very few get close to that much—either, as in Linleigh Hawk's case, because they're actively fighting sleep, or because they're so **jazzed** from caffeine that they can't settle down at bedtime. The downside: "I'm exhausted. I can't remember simple things," Hawk says. But she gets the work done.

jazzed
excited

14   Indeed, lack of sleep interferes with **concentration**, says William Kohler, **medical** director of the Florida Sleep Institute in Spring Hill. It also can make kids fidgety. Since inattention and restlessness are signs of attention deficit hyperactivity disorder as well, sleep researchers increasingly believe that some kids diagnosed with ADHD are actually sleep deprived.

fidgety
moving your hands or feet, especially because you are bored or nervous

15   The caffeine itself makes kids **fidgety**, too, of course. Just ask Maya Thompson, a Sacramento, Calif., mother. "It's like two totally different extremes," she says of how much more aggressive her son Jordan, 12, becomes with even a sip of a caffeinated drink. Jordan, for his part, says that lots of kids in his sixth-**grade** class pull Monster or Rock Star **energy** drinks out of their backpacks and drink them before PE class. "Oh my gosh!" says Maya, 30. "I'm shocked by that—that is crazy!"

16   The young adult crowd who favor caffeine with their alcohol appear to be putting themselves at some risk, too. The stimulant does mitigate the effects of alcohol by improving **response** time, according to Mark Fillmore, a psychologist at the University of Kentucky who has been testing the combination on student volunteers. But it fails to reduce the number of errors that a person under the influence makes. "Caffeine seems to **restore** the speed of your behavior but not the accuracy," Fillmore says.

Reading Comprehension Check

1. In the first sentence of the article, "Linleigh Hawk starts the day at 5:30 a.m. by downing her first cup of coffee," the word *downing* means
   a. putting down.
   c. drinking.
   b. rejecting.
   d. sipping.

2. Doctors are getting worried (as mentioned in paragraph 2) because
   a. coffee drinking is on the decline.
   b. the number of young adults drinking coffee has increased dramatically.
   c. young people do not consider their health enough.
   d. both a and b

3. What is Jeremy Freer's idea in paragraph 3?
   a. He tries to go home early.
   b. Caffeinated drinks are very harmful.

  c. none of the above

  d. He would fall asleep when he went out with his friends if he didn't consume caffeinated drinks.

4. What are two negative consequences of high caffeine intake mentioned in the article?

  a. rapid heartbeat and fatigue
  c. accelerated speech and decay
  b. rapid heartbeat and nausea
  d. nausea and drug intake

5. When Nora Volkow, a psychiatrist, says, "We really have no idea how it affects development long term," what does *it* refer to? (paragraph 6)

  a. high caffeine consumption by kids
  b. guinea pigs consuming
  c. education and drinking
  d. bad parenting

6. The term *appeal*, in the sentence "The appeal to kids of high-octane energy drinks has some officials concerned . . . ," (paragraph 7) could be replaced by

  a. response.
  c. attraction.
  b. effort.
  d. resistance.

7. In the sentence "Caffeine also heads off migraines by contracting blood vessels in the brain," (paragraph 11) the expression *heads off* means

  a. increases.
  c. causes.
  b. stops.
  d. deducts.

8. Heart palpitations, risk of miscarriage, and stomach pain are all mentioned as possible side effects of

  a. soda consumption.
  c. drug dependency.
  b. caffeine intake.
  d. both b and c

9. William Kohler, a medical director, believes there is a connection between

  a. soda consumption and concentration.
  b. caffeine intake and lack of sleep.
  c. lack of sleep and concentration.
  d. concentration and caffeine intake.

10. The word *mitigate*, in the sentence "The stimulant does mitigate the effects of alcohol by improving response time," (paragraph 16) could be replaced by

  a. sideline.
  c. increase.
  b. moderate.
  d. cause.

SKILL FOCUS
Identifying the Main Idea and Topic

When you are asked to find the *main idea* of a sentence or a paragraph, you are really being asked to identify the most important point the author wants to convey to the reader.

Movie Analogy: Understanding the Concept of *Main Idea*

Imagine a friend calls you and says she is in a hurry on the way to the movies and would like you to recommend a film. You tell your friend the name of the film you think she should see and she asks you to tell her in a sentence (there is no time to lose!) what the film is about.

ESL Annotation

2.8 ESL The concept of main idea is culturally constructed. In some East Asian cultures, it is considered rude to focus quickly on a main point, but rather to first focus attention on the details building up to a text's message.

© Pearson Education, Inc.

You say, "*Freedom Writers* is about a dedicated female teacher who inspires her underprivileged students to express themselves through writing." As you may have guessed by now, you've just offered your friend the main idea of the movie!

Main Idea versus Topic

Another way to understand the concept of *main idea* is to compare it with the idea of *topic*.

A topic is a word, name, or phrase that tells what an author is writing about. It is more *general* than a main idea.

Examine the paragraph example below.

Not too long ago, when you went to the supermarket to pick eggs you mainly had a choice between a few brands. But nowadays consumers are faced with a host of choices when purchasing a carton of eggs. There are eggs from cage-free chickens, organically grown eggs, and the traditional farm-raised eggs.

The topic, or what the general category the author is writing about in the above paragraph, would be:

Buying eggs

The main idea, however, is more specific and could be stated as:

Modern day consumers have more choices in purchasing eggs than in the past.

So we can see from a comparison of the topic and the main idea, we are moving from general to more specific.

Topic	*Main Idea*
Buying eggs	Modern day consumers have more choices in purchasing eggs than in the past.

We can see this relationship expressed on a continuum; see the one below. This can be very helpful when trying to locate the main idea in a reading.

Too general	X	Too specific
Topic	Main Idea	Details/Examples

Stated Main Idea versus Implied Main Idea

Every textbook paragraph has a main idea. Sometimes the main idea is stated directly—that is, the author's most important point is stated in a sentence (for example, "Russia must do something to save its economy," OR "The exact nature of the five stages of death has been disputed." Other times, the author gives you the information needed to understand the main point without stating it directly as a single sentence. This is called an *implied main idea* because you the reader must use information contained in the paragraph to infer (reason out) what the author's main point is.

We will return to the key reading skill terms of *inference* and *implication* in later chapters. For now, let's practice distinguishing between topic and main idea in paragraph contexts.

BIOGRAPHICAL PROFILE

Robert Atkins

Robert Atkins is best known for his controversial low-carbohydrate diet, which had a great influence on the way the American people made conscious decisions about nutritional choices.

He was born on October 17, 1930. He was an American cardiologist who received his medical degree from Cornell Medical College in 1955. Dr. Atkins revolutionized the food industry with his unique Atkins Nutritional Approach, also known as "the Atkins Diet." He recommended eliminating all carbohydrates from the diet, especially simple ones such as bagels and donuts, and consuming mostly proteins along with salads and vegetables. Convinced by his unique approach to nutrition, many health-conscious Americans began to reduce their intake of carbohydrates and reported significant weight loss after being on the Atkins Diet for several months. His controversial diet caused panic amongst food manufacturers who produced and marketed mostly carbohydrate-based food items.

During his illustrious career, Dr. Atkins wrote several books on healthy living. Although he became an internationally renowned figure and changed the lives of hundreds of thousands of people, his own life ended tragically when he sustained serious injuries to his head after falling in front of his office in New York City on April 8, 2003. Some critics argued that his accident may have been connected to his being somewhat overweight. He succumbed to his injury on April 17, 2003. However, his legacy lives on, as thousands of people around the world continue to follow the Atkins Diet.

Some Questions for Group Discussion

1. Why do you think the Atkins Diet stirred up so much controversy? In other words, what was it about his recommended diet that raised many eyebrows?
2. Discuss why scores of people put so much faith in a dietary concept created by one person. Would you change your dietary habits based on an expert's advice?
3. Do you agree with the critics that Dr. Atkins's premature death was caused by his obesity? Do research on the Internet to determine whether it was his being overweight that ended his life.

Biographical Internet Research

Find out about another prominent figure in Health and Nutrition online, selecting one from the list below, and share a biographical profile with your classmates:

- Jenny Craig
- Deepak Chopra
- Michio Kushi
- Bernard Jensen
- Michael Pollen

ESL Annotation

2.9 ESL Many ESL students have never heard of the Atkins Diet and may not know much about "high-profile" diets.

PRACTICING THE SKILL
Practice 1

Identifying Topic and Main Idea

Read the following short paragraphs and practice distinguishing between topic and main idea.

Passage 1

How much sleep is necessary to maintain a healthy lifestyle? Many people say they need at least eight hours to feel refreshed in the morning. Researchers say the amount of sleep one needs depends on the individual.

© Pearson Education, Inc.

Some can thrive on as little as six hours of sleep while others lag behind if they sleep less than eleven.

Topic	Main Idea
Sleep	The amount of sleep one needs depends on the individual.

Passage 2

Swimming is one of the healthiest activities for your body. Unlike running or weight lifting, it will put little physical strain on your system. The water helps support your body and allows you to both build muscle tone and get the cardiovascular workout you need.

Topic	Main Idea
Swimming	Swimming is one of the healthiest activities for your body.

Passage 3

Mad Cow Disease is a fatal brain disorder caused by a prion, which is an abnormal form of protein. Prions influence other proteins to take on their abnormal shape, and these abnormal proteins cause brain damage. Mad Cow Disease is also called bovine spongiform encephalopathy (BSE). The disease eats away at a cow's brain, leaving it full of spongelike holes. Eventually the brain can no longer control vital life functions, and the cow literally "goes mad."

(From *Nutrition: An Applied Appproach* by Janice Thompson and Melinda Manore, p. 216)

Topic	Main Idea
Mad Cow Disease	Mad Cow Disease is a fatal brain disorder that inflicts itself on cows.

Passage 4

A classic study done by researchers at Laval University in Quebec, Canada, shows how genetics plays a role in our responses to overeating (Bouchard et al. 1990). Twelve pairs of male identical twins volunteered to stay in a dormitory where they were supervised 24 hours a day for 120 consecutive days. Researchers measured how much energy each man needed to maintain his body weight at the beginning of the study. For 100 days the subjects were fed 1,000 kcal more per day than they needed to maintain body weight. Daily physical activity was limited, but each person was allowed to walk outdoors for 30 minutes each day, read, watch television and videos, play cards and video games. The research staff stayed with these men to ensure that they did not stray from the study protocol.

(From *Nutrition: An Applied Appproach* p. 395)

Topic	*Main Idea*
Genetics and overeating	An experiment was conducted to study the relationship between genetics and overeating.

Practice 2

Identifying Main Idea and Topic

Let's practice identifying main idea and topic by revisiting Reading Selection 1. Work with a partner to restate the main idea of the selected paragraphs provided below, using your own words.

Collaboration

Passages: Excerpts from "Fat Chance"

1   If you had to choose, would you rather be fat or blind? When a researcher asked that question of a group of formerly obese people, 89 percent said they would prefer to lose their sight than their hard-won slimness. "When you're blind, people want to help you. No one wants to help you when you're fat," one explained. Ninety-one percent of the group also chose having a leg amputated over a return to obesity.

What is the main idea?

In a survey, most people said

they would rather be blind

than obese.

2   This is shocking. But it seems less so by the end of "Rethinking Thin," a new book about obesity by Gina Kolata, a science reporter for the *New York Times*. Kolata argues that being fat is not something people have much control over. Most people who are overweight struggle to change their shape throughout their lives, but remain stuck within a relatively narrow weight range set by their genes. For those determined to foil biology, strict dieting is a life sentence. "I am a fat man in a thin man's body," an MIT obesity researcher who shed his unwanted pounds years ago tells Kolata.

What is the topic here?

Obesity and dieting

3   He's one of the lucky and single-minded few. Study after study, Kolata notes, has shown that for most fat people the long-term rewards of dieting are modest at best. Yet as obesity rates have skyrocketed, exhortations to eat right, exercise and shed pounds have gone from loud to shrill. Kolata's understandable sympathy for those caught between the ever intensifying pressure to be thin and the stubborn size of their bodies, however, leads her to flirt with an unlikely conclusion: Maybe the outcry over obesity is itself supersized, and being fat isn't really unhealthy after all.

4   Kolata follows a two-year clinical trial at the University of Pennsylvania designed to test the low-carbohydrate, high-fat Atkins diet against a traditional low-calorie, low-fat one. Kolata wrote her book before she had the results for the trial, though a different study, published in March in the *Journal of the American Medical Association*, found that Atkins beats the low-cal diet for keeping off weight. The diet-versus-diet contest, however, isn't her real story.

What is the main Idea?

A journalist investigated

clinical trials that focused on

various diets

© Pearson Education, Inc.

Practice 3

Identifying Stated Main Idea

In the following passages about health and nutrition from the *New York Times*, try to locate which sentence contains the *stated main idea*, and underline it. To help guide you toward recognition of the main idea sentence, consider which sentence does the following:

- States the single most important point about the topic
- Is general enough to cover all the information in the paragraph
- Is explained, focused on, and supported by the other sentences

Underline the stated main idea in each of the examples below.

Passage 1

America has become weirdly polarized on the subject of weight. On the one hand, we've been told with almost religious certainty by everyone from the surgeon general on down, and we have come to believe with almost religious certainty, that obesity is caused by the excessive consumption of fat, and that if we eat less fat we will lose weight and live longer. On the other, we have the ever-resilient message of Atkins and decades' worth of best-selling diet books, including "The Zone," "Sugar Busters" and "Protein Power" to name a few. All push some variation of what scientists would call the alternative hypothesis: it's not the fat that makes us fat, but the carbohydrates, and if we eat less carbohydrates we will lose weight and live longer.

From Gary Taubes, "What if It's All Been a Big Fat Lie?" *New York Times*, July 7, 2002

Passage 2

Americans are eating more fresh fruits and vegetables, and that is a healthy development. But a recent outbreak of hepatitis in western Pennsylvania is a reminder that in order to ensure the safety of our food supply chain, changes in our eating patterns require similar adjustments in our vigilance. Traditionally, concerns about food-borne illnesses focused on meat and poultry, foods inspected by the Department of Agriculture. Fresh produce, overseen by the Food and Drug Administration, is increasingly seen as a potential source of disease. Yet the FDA lacks the resources and policing authority of the Agriculture Department. An ever-growing reliance on imported produce compounds the challenge. The recent hepatitis outbreak was traced to one restaurant's imported green onions.

From "Fresh Produce, the Downside." From *The New York Times*, December 1, 2003. © 2003 *The New York Times*. All rights reserved. Used by permission and protected by the Copyright Laws of the United States. The printing, copying, redistribution, or retransmission of the Material without express written permission is prohibited. www.nytimes.com

Passage 3

For decades, the beauty industry was described as—or accused of—selling "hope in a jar." Now, a marketing blitz with a budget estimated at more than

$150 million in the first year will try to persuade dieters to seek hope in a pill bottle despite widespread skepticism about the grandiose promises of diet pills, plans and potions. A campaign for the drug Alli is being waged on many fronts by seven agencies. Its first-year budget is estimated at more than $150 million. The campaign, being introduced in stages by seven agencies, promotes a product from GlaxoSmithKline called Alli—pronounced, not coincidentally, like "ally," as in a helper or associate. Alli is the first weight-loss drug to be approved by the Food and Drug Administration for sale in the United States over the counter, no prescription necessary. It works by preventing the body from absorbing some of the fat one eats.

From Stuart Elliott, "Telling Dieters a Pill Works Only if They Work, Too." From *The New York Times*, May 9, 2007. © 2007 The New York Times. All rights reserved. Used by permission and protected by the Copyright Laws of the United States. The printing, copying, redistribution, or retransmission of the Material without express written permission is prohibited. www.nytimes.com

Passage 4

In the debate over whether organic food is better than conventionally raised food, advocates for organic produce say it contains fewer harmful chemicals and is better for the earth, and some claim that it is more nutritious. And recent preliminary evidence suggests that the levels of certain nutrients, especially vitamin C, some minerals and some polyphenols—naturally occurring antioxidants that may help bolster the immune system—are higher in organically grown crops. As a result of this preliminary evidence and the Agriculture Department's adoption in 2000 of standards for organic foods, the Organic Trade Association has created the nonprofit Center for Organic Education and Promotion to finance research that could verify what small-scale research may suggest: organic food may provide greater health benefits than conventional food.

2.10 The last sentence may also be considered a possible answer.

From Marian Burros, "Eating Well: Is Organic Food Provably Better?" From *The New York Times*, July 16, 2003. © 2003 The New York Times. All rights reserved. Used by permission and protected by the Copyright Laws of the United States. The printing, copying, redistribution, or retransmission of the Material without express written permission is prohibited. www.nytimes.com

Passage 5

Mothers who are depressed or anxious are more likely to take their children to doctors for stomachaches and abdominal pains, a new study has concluded. The study found that mothers with the highest levels of depression were twice as likely as mothers with the lowest levels to seek medical help for abdominal pain reported by their children. The gap persisted even when the figures were adjusted to account for different levels of pain. Dr. Rona L. Levy, a psychologist at the University of Washington School of Social Work, presented the findings to a conference of the Society of Behavioral Medicine in Salt Lake City late last month.

From John O'Neil, "Vital Signs: Mental Health; Mothers' Minds and Babies' Bellies." From *The New York Times*, April 8, 2003. © 2003 The New York Times. All rights reserved. Used by permission and protected by the Copyright Laws of the United States. The printing, copying, redistribution, or retransmission of the Material without express written permission is prohibited. www.nytimes.com

© Pearson Education, Inc.

Identifying the Main Idea

Sometimes the main idea of a reading passage is not directly stated, but implied. It is the reader's responsibility to read between the lines and figure out the author's implied main idea. Consider the following example.

Example

Why do so many people take dietary supplements? Many people believe they cannot consume adequate nutrients in their diet, and they take a supplement as extra nutritional insurance. Others have been advised by their health care provider to take a supplement due to a given health condition. There are people who believe that certain supplements can be used to treat illness or disease. There are also people who believe that supplements are necessary to enhance their physical looks or athletic performance.

(From *Nutrition: An Applied Approach*, p. 302)

After reading the passage above, you realize that the main idea is not directly stated. However, when you pay attention to the details that are offered, you will notice that all of the supporting sentences discuss the many reasons people take dietary supplements. Thus, the main idea of the passage is that *people take dietary supplements for different reasons.*

Practice 4

Identifying the Implied Main Idea

Passage 1

For most of her life, Darcy had thoroughly enjoyed good food. Her husband bragged about her being a gourmet cook. But a few weeks after learning she was pregnant, her appetite seemed to disappear. She would wander through the aisles of the grocery store with an empty cart, knowing she should be choosing nutritious foods for her growing baby but feeling unable to find a single food that appealed to her. Eventually she'd return home with a few things for her husband. . . . and a large bag of ice.

(From *Nutrition: An Applied Approach*, p. 548)

What is the implied main idea?

Darcy was conflicted between satisfying her growing baby's appetite and dealing with her own loss of appetite.

Passage 2

Strong proponents of veganism state that any consumption of animal products is wrong and that feeding animal products to children is forcing them into a life of obesity, clogged arteries, and chronic diet-related diseases. In addition, many people who consume a vegan diet feel that consumption of animal products wastes natural resources and contributes to environmental damage and is therefore morally wrong. In contrast, strong antagonists of veganism emphasize that feeding a vegan diet to young children deprives them of essential nutrients that can only be found in animal products. Some people even suggest that veganism for young children is, in essence, a form of child abuse.

(From *Nutrition: An Applied Approach* , p. 482)

What is the implied main idea?

Feeding a vegan diet to young children is a controversial issue.

Passage 3

"You know I never thought I needed to take a multivitamin because I am healthy and I eat lots of different kinds of foods. But now I have learned in my nutrition course about what all these vitamins and minerals do in the body, and I'm thinking, heck, maybe I should take one just for insurance. I mean, I use up a lot of fuel playing basketball and working out. Maybe if I popped a pill every day, I'd have an easier time keeping my weight up!"

(From *Nutrition: An Applied Approach*, p. 372)

What is the implied main idea?

The writer is considering whether or not it is worth it to take a multivitamin.

Recommended Debate Topic: Should unhealthy foods such as soda, high-caffeine drinks, candy, and fast food be available in public school and college campuses? Brainstorm other debate topics related to health and nutrition with your peers, and present your ideas to your instructor for approval.

 **DEBATABLE TOPIC**

Your suggested debate topics:

a. _____

b. _____

c. _____

The following article and subsequent letter response will help prepare you for the debate activity as it examines the issue of soft drink bans in public schools. You will also receive more practice in recognizing main ideas and topics.

READING

Reading Selection **3A**

Newspaper Article

Bottlers Agree to a School Ban on Sweet Drinks

Pre-Reading Questions

2.11 Flesch-Kincaid Grade Level 12.0

Collaboration

Discuss these questions in small groups.

1. What kinds of drinks do you usually consume
   a. early in the morning?
   b. during the school/workday?
   c. in the evening?

© Pearson Education, Inc.

2. What types of drinks are most readily available in vending machines at your college?

3. Do you agree with the common view that young people consume too much sugar every day?

4. If you had to reduce your sugar intake for health reasons, what food item would be most difficult for you to sacrifice? Explain.

Bottlers Agree to a School Ban on Sweet Drinks

By Marian Burros and Melanie Warner, the *New York Times*

May 4, 2006

1   The country's top three soft-drink companies announced yesterday that beginning this fall they would start removing sweetened drinks like Coke, Pepsi and iced teas from school cafeterias and vending machines in **response** to the growing threat of lawsuits and state **legislation**.

2   Under an agreement between beverage makers and health advocates, students in elementary school would be served only bottled water, low-fat and nonfat milk, and 100 **percent** fruit juice in servings no bigger than eight ounces. Serving sizes would increase to 10 ounces in middle school. In high school, low-calorie juice drinks, sports drinks and diet sodas would be permitted; serving sizes would be limited to 12 ounces.

3   The agreement, which includes parochial and private schools contracts, is voluntary, and the beverage industry said its school sales would not be affected because it expected to replace sugary drinks with other ones.

4   "This is a **voluntary policy**, but I think schools will want to follow it," said Susan K. Neely, president of the American Beverage Association. Still, about 35 million public school children would be affected by the agreement, which would apply to extended school functions like band practice but would not apply to events likely to be attended by parents, like evening plays or interscholastic sports. An additional 15 million students attend schools that operate under stricter **regulations**, where the **guidelines** would not apply.

5   Last week, for example, Connecticut banned all sodas, including diet drinks and sports drinks like Gatorade, in its schools; New York City schools permit only low-fat milk, water and 100 **percent** fruit juice, which is sold under an exclusive **contract** with Snapple. Contracts between schools and bottlers would be updated under the deal, and changes would not go into effect before the next school year.

brokered
arranged and managed

6   The agreement was **brokered** by the Alliance for a Healthier Generation, a collaboration between the William J. Clinton Foundation and the American Heart Association. It is **similar** to an arrangement that the industry had been negotiating with a coalition of lawyers and the Center for Science in the Public Interest, an advocacy group, that had threatened to sue if an agreement

Marian Burros and Melanie Warner, "Bottlers Agree to a School Ban on Sweet Drinks." From *The New York Times*, May 4, 2006. © 2006 The New York Times. All rights reserved. Used by permission and protected by the Copyright Laws of the United States. The printing, copying, redistribution, or retransmission of the Material without express written permission is prohibited. www.nytimes.com

could not be reached. The terms were accepted by the three biggest soft-drink companies, Coca-Cola, PepsiCo Inc. and Cadbury Schweppes (whose products include Dr Pepper and Snapple), which together control more than 90 **percent** of school sales.

7   At a news **conference** at his office in Harlem, Mr. Clinton called the beverage industry "courageous" for agreeing to switch to lower-calorie drinks. Mr. Clinton, who has made obesity a **major** issue of his post-presidency agenda, was joined by Gov. Mike Huckabee of Arkansas, a vocal **proponent** of fitness.

proponent
a supporter or advocate of something

8   Later in the day, Mr. Clinton said it was more than the threat of lawsuits that spurred the agreement.

9   "We've been talking to them for months and months, and they may have liked the way we were working with them, not just singling them out," he said in a telephone interview. "I'm glad we did it without litigation and could accelerate the **process**."

10   It will take three years for the agreement to be put fully into effect. The industry has agreed at the end of each school year starting in 2007 to disclose the progress toward fulfilling the agreement. The new standards are expected to be in place in 75 **percent** of schools by the summer of 2008 and all by 2009. The success of the program depends on schools' willingness to amend existing contracts, industry representatives said. The majority of school contracts with Pepsi Bottling Group, Pepsi's largest bottler, for **instance**, are for three to five years, said its spokeswoman, Kelly McAndrew, who said Pepsi would encourage schools to renegotiate their contracts.

11   "We're doing our part to communicate this new **policy**," she said.

12   Mirroring **overall** beverage consumption in the United States, bottled water and sports drinks have become increasingly popular in schools in recent years. But in a **survey** released in August, the American Beverage Association said 45 **percent** of all school vending sales were sweetened soda.

13   While the soft-drink industry was negotiating the deal, it was discussing a **similar accord** with the Center for Science in the Public Interest and a group of lawyers who had successfully sued tobacco companies.

accord
an agreement

14   Richard A. Daynard, associate dean at Northeastern University School of Law, a tobacco-lawsuit veteran, called the agreement "the first **major** victory for the obesity-litigation strategy."

15   "This would not have happened but for the threat of litigation," Professor Daynard said.

16   Beverage-industry officials **acknowledged** discussions with the lawyers but would not comment further.

17   Dr. Michael Jacobson, executive director of the Center for Science in the Public Interest, applauded the agreement, but said, "I'd like to get rid of the Gatorades and diet soft drinks completely."

18   Nutritionists and parent groups have pressured schools and the beverage industry for some time to restrict sales. Several states, including California, and some local school districts have banned soft-drink sales, and other states are considering **similar** crackdowns. In **response**, the beverage association last year announced a **policy** that would have cut back on the sale of certain soft drinks in schools. But critics said the plan was unenforceable.

© Pearson Education, Inc.

19   Gary Ruskin, executive director of Commercial Alert, a nonprofit public-health group, said the new agreement might prove to have the same problem. Mr. Ruskin criticized it, too, because it did not address soft-drink advertising in schools and did not stop bottlers from advertising on Channel One, which is shown to seven million schoolchildren a day. Mr. Clinton said there remained "an **enormous** amount to be done" about childhood obesity.

single out
select from a group

20   "You can't **single out** one cause of this problem," he said. "But if an 8-year-old child took in 45 less calories per day, by the time he reached high school, he would weight 20 pounds less than he would have weighed otherwise."

READING

Reading Selection **3B**

A Letter of Response

ESL Annotation

2.12 ESL In many cultures it may be considered "out of place" for a 16-year-old high school student to offer blunt criticism in a public venue. This may be worth some class discussion.

preposterous
completely unreasonable or silly

My Soda, My Choice

Monday, May 15, 2006

This is a response to the article in Reading Selection 3A.

To the Editor:

Re "Bottlers Agree to a School Ban on Sweet Drinks" (front page, May 4): As a 16-year-old high school student, I strongly object to the lobbying by state legislatures to **deny** students the right to buy certain soft drinks in school.

     It is **preposterous** that by the middle of my senior year, I will have the right to vote, but the state will consider me unable to make proper lifestyle choices. Although some lawmakers believe that they are endowed with the wisdom to make daily choices for others, I would prefer personal freedom.

JONATHAN PANTER
Palisades, N.Y., May 6, 2006

Reading Comprehension Check

1. According to the article, what motivated the top three soft-drink companies to remove their sweetened drinks from vending machines?
   a. fear of bad press   c. general altruism
   b. fear of being sued   d. exponential sales

2. What is the topic of the article?
   a. public schools
   b. Due to increasing pressure, the top three bottlers agreed to a ban on soda in public schools.
   c. soft drinks in schools
   d. It will take three years for the ban to go into effect.

3. The agreement of replacing sweetened drinks was
   a. mandatory.   c. voluntary.
   b. compulsory.   d. sanctioned by law.

4. What is the main idea of the article?
   a. schools and soda bans
   b. Large soda companies feared being sued.
   c. Giving in to heavy pressure, the top soda companies have agreed not to sell soft drinks in schools.
   d. Some states offer stricter policies than others.

5. Find the sentence in paragraph 7 that states: "Mr. Clinton, who has made obesity a major issue of his post-presidency agenda . . ." From this sentence we can derive that Mr. Clinton focused on the obesity issue mostly
   a. before he was president.
   b. while he was president.
   c. after he was president.
   d. both b and c

6. According to the American Beverage Association, what percentage of vending machine sales were from sweetened soda?
   a. exactly half
   b. almost half
   c. about a quarter
   d. 30 percent

7. What is Mr. Clinton's idea in the last paragraph of the article?
   a. Every child must deal with obesity-related illnesses such as diabetes.
   b. A few calories less a day for a child could make a big difference in the long run.
   c. By the time an 8-year-old reaches high school, it is too late to change his drinking habits.
   d. Health is a national issue of great concern.

8. In the letter that responds to the article, who is criticized for their lobbying efforts?
   a. a 16-year-old student
   b. the school system
   c. politicians
   d. none of the above

9. What is the topic of the letter?
   a. personal freedom and soda bans
   b. teenage disagreement
   c. the value of today's soft drinks
   d. A student wants to change the regulations of the soda ban.

10. The writer uses the term *personal freedom* at the end of his letter to express
    a. his outrage at the schools.
    b. his belief in the value of soft drinks.
    c. his right to choose what he wants to drink.
    d. the freedom that teenagers have.

Connecting Reading Skills with Standardized Testing

Finding the Main Idea versus Identifying the Topic

On standardized reading exams, it is easy to confuse questions that focus on the main idea with questions that ask for the topic of a reading selection. Students often answer a "main idea" question with a multiple-choice option that offers the

© Pearson Education, Inc.

"topic," and vice versa. Pay attention to the relationship between the questions given and the answer choices offered. Below we can see some sample questions.

You are being asked the main idea when the question is worded in the following ways:

- The author's main point is that . . .
- The principal idea of the passage is . . .
- Which of the following best expresses the main point of the entire passage?
- Which of the following best expresses the main idea of the second paragraph?

You are being asked to identify the topic of a passage when the test question begins as follows:

- The best title for the selection is . . .
- The passage discusses . . .
- The passage focuses mainly on . . .
- This passage is about . . .
- This passage concerns . . .
- The problem the author is discussing in this passage is . . .
- The author is explaining the nature of . . .

Read the following article and practice with *main idea* and *identifying topic* questions.

READING

Reading Selection **4**

Online Magazine Article

2.13 Flesch-Kincaid Grade Level 11.5

The 9 Most Common Kitchen Mistakes Even Healthy Women Make . . . and Why They're Robbing Your Food of Nutrients

---

Pre-Reading Questions

Collaboration

Answer these questions in small groups.

1. How often do you (or someone in your family) go grocery shopping? Do you buy grocery in small batches for a few days, or do you purchase foods in big batches for longer durations? Give specific reasons for your answers.

2. When you go grocery shopping at a supermarket, what criteria do you use to select the food items? For example, do you consider the nutritional value of the foods you purchase? Give specific examples.

3. Do you think that most supermarkets provide the nutritional information and shelf life of the agricultural produce they sell? If not, then should the government require them to provide this information to the consumer? Explain why.

The 9 Most Common Kitchen Mistakes Even Healthy Women Make . . . and Why They're Robbing Your Food of Nutrients

By Amanda Pressner

Shape.com, http://www.shape.com/healthyeating/8018

1   There's something empowering about **hitting** the supermarket to shop for your week's meals. Rather than putting yourself at the mercy of the local Chinese take-out restaurant or succumbing to the lure of the drive-through, you're taking dinner—and your waistline—into your own hands. "Eating out less and cooking more may be one of the most effective things you can do to keep fat and calories in check," says Cheryl Forberg, R.D., author of *Stop the Clock! Cooking.* "Plus, building your diet around produce, whole grains, beans, and lean protein practically guarantees you'll reach your recommended targets for most vitamins and minerals." But while we may be tossing the freshest, most wholesome foods into our carts, many of us are storing and preparing them in ways that rob them (and our bodies) of the very nutrients we're seeking. Nutritionists and food-safety experts point to nine typical kitchen blunders that negatively **impact** the quality of our diets. Fortunately, you can **sidestep** all of them easily. Follow this advice to make your next meal healthier.

hitting
going to or visiting

What is the main Idea?
Most women are not aware of the nine mistakes they make storing and preparing foods that deprive them of their nutrients

Mistake #1   *You're overloading on produce*

2   Sure, making one big grocery run at the start of the week seems like a no-fail way to get your five a day. After all, if those carrots, greens, apples, and berries are around, you'll eat more of them and therefore get more nutrients, right? Wrong. "The vitamins and minerals in fruits and vegetables begin to diminish the moment they're harvested," says Geri Brewster, R.D., a wellness consultant at Northern Westchester Hospital in Mt. Kisco, New York. That means the longer you store produce, the fewer nutrients it will contain. After about a week in the fridge, for example, spinach retains just half of its folate and around 60 **percent** of its lutein (an antioxidant associated with healthy eyes), concludes a study in the *Journal of Food Science.* Broccoli loses about 62 **percent** of its flavonoids (antioxidant **compounds** that help ward off cancer and heart disease) within 10 days, according to a study in the *Journal of Agricultural and Food Chemistry.* "You're better off buying smaller batches at least twice a week," says Brewster. If you can't shop every few days, pick up frozen produce. These fruits and veggies are harvested at their peak and are flash-frozen immediately. Because the produce isn't exposed to oxygen, the nutrients stay stable for a year, according to researchers at the University of California, Davis. Just be sure to avoid frozen products packed in sauces or syrups. These additions can mean extra calories from fat or sugar, and sometimes they're high in sodium as well.

sidestep
to avoid a difficult question or decision

What's the topic of this paragraph?
Freshness factors for fruits and vegetables

© Pearson Education, Inc.

stashing
keeping something in a safe, often secret, place

What's the main idea?

Rather than keeping milk and

grain products in clear

containers where they may be

exposed to light and lose their

nutrients, it is better to store

them in cardboard cartons

and opaque containers.

opaque
not transparent or translucent

Mistake #2 *You're stashing foods in see-through containers*

3   If you're still buying your milk in clear plastic jugs, consider switching to cardboard cartons. Milk is rich in the B vitamin riboflavin; when exposed to light, a **chemical reaction** is kicked off that reduces the vitamin's potency, according to researchers from Ghent University in Belgium. Other nutrients, such as amino acids (the building blocks of protein) and vitamins A, C, D, and E, are also affected. And because lowfat and nonfat milk varieties are thinner than whole milk, light can penetrate them more easily. "This **process**, known as photooxidation, can change the flavor of the milk and **create** disease-causing free radicals," says Susan Duncan, Ph.D., a food scientist at Virginia Tech. Since grain products (especially whole grains) are also high in riboflavin, they too are susceptible to this breakdown of nutrients and production of free radicals. Duncan recommends avoiding the practice of storing dry goods like pasta, rice, and cereals in clear containers on your countertop. Instead, keep them in their original boxes or in **opaque** containers and stash them in your kitchen cabinets, where they'll be shielded from light.

pungent
sharply affecting the organs of taste or smell

What's the topic of this paragraph?

cooking garlic and health

Mistake #3 *You're too quick to cook your garlic*

4   Legend has it that these **pungent** little bulbs can ward off vampires, but science shows that if you cook them correctly, they may have the power to fight off an even more frightening villain: cancer. "Chop, slice, or crush your cloves, then set them aside for at least 10 minutes before sautéing," says John Milner, Ph.D., chief of the nutritional science **research** group at the National Cancer Institute in Rockville, Maryland. "Breaking up garlic triggers an enzymatic **reaction** that releases a healthy compound called allyl sulfur; waiting to cook garlic allows enough time for the full amount of the compound to form."

What's the main point here?

Avocados are a healthier

substitute for butter because

they are rich in

monounsaturated fat.

Mistake #4 *The only time you eat avocados is in guacamole*

5   Adding this green fruit to salads and sandwiches is an easy way to raise your nutritional bar. Avocados are exceptionally rich in folate, potassium, vitamin E, and fiber. It's true that they're also high in fat, but it's the heart-healthy monounsaturated kind. And half an avocado has just 153 calories. One novel way to work them into your diet is to use them as a fat substitute in baking. Many of us have been using applesauce or puréed prunes in place of butter and oil in brownie and cookie recipes for years. Researchers at Hunter College in New York City wanted to see if avocado could work in the same way without affecting the taste. They replaced half of the butter in an oatmeal cookie recipe with puréed avocado. Not only did this swap cut the total fat count by 35 **percent** (avocados have fewer fat grams per tablespoon than butter or oil), it also made the resulting treats softer, chewier, and less likely to crumble than cookies made according to the original recipe. If you're still wary of using such a nontraditional ingredient in sweets, try adding it to savory baked **items**, such as quick breads and muffins.

Mistake #5   *You skimp on seasonings*

6   Herbs and spices not only enhance the flavor of your cooking without adding fat or sodium, many of these fragrant ingredients also protect you from food poisoning. After testing 20 common seasonings against five strains of bacteria (including E. coli, staphylococcus, and salmonella), researchers at the University of Hong Kong found that the higher the antioxidant value of the spice, the greater its ability to inhibit bacterial activity. Cloves, cinnamon sticks, and oregano were the most effective at fighting off these food-borne pathogens. A separate study **published** in the *Journal of Agricultural and Food Chemistry* shows that rosemary, thyme, nutmeg, and bay leaves are also antioxidant-rich. Of course, you can't ignore standard food-safety practices, but adding half a teaspoon of herbs or spices to salads, vegetables, and meats can give you extra peace of mind and boost your intake of disease-fighting antioxidants.

skimp on
to supply inadequately

What's the main focus here?

Herbs and spices such as

cloves and cinnamon sticks

are rich in antioxidants and

adding them to salads and

vegetables can help us fight

disease.

Mistake #6   *You're a serial peeler*

7   Most of the antioxidants and polyphenols in produce are located very close to the surface of the skin or in the skin itself. A study **published** in the **journal** *Nutrition Research* found that most fruit peels exhibited two to twenty-seven times more antioxidant activity than the pulp of the fruit. "Many of us remove the skins from eggplant, bell peppers, peaches, apples, and nectarines while preparing recipes, but we're really just tossing away nutrients and fiber," says nutritionist Forberg. She recommends gently scrubbing potatoes and carrots rather than removing their skin, and using a vegetable peeler or sharp knife to pare away as thin a **layer** as possible from fruits and veggies that must be peeled.

What's the main idea of this paragraph?

Excessive peeling of most

fruits results in diminishing

disease-fighting antioxidants.

Mistake #7   *You're simmering away vitamins and minerals*

8   Boiling may seem like a simple, no-fuss way to prepare vegetables without adding oil, but this cooking **method** can cause up to 90 **percent** of a food's nutrients to leech out, says Karen Collins, R.D., a nutrition advisor to the American Institute for Cancer Research in Washington, D.C. "Minerals like potassium and watersoluble vitamins like B and C end up getting tossed out with the water," she says. To keep these essentials from draining away during the cooking **process**, try steaming (use a **minimal** amount of water with a steamer basket), microwaving, or stir-frying. A study from the University of Essex in England showed that when certain vegetables were prepared using these **techniques**, most of the nutrients they contained were spared. And stir-frying scores even more points when you're cooking dark green or orange vegetables. These are rich in beta-carotene, and the oil you use in stir-frying them can increase the amount of the antioxidant you absorb by up to 63 **percent**, according to a study **published** in the **journal** *Molecular Nutrition & Food Research*. You don't need to use a lot of oil; even just a tablespoon will do.

What is the focus of this paragraph?

Boiling vegetables deprives

them of their nutrients. It is

much better to steam or

stir-fry them in order to

increase the amount of

antioxidants.

© Pearson Education, Inc.

Mistake #8   *You don't wash all your produce before eating it*

What is the topic of this paragraph?

Washing fruits before peeling

and eating them to avoid

bacterial activity.

9   Most of us remember to rinse plums and berries before noshing on them, but when was the last time you doused a banana, orange, cantaloupe, or mango with water? It may seem strange to wash peel-and-eat produce, but harmful bacteria lingering on the surface could be transferred to your hands or even to the inside of the fruit when you cut into it. To clean produce, simply run each piece under the tap and gently scrub. "Using your hands to rub fruits like oranges, bananas, and peaches under water is **sufficient**," says Ruth Frechman, R.D., a dietitian in Burbank, California, and a spokeswoman for the American Dietetic Association. When you're done, dry the **items** with a clean cloth or paper towel. It's important to wash your hands with soap and warm water for at least 20 seconds before and after you handle the **items** to further reduce the spread of bacteria. Frechman also suggests throwing out the outer leaves of greens like cabbage and lettuce before washing, as they've been handled the most and can have the highest levels of bacterial contamination.

Mistake #9   *You're not pairing foods properly*

lethargic
drowsy, sluggish

What is the topic of this paragraph?

Increasing our iron intake by

pairing whole-grain cereal

and leafy greens with

vitamin C-rich foods.

10   Many of us think about getting enough iron only when we feel **lethargic** or fatigued. But we should pay attention to our iron intake every day, before symptoms **occur**. Our bodies absorb about 15 to 35 **percent** of heme iron (found in meats and seafood), but just 2 to 20 **percent** of non-heme iron (from beans, whole-grain cereal, tofu, and dark, leafy greens). We can maximize how much iron we take in by pairing the latter group with vitamin C-rich foods and beverages, such as citrus fruits and juices, tomatoes, hot and sweet peppers, strawberries, and melons. On the other hand, drinking tea or coffee at meals can inhibit how much iron we absorb by up to 60 **percent**, says Marla Reicks, R.D., a professor of nutrition at the University of Minnesota in St. Paul. That's because these beverages contain **compounds** called polyphenols that bind to the iron. Wait until you've completely finished your meal before putting the kettle on to boil.

From Reading to Writing: Making an Outline

Overview

You may have noticed that the reading selections in this chapter are coherent and flow smoothly. The reason for this is that there are logical relationships between the main ideas and the supporting details that make those ideas clear and easy to understand. However, sometimes you may be required to read complex texts in which the ideas are not that easy to follow. *Outlining*, in this sense, is an important skill that helps the reader see how the different ideas are organized logically in the original text. One of the main purposes of outlining is to first identify how the author develops the argument by using several ideas with supporting evidence. Then, you can use your outline to discuss the ideas elaborating on the specific topic of the text, orally and in writing.

Preparing an Outline

The first step toward preparing an outline is to write down the title and the author of the original text. The next step is to write the author's main idea, which can usually be found in the introductory paragraph. Keep in mind that an outline does not necessarily have to contain complete sentences. Your task, however, is to retain the original meaning, yet use your own words. We have provided a worksheet (see below) to make outlining a fruitful and enjoyable exercise.

As you begin the process of outlining, constantly frame these questions in the back of your mind:

- What is the author's main idea?
- What specific bits and pieces of evidence does he or she present to support the main idea?

You will need to read the entire text carefully to answer these questions. While reading the text, focus on identifying the logical connections between the different ideas and the overall structure and content.

Once you have prepared a rough outline, read it carefully, and read the original text a second time to fill in the information gaps. You will notice that during a second reading you comprehend the text more clearly, as you search for and find the missing pieces of information. As you can see, outlining will enable you to recall information later when you discuss the reading selection with your peers in class and submit your outline to your instructor in written form.

Implications for Your Learning

While it is not necessary to prepare an outline of every single reading selection in your textbook, practicing outlining regularly will improve your ability to read, review, and discuss information related to the general and specific ideas contained in the original text. Moreover, outlining has implications for writing as well. You can prepare an outline of the main ideas you want to present in a speech or in written communication. You can also apply the skill of outlining to writing well-organized paragraphs of your own. Once you have outlined the main ideas, you can expand them in a logical and coherent manner as you write the paragraph. As you can see, there are many advantages to outlining information.

Sample Outline

Here is a sample outline of Reading Selection 3A on p. 90 as a model for your outlining practice. Notice how the major details are followed by the minor details supporting the main idea.

Title: Bottlers Agree to a School Ban on Sweet Drinks

Author: Marian Burros and Melanie Warner

The *New York Times*, May 4, 2006

© Pearson Education, Inc.

Main idea: Owing to growing pressure of lawsuits and state legislation, three leading soft-drink companies have decided to eliminate sweetened drinks such as Coke and Pepsi from school cafeterias and vending machines.

I. There is an agreement between soft drink makers and health advocates.

   A. Students would be served water, nonfat milk, and 100 percent fruit juice.

   B. Serving sizes would increase to 10 ounces in middle school.

   C. The companies' profits would not be affected.

   D. This agreement is voluntary.

II. Many public school students will be affected by this agreement.

   A. The ban would be limited to some school functions.

   B. Many schools have stricter soda ban policies.

   C. Connecticut banned all soda, even Gatorade.

   D. New York allows only low-fat milk, water, and fruit juice.

III. The agreement was brokered by an alliance, a foundation, and the American Heart Association.

   A. The terms were accepted by the largest three soft-drink companies.

   B. Mr. Clinton applauded the agreement.

   C. It will be three years before the agreement is fully implemented.

IV. There has been a push in recent years by nutritionists and parent groups to limit soda sales in schools.

   A. California has already banned soft-drink sales.

   B. Owing to pressure, the beverage association has modestly cut back on soda sales.

   C. Critics argue that the agreement has not addressed the issue of marketing soda products to students on Channel One.

 EXERCISE 6

Outlining

Now that you have looked at a sample outline, try to make an effective outline for Reading Selection 4, "The 9 Most Common Kitchen Mistakes Even Healthy Women Make . . . and Why They're Robbing Your Food of Nutrients," which begins on page 95 of this chapter. Use the worksheet below to prepare your outline. When you are finished, submit your outline to your instructor for feedback.

Outline Worksheet

Read the original text thoroughly at least once. If you are reading a lengthy selection, it is likely that the text includes many paragraphs containing several ideas. Write the title and author of the text, then the main idea, which is usually found in the introductory paragraph, followed by other ideas related to the main idea and the supporting details as follows.

Title: The 9 Most Common Kitchen Mistakes Even Health Women
      Make . . . and Why They're Robbing Your Food of Nutrients

Author: Amanda Pressner

Your name _____

Main idea: (Write the main idea of the original text in your own words here.)
Most women are not aware of the nine mistakes they make storing and
preparing foods that deprive them of their nutrients.

  I. Idea I supporting the main idea
    Most agricultural produce begins to lose nutrients from the time they
    are harvested.

Supporting details

    A. *After about a week in the fridge, spinach retains half of its folate and*
       around 60 percent of its lutein.

    B. *Broccoli loses about 62 percent of its flavonoids within 10 days.*

 II. Idea II supporting the main idea
    Rather than keeping milk and grain products in clear containers where
    they may be exposed to light and lose their nutrients, it is better to store
    them in cardboard cartons and opaque containers.

Supporting details

    A. *When exposed to light, a chemical reaction reduces milk's vitamin B*
       potency.

    B. *Exposure to light also affects amino acids and vitamin A, C, D, and*
       E in milk.

    C. *Grain products such as whole grains can also lose their nutrients*
       when exposed to light.

III. Idea III supporting the main idea
    Waiting at least ten minutes to cook garlic after chopping the cloves
    is much healthier.

Supporting details

    A. *If garlic is cooked correctly, it has the power to ward off cancer.*

    B. *Waiting to cook garlic allows the time for an enzymatic reaction to*
       release a healthy compound called allyl sulfur.

IV. Idea IV supporting the main idea
  Avocados are a healthier substitute for butter because they are rich in
  folate, potassium, fiber, and monounsaturated fat.

Supporting details

    A. *Half an avocado has only 153 calories.*

    B. *They can be used as a fat substitute in baking.*

    C. *Researchers at Hunter College found that using avocados for baking*
       resulted in softer and chewier cookies.

© Pearson Education, Inc.

If the text is really lengthy, and you find that there are more ideas expounding on the main idea, continue in the same manner and outline the information until you reach the concluding paragraph.

Self-evaluation of Outlining

After preparing the outline, answer the following questions based on your experience. Your instructor may ask you to share your answers with your peers or to submit this self-evaluation form.

┌ESL Annotation

2.14 ESL In many cultures students are taught from day one that only teachers/experts have the skills to evaluate students. Students do not evaluate students.

Title _____

Author _____

Your name _____

1. How did you organize the main ideas of the original text? Did you find this exercise easy, or did you find it difficult?

    _____

    _____

    _____

2. Did you manage to include all the main ideas and supporting details of the original text the first time? If not, what specific bits and pieces of information did you miss?

    _____

    _____

    _____

3. Did you read the text a second time? If you did, what additional pieces of information did you find?

    _____

    _____

    _____

4. Do you think this exercise helped you identify the logical relationships between the main ideas and the supporting details more easily?

    _____

    _____

    _____

5. Do you think outlining can help you present your ideas orally and in written form more logically and clearly?

    _____

    _____

    _____

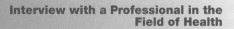

Janice Thompson

Profession: Professor of Public Health Nutrition, Ph.D., FACSM, University of Bristol, England

How did you choose your current profession?

I never planned to become a professor or work in academia. I came from a family where no one had gone to university, and my sister and I were the only two from our immediate family to get a university degree. I always loved learning, and I decided to attend a community college after high school as I wanted to play sports and take some courses because I had no idea what I wanted to do with my life. While there I became very interested in physiology and how the body works (or sometimes does not work). There was a new discipline emerging at that time, exercise physiology, and I decided to transfer to a four-year university and major in that area. As I learned more I became very interested in how exercise and nutrition work together to play important roles in affecting our body weight and our general health.

After I graduated with my bachelor's degree I applied for a Master's degree program at the university where I earned my Bachelor's degree and was able to get a job as a teaching assistant. My primary advisor at that time encouraged me to apply for a PhD program. I was shocked as I did not think I was smart enough to get a PhD! He encouraged me to go for it, and his support and encouragement were the reasons I started to think about pursuing a career in academia.

Once in my PhD program I was able to focus on doing research and taking courses in both nutrition and exercise Physiology. To this day all of my work focuses in both of these areas. I knew when I was getting my PhD that academia was perfectly matched to my personality and career interests, as I love to learn new things each day, I enjoy teaching and working with students, and I deeply value the flexibility that we have in our jobs at the university. It has been a long and often unclear career path with unexpected challenges and results. However I would not change anything and feel very fortunate to have such an interesting and rewarding career.

How did you prepare to reach your goal of becoming a professor of nutrition?

I spent a great deal of time and my own money getting the degrees needed to work in academia. In total it took me almost twelve years to earn my BS, MS, and PhD degrees. I then spent three years working at Stanford University as a postdoctoral fellow. This was a research training job that taught me how to write successful grant proposals to fund my research, and I also learned a great deal about what it means to be a scientist and how to conduct very high quality research. This was an unplanned career decision and one that did not pay very well. I wasn't sure if it was the right thing to do as I had student loan debts to pay and I was not sure if I could succeed at such a top-notch academic institution. But it was the right thing to do, as it is probably the experience that has contributed most to my success in academia. It not only provided me with critically important skills, it also taught me about the dedication and focus needed to be a successful researcher and I met one of my most inspiring mentors while working there. To this day I am so grateful I took the opportunity to do my postdoctoral fellowship there, as it opens many doors for me because of Stanford's excellent academic reputation.

What did you struggle with most when preparing to become a professor?

Lack of money was always my biggest challenge. I come from a family that provides lots of love and emotional support, but there was no extra money to pay for a university education. So I worked the entire time to earn enough money to pay both my living expenses and to pay for my tuition and books. My family was great and helped whenever they could, but I can look back now and see how much I wanted to succeed because I was willing to work and go to school full-time even though it was quite often very difficult and tiring.

How did you get through this struggle?

I'm the type of person who doesn't plan very far ahead, and I think this really helped me make it through the challenges of so much school and work. I took my life one semester and one degree at a time, and I also did not take any classes during the summer months. I would work during the summer to save money, and during this time, even though I was working, I found fun jobs to do and made lots of amazing and interesting friends. This helped me to stay focused and also helped me to have fun while working very hard. I also had a great deal of positive support from my family and friends, which was helpful. By working so many odd jobs I gained really useful skills, which helped me to be well-rounded and maintain common sense. I also learned so much about the types of work that I hated or found rewarding. These lessons have been invaluable and they helped me to stay focused on getting my PhD, as I knew there were so many jobs that I could do for a brief period of time but I had no desire to do them for the rest of my life!

What do you enjoy most about your work?

I love working with people. So I enjoy teaching students of all ages and backgrounds. I also love doing research as I learn new things and it challenges me to use my imagination. I love

© Pearson Education, Inc.

(Continued)

that every day is different for me, as I really love variety and a chance to try new things on a regular basis.

What advice do you have for a student considering a career in nutrition?

For students interested in nutrition, I suggest keeping an open mind as there are so many exciting and interesting career opportunities now available. As we continue to understand more about the importance of nutrition in health and disease, there will be more and more career opportunities available. Nutrition also complements many other disciplines (such as medicine, physiology, biochemistry), and it can be a good starting point into non-nutrition-based careers. For students interested in working in academia, I encourage you to remember that there will always be plenty of challenges and difficulties as you work through your various degrees. Stay focused on what it is you really want to do for a living, and remember that you will not be in school forever! By

achieving your goals you will end up with an incredibly rewarding, stimulating, and flexible job that provides continuing opportunities to learn new things, travel to interesting places, and meet new people.

In your opinion what were the three most interesting points made by the interviewee? Discuss your choices with the class.

- _____
  _____

- _____
  _____

- _____
  _____

Textbook Application

Read the following section from Chapter 1 of *Nutrition: An Applied Approach* and try to accurately answer the multiple-choice questions. You may want to highlight key points in the reading as you navigate the passage.

Reading Selection 5

Textbook

2.15 Flesch-Kincaid Grade Level 12.0

Collaboration

The Role of Nutrition in Our Health

Pre-Reading

Before you read the chapter on nutrition, discuss the following questions in small groups.

1. In your opinion, why is nutrition important? Do you think that proper nutrition can contribute to wellness?

2. Nutritionists believe that a healthful diet can prevent many diseases and reduce your risk for others. Do you agree with this view? Why, or why not?

3. It is important to develop a dietary plan that is nutritionally adequate? Have you ever consulted with a nutritionist to find out whether your nutrient needs are met? If you were to see a nutritionist, how would you go about finding one who is credentialed and trustworthy?

4. You receive a phone call from your mother, who is excited about a research study claiming that consuming a moderate amount of chocolate can reduce

the risk of heart disease in older women. You ask your mother who funded the research study, but she does not know and asks you why it is important at all. Explain to your mother why such information is important before one takes the findings of a study for granted.

Chapter 1: The Role of Nutrition in Our Health

What Is Nutrition?

If you think that the word *nutrition* means pretty much the same thing as *food,* you're right—partially. But the word has a broader meaning that will gradually become clear as you make your way in this course. **Specifically, nutrition** is the science that studies food and how food nourishes our bodies and influences our health. It encompasses how we consume, digest, metabolize, and store nutrients and how these nutrients **affect** our bodies. Nutrition also involves studying the **factors** that influence our eating patterns, making recommendations about the amount we should eat of each type of food, attempting to maintain food safety, and addressing **issues** related to the **global** food supply. You can think of nutrition, then, as the discipline that encompasses everything about food.

Nutrition is a relatively new scientific discipline. Although food has played a defining **role** in the lives of humans since the **evolution** of our species, the importance of nutrition to our health has only been formally recognized and studied over the past 100 years or so. Early **research** in nutrition focused on making the link between nutrient deficiencies and illness. For instance, the cause of scurvy, which is a vitamin C deficiency, was discovered in the mid-1700s. At that time, however, vitamin C had not been identified—what was known was that some ingredient found in citrus fruits could prevent scurvy. Another example of early discoveries in nutrition is presented in the accompanying Highlight box on early nutrition **research** into a disease called pellagra. As is the case with scurvy and vitamin C, this early **research** was able to pinpoint a deficiency disease and foods that could prevent it; it would only be later in the 20th century that the exact nutrient responsible for the deficiency symptoms would be discovered. Thus, unlike sciences such as physics and mathematics, the majority of discoveries in the field of nutrition are relatively recent, and we still have much to learn.

Why Is Nutrition Important?

Think about it: if you eat three meals a day, then by this time next year, you'll have had more than a thousand chances to influence your body's makeup! As you'll learn in this **text,** you are what you eat: the substances you take into your body are broken down and reassembled into your brain cells, bones, muscles—all of your tissues and organs. The foods you eat also provide your body with the **energy** it needs to **function** properly. In addition, we know that proper nutrition can help us improve our health, prevent certain diseases, **achieve** and maintain a desirable weight, and maintain our **energy** and vitality. More surprisingly, in the Nutrition Debate at the end of this **chapter** you'll find out that food can influence not only your own health but also the health of any children you might have. Let's take a closer look at how nutrition supports health and wellness.

nutrition The science that studies food and how food nourishes our bodies and influences our health.

Nutrition is the science that studies all **aspects** of food.

From Janice Thompson and Melinda Manore, *Nutrition: An Applied Approach,* pp. 4–15. Copyright © 2006 by Pearson Education, Inc. Reprinted by permission.

© Pearson Education, Inc.

HIGHLIGHT

Early Nutrition Research: Solving the Mystery of Pellagra

In the first few years of the 20th century, Dr. Joseph Goldberger successfully controlled outbreaks of several fatal infectious diseases, from yellow fever in Louisiana to typhus in Mexico. So it wasn't surprising that, in 1914, the Surgeon General of the United States chose him to tackle another disease thought to be infectious that was raging throughout the South. Called pellagra, the disease was characterized by a skin rash, diarrhea, and **mental** impairment. At the time, it afflicted more than 50,000 people each year, and in about 10% of cases, it resulted in death.

Goldberger began studying the disease by carefully observing its occurrence in groups of people. He asked, if it is infectious, then why would it **occur** in prison inmates, yet leave their guards unaffected? Why, in fact, did it overwhelmingly **affect** impoverished Southerners, while leaving their affluent (and well-fed) neighbors healthy? Could a dietary deficiency cause pellagra? Before he could confirm his hunch, he first had to prove that pellagra was not spread by germs. To do so, he and his **colleagues** deliberately injected or ingested patients' scabs or bodily fluids. When he and his team remained healthy, he conducted a series of experiments in which he fed his patients different nutrient-rich foods. Finally he found an inexpensive and widely available substance—brewer's yeast—that cured the disease. Shortly after Goldberger's death in 1937, scientists identified the precise nutrient that was deficient in the diet of pellagra patients: niacin, one of the B vitamins, which is plentiful in brewer's yeast.

Source: Based on Markel, H. 2003. The New Yorker who changed the diet of the South. *New York Times,* August 12, section D5.

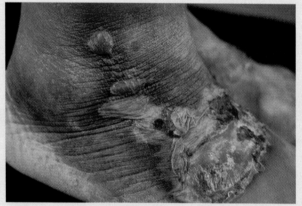

Pellagra is often characterized by a scaly skin rash.

Nutrition Is One of Several Factors Contributing to Wellness

wellness A multidimensional, lifelong **process** that includes **physical**, emotional, and spiritual health.

Wellness can be defined in many ways. Traditionally considered simply the absence of disease, wellness has been redefined as we have learned more about our bodies and what it means to live a healthful lifestyle. Wellness is now considered to be a multidimensional **process**, one that includes **physical**, emotional, social, **occupational**, and spiritual health (FIGURE 1.1). Wellness is not an endpoint in our lives, but is an active process we work on every day.

In this book, we **focus** on two critical **aspects** of **physical** health: nutrition and **physical** activity. The two are so closely related that you can think of them as two sides of the same coin: our **overall** state of nutrition is influenced by how much **energy** we expend doing daily activities, and our level of **physical** activity has a **major impact** on how we use the nutrients in our food. We can perform more strenuous activities for longer periods of time when we eat a nutritious diet, **whereas** an inadequate or excessive food intake can make us lethargic. A poor diet, inadequate or excessive **physical** activity, or a combination of these also can lead to serious health problems. Finally, several studies have suggested that healthful nutrition and regular **physical** activity can increase feelings of well-being and reduce feelings of anxiety and **depression**.

In other words, wholesome food and **physical** activity just plain feel good!

A Healthful Diet Can Prevent Some Diseases and Reduce Your Risk for Others

Early work in the **area** of nutrition focused on nutrient deficiencies and how we can prevent them. As you read in the Highlight box on pellagra, nutrient deficiencies can cause serious, even life-threatening diseases; scurvy, goiter, and rickets are other examples discussed in this book. The discoveries of the causes of such diseases have helped nutrition experts develop **guidelines** for healthful diets that can prevent them. An ample food supply and fortifying foods with nutrients have ensured that the majority of nutrient deficiency diseases are no longer of concern in developed countries. However, these diseases are still **major** problems in many developing nations.

FIGURE 1.1   Many **factors** contribute to an individual's wellness. **Primary** among these are a nutritious diet and regular **physical** activity.

In addition to preventing nutrient deficiency diseases, a healthful diet can reduce your risk for *chronic* diseases, that is, diseases that come on slowly and persist for years (if not for life), often **despite** treatment. Nutrition is strongly associated with four chronic diseases that are among the top ten causes of death in the United States (Table 1.1): heart disease, cancer, cerebrovascular disease (which causes strokes), and type 2 diabetes. Obesity, which increases our risk for all of these diseases, is significantly affected by nutrition and activity: consuming too much food and exercising too little are **factors** in obesity. In the United States and many developed nations, the prevalence of obesity (FIGURE 1.2) and these four chronic diseases has dramatically increased over the past 16 years. Throughout this **text**, we will discuss in more detail how nutrition and **physical** activity **affect** the development of obesity and other chronic diseases.

TABLE 1.1   Ten Leading Causes of Death in the United States for People of All Ages

Rank	Cause of Death	Number of Deaths
1	Heart disease	696,947
2	Cancer	557,271
3	Stroke	162,672
4	Chronic lower respiratory disease	124,816
5	Accidents (unintentional injuries)	106,742
6	Diabetes	73,249
7	Influenza/pneumonia	65,681
8	Alzheimer's disease	58,866
9	Nephritis, nephrotic syndrome, and nephrosis	40,974
10	Septicemia	33,865

Source: National Center for Health Statistics. 2004. Fast Stats A to Z. Deaths—Leading Causes. www.cdc.gov/nchs/fastats/lcod.htm.

© Pearson Education, Inc.

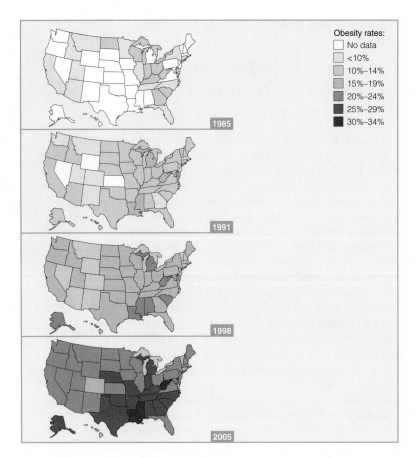

FIGURE 1.2   These diagrams illustrate the increase in obesity rates across the United States from 1985 to 2005 as documented in the Behavioral Risk Factor Surveillance Survey. Obesity is defined as a body mass index greater than or equal to 30, or approximately 30 pounds overweight for a 5'4" woman. (Data from Mokdad, A. H., et al. 1999. *JAMA* 282:16; Mokdad, A. H., et al. 2001. *JAMA* 286:10. Graphics from Centers for Disease Control and Prevention, U.S. Obesity Trends 1985 to 2005.)

In short, nutrition appears to play a **role** in a variety of diseases. Its **role** can vary from mild influence, to a strong association, to directly causing a disease (FIGURE 1.3). The strength of the association between nutrition and various diseases will continue to be **modified** as nutrition **research** continues.

RECAP: *Nutrition is the science that studies food and how food affects our body and our health. Nutrition is an important component of wellness and is strongly associated with* **physical** *activity. One goal of a healthful diet is to prevent nutrient deficiency diseases such as scurvy and pellagra; a second goal is to lower the risk for chronic diseases such as type 2 diabetes and heart disease.*

What Are Nutrients?

A glass of milk or a spoonful of peanut butter may seem to be all one substance, but in reality most foods are made up of many different chemicals. Some of these chemicals are not useful to the body, **whereas** others are critical to human

Diseases in which nutrition plays some role	Osteoporosis Osteoarthritis Some forms of cancer
Diseases with a strong nutritional component	Type 2 diabetes Heart disease High blood pressure Obesity
Diseases caused by nutritional deficiencies or toxicities	Pellagra Scurvy Iron-deficiency anemia Other vitamin and mineral deficiencies Nutrient toxicities

FIGURE 1.3 The relationship between nutrition and human disease. Notice that, whereas nutritional factors are only marginally implicated in the diseases of the top row, they are strongly linked to the development of the diseases in the middle row, and truly causative of those in the bottom row.

growth and **function**. These latter chemicals are referred to as **nutrients.** The six groups of nutrients found in the foods we eat are (FIGURE 1.4):

- carbohydrates
- fats and oils (two types of lipids)
- proteins
- vitamins
- minerals
- water

nutrients Chemicals found in foods that are critical to human growth and function.

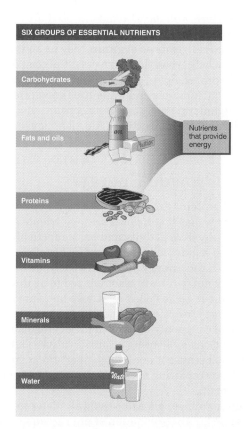

FIGURE 1.4 The six groups of essential nutrients found in the foods we consume.

© Pearson Education, Inc.

HIGHLIGHT

HIGHLIGHT HIGHLIGHT HIGHLIGHT HIGHLIGHT

What Is a Kilocalorie?

Have you ever wondered what the difference is between the terms *energy*, *kilocalories*, and *calories*? Should these terms be used interchangeably, and what do they really mean? The **brief** review provided in this highlight should broaden your understanding. First, some **precise** definitions:

- *Energy* is defined as the **capacity** to do work. We derive **energy** from the **energy**-containing nutrients in the foods we eat, namely, carbohydrates, fats, and proteins.
- A *kilocalorie* (kcal) is the amount of heat **required** to raise the temperature of 1 kilogram (about 2.2 pounds) of water by 1 degree Celsius. It is a unit of measurement we use to quantify the amount of **energy** in food that can be supplied to the body.

For **instance**, we can say that the **energy** found in 1 gram of carbohydrate is equal to 4 kcal.

- A *calorie* (cal) is also a unit of measurement: technically, 1 kilocalorie is equal to 1,000 calories. *Kilo-* is a prefix used in the metric system to indicate 1,000 (think of *kilometer* or *kilobytes*). However, for the sake of simplicity, nutrition labels use the term *calories* to indicate kilocalories. Thus, if the wrapper on an ice cream bar states that it contains 150 calories, it actually contains 150 kilocalories.

In this textbook, we use the term *energy* when referring to the general concept of **energy** intake or **energy** expenditure. We use the term *kilocalories* (or *kcal*) when discussing units of **energy**. We use the term *calories* only when reviewing information about food labels.

As you may know, the term *organic* is commonly used to describe foods that are grown without the use of non-natural fertilizers or chemicals. But when scientists describe **individual** nutrients as **organic**, they mean that these nutrients contain an element called carbon that is an essential component of all living organisms. Carbohydrates, lipids, proteins, and vitamins are organic because they contain carbon. Minerals and water are **inorganic** because they do not contain carbon. Organic and inorganic nutrients are equally important for sustaining life but differ in their structures, functions, and basic chemistry.

organic A substance or nutrient that contains the element carbon.

inorganic A substance or nutrient that does not contain carbon.

Carbohydrates, Fats, and Proteins Are Nutrients That Provide Energy

Carbohydrates, fats, and proteins are the only nutrients that provide **energy**. By this we mean that our bodies break down these nutrients and reassemble into a fuel that supports **physical** activity and basic functioning. Although taking a multivitamin and a glass of water might be beneficial in other ways, it will not provide you with the **energy** you need to do your 20 minutes on the stair-climber! The **energy** nutrients are also referred to as **macronutrients.** *Macro* means "large," and our bodies need relatively large amounts of these nutrients to support **normal function** and health.

Alcohol is a **chemical** commonly consumed in beverage form and may also be added to some foods as a flavoring or preservative—but it is not considered a nutrient. This is because it does not support the regulation of body functions or the building or repairing of tissues. In fact, alcohol is considered to be both a drug and a toxin.

We express **energy** in units of *kilocalories* (kcal). Refer to the Highlight box What Is a Kilocalorie? for an explanation of **energy** and kilocalories. Both

Carbohydrates are the **primary** source of fuel for our bodies, particularly for our brain.

carbohydrates and proteins provide 4 kcal per gram, alcohol provides 7 kcal per gram, and fats provide 9 kcal per gram. Thus, for every gram of fat we consume, we obtain more than twice the **energy** as compared to a gram of carbohydrate or protein. Refer to the You Do the Math box on page 10 to learn how to calculate the **energy contribution** of carbohydrates, fats, and proteins in a given food.

macronutrients Nutrients that our bodies need in relatively large amounts to support **normal function** and health. Carbohydrates, fats, and proteins are macronutrients.

Carbohydrates Are a Primary Fuel Source

Carbohydrates are the **primary source** of fuel for our bodies, particularly for our brain and during **physical** exercise (FIGURE 1.5). A close look at the word "carbohydrate" reveals the **chemical structure** of this nutrient. *Carbo-* refers to carbon, and -*hydrate* refers to water. You may remember that water is made up of hydrogen and oxygen. Thus, carbohydrates are composed of chains of carbon, hydrogen, and oxygen.

Carbohydrates encompass a wide variety of foods; rice, wheat, and other grains as well as vegetables are carbohydrates, and fruits contain natural sugars that are carbohydrates. Carbohydrates are also found in legumes (including lentils, dry beans, and peas), milk and other dairy products, seeds, and nuts. Carbohydrates and their role in health are the subject of Chapter 4.

carbohydrates The **primary** fuel source for our bodies, particularly for our brain and for **physical** exercise.

Fats Provide Energy and Other Essential Nutrients

Fats are another important **source** of **energy** for our bodies (FIGURE 1.6). They are a type of *lipids*, a diverse group of organic substances that are insoluble in water. Like carbohydrates, fats are composed of carbon, hydrogen, and oxygen; however, they contain proportionally much less oxygen and water than carbohydrates do. This quality allows them to pack together tightly, which explains why they yield more **energy** per gram than either carbohydrates or proteins.

Fats are an important **energy source** for our bodies at rest and during low-**intensity** exercise. Our bodies are **capable** of storing large amounts of fat as

fats An important **energy** **source** for our bodies at rest and during low-**intensity** exercise.

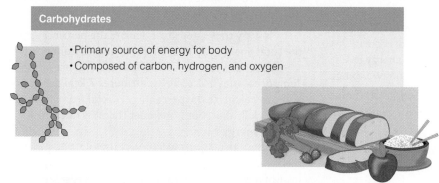

Carbohydrates
- Primary source of energy for body
- Composed of carbon, hydrogen, and oxygen

FIGURE 1.5 Carbohydrates are a **primary source of energy** for our bodies and are found in a wide variety of foods.

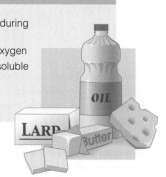

Fats and oils
- Important source of energy at rest and during low-intensity exercise
- Composed of carbon, hydrogen, and oxygen
- Foods containing fats also provide fat-soluble vitamins and essential fatty acids

FIGURE 1.6 Fats are an important **energy source** during rest and low-**intensity** exercise. Foods containing fat also provide other important nutrients.

© Pearson Education, Inc.

YOU DO THE MATH

Calculating the Energy Contribution of Carbohydrates, Fats, and Proteins

The **energy** in food is used for everything from maintaining **normal** body functions—such as breathing, digesting food, and repairing damaged tissues and organs—to enabling you to perform **physical** activity and even to read this **text**. So how much **energy** is produced from the foods you eat?

Carbohydrates are the main **energy source** for your body and should make up the largest percentage of your nutrient intake, about 45–65%; they provide 4 kcal of **energy** per gram of carbohydrate consumed. Proteins also provide 4 kcal of **energy** per gram, but they should be limited to no more than 10–35% of your daily **energy** intake. Fats provide the most **energy**, 9 kcal per gram. Fats should make up approximately 20–35% of your total **energy** intake per day. In order to figure out whether you're taking in the **appropriate** percentages of carbohydrates, fats, and proteins, you will need to use a little math.

1. Let's say you have completed a personal diet **analysis**, and you consume 2,500 kcal per day. From your diet **analysis** you also find that you consume 300 g of carbohydrates, 90 g of fat, and 123 g of protein.

2. To calculate your percentage of total **energy** that comes from carbohydrate, you must do two things:

   a. Take your total grams of carbohydrate and multiply by the **energy** value for carbohydrate to give you how many kcal of carbohydrate you have consumed.

   300 g of carbohydrate × 4 kcal/g
   = 1,200 kcal of carbohydrate

   b. Take the kcal of carbohydrate you have consumed, divide this number by the total number of kcal you consumed, and multiply by 100. This will give you the percentage of the total energy you consume that comes from carbohydrate.

   (1,200 kcal/2,500 kcal) × 100 = 48% of total energy comes from carbohydrate

3. To calculate your percentage of total **energy** that comes from fat, you follow the same steps but incorporate the **energy** value for fat:

   a. Take your total grams of fat and multiply by the **energy** value for fat to find the kcal of fat consumed.

   90 g of fat × 9 kcal/g = 810 kcal of fat

   b. Take the kcal of fat you have consumed, divide this number by the total number of kcal you consumed, and multiply by 100 to get the percentage of total **energy** you consume that comes from fat.

   (810 kcal/2,500 kcal) × 100 = 32.4% of total **energy** comes from fat

Now try these steps to calculate the percentage of the total **energy** you consume that comes from protein.

Also, have you ever heard that alcohol provides "empty calories"? Alcohol contributes 7 kcal per gram. You can calculate the percentage of kcal from alcohol in your daily diet, but remember that it is not considered an **energy** nutrient.

These calculations will be very useful throughout this course as you learn more about how to design a healthful diet and how to read labels to assist you in meeting your nutritional goals. Later in this book, in Chapter 11, you will learn how to **estimate** your unique energy needs and determine the ideal amount of **energy** you need from carbohydrates, fats, and proteins.

adipose tissue. These fat stores can then be broken down for **energy** during periods when we are not eating; for example, while we are asleep. Foods that contain fats are also important in providing fat-soluble vitamins and essential fatty acids.

Dietary fats come in a variety of forms. Solid fats include such things as butter, lard, and margarine. Liquid fats, referred to as *oils,* include vegetable oils such as canola and olive oils. Cholesterol is a form of lipid that our bodies can make independently, and it can also be consumed in the diet. Chapter 5 provides a thorough discussion of lipids.

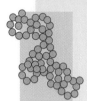

Proteins

- Support tissue growth, repair, and maintenance

- Composed of carbon, hydrogen, oxygen, and nitrogen

FIGURE 1.7 Proteins contain nitrogen in addition to carbon, hydrogen, and oxygen. Proteins support the growth, repair, and **maintenance** of body tissues.

Proteins Support Tissue Growth, Repair, and Maintenance

Proteins also contain carbon, hydrogen, and oxygen, but they are different from carbohydrates and fats in that they contain the element *nitrogen* (FIGURE 1.7). Within proteins, these four **elements** assemble into small building blocks known as amino acids. We break down dietary proteins into amino acids and reassemble them to build our own body proteins—for **instance**, the proteins in our muscles and blood.

Although proteins can provide **energy**, they are not a **primary source** of **energy** for our bodies. Instead, the main **role** of proteins is in building new cells and tissues, both for growth and for repair. Proteins are also important in regulating the breakdown of foods and our fluid balance.

Proteins are found in many foods. Meats and dairy products are our **primary** sources, but we also obtain small amounts of protein from vegetables and whole grains. Seeds, nuts, and legumes are good sources of protein. Proteins are reviewed in detail in Chapter 6.

> RECAP: *The six essential nutrient groups found in foods are carbohydrates, fats, proteins, vitamins, minerals, and water. Carbohydrates, fats, and proteins are referred to as the **energy** nutrients, as they provide our bodies with the **energy** necessary to thrive. Carbohydrates are the **primary energy source** for our bodies; fats provide fat-soluble vitamins and essential fatty acids and act as **energy** storage molecules; and proteins support tissue growth, repair, and **maintenance**.*

Vitamins Assist in the Regulation of Biological Processes

Vitamins are organic **compounds** that help regulate our bodies' functions. Contrary to popular belief, vitamins do not contain **energy** (or kilocalories); however, they are essential to **energy metabolism,** the **process** by which the macronutrients are broken down into smaller molecules that our body can absorb and use. As you'll learn in Chapter 10, vitamins assist with releasing and using the **energy** found in all three macronutrients: carbohydrates, fats, and proteins. They are also critical in building and maintaining healthy bone, muscle, and blood, supporting our immune system so we can fight infection and disease, and ensuring healthy **vision**. Because we need relatively small amounts of these nutrients to support **normal** health and body functions, the vitamins (in addition to minerals) are referred to as **micronutrients.**

Vitamins are classified as two types: **fat soluble** and **water soluble** (Table 1.2). This classification is based upon their solubility in water, which affects how vitamins are absorbed, transported, and stored in our bodies. As our bodies cannot synthesize most vitamins, we must consume them in our

Fat-soluble vitamins are found in a variety of fat-containing foods, including dairy products.

proteins The only macronutrient that contains nitrogen; the basic building blocks of proteins are amino acids.

vitamins Organic compounds that assist us in regulating our bodies' processes.

metabolism The **process** by which large molecules such as carbohydrates, fats, and proteins are broken down via chemical reactions into smaller molecules that can be used as fuel, stored, or assembled into new **compounds** the body needs.

© Pearson Education, Inc.

TABLE 1.2   Overview of Vitamins

Type	Names	Distinguishing Features
Fat soluble	A, D, E, and K	Soluble in fat Stored in the human body Toxicity can **occur** from consuming excess amounts, which accumulate in the body
Water soluble	C, B vitamins (thiamin, riboflavin, niacin, vitamin B_6, vitamin B_{12}, pantothenic acid, biotin, and folate)	Soluble in water Not stored to any extent in the human body Excess excreted in urine Toxicity generally only occurs as a result of vitamin supplementation

TABLE 1.3   Overview of Minerals

Type	Names	Distinguishing Features
Major minerals	Calcium, phosphorus, sodium, potassium, chloride, magnesium, sulfur	Needed in amounts greater than 100 mg/day in our diets Amount present in the human body is greater than 5 g (or 5,000 mg)
Trace minerals	Iron, zinc, copper, manganese, fluoride, chromium, molybdenum, selenium, iodine	Needed in amounts less than 100 mg/day in our diets Amount present in the human body is less than 5 g (or 5,000 mg)

micronutrients Nutrients needed in relatively small amounts to support **normal** health and body functions. Vitamins and minerals are micronutrients.

fat-soluble vitamins Vitamins that are not soluble in water, but are soluble in fat. These include vitamins A, D, E, and K.

water-soluble vitamins Vitamins that are soluble in water. These include vitamin C and the B vitamins.

minerals Inorganic substances that are not broken down during digestion and absorption and are not destroyed by heat or light. Minerals assist in the regulation of many body processes and are classified as **major** minerals or **trace** minerals.

diets. Both types of vitamins are essential for our health and are found in a variety of foods. Learn more about vitamins in the *In Depth* look on pages 252–263. Chapters 7 through 10 discuss **individual** vitamins in detail.

Minerals Assist in the Regulation of Many Body Functions

Minerals are inorganic substances, meaning that they do not contain carbon. Some important dietary minerals include sodium, potassium, calcium, magnesium, and iron. Minerals are different from the macronutrients and vitamins in that they are not broken down during digestion or when our bodies use them to **promote normal function**; they are also not destroyed by heat or light. Thus, all minerals maintain their **structure** no matter what **environment** they are in. This means that the calcium in our bones is the same as the calcium in the milk we drink, and the sodium in our cells is the same as the sodium in our table salt.

Minerals have many important functions in our bodies. They assist in fluid regulation and **energy** production, are essential to the health of our bones and blood, and help rid our body of harmful by-products of metabolism.

Minerals are classified according to the amounts we need in our diet and according to how much of the mineral is found in our bodies. The two categories of minerals in our diets and bodies are the **major minerals** and the **trace minerals** (Table 1.3). Learn more about minerals in the *In Depth* look on pages 252–263. Chapters 7 through 10 discuss **individual** minerals in detail.

Now that you have read a **chapter** from an authentic content-focused textbook, try to answer a few True or False review questions taken from the Nutrition **text**. This exercise will give you an opportunity to practice discussion skills pivotal to success in a college course. Next, test your knowledge by answering a larger set of multiple-choice questions related to the **text**.

True or False Questions

Read the following statements carefully. Write the letter T next to the sentence if the statement is true and the letter F if the statement is false. Discuss these statements with a partner.

Collaboration

1. Nutrition is the science that studies food and how food nourishes our body and influences health. _T_

2. Proteins are a primary energy source for our bodies. _F_

3. All vitamins must be consumed daily to support optimal health. _F_

4. The Recommended Dietary Allowance is the maximum amount of nutrient that people should consume in order to support normal body functions. _F_

5. Federal agencies in the United States are typically poor sources of reliable nutrition information. _F_

Reading Comprehension Check

Vocabulary in Context

1. A definition of nutrition is given in
   a. the first sentence.
   b. the second sentence.
   (c.) the third sentence.
   d. the whole first paragraph.

Supporting Details

2. The example of scurvy is given in paragraph 2 to
   a. show the relationship between history and research.
   (b.) show that early nutrition research focused on nutrient deficiencies and illness.
   c. demonstrate the importance of vitamin C.
   d. illustrate how dangerous diseases are formed.

Supporting Details

3. Read the section Why Is Nutrition Important? Thousands of years ago some cultures believed that a proper diet could
   a. cure cancer.
   b. invite in devils.
   (c.) connect us with God.
   d. none of the above

Main Idea

4. Read Solving the Mystery of Pellagra. What is the main idea of the passage?
   (a.) Thanks to Dr. Joseph Goldberger, a cure was found for a disease called pellagra.

© Pearson Education, Inc.

b. Through his research Dr. Goldberger proved pellagra was not infectious.

c. The U.S. Surgeon General chose Dr. Goldberger to help fight pellagra.

d. nutrient deficiency and illness

Supporting Details

5. Read the section A Healthful Diet Can Prevent. . . . We learn that efficiency diseases
   a. are no longer an issue in the modern world.
   b. are still a major problem in every country.
   (c.) are still a major problem in developing nations.
   d. kill more now than ever.

Graphic Analysis

6. Examine Figure 1.2 from the text. From the diagrams we learn that
   a. obesity rates have increased in certain states.
   (b.) in recent decades, obesity rates have increased across America.
   c. Florida has the highest obesity rate.
   d. mostly the western states have had a dramatic rise in obesity.

Patterns of Organization

7. What pattern of organization is used to describe a combination as a factor in increasing the risk of obesity and certain diseases?
   (a.) cause and effect   c. classification
   b. comparison and contrast   d. chronological order

Graphic Analysis

8. Examine Figure 1.3 from the textbook chapter on page 109. What is the difference between the diseases listed in the top column from those listed in the middle?
   a. The level of toxicities differs.
   (b.) Those at the top are more connected with dietary habits.
   c. Those in the middle are more connected with dietary habits.
   d. Obesity is in the middle column.

Graphic Analysis

9. Examine Figure 1.4. on page 109. The groups of essential nutrients are listed
   a. in order of importance.
   b. in alphabetical order.
   c. in order of quantity.
   (d.) The logic of the ordering is not apparent from the chart.

Vocabulary in Context

10. Read the section Carbohydrates, Fats, and Proteins Are Nutrients That Provide Energy. Alcohol is defined as
    a. an energy provider, but not an essential nutrient.
    b. a chemical found in food.
    c. a drug and toxin.
    (d.) all of the above

Supporting Details

11. Read the section Fats Provide Energy. . . . When are fats most important to us?

    a. when we do heavy exercise   c. while we are speaking

    (b.) while we are asleep   d. all of the above

Supporting Details

12. Read the section Proteins Support Tissue Growth. . . . Proteins are

    a. a primary source of energy.

    b. amino acids.

    (c.) critical for building new cells and tissues.

    d. like drugs.

Supporting Details

13. Which of the following is **not** mentioned as a role for proteins?

    a. repairing damaged structures   c. building new cells and tissues

    (b.) curing illnsses   d. regulating metabolism

Patterns of Organization

14. Read the section entitled Vitamins Assist in the Regulation of Bodily Processes. What is the overall pattern of organization of the passage?

    a. process   (c.) comparison and contrast

    b. listing   d. classification

Graphic Analysis

15. Examine Table 1.2. This table shows

    a. how fat soluble and water-soluble vitamins are different.

    (b.) examples of both fat-soluble and water-soluble vitamins and how the types of vitamins are different.

    c. examples of both fat-soluble and water-soluble vitamins.

    d. the similarities of the two groups.

Study: Ban on Fast-Food TV Ads May Cut Obesity

READING

Reading Selection **6**

Additional Reading

Magazine Article

2.16 Flesch-Kincaid Grade Level 12.0

Collaboration

Pre-Reading Questions

Before reading the article, discuss the following questions in small groups and share your answers with your classmates.

1. In your opinion, do you think your eating habits are influenced by TV ads for fast food? If yes, can you think of a TV ad that prompted you to buy the food product?

2. Do you think young children below the age of 10 beg their parents to purchase food items that they see on TV commercials? Discuss how parents can educate their young children about the consequences of unhealthy eating.

© Pearson Education, Inc.

3. Some people argue that the government is being irresponsible by allowing fast-food companies to advertise their unhealthy product on TV. In your opinion, should the government ban fast-food TV ads?

Study: Ban on Fast-Food TV Ads
May Cut Obesity

USA Today

November 20, 2008

dent
a reduction in the amount
of something

1   ATLANTA (AP)—A little less "I'm Lovin' It" could put a **significant dent** in the problem of childhood obesity, suggests a new study in the U.S. that attempts to measure the effect of TV fast-food ads.

2   A ban on such commercials would reduce the number of obese young children by 18%, and the number of obese older kids by 14%, researchers found.

3   They also suggested that ending an advertising expense tax **deduction** for fast-food restaurants could mean a slight reduction in childhood obesity.

4   Some experts say it's the first national study to show fast-food TV commercials have such a large effect on childhood obesity. A 2006 Institute of Medicine report suggested a **link**, but concluded proof was lacking.

5   "Our study provides **evidence** of that **link**," said study co-**author** Michael Grossman, an economics professor at City University of New York.

6   The study has important **implications** for the effectiveness of regulating TV advertising, said Lisa Powell, a researcher at the University of Illinois at Chicago's Institute for Health Research and Policy. She was not **involved** in the **research** but was familiar with it.

7   The percentage of U.S. children who are overweight or obese rose steadily from the 1980s until recently, when it leveled off. About a third of American kids are overweight or obese, according to U.S. Centers for Disease Control and Prevention estimates.

pondering
thinking carefully and seriously

8   The causes of childhood obesity are complicated, but for years researchers have been **pondering** the effects of TV advertising. Powell, for example, found fast-food commercials account for as much as 23% of the food-related ads kids see on TV. Others have estimated children see fast-food commercials tens of thousands of times a year.

9   The new study is based in part on several years of government **survey data** from the late 1990s that **involved** in-person interviews with thousands of U.S. families.

10   The researchers also looked at information about local stations in the 75 largest TV markets, including locally seen fast-food commercials and the size of viewing audiences. The researchers used a statistical test that **presumes** TV ads lead to obesity but made calculations to address other influences such as **income** and the number of nearby fast-food restaurants. They also took

presumes
thinks something is true without
certainty

Associated Press, "Study: Ban on Fast-Food TV Ads May Cut Obesity," *USA Today*, November 20, 2008. Used with permission of The Associated Press. Copyright © 2008. All rights reserved.

steps to account for the possibility that some children may already have been overweight and inactive regardless of their TV-watching habits.

11   The study is being **published** this month in the *Journal of Law & Economics*.

12   The authors, funded by a **federal** grant, included Grossman and researchers from Lehigh University and Georgia State University. The authors stopped short of **advocating** an advertising ban or eliminating the advertising tax **deduction**.

advocating
supporting someone or something

13   Grossman said it is possible that some families **benefit** from advertising by finding out what restaurants are nearby and what they're serving. "A lot of people consume fast food in **moderate** amounts and it doesn't harm their health," he said.

moderate
neither big nor small

14   McDonald's Corp., the giant fast-food chain responsible for the widely seen "I'm Lovin' It" ad campaign, referred questions about the study to the National Council of Chain Restaurants. Officials with that organization could not be reached Wednesday evening.

Reading Comprehension Check

1. What is the topic of the article?
   a. Less advertising on TV will result in fewer consumers wanting junk food.
   b. fast-food and TV advertising
   c. TV advertising
   d. McDonald's offers TV ads.

2. What does research data suggest in the second paragraph?
   a. A fast-food TV ad ban would result in a lower obesity rate for both older and younger children.
   b. A ban on fast-food TV ads would result in lower obesity rates for older children, but not for younger ones.
   c. There is no relationship between fast-food TV ads and childhood obesity.
   d. none of the above

3. In the sentence "The study has important implications for the effectiveness of regulating TV advertising . . . " (paragraph 6), the word *implications* could be replaced by
   a. negativity.   c. meanings.
   b. causes.   d. corrosive.

4. According to the article, what percentage of American kids is overweight or obese?
   a. 50 percent   c. 75 percent
   b. 14 percent   d. 33 percent

5. The main idea of the article is that
   a. fast-food TV advertising is the sole cause of childhood obesity.
   b. the majority of American children eat unhealthy food.
   c. a study suggests that fast-food TV advertising has a significant effect on childhood obesity rates.
   d. both b and c

© Pearson Education, Inc.

6. Besides fast-food TV advertising, the study researchers also looked at other possible factors related to childhood obesity such as
   (a.) family income and proximity of fast-food restaurants.
   b. how many fast-food restaurants were nearby and parental habits.
   c. peer pressure and family income.
   d. cigarette smoking and sugar consumption.

7. Michael Grossman, one of the study's coauthors, believes that
   a. there should be an absolute ban on fast-food TV advertising.
   b. many families consume fast-food in moderate amounts.
   c. some families may benefit from these ads as they learn what some local restaurants have to offer.
   (d.) both b and c

8. In the sentence "They also took steps to account for the possibility that some children may already have been overweight . . ." the expression *to account for* could be replaced by
   a. to deliver.   (c.) to find an explanation for.
   b. to add.   d. to open up an account.

9. In the sentence "The authors stopped short of advocating an advertising ban or eliminating the advertising tax deduction," the expression *stopped short* means
   a. agreed to.
   (b.) not go so far as to do or say something.
   c. stepped on the breaks early.
   d. inquired.

10. What is the main point of the last paragraph?
    a. McDonald's Corp. is pleased by the findings of the study.
    b. McDonald's Corp. is protesting the results of the study.
    (c.) McDonald's Corp is looking further into the study results before offering comment.
    d. both b and c

Suggested Resources

Books

1. *Fast Food Nation* by Eric Schlosser. Harper Perennial. This nonfiction exposition of the fast-food industry is both informative and shocking. Schlosser investigates how America's voracious appetite for quick and cheap fast food has led to unhealthy eating habits.

2. *Foods that Heal* by Bernard Jensen. Avery; 2nd revised edition. In this book, Dr. Bernard Jensen provides a list of therapeutic foods that one should eat to remain healthy and live a long life.

Movies

1. *Supersize Me* (2004). A filmmaker conducts an experiment in which he eats only McDonald's food for a whole month only to find out that his health has deteriorated drastically.
2. *Fast Food Nation* (2006). This is a fictionalized version of Eric Schlosser's book, which shows illegal immigrants working in the meat-packing industry and the unhygienic conditions under which burgers are made.

Internet Sites

1. www.nutrition.gov

   This is the U.S. federal guide offering access to all government Web sites with reliable and accurate information on nutrition and dietary guidance.
2. www.sne.org

   Society for Nutrition Education (SNE). Go to this site for further information about the Society for Nutritional Education and its goals to educate individuals, communities, and professionals about nutrition education and influence policy makers about nutrition, food, and health.

© Pearson Education, Inc.

Active Reading: Highlighting and Annotating Relevant Text

There are a number of productive ways of interacting with text. We have already discussed the role of outlining. Active readers can also incorporate the critical skills of highlighting and annotation to improve their ability to comprehend reading material.

Highlighting

Overview

Highlighting key terms and concepts in a reading passage with a brightly colored highlighter serves a number of purposes. First, it motivates the reader to seek out the most relevant points in a given section of a text upon first read (a very similar skill to note taking when listening to a lecture!). Second, when exam time approaches, highlighted text will guide you toward the key terms and concepts that you need to review.

Some hints about highlighting:

- Highlight main ideas, not minor points
- Highlight key terms that connect to important concepts
- Highlight points that you feel would be helpful to remember upon review

Challenge Activity

Let's turn to the biographical profile of Dr. Robert Atkins in Chapter 2. Using a highlighter, try to highlight the key points in the text.

Biographical Profile: Dr. Robert Atkins

Robert Atkins is best known for his controversial low-carbohydrate diet which had a great influence on the way the American people made conscious decisions about nutritional choices.

He was born on October 17, 1930. He was an American cardiologist who received his medical degree from Cornell Medical College in 1955. Dr. Atkins revolutionized the food industry with his unique Atkins Nutritional Approach, also known as the Atkins Diet. He recommended eliminating all carbohydrates from the diet, especially simple ones such as bagels and donuts, and consuming mostly proteins along with salads and vegetables. Convinced by his unique approach to nutrition, many health-conscious Americans began to reduce their intake of carbohydrates and reported significant weight loss after being on the Atkins Diet for several months. His controversial diet caused panic amongst food manufacturers who produced and marketed mostly carbohydrate-based food items.

During his illustrious career, Dr. Atkins wrote several books on healthy living. Although he became an internationally renowned figure and changed the lives of hundreds of thousands of people, his own life ended tragically when he sustained serious injuries to his head after falling in front of his office in New York City on April 8, 2003. Some critics argued that his accident may have been connected to his being somewhat overweight. He succumbed to his injury on April 17, 2003. However, his legacy lives on, as thousands of people around the world continue to follow the Atkins Diet.

Compare what you highlighted with a colleague, and discuss your choices.

Learning Implications

The more you interact with a text, the more connected you will feel to the ideas and information contained within it. Highlighting provides a visual aid for a later review of a text and gives the reader an opportunity to distinguish between major and minor points offered in a reading. This is especially helpful with high-level reading that is hard to comprehend. Highlighting is a way of breaking a text down into comprehensible points.

Annotation

Overview

Reading is often thought of as a passive activity whereby the reader simply reads sentences in silence. Contrary to popular belief, reading is actually a complex process, and active readers are fully aware of the fact that they must use their writing skills while reading. Annotating your textbook is an effective way to respond to what you are reading. Annotating involves adding notes to the text, explaining difficult concepts, and commenting on controversial issues for future reference. As you read your textbook, write notes in the margin of the textbook, underline main ideas and supporting details, circle unfamiliar vocabulary items, and put a question mark next to a statement you find confusing. As you get used to making annotations, you will notice that your attention, concentration, and reading comprehension has improved significantly. Annotating a text enables you to revisit the reading selection and understand the main idea, key concepts, and review the material with relative ease.

There are various ways to annotate a text. Here are a few techniques, but you can create your own techniques to mark your textbook for clarification and further reflection.

- Use a marker to highlight the main ideas, key concepts, numbered items, definitions, and examples. You may use different colors for different purposes. For example, you may use a blue marker for the main idea and a green marker for vocabulary.
- You also may underline terms and their definitions.

© Pearson Education, Inc.

Collaboration

- Put a question mark next to a sentence, an unfamiliar word, or a confusing passage. You can always go back to the passage later. The question mark will remind you that you had difficulty understanding something.

- Highlight key concepts with an asterisk or a check.

- If the author has used the process analysis pattern of organization, use numbers to denote the steps in a process.

- As you read the text, write questions in the margin for further analysis. These recall questions will help you comprehend the material.

- As mentioned previously, reading is an active process. Unlike watching TV, where you do not need to get involved, active reading requires your involvement. Feel free to disagree with the author and write in the margin your thoughts. When you get used to annotating a text, you will reap the many rewards of active reading.

- Finally, if you are reading a long selection, write a summary including the main idea and a few major details.

Example of an Annotated Text

What follows is a passage from a nutrition textbook for college students. Notice how the text has been annotated. Keep in mind that there is no single way of annotating a text. Depending on what works for you best, you may develop your own technique of annotating a text.

What is fiber?

What are some of the digestive and chronic diseases?
Chronic: *lasting for a long time*

How does fiber consumption help us?

Fiber Helps Us Stay Healthy

Although we cannot digest fiber, it is still an important substance in our diet. Research indicates that it helps us stay healthy and may prevent many digestive and chronic diseases. The potential benefits of fiber consumption include the following:

1. - May <u>reduce the risk of colon cancer</u>. While there is still some controversy surrounding this issue, many researchers believe that fiber binds cancer-causing substance and speeds their elimination from the colon. However, recent studies of colon cancer and fiber have shown that their relationship is not as strong as previously thought.

2. - Helps <u>prevent hemorrhoids, constipation, and other intestinal problems</u> by keeping our stool moist and soft. Fiber gives gut muscles "something to push on" and make it easier to eliminate stools.

3. - Reduces the risk of *diverticulosis*, a condition that is caused in part by trying to eliminate small, hard stools. This increased pressure weakens intestinal walls, causing them to **bulge** outward and form pockets, which become infected and **inflamed**. This is a painful condition that must be treated with antibiotics or surgery.

Bulge: a protruding part or swelling

Inflamed: causing pain, redness, and swelling because of an infection

4. - May <u>reduce the risk of heart disease</u> by delaying or blocking the absorption of dietary cholesterol into the bloodstream. Fiber also contributes small fatty acids that may lower the amount of low-density lipoprotein (or LDL) to healthful levels in our bodies.

■ May <u>enhance weight loss</u>, as eating a high fiber diet causes a person to feel 5
more full. Fiber absorbs water, expands in our intestine, and slows the movement of food through the upper part of the digestive tract. People who eat a
fiber-rich diet tend to eat fewer fatty and sugary foods.

■ May <u>lower the risk of type 2 diabetes</u>. In slowing digestion, fiber also slows 6
the release of glucose into the blood. It thereby improves the body's regulation
of insulin production and blood glucose levels.

(From *Nutrition: An Applied Approach*, p. 132)

Challenge Activity

Re-read the last article, Study: Ban on Fast-Food TV Ads May Cut Obesity on
p. 118, and annotate the text. Use the techniques mentioned above, or refer to
the annotated text above, or create your own to mark the text. Underline or
circle main ideas, unfamiliar words, write in the margin, place question marks
next to something you do not understand, write open-ended questions about the
content. You can discuss these questions with your peers and instructor to
understand the story more clearly.

Learning Implications

As you annotate a text, you interact with the material. Furthermore, you take a
multisensory approach to reading—kinesthetic and visual learning. Annotating
your textbook will help you improve your attention, concentration, and reading
comprehension. Keep annotating the text, and you will gradually develop a
consistent marking system, which will become an effective study aid for you.

© Pearson Education, Inc.

ENVIRONMENTAL SCIENCE
Global Warming

Chapter 3

"America has not led but fled on the issue of global warming."

SENATOR JOHN KERRY

Objectives

IN THIS CHAPTER YOU WILL LEARN . . .

- ✓ About the issue of global warming
- ✓ How to recognize supporting details within a paragraph
- ✓ How to distinguish between major and minor details
- ✓ How to take effective notes from a lecture

Making Predictions

Consider this chapter's topic of Environmental Science. What subtopics relate to this field? (See Fig. 3.1.)

■ Figure 3.1

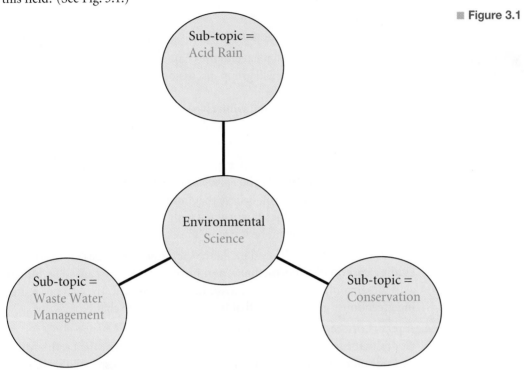

Introduction to the Discipline of Environmental Science

Environmental science is the study of interactions among physical, chemical, and biological components of the environment. Environmental scientists use their knowledge of the physical makeup and history of the earth to protect the environment. A major focus in the field is on locating energy resources, predicting geologic hazards, and providing environmental site assessments and advice in such areas as indoor air quality and hazardous waste cleanup. The great scale and complexity of environmental problems are creating a growing need for scientists with rigorous, interdisciplinary training in Environmental Science. Many environmental scientists work at consulting firms, helping businesses and government agencies comply with environmental policy. They are usually hired to solve problems. There are environment-related jobs in industry, environmental protection agencies, local/central government, media, international organizations, and environmental consultancy. The opportunities are endless. Environmental Science graduates could be managing tropical rainforests, monitoring coral reef biodiversity, or practicing environmental law. This chapter focuses primarily on one of the greatest challenges facing not only environmental scientists, but all of us who inhabit the earth: global warming. You will read about some of the devastating effects global warming has already caused and will cause to our ecosystem. This chapter will also explore some innovative approaches to dealing

© Pearson Education, Inc.

with global warming, green roofs being one example. The role of the government in placing stricter controls on energy consumption is a critical question, and one that serves as this chapter's subject for debate.

Preview Questions

Collaboration

The following questions are all related to the chapter focus area of Environmental Science. Share your views in small group discussion.

1. Do you feel that summers and winters are usually warmer than they used to be during your childhood? If so, then what do you think is causing the climate change?

2. Scientists studying climate change believe that human activities are dangerously warming the earth. Do you agree with their view that global warming is caused by humans, or do you believe that human activities have absolutely no impact on global warming? If you agree with the scientists, describe specific human activities that might be warming the earth. If you don't agree, why?

3. Climate scientists have found evidence that greenhouse gas emissions, including carbon dioxide, methane, and nitrous oxide, are caused by human activities, mainly the burning of fossil fuels. Discuss effective ways of reducing greenhouse gas emissions that have driven climate change recently.

4. A report of the Intergovernmental Panel on Climate Change (IPCC) concludes that further climate change is inevitable, and that the earth's future depends on how humans treat it. Is it the government's responsibility to make people aware of how their activities are harming the earth? If so, how can the government best educate citizens to become more environmentally friendly?

Interpreting a Cartoon

■ **Figure 3.2**

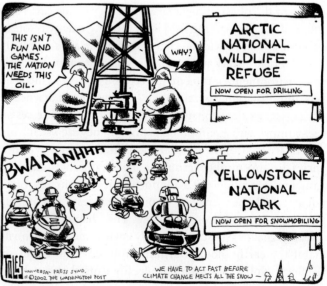

ESL Annotation

3.1 ESL Many ESL students might not know of Yellowstone National Park or the Arctic Wildlife Refuge.

Examine the cartoon and answer the following questions in pairs:

1. What is amusing about this cartoon?

2. In your opinion, what message is the cartoonist trying to convey to the reader?

Collaboration

Discipline-specific Terminology Bank

atmosphere	ecosystems	glacial melts	mitigate
deforestation	emissions	greenhouse gases	ozone
degrade	energy-efficient	habitats	precipitation
depleting	erosion	incineration	ramifications
disrupt	fossil fuels	industrialized	renewable

Sample Paragraph

Read the following paragraph containing some of the discipline-specific terminology you will come across in the reading selections in this chapter. See how many of the highlighted words you can understand, or derive the meaning of, from the context.

Many environmental scientists argue that life on earth is in peril. Some point to the rapid **deforestation** of the Amazon. Others emphasize our **depleting** natural resources, the **erosion** of our coastlines, and the frightening lack of **precipitation** in geographic zones that were once fertile. These scientists consider the short- and long-term **ramifications** of climate change and many wonder if it is too late to **mitigate** what has become a global crisis. Many seek to find **renewable** energy sources that will not **disrupt** natural **habitats** and further **degrade** life on earth.

EXERCISE 1

Matching Column A and Column B

Match the word in Column A with the definition in Column B. Put the letter representing the correct definition in the space preceding each word.

Column A

Column B

Word

Definition

1. __j__ depleting

a. slowly destroying the surface through the wind or rain

2. __f__ ramifications

b. to make something less harmful

3. __b__ mitigate

c. can be replaced naturally

4. __h__ deforestation

d. places where plants and animals are found

© Pearson Education, Inc.

5. __g__ degradation   e. the amount of rain or snow that falls

6. __i__ disruption   f. unexpected results of an action or decision

7. __e__ precipitation   g. the process of something being damaged

8. __c__ renewable   h. the act of cutting down trees

9. __d__ habitats   i. to keep something from moving or growing

10. __a__ eroding   j. reducing something to an insufficient amount

EXERCISE 2

Fill in the Blanks

In the following sentences, fill in the blank with a word from the terminology bank that makes the sentence grammatically correct and meaningful.

deforestation	degradation	depleting	disruption	eroding
habitats	mitigate	precipitation	ramifications	renewable

1. The southern coastline has been gradually ___eroding___ because of the torrid waves of the sea, making the foundations of several beach houses weaker.

2. Earth's natural resources are ___depleting___ as a result of harmful human activities such as burning fossil fuels and excessively cutting down trees.

3. The Environmental Protection Agency has recommended planting thousands of trees to ___mitigate___ the severity of soil erosion on the southern coast.

4. Our excessive reliance on gasoline has caused its price to skyrocket, prompting environmental scientists to look for ___renewable___ sources of energy such as wind and solar power.

5. People for the Ethical Treatment of Animals (PETA) has protested the destruction of the natural ___habitats___ of wildlife in the Antarctica.

6. Incessant rains throughout this year increased annual ___precipitation___ in the southern areas of the country.

7. Scientists studying climate change are convinced that human activities are bound to have serious ___ramifications___ for life on earth in the imminent future.

8. Several wild species are on the verge of extinction because of the continued environmental ___degradation___ caused by profit-driven corporations recklessly exploiting earth's natural resources.

9. Large-scale illegal ___deforestation___ in the Amazon has been increasing at an alarming rate, causing the Brazilian government to take strict measures to protect the natural habitat of wildlife.

10. Environmental scientists believe that if we do not treat our planet with care and respect, then ___disruption___ of climate patterns and water supplies will continue.

Collaboration

EXERCISE **3**

Pair Activity

Choose five words you have just learned, and make complete sentences with them.

1. _____

_____

2. _____

_____

3. _____

_____

4. _____

_____

5. _____

_____

Graphic Analysis

The graph in Figure 3.3 indicates that the earth's temperature has risen steadily over the last 150 years as a result of increasing levels of atmospheric carbon dioxide. As you know, environmental scientists believe that human activities such as burning fossil fuels and transport are warming the earth. Study the graph carefully with a partner, paying attention to the rising levels of atmospheric temperature, and answer the questions.

Collaboration

■ **Figure 3.3**

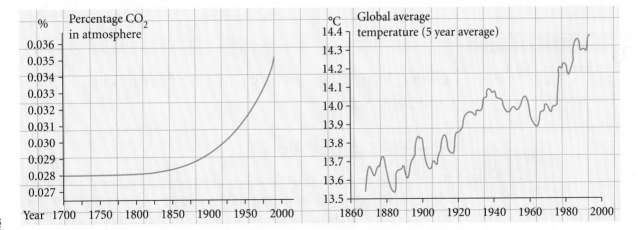

1. What was the percentage CO_2 in the atmosphere in the year 1700?
   _____.028_____

2. For how many years did the percentage CO_2 remain more or less the same? _____75_____

3. Which year saw the highest levels of carbon dioxide in the atmosphere?
   _____1990_____

4. Which year saw a sudden rise in the CO_2 levels? _____1850_____

5. When was the global average temperature the highest? _____1990_____

6. What was the change in world temperatures in centigrade between 1870 and
   1940? _____.6_____

In-class Survey: Personal Connection to Environmental Issues

ESL Annotation

3.2 ESL Environmental concerns are discussed regularly on American televisions and in newspapers. In some cultures, there is little focus in daily life on environmental issues. If you have ESL students, be sure to discuss this point.

Refer to the following questions to interview at least two classmates. Please take notes on a separate piece of paper as they respond to your questions, and orally report your findings.

Question	Respondent 1	Respondent 2
1. How would you describe the air quality in your neighborhood? If it is not very clean, what is causing the air pollution?		
2. How often do you recycle the paper, glass, and plastic products that you use? What kinds of items do you recycle? Which ones do you dispose of?		
3. Considering your neighborhood, in what ways do you see people acting in ways that are harmful to the environment?		

READING

Reading Selection 1

Magazine Article

3.3 Flesch-Kincaid Grade Level 12.0

Collaboration

Global Warming Already Causing Extinctions, Scientists Say

Pre-Reading Questions

Before reading the following article, answer these questions in pairs or small groups. Discussing the questions will help prepare you to analyze the text with relative ease.

1. How do you think the melting of the polar caps at the earth's poles can affect wildlife?

2. What are some factors that affect the survival of the polar bear? Read the first reading below and practice your reading comprehension with the set of ten multiple-choice questions that follow. Make predictions through question formation for the first group of paragraphs.

Global Warming Already Causing Extinctions, Scientists Say

By Hannah Hoag, *National Geographic News*

November 28, 2006

1 No matter where they look, scientists are finding that **global** warming is already killing species—and at a much faster rate than had originally been **predicted**.

2 "What surprises me most is that it has happened so soon," said biologist Camille Parmesan of the University of Texas, Austin, lead **author** of a new study of **global** warming's effects.

3 Parmesan and most other scientists hadn't expected to see species extinctions until 2020.

4 But populations of frogs, butterflies, ocean corals, and polar birds have already gone extinct from **global** warming because of climate change, Parmesan said.

5 Scientists were right about which species would suffer first—plants and animals that live only in narrow temperature ranges and those living in cold climates such as Earth's Poles or mountaintops.

6 "The species dependent on sea ice—polar bear, ring seal, emperor penguin, Adélie penguin—and the cloud forest frogs are showing massive extinctions," Parmesan said.

7 Her review compiles 866 scientific studies on the effects of climate change on terrestrial, marine, and freshwater species. The study appears in the December issue of the *Annual Review of Ecology, Evolution, and Systematics*.

?_____

_____

_____

_____

?_____

_____

_____

© Pearson Education, Inc.

Global Phenomenon

8 Bill Fraser is a wildlife ecologist with the Polar Oceans **Research** Group in Sheridan, Montana.

9 "There is no longer a question of whether one species or ecosystem is experiencing climate change. [Parmesan's] paper makes it evident that it is almost **global**," he said.

10 "The scale now is so vast that you cannot continue to ignore climate change," added Fraser, who began studying penguins in the Antarctic more than 30 years ago. "It is going to have some severe **consequences**."

11 Many species, for example, have shifted their ranges in **response** to rising temperatures. A number of butterflies and birds from temperate climates have kept pace with the changes by moving to higher latitudes or altitudes where the temperatures remain within their comfort zones.

12 "Sweden and Finland are actually gaining species **diversity** because of butterflies coming up from the continent that they never had before," Parmesan said.

13 But many species have run out of suitable habitat or fallen prey to pests and disease, while others are suffering from extreme weather events such as El Niños—**global** climate disruptions that have increased in **intensity** and severity since the early 1900s.

14 One El Niño in 1997–1998 caused 16 **percent** of **global** corals to go extinct, which in turn threatened many fish species.

15 "Fish depend on the **structure** coral reefs provide" said biologist Boris Worm of Dalhousie University in Halifax, Canada.

16 For species such as coral, the extreme swings in temperature that can be caused by global warming are more of a concern than the rising average temperatures, Worm said.

17 Harlequin frogs native to the cloud forests of Costa Rica have been hit especially hard.

18 In January J. Alan Pounds, a **resident** scientist at Costa Rica's Monteverde Cloud Forest Preserve, reported that about two-thirds of the 110 known harlequin frog species had been killed off by a disease-causing fungus.

19 The fungus thrives in warmer temperatures, which also make frogs more susceptible to infection.

On Thin Ice

20 In the Antarctic, three **decades** of declining sea ice have led to a reduction of ice algae. This, in turn, has reduced the number of krill, an essential food for many fish, marine mammals, and seabirds, including penguins.

21 "We've **predicted** that the Adélie penguin will soon be locally extinct," Fraser, of the Polar Oceans **Research** Group, said.

22 The species has already nearly disappeared from its northernmost sites in the Antarctic. The population on Anvers Island, for example, has declined more than 70 **percent**, from 16,000 breeding pairs 30 years ago to 3,500 today.

23 And this year the Adélie population on Litchfield Island disappeared.

24   "It is the first time in 700 years that the island does not have penguins on it," Fraser said.

25   Arctic polar bears living in Canada's Hudson Bay, at the southern end of the species' **range**, are fewer in number and scrawnier because they lack the ice they require to feed from.

26   "The arctic ice is reducing in **area** and thickness—some places are just too thin to support a polar bear," the University of Texas's Parmesan said.

27   Such animal **woes** may hint at hard times ahead for humans, Fraser added.

woes
problems that are affecting someone; great sadness

28   "The planet has warmed and cooled in the past, but never have we seen the type of warming that is occurring now, **accompanied** by the presence of 6.5 billion people who depend on these ecosystems," he said.

29   "Whether we want to admit it or not, we are completely and totally dependent on them."

Reading Comprehension Check

1. Biologist Camille Parmesan is surprised because
   a. global warming is a problem.
   b. she did not expect to see global warming killing off species so quickly.
   c. she thought species extinction would happen sooner.
   d. polar bears are somehow surviving.

2. The term *extinct* in the phrase "But populations of frogs, butterflies, ocean corals, and polar birds have already gone extinct" means
   a. having no living members left in a species.
   b. on a journey.
   c. temporary movement.
   d. downriver.

3. What is the topic of this article?
   a. Something must be done to save the polar bears.
   b. global warming and animal extinction
   c. Global warming is causing the extinction of many animal species.
   d. biodiversity

4. According to Bill Fraser, a wildlife ecologist, what will happen if changes in the earth's climate are ignored?
   a. All animal species will die out.
   b. No significant changes will occur.
   c. There will be severe consequences.
   d. Temperatures will go down.

5. What are "El Niños"?
   a. Spanish weather radars
   b. polar freezes
   c. severe climate increases
   d. global climate disruptions that have increased in intensity and severity since the early 1900s

© Pearson Education, Inc.

6. What were two consequences of an El Niño that occurred in 1997–1998?
   a. Corrals declined and winds increased.
   b. Fish species were threatened with an increase of global corrals.
   c. Sixteen percent of global corals went extinct and fish species were threatened.
   d. none of the above

7. The word *susceptible* as used in the phrase "which also make frogs more **susceptible** to infection" could be replaced by
   a. vulnerable.   c. protected.
   b. pertinent.   d. indentured.

8. Krill is an essential food for all but the following animal species.
   a. penguins   c. hawks
   b. marine mammals   d. fish

9. Hudson Bay, Litchfield Island, and Anvers Island are mentioned as
   a. locations where penguins have gone extinct.
   b. examples of places which have seen sharp declines or the complete disappearance of particular animal species.
   c. safe havens for animals.
   d. none of the above

10. The main idea of the article is that
    a. global warming must be stopped.
    b. climate change is killing off animal species at an alarming rate.
    c. polar bears and penguins have been the most threatened.
    d. global warming

READING

Reading Selection 2

Newspaper Article

3.4 Flesch-Kincaid Grade Level 9.6

Collaboration

To Fight Global Warming, Some Hang a Clothesline

Pre-Reading Questions

Answer the following questions in small groups.

1. Have you ever hung laundry outside to dry? Do you think there are any advantages to doing this instead of throwing your clothes in a dryer?

2. Is the latest, up-to-date technology always better than what we used in the past? For example, do you think modern-day cell phones are an improvement over rotary phones? Consider other technologies.

3. Would you be willing to sacrifice your state-of-the-art premium dryer for the sake of a cleaner environment? Explain.

To Fight Global Warming, Some Hang a Clothesline

By Kathleen A. Hughes, the *New York Times*

April 12, 2007

1   As a child, I helped my mother hang laundry in our backyard in Tamaqua, Pa., a small coal mining town. My **job** was handing up the clothespins. When everything was dry, I helped her fold the sheets in a **series** of moves that resembled ballroom dancing.

2   The clothes and linens always smelled so fresh. Everything about the laundry was fun. My brother and I played hide-and-seek in the rows of billowing white sheets.

3   I remember this as I'm studying **energy**-saving tips from Al Gore, who says that when you have time, you should use a clothesline to dry your clothes instead of the dryer.

4   A clothesline. It **strikes me** that I haven't seen one since 1991, when I moved to Rolling Hills, Calif., a gated **community** about an hour south of Los Angeles. There are rolling hills, ranch houses, sweeping views of the ocean and rocky cliffs—plenty of room—but not a single **visible** clothesline.

5   I decide **to rig** a clothesline as an experiment. My mother died many years ago and the idea of hanging laundry with my own daughter, Isabel, who is 13 and always busy at the **computer**, is oddly appealing. I'm also hoping to use less **energy** and to reduce our monthly electric bills, which hit the absurdly high level of $1,120 last summer.

6   That simple decision to hang a clothesline, however, catapults me into the laundry underground. Clotheslines are banned or **restricted** by many of the roughly 300,000 homeowners' associations that set rules for some 60 million people. When I called to ask, our Rolling Hills **Community** Association told me that my laundry had to be completely hidden in an enclosure approved by its board of directors.

ESL Annotation

3.5 ESL In many countries around the globe, hanging wet clothes is the default setting, and is not considered a "lifestyle choice" or seen as an "exotic" activity.

strikes me
to come to the realization/to understand

to rig
to arrange something so that it will do something in a particular way

Kathleen A. Hughes, "To Fight Global Warming, Some Hang a Clothesline." From *The New York Times*, April 12, 2007. © 2007 The New York Times. All rights reserved. Used by permission and protected by the Copyright Laws of the United States. The printing, copying, redistribution, or retransmission of the Material without express written permission is prohibited. www.nytimes.com

© Pearson Education, Inc.

7   I briefly considered hanging our laundry in the front yard, just to see what would happen, but my family vetoed this idea. Instead, I settled on stringing two lines in a corner of the backyard, a spot not **visible** to neighbors or officials. I'm supposed to submit a **site** plan of our property and a photograph of my laundry enclosure. But I don't have an enclosure, unless the hedge qualifies.

8   Looking for fellow clothesline fans, I came across the Web **site** of Alexander Lee, a lawyer and 32-year-old clothesline activist in Concord, N.H. In 1995 Mr. Lee **founded Project** Laundry List, a nonprofit organization, as a way to champion "the right to dry." His Web **site**, laundrylist.org, is an encyclopedia on the **energy** advantages of hanging laundry.

9   Mr. Lee sponsors an **annual** National Hanging Out Day on April 19. He plans to string a clothesline at the State House in Concord, N.H., this Saturday as part of a Step It Up 2007 rally on climate change, where he will hang T-shirts and sheets with the slogan "Hang Your Pants. Stop the Plants."

10   Inspired, I moved forward with my **project** without submitting the **site** plan and photograph for approval. My daughter agreed to help me hang the first load.

11   "It looks beautiful," she said when we stepped back. "It looks like we care about the earth."

12   The experiment was off to a good start. The first load dried in less than three hours. The clothes smelled like fresh air and wind. As we took them down, the birds were chirping and the sun was shining.

13   But there was a downside. "The towels are like sandpaper," said my husband, Dan, after stepping out of the shower.

14   Not only that. Heading outside to the clothesline and hanging each load takes about 7 minutes—6 minutes and 30 seconds longer than it takes to stuff everything into the dryer.

15   As the months rolled by, no one from the **community** association complained. Of course, since the clotheslines are in a lowered corner of the backyard surrounded by hedges, they cannot be seen from the street, the neighbors' houses or even our own house. But the rope lines started to sag, allowing the sheets and heavy wet towels to drag in the dirt. The wooden clothespins soon became weathered and fell apart.

dashing my hope
erasing hope

16   Meanwhile, my daughter lost interest after the first load, **dashing my hope** of recreating the happy times I spent hanging clothes with my own mother.

17   I briefly gave up—the dryer was so much easier—but then tried again. I bought stronger lines, plastic instead of rope, and switched to plastic clothespins. I also learned that tossing the clothes in the dryer for just a few minutes after they have dried on the line makes them softer.

18   Everyone now seems happy enough with the fresh smelling laundry, which is just slightly stiff. Of course, I still haven't asked our local board of directors for approval. If they object, I could be forced to take my laundry down or build an enclosure, an inconvenient confrontation I'm simply avoiding. In the meantime, our electric bill has dropped to $576 in March from its high last summer, reflecting a **series** of efforts to cut **energy**. (That's still too high, so we're about to try fluorescent bulbs.)

19   There were more than 88 million dryers in the country in 2005, the latest count, according to the Association of Home Appliance Manufacturers. If all Americans line-dried for just half a year, it would save 3.3% of the country's total residential **output** of carbon dioxide, experts say.

20   "It's a huge waste of **energy** to tumble dry your clothes," said Tom Arnold, chief environmental officer of TerraPass, a San Francisco company that sells carbon offsets, which aim to reduce **greenhouse gases** to compensate for one's activities. "It's one of the simplest things to do to help with **global** warming.

greenhouse gases
those, especially carbon dioxide or methane, that trap heat above the earth and cause the greenhouse effect

21   The laundry underground is a mixed group. It includes the frugal, people without dryers, and people from countries where hanging laundry is part of the culture. Many people hang a few delicate **items**. Tim Eames, a British designer who lives in Los Angeles, does not own a dryer. "The thought of getting a machine to do something as simple as drying my laundry is totally inconceivable," he said.

22   For those in colder climates, going without a dryer can be a **challenge**. Tom Stokes, a **global** warming activist in Stockbridge, Mass., managed to fit six clotheslines in a large downstairs bathroom, and he now hangs all of his laundry there in the winter. "It's relatively easy in the summer. It takes more determination to string up a line and hang laundry year round," he says.

23   Indeed, Annalisa Parent, a photographer who grew up in New Hampshire, said that when she was a child, her family hung all their laundry outside, even in the snow. Her father, an engineer, built a one-of-a-kind clothesline with an arched roof above it. She recalls standing her frozen jeans on the furnace to thaw them before school and wishing that her family could be like the families with dryers.

24   Now, at 32, she still doesn't own a dryer. She hangs all of her laundry inside her town house in South Burlington, Vt. Ms. Parent says she was inspired to see "the beauty in a clothesline" by Mr. Lee, a friend from college. She has taken more than 500 photographs of clotheslines and her work, featured on his Web **site**, shows clotheslines by the sea, clotheslines in Romania and even close-ups of clothespins.

25   In Hollywood movies, however, clotheslines often appear in scenes depicting dire poverty. Jennifer Williams, a set decorator, says she hung clotheslines to help convey that in the films "Angela's Ashes," "Children of Men" and "Pearl Harbor."

26   That **image** could limit the comeback of the clothesline. "People see laundry as an ugly flag of poverty," said Mr. Lee. "It's a reminder to some people of where they grew up." For me, that was Tamaqua, Pa., where my father worked for a company that made explosives for the mines. Clotheslines are still popular in Tamaqua, where the average home price is $64,400. Linda Yulanavage, head of the local Chamber of Commerce, says more than half of the town's 11,000 residents use clotheslines because they like the smell of fresh air in their laundry and because it saves **energy**. "People see it as a **normal**, everyday thing to see clothes hanging on the line," she says. "It gives a homey, close neighborhood feeling."

carbon footprint
the amount of harmful carbon dioxide that a person, company, industry, etc. produces when doing normal activities, such as driving a car, heating a building, or producing goods

27   I completely agree, although I seem to have the only clothesline in Rolling Hills. Maybe others will join. Meanwhile, my **carbon footprint** is shrinking and our clothes smell like the great outdoors.

Reading Comprehension Check

1. What does the author compare ballroom dancing with?
   a. hanging the laundry
   (b.) her movements folding sheets
   c. her mother's footsteps
   d. the feeling of her backyard

© Pearson Education, Inc.

2. The word *billow* in the second paragraph ("My brother and I played hide-and-seek in the rows of *billowing* white sheets.") could be replaced by
   a. dirty.
   b. endless.
   (c.) fluttering.
   d. descending.

3. What is the main idea of paragraph 4?
   a. Hanging clothes is fashionable.
   b. The author misses hanging clothes.
   (c.) There are no clotheslines in the author's gated community.
   d. The author thinks hanging clothes is fresher than using a machine.

4. Which reason is NOT given for why the author wanted to try using a clothesline?
   a. It could save her money.
   b. It could save time.
   (c.) She wanted to show off to her neighbors.
   d. She is sentimental about sharing her mother's tradition with her daughter.

5. In the first sentence of paragraph 6, "That simple decision to hang a clothesline, however, *catapults* me into the laundry underground," a synonym for the word *catapults* could be
   a. considers.
   b. deceives.
   (c.) hurls.
   d. promotes.

6. What is Alexander Lee's relation to the author?
   a. He is her brother.
   b. He is her leader.
   c. He is against her plan.
   (d.) He is an inspiration for her to hang her clothes out to dry.

7. What is the main point made by Tom Arnold, chief environmental officer of TerraPass?
   (a.) Using a clothesline is an easy way to help the environment.
   b. Using a clothesline is the main solution to global warming.
   c. It's fine to use a dryer when you really need to.
   d. A lot of what we do wastes energy.

8. The word *inconceivable*, as used in paragraph 21 in the sentence "The thought of getting a machine to do something as simple as drying my laundry is totally inconceivable," could be replaced by
   a. realistic.
   (b.) unimaginable.
   c. thoughtless.
   d. durable.

9. According to the author, how are clotheslines depicted in Hollywood movies?
   a. as inconvenient
   (b.) as a sign of poverty
   c. as attractive
   d. as environmentally sensitive

10. In the last paragraph, the author completely agrees with which of the following statements?
    a. Hanging laundry is worth the effort.
    b. Hanging laundry is an ugly flag of poverty.
    (c.) Hanging clothes makes her neighborhood feel more like home.
    d. There are advantages and disadvantages to hanging laundry.

Al Gore

Al Gore is a prominent environmental activist who shared the 2007 Nobel Peace Prize with the Intergovernmental Panel on Climate Change "for their efforts to build up and disseminate greater knowledge about man-made climate change, and to lay the foundations for the measures that are needed to counteract such change."

Gore was the forty-fifth Vice President of the United States, serving from 1993 to 2001 under President Bill Clinton. Before that, Vice President Gore served in the U.S. House of Representatives (1977–85) and the U.S. Senate (1985–93), representing Tennessee.

Albert Arnold Gore, Jr. was born on March 31, 1948 in Washington, D.C., where his father, Albert Gore, Sr., was serving as a Democrat in the U.S. House from Tennessee. Gore's mother, Pauline LaFon Gore, was one of the first women to graduate from Vanderbilt Law School.

In 2006, Gore published the book and Oscar-winning documentary film *An Inconvenient Truth* as part of a campaign against climate change. His goal was to educate the public to the fact that global warming, which is caused by greenhouse gases, is raising sea levels and leading to storms, droughts, and other climate disruptions. Gore's message is that human action can slow the consequences of global climate change. In the documentary, Gore states, "The scientists are virtually screaming from the rooftops now. The debate is over! There's no longer any debate in the scientific community about this. But the political systems around the world have held this at arm's length because it's an inconvenient truth, because they don't want to accept that it's a moral imperative."

Under his leadership, one of Gore's organizations, Save Our Selves, organized the July 7, 2007 benefit concert Live Earth in an effort to raise awareness about climate change.

"He is probably the single individual who has done most to create greater worldwide understanding of the measures that need to be adopted," the Norwegian Nobel Committee said of Gore.

Some Questions for Group Discussion

1. Carefully read Gore's quote at the bottom of the fourth paragraph. What is his main point?
2. Gore had a long and successful career as a politician, serving in the House, the Senate and as Vice President. What do you think motivated him to become a leader in the environmental movement?
3. As stated in the biographical profile, Gore was awarded the Nobel Peace Prize in 2007 for his work on climate change. Do you think it makes sense to give a peace prize to an environmentalist? Is there a connection between Gore's work and world peace? Explain.

Biographical Internet Research

Research another great figure in Environmental Studies, taken from the list below, and share a biographical profile with your fellow students:

- Rachel Carson
- John Muir
- John James Audobon
- David Brower
- Aldo Leopold

SKILL FOCUS
Identifying Supporting Details

Supporting details are a key element in a reading passage as they provide additional information to explain, illustrate, or prove the main idea of a particular paragraph. Supporting details answer the questions readers naturally formulate as they interact with a given text. Imagine you are reading a textbook paragraph and the first sentence is "When winter arrives, the Alaskan grizzly must adapt to this harsh, new environment." Clearly this is the main point of the paragraph. The reader then predicts how the paragraph will follow—in other words, what supporting details the paragraph will consist of, by formulating questions.

© Pearson Education, Inc.

Main idea: *When winter arrives, the Alaskan grizzly must adapt to this harsh, new environment.*

Questions: How/In what particular ways does the Alaskan grizzly adapt to winter?

What are some characteristics of a harsh Alaskan winter?

Following through with the full paragraph, the reader's questions are answered.

When winter arrives, the Alaskan grizzly must adapt to this harsh, new environment. Temperatures in the Alaskan plains often dip to −30° F and winds can be very strong. The grizzly adapts first through bodily change, putting on as many as one hundred extra pounds through a heavy autumn eating season. In the heart of the winter, grizzlies hibernate to maintain a healthy body temperature.

Types of Supporting Details

Supporting details most often come in the form of:

- Characteristics (Three characteristics of gene mutation are . . .)
- Steps (First, the kangaroo emerges from its hiding place. Then, it . . .)
- Examples (Another example of dyslexic behavior is . . .)
- Reasons (These religions are often in conflict because . . .)
- Results (A consequence of this action is that the night owl . . .)
- Descriptions (Sharp, rocky coasts contrast with the smooth blue Aegean Sea.)
- Dates (The battles that occurred in the winter of 1943 and summer of 1944 were critical.)
- Places (Some cities with high rates of violence include Washington, Miami, and Detroit.
- Names (Such leaders as Franklin, Washington, and Hamilton are most remembered from this period.)
- Statistics (Americans consume nearly a quarter of the world's energy supply.)

Let's practice predicting supporting details by trying to formulate questions from main idea sentences related to our chapter theme.

EXERCISE 4

Predicting Supporting Details

Collaboration

Work with a partner to formulate who/what/ why/ where/how questions about the main ideas offered. The first one has been done for you.

1. **Main Idea:** The president's proposal to drill for oil in Alaska has been defeated by Congress.

    Questions: a. Why did Congress reject the president's proposal?
    b. What prompted the president to offer this proposal?
    c. What were the exact details of the drill-for-oil project?

2. **Main Idea:** A basic law of thermodynamics is that energy is never completely efficient.

> **Questions: a.** *What is thermodynamics?*
>
> **b.** *What keeps energy from being completely efficient?*

3. **Main Idea:** In the 1940s the properties of the new insecticide DDT seemed close to miraculous.

> **Questions: a.** *Who invented DDT?*
>
> **b.** *Why was the new insecticide DDT invented?*
>
> **c.** *What made the properties of the new insecticide so miraculous?*

4. **Main Idea:** Chains of carbon atoms form the framework of all organic molecules, the building blocks of life.

> **Questions: a.** *How are the chains of carbon atoms formed?*
>
> **b.** *What is the function of organic molecules?*

5. **Main Idea:** Many of the environmental problems that plague modern society have resulted from human interference in ecosystem function.

> **Questions: a.** *What are the environmental problems?*
>
> **b.** *What human activities are causing these problems?*
>
> **c.** *Where are these problems occurring?*
>
> **d.** *What is the impact of these problems?*

6. **Main idea:** Many scientists believe that global warming is already affecting our ecosystem.

> **Questions: a.** *What evidence of global warming do these scientists have?*
>
> **b.** *How is global warming affecting our eco system?*
>
> **c.** *What can be done to reduce the impact of global warming?*

Major and Minor Details

As we have stated earlier, *supporting details* are used by a writer to explain, illustrate or prove the main idea of a particular paragraph. So, for example, if the main focus of a paragraph is "There are several different kinds of colleges," a supporting detail could be an example of one kind of college. For example:

"A community college offers two-year Associate Degrees."

This kind of detail is known as a *major detail* as it directly supports the main idea.

If the paragraph continues, however, by explaining more about the major detail, in this case about community colleges, then the following would be considered *minor details* (as they relate to the major detail):

For many students a community college is an introduction to higher education. Many community colleges feed their graduating students into four-year schools.

© Pearson Education, Inc.

This relationship between main point and major and minor details is diagrammed below.

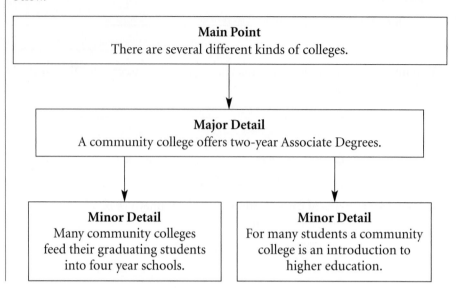

Main Point
There are several different kinds of colleges.

Major Detail
A community college offers two-year Associate Degrees.

Minor Detail
Many community colleges feed their graduating students into four year schools.

Minor Detail
For many students a community college is an introduction to higher education.

Predicting Supporting Details

Collaboration

With a partner, imagine some logical details that follow from the main point offered below. Turn the questions you might have into statements, providing the details in the table below.

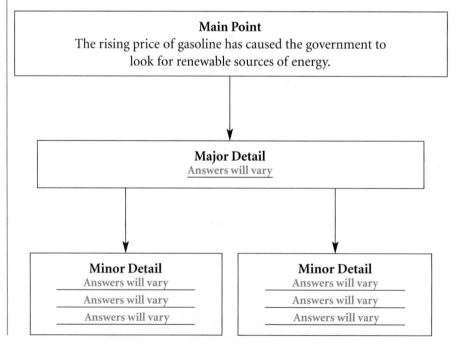

Main Point
The rising price of gasoline has caused the government to look for renewable sources of energy.

Major Detail
Answers will vary

Minor Detail
Answers will vary
Answers will vary
Answers will vary

Minor Detail
Answers will vary
Answers will vary
Answers will vary

Collaboration

EXERCISE 6

Practice Identifying Major and Minor Details

In the following short paragraphs, work with a partner to identify both the major and minor details. Underline the major details and circle the minor ones. The first one has been done for you.

1. During aggressive displays, animals may exhibit weapons such as claws and fangs and they often do things to make them appear larger. <u>Competitors often stand upright and erect their fur, feathers, ears, or fins.</u> The displays are typically accompanied by intimidating sounds (growls, croaks, roars, chirps) whose loudness can help decide the winner. Fighting tends to be a last resort when displays fail to resolve a dispute.

   (Teresa Audesirk, Gerald Audesirk, and Bruce E. Byers, pp. 570-577 from *Biology: Life on Earth* 8th ed. Copyright © 2008 by Pearson Education, Inc. Reprinted by permission.)

2. <u>In addition to observing natural selection in the wild, scientists have also devised numerous experiments that confirm the action of natural selection.</u> For example, one group of evolutionary biologists released small groups of Anolis sagrei lizards onto fourteen small Bajamian islands that were previously uninhabited by lizards. The original lizards came from a population on Staniel Cay, an island with small vegetation, including plenty of trees. In contrast, the islands to which the small colonial groups were introduced had few or no trees and were covered mainly with small shrubs and other low-growing plants.

   (From *Biology: Life on Earth*, p. 291)

3. <u>The scientific name of an organism is formed from the two smallest categories, the genus and the species.</u> Each genus includes a group of closely related species, and each species within a genus includes populations of organisms that can potentially interbreed under natural conditions. Thus, the genus Sialia (bluebirds) includes the eastern bluebird (Sialia sialis), the western bluebird (Sialis mexicana), and the mountain bluebird (Sialus currucoides)—very similar birds that normally do not interbreed.

   (From *Biology: Life on Earth*, p. 358)

4. <u>Chemical reactions fall into two categories.</u> In exergonic reactions, the reactant molecules have more energy than do the product molecules, so the reaction releases energy. In endergonic reactions, the reactants have less energy than do the products, so the reaction requires an input of energy. Exergonic reactions can occur spontaneously; but all reactions, including exergonic ones, require an initial input of energy to overcome electrical repulsions between reactant molecules.

   (From *Biology: Life on Earth*, p. 114)

© Pearson Education, Inc.

5. Paleontologists (scientists who study fossils) have cataloged the extinction of approximately 70 percent of all living species by the disappearance of their fossils at the end of the Cretaceous Period. In sites from around the globe, researchers have found a thin layer of clay deposited around 65 million years ago; the clay has about 30 times the typical levels of a rare element called iridium, which is found in high concentrations in some meteorites.

(From *Biology: Life on Earth*, p. 130)

EXERCISE 7

More Practice with Supporting Details

The following excerpts are taken from an introductory biology text. Read the following paragraphs carefully and answer the multiple-choice questions that follow, by circling the letter of the correct answer. Remember to apply the skills you learned earlier to identify the major and minor details supporting the main idea.

Passage 1

Biodiversity refers to the total number of species within an ecosystem and the resulting complexity of interactions among them; in short, it defines the biological "richness" of an ecosystem. Rain forests have the highest biodiversity of any ecosystem on Earth. Although rain forests cover only 6% of Earth's total land area, ecologists estimate that they are home to between 5 million and 8 million species, representing half to two-thirds of the world's total. For example, a recent survey of a 2.5 acre site in the upper Amazon basin revealed 283 different species of trees, most of which were represented by a single individual. In a 3-square-mile (about 5-square-kilometer) tract of rain forest in Peru, scientists counted more than 1300 butterfly species and 600 bird species. For comparison, the entire U.S. is home to only 400 butterfly and 700 bird species.

(From *Biology: Life on Earth*, p. 588)

1. The main idea of the passage is
   a. There are 400 butterflies and 700 birds in the United States.
   b. The Amazon basin has 283 tree species.
   c. The rich flora and fauna of an ecosystem is called biodiversity.
   d. Rain forests have approximately 8 million species.

2. The first major detail presented in the passage is which of the following?
   a. A survey of a large area in the Amazon basin was recently conducted.
   b. Rain forests cover 6% of Earth's land area.
   c. Scientists found 1300 butterflies and 600 birds in Peru.
   d. The highest biodiversity is found in the rain forests.

3. Which of the following is a minor detail?
    a. Biodiversity refers to the complex interactions between plants and animals in an ecosystem.
    b. Biodiversity is a term used to define the richness of an ecosystem.
    c. The Amazon basis has 283 different species of trees.
    d. Rain forests have the highest biodiversity of an ecosystem.

Passage 2

Because of infertile soil and heavy rains, agriculture is risky and destructive in rain forests. If the trees are carried away for lumber, few nutrients remain to support crops. If the nutrients are released to the soil by burning the natural vegetation, the heavy year-round rainfall quickly dissolves and erodes them away, leaving the soil depleted after only a few seasons of cultivation. The exposed soil, which is rich in iron and aluminum, then takes on an impenetrable, bricklike quality as it bakes in the tropical sun. As a result, secondary succession on cleared rain-forest land is slow; even small forest cuttings take about 70 years to regenerate. Despite their unsuitability for agriculture, rain forests are being felled for lumber or burned down for ranching or farming at an alarming rate. The demand for biofuels (fuels produced from biomass, including palm and soybean oil) is driving rapid destruction of rain forests to grow these crops. Estimates of rain-forest destruction range up to 65,000 square miles (42 million acres, or about 170,000 square kilometers) per year, or about 1.3 acres each second. In recent years Brazil alone has lost about 10,000 square miles (6000 square kilometers) annually. For comparison, the state of Connecticut occupies about 5000 square miles.

(From *Biology: Life on Earth*, pp. 589–590)

1. Which of the following is the main idea of the passage?
    a. Agriculture can thrive in rain forests.
    b. Heavy rains have caused a boom in Brazil's agricultural growth.
    c. Rain forests are unsuitable for agriculture.
    d. Infertile soil helps the natural vegetation to grow rapidly.

2. According to the passage, which of the following statements is not true?
    a. Deforestation deprives the soil of its rich nutrients.
    b. Heavy rains deplete the soil.
    c. Humans' cutting down rain forests for lumber and farming is a cause for concern.
    d. Brazil has lost approximately 10,000 square miles of rain forests biannually.

3. According to the passage, biofuels
    a. have sparked an interest in protecting rain forests.
    b. are not in demand at all.
    c. have saved 42 million acres of rain forests.
    d. have accelerated deforestation.

© Pearson Education, Inc.

Passage 3

Although they are as diverse as terrestrial ecosystems, aquatic ecosystems share three general features. First, because water is slower to heat and cool than air, temperatures in aquatic ecosystems are more moderate than those in terrestrial ecosystems. Second, water absorbs light; even in very clear water, below 650 feet (200 meters) little light is left to power photosynthesis. Suspended sediment (nonliving particles carried by a moving water) or microorganisms greatly reduce light penetration. Finally, nutrients in aquatic ecosystems tend to be concentrated near the bottom sediments, so where nutrients are highest, the light levels are lowest. Of the four requirements for life, aquatic ecosystems provide abundant water and appropriate temperatures. Thus, the availability of energy and nutrients largely determines the quantity of life and the distribution of life in aquatic ecosystems.

(From *Biology: Life on Earth*, p. 598)

1. Which of the following sentences best states the main idea of the passage?
   a. Terrestrial ecosystems are incredibly diverse.
   b. Energy and nutrients influence the quantity of life in aquatic ecosystems.
   c. There are three characteristics that distinguish aquatic ecosystems from terrestrial ecosystems.
   d. Water absorbs light in clear water.

2. The first major detail is
   a. the diversity of terrestrial ecosystems.
   b. three general features of aquatic ecosystems.
   c. that water is slower to heat.
   d. that aquatic ecosystems have lower temperatures than terrestrial ecosystems do.

3. The second major detail discussed by the author is that
   a. aquatic ecosystems have insufficient light for photosynthesis.
   b. aquatic ecosystems have moderate temperatures.
   c. there are four requirements for life in aquatic ecosystems.
   d. water is cooler than air.

4. The third major detail that the author discusses is
   a. microorganisms greatly reduce light penetration.
   b. photosynthesis does not occur in aquatic ecosystems.
   c. aquatic ecosystems contain nutrients near the bottom.
   d. aquatic ecosystems provide plenty of water and temperatures.

5. Which of the following is not a major detail?
   a. Aquatic ecosystems have three general features.
   b. It is difficult to power photosynthesis in aquatic ecosystems.

c. Nutrients are found near the bottom sediments in aquatic ecosystems.

d. Nonliving particles reduce light penetration.

The next Reading Selection allows you to apply the skills you have just learned.

READING

Reading Selection **3**

Online News

3.6 Flesch-Kincaid Grade Level 11.5

Collaboration

Going Green on Top

Pre-Reading Questions

Work with a partner by first discussing some pre-reading questions. Then connect the article's main points with their supporting details by answering the questions following the reading.

1. Have you ever seen a "green roof"? If yes, what was your impression? If no, do you know of any green roofs in your community or in your county?

2. What do you think might be some advantages of a building having a "green roof?" Explain.

3. Can you think of other ways to increase the amount of "green space" in our communities? Share your ideas.

Going Green on Top (excerpt)

By Bryn Nelson, MSNBC

April 16, 2008

1   The Washington Nationals' new baseball stadium opened the 2008 season with one. Vancouver's 2010 Winter Olympics will feature many more. And earlier this year Minneapolis decreed that the city's voluminous **Target** Center arena will have one too.

2   Suddenly, green roofs are **sprouting** across North America. Designed to curb air pollution, decrease **energy** expenses and reduce storm runoff, the environmentally friendly assemblies are adding a decidedly earthy element to urban skylines—a sign that the green roof industry is rapidly **coming into its own**.

3   Particularly in cities, the rise of roof-topping grasses, succulents and other vegetation is fueling a boom for landscape architects, growers, builders and consultants **in the know**. As the roofs bloom in size and number, cities are weighing new incentives to developers and owners to install the admittedly costly growing **medium** and plant life as a long-term **investment** that could **benefit** both businesses and surrounding communities. And with a strengthening **infrastructure** to support them, designers are branching out in new directions.

sprouting
starting to grow, or produce new leaves, buds, or shoots

coming into its own
becoming an individual entity, no longer dependent

in the know
privy to special or secret information

© Pearson Education, Inc.

4   Steven Peck, founder and president of the Toronto-based industry association Green Roofs for Healthy Cities, said the industry's "mother ship" hails from Europe, particularly Germany. **Research** there in the 1970s on lightweight, low-**maintenance** green roof systems dominated by hardy sedum grasses, he said, "opened up thousands of miles of roofscapes that had been unavailable to any sort of greenery."

5   German policymakers quickly took notice of the advantages, including the **potential** to reduce both stormwater runoff and the urban heat island effect associated with asphalt, concrete and metal surfaces. In **response**, they created dozens of incentives and **regulations** encouraging more green roof **construction**. In the mid-'90s, a European industry mostly dominated by French and German firms began expanding into North America and introducing the basic concepts to a new **generation** of specialists. Peck, himself introduced to the idea in 1997, was tasked with leading a **federal** study on its benefits and barriers in Canada, only to find that there was little scientific information available for North America. "There was no proof, it was all in German **academic** studies," he said.

6   One of his committee member spent hours translating many of the studies into English. And even those reports sidestepped **analysis** of **big-picture** benefits that had been largely taken for **granted**. A decade later, the industry has been **buttressed** by **research** and case studies detailing both **individual** benefits like savings on cooling costs and enhanced commercial values, and bigger-picture pluses like reduced air pollution and storm water overflows. Another essential element has been building expertise across a talent pool that remains unevenly distributed. Peck's group has been working for five years on an accreditation program modeled in part on LEED certification (Leadership in Environmental **Energy** and **Design**). The new Green Roof **Professional**, or GRP system, should roll out sometime next year, he said. In the meantime, Green Roofs for Healthy Cities

big-picture
the larger context

buttressed
strengthened or supported

has grown to include more than 80 **corporate** members and has trained more than 4,500 individuals. "You can't have an industry unless you can have people who can **design** and deliver," he said.

7   Most green roofs still feature sedum and ice plant succulents, which can tolerate harsh growing conditions and are ideally suited for low-**maintenance** rooftops. These "extensive" roofs, as they're known, require only a few inches of growing **medium**, reducing **overall** weight and cost.

8   John Shepley, co-owner of Maryland's Emory Knoll Farms with industry leader Ed Snodgrass, said business is booming at their green roof plant nursery, based on a former dairy farm. "We're probably growing 50 **percent** annually without trying," Shepley said. Although Washington, D.C., and New York City remain big markets, he said, the **federal** government has been coming on strong with new mandates for green buildings. In mid-March, Shepley delivered pregrown sedum plugs to cover a concessions **area** at the new Washington Nationals baseball stadium. Two years ago, the business helped install thousands more grass plugs on a massive green roof for a Library of Congress facility in Culpepper, Va.

9   As green roof **technology** matures, new projects have begun unveiling increasingly varied designs, including "intensive" roofs that require deeper growing depths and considerably more **investment** but can deliver more aesthetic, conservation and other benefits. Chicago's $480 million Millennium Park, a 24.5-acre cap over rail yards and a parking garage, is one of the world's largest intensive green roofs to date. An award winner from Green Roofs for Healthy Cities, the **project** has all the advantages of a **major** urban park, Peck maintains.

10   Considered the industry frontrunner among North American cities, Chicago used a mix of intensive and extensive vegetation to cover 20,000 square feet atop its City Hall in 2001. In August of that year, researchers recorded a rooftop temperature of 119 degrees in the planted **area**, compared with a blistering 169 degrees on an adjoining black tar roof. Since then, the green roof has saved the city an estimated $3,600 in **annual** cooling and heating costs. If all Chicago roofs were similarly **clad**, city officials believe peak **energy** demand could be cut by 720 megawatts, or enough electricity for 750,000 consumers. Similarly, the load on the city's storm sewer system could be slashed by roughly 70 **percent**. Chicago is now adding green roofs to everything from office buildings to fire stations, and city governments in Toronto, Minneapolis and Seattle are **following suit**. Other city-based incentives, popular in Chicago and Portland, give developers extra floor space if they add green roofs, and fast-track programs are rewarding environmentally conscious projects with a front-of-the-line approval **process**. Washington, D.C., which has long struggled to control storm-water overflows into the Potomac and Anacostia Rivers, is moving toward a system that will account for impervious building surfaces that increase runoff when assessing water consumption **fees**. Adding more water-retaining surfaces, including green roofs, will effectively lower a building owner's city **fees**. Beyond relieving the **impact** of development, the measure is designed to encourage both public and private-**sector investment** into runoff-reduction **technology**.

clad
wearing or covered in a particular thing

following suit
imitating a previous action

© Pearson Education, Inc.

thwart
to prevent someone from doing
something

11   **Nevertheless,** Mark Thomann, **design** director at the New York landscape **design** firm Balmori Associates, said high **construction** costs, a lack of government support, and limited **expert** availability are still combining to **thwart** many ambitious green roof plans. "We imagined doing 50 of these a year, and the reality is we do one to two a year" he said.

Reading Comprehension Check

1. A baseball stadium, an Olympic facility and a Minneapolis arena are all given as examples of
   a. 2008 season locations.
   (b.) green roof sites.
   c. environmentally safe sites.
   d. both a and b

2. All of the following are offered as benefits of green roofs in paragraph 2 EXCEPT
   a. reduces storm runoff.
   b. curbs air pollution.
   (c.) increases pollination.
   d. decreases energy expenses.

3. Green roofs might be a good long-term investment for
   a. surrounding communities.
   b. businesses.
   c. schools.
   (d.) both a and b

4. Germany is pointed to in paragraph 4 as
   a. a ship.
   (b.) a pioneer in green roof research.
   c. a lightweight system.
   d. a failed experiment in green-roofing.

5. In paragraph 5 we learn that Peck, founder of a green roof's organization, once worked on a federal study in
   a. Germany.
   b. North America.
   (c.) Canada.
   d. the United States.

6. The fact that GRP system has 80 corporate members and over 4,500 trained individuals is mentioned in paragraph 6 to show
   (a.) how much this company has grown.
   b. the role of environmental groups.
   c. the importance of good design.
   d. all of the above

7. Two characteristics of sedum and ice plant succulents are that they
   a. are extensive and green.
   b. can tolerate difficult growing conditions and are more expensive.
   (c.) can tolerate difficult growing conditions and well-suited for low-maintenance rooftops.
   d. cost less and reduce carbon dioxide.

8. "Intensive" roofs are mentioned in paragraph 9 to illustrate
   a. the cost of green roofs.
   (b.) that green roof technology has spawned various designs.
   c. how the Chicago's Millennium Park was organized.
   d. none of the above

9. Developers are sometimes given extra floor space and a faster approval process to
   a. punish those who are environmentally unsafe.
   b. be more effective.
   (c.) to reward them for adding green roofs.
   d. make cities more energy efficient.

10. Which is NOT mentioned in paragraph 11 as an obstacle to the growth of green roof plans?
    a. limited expert availability
    b. a lack of government support
    (c.) an increase in the price of natural gas
    d. high construction costs

READING

Reading Selection **4**

Letter to Newspaper

3.7 Flesch-Kincaid Grade Level 11.5

Read the following response letters, paying particular attention to the types of supporting details each writer includes in making his or her point. First, determine the main idea. Then decide for each letter which supporting detail in your opinion is the most effective (Hint: specific examples help strengthen a writer's main argument).

New York Times Readers Respond to "The Evidence for Global Warming"

July 8, 2006

Ralph Deeds, Birmingham, Michigan:

1 It appears to me that the politics of **global** warming is more difficult than the science. For example, existing automobile **technology** could produce a huge savings in oil if our Congress would stop debating flag burning and pass **legislation** to encourage more fuel-efficient motor vehicles. This could easily be done by gradually increasing the gasoline tax to bring pump prices up to European levels. Phasing in the tax increase over several years would give drivers and car companies time to adjust to the production and sale of smaller, more fuel-efficient cars. The downside of a big gas tax increase is that it would be regressive, bearing most heavily on those least able to afford it. An **alternative** would be a **vehicle** weight and/or horsepower tax. **Likewise, technology** exists for cleaner power production if there were the political will to require the power companies to use it.

Main Point: _The politics of global warming is more difficult than the science._

Most effective supporting detail: _Existing automobile technology could produce a huge savings in oil if our Congress would stop debating flag burning and pass legislation to encourage more fuel-efficient motor vehicles._

Jill E. Burwell, Mt. Morris, Michigan:

2 Mr. Boffey, thank you for a perfect Talking Points article. Finally, someone has gathered the **evidence** from both sides of the fence and laid it out in terms

© Pearson Education, Inc.

grasp of
To take and hold something firmly; to completely understand a fact or an idea, especially a complicated one

everyone can understand. I now feel I have a much better **grasp of** the **issues** and the differing viewpoints and can hold an intelligent conversation on the subject. And it appears to me that's the most important thing we have to do right now—keep the subject under discussion. The gamble you mention in your **conclusion** is one with **stakes too high** to be **ignored**.

stakes too high
the situation is critical

> **Main Point:** *The reader feels she has a much better grasp of the issues and the differing viewpoints and can hold an intelligent conversation on the subject.*
>
> **Most effective supporting detail:** *And it appears to me that the most important thing we have to do right now is to keep the subject under discussion.*

Eugene I. Gordon, Mountainside, New Jersey:

one-sided
showing only one side of a question, subject, etc. in a way that is unfair

3   Mr. Boffey's article is **one-sided** concerning the cause of the current **global** warming. Mr. Boffey mentions the cooling experienced during a minor ice age a few hundred years ago but neglects to mention that it was **accompanied** by a virtual disappearance of the 11-year sunspot **cycle**, the Maunder **Minimum**. It is known that high sunspot activity increases the thermal flux incident on the Earth from solar radiation and high-energy particles. Currently we are experiencing a **maximum** in sunspot activity that **virtually** perfectly parallels the increasing **global** temperature average including up and down variations. Fortunately, the sunspot activity has begun to decrease and we should get relief independent of what else we do. In addition, Mr. Boffey completely ignores the fact that the **dominant** greenhouse gas is water vapor, which is 50 times more complicit in retaining IR [infrared] radiation than carbon dioxide. Anthropogenic carbon dioxide plays but a tiny **role** in the total greenhouse gas picture. Were it not for water vapor, the average temperature of the earth would be about 0 degrees Fahrenheit rather than 58 and there would be **virtually** no life on Earth. We should be glad for the water vapor and not worry so much about carbon dioxide. One has to be suspicious of the motives or capability of scientists who **reach a consensus** without even mentioning sunspots or water vapor. The proper scientific **method** to advance anthropogenic CO_2 as the cause requires that the effects of sunspots and water vapor be explained and discounted if possible. In the absence of doing that the **so-called** consensus experts need to be viewed with great care. Mr. Boffey disparages oil interests without examining the interests of the scientific **community** that reaches a consensus while ignoring basic physics and the record.

reach a consensus
to come to an agreement

so called
used in order to show that you think the name that someone or something is called is wrong

> **Main Point:** *Mr. Boffey's article is one-sided concerning the cause of the current global warming.*
>
> **Most effective supporting detail:** *Mr. Boffey mentions the cooling experienced during a minor ice age a few hundred years ago but neglects to mention that it was accompanied by a virtual disappearance of the 11-year sunspot cycle, the Maunder Minimum.*

Dennis Wheeler, Coeur d'Alene, Idaho:

4   Phillip Boffey's article seems balanced and **objective**. The real issue is, Where is most CO_2 pollution coming from? Seems like finger points to China and

Asian continent. Therein lies the **dilemma**. U.S. citizens should neither pay for nor be penalized through loss of jobs from more **regulations** if the real cause rests with other countries. **Radical** environmentalists and liberals always want us to pay for everything so they paint the U.S.A. as the bad guys. We need the unbiased answers.

dilemma
a situation in which you have to make a difficult choice between two or more actions

Main Point: _The real issue is, Where is most CO₂ pollution coming from?_

Most effective supporting detail: _U.S. citizens should neither pay for nor be penalized through loss of jobs from more regulations if the real cause rests with other countries._

Jacob Silver, Negaunee, Michigan:

5 This is a very good essay, well researched, and covering a wide **area** of the **phenomenon**. However, you did not mention what the **implications** of the melting of the southern Greenland ice sheets are for the Gulf Stream. If the **transfer** of heat from the equator to the arctic regions **ceases**, it will have severe and differentiated **consequences**, would it not?

Main Point: _You did not mention what the implications of the melting of the southern Greenland ice sheets are for the Gulf Stream._

Most effective supporting detail: _If the transfer of heat from the equator to the arctic regions ceases, it will have severe and differentiated consequences, would it not?_

Rebecca Shipman, Woodbury, Minnesota:

6 Your **talking points** article does a great service. It is vital to have **data** that is rock-solid and to be intellectually honest, else the **global** warming **naysayers** will pick out the one questionable argument, use it as proof of zealotry on the part of the opposition, and then call for dismissal of the danger of **global** warming as a whole. I fear the **response** will be **too little, and too late**. Currently, there are no **economic consequences** to behavior that increases CO_2 levels in the atmosphere, and, on the **contrary**, much wealth to be gained. Economics and those with a vested interest in the current system are against changes that would **mitigate global** warming. History shows that rapid change in climate causes drastic changes in population. Some species are advantaged but many become extinct. Are we prepared for this to happen to humans based on where they happen to live and what **resources** they have **available**?

talking points
key focus issues

naysayer
a person who habitually expresses negative or pessimistic views

too little, and too late
inadequate as a remedy, not in time to be effective

mitigate
to make a situation or the effects of something less harmful or serious

Main Point: _The response to global warming is too little, too late . . ._

Most effective supporting detail: _Economics and those with a vested interest in the current system are against changes that would mitigate global warming._

© Pearson Education, Inc.

DEBATABLE TOPIC

Recommended Debate Topic: Should the government place stricter controls on energy consumption?

Brainstorm other debate topics related to global warming with your peers, and present your ideas to your instructor for approval.

Your suggested debate topics:

a. _____

b. _____

c. _____

The following article will help prepare you for the debate activity by offering a counterargument to the more popular environmentalist position.

READING

Reading Selection 5

Newspaper Editorial

3.8 Flesch-Kincaid Grade Level 12.0

Collaboration

My Nobel Moment

Pre-Reading Questions

Discuss these with a small group of classmates.

1. It is never easy to defend a position/idea that goes against what most people believe. Why is it important for someone to do so? What type of person is willing to argue against the majority view?

2. If global warming is a myth, how else can glacial meltdowns, animal extinctions, and rising temperatures be explained?

3. Some critics argue that the government has denied the phenomenon of global warming and finds experts to side with their view mostly because they don't want to pay the high cost of remedying the problem? Would you agree that past governments have played the role of "naysayer" on global warming for economic reasons, or might there be another explanation?

My Nobel Moment

By John R. Christy, *The Wall Street Journal*

November 1, 2007

John Christy is director of the Earth System Science Center at the University of Alabama in Huntsville and a participant in the UN's Intergovernmental **Panel** on Climate Change, corecipient of the 2007 Nobel Peace Prize.

1   I've had a lot of fun recently with my tiny (and unofficial) slice of the 2007 Nobel Peace Prize awarded to the Intergovernmental **Panel** on Climate Change (IPCC). But, though I was one of thousands of IPCC participants, I don't think I will add "0.0001 Nobel Laureate" to my resume.

2   Both halves of the award honor promoting the message that Earth's temperature is rising due to human-based emissions of greenhouse gases. The Nobel committee praises Mr. Gore and the IPCC for alerting us to a **potential catastrophe** and for spurring us to a carbonless economy.

catastrophe
a sudden and widespread disaster

3   I'm sure the majority (but not all) of my IPCC **colleagues** cringe when I say this, but I see neither the developing catastrophe nor the **smoking gun** proving that human activity is to blame for most of the warming we see. Rather, I see a **reliance** on climate models (useful but never "proof") and the coincidence that changes in carbon dioxide and **global** temperatures have loose similarity over time.

smoking gun
definite proof of who is responsible for something bad or how something really happened

4   There are some of us who remain so humbled by the **task** of measuring and understanding the extraordinarily **complex** climate system that we are skeptical of our ability to know what it is doing and why. As we build climate **data** sets from scratch and look into the guts of the climate system, however, we don't find the alarmist theory matching observations. (The National Oceanic and Atmospheric **Administration** satellite **data** we analyze at the University of Alabama in Huntsville does show modest warming—around 2.5 degrees Fahrenheit per century, if current warming trends of 0.25 degrees per decade continue.)

5   It is my turn to cringe when I hear overstated-confidence from those who describe the projected **evolution** of **global** weather patterns over the next 100 years, especially when I consider how difficult it is to accurately predict that system's behavior over the next five days.

6   Mother Nature simply operates at a level of complexity that is, at this point, beyond the mastery of mere **mortals** (such as scientists) and the tools **available** to us. As my high-school physics teacher admonished us in those we-shall-conquer-the-world-with-a-slide-rule days, "Begin all of your scientific pronouncements with 'At our present level of ignorance, we think we know . . .'"

mortals
relating to humankind

7   I haven't seen that type of climate humility lately. Rather I see jump-to-conclusions advocates and, unfortunately, some scientists who see in every weather anomaly the specter of a **global**-warming apocalypse. Explaining each **successive phenomenon** as a result of human action gives them comfort and an easy answer.

8   Others of us scratch our heads and try to understand the real causes behind what we see. We discount the possibility that *everything* is caused by

© Pearson Education, Inc.

human actions, because everything we've seen the climate do has happened before. Sea levels rise and fall continually. The Arctic ice cap has shrunk before. One millennium there are hippos swimming in the Thames, and a geological blink later there is an ice bridge linking Asia and North America.

9   One of the challenges in studying **global** climate is keeping a **global perspective**, especially when much of the **research** focuses on **data** gathered from spots around the globe. Often observations from one **region** get more attention than equally valid **data** from another.

10   The recent CNN report "Planet in Peril," for **instance**, spent **considerable** time discussing shrinking Arctic sea ice cover. CNN did *not* note that winter sea ice around Antarctica last month set a record **maximum** (yes, **maximum**) for coverage since aerial measurements started.

11   Then there is the **challenge** of translating **global** trends to local climate. For **instance**, hasn't **global** warming led to the five-year drought and fires in the U.S. Southwest?

12   Not necessarily.

it would be a stretch
it is probably not true, a logical leap

13   There has been a drought, but **it would be a stretch** to **link** this drought to carbon dioxide. If you look at the 1,000-year climate record for the western U.S. you will see not five-year but 50-year-long droughts. The 12th and 13th centuries were particularly dry. The inconvenient truth is that the last century has been fairly benign in the American West. A return to the region's long-term "**normal**" climate would present huge challenges for urban planners.

14   Without a doubt, atmospheric carbon dioxide is increasing due primarily to carbon-based **energy** production (with its undisputed benefits to humanity) and many people ardently believe we must "do something" about its alleged consequence, **global** warming. This might seem like a legitimate concern given the **potential** disasters that are announced almost daily, so I've looked at a **couple** of ways in which humans might reduce CO_2 emissions and their **impact** on temperatures.

15   California and some Northeastern states have decided to force their residents to buy cars that average 43 miles-per-gallon within the next decade. Even if you applied this law to the entire world, the net effect would reduce projected warming by about 0.05 degrees Fahrenheit by 2100, an amount so minuscule as to be undetectable. **Global** temperatures vary more than that from day to day.

making a dent
having a modest effect

16   Suppose you are very serious about **making a dent** in carbon emissions and could replace about 10% of the world's **energy** sources with non-CO_2-emitting **nuclear** power by 2020—roughly **equivalent** to halving U.S. emissions. Based on IPCC-like projections, the **required** 1,000 new **nuclear** power plants would slow the warming by about 0.2176 degrees Fahrenheit per century. It's a dent.

17   But what is the **economic** and human price, and what is it worth given the scientific uncertainty?

18   My experience as a missionary teacher in Africa opened my eyes to this simple fact: Without **access** to **energy**, life is brutal and short. The uncertain impacts of **global** warming far in the future must be weighed against disasters at our doorsteps today. Bjorn Lomborg's Copenhagen Consensus 2004, a cost-**benefit** analysis of health **issues** by leading economists (including three Nobelists), calculated that spending on health **issues** such as micronutrients for children, HIV/AIDS and water purification has benefits 50 to 200 times those of attempting to marginally limit "**global** warming."

19   Given the scientific uncertainty and our relative impotence regarding climate change, the moral imperative here seems clear to me.

Reading Comprehension Check

1. In the fourth paragraph Christy argues that there is no evidence that
   a. humans are to blame for climate change.
   b. human life existed for as long as most scientists say.
   c. animal species are dying.
   d. Al Gore deserved an award.

2. Christy uses the example of how difficult it is to predict climate change over the next five days to prove
   a. that global warming has ample evidence on its side.
   b. how much more difficult it is to predict climate change over the next one hundred years.
   c. that most scientists haven't considered the patterns of climate change.
   d. both a and b

3. Christy mentions his high school Physics teacher
   a. to show how wrong teachers can be.
   b. to illustrate the effects of global warming.
   c. as an example of someone who took a humble approach to scientific knowledge.
   d. as someone he learned a lot from.

4. Christy argues that many scientists
   a. are quick to jump to conclusions.
   b. look for easy answers to a complex problem.
   c. are not well-educated.
   d. both a and b

5. Arctic ice caps shrinking and sea levels rising and falling are offered as examples of
   a. crises that need immediate attention.
   b. climate dipping.
   c. phenomena that have happened before.
   d. evidence of global warming.

6. Christy cites a maximum level of winter sea ice around Antarctica to make the point that
   a. the media ignores important evidence in the global warming story.
   b. global warming does not get enough media coverage.
   c. polar bears are in peril.
   d. none of the above

7. Christy argues that California's and some Northeastern states' forcing people to drive cars with high gas mileage
   a. will make a big difference in slowing global warming.
   b. will have little effect on climate change.
   c. makes a lot of sense.
   d. both b and c

© Pearson Education, Inc.

8. Christy mentions his missionary teaching experience in Africa to make the point that
   a. limiting access to energy is important.
   b.) access to energy makes a big difference in people's lives.
   c. we have to put climate control over the daily concerns of the earth's people.
   d. none of the above

9. Micronutrients for children, HIV/AIDS and water purification are given as examples of
   a. life-threats due to global warming.
   b. exaggerated concerns.
   c.) global concerns which are more important than climate control.
   d. UN issues.

10. What is the main idea of this editorial?
    a.) Scientists should not exaggerate both the existence and the human causation of global warming.
    b. Global warming is a completely made-up phenomenon.
    c. Climate change needs our immediate attention.
    d. If we study the facts, we can see that climate change is happening faster than we expected.

Connecting Reading Skills with Standardized Testing

Identifying Supporting Details

Questions focusing on supporting details within a passage are common on standardized reading exams. These types of questions explore whether you can identify and make sense of specific information included in a passage.

You are being asked about supporting details when the question includes such phrases as:

- Which of the following statements is best supported by the passage?
- According to the information in the passage . . .
- Which of the following is not cited in the passage?
- The author states . . .

Questions focusing on supporting details often refer to specific information in a passage (and ask about the who/what/why/where and how):

- The Mongoose is found in which type of habitat?
- The second most common application of genetic engineering is . . . ?
- Tomatoes are not considered as vegetables because . . .
- The last leader of the Ottoman Empire was . . .

Helpful Hints: Test Questions on Supporting Details

- Don't be fooled by answer choices that use words like *all* or *none*, or *always* and *never*. Less absolute terms, such as *some*, *often*, or *few* more often apply as correct multiple-choice answers.

- Be on the lookout for negative questions. If you are asked "Which of the following is **not** a characteristic of the Pax Romana?," you need to first go through the text and identify which characteristics in your list of multiple-choice answers *are* mentioned in the text. Then you can zero in on which is not mentioned.

- Determine what type of information you need by considering the categories of supporting details outlined earlier in the chapter (see page 142):

Characteristics	Descriptions
Steps	Dates
Examples	Places
Reasons	Names
Results	Statistics

- Pay attention to signal words such as *first, second, next, also, another, finally,* etc., which often introduce supporting details.

"Meltwater" and "Give and Take" —Two Environmental Poems

READING

Reading Selection **6**

Poetry

3.9 Flesch-Kincaid Grade Level 4.7

Read the following poems and practice with the *identifying supporting details–*type questions that follow each of the poems.

Meltwater

By Maggie Butt, from *Feeling the Pressure: Poetry and Science of Climate Change,* ed. Paul Munden. Berne, Switzerland: British Council, 2008.

ESL Annotation

3.10 ESL Most ESL Students may not know that poems have symbolic and intended meaning. They also may not be familiar with literary terms such as metaphors, simile, tone, and alliteration.

my time is coming, smell it on the wind
watch raindrops winnowing down glass

touch ice-cube to your lips and tongue
feel the cool chemistry of meltwater.

see me submerge fields and swallow crops
spill out of wells to infiltrate your graves

raising the dead; firm ground will swamp
to ooze and squelch and slip, mud-symphony.

hear gurgles, trickles, runnels in your sleep
reach for the drifting flotsam of your dreams.

sweep river-sludge and sewage from the rug
swell my boundaries with your salt tears;

heave seas, wide breaths to rear up hills
waves come to claim their lost inheritance

listen to the future: rain-rocked, lake-like
nothing divides the waters from the waters.

© Pearson Education, Inc.

Reading Comprehension Check

1. *Lips and tongue* are mentioned
   a. as raindrops.
   b. as what you touch a melting ice cube with.
   c. to compare with the wind.
   d. as coolers.

2. The words *spill, ooze, slip* and *trickles* all refer to what natural resource?
   a. wind
   b. the sea
   c. water
   d. the air

3. *Sweeping river sludge and sewage* and *waves come to claim their lost inheritance* offer promises of
   a. a global water crisis.
   b. a better world.
   c. a shortage.
   d. a balanced state.

Give and Take

By Roger McGough, from *Feeling the Pressure: Poetry and Science of Climate Change,*
ed. Paul Munden

3.11 Flesch-Kincaid Grade Level 7.4

I give you clean air
You give me poisonous gas
I give you mountains
You give me quarries

I give you pure snow
You give me acid rain
I give you spring fountains
You give me toxic canals

I give you a butterfly
You give me a plastic bottle
I give you a blackbird
You give me a stealth bomber

I give you abundance
You give me waste
I give you one last chance
You give me excuse after excuse after excuse.

Reading Comprehension Check

1. Plastic bottles, acid rain and toxic canals are mentioned to contrast
   a. negative things.
   b. both positive and negative things.

c. the positive things that are given.

d. water.

2. What evidence do we have of the Giver's patience?

a. the offering of spring fountains

b. the offer of a last chance

c. The Giver shows no patience.

d. butterflies and abundance

From Reading to Writing: Taking Notes

Overview

In the previous chapter, you learned how to prepare an outline of a full-length article or essay. In this chapter, you will focus on developing note-taking skills. In most mainstream courses in college, your instructor is likely to give a lecture on a specific topic. Depending on the subject of the course, he or she also may invite an expert from a discipline, a government official, the president of a non-profit organization, or a celebrity to deliver a lecture. (Sometimes your instructor may play an audio lecture and ask you to take specific notes for an activity or brief assignment afterward.)

It will be important for you to listen to the speaker carefully and write down the main idea and supporting details (including both major and minor details) quickly. You will need to rely solely on your listening ability and, of course, knowledge of the subject matter to take good, useful notes. Remember that unlike an audio lecture, which can be rewound and played again for further clarification, you only have one opportunity to listen to the speaker carefully and obtain information in the form of notes. It is, therefore, important that you pay attention to the speaker's main idea and relevant, supporting examples. Imagine that you are attending an important meeting where main ideas are only offered once, and participants usually do not repeat their points unless they are asked for clarification. Paying close attention to the lecture while taking brief notes quickly will enable you to understand the general idea of the content and some of the key concepts.

How to Take Notes

The lecturer will most likely be speaking at a fast pace, and it will not be possible for you to write complete sentences. If you try to write down everything, you will have a great deal of difficulty keeping up with the lecturer. The following note-taking tips will help you gather as much information as possible while listening to the lecturer.

1. Ask questions

As the lecturer speaks and you take brief notes, search for answers to the following questions: HOW? WHY? WHAT? WHERE? WHEN? Framing questions such as what is the main focus of this lecture, who introduced this concept, when did this event happen, and where did this event/incident take place, etc. will help you

ESL Annotation

3.12 ESL In many cultures the tradition of note-taking involves copying everything one hears during a professor's lecture. Make sure to point out clearly that the norm in America diverges from this practice.

© Pearson Education, Inc.

understand the lecturer's movement of thoughts and follow the main idea and supporting details easily.

2. Use abbreviations and symbols

In listening to a lecture, your primary goal is to capture the main idea and supporting details. However, you may realize that sometimes a certain word is difficult to spell. In order to keep up with the lecturer, it is recommended that you use abbreviation and symbols to catch the main idea. If, for instance, the lecturer mentions, "The polar bear has become an endangered species," then you only need to write "p bear," and "in danger." Keep in mind that as you take notes you will also be taking mental notes, and that you can always revisit your notes to recall information. When you reflect on your notes, you will remember that by "p bear," you meant "polar bear." As mentioned previously, writing complete sentences will make the note-taking task more difficult. Simply look for the main ideas and supporting details while taking notes. The following table shows a few abbreviations and symbols that will help you note the content of a lecture easily. Keep in mind that this is not an exhaustive list, and that you can always create your own symbols as you try to understand the lecture.

Abbreviations	*Symbols*
EPA = Environmental Protection Agency	+ = growth, surplus, increase, progress
CO_2 = carbon dioxide	− = reduce, deduction, decrease
UN = United Nations	= = equal, similar to something
US = United States	$ = income, salary, money, revenue, profit, sales, dollar.
KP = Kyoto Protocol	
IPCC = Intergovernmental Panel on Climate Change	% = percent, percentage, approximate
RH = Rolling Hills	# = number of people, countries, etc.
CA = California	& = and, extra, in addition
AHAM = Association of Home Appliance Manufacturers	< smaller than, shorter than, less than
GG = greenhouse gases	> larger than, greater than

Why Take Notes

After reflecting on your notes, you will realize that you understand the content of the lecture more clearly compared to when you heard it the first time. You may want to compare your notes with those of your classmates' and fill in any information gaps. By sharing your notes with your classmates and answering their questions, you will circle in on the information that the lecturer presented. As you develop your note-taking skills, you will also improve your reading and listening ability. In fact, your note-taking skills have implications for your ability to write well-organized essays as well. Before you begin to write an essay, you can brainstorm main ideas and supporting details, making specific notes. You will then be able to write coherent paragraphs. It is clear that taking good, brief notes is important to improving reading, writing, listening, and speaking skills.

Note-taking Exercise

Your instructor will deliver a short lecture on a reading at the end of the chapter, entitled "The World's Water Crisis." As you listen to the lecture, use the following worksheet to take specific notes following the instruction outlined in the above lesson.

3.13 Read the first six paragraphs of the article, The World's Water Crisis (on p. 184 of the text) out loud to the class.

Note-Taking Worksheet

If you feel you need more space to take effective notes, do not hesitate to use your notebook for this exercise.

Title: _____

Main Idea: _____

_____

_____

1st Major Detail _____

_____

_____

Minor Detail: _____

_____

_____

2nd Major Detail _____

_____

_____

Minor Detail _____

_____

_____

3rd Major Detail _____

_____

_____

(Continued)

© Pearson Education, Inc.

Minor Detail _____

_____

_____

4th Major Detail _____

_____

_____

Minor Detail _____

_____

_____

5th Major Detail _____

_____

_____

Minor Detail _____

_____

_____

6th Major Detail _____

_____

_____

Minor Detail _____

_____

_____

If the lecture contains more major details, continue in the same manner and add them to the worksheet.

Conclusion _____

_____

_____

Questions: Write any questions you may have about the lecture and ask your instructor for clarification.

1. _____

2. _____

3. _____

Marcus Zobrist and his wife Kathy Hurld

Professions: Mr. Zobrist is an environmental engineer. Ms. Hurld is a biologist. They both work for the U.S. Environmental Protection Agency's Office of Water in Washington, D.C.

How did you choose your current profession?

Kathy: I've always had a fascination and love for the water, especially the deep ocean. I went off to college with the goal of becoming an oceanographer and college professor. During my junior year of college, I decided this was not the career path for me as I did not enjoy lab work enough to do it all day everyday; I did not want to be a "lab rat." I still wanted to protect the environment, so I set my sights on political science and becoming an environmental lawyer. After college I interned at the EPA, and then worked as an environmental consultant. These experiences showed me a professional field that satisfied both the scientist and the big-picture policy wonk within me. Upon returning from the Peace Corps, I resettled in Washington, D.C., and looked for a job that put my biology and political science training to work. Fourteen years later, I still enjoy the issues and challenges in drafting federal regulations, crafting national policies, conducting research, assisting states and tribes to protect their resources and negotiating international treaties.

Marcus: I originally headed off to college to study aerospace engineering, and was so sure of my choice that I had limited my college search to schools that offered that somewhat rare specialty. My college offered monthly seminars where people working in the field, mostly recent graduates of the school, would come in and talk to the students about what they were working on. While the projects they were working on all sounded fascinating, all of the practicing engineers who spoke to us were working in the defense industry. I did some research on my chosen profession and realized that there were relatively few jobs working in civil aeronautics working on things like the space probes or the Space Shuttle. I am idealistic, and I quickly realized that I wanted to use my professional training to make a difference, and thought that working on weapons would not give me such satisfaction, so I transferred schools and switched to environmental engineering. It was a choice that I have not regretted—I am motivated by my work that involves developing new policies and guidance on addressing challenging environmental problems.

How did you prepare to reach your goal of becoming a scientist/engineer?

Marcus: I don't know that I ever prepared myself. While in the first couple years of engineering school, the curriculum is all about learning "core" skills—mathematics, applied physics, chemistry, statistics, etc. and not about the more exciting specialty topics such as watershed management, or wastewater treatment plant processes and design. I know during those early years that I simply needed to gain a solid foundation on the core knowledge, and that knowledge would serve me well in tackling the challenges of my specialty.

Kathy: To prepare myself, I started in high school; I took every opportunity to learn and be part of projects that would expand my knowledge and expose me to various aspects of scientific research. I took courses like microbiology and attended summer camps on environmental and ocean issues. Over the years I took a diversity of jobs within the scientific field including work as laboratory bench scientist, as a lab technician in a genetics laboratory (raising rats), collecting field samples and managing a lab. I kept an open mind regarding what my career would look like as opportunities open up where you least expect them. I have always been open to trying various positions and understood that I'd probably have to work my way up or take a job like catering while looking for a position in my chosen career field.

What did you struggle with most when preparing to become a scientist/engineer?

Marcus: In engineering school, one would think it's all about the ability to do math or physics, engineers are notorious "geeks" with poor communication skills, right? To my surprise, both of the schools I attended emphasizing good oral and written communications skills in addition to the engineering skills. To my surprise and chagrin, in addition to doing the math or physics, engineering students were also expected to be able to write lab reports or other papers that were not just technically correct, but also clear, concise, and well written. A technically excellent but poorly written report just was not worthy of a high or even decent grade. I, like many of my fellow students, originally bristled at the attention paid to communications skills, we preferred to think of ourselves as the brilliant but slightly mad scientist type—our sheer ability to do complex math problems was all we needed to be successful. I, like many of my fellow students, really struggled with the required technical writing classes and the expectation that all of our class work was to be both technically correct and well written.

Kathy: My biggest struggle was taking written tests. I have known since high school that I learn best directly from others. I comprehend the material better and can more effectively apply concepts to problems when the information is imparted to me orally or through hands-on experience. What I did not know is that I had difficulty translating what I learned through books onto written exams. In high school, exams really were not a challenge for me as most if not all the exam material was covered in class, whereas in college, it was

© Pearson Education, Inc.

(Continued)

a very different story. I knew the material, even my professors knew I knew the material. Case in point, I went in to ask the professor a few questions prior to a physics exam. Right before I left his office he asked me to solve an equation, which I did. When he returned our exams he looked at me and asked what happened, a very similar question was on the exam but I got it wrong. I knew the material, he knew I knew the material, yet I could not translate it onto the paper.

How did you overcome/get through this struggle?

Marcus: One of the reasons I bristled at the expectation to write labs summaries and similar projects in a clear manner is that clear technical writing is not easy to do. I quickly realized that being a good technical writer is challenging and something to be proud of, and I quickly began to appreciate the writing skill necessary to write a clear set of operating instructions for a machine, let alone an article on physics worthy of a publication in science magazine. For me, technical writing was as challenging as some of the math, and learning to do it well was personally rewarding. Today, I find the ability to communicate effectively to be immensely valuable to my job.

Kathy: I overcame this issue by finding new and multiple ways to study. For one class I was a tutor for others in the class. That had me thinking of questions for them to answer so I was less tense when I took the exam myself. I took every opportunity to get help on physics—tutor, weekly sessions with the professor, and attending study labs. For other classes I found study groups really helped me. The lesson really is to find people who can help you and to keep trying until you find something that works. For each class it was a different solution. What helped me was the confidence of the professor who said "I know you know the material, I won't/can't fail you." Oh great, I thought, I've a guaranteed D+. While I did much better than a D+, the reassurance of that teacher alleviated some of the stress in taking tests and I was able to demonstrate my knowledge much more effectively on paper. This is one thing I will always thank this professor for.

What do you enjoy most about your work?

Marcus: I enjoy the opportunity to use my skills to make a difference. As a team leader at the EPA, I also enjoy helping the members of my team to do their best. The team is made of many junior staff, helping them to achieve their best and

maximize their efforts to achieve environmental protection is one of the most valuable things I do.

Kathy: There are three things I really appreciate about my job: (1) the opportunity to affect change on a national and international level; (2) the opportunity to combine and use knowledge from my scientific and public policy degrees; and (3) the diversity of my job. On any given day, I could be briefing management on a complex scientific issue, planning a national conference, speaking to students, working with an intern, coordinating with my state and tribal partners on ways to protect our wetlands, or preparing to travel overseas to negotiate international treaties. Each of these activities requires different skills and presents different challenges and rewards. No two days are the same.

What advice do you have for a student considering a career in teaching?

Kathy: The advice I have is love what you do. No matter the day or the job, find something that gets you jazzed. You will not love it all the time, you may not even like some aspects at all, but the good should outweigh the bad. Teaching is one of the most important professions, teaching others to appreciate, discover, wonder, and share is truly a calling and very rewarding. I know I enjoy teaching others about the environment. If you choose a career in teaching you will be uniquely positioned to watch the awe, knowledge, and curiosity grow in others.

Marcus: I think of the role of developing the ability and effectiveness of my team as something akin to being a teacher. I try to transfer my knowledge and experience to the more junior members, which is very satisfying.

In your opinion what were the three most interesting points made by the interviewee? Discuss your choices with the class.

- _____
  _____
- _____
  _____
- _____
  _____

Textbook Application

The following reading section is taken from an introductory book on Environmental Science. You will notice that the language used in the chapter is a bit more challenging than the one you encountered in the previous readings. Read the chapter carefully and answer the multiple-choice questions accurately.

READING

Reading Selection **7**

Textbook Reading

3.14 Flesh-Kincaid Grade Level 11.0

How Do Ecosystems Work?

(Excerpt from *Biology: Life on Earth,* Chapter 28, pp. 570–577)

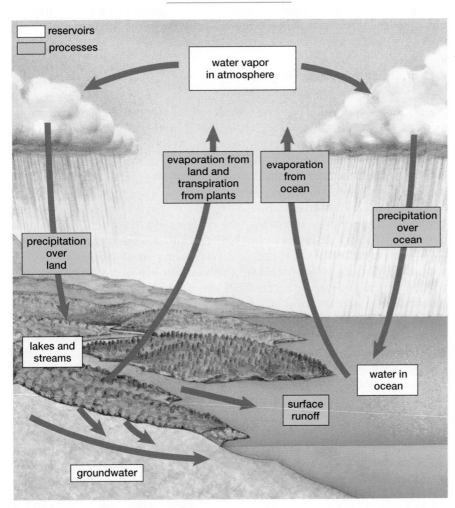

FIGURE 28-11 **The hydrologic cycle**

Most Water Remains Chemically Unchanged During the Hydrologic Cycle

The water **cycle**, or **hydrologic cycle** (FIG. 28-11), differs from most other nutrient cycles in that most water remains in the form of water throughout the **cycle** and is not used in the synthesis of new molecules. The **major** reservoir of water is the ocean, which covers about three-quarters of Earth's surface and contains more than 97% of Earth's water. Another 2% is trapped in ice, leaving only 1% as liquid fresh water. The hydrologic **cycle** is driven by solar **energy**, which evaporates water, and by gravity, which draws it back to Earth in the form of precipitation (rain, snow, sleet, and dew). Most evaporation occurs

© Pearson Education, Inc.

from the oceans, and much water returns directly to them as precipitation. Water falling on land takes various paths. Some is evaporated from the soil, lakes, and streams. A **portion** runs off the land back to the oceans, and a small amount enters underground reservoirs. Because the bodies of living things are roughly 70% water, some of the water in the hydrologic **cycle** enters the living communities of ecosystems. It is absorbed by the roots of plants; much of this water is evaporated back to the atmosphere from plants' leaves. A small amount is combined with carbon dioxide during photosynthesis to produce high-**energy** molecules. **Eventually** these molecules are broken down during cellular respiration, releasing water back to the **environment**. Consumers get water from their food or by drinking.

Lack of Access to Water for Irrigation and Drinking Is a Growing Human Problem

As the human population has grown, fresh water has become scarce in many regions of the world. Additionally, contaminated, untreated drinking water is a **major** problem in developing countries, where over 1 billion people drink it. Impure water spreads diseases that kill millions of children each year. In both Africa and India, where water contamination poses **significant** threats, people are starting to use sunlight to kill disease-causing organisms. They place water in plastic bottles and shake them to increase the oxygen levels in the water. Then they put the bottles in a sunny spot, allowing the combination of oxygen, warmth, and ultraviolet (UV) light to **create** free radicals that kill bacteria. With no **technology** other than plastic bottles, these people are generating safe drinking water.

Currently, about 10% of the world's food is grown on cropland irrigated with water drawn from aquifers, which are natural underground reservoirs. Unfortunately, in many areas of the world—including China, India, Northern Africa, and the midwestern United States—this groundwater is being "mined" for agriculture; that is, it is **removed** faster than it is replenished. Parts of the High Plains aquifer, which extends from the Texas Panhandle north to South Dakota, have been depleted by about 50%. In India, two-thirds of crops are grown using underground water for irrigation, draining aquifers far faster than they are being replenished. One promising solution is to devise ways of trapping the heavy monsoon rains, whose water usually pours into rivers and **eventually** into the ocean. People of a village in India have found that by digging a **series** of holding ponds, they can capture rainwater that would formerly run off. Their system allows the water to percolate down into the soil and helps replenish the underground water supplies. During the dry season, the people can then tap these supplies for irrigation.

28.4   WHAT CAUSES "ACID RAIN"?

Many of the environmental problems that plague modern society have resulted from human interference in ecosystem **function**. Primitive peoples were sustained **solely** by the **energy** flowing from the sun, and they produced wastes that were readily taken back into the nutrient cycles. But as the population grew and **technology** increased, humans began to act more and more independently of these natural processes. The Industrial **Revolution**, which began in earnest in the mid-nineteenth century, resulted in a tremendous increase in our **reliance** on **energy** from fossil fuels (rather than from sunlight) for heat, light, transportation, industry, and agriculture. In mining and transporting these fuels, we have exposed ecosystems to a variety of substances that are foreign and often toxic to them (**FIG. 28-12**). In the following sections, we describe two environmental problems of global proportion that are primarily a direct result of human reliance on fossil fuels: acid deposition and global warming.

FIGURE 28-12 **A natural substance out of place**
This bald eagle was killed by an oil spill off the coast of Alaska.

Overloading the Sulfur and Nitrogen Cycles Causes Acid Deposition

Although volcanoes, hot springs, and decomposer organisms all **release** sulfur dioxide, human industrial activities, primarily burning fossil fuels in which sulfur is trapped, account for about 75% of the sulfur dioxide emissions worldwide. This is far more than natural ecosystems can absorb and recycle. The nitrogen **cycle** is also being overwhelmed. Although natural processes—such as the activity of nitrogen-fixing bacteria and decomposer organisms, fires, and lightning—produce nitrogen oxides and ammonia, about 60% of the nitrogen that is **available** to Earth's ecosystems now results from human activities. Burning of fossil fuels combines atmospheric nitrogen with oxygen, producing most of the emissions of nitrogen oxides. On farms, ammonia and nitrate are often supplied by **chemical** fertilizers produced by using the **energy** in fossil fuels to convert atmospheric nitrogen into **compounds** that plants can use.

© Pearson Education, Inc.

Excess production of nitrogen oxides and sulfur dioxide was **identified** in the late 1960s as the cause of a growing environmental threat: *acid rain*, more accurately called **acid deposition**. When combined with water vapor in the atmosphere, nitrogen oxides and sulfur dioxide are **converted** to nitric acid and sulfuric acid, respectively. Days later, and often hundreds of miles from the **source**, these acids fall to Earth with rainwater, eating away at statues and buildings (**FIG. 28-13**), damaging trees and crops, and rendering lakes lifeless. Sulfuric acid may form particles that visibly cloud the air, even under dry conditions. In the U.S., the Northeast, Mid-Atlantic, Upper Midwest, and West regions, as well as the state of Florida, are the most vulnerable, because the rocks and soils that predominate there are less able to buffer acids.

FIGURE 28-13 **Acid deposition is corrosive**
This limestone statue at Rheims Cathedral in France is being dissolved by acid deposition.

Acid Deposition Damages Life in Lakes and Forests

In the Adirondack Mountains, acid rain has made about 25% of all the lakes and ponds too acidic to support fish. But by the time the fish die, much of the food web that sustains them has been destroyed. Clams, snails, crayfish, and insect larvae die first, then amphibians, and finally fish. The result is a crystal-clear lake—beautiful but dead. The **impact** is not limited to aquatic organisms. Acid rain also interferes with the growth and yield of many farm crops by leeching out essential nutrients such as calcium and potassium and killing decomposer microorganisms, thus preventing the return of nutrients to the soil.

Plants, poisoned and deprived of nutrients, become weak and vulnerable to infection and insect attack. High in the Green Mountains of Vermont, scientists have witnessed the death of about half of the red spruce and beech trees and one-third of the sugar maples since 1965. The snow, rain, and heavy fog that commonly cloak these eastern mountaintops are highly acidic. At a **monitoring** station atop Mount Mitchell in North Carolina, the pH of fog has been recorded at 2.9—more acidic than vinegar (**FIG. 28-14**).

Acid deposition increases the **exposure** of organisms to toxic metals, including aluminum, mercury, lead, and cadmium, which are far more soluble in acidified water than in water of **neutral** pH. Aluminum dissolved from rock may inhibit plant growth and kill fish. The tap water in some households has been found to be dangerously contaminated with lead dissolved by acidic water from lead solder in old pipes. Fish in acidified water often have dangerous levels of mercury in their bodies, because mercury is subject to *biological magnification* as it is passes through trophic levels (see "Earth Watch: Food Chains Magnify Toxic Substances").

FIGURE 28-14 Acid deposition can destroy forests
Acid rain and fog have destroyed this forest atop Mount Mitchell in North Carolina.

The Clean Air Act Has Significantly Reduced Sulfur, but Not Nitrogen, Emissions

In the U.S., amendments to the Clean Air Act in 1990 resulted in substantial reductions in emissions of both sulfur dioxide and nitrogen oxides from power plants. **Overall** sulfur emissions have decreased considerably throughout the U.S., improving air quality and rain acidity in some regions. Nitrogen oxide and ammonia **release** is not as strictly limited under the Clean Air Act. Although emissions of nitrogen oxides have dropped in some regions, atmospheric nitrogen **compounds** have shown a small **overall** increase, primarily because more gasoline is being burned by automobiles. Release of ammonia (NH_3) mostly from livestock and fertilizers, has increased by about 19% in the U.S. since 1985.

Unfortunately, damaged ecosystems recover slowly. A recent **survey** of Adirondack lakes found hopeful signs that about 60% of them are becoming less acid, although full **recovery** is still **decades** away. Some southeastern soils

© Pearson Education, Inc.

have become saturated with acid-releasing substances, and in these areas freshwater acid levels are increasing. High-elevation forests remain at risk throughout the U.S. Many scientists believe that **considerable** additional reductions in emissions, with far stricter controls on nitrogen emissions, will be needed to prevent further deterioration and allow the **recovery** of damaged ecosystems.

28.5   WHAT CAUSES GLOBAL WARMING?

Interfering with the Carbon Cycle Contributes to Global Warming

Between 345 million and 280 million years ago, huge quantities of carbon were diverted from the carbon **cycle** when, under the warm, wet conditions of the Carboniferous **period**, the bodies of prehistoric organisms were buried in sediments, escaping decomposition. Over time, heat and pressure **converted** their bodies, with their stored **energy derived** from the sun, into fossil fuels such as coal, oil, and natural gas. Without human **intervention**, this carbon would have remained underground. Beginning with the Industrial **Revolution**, however, we have increasingly relied on the **energy** stored in these fuels. One researcher estimates that a typical gas tank holds the transformed remains of 1000 tons of prehistoric life, largely microscopic phytoplankton. As we burn fossil fuels in our power plants, factories, and cars, we harvest the **energy** of prehistoric sunlight and **release** CO_2 into the atmosphere. Since 1850, the CO_2 content of the atmosphere has increased from 280 parts per million (ppm) to 381 ppm, or almost 36%. According to recent **analysis** of gas bubbles trapped in ancient Antarctic ice, the atmospheric CO_2 content is now about 27% higher than at any time during the past 650,000 years, and CO_2 is increasing at an unprecedented rate of about 1.5 parts per million yearly. Burning fossil fuels accounts for 80–85% of the CO_2 added to the atmosphere each year.

A second **source** of added atmospheric CO_2 is **deforestation**, which destroys tens of millions of forested acres annually and accounts for 15–20% of CO_2 emissions. Deforestation is occurring principally in the Tropics, where rain forests are rapidly being **converted** to **marginal** agricultural land. The carbon stored in the massive trees in these forests returns to the atmosphere (primarily through burning) after they are cut.

Collectively, human activities **release** almost 7 billion tons of carbon (in the form of CO_2) into the atmosphere each year. About half of this carbon is absorbed into the oceans, plants, and soil, while the remaining 3.5 billion tons remains in the atmosphere, fueling **global** warming.

Greenhouse Gases Trap Heat in the Atmosphere

Atmospheric CO_2 acts something like the glass in a greenhouse; it allows solar **energy** to enter, then absorbs and holds that **energy** once it has been **converted** to heat (**FIG. 28-15**). Several other **greenhouse gases** share this property, including nitrous oxide (N_2O) and methane (CH_4) which are both released by agricultural activities, landfills, wastewater treatment, coal mining, and burning fossil fuels. The **greenhouse effect**, which is the ability of greenhouse gases to trap the sun's **energy** in a planet's atmosphere as heat, is a natural **process**. By keeping our atmosphere relatively warm, the greenhouse effect allows life on Earth as we know it. However, there is

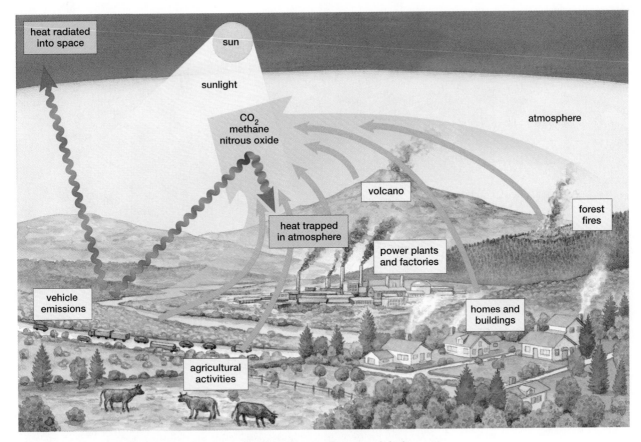

FIGURE 28-15 Increases in greenhouse gas emissions contribute to global warming
Incoming sunlight warms Earth's surface and is radiated back to the atmosphere.
Greenhouse gases, released by natural processes but tremendously increased by
human activities, absorb some of this heat, trapping it in the atmosphere.

overwhelming consensus among atmospheric scientists that human activities
have amplified the natural greenhouse effect, producing a **phenomenon**
called **global warming**.

Historical temperature records have **revealed** a **global** temperature increase paralleling the rise in atmospheric CO_2 (**FIG. 28-16**). Nineteen of the
twenty hottest years on record have occurred since 1980, and the six hottest
years happened between 1998 and 2005, which set an all-time record.

If greenhouse gas emissions are not curtailed, the Intergovernmental Panel
on Climate Change (IPCC) predicts that average **global** temperatures will rise
from the current average of about 58°F (14.4°C) to between 61.5°C (16°C) and
66°C (19°C) by the year 2100 (**FIG. 28-17**).

Seemingly small **overall** temperature changes can have **enormous** impacts.
For example, average air temperatures during the peak of the last Ice Age
(20,000 years ago) were only about 5°C lower than at present. The **predicted**
rapid temperature increase is of particular concern because it is likely to **exceed**
the rate at which natural selection can allow most organisms to adapt. The temperature change will not be distributed evenly worldwide; temperatures in both
the arctic and parts of the U.S., for example, are **predicted** to increase considerably faster than the **global** average.

© Pearson Education, Inc.

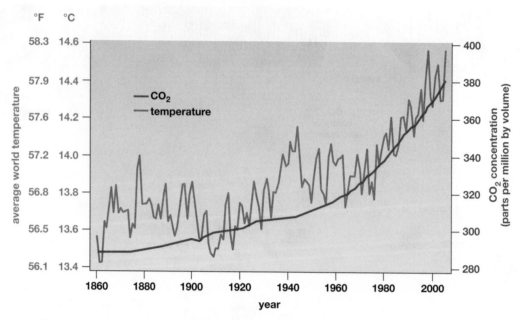

FIGURE 28-16 Global warming parallels CO_2 increases
The CO_2 concentration of the atmosphere (blue line) has increased steadily since 1860.
Average global temperatures (red line) have also increased, roughly paralleling the increasing
atmospheric CO_2.

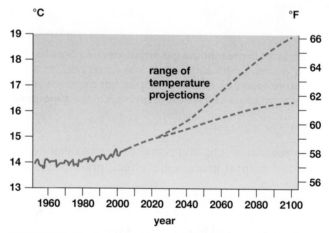

FIGURE 28-17 Projected range of temperature increases

Global Warming Will Have Severe Consequences

As geochemist James White at the University of Colorado quipped, "If the Earth
had an operating **manual**, the **chapter** on climate might begin with the caveat that
the system has been adjusted at the factory for optimum comfort, so don't touch
the dials." Earth has begun to experience the **consequences** of **global** warming,
and all indications are that they will be severe and, in some regions, catastrophic.

A Meltdown Is Occurring

Throughout the world, ice is melting (see "Earth Watch: Poles in Peril").
Worldwide, glaciers are retreating and disappearing (**FIG. 28-18**). In Glacier
National Park, where 150 glaciers once graced the mountainsides, only 35
remain, and scientists **estimate** that these may all disappear within the next

FIGURE 28-18 Glaciers are melting
Photos taken from the same vantage point in 1941 (top) and 2004 (bottom) document the retreat of Muir Glacier in Glacier Bay, Alaska.

30 years. Greenland's ice sheet is melting at twice the rate of a decade ago, releasing 53 cubic miles (221 cubic kilometers) of water into the Atlantic annually. As polar ice caps and glaciers melt and ocean waters expand in **response** to atmospheric warming, sea levels will rise, threatening coastal cities and flooding coastal wetlands. Alaskan permafrost is melting, dumping mud into rivers, destroying salmon spawning grounds, and releasing CO_2 into the atmosphere as trapped organic matter decomposes. In Siberia, a **region** of frozen peat the size of France and Germany combined is melting, creating giant bogs that could **release** billions of tons of methane (a far more powerful heat-trapping gas than CO_2) into the atmosphere. Permafrost melting provides an example of positive feedback, in which an outcome of **global** warming, in this case the **release** of additional greenhouse gases, accelerates the warming **process**.

© Pearson Education, Inc.

EARTH WATCH   Poles in Peril

BIOETHICS

On Earth's opposite poles, Arctic and Antarctic ice is melting. The Antarctic Peninsula is uniquely vulnerable to **global** warming because its average year-round temperature hovers close to the freezing point of water. Over the past 50 years, the temperature around the peninsula has increased by about 4.5°F (about 2.5°C), far faster than the **global** average. Since 1995, over 2000 square miles of the ice shelf off the Antarctic Peninsula have disintegrated; based on ice **core** samples, scientists believe that these shelves had persisted for thousands of years. The loss of floating ice shelves has far-reaching **consequences**. The sea ice creates conditions that favor abundant growth of phytoplankton and algae. These **primary** producers provide food for larval krill, shrimplike crustaceans that are a keystone species in the Antarctic food web. Krill **comprise** a **major portion** of the diet of seals, penguins, and several species of whales. But over the past 30 years, krill populations in the southwest Atlantic have plummeted by about 80%. Researcher Angus Atkinson of the British Antarctic **Survey** hypothesizes that the **decline** is linked to the loss of sea ice. One likely **scenario** is that as the ice shelves shrink, algae that grows on the underside of the ice dwindles, and the krill that rely on it starve. Researchers are concerned that the **impact** of the krill loss may reverberate up the food chain, starving whales and seals and perhaps penguins as well. Adélie penguins spend their winters on the Antarctic ice shelves, feeding on krill. Although most Antarctic penguin populations remain healthy, researcher William Fraser, who has been studying Antarctic penguins for 30 years, reports that the Adélie penguin population in the western Antarctic Peninsula has lost about 10,000 breeding pairs since 1975.

At the far end of Earth, arctic temperatures have risen almost twice as rapidly as the world average, causing a 20–30% decrease in late-summer arctic sea ice during the past 30 years. Larger changes are projected for the next century, including temperature increases of about 7°F–14°F (4°C–8°C). In a disturbing example of **positive** feedback, melting ice will accelerate warming, because ice reflects 80–90% of the solar **energy** that hits it, but the ocean water exposed when ice disappears absorbs most solar energy, converting it to heat.

Arctic sea ice is critical for polar bears and for ringed seals, their **major** food **source**. Complete loss of sea ice, which some scientists predict within the next century,

would mean almost certain extinction for polar bears in the wild. In Canada's Hudson Bay, sea ice is breaking up 3 weeks earlier than it did 30 years ago, depriving the bears of a **prime** opportunity to hunt ringed seals on the ice (**FIG. E28-2**). As a result, Hudson Bay polar bears now start their summers with 15% less weight (150 pounds for an adult male). Leaner females are producing fewer cubs with a lower survival rate, and the local bear population has declined by 22% since 1987. Hungry polar bears are increasingly invading northern Canadian and Alaskan towns, where they are sometimes shot. Polar bears are powerful swimmers; but as the ice floes have retreated, they have now been seen swimming 60 miles offshore, a far greater distance than usual for them. Several bears were spotted floating dead after a storm and are believed to have drowned, being too far out at sea to swim to safety.

The Arctic National Wildlife Refuge is the **site** of the largest number of onshore polar bear dens in Alaska. In late fall, polar bears congregate along the refuge shoreline. More bears are gathering there as ice retreats farther from the shoreline. Yet there is continuing political pressure in the U.S. to open the refuge to oil drilling. Ironically, polar bears are threatened not only with climate change, but with drilling for yet more oil to fuel the country's voracious appetite for fossil fuels, which will contribute to future **global** warming.

FIGURE E28-2 Polar bears on thin ice
The loss of arctic sea ice threatens the survival of polar bears.

More Extremes in Weather Are Predicted

Many scientists believe that **global** warming is already affecting our weather. Recent studies have documented that during the past 35 years, both the **intensity** and **duration** of hurricanes have increased by 50%, doubling the number in the

LINKS TO LIFE   Making a Difference

With less than 5% of the world's population, the U.S. is responsible for about 25% of world's greenhouse gases. The total greenhouse gas emissions produced by the U.S. amount to about 6 tons (5 metric tonnes) of carbon per person each year—more than any other country on Earth.

Can one person's actions make a difference? Jonathan Foley of the University of Wisconsin thinks so. He is on the cutting edge of climatological **research**, having led a **team** that developed one of the first **computer** models of **global** climate change to consider the **impact** of biological systems and human land use (such as converting forests to cropland) on climate. In 1998 Jon and his wife, Andrea, recognizing that greenhouse gas emissions and the resulting climate change can be significantly impacted by **individual** decisions and choices, made a choice of their own: to cut their family's **energy** use and carbon dioxide emissions in half. The Foleys and their young daughter lived in a five-bedroom house 30 miles from their work; Jon and Andrea each used a separate car to commute about 60 miles daily. First, they moved to a smaller house much closer to work. A visitor to the Foleys' new home—warm and cozy in winter and cool in summer—would never realize how little **energy** it consumes. Cracks have been sealed and the attic insulated. Every appliance has been chosen for **energy** efficiency. Compact fluorescent bulbs, using 75% less energy than incandescents, shed light throughout. Decorative ceiling fans reduce the need for summer air conditioning. Solar collectors supply over two-thirds of the family's water heating needs, while low-emittance window glass lets sunlight in while reducing heat loss in winter. The Foleys can now ride bicycles or take the bus to work, but they also enjoy their Toyota Prius hybrid gas/electric car—which gets nearly 50 mpg in city driving. Have they reached their **goals**? Within two years of their **resolution**, the Foleys, who now have two daughters, cut their **energy** use by roughly 65%. Foley says:

> Cutting your greenhouse gas emissions doesn't have to be a "sacrifice" at all. We have cut our emissions more than 50%, and we now have lower **energy** bills, a more comfortable house, more time to spend with our family, and a higher quality of life. Americans have a lot to gain by cutting fossil fuel use: reduced greenhouse gas emissions, improved air quality in our cities, less dependence on foreign oil supplies, and so on. This is a win-win **scenario**, so why not go for it?

Recently, innovative programs throughout the world (such as Carbonfund.org) are providing additional ways for individuals to "go for it." *Carbon **offset*** initiatives allow people to help compensate for the carbon they **release** by investing in projects that encourage energy efficiency, renewable **energy** use, and reforestation. For example, if your car gets 30 mpg and you drive 12,000 miles/yr, your car will **release** about 3.5 tons of CO_2 (or about 1 ton of carbon). Carbonfund.org allows you to **select** projects where your **investment** will reduce CO_2 emissions for about $5 per ton. This and many other carbon **offset initiatives** (search "Carbon offsetting" at http://www.ecobusinesslinks.com) provide a great way to augment personal lifestyle choices and further reduce your **impact**. Can you make a difference? The answer is an unequivocal "Yes!"

highest **categories** of wind speed and destruction (**Categories** 4 and 5), such as Hurricane Katrina, which devastated New Orleans in 2005. As the world warms, experts predict that droughts will last longer and be more severe, while other regions experience flooding. Scientists at the National Center for Atmospheric **Research** report that since the 1970s, the **area** of Earth impacted by severe drought has doubled from about 15% to about 30% as a result of increased temperatures and local decreases in rainfall. Agricultural disruption resulting from such extremes in weather could be disastrous for nations that are barely able to feed themselves.

Wildlife Is Affected

Biologists worldwide are documenting changes in plant and animal wildlife related to warming. The **impact** of **global** warming on forests could be profound. Fires, fuelled by drought and overly dense forests resulting from fire suppression in the past, have swept through large areas of the western U.S. and Alaska, releasing still more carbon dioxide into the atmosphere. As the world warms, tree distributions will change, based on their tolerance for heat. For example, sugar maples may disappear from northeastern U.S. forests, while some southeastern forests could be replaced by grasslands. Coral reefs, already stressed by

© Pearson Education, Inc.

CASE STUDY REVISITED WHEN THE SALMON RETURN

Researchers investigating the sockeye salmon's return to an Alaskan stream witness an awesome sight. Hundreds of brilliant red bodies writhe in water so shallow it barely covers them. A female beats her tail, excavating a shallow **depression** in the gravel where she releases her coral-colored eggs; meanwhile, a male showers them with sperm. But after their long and strenuous **migration**, these adult salmon are dying. Their flesh is tattered, their muscles wasted, and the **final** act of reproduction saps the last of their **energy**. Soon the stream is clogged with dying, dead, and decomposing bodies—an abundance of nutrients unimaginable at any other time of the year. Eagles, grizzly bears, and gulls gather to gorge themselves on the fleeting bounty. Flies breed in the carcasses, feeding spiders, birds, and trout. The breeding cycles of local mink populations have evolved around the event; females lactate just when the salmon provide them with abundant food. Isotope studies reveal that up to one-fourth of the nitrogen **incorporated** into the leaves of trees and shrubs near these streams comes from the bodies of salmon. Historically, researchers **estimate** that 500 million pounds of salmon migrated upstream in the U.S. Pacific Northwest each year, contributing hundreds of thousands of pounds of nitrogen and phosphorus to the Columbia River watershed alone. Now, due to **factors** including overfishing, river damming, diversion of water for irrigation, runoff from agriculture, and pollution of the estuaries (where several salmon species spend a **significant** part of their life cycle), migratory salmon populations in the **region** have declined by over 90% in the past century. The web of life that relied on the mighty **annual** upstream flow of nutrients has been disrupted.

Consider This Some salmon populations have been so thoroughly depleted that they qualify for protection under the Endangered Species Act. Some people argue that because these salmon are also raised commercially in hatcheries and artificial ponds, they should not be afforded this protection. Meanwhile, researchers studying chinook salmon raised in hatcheries noted a 25% **decline** in the average size of eggs of hatchery-reared fish over just four generations. These eggs produce smaller juvenile fish. Based on this information, explain why ecologists and conservationists are arguing for protection of wild salmon.

human activities, are likely to suffer further damage from warmer waters, which drive out the symbiotic algae that provide them with **energy**. Corals are further threatened because, as the oceans absorb more CO_2, their waters are becoming more acidic, making it more difficult for corals to form their limestone skeletons.

Reports of changes keep coming in from throughout the world. The growing season in Europe has increased by more than 10 days over the past 28 years. Mexican Jays in southern Arizona are nesting 10 days earlier than they did in 1971. Many species of butterflies and birds have shifted their ranges northward. In the United Kingdom and the northeastern U.S., spring flowers are blooming earlier. While individual cases could be due to other **factors**, the cumulative weight of **data** from diverse sources worldwide provides strong **evidence** that warming-related biological changes have begun. **Global** warming is also **predicted** to increase the **range** of tropical disease-carrying organisms, such as malaria-transmitting mosquitoes, with **negative consequences** for human health.

How Are People Responding to the Threat?

Under the landmark Kyoto Treaty, negotiated in 1997 and implemented in 2005, thirty-five industrialized countries have pledged to reduce their collective emissions of greenhouse gases to levels 5.2% below 1990 levels. The treaty exempts developing countries (where most of the world's population resides), whose emissions per person are extremely low, and whose attempts to increase living standards cannot currently be implemented without increases in greenhouse emissions. Although 159 countries have ratified (agreed to implement) the treaty, the U.S.—the world's largest generator of greenhouse gases—has refused (as of this writing) to do so. Encouragingly, several U.S. states (including California) and many city mayors have pledged to adopt Kyoto-type standards independently. Although worldwide efforts are essential, our **individual** choices, collectively, can also have a big **impact**, as described in "Links to Life: Making a Difference."

Reading Comprehension Check

Statistical Analysis

1. What percentage of the earth's surface does the ocean cover?
   a. 97%
   b. half
   (c.) about 75%
   d. none of the above

Vocabulary

2. Read the section Lack of "Access for Water Irrigation and Drinking Is a Growing Human Problem." What are *aquifers*?
   a. man-made water holes
   (b.) natural underground reservoirs
   c. cropland irrigation
   d. depleted soil

Supporting Details

3. Read the section "What Causes Acid Rain?" *Primitive Peoples* are mentioned to illustrate
   a. the technological progress humans have made over time.
   b. that they are to blame for our current environmental problems.
   (c.) that earlier in human history people produced only natural wastes.
   d. the concept of nutrient cycles.

Negative Question

4. Read the section "Overloading the Sulfur and Nitrogen Cycles Causes Acid Decomposition." Which is **not** mentioned as a negative effect of acid rain?
   a. tree and crop damage
   b. lifeless lakes
   (c.) the death of whole human populations
   d. damage to statues and buildings

Vocabulary

5. Read the section "Acid Decomposition Damages Life in Lakes and Forests." In the sentence "Acid rain also interferes with the growth and yield of many farm crops by leeching out essential nutrients such as . . . ," the term *leeching out* could be replaced with
   (a.) destroying.
   b. adding.
   c. identifying.
   d. complementing.

Supporting Details

6. Read the section "What Causes Global Warming: Interfering with the Carbon Cycle . . . ." Deforestation is given as an example of
   a. a naturally occuring process.
   (b.) a source of added atmospheric CO_2.

© Pearson Education, Inc.

    c. a phenomenon of the past.
    d. a carbon gain

Graphic Analysis

7. Read the section "Greenhouse Gases Trap Heat in the Atmosphere." Figure 28-15 illustrates
    a. why vehicles emissions are a growing problem.
    b. how greenhouse gases get trapped in the atmosphere.
    c. the natural processes that heal the earth.
    d. how power plants and factories relate to volcanic activity.

Graphic Analysis

8. Figure 28-16 shows the relationship between global temperature increase and the rise of atmospheric CO_2 as
    a. inverse.
    b. parallel.
    c. bearing no relation.
    d. none of the above

Graphic Analysis

9. Read the section "A Meltdown is Occurring." The two photos of Carroll Glacier (Fig. 28-18) are given to show
    a. how in the past glaciers were disappearing.
    b. how much more beautiful the glacier is today.
    c. how glaciers are retreating.
    d. both b and c

Supporting Details

10. Read the section "More Extremes in the Weather are Predicted." What examples are given of how global warming is affecting our weather?
    a. hurricanes, droughts, flooding, and agricultural disruption
    b. hurricanes and flooding
    c. hurricanes, tornadoes, and agricultural disruption
    d. hurricanes, droughts, and earthquakes

Vocabulary

11. Read the section "Wildlife Is Affected." In the final paragraph, in the phrase "the cumulative weight of data from diverse sources worldwide . . . ," a synonym for *cumulative* is
    a. subtracted.
    b. combined.
    c. connecting.
    d. damaging.

Main Idea

12. Read the section "How Are People Responding to the Threat?" What is the main idea of this section?
    a. The United States is leading the world in greenhouse emissions control.
    b. 159 countries have ratified the Kyoto Protocol.

c. The world's greatest polluters are the ones who won't sign on to the Kyoto accord.

d. none of the above

Main Idea

13. Read the section "Earthwatch, Poles in Peril." What is the main idea of this reading?

a. The Polar bears' survival is threatened by loss of arctic sea ice.

b. The Arctic National Wildlife Refuge is a home to many polar bears.

c. Arctic temperatures have risen almost twice that of the rest of the world's average.

d. Polar bears have the skills to survive these climactic changes.

Supporting Detail

14. Read the section "Links to Life: Making a Difference." Jonathan Foley is mentioned as an example of

a. someone who solved the global warming crisis.

b. how one person's actions can make a difference in fighting climate change.

c. how one person's actions can make a difference in biological systems.

d. how together with his wife he moved to a smaller house.

Author's Purpose

15. Read the section "Case Study Revisited, When the Salmons Return." The main purpose of this reading is

a. to demonstrate the stages of salmon migration.

b. to give an example of how greenhouse gases function.

c. to discuss the relationship between salmon migration and the breeding cycles of local minks.

d. to describe how salmon migration has been negatively affected by environmental factors.

READING

Reading Selection 8

Additional Reading

Online Magazine Article

The World's Water Crisis

3.15 Flesch-Kincaid Grade Level 12.0

Pre-Reading Questions

Share your thoughts on the following questions with a classmate.

1. What are some of the possible consequences if the world's water supply runs out?

2. What can governments do to help avoid a water shortage crisis?

Collaboration

© Pearson Education, Inc.

The World's Water Crisis

By Brian Howard, *E/The Environmental Magazine*

Sept–Oct, 2003

ESL Annotation

3.16 ESL In many countries, water scarcity is not a new subject, but a central part of daily life. Water use is regulated and water waste is unheard of.

1   At the G8 summit in Evian, France, delegates met to discuss, among other **issues,** how to provide safe drinking water to the 1.5 billion of the world's citizens who live without it. Everyone within the summit gates enjoyed the free and plentiful bottled mineral water. "It's obscene," says one journalist who attended the **conference,** held near the **source** of one of the world's most famous bottled water brands. "How can they not see that holding the summit in this place and talking about water in Africa is tasteless. It's beyond comprehension."

2   In fact, although many people might agree philosophically with Mikhail Gorbachev when he said, "Clean water is a universal human right," the world is sharply divided in terms of **access** to safe hydration. Those who can afford it are guzzling ever-increasing numbers of designer water bottles, while half the world's population lacks basic sanitation facilities, according to the United Nations (UN). Diseases caused by unsanitary water kill five to 12 million people a year, most of them women and children. A child dies every eight seconds from a preventable water-borne disease.

3   Only one-hundredth of one **percent** of the blue planet's water is readily accessible for human use. The World **Resources Institute** (WRI) estimates that 2.3 billion people currently live in "water-stressed areas." Hydrologists cite much of Africa, northern China, pockets of India, Mexico, the Middle East and parts of western North America as regions facing severe water shortages. Some of the world's largest cities, including Mexico City, Bangkok and Jakarta, have severely over-pumped their groundwater aquifers.

scarcity
a situation in which there is not enough of something

4   As world population continues to increase, water **scarcity** will **affect** two out of every three people by 2025, according to UN estimates. In the 20th century, demand for fresh water grew twice as fast as population. This imbalance is largely due to industrial agriculture, but is also a product of unequal development in standards of living versus sound water management.

5   Additionally, scientists at Harvard University point out that **global** warming could significantly harm water availability. A warmer atmosphere could lead to higher rates of evaporation, causing droughts and more severe weather. Faster runoff rates and slower infiltration of groundwater could follow. Warmer water may also **promote** detrimental algal and microbial blooms, which may lead to more water-borne illnesses. And ironically, as the climate heats up, people will want to use more water for drinking, bathing and watering plants.

squabbled over
to be in conflict about something

6   "The next world war will be over water," says Vice President Ismail Serageldin of the World Bank. Even now, some competition is beginning to build between (and within) nations over **finite** water **resources.** Egypt has watched warily as Ethiopia has built hundreds of dams on the Nile. Syria and Iraq have **squabbled over** water projects with Turkey, and some of Israel's many conflicts with Jordan and the Palestinians have been over water **issues.** Botswana raised a public outcry after Namibia announced emergency drought plans to divert water from the Okavango River.

7   Certain regions of the United States, including the Colorado and Rio Grande River Basins, also suffer ominous shortages. Much of the West's **integral** agriculture, livestock and recreation industries have been seriously threatened by water scarcity, and the **region** has endured catastrophic wildfire seasons. At the same time, sprawling development is threatening critical watershed areas throughout the world. Elizabeth Ainsley Campbell, executive director of the Nashua River Watershed Association, warns, "Unless we become more proactive in planning for growth and setting aside open space, our drinking water will be increasingly vulnerable to pollution from fertilizers, insecticides, fuel byproducts and other chemicals associated with commercial and residential development."

8   Groundwater is similarly **under siege**. Over-pumping and rising sea levels have resulted in falling, and saltwater-invaded, water tables. **Initial** remediation of the 300,000 contaminated groundwater sites in the U.S. will cost up to $1 trillion over the next 30 years, according to the National **Research** Council. Water scarcity is also a serious threat to natural ecosystems. "Watersheds with the highest biological value, as measured by the number of endemic bird and fish species, are also generally the most degraded," says Carmen Revenga of the WRI. "Many biologically rich watersheds—particularly in Southeast Asia and China—also have high population densities, high levels of **modified** and irrigated land, and high rates of deforestation, especially in tropical areas," she says. In the U.S., 37 **percent** of freshwater fish are at risk of extinction, 51 **percent** of crayfish and 40 percent of amphibians are imperiled or vulnerable, and 67 **percent** of freshwater mussels are extinct or vulnerable to extinction.

under siege
being attacked

Fleecing the Third World

9   In much of the Third World, municipal water systems often serve only cities or primarily upper- and middle-class residents (who typically pay very low **fees** for use), while recurrent **revenue** problems inhibit increases or upgrades in service. As a result, as Christian **Aid** journalist Andrew Pendleton puts it, "The only water that is **available** to many poor people free of charge lies in festering pools and contains killer diseases such as cholera." Pendleton continues, "If poor parents want to **ensure** their children will not die as a result of diarrhea, they must pay through the nose for water from private vendors or tankers."

10   Some people in developing countries are increasingly turning to bottled water to meet their daily needs, **a red flag** for some critics. World consumption of bottled water is growing at seven **percent** a year, with the largest increases in the Asia Pacific **region**. U.S. News & World Report recently concluded, "The drive toward bottled water and filters will, however, widen the gap between the haves and have-nots." For one thing, as Pendleton points out, poor people in need may be charged more per gallon of clean water than those in developed nations. Many families in Ghana spend 10 to 20 **percent** of their **income** on water.

a red flag
something that shows or warns you that something might be wrong, illegal, etc.

11   Also, since many countries lack the **infrastructure** to recycle used water bottles, the containers end up further polluting the local water sources. In Nepal, for example, water bottles tossed aside by trekkers have caused a serious litter problem, since the government can't afford to cart them out of remote areas. Many activists have also protested aggressive bottling operations in the developing world. In Brazil, Nestle offers Latin Americans a brand of

© Pearson Education, Inc.

bottled water called Nestle Pure Life. But as Paul Constance of the Inter-American Development Bank points out, "Though it looks much like the bottled mineral water long offered in restaurants and upscale supermarkets, Pure Life is different. It is drawn from local water sources, has an aggressively low price, and is marketed specifically 'to meet the needs of people who have daily difficulty in **access** to quality water.'" One Pure Life bottling plant was **established** on a popular and ecologically sensitive mineral spring, prompting fierce opposition.

12   In Haiti's capital, Port-au-Prince, only 10 **percent** of homes have tap water, even though the local groundwater reserves are thought to host enough **capacity** for every **resident**. The public water system struggles from serious disrepair and a chronic lack of funding. Recently, some entrepreneurs began drawing water from a **network** of private wells and trucking it to tank owners, who then sell the precious liquid to families at a huge profit. Constance says it is not uncommon for "**legal** or illegal private providers to make handsome profits by trucking or carting water into the poorest neighborhoods." Many people have to carry water bottles great distances.

13   Clearly, the world is approaching a water crisis. Watersheds and municipal systems must be secured from rising threats. And some wonder if bottled water quenches human greed far better than human thirst.

COPYRIGHT 2003 Earth Action Network, Inc.

Reading Comprehension Check

1. What two things are contrasted in the second paragraph?
   a. rich people and safe drinking water
   b. wealthy people drinking designer water and poor people lacking any clean water
   c. clean water and poor people
   d. none of the above

2. In the third paragraph, which area of the world is NOT mentioned as lacking in clean drinking water?
   a. India
   b. Mexico
   c. much of Africa
   d. Canada

3. What is the topic of this article?
   a. Many poor people around the world do not have sufficient access to clean drinking water
   b. Sub-Saharan Africa
   c. access to clean drinking water around the world
   d. the discussion of G-8 leaders on the world's energy crisis

4. The word *scarcity* in paragraph 4 ("water scarcity will affect two out of every three people by 2025 . . .") means
   a. surplus.
   b. shortage.

  c. delay.
  d. capacity.

5. What is Vice President Ismail Serageldin of the World Bank's main point?
  a. Competition is growing over water as a finite resource.
  b. Peace in the world is impossible.
  c. Egypt is a hot spot.
  d. We should continue to work for peace in the world.

6. Over-pumping and rising sea levels are mentioned as causes of
  a. global warming.
  b. the threat to groundwater.
  c. water conflicts.
  d. both a and b

7. In the sentence "the only water that is available to many poor people free of charge lies in festering pools . . . ," the word *festering* could be replaced by
  a. fresh.
  b. growing.
  c. rotting.
  d. lowly elevated.

8. According to the article, many people in the African country of Ghana spend _____ percent of their income on bottled water.
  a. 5
  b. 30
  c. 10–20
  d. 50

9. In the second to last paragraph, the word *chronic* in the sentence "The public water system struggles from serious disrepair and a chronic lack of funding" means
  a. continual.
  b. vacant.
  c. sporadic.
  d. inevitable.

10. What is the main idea of this article?
  a. Access to clean drinking water is a serious global problem, especially for the world's poor.
  b. There is a threat of serious drought in the next few years.
  c. Africa is in crisis over a lack of access to water.
  d. The world's richest countries must work together to solve the water crisis.

Suggested Resources

Books

1. *Cool It: The Skeptical Environmentalist's Guide to Global Warming* by Bjørn Lomborg. Lomborg's book on global warming is ideal for anyone who is interested in learning about the phenomenon from an objective perspective. As a political scientist and economist, he offers feasible solutions to the real problems of global warming in this book.

© Pearson Education, Inc.

2. *An Inconvenient Truth: The Planetary Emergency of Global Warming and What We Can Do About It* by Al Gore. In his book on global warming, Al Gore makes a clear call to action and urges the American people to take a proactive role in reducing CO_2 emissions to make the earth a cleaner and healthier planet for generations to come.

Movies

1. *An Inconvenient Truth* (2006). This informative documentary highlights the urgency of acting now to reduce the effects of global warming or face the consequences of harmful human activities. Using concrete examples and information, Gore inspires the viewers to protect the living planet by being environmentally friendly.

Internet Sites

1. www.epa.gov

   This is the U.S. Environmental Protection Agency's official site. Here You can find up-to-date information on such environmental topics as recycling and acid rain. You can also interact with the site by submitting letters stating your viewpoint on a particular issue.

2. www.niehs.gov

   The National Institute of Environmental Health Sciences' Web site. This site explores the relationship between the environment and health concerns such as lead poisoning, asthma, and breast cancer.

Skimming and Scanning

Overview

Skimming and *scanning* are two reading techniques that enable you to read a passage quickly and determine the main idea and specific bits and pieces of information without having to read the function words such as prepositions, articles, conjunctions, etc. First, we will look at the technique of skimming. Then we will discuss how scanning can help you find specific information.

Skimming

When you skim a passage, you read it quickly to find out what the main idea is. Your goal is to understand the main idea of the passage without reading every single word. As mentioned above, while skimming, skip the function words such as prepositions (*to, into, on, at*), articles (*a, an, the*), and conjunctions (*so, but, yet, and*), and pay attention to the content words such as nouns (*government, policy, citizens, law*), verbs (*approve, penalize, allow*), adjectives (*mandatory, strict, legitimate*) and adverbs (*temporarily, permanently, momentarily*). You will notice that function words are not that important, and that content words carry the meaning. When you skim, follow these steps to determine the main idea:

1. Skim the introductory paragraph quickly without reading every single word. Usually the main idea is found in the first paragraph. Sometimes, the main idea may not be in the first paragraph, in which case you will need to skim the first two paragraphs. Keep in mind, however, that in some cases the main idea is offered in the final paragraph of a text.

2. While skimming, pay attention to the content words such as nouns and verbs. These will give you a clue as to what the main idea of the entire passage is.

3. Go all the way to the last paragraph and read it quickly. Most authors usually summarize the main ideas in the last paragraph.

4. Focus on some key words as you skim, and find the main idea. Keep in mind that skimming will help you get a general sense of what the reading is about. It will not help you find specific details. For that purpose, you will need to use another reading technique called scanning, but let's first focus on skimming.

Challenge Activity

Use skimming as a reading technique to find the main idea of the following passage. Read the passage carefully, delete the function words such as articles, prepositions, and conjunctions, and underline the main idea. Keep in mind that when you skim, you need to read slowly and carefully.

Yes, a mighty change is coming. With temperatures warming, snow evaporating and portions of the Alps melting away, forecasts suggest we're looking ahead to a tourism revolution. Warming weather is shrinking prospects at most low- and even mid-altitude ski resorts, from the Rockies to the Pyrenees, while increasingly violent weather is destabilizing

© Pearson Education, Inc.

traditional beach paradises from the Mediterranean to Southeast Asia and the Caribbean. "[Global warming] will have important consequences on the whole tourism chain, from the choice of destination to transportation and accommodation," says Jürgen Bachmann, of the Association of French Tour Operators. Hordes of northern European tourists may descend on Spain's Costa del Sol as long as the average August temperature sticks around 35 degrees Celsius, but if it rises to 40 degrees they might just shift toward the country's more temperate Basque coastline. Ski resorts that increasingly rely on snow cannons still need cold enough temperatures to use them. Indeed, weather-dependent destinations are increasingly facing a harsh Darwinian choice: adapt to the new climate realities or disappear.

(From Eric Pape, "The Costa del Norte." From *Newsweek*, April 16, 2007. © 2007 *Newsweek*, Inc. All rights reserved. Used by permission and protected by the Copyright Laws of the United States. The printing, copying, redistribution, or retransmission of the Material without express written permission is prohibited. www.newsweek.com)

Scanning

Unlike skimming, which is used to find the main idea, scanning is used to find specific details. Try to focus on the content words such as nouns, verbs, adjectives, etc. and find the specific bits and pieces of information you need to answer a question about the passage. Take the following steps to scan a passage:

1. First, read the title and subtitle of the passage. Then read the sections and subheadings, if any, to focus your search for specific details.

2. As you scan the passage, constantly ask yourself questions you need to answer. For example, ask *who* if you are looking for names, *where* if you need to know the place where something happened such as a meeting or an accident, *what* if you want to know what actually happened, *when* if your focus is the time of an event or an incidence, and *why* if you are looking for reasons.

3. Keep scanning and look for specific words that answer the above questions.

4. Stop scanning and read the passage slowly to understand the context better. You will notice that most of your questions were answered through scanning.

The following questions will help you scan a passage and find the answers. Keep in mind that these are just a few questions to help you scan with relative ease and success. You can most certainly create your own questions to scan. Remember that the questions you will ask will depend on the context, so some of these questions may not be relevant to the reading selection.

1. Why did something (an event, incident, accident, natural calamity) happen?
2. How does something (passing an exam, writing a good essay) happen?
3. How much time or money is involved in this process?
4. Which of the two options/topics/decisions is more appropriate?
5. When does something (a semester, a sports event, a political event) happen?
6. How often does (an event, a publication, a grant or scholarship, an award) something happen?

7. Where did/does this (an important political meeting, an international event, a violent crime) happen?

8. Who did/does this (a criminal, a teaching assistant, director of a foundation, an author, a university professor)?

Challenge Activity

Now use scanning as a reading technique to look for supporting details. When you read the following passage, ask some of the questions listed above. Depending on the topic of the passage, you may have to ask a different set of questions. Once again, skip the function words such as the articles, prepositions, and conjunctions, and focus on the content words such as nouns, verbs, adjectives, and adverbs. After you read the passage, try to answer the questions that follow.

A decade ago, the open-strip lignite pits of East Germany were an environmental disaster zone: hundreds of square kilometers of degraded land, toxic residues and acid lakes. Since then, a €7.8 billion renaturalization project has brought back clean lakes, verdant meadows and restored "wilderness." With a little help from biologists—such as importing seeds from species-rich regions—biodiversity has skyrocketed. Rare species have taken over the once-dead land, including wild orchids, hoopoe birds and wolves. As ever-fewer pockets of true wilderness remain in many parts of the world, scientists and activists are beginning to shift their attention from conserving "real" nature to restoring or improving degraded ecosystems. Scientists have gotten better at artificially balancing the needs of different flora and fauna. And activists are less ideologically pure about preserving nature in the wild. Some environmentalists fear that a focus on restoration will distract from efforts to stave off the destruction of wilderness and species. "But in some countries there's so little left to protect that you first have to restore something so you can protect it," says Norbert Hölzel, a restoration biologist at Germany's Giessen University.

(Stefan Theil, "Conservation: Coming Back from the Brink," *Newsweek,* October 16, 2006)

Did you understand the passage completely? Scan the passage a second time and answer the following questions.

1. Who has helped biodiversity grow? *biologists*

2. Scientists are shifting their attention from what to what? *from conserving real nature to restoring degrading ecosystems*

3. What are some environmentalists afraid of? *Restoration efforts will distract from saving the threatened wilderness*

© Pearson Education, Inc.

E-COMMERCE
Internet Marketing

> *"The Internet is
> becoming the town
> square for the global
> village of tomorrow."*
>
> BILL GATES

Objectives

IN THIS CHAPTER YOU WILL LEARN . . .

- About the academic area of e-commerce
- About the future of Internet marketing
- How to make inferences based on facts
- How to focus on details to arrive at a logical conclusion
- How to write a concise memorandum

Making Predictions

Consider this chapter's theme of E-Commerce. What subtopics relate to this field? (See Fig. 4.1.)

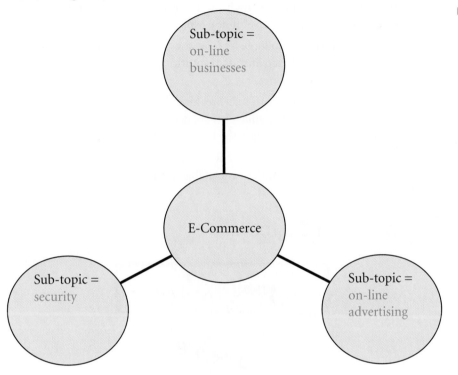

Introduction to the Discipline of E-Commerce

The discipline of Electronic Commerce, most commonly known as E-commerce, focuses on the buying and selling of products and services over the Internet and other computer networks. Since the advent of the Internet, both small and large businesses have made their presence known in the virtual world. The cost of marketing on the Internet is rather inexpensive, so more and more businesses brand their products and services on the Web, reaching out to potential customers worldwide. It is beyond the scope of this chapter to cover everything related to e-commerce. Instead, it focuses on one of its subtopics: Internet marketing.

This chapter will introduce you to the various approaches businesses use to sell their products on the Internet. The reading selections cover topics such as ordering food online, gender difference in Internet use, Web sites competing for TV's advertising revenue, and the popularity of Internet marketing in China. It is our hope that after completing this chapter, you will come to a better understanding of how e-commerce facilitates the payment aspects of the business transactions on the Internet.

© Pearson Education, Inc.

Preview Questions

Collaboration

1. How often do you purchase products and services online? What types of items do you usually buy through the Internet? Has your online shopping experience mostly been positive? If not, explain the drawbacks of e-commerce.

2. Do you know anyone who has ever been a victim of online identity theft? If yes, describe the incidence and its resolution. Discuss ways of preventing identity theft on the Internet.

3. Do you believe that e-commerce is breaking down international boundaries and creating a truly global village? If so, does everyone benefit from doing business in cyberspace? Who are the losers in this virtual enterprise?

4. In your opinion, what types of action can the government take to protect traditional businesses from their inevitable decline in the wake of aggressive Internet marketing?

Interpreting a Cartoon

■ **Figure 4.2**

mattbuck.com

Examine the cartoon shown here and answer the following questions in pairs.

Collaboration

1. What is amusing about this cartoon?

2. In your opinion, what is the cartoonist's message?

Discipline-specific Terminology Bank

acquisition	copyright	database	governance
blogs	corporate	digital	legislation
cookies	cyberspace	forecast	online

| processing | regulation | track | Web site |
| prohibiting | subsidiary | traffic | |

ESL Annotation

4.1 ESL Students find these kinds of thematically-focused vocabulary lists particularly useful.

Sample Paragraph

Nowadays more and more **Web sites** sell products and services to both consumers and businesses. Millions of consumers around the world conveniently choose from a wide range of products and purchase them **online**. Internet marketing experts **forecast** that the **trend** will continue, as **blogs** where consumers share their experiences with each other recommending and criticizing products grow in number.

EXERCISE 1

Matching Column A and Column B

Match the word in Column A with the definition in Column B. Put the letter representing the correct definition in the space preceding each term.

Column A

Word

1. _e_ traffic
2. _g_ forecast
3. _f_ corporate
4. _h_ cyberspace
5. _a_ blogs
6. _i_ cookies
7. _d_ track
8. _c_ copyright
9. _j_ online
10. _b_ regulation

Column B

Definition

a. personal Web sites to share activities and opinions
b. an official rule made by a government
c. the legal right to publish or broadcast
d. to follow progress or development
e. the movement of messages electronically
f. shared by members of a group
g. saying what will happen in the future
h. an imaginary space where electronic messages exist
i. a computer file with information in it
j. connected to the Internet

EXERCISE 2

Fill in the Blanks

In the following sentences, fill in the blank with a word from the terminology bank below that makes the sentence grammatical and meaningful.

| blogs | cookies | copyright | corporate | cyberspace |
| forecast | online | regulation | track | traffic |

© Pearson Education, Inc.

1. ___Cyberspace___ has become an extremely busy information highway where people using computers exchange electronic messages.

2. The government has announced a new ___regulation___ strictly controlling the marketing and selling of products on the Internet.

3. Responding to the growing needs of businesses interested in knowing how many potential consumers are visiting their Web sites, IBM is launching a state-of-the-art server that will manage global Internet ___traffic___.

4. Some Web browsers block ___cookies___ to prevent a computer user's personal information from being sent to the central server each time he or she surfs the Internet.

5. Internet marketing experts ___forecast___ that the number of people buying goods and services from the Internet will quadruple by the year 2010.

6. It is the CEO and Board of Directors' ___corporate___ responsibility to ensure that the business transaction on their Web site is carried out in a secure manner.

7. Unlike the traditional bricks-and-mortar businesses, most small businesses nowadays offer their products and services ___online___.

8. ___Blogs___ have become a popular forum where people share their activities, opinions, and travel experiences with others.

9. Most online businesses use software programs to ___track___ the number and demographics of consumers visiting their Web sites.

10. A group of British singers has sued an online business selling their music without their knowledge and consent for ___copyright___ infringement.

EXERCISE 3

Pair Activity

Collaboration

Working with a partner, choose five words you have just learned, and make complete sentences with them.

1. _____

   _____

2. _____

   _____

3. _____

   _____

4. _____

   _____

5. _____

   _____

Graphic Analysis

The pie chart shown in Figure 4.3 represents ad spending by various media sources in terms of percentage in July 2007. The smaller pie chart represents other medium comprising 10.4 percent of ad spending. As you can see, Cable Television is the most popular medium (20.7%) for ad spending followed by other media sources such as Network Television, Local Television, etc. Working with a partner, study the graph carefully and answer the questions. Keep in mind that some questions may ask you to predict the trend in the future.

Collaboration

■ **Figure 4.3**

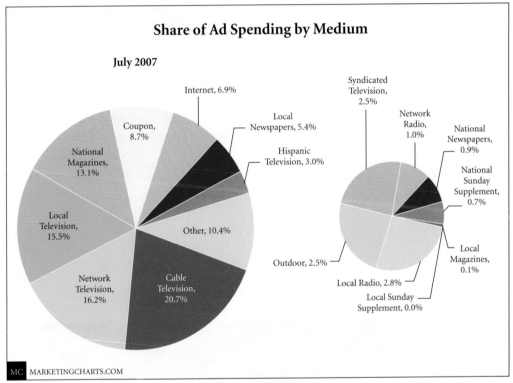

Share of Ad Spending by Medium

July 2007

Internet, 6.9%
Coupon, 8.7%
National Magazines, 13.1%
Local Television, 15.5%
Network Television, 16.2%
Cable Television, 20.7%
Other, 10.4%
Local Newspapers, 5.4%
Hispanic Television, 3.0%

Syndicated Television, 2.5%
Network Radio, 1.0%
National Newspapers, 0.9%
National Sunday Supplement, 0.7%
Local Magazines, 0.1%
Local Sunday Supplement, 0.0%
Local Radio, 2.8%
Outdoor, 2.5%

MC MARKETINGCHARTS.COM

Source: Nielsen/NetRatings AdAcross

1. How many sources of media have less than 10 percent share of ad spending?

   Four: Hispanic Television, Local Newspapers, Internet, and Coupon.

2. What is the combined percentage share of ad spending by print media?

   28.9% (Local Newspapers 5.4%, Coupon 8.7%, National Magazines 13.1%,

   National Newspapers 0.9%, National Sunday Supplement 0.7%, Local

   Magazines 0.1%).

3. What is the third most popular source of media for ads?

   Local Television, 15.5%.

4. Do you think Cable Television will still have the highest share of ad spending in July 2017, or do you think some other medium will take over it? If you think another medium will outdo Cable Television, what will bring about the change? Explain. *Answers will vary.*

© Pearson Education, Inc.

READING

Reading Selection **1**

Newspaper Article

4.2 Flesch-Kincaid Grade Level 9.9

Collaboration

www.FriesWithThat?.com

Pre-Reading Questions

Before you read the following reading selection, get into small groups of three or four and discuss these questions.

1. Have you ever ordered your lunch or dinner online? If not, explain why. If you have, share what prompted you to place your food order online instead of ordering your food by phone and driving to a restaurant to pick it up.

2. Do you think more and more people will eventually be ordering food on-line? Discuss the factors that will change the ways in which people purchase commercial food.

3. In your opinion, as online food businesses gain popularity, what role should government regulatory agencies play to ensure that the food items sold on-line are safe for consumption?

Read the following article and answer the multiple-choice questions that follow it. Try to be an "information predictor" for the first part of the reading.

www.FriesWithThat?.com

By **Stephanie Rosenbloom, the** *New York Times*

August 5, 2007

ESL Annotation

4.3 ESL In many countries ordering food on-line is not a reality, so the topic may not be considered worthy of discussion.

Curb service: Kwany Spinks checks out the order he placed with Outback Steakhouse on West 23rd Street in Manhattan.

Stephanie Rosenbloom, "www.FriesWithThat?.com." From *The New York Times*, August 5, 2007. © 2007 The New York Times. All rights reserved. Used by permission and protected by the Copyright Laws of the United States. The printing, copying, redistribution, or retransmission of the Material without express written permission is prohibited. www.nytimes.com

1   Who has never been put on hold while trying to order pizza, hot wings or moo shu pork? Who has never opened a delivery bag and discovered a Coke instead of a Diet Coke, or that the brown rice is as white as the napkins the restaurant neglected to include?

2   "I hate calling up to order food," said Lewis Friedman, a Manhattan real **estate** broker. "It **throws me over the edge.** They put you on hold. They get the order wrong. It's always **a crap shoot**."

3   But all that changed last month when he saw a sign in the window of Lenny's, a chain of sandwich shops in Manhattan, encouraging customers to orders online. Mr. Friedman returned to his office, logged on and, at long last, felt in control of his gustatory future.

4   "I'm **in the driver's seat**," he said. "I can click that I use skim milk. I can click that I like light skim milk. I can click for Equal as opposed to Sweet 'n Low or Splenda."

5   The comedian Jim Gaffigan has teased Americans about how fast they want their food. "That's why we really love those value meals," he said. "You just have to say a number: 'Two!' Soon you won't have to speak. It will just be a noise. 'Ennnghhh!'"

6   Mr. Gaffigan must **have a crystal ball**. Small and large chains, even **individual** restaurants, are now enabling customers to order without speaking: They can order online before pulling into a drive-through; they can **text**-message an order, and soon, they will be able to experience one-click ordering on their cell phones, for pickup or delivery. Push a button, and a hoagie is on the way.

7   The restaurant industry is investing in such **technology** to woo the thousands of consumers like Mr. Friedman who fly through life with their thumbs on their BlackBerrys.

8   Hoping to make ordering a burger as routine as ordering a book from Amazon, a number of chains are emphasizing the dot-com after their **corporate** name to lure the hungry and time-pressed to their Web sites.

9   As for all those supposed concerns about unhealthy eating and the retreat from home cooking—who are we fooling? The average American 18 and older buys a snack or a meal from a restaurant five times a week on average, according to a 2006 **survey** by the National Restaurant Association. More people eat at their desks and in their cars. And children are weaned on drive-through, pickup and delivery.

10 The biggest regret Americans seem to have about fast food is that it isn't snappier: A **survey** last year by QSR magazine, a restaurant industry **publication**, found that 68 **percent** of people are willing to wait no more than five minutes in a drive-through line. And in an age where everything from sneakers to cars is customizable, people think they should be able to get exactly what they want, when they want it.

11 "It has really, really exploded in the past year or two," said J. Patrick Doyle, the executive vice president of **Team** USA, the name Domino's Pizza uses for its corporately owned locations. "I predict pizza will be one of the top 10 **items** purchased online within the next 12 to 24 months."

12 Though online ordering has been around at some locations for about five years, most people still call in or wait in lines to place their orders. About 13 **percent** of Americans placed online food orders from a restaurant last year,

? _____
_____
_____
_____

throws me over the edge
something that really annoys

a crap shoot
left up to chance; up against the odds

in the driver's seat
to be in a controlling position

? _____
_____
_____
_____

have a crystal ball
have a means of predicting the future

? _____
_____
_____
_____

© Pearson Education, Inc.

according to the National Restaurant Association, up from about 10 percent in 2004.

13   But Philip DeSorbo Jr., a **project** leader for the retail **technology** department at Subway, which has nearly 28,000 restaurants in 87 countries, said these days many people would rather send an e-mail message than leave a voice mail message. "I think online will **eventually** surpass picking up the phone," he said.

14   Igniting the **trend** are consumers like Mr. Friedman, who may seem like the **finicky** protagonist of Dr. Seuss's "Green Eggs and Ham," but who is just your average **multitasking**, high-speed wireless American.

15   Now each weekday morning he places an online order with Lenny's. Soon an iced coffee and an Atkin's Special (egg whites, turkey, onion, tomato, roasted red pepper) are made to his typed specifications and delivered to the reception desk.

16   "I'm saving time," said Mr. Friedman, who orders breakfast and lunch online. "I'm so adept at it now that I can actually do business on the phone while I'm placing my food order."

17   People like him see advantages to online and **text** ordering. It is faster; there is no being placed on hold or inadvertently hung up on; and you need not ask about the specials or explain that the jalapenos should be on the side. It is more **accurate**; you type in the order and delivery address yourself. There is no need for cash. Favorite orders and **credit** card information can be saved so re-ordering is a matter of a few mouse clicks. A delivery can be scheduled days in advance. And thanks to electronic menus, there is more drawer space in the kitchen.

18   Yet as recently as 2001, Jim Kargman, the president of QuikOrder, a company that provides the **technology** for online ordering, found some fast food chains **reluctant** to adopt online ordering. "Now it's basically become mainstream," said Mr. Kargman, whose clients now include Pizza Hut and Domino's.

19   Industry executives have found that those inclined to use online or **text** ordering are less defined by race or age than by whether or not they have **access** to high-speed Internet connections.

20   Online orders on **corporate** Web sites or sites like SeamlessWeb.com, an **aggregate site** for restaurant ordering, come from working parents in search of no-fuss family dinners, ravenous college students and professionals working overtime.

21   "The heavy user for fast food is the heavy user for computers and handheld devices," said David Palmer, a restaurant analyst for UBS, the **financial** services company.

22   For that reason, perhaps no group understands the benefits of new ordering methods better than college students, who grew up zooming through cyberspace. In **response** to student demand for a way to **text** food orders to restaurants in between classes, Campusfood.com, an online **network** of restaurants **available** on more than 300 campuses, began offering **text** and SMS message ordering in April. The first big push for the service will be this fall.

23   "It's exactly like sending a regular **text** message like I do with my friends all the time," said Rebecca Minsky, 21, a junior at Cornell University who has been using Campusfood.com since her freshman year. When she leaves the gym she texts her order; by the time she arrives home, dinner is ready.

24   In fact, Ms. Minsky used Campusfood.com so often that she ended up interning for the company this summer.

finicky
liking only a few kinds of food, clothes, music, etc.; difficult to please

multitasking
doing several things all at once

25   "What they like is it's really on their own terms," said Jim Ensign, the vice president for marketing communications for Papa John's International.

26   The advantages for restaurants include fewer phone calls to answer, higher sales prices (the average pizza sale is $2 to $5 higher than over the phone, said Mr. Kargman of QuikOrder), and **access** to the e-mail addresses of thousands of customers.

27   What is good for the industry, though, is not necessarily good for the **consumer**. "I'm sure it will be popular among the heavy users of fast food who will be encouraged to eat even more of it," said Marion Nestle, a professor of nutrition, food studies and public health at New York University and the **author** of "Food Politics: How the Food Industry Influences Nutrition and Health" and "What to Eat." "And that's too bad," she said, "because there are healthier eating options, obviously."

28   Still, she said, the industry is giving people what they want: "How clever of them to take advantage of that kind of **technology**." Ms. Nestle also pointed out that **consumer** interest in these new ways of ordering is an intriguing commentary on class, as it shows how **reluctant** people are to speak with fast food workers—often teenagers and immigrants with accents.

reluctant
unwilling, disinclined

29   Pizza is the nation's most delivered food category, Mr. Kargman said, so it is not surprising that the world's three largest pizza chains (Pizza Hut, Domino's and Papa John's) are at the forefront of electronic ordering. Nation-wide, nearly 30 online orders on average are placed every minute at Pizza Hut, and the company said in June that its online ordering business grew six fold in the last three years.

30   The **major** national pizza chains have about 41 **percent** of the pizza-restaurant business, according to the Associated Press.

31   "This is one way among many that the chains are trying to grow within this **mature** market," said Mr. Palmer of UBS. "Other ways include offering breakfast, staying open later, introducing premium **items**, or **credit** card payment capability, offering wi-fi."

32   "I only order online," said Andy Claude, 31, who works in the **investment** industry in San Diego and who has been ordering from Papa John's for about five years. "When you order on the phone, sometimes you say 'extra cheese' or 'half pepperoni' and it doesn't always come that way."

33   Pizza, however, is not the only cuisine that has gone digital. A little more than a year ago, Chipotle, the Mexican chain, began offering online ordering, which it calls DSL (Don't Stand in Line). In the first six months of this year it did 350,000 transactions online, up from 250,000 in the first half of last year, said Chris Arnold, a spokesman.

34   About three months ago, an Outback Steakhouse on West 23rd Street in Manhattan began offering curbside take away, said Chris Eldridge, the proprietor. Customers place an order online and type in the make and color of their car. When they pull up to the restaurant, their food is carried out to them.

35   Of course there are consumers who have ordered online only to have their food never arrive or arrive with fixings they won't so much as poke at. **Nonethe-less**, industry professionals generally agree that online orders are more **accurate**.

36   Restaurants like Subway and Papa John's are experimenting with **text** messaging. At the National Restaurant Association show in May, Mr. Kargman of

© Pearson Education, Inc.

QuikOrder announced that he had acquired patented **technology** called FavOrder that will allow customers to place orders on Web sites and **via** cellphones and PDAs with a single click. Cellphone one-click ordering will be **available** to the public later this year.

37 "The reality of it is, there's a lot of us that are resistant to change," said Tom Santor, a spokesman for Donatos Pizza, a chain with 176 restaurants in the United States. "But guess what? It ain't doing us any good. This train has done left the station."

38 People like Alison Strianse of Brooklyn are riding it into the future.

39 "I'm hooked on Delivery.com," she said, which she uses to order lunch. "You literally don't have to leave your desk."

40 When she learned about the Web **site** from a friend a few weeks ago she looked at him and thought: "You've changed my life."

Reading Comprehension Check

1. As used in the sentence in paragraph 3 "Mr. Friedman returned to the office, logged on and, at long last, felt in control of his gustatory future," the word *gustatory* means
   a. the art of cooking.
   b. a gust of wind.
   c. related to eating.
   d. buying food online.

2. A Manhattan real estate broker, Lewis Friedman's main point about ordering food online is that
   a. he prefers calling up restaurants to order food.
   b. restaurant Web sites offer unhealthy food.
   c. it is inconvenient to order food from a computer.
   d. he is completely in control of what he wants to eat.

3. In making fun of the American people, the comedian Jim Gaffigan's main point in paragraph 5 is that
   a. they do not mind waiting for hours to have their food delivered.
   b. the restaurant industry's push for online food will not become popular.
   c. they prefer convenience to quality.
   d. they are overly conscious about healthy food.

4. In the sentence "The restaurant industry is investing in such technology to *woo* the thousands of consumers like Mr. Friedman who fly through life with their thumbs on their BlackBerrys" (paragraph 7), the word *woo* could be replaced with
   a. solicit.   c. discourage.
   b. distract.   d. sanction.

5. 18-year-old Americans buying commercial food at least five times a week is offered as an example of
   a. young Americans' tendency to prefer homemade food.
   b. Americans clamoring for healthier eating options.
   c. fewer Americans eating while commuting to work.
   d. young Americans withdrawing from homemade food.

6. Thirteen percent of Americans purchasing food from restaurant Web sites is mentioned to support the point that
   a. the number of people placing online food orders has decreased.
   (b.) most people still purchase food the conventional way.
   c. those who purchase food online are dissatisfied with the quality.
   d. those who purchase food online are satisfied with the quality.

7. The main idea of the article is that
   a. most people eat while commuting to work or at their desks.
   b. it is much easier to order food by phone than it is to purchase it online.
   c. pizza is the most popular food item purchased online.
   (d.) the restaurant industry is capitalizing on the American people's tendency to want food fast.

8. In the sentence in paragraph 19 "Industry executives have found that those inclined to use online or text ordering are less defined by race or age than by whether or not they have access to high-speed Internet connections," the word *inclined* means
   a. feel repelled.
   b. disenchanted.
   (c.) having tendency.
   d. not in favor of (using).

9. A professor of nutrition, food studies, and public health at New York University, Ms. Marion Nestle's main point about restaurant Web sites becoming popular among fast food users is that
   a. consumers will gain health and longevity from purchasing food online.
   b. restaurant Web sites are extremely good for the consumer.
   (c.) the popularity of online food purchases is good for the restaurant industry.
   d. consumers do not have many healthier options left.

10. What advantage is mentioned to ordering food online?
   a. The food is more delicious and healthier.
   b. The food is inexpensive.
   (c.) The service is accurate.
   d. Side dishes are free.

Internet's Gender Gap Narrows

READING

Reading Selection **2**

Online Magazine Article

4.4 Flesch-Kincaid Grade Level 11.9

Collaboration

Pre-Reading Questions

Discuss the following questions in small groups before reading the article.

1. If you are female, how often and for what purposes do you use the Internet? If you are male, what prompts you to navigate the Internet? Discuss if there are gender differences in Internet usage and give specific examples to support your answer.

© Pearson Education, Inc.

2. Do you think men outnumber women in terms of browsing the Internet, or do you think the number of men and women surfing the Internet is equal? Give specific reasons for your answer.

3. In your opinion, how do marketers study male and female online behavior to target the two sexes for profit? Think of some of the Web sites you have visited that are specifically geared toward women and discuss the strategies marketers use to draw more female Internet users.

Internet's Gender Gap Narrows

By Joanna Glasner, wired.com

March 21, 2006

ESL Annotation

4.5 ESL Many students new to American culture may not be familiar with the fact that studies focusing on gender comparisons are commonplace in the US.

1   A few years ago, you could get an idea, **accurate** or not, about the difference between women's and men's online behavior by looking at their respective **domain** names.

2   Women.com has been a portal **site** for women for the past decade, featuring articles on topics like fitness, fashion and romance. Men.com, for most of that time, posted adult content.

3   Today, however, the differences are far more subtle. Both Men.com and Women.com are now **gender**-targeted health and lifestyle sites with mostly PG-rated content. Their advertisers are **established** Internet sites and **consumer**-goods companies. They organize content into **similar** subject areas like health and entertainment.

drill down
to **focus** on the details

4   You have to **drill down** to some of the subtopics to spot where they diverge. (Women.com links to a special report on "this season's sexiest shoes." Men.com links to the all-female anchors of Naked News.)

5   As Men.com and Women.com have come to mirror each other more closely over the years, so have the online activities of men and women. Once a **medium** dominated by men, the Internet now draws approximately equal proportions of male and female users in the United States. Top search engines and portal sites draw about the same numbers of men and women. A recent Pew **Research** Center study found that men and women are about equally likely to go online to buy things, make travel arrangements or do their banking.

6   Even so, it's the differences between the sexes' behavior online that intrigues marketers.

impetus
an influence that makes something happen, or happen more quickly

7   The desirability of the "female **target** market" was the **impetus** behind NBC Universal agreeing to pay $600 million earlier this month to buy iVillage, which runs a **network** of female-oriented Internet domains, including Women.com. In a written statement, NBC described the deal as a way to "engage millions of loyal iVillage users, a **community** which mirrors a key demographic of the NBC Universal audience—women."

8   Companies that make money selling advertising want to attract women for many reasons. Not least is the fact that women **comprise** more than half the U.S. population and control a large and growing share of national **income** and wealth.

Joanna Glasner, "Internet's Gender Gap Narrows." http://www.wired.com/techbiz/startups/news/2006/03/70441. Copyright © 2008 Condé Nast Publications. All rights reserved. Originally published in Wired.com. Reprinted by permission.

9   That said, women-oriented portals haven't been standup investments. iVillage and Women.com (which iVillage acquired in 2001) both went public to much fanfare in 1999, the heart of the dot-com startup boom. Shortly afterward, shares of both plummeted, with iVillage hitting a low of 38 cents in 2001. The web publisher has since recovered, and is now a profitable business with a share price over $8.

10   But while iVillage's fortunes have improved, experts in marketing to women aren't **convinced** advertisers and publishers trying to reach females online need a "women's portal" to do so.

11   "There's a lot of what I call 'pink thinking,' when marketing is just **scratching the surface** of what women want," said Lisa Johnson, CEO of the marketing consultancy ReachWomen and co-**author** of *Don't Think Pink*. Pink thinking refers to the idea that adding pastels or "lighter" versions of the original will make a product more appealing to women. Such an **approach** might work for products like makeup or women's shoes, but not for most things.

scratching the surface
treating something superficially

12   So what do women want? It's a question that dumbfounded the father of psychoanalysis, Sigmund Freud.

13   Marketing consultants and demographic researchers believe they have found some answers. In the online world, at least, their findings **indicate** that although men and women behave similarly, some distinctions exist. Websites that fail to draw a sizable female audience, they say, ought to incorporate the following:

- More sources of information: Typically, women have a longer wish list of what they want from a website than men, says Johnson. Preferences include having information put in the **context** of a story and getting information on a **topic** from multiple sources in one place. These are qualities men like, too, Johnson says, but about which women are usually pickier.

- A sense of connection: Websites and online advertisers appeal more to women when they **create** an emotional connection, says Catherine Stellin, vice president of **research** at The **Intelligence** Group, a marketing consultancy. That doesn't mean bonding with the Energizer bunny. It's a bit more subtle, says Stellin, who cites as an example **financial**-planning companies that include profiles of executives or successful retirees in their ad campaigns.

- Time-saving **features**: Male and female shoppers typically behave in opposite ways online and offline, says Marty Barletta, **author** of *Marketing to Women*. In brick-and-mortar stores, Barletta says, women are more apt to spend time browsing and men are more likely to quickly make a **purchase**. Online, that behavior reverses itself, with men likely to spend more time perusing and women tending to make a **purchase** quickly.

- Better explanations: Barletta has much disdain for the way automobile and PC sites sell their wares. Her **primary** objection is that most presume a prospective customer already understands the **technical** details of the product she's eyeballing. In reality, customers may not know whether it's worth paying extra for a 1.7-GHz PC over a 1.4-GHz model, or why axle ratio is important. "They **assume** an engineer's knowledge," Barletta said.

14   **Overall**, women outpace men in a small number of online areas, including health, medicine and religion, according to Pew **Research** Center. Women,

© Pearson Education, Inc.

according to Pew analyst Deborah Fallows, are also more likely to use the Internet for e-mail, maps and getting directions.

15   Men, by comparison, are more likely to use the Internet to check the weather, get news, find sports information and download software or music files, among other things, according to Fallows.

16   Of course, these are generalities, based on trends delineated from massive surveys. In the real world, millions of men use Internet mapping sites, and women download software and music files.

17   Still, it's always entertaining, if nothing else, to see what **perceived** demographic we belong to based on the **media** we consume.

18   The demographic compartmentalization is fairly **obvious** online. At iVillage, low-calorie foods and skin-care products rule the ad space. At Men.com, it's eMusic, the Weather **Channel** and car-**data site** Edmunds.

19   Even so, the distinctions are not so stark as on television, where it's predictable that a steamy nighttime soap will be punctuated with ads for beauty and hair-care products. On the opposite end, viewers of evening **network** news broadcasts are **prime** candidates for the kinds of pharmaceuticals expressly *not* to be taken by female patients.

Joanna Glasner is a freelance writer based on the West Coast. She has been writing for Wired News since Internet stock offerings were hot, cell phones wouldn't fit in your pocket, and everyone still had a dialup connection at home.

Reading Comprehension Check

1. As used in the sentence (paragraph 3) "Today, however, the differences are far more subtle. Both Men.com and Women.com are now gender-targeted health and lifestyle sites with mostly PG-rated content," the word *subtle* means
   a. obvious.
   b. explicit.
   c. slight.
   d. clear.

2. In the sentence (paragraph 4) "You have to drill down to some of the subtopics to spot where they diverge. (Women.com links to a special report on 'this season's sexiest shoes.' Men.com links to the all-female anchors of Naked News.)," the word *diverge* can be replaced with
   a. differ.
   b. agree.
   c. arrive.
   d. move toward.

3. In the sentence (paragraph 6) "Even so, it's the differences between the sexes' behavior online that intrigues marketers," the word *intrigues* most nearly means
   a. disturbs.
   b. attracts.
   c. repels.
   d. frustrates.

4. Which of the following sentences is the best statement of the main idea of the article?
   a. American men outnumber American women in terms of browsing the Internet.

b. The number of American women surfing the Internet far exceeds that of American men.

c. The number of male and female Internet users in the United States is almost equal nowadays.

d. The gender gap in Internet usage is constantly widening.

5. NBC agreed to pay $500 million to acquire iVillage because
   a. it wanted to draw a sizeable male audience.
   b. the company was interested in building a gated community.
   c. it had a huge surplus and had to spend it somehow.
   d. the company was interested in targeting the female market.

6. Lisa Johnson, CEO of the marketing consultancy ReachWomen and coauthor of *Don't Think Pink* says, "There's a lot of what I call 'pink thinking,' when marketing is just scratching the surface of what women want." (paragraph 11). *Pink thinking* is a marketing term referring to the idea that
   a. adding pastels to products usually aggravates potential female customers.
   b. most women find products with strong color unattractive.
   c. most female buyers find products painted in soft colors attractive.
   d. marketers targeting female Internet users wear pink hats.

7. Marketing consultants and demographic researchers believe that though male and female Internet users behave almost similarly, women gravitate toward the Web sites that provide
   I. limited information.
   II. information from multiple sources.
   III. reasonable prices.
   IV. a sense of bonding.
   a. I and II   c. II and III
   b. I and III   d. II and IV

8. Marty Barletta, author of *Marketing to Women*, uses the example of men and women shopping in stores and online to support the fact that
   a. male and female shoppers spend equal amounts of time in bricks-and-mortar stores.
   b. male and female shoppers spend equal amounts of time buying products online.
   c. male and female shoppers behave differently shopping online and offline.
   d. There is no gender difference in male and female shoppers online and offline.

9. Women are more frequent users than men in all of these online areas EXCEPT
   a. health.   c. getting directions.
   b. medicine.   d. entertainment.

10. Which of the following statements explains why it is worthwhile to study gender differences in the two sexes' shopping behavior?
    a. It is a losing proposition for the marketers.
    b. It is frustrating for the consumers.
    c. It is amusing to examine the differences in male and female shopping behavior.
    d. It causes a sluggish economy.

© Pearson Education, Inc.

Larry Page and Sergei Brin

While pursuing his PhD in computer science at Stanford University, Larry Page met Sergei Brin, a Russian immigrant who was also pursuing a PhD in computer science there, and together they founded the Google search engine in 1998. Since then, Google has become the largest search engine in the world, highly frequented by Internet surfers looking for various Web sites. Both Larry Page and Sergei Brin have suspended their doctoral studies indefinitely while they are both working at Google.

Larry Page was born on March 26, 1973, in Lansing, Michigan into a family of educators. His father, Dr. Carl Victor Page, was a professor of computer science at Michigan State University, and his mother, Gloria Page, taught computer programming at the same university. Sergei Brin was born on August 21, 1973, in Moscow in the Soviet Union. Like Larry Page, Sergei Brin also grew up in an educational environment. His father, Michael Brin, taught mathematics at the University of Maryland, and his mother was an economist.

Before Sergei Brin met Larry Page at Stanford University, he had written several papers on data mining and pattern extraction. He coauthored a seminal paper with Larry Page, entitled "The Anatomy of a Large-Scale Hypertextual Web Search Engine." Their paper has become the tenth most widely read scientific article at Stanford University.

Larry Page has a net worth of slightly more than $18 billion, which makes him the world's twenty-sixth richest person. Sergei Brin's net worth is $18.5 billion, making him the world's twenty-fifth richest person. Larry Page and Sergei Brin recently purchased a Qantas Boeing 767 for business and personal purposes. Both of them appeared on the list of the 50 most important people on the Internet by PC World in 2006. Prior to that, they were named "Persons of the Week" by ABC *World News Tonight* in 2004. In 2005, Sergei Brin was considered to be one of the "Young Global Leaders" by the World Economic Forum.

Page is heavily invested in Tesla Motors, a company that is designing the Tesla Roadster, a battery electric vehicle. Sergei Brin drives a Toyota Prius, a hybrid car that uses both gasoline and electrical energy.

Some Questions for Group Discussion

1. Do you think that Larry Page and Sergei Brin's tremendous success had something to do with the fact that both of their parents were educators? In other words, do highly educated parents determine and influence their children's financial success? Support your answer with specific examples.
2. The parents of Larry Page and Sergei Brin were university professors, not business icons. What do you think motivated Larry Page and Sergei Brin to become world leaders in the area of Internet marketing?
3. Larry Page, the world's twenty-sixth richest person, has invested in a company that is developing a battery electric vehicle. His partner, Sergei Brin, who is the world's twenty-fifth richest individual, drives a Toyota Prius while he can easily afford the most expensive cars in the world. Discuss why you think Larry Page and Sergei Brin have gone "green."

Biographical Internet Research

Research another leader in Internet Marketing from the list below, and share his biographical profile with your peers. Discuss what set them apart from others in the business world.

- Jeff Bezos
- Pierre Omidyar
- Michael Dell
- David Filo
- Jerry Yang

SKILL FOCUS
Making Inferences

When good readers make an *inference*, they draw logical conclusions based on facts. It is important to remember that the reader must avoid inferring on the basis of opinion, as sometimes authors present information that is not clearly stated. In other words, information is implied, so the reader has to examine facts and details closely to make a conclusion that is factual and logical.

Look at the following sample exercise to understand clearly that inferences must be based on facts.

Example

When people ask me what I do for a living, and I tell them that I am a linguist, they respond with a blank stare.

What can you infer from the above statement?

　　a. Linguists are extremely popular nowadays.

　　b. Linguistics can be a rewarding career.

　　c. Most people are not familiar with the field of linguistics.

　　d. Linguists are in great demand.

If you read the sentence carefully, you will notice that Choice (a) is exactly the opposite. If linguists were that popular, then people would not give the author "a blank stare." So, Choice (a) is not correct. Choice (b) is also incorrect, because if linguistics were such a rewarding career, then most people would be aware of the discipline. Choice (c) is a logical conclusion because most people respond to the author with "a blank stare" not knowing what a linguist does for a living. Choice (c), therefore, is the correct answer. In contrast, Choice (d) cannot be true either because the sentence does not give the impression that linguists are indeed in demand. An effective technique to make correct inferences on a multiple-choice test is to determine how many statements are false. Think about the question as if the choices were true/false questions. Read the four choices carefully, and then reread the passage to determine which statements are false. If you focus on the facts and clues presented in the passage, you will notice that there is always only one statement that is true, and thus the correct conclusion. The following example will make this point clear. Read the sentence carefully and answer the question that follows.

Example

Shakespeare isn't far from truth when he wrote, "The first thing we do, let's kill all the lawyers." *(Henry VI)*

It can be inferred from the above statement that

　　a. Shakespeare killed many lawyers.

　　b. the author murdered several lawyers.

　　c. the author is not too fond of lawyers.

　　d. the author is seriously considering killing all the lawyers.

Choice (a) is not true, since the above sentence is taken from Shakespeare's famous play *Henry VI,* in which a character says this line. It does not mean that Shakespeare himself killed many lawyers. We know that the author agrees with Shakespeare's statement, but we do not know if he murdered several lawyers. Choice (b), therefore, is not correct. The author writes, "Shakespeare couldn't be further from truth . . . [supporting the statement that all the lawyer should be killed]". Choice (c) says that the author is not too fond of lawyers. We can

© Pearson Education, Inc.

make this inference correctly on the basis of the statement. It is reasonable and logical to infer that the author most probably dislikes lawyers. Otherwise, he would not agree with Shakespeare. Choice (c) is the correct answer. Choice (d) is false because the author simply affirms that Shakespeare was right in condemning all the lawyers. The statement does not indicate that the author is actually planning to kill all the lawyers.

When making inferences, think like a detective, read the main idea, and look at the details closely. It is important that you abstain from forming your own opinion of the topic, and that you focus on what is stated. By relying on the facts and details in the passage, you will arrive at a logical conclusion.

Let's look at another example to understand how inferences are made. Read the brief passage below and answer the question, paying close attention to the facts to arrive at a logical conclusion.

Example

Jennifer entered a house. Upon hearing the door, Jimbo, the dog, snarled, thinking it was an intruder. However, when Jimbo saw Jennifer, it rolled over, wagging its tail.

A logical conclusion drawn from this passage is

    a. Jennifer is Jimbo's veterinarian.

    b. Jennifer is Jimbo's owner.

    c. Jimbo is Jennifer's Seeing Eye dog.

    d. Jimbo knows Jennifer.

Let's read each of the choices carefully and determine which statement is true and which one is false.

There is nothing in the passage that leads us to conclude that Jennifer is a veterinarian. The passage does not give us any information about Jennifer's profession. Choice (a), therefore, is not a logical conclusion. (False) Choice (b) is not a correct conclusion either, because we cannot find anything in the passage that establishes the fact that Jennifer is indeed Jimbo's owner. The passage begins with "Jennifer entered a house," not "Jennifer entered her house." It is probably true that Jimbo lives in the house, but we cannot tell if Jennifer owns the house. (False) Is there any information in the passage that supports the idea that Jennifer is blind? Seeing Eye dogs are usually owned by people who are blind. We do not know if Jennifer is blind, so we cannot say Choice (c) is true. (False) What we do know from the passage is that Jimbo rolled over after seeing Jennifer. It is unusual for a dog to roll on its back, asking a stranger to scratch its tummy, but Jimbo does that to Jennifer. This is the only piece of fact that is presented in the above passage, and the information is implied that Jimbo wants Jennifer to rub its stomach. We can safely conclude that Choice (d) is the correct inference. (True)

PRACTICING THE SKILL

Collaboration

Practice making inferences by reading the following passages with a classmate and arrive at a logical conclusion based on the facts. Underline the sentence, or sentences, that clue you in to the correct answer.

Passage 1

Many sites exist primarily to inform and influence target audiences favorably about the owner of the site. Such sites typically emphasize a firm or organization's mission, size, scope, services, revenue, profitability, stock market success, industry relationship, and so forth—in much the same way as an annual financial report would. In fact, much of what you find on corporate identity sites is there to influence Wall Street, stockholders, and investors, and to instill a sense of pride among company employees.

(Barbara G. Cox and William Koelzer, Internet Marketing. *Upper Saddle River: Pearson Prentice Hall, 2004, p. 5)*

It can be inferred from this passage that

    (a.) the primary purpose of corporate identity sites is marketing.

    b. company employees are frustrated with the corporate identity sites.

    c. owners of the sites are proud of their employees.

    d. there is no difference between the sites and an annual financial report.

Passage 2

Similar to corporate identity sites, product or service information sites emphasize positioning products or services more than selling them. Some of these sites are posted by businesses that really do intend to sell their products directly, but haven't mastered the Internet marketing elements they need to use to accomplish that goal. These sites are akin to product brochures. They may give the business telephone number and perhaps the e-mail address, but they do not provide the interactive tools that are central to the Web's capacity for direct selling. These information-oriented Web sites reflect a product focus, but usually do not communicate urgency or establish a two-way information exchange with site visitors.

(From *Internet Marketing*, p. 6)

It can be inferred from this passage that

    a. information-oriented Web sites are not interested in selling their products.

    b. these sites are primarily concerned with the owner's identity.

    c. information-oriented Web sites do not provide their contact information.

    (d.) some businesses providing information-oriented sites have poor Internet marketing skills.

Passage 3

Online banking was among the earliest and most successful Web-based services. Not only can users get information about bank offices and hours and locations, types of accounts, rates, terms, and other bank products, but they can also access their account information; transfer funds; pay bills; plan a reinvestment, retirement, or home loan refinance; and communicate with the bank. Investors can learn about bank assets and liabilities, stability, size, and investments.

(From *Internet Marketing*, p. 8)

© Pearson Education, Inc.

We can conclude from this passage that
    a. online banking is not successful nowadays.
    b. customers shy away from online banking because of the hidden charges.
    c. customers can access many useful pieces of information about their bank accounts from their homes.
    d. customers must attend a series of workshops before using online banking.

Passage 4

News and entertainment sites are usually tied to another media, such as television, films, magazines, or newspapers. Cnn.com, tvguide.com, Hollwood.com, usatoday.com, and austindailyherald.com are all examples. These sites keep visitors returning day after day for updates and current information, as well as for customer service regarding subscription, delivery, or other services. What do they gain by providing all this information? Increased ratings, circulation, and physical sales—which, in turn, help increase advertising sales.

(From *Internet Marketing*, p. 8)

A correct conclusion drawn from the above passage is that
    a. news and entertainment sites provide useless information.
    b. these sites work independently of other media sources such a TV and films.
    c. visitors are satisfied with the information and services news and entertainment sites provide.
    d. providing information and services causes advertising sales to plummet.

Passage 5

Some large stores and manufacturers are finding ways to personalize their Web sites. These sites usually encourage visitors to sign in or register for something or otherwise provide a name or nickname that the site can use when the visitor returns in the future. Amazon.com, for example, displays "Welcome back, [visitor name]." The entry page has "New books for [visitor name]" based on searches or purchases the visitor made on previous visits.

(From *Internet Marketing*, p. 8)

It can be inferred from the above passage that
    a. some manufacturers want to prevent potential customers from visiting their Web sites.
    b. some large stores are writing their customers' names on signboards.
    c. most people appreciate it when they are addressed by their names.
    d. many Web sites offer their customers free cookies when they sign in.

The next Reading Selection allows you to apply the skills you have just learned. Now that you have read brief passages and have drawn logical conclusions, let's practice reading full-length articles to make inferences based on facts and details.

Web Sites Go Fishing in TV's Advertising Revenue Stream

READING

Reading Selection **3**

Newspaper Article

4.6 Flesch-Kincaid Grade Level 11.5

Collaboration

Pre-Reading Questions

1. Do you watch popular television series online? If you do, tell what factors influenced your decision to move from a television to the Internet? If you do not, would you consider watching a television series online?

2. Some experts believe that Web sites will take a major bite out of the television advertising revenue stream. Discuss what television companies should do to compete with the Web sites and maintain a steady stream of advertising revenue.

3. Some Web sites show video material from established television providers and are accused of copyright infringement. YouTube, for example, has popularized home movie clips and continues to add video clips produced by television companies. Discuss what the government should do to protect traditional TV's copyright.

Web Sites Go Fishing in TV's Advertising Revenue Stream

By Eric Pfanner, the *New York Times*

November 19, 2007

1 LONDON, Nov. 18—Web sites have been "draining the life out of newspapers and radio for years," according to one of the founders of an Internet video **site**, and now they are going after the advertising **revenue** stream of television as well.

2 Simon Assaad, a co-founder of Heavy.com called television "the last part of the market that we haven't punctured."

3 And, although other Web sites may not have laid out the battleground quite as **explicitly,** their content is starting to look a lot more like **traditional** TV, including the commercials.

explicitly
fully and clearly expressed or demonstrated

4 Video is **proliferating** on the Internet, and it is no longer limited to short clips of cats flushing toilets, breath mints reacting explosively with carbonated sodas and other user-**generated** content of the kind that captured the anarchic spirit of the early Web 2.0 days.

proliferating
increasing in number or spreading rapidly

5 Hulu.com, a joint venture controlled by NBC Universal and the Fox TV business of the News Corporation, started showing television **series** like "The Office," "Prison Break" and "24" this fall to online viewers in the United States.

6 Other Internet video services, including Joost, Blinkx and Babelgum, have started or are planning television like offerings from a variety of sources. YouTube, the Google-owned company that popularized home movie clips,

Eric Pfanner, "Web Sites Go Fishing in TV's Advertising Revenue Stream." From *The New York Times*, November 19, 2007. © 2007 The New York Times. All rights reserved. Used by permission and protected by the Copyright Laws of the United States. The printing, copying, redistribution, or retransmission of the Material without express written permission is prohibited. www.nytimes.com

© Pearson Education, Inc.

has been adding video material from **established** television providers, even as it tries to fend off allegations of copyright infringement from Viacom.

7   Social networking sites, which have some of the largest and fastest-growing audiences on the Internet, are also trying to get in the picture and **make a grab** for ad **revenue**. Bebo, a social network popular in Britain among teenagers and young **adults**, introduced a service last week that lets content partners show their videos, and ads, to Bebo users.

make a grab
to go after something

8   "The Internet is at an interesting stage—it's getting both more and less interactive," said John Barrett, **research** director at Parks Associates, a company in Dallas that studies the use of digital **technology**.

9   "At one end of the spectrum, you've got things like social networking. At the other end, there's more video that people just click, download and watch," Mr. Barrett said. "The **passive** end of the spectrum gets more like radio and TV every day, and that's an **environment** that advertisers are comfortable with."

10   But as with many **media** offerings on the Web, turning audiences into earnings is difficult. Internet users have come to expect online **media** to be free, so trying to charge for Web videos is probably futile, with the exception of live sports or high-profile movies. Instead, the predominant **revenue** producer for Web video will probably be advertising, experts say.

11   Many advertisers, particularly the makers of **consumer** goods that dominate television advertising, remain wary about the Internet, partly out of fear of undermining their brand **image** by associating with provocative Web fare.

12   While Procter & Gamble spends more than any other company on advertising offline, only about 1 **percent** of its ad budget was allocated to the Internet last year, according to eMarketer, a **research** firm.

13   And while many marketers have spent heavily on ads linked to searches on Google and other search engines, some mainstream brands have shied away from online **display** ads like banners. In the first half of 2007, the leading spenders on online **display** ads in the United States were Experian, the **consumer credit** reporting service, and NexTag, a comparison shopping site, according to Nielsen Online.

14   Could television-style video persuade more mainstream brands to embrace Internet advertising?

15   EMarketer estimates that by 2011 online video ads will generate $4.3 billion, or about 10 **percent**, of **overall** Internet ad **revenue** in the United States, up from $410 million, or 2.4 **percent**, last year.

16   Online video content and advertising will not necessarily grow at the same rates. On the Internet, unlike many **traditional media**, advertising formats can be mixed and matched.

17   While some advertisers are using television-style 15- or 30-second ads before, during or after a video program, such ads can also appear in the middle of a block of **text**. Joost, YouTube and other online video providers are using fixed advertising "overlays" that appear on part of a video screen from time to time, allowing users to click through to a marketer's Web **site** or advertising video.

18   Web video services say some of their advertising formats are more effective than other kinds of Internet ads, like banners. Suranga Chandratillake, chief executive of Blinkx, said that about 5 **percent** of viewers typically clicked on a video overlay ad; with banners, advertisers are lucky to get 1 **percent** of viewers to click through.

19   Joanna Lyall, who helps marketers plan digital ad strategies at Mindshare, a **media** buying agency owned by WPP Group, said that paid televisionlike spots might not be as effective as other, less conventional forms of Internet marketing. Some of the most memorable online ads have been videos that were posted on social sharing sites like YouTube, at no cost, but spread virally because of their entertainment quality.

20   "The reason advertising works online at the moment is because it's not like TV," she said. At the same time, with more and more people making their own clips and posting them on the Web, it is becoming harder for would-be rivals to be noticed, said Caroline Slootweg, the head of new **media** at Unilever.

21   "The days of just putting something up there and hoping it goes are pretty much over," she said.

Reading Comprehension Check

1. "Web sites have been 'draining the life out of newspapers and radio for years,' according to one of the founders of an Internet video site, and now they are going after the advertising revenue stream of television as well."

   It can be inferred from the above statement that
   a. newspapers and radio will regain their advertising revenue.
   b. Web sites have helped newspapers and radio increase their advertising revenue.
   c. TV's advertising revenue will be affected by Internet video sites.
   d. television will see exponential growth in its advertising revenue.

2. "And, although other Web sites may not have laid out the battleground quite as explicitly, their content is starting to look a lot more like traditional TV, including the commercials."

   Which of the following conclusions can be drawn from the above passage?
   a. Most Internet video sites are unaware of the potential of advertising online.
   b. Internet video sites understand that advertising online can be profitable.
   c. Other Web sites have no plans to compete with television commercials.
   d. The television industry is not concerned about the Internet's recent initiative.

3. What does the following statement suggest about the future of video on the Internet?

   "Video is proliferating on the Internet, and it is no longer limited to short clips of cats flushing toilets, breath mints reacting explosively with carbonated sodas and other user-generated content of the kind that captured the anarchic spirit of the early Web 2.0 days."
   a. Internet video sites will only show clips of cats flushing toilets and breath mints reacting explosively.
   b. Short video clips on the Internet were not popular among Web users.
   c. Internet video sites received a warm welcome from Web users.
   d. Internet video sites have no future.

© Pearson Education, Inc.

4. "YouTube, the Google-owned company that popularized home movie clips, has been adding video material from established television providers, even as it tries to fend off allegations of copyright infringement from Viacom."

   According to the passage, which of the following conclusions CANNOT be true?
   a. YouTube made home movie clips extremely popular.
   b. YouTube has begun to show video material from television providers.
   c. Viacom filed a lawsuit against YouTube for copyright infringement.
   d. YouTube signed a contractual agreement with Viacom to show its video material on the Internet.

5. "Social networking sites, which have some of the largest and fastest-growing audiences on the Internet, are also trying to get in the picture and make a grab for ad revenue."

   According to the passage, which of the following conclusions is logical?
   a. Social networking sites are losing their audiences.
   b. They are planning to charge their audiences to view their video content.
   c. Social networking sites believe that they can make inroads into the Internet advertising revenue stream.
   d. The number of Web users visiting social networking sites is fast decreasing.

6. What can be inferred from the following statement?

   "Internet users have come to expect online media to be free, so trying to charge for Web videos is probably futile, with the exception of live sports or high-profile movies."
   a. Most Web users are more than willing to pay for video material on the Internet.
   b. Internet video sites will have a difficult time charging their audiences for online media.
   c. Most Web sites will easily turn audiences into earnings by showing them catchy video content.
   d. Most Internet users usually prefer not to watch Web videos.

7. "Many advertisers, particularly the makers of consumer goods that dominate television advertising, remain wary about the Internet, partly out of fear of undermining their brand image by associating with provocative Web fare."

   Which of the following conclusions can be drawn from the above passage?
   a. Many advertisers are wholeheartedly embracing the Internet.
   b. Only the manufacturers of consumer goods are amenable to the idea of advertising on the Internet.
   c. Many advertisers feel comfortable promoting their products on television.
   d. Most of the advertisers are least concerned about their image.

8. "And while many marketers have spent heavily on ads linked to searches on Google and other search engines, some mainstream brands have shied away from online display ads like banners."

   Which of the following is a logical conclusion from the above passage?
   a. Most marketers avoid spending substantial amounts of money on advertising on the Internet.
   b. Some advertisers are wary of spending heavily on online banners.

c. Many advertisers prefer not to link their ads to search engines.

d. Some major companies are thrilled about banners.

9. "EMarketer estimates that by 2011 online video ads will generate $4.3 billion, or about 10 percent, of overall Internet ad revenue in the United States, up from $410 million, or 2.4 percent, last year."

According to the passage, it is logical to infer that

a. online video ads will not generate significant revue in the coming years.

b. EMarketer's prediction of Internet advertising revenue in 2011 is completely inaccurate.

c. more mainstream brands are likely to embrace Internet advertising in the next few years.

d. Internet advertising revenue will grow 10 percent every year.

10. "Joanna Lyall, who helps marketers plan digital ad strategies at Mindshare, a media buying agency owned by WPP Group, said that paid televisionlike spots might not be as effective as other, less conventional forms of Internet marketing."

A logical conclusion to draw from Joanna Lyall's statement is that

a. televisionlike commercials on the Internet will be more successful than commercials on traditional media.

b. paid commercials on the Internet will be less financially rewarding than those on television.

c. televisionlike spots will be as successful as those on traditional media.

d. online advertising revenue will grow more exponentially than television advertising revenue in the next few years.

Recommended debate topic: Should all companies be allowed to advertise online, or should the government regulate the types of businesses that are permitted to do Internet marketing?

Brainstorm some controversial topics related to e-commerce with your classmates and instructor for the debate activity.

Your suggested debate topics:

DEBATABLE TOPIC

a. _____

b. _____

c. _____

IM has more information about conducting a debate with your students.

Got a Search Engine Question? Ask Mr. Sullivan

Pre-Reading Questions

Before you read the following article, discuss these questions in small groups and share your answers with your classmates.

© Pearson Education, Inc.

Collaboration

1. Do you use search engines such as Google, Yahoo, and Dogpile? If yes, which search engine do you usually use to find information on the Internet? How does your favorite search engine compare with others?

2. What kind of information do you search for on the Internet? In your opinion, how reliable and accurate is the information search engines provide to Internet users?

3. Some critics think that search engines tend to be invasive, as they make people's personal information accessible to the public. Do you think the government should protect people's privacy and mandate what kind of information is made available to the Internet users?

Got a Search Engine Question? Ask Mr. Sullivan

By Jefferson Graham, *USA TODAY*

August 1, 2006

Danny Sullivan, who lives in a remote village about four hours from London, makes a living analyzing online search and organizing search conferences. The next one opens Monday in San Jose, Calif.

1   SALISBURY, England—Google's Matt Cutts considers Danny Sullivan's Search Engine Watch website "must reading." To Yahoo's Tim Mayer, it's simply the "most authoritative **source** on search."

2   His readers would naturally **assume** that Sullivan, the self-described "world-renowned search **authority**," is the ultimate Silicon Valley insider. He is. But he does it all some 4,000 miles away—near here, in the remote little village of Chitterne, about four hours southwest of London.

Jefferson Graham, "Got a Search Engine Question? Ask Mr. Sullivan," *USA Today*, August 1, 2006. Reprinted with permission.

3   When the world he writes about arrives at work in Silicon Valley, Sullivan has just finished dinner with his wife and two boys. He then retires to his den, parks himself in front of three **computer** monitors and spends the remaining evening hours trying to decipher the mystery of how online search engines rank listings.

4   "That he can do what he does from so far away is just wild," says Cutts, a Google engineer who is a regular on Sullivan's online podcasts.

5   The website takes up much of Sullivan's time. But his biggest **income** producer is the Search Engine **Strategies conference** (SES), which he stages six times a year. The next one opens in Silicon Valley's San Jose, Calif., on Monday. The conferences attract 1,500 to 6,000 attendees who pay nearly $2,000 each to hear tips about how to get websites to the top of search queries.

6   Sullivan's conferences attract some of the search industry's biggest players. Next week's **features** an address by Google CEO Eric Schmidt. Past sessions attracted IAC/InterActive CEO Barry Diller, Yahoo co-founder Jerry Yang and Google founders Sergey Brin and Larry Page.

7   SES is attended by owners of small and large businesses, their employees and independent operators who call themselves search engine optimizers. SEOs work with companies to make their websites more likely to be found on Google and rival Yahoo.

8   Sullivan says SES attracts executives in newly created positions for vice presidents of search at companies such as Coca-Cola, Citigroup and *The New York Times.*

9   For smaller ventures, the type of information discussed at SES is "life or death" advice, says Rand Fishkin, CEO of SEOmoz.org, a Seattle SEO firm.

10   "If I'm a small company and get five inquiries a day from people who found me in search engines, suddenly I am lifted out of obscurity and in the **prime** real **estate** for this new way of advertising," he says.

11   The search advertising market—those little **text** ads **published** near search listings—is one of the fastest-growing areas of advertising. It's expected to grow to $26 billion in 2010 from $17.4 billion this year, according to market tracker Forrester **Research.**

Falling into a new industry

12   Sullivan, 40, says he shares common roots with employees at Google and Yahoo, even though he works thousands of miles away. He recalled his life over a lunch of soup and crisps (potato chips) at a small pub on a tiny, lush country lane with lots of sheep and barely enough room for one car.

13   He was born and raised in Newport Beach, Calif. After graduating from the University of California, Irvine, he spent a year in England, where he was hired by the BBC to type articles for reporters.

14   He met his future wife, Lorna, at the BBC. They married and moved back to California, where Sullivan worked at the *Los Angeles Times* and *The Orange County Register* in their graphics departments.

15   Then search came into his life. At the time, a friend had put up a website and couldn't make sense of how to be found in search listings. Sullivan

© Pearson Education, Inc.

tried to help him and was so successful, he went to work with his friend help-ing others with their sites.

16   Meanwhile, Lorna missed home, and Sullivan agreed to leave California behind for this village near her family. Chitterne is so small that it got high-speed Internet **access** only last year.

17   While trying to figure out what to do for a **job** in England, he posted a Web page with tips for how to rise to the top of search engine results. **Response** was so great, he decided to turn his Web page into an online resource. That was in 1996. "And I've never looked back since," Sullivan says.

18   Within a year, he sold his website for an undisclosed price to Meckler-Media (now Jupitermedia), which kept him on as an independent contractor and expanded into trade shows. The business was sold again this year to Inci-sive **Media** for $43 million.

19   Sullivan is still a contractor, but he profits from the trade shows, based on attendance.

20   Yahoo's Mayer, a product manager in the search division, remembers attending Sullivan's earliest shows, when just a few hundred came. These days, "It's just insane," he says. "I'm always amazed at how many people now attend. It just shows how many people are making their living through search engine advertising."

21   On top of the ticket prices, the conferences also attract other **fees** from sponsorships and exhibitions, starting at about $5,000.

22   Rory Brown, who oversees the show as managing director for Incisive, says Sullivan has nothing to do with that side of the business. The sepa-ration between editorial and business "is carefully guarded," Brown says. Sullivan has completely free rein "to program the **conference** however he wishes."

23   Sullivan says he likes it this way. "I would hate having to call Google and ask them to sponsor the show. It would be too much of a **conflict**."

24   Sullivan says he has no regrets about selling Search Engine Watch be-fore companies such as Google and Yahoo became household names and started generating billions of dollars in **revenue**.

25   "The sale did not make me a millionaire, but it helped me into a new house, and I've done well by the **site** and **conference** since," he says.

No illusions about fame

harbors no illusions
has no wrong ideas about something

26   He may not have a fortune, but in his own little world, "Danny is the rock star of our industry," says Brown, who sells him that way to **potential** attendees of shows.

niche
a job or activity that is perfect for the skills, abilities, and character that you have

27   Sullivan holds well-attended Q&A sessions, where he takes questions from the audience for several hours.

28   But he **harbors no illusions** about how large his **niche** fame actually is.

get swamped
be overwhelmed with, have too much to handle

29   "Sure, you can **get swamped** at the show," he says. "A lot of people want to talk to you. But then I'll stand next to Matt Cutts, and he'll get masses of people **vying for** his attention."

vying for
competing for the same thing

30   Sullivan calls this fame within a small group of people. "Here in England, where people ask what I do, and I tell them about search marketing, they respond with **a blank stare**. That says it all."

a blank stare
indication of uncertainty of what is being said

Reading Comprehension Check

1. "Google's Matt Cutts considers Danny Sullivan's Search Engine Watch Web site 'must reading.' To Yahoo's Tim Mayer, it's simply the 'most authoritative source on search.'"

   Which of the following conclusions can be drawn from the passage?
   a. Danny Sullivan's Web site is specifically designed for students enrolled in remedial reading courses.
   b. His Web site is authoritarian.
   c. Yahoo's Tim Mayer has formed a strategic alliance with Danny Sullivan.
   d. The information the Search Engine Watch Web site provides is reliable.

2. "His readers would naturally assume that Sullivan, the self-described 'world-renowned search authority,' is the ultimate Silicon Valley insider. He is. But he does it all some 4,000 miles away—near here, in the remote little village of Chitterne, about four hours southwest of London."

   According to the passage, which of the conclusions CANNOT be true?
   a. Danny Sullivan is a Silicon Valley insider.
   b. Sullivan flies 4000 miles to his office in Silicon Valley, California from London to meet with his clients.
   c. Sullivan does most of his work in a little-known village in England.
   d. He describes himself as the "world-renowned search authority."

3. What can be inferred from the following statement?

   "The [SES] conferences attract 1,500 to 6,000 attendees who pay nearly $2,000 each to hear tips about how to get websites to the top of search queries."
   a. Attendees do not find the SES conferences worth their while.
   b. Sullivan's Search Engine Watch Web site is not a profitable enterprise.
   c. These attendees believe that the information they receive at the conferences will help them make their Web sites more accessible to the Internet users.
   d. The SES conferences are a losing proposition.

4. What does the following statement suggest about smaller businesses?

   "'If I'm a small company and get five inquiries a day from people who found me in search engines, suddenly I am lifted out of obscurity and in the prime real estate for this new way of advertising,' he says."
   a. People have difficulty finding smaller businesses on the Internet.
   b. Most search engines usually ignore smaller companies.
   c. Smaller companies largely depend on search engines to be recognized by potential customers.
   d. People find smaller businesses without using search engines.

5. "The search advertising market—those little text ads published near search listings—is one of the fastest-growing areas of advertising. It's expected to grow to $26 billion in 2010 from $17.4 billion this year, according to market tracker Forrester Research."

   Which of the following inferences can be made from this projection?
   a. Forrester Research believes that the search advertising market will continue to decline in the coming years.
   b. The market for Internet advertising will most likely shrink rapidly.

© Pearson Education, Inc.

(c.) The market tracker company thinks that the search advertising market will grow exponentially in the future.

d. Forrester Researcher's projection cannot be trusted.

6. "Meanwhile, Lorna missed home, and Sullivan agreed to leave California behind for this village near her family. Chitterne is so small that it got high-speed Internet access only last year."

A logical conclusion drawn from this passage is that

a. Sullivan left California because he was not getting along with his clients in Silicon Valley.

(b.) Sullivan cares about Lorna's feelings.

c. Sullivan and Lorna did not have a comfortable house in California.

d. Sullivan moved to Chitterne because of high-speed Internet access.

7. Which of the conclusions listed below can be drawn from the following statement?

"While trying to figure out what to do for a job in England, he posted a Web page with tips for how to rise to the top of search engine results. Response was so great, he decided to turn his Web page into an online resource."

a. Sullivan's tips on search engine results were poorly received.

(b.) Sullivan's tips on search engine results were well received.

c. Sullivan got most of his ideas for his Web page from his wife.

d. Most smaller businesses could care less about search engine results.

8. "Within a year, he sold his website for an undisclosed price to MecklerMedia (now Jupitermedia), which kept him on as an independent contractor and expanded into trade shows."

It can be inferred from the passage that MecklerMedia maintained its business relation with Sullivan because

a. it incurred huge losses after buying his Web site.

b. it paid a very small amount of money to Sullivan for his Web site.

(c.) the company thought it could use Sullivan's expertise to generate revenue.

d. Sullivan resisted the idea of the company's expansion into trade shows.

9. "Sullivan says he has no regrets about selling Search Engine Watch before companies such as Google and Yahoo became household names and started generating billions of dollars in revenue."

Based on this passage, we can conclude that

a. Sullivan has second thoughts about selling his popular Web site.

b. Sullivan wishes he had not sold Search Engine Watch.

(c.) Sullivan is satisfied with his decision to sell Search Engine Watch.

d. Sullivan wonders if his Web site could have generated billions of dollars in revenue.

10. "Sullivan calls this fame within a small group of people. 'Here in England, where people ask what I do, and I tell them about search marketing, they respond with a blank stare. That says it all.'"

It can be inferred from Mr. Sullivan's statement that

a. he is extremely popular in England.

(b.) most people in England are not aware of what Mr. Sullivan does for a living.

c. he is the rock star of the search marketing industry in England.

d. Mr. Sullivan has reached the status of a cult figure in England.

From Reading to Writing: How to Write Better Memos

The following is by Harold K. Mintz, as it appeared in *Strategies for Business and Technical Writing*, Fifth Edition, ed. Kevin J. Harty.

Memos—interoffice, intershop, interdepartmental—are the most important medium of in-house communication. This article suggests ways to help you sharpen your memos so that they will more effectively inform, instruct, and sometimes persuade your coworkers.

Memos are informal, versatile, free-wheeling. In-house they go up, down or sideways. They can even go to customers, suppliers, and other interested outsiders. They can run to ten pages or more, but are mostly one to three pages. (Short memos are preferable. Typed single-space and with double-space between paragraphs, Lincoln's Gettysburg Address easily fits on one page, and the Declaration of Independence on two pages.) They can be issued on a one-shot basis or in a series, on a schedule or anytime at all. They can cover major or minor subjects.

Primary functions of memos encompass, but are not limited to:

- Informing people of a problem or situation.
- Nailing down responsibility for action, and a deadline for it.
- Establishing a file record of decisions, agreements and policies.

Secondary functions include:

- Serving as a basis for formal reports.
- Helping to bring new personnel up-to-date.
- Replacing personal contact with people you cannot get along with. For example, the Shubert brothers, tyrannical titans of the American theatre for 40 years, often refused to talk to each other. They communicated by memo.
- Handling people who ignore your oral directions. Concerning the State Department, historian Arthur Schlesinger quoted JFK as follows: "I have discovered finally that the best way to deal with State is to send over memos. They can forget phone conversations, but a memorandum is something which, by their system, has to be answered."

Memos can be used to squelch unjustified time-consuming requests. When someone makes what you consider to be an unwarranted demand or request, tell him to put it in a memo—just for the record. This tactic can save you much time.

Organization of the Memo

Memos and letters are almost identical twins. They differ in the following ways: Memos normally remain in-house, memos don't usually need to "hook" the reader's interest, and memos covering a current situation can skip a background treatment.

© Pearson Education, Inc.

ESL Annotation

4.8 ESL Many ESL students come from cultures where the expectation is to use formal salutations and very formal language in professional communications. The proper business etiquette in the US is clearly worth some class focus

Overall organization of a memo should ensure that it answer three basic questions concerning its subject:

- What are the facts?
- What do they mean?
- What do we do now?

To supply the answers, a memo needs some or all of the following elements: summary, conclusions and recommendations, introduction, statement of problem, proposed solution, and discussion. Incidentally, these elements make excellent headings to break up the text and guide the readers.

In my opinion, every memo longer than a page should open with a summary, preferably a short paragraph. Thus, recipients can decide in seconds whether they want to read the entire memo.

Two reasons dictate placing the summary at the very beginning. There, of all places, you have the reader's undivided attention. Second, readers want to know, quickly, the meaning or significance of the memo.

Obviously, a summary cannot provide all the facts (see Question 1, above), but it should capsule their meaning, and highlight a course of action.

When conclusions and recommendations are not applicable, forget them. When they are, however, you can insert them either right after the abstract or at the end of the memo. Here's one way to decide: If you expect readers to be neutral or favorable toward your conclusions and recommendations, put them up front. If you expect a negative reaction, put them at the end. Then, conceivably, your statement of the problem and your discussion of it may swing readers around to your side by the time they reach the end.

The introduction should give just enough information for the readers to be able to understand the statement of the problem and its discussion.

Literary Qualities

A good memo need not be a Pulitzer Prize winner, but it does need to be clear, brief, relevant. LBJ got along poorly with his science adviser, Donald Hornig, because Hornig's memos, according to a White House staffer, "were terribly long and complicated. The President couldn't read through a page or two and understand what Don wanted him to do, so he'd send it out to us and ask us what it was all about. Then we'd put a short cover-memo on top of it and send it back in. The President got mad as hell at long memos that didn't make any sense."

Clarity is paramount. Returning to the asterisked sentence in the second paragraph of the introduction, I could have said: "Memoranda are endowed with the capability of internal perpendicular and lateral deployment." Sheer unadulterated claptrap.

To sum up, be understandable and brief, but not brusque, and get to the point.

Another vitally important trait is a personal, human approach. Remember that your memos reach members of your own organization; that's a common bond worth exploiting. Your memos should provide them with the pertinent information they need (no more and no less) and in the language they understand. Feel free to use people's names, and personal pronouns and adjectives: you-your, we-our, I-mine. Get people into the act; it's they who do the work.

Lastly, a well-written memo should reflect diplomacy or political savvy. More than once, Hornig's memos lighted the fuse of LBJ's temper. One memo, regarded as criticizing James E. Webb (then the head of NASA), LBJ's friend, infuriated the President.

Another example of a politically naive memo made headlines in England three years ago. A hospital superintendent wrote a memo to his staff, recommending that aged and chronically ill patients should not be resuscitated after heart failure. Public reaction exploded so overwhelmingly against the superintendent that shock waves even shook Prime Minister Wilson's cabinet. Result? The Health Ministry torpedoed the recommendation.

Two other courses of action would have been more tactful for the superintendent: make the recommendation orally to his staff or, if he insisted on a memo, stamp it "private" and distribute it accordingly.

Literary style is a **nebulous** subject, difficult to pin down. Yet if you develop a clear, taut way of writing, you may end up in the same happy predicament as Lawrence of Arabia. He wrote "a violent memorandum" on a British-Arab problem, a memo whose "acidity and force" so impressed the commanding general that he wired it to London. Lawrence noted in his *Seven Pillars of Wisdom* that, "My popularity with the military staff in Egypt, due to the sudden help I had lent . . . was novel and rather amusing. They began to be polite to me, and to say that I was observant, with a **pungent** style. . . ."

nebulous
hazy, vague, indistinct, or confused

pungent
sharply affecting the organs of taste and smell

Format of the Memo

Except for minor variations, the format to be used is standard. The memo dispenses with the addresses, salutations, and complimentary closes used in letters. Although format is a minor matter, it does rate some remarks.

To and From Lines—Names and departments are enough.

Subject—Capture its essence in ten words or less. Any subject that drones on for three or four lines may confuse or irritate readers.

Distribution—Send the memo only to people involved or interested in the subject matter. If they number less than say, ten, list them alphabetically on page 1; if more than ten, put them at the end.

Text—Use applicable headings listed after the three questions under "Organization."

Paragraphs—If numbering or lettering them helps in any way, do it.

Line Spacing—Single space within paragraphs, and double space between.

Underlines and Capitals—Used sparingly, they emphasize important points.

Number of Pages—Some companies impose a one-page limit, but it's an impractical restriction because some subjects just won't fit on one page. As a result, the half-baked memo requires a second or third memo to beef it up.

Figures and Tables—Use them; they'll enhance the impact of your memos.

© Pearson Education, Inc.

Conclusions

Two cautions are appropriate. First, avoid writing memos that baffle people, like the one that Henry Luce once sent to an editor of *Time*. "There are only 30,000,000 sheep in the U.S.A.—same as 100 years ago. What does this prove? Answer???"

Second, avoid "memo-itis," the tendency to dash off memos at the drop of a pen, especially to the boss. In his book, *With Kennedy*, Pierre Salinger observed that "a constant stream of memoranda" from Professor Arthur Schlesinger caused JFK to be "impatient with their length and frequency."

Sample Memorandum

Read the sample memorandum below carefully. You will be asked later to write your own memo, so pay attention to the format and organization of the memorandum as you read the document.

MEMORANDUM

TO: Investor Relations
FROM: Melanie Edwards
DATE: September 23, 2007
SUBJ: Annual Meeting

Our fiscal year is coming to an end, and our editing team is proofreading the 2007 Annual Report for accuracy and distribution.

Please verify the mailing addresses of all of our shareholders and send the Annual Report to them no later than September 30. Be sure that the Annual Report includes the proxy form for the upcoming elections of Board of Directors and CFO.

If you have any questions about the annual meeting or have suggestions, please do not hesitate to contact me via e-mail or phone.

cc: Kate Craig, CFO
        David Demarcos, President
        Tom Rothman, Vice President

EXERCISE 4

Writing a Memo

Pretend that you are Danny Sullivan, and you are organizing a Search Engine Strategies conference (SES) in a major city. You want as many CEOs of large businesses to attend your conference as possible since they will be your paying customers. Write a memo to your employees, asking them to contribute exciting business ideas to make the upcoming conference attractive to your prospective clients. As you write your memo, adhere to the format and organization of the document.

Connecting Reading Skills with Standardized Testing

Making Inferences

Most standardized reading exams include questions on inferences and logical conclusions. These questions test your ability to differentiate between true and false statements and arrive at a logical conclusion based on the reading passage. You can tell the question is inference-based when it is phrased as:

- A conclusion that can be drawn from . . .
- Based on the passage, which of the following conclusions is logical?
- According to the passage, which of the following conclusions cannot be true?
- It can be concluded from the above passage that . . . It can be inferred from the passage that . . .

Remember that inferences are based on facts, not on opinion. In other words, you are to draw a logical conclusion based on the facts and details presented in the passage.

Helpful Hints: Test Questions on Making Inferences

Here are a few tips on drawing a logical conclusion from a passage:

- Focus on the facts and details presented in the passage. Pay close attention to the facts. Also, the details are clues that will lead you to a logical conclusion.
- Read each of the choices carefully and think of them as true/false questions. After reading each question, ask yourself if it is a true or false statement.
- After reading the choices, reread the passage to see how many of them are true or false. Refer to the passage again to differentiate between true and false statements. You will notice that false statements are not mentioned in the passage.
- Avoid forming your own opinion and pay close attention to what is stated in the passage. Your opinion is just that—your opinion. Focus on what is presented in the passage.
- Use your background knowledge of the topic to arrive at a correct conclusion. Sometimes the facts are not directly stated. Instead, they are implied, and you will need to rely on your knowledge of the topic to make the correct inference.

© Pearson Education, Inc.

Textbook Application

The following reading is taken from an introductory book on Internet Marketing. The purpose of this reading exercise is to give you an opportunity to practice reading authentic text and apply what you have learned. Read the chapter excerpt carefully and answer the multiple-choice questions that follow.

READING

Reading Selection **5**

Textbook Reading

4.9 Flesch-Kincaid Grade Level 8.3

Types of Businesses, Types of Sites: Introduction to E-Commerce

Business Web Sites: B2C, B2B, C2C

Sites that market or sell products and services, whether order-takers or more person-oriented, generally fall into one of three business Web **categories**: business-to-**consumer**, business-to-business, or **consumer**-to-**consumer**. Some sell to both consumers and businesses.

BUSINESS-TO-CONSUMER SITES (B2C)

Business-to-**consumer** sites are probably the ones most familiar to the Web-using public. These sites, in almost every possible industry, market goods and services to you. Many stores—department, variety, books, cars, fabric, music, electronics, clothing, food, hardware, and many other types—that you know from in-person experience also have **Web** sites to sell merchandise. Other business-to-**consumer** sites have no "brick-and-mortar" facilities; they sell exclusively over the Internet. And not all business-to-**consumer** sites sell online. Some of them market goods and services that consumers **purchase** by telephone or from a local store or office. Examples include amazon.com and barnes&noble.com (books and related **items**), bloomingdales.com and nordstrom.com (department stores), pontiac.com and lincoln.com (vehicles), staples.com and officemax.com (office supplies), and a host of others.

How much selling do business-to-**consumer** sites carry out? U.S. consumers spent $10.8 billion online in 2000, a 54 **percent** increase over the $7 billion spent in 1999, according to a **survey** by online **research** firm Jupiter **Media** Metrix. During the 2000 holiday season, about 36 million consumers purchased online and spent an average of $304. About 35 **percent** of online buyers surveyed said they shopped at so-called "pure play" (sell **solely** online) retailers, while 37 **percent** said they shopped online with companies that also have **physical** stores or catalog services.

Tower Group projects that, by 2005, **consumer**-to-business (C2B) payments online will **exceed** 31 billion transactions—nearly eight times the projected person-to-person sales **volume** for that year. Tower expects the

From Barbara G. Cox and William Koelzer, *Internet Marketing* (NetEffect Series), 1st ed., pp. 10–15, © 2004. Reproduced in print and electronic formats by permission of Pearson Education, Inc., Upper Saddle River, New Jersey.

C2B market to account for 88 **percent** of **consumer**-initiated online payments and 68 **percent** of **corresponding** value.

According to NFO Interactive's (NFO) report, *The 2000 Online Retail Monitor*, in the United States, 42 **percent** of online shoppers are men and 52 **percent** are women. (The remaining 6 **percent** are not identified.) Eighty **percent** of all U.S. Internet users have participated in at least one transaction online. NFO also reports that one-fourth of the online shopping population in the United States accounts for three-fourths of all online purchases. The remaining 75 **percent** of online shoppers **purchase** less frequently and tend to buy less expensive **items**. eMarketer concluded that in 2000, 37 **percent** of online shoppers were "regular buyers" who **purchase items** online at least every three months; 62.7 percent were buyers who bought at least one item online within the previous year.

Online shopping is increasing in part simply because the number of household computers is growing. A recent Employment **Policy Foundation** (EPF) report indicated that 51 **percent** (54.5 million) of U.S. households have at least one **computer**. Of those households 43.5 million have Internet **access**. The EPF predicts that by November 2002, 68 million U.S. households will have computers, and 66 million will also have Internet access.

Many high-ticket **items** are now purchased with online help. According to automotive industry **research** company Polk (http://www.polk.com), 60 **percent** of U.S. car buyers used the Internet to help with their **purchase** in 2000—up from 46 **percent** in 1999.

BUSINESS-TO-BUSINESS SITES (B2B)

The B2B market is growing at an astonishing rate. **Despite** the **economic** downturn at the beginning of 2001 and a generally gloomy outlook for the dot-world at that time, companies around the globe will increase their spending on business-to-business (B2B) e-marketplaces (exchanges, auctions, etc.) from U.S. $2.6 billion in 2000 to $137.2 billion by 2005, according to Jupiter **Research**. Goldman Sachs' estimates are more aggressive: it predicts that worldwide B2B spending will reach $4,500 billion by 2005—out of total online commerce spending of $60 trillion by that year. **Furthermore**, Goldman Sachs expects that 80 **percent** of B2B commerce worldwide will be conducted online over the next 20 years.

According to ActivMedia **Research**, "Most B-to-B websites are **established** for a dual purpose: to both sell products and services, either directly or indirectly (98%), and to provide information (73%). The **primary** means for creating a sale for 77% of sites is by stimulating customers to make an offline **contact**. Most B-to-B sites also provide pre-sale support and purchasing information (62%) and generate leads for staff to follow-up (60%) as ways to make a sale through their website."

The same article claims the following B2B **site function** proportions:

- 33 **percent** of B2B sites market, but do not sell, products online
- 25 **percent** of B2B sites offer **professional** services
- 15 **percent** of B2B sites sell products at the **site** to business end-users

© Pearson Education, Inc.

AUCTION TIP!	**BE SPECIFIC**

To a great extent, a firm's success with auction sites depends on how clearly it describes product functions, **features**, and benefits—not only from a **technical** standpoint, but from a marketing **perspective** as well.

TIP!	**TORTURED TERMINOLOGY**

The terms *e-marketplace*, *B2B exchange* **site** and, frequently, *B2B auction site* were **virtually** interchangeable in the Spring of 2001, because many e-marketplace sites (designed specifically for businesses to sell to businesses) each **incorporated** many different selling methods. These methods ranged from simple buy/sell transactions to open auction, bid or sealed auction, barter, and other forms of commerce. The prevalent term, however, was *B2B exchange,* with *e-marketplace* becoming the generic term for any site dealing as a platform for B2B selling.

B2B SELLING ON AUCTION SITES

B2B auctions require precision of product description and specifications. Auction sites cannot succeed unless suppliers are clear about the products or services a buyer needs and the terms under which they are to be delivered. Many industrial products are technically **complex**. Many large exchange sites work closely with members of each client's purchasing organization to help specify their needs in detail and communicate them clearly to bidders before each auction.

B2B auction sites vary widely. Some are narrowly focused, such as TekSell.com (http://www.teksell.com), which provides an online marketplace for serious IT (information **technology**) professionals to buy and sell new, remanufactured, and previously owned data, video, and voice **equipment**. Another niche auction/exchange site is operated by Tradeloop Corporation (http://www.tradeloop.com), an online marketplace for **computer** resellers, value-added resellers (VARs), brokers, and distributors.

Although most B2B auction sites operate in narrowly defined business segments, some span several broad segments. A pioneer in this realm is FreeMarkets (http://www.freemarkets.com). The firm conducts online auctions for industrial parts, raw materials, commodities, and services. In these auctions, suppliers compete in real time for the **purchase** orders of large buying organizations by lowering their prices until the auction is closed.

E-MARKETPLACES—B2B EXCHANGE SITES

While the year 2000 saw thousands of exchange sites appear almost overnight, the numbers **diminished** quickly. According to eMarketer (http://www.emarketer.com) analyst Steve Burtler, "Deloitte Consulting pegs the total at 1,500 exchanges worldwide, predicting that less than 500 will remain in three years' time. Forrester **Research** believes that only 181 B2B exchanges will exist by 2003."

According to an October 2000 report by The Boston Consulting Group (BCG), total U.S. e-marketplace revenues will **approach** $9 billion in the next four to five years, pointing to solid long-term **revenue** prospects for **individual** e-marketplaces. "In five years' time, e-market-places serving America's largest industries should be expected to gener-ate $350 million to $450 million in **annual** revenues, while e-marketplaces in most other industries will generate revenues of much less than $100 million. Only a small number of top performers will be able to **exceed** these **revenue** projections," says BCG in its report, "The B2B Opportunity: Creating Advantage Through E-Marketplaces." BCG also forecasts that, by 2004, business-to-business e-commerce will gener-ate productivity gains **equivalent** to 1 to 2 **percent** of sales; by 2010, this figure could grow to 6 **percent**, or roughly $1 trillion. **Nonetheless**, the market will only support one to three major e-marketplaces within any given industry segment.

"Today, there are more than 700 e-marketplaces currently in operation. Most of them face an uphill battle to **survive**," says BCG Vice President Jim Andrew. "**Ultimately**, the U.S. B2B market will be characterized by a handful of e-marketplace giants that serve the **overall** needs of an industry; and scores of niche players serving a special segment within an industry or providing a specialized **function** across many industries."

BCG notes that, in order to **survive** among so many competitors, e-marketplaces (B2B exchanges) will need to prove to **potential** participants that they have staying power and offer the best opportunity to maximize competitive advantage. BCG's report outlines five success **factors** that e-marketplaces need to **create** the critical mass or liquidity **required** of a viable business:

- Leave room for companies to differentiate themselves
- Stay cost-effective and focused on execution
- Clearly communicate to buyers and sellers the value that the e-market-place creates
- Extend the offering to **medium** and small companies
- Be flexible about changing the business model

BCG's report, titled "The U.S. B2B Landscape Through 2004," is avail-able in PDF **format** online at http://www.bcg.com/publications/files/ B2BResearch.pdf.

What do you need to do if you intend to sell through online ex-changes? Carefully review those serving your industry to be sure that the one or more that you choose will **survive** an exchange shakeout, should that happen. How? Talk to other firms that appear in those sites, interview owners of such sites, read industry news on e-marketplace sites, and talk to the executive directors of trade associations that serve your **target** audiences'

© Pearson Education, Inc.

industries. A B2B yellow pages (http://www.B2Byellowpages.com) helps users locate B2B Web sites. Its directory allows businesses to **aggregate**, locate, and publicize Web sites to other businesses.

CONSUMER TO CONSUMER (C2C)

CONSUMER AUCTION SITES

Most **consumer**-to-**consumer** sales take place through auction sites. In a Harris Interactive **survey** sponsored by The National Consumers League (NCL; see http://www.natlconsumersleague.org), 83 **percent** of online auction bidders have bought something in an online auction. The report says that 75 **percent** of those buyers have spent an average $100 or less, and 21 **percent** have spent between $101 and $500.

In general, auction sites are just what you think they are. Sellers post **items** to sell and buyers post bids on them. The highest bidder wins the item that is for sale, assuming the bid meets an **established minimum** amount. The auction **site** takes a small **commission** from the seller's **credit** card account for each item sold. Buyers generally pay nothing to the auction **site** itself.

EBAY

The largest C2C auction **site** today is eBay at http://www.eBay.com. It has been the model for auction sites that followed, including many now emerging to help *businesses* **conduct** e-commerce. Even though eBay is primarily a C2C service, its simplicity is well worth study by any business planning to buy or sell products in a B2B auction **site**.

At eBay and most other auction sites, users register and, if they intend to sell on the site, set up a means of payment, typically a **credit** card or a **financial** account enabling transfers of **funds**. Buyers explore a directory of **categories** or enter identifying words into the site's search engine and the **site** displays a list of such products for sale. Sellers pay for listing and selling **items**. eBay charges an insertion fee, usually between 25 cents and $2.00, depending on the opening bid, and a fee at the end of the auction, ranging from 1.25 **percent** to 5 **percent** of the **final** selling price. Additional **fees** also apply for enhancements such as bold font or featured placement. See http://pages.ebay.com/help/sellerguide/selling-**fees**.html for a complete explanation.

In November 2001, we searched for "scissors" and eBay displayed a list of 851 (up from 729 the **previous** June) auctions with the word "scissors" in the title and 3,876 (up from 2,965 the **previous** June) auctions with "scissors" in either the title or the description or both (Fig. 1.2). Most B2B exchange sites **function** much like eBay, although many B2B auctions are not conducted within a fixed time frame.

eBay's tutorial is excellent. Businesses planning to buy or sell in a B2B auction or exchange **site** will **benefit** by having the planning staff review the tutorial and even buy and sell some **items** on eBay. They will become familiar with the basic auction **process**, but will do so at far less monetary risk than they would incur in large "for-real" transactions involving B2B **items** costing thousands of dollars.

Reading Comprehension Check

Vocabulary in Context

1. As used in the sentence "Many stores—department, variety, books, cars, fabric, music, electronics, clothing, food, hardware, and many other types—that you know from in-person experience also have Web sites to sell merchandise," the word *merchandise* means
   a. refined goods.
   b. agricultural produce.
   (c.) products.
   d. Internet sites.

Vocabulary in Context

2. "Other business-to-consumer sites have no "brick-and-mortar" facilities; they sell exclusively over the Internet." (p. 228)

   The term *brick-and-mortar* could be replaced with
   (a.) physical entity.
   b. real estate Web sites.
   c. Information Technology.
   d. customer service.

Vocabulary in Context

3. In the sentence "Tower Group projects that, by 2005, consumer-to-business (C2B) payments online will exceed 31 billion transactions—nearly eight times the projected person-to-person sales volume for that year," a synonym for the word *exceed* is
   a. deteriorate.
   (b.) surpass.
   c. decline.
   d. regress.

Vocabulary in Context

4. As used in the sentence "A recent Employment Policy Foundation (EPF) report indicated that 51 percent (54.5 million) of U.S. households have at least one computer," an antonym for the word *indicated* is
   a. demonstrated.
   b. exaggerated.
   (c.) suggested.
   d. concealed.

Main Idea

5. What is the main point of the following passage?

   "Despite the economic downturn at the beginning of 2001 and a generally gloomy outlook for the dot-world at that time, companies around the globe will increase their spending on business-to-business (B2B) e-marketplace (exchanges, auctions, etc.) from U.S. $2.6 billion in 2000 to $137.2 billion by 2005, according to Jupiter Research." (p. 229)
   a. The chances of B2B sites generating significant revenue are slim.
   (b.) Companies are spending substantial amounts of money on B2B e-marketplace because they believe it will maximize their profits.
   c. These companies are increasing their spending because of the economic downturn in 2001.
   d. B2B sites project a gloomy outlook for Internet marketing.

© Pearson Education, Inc.

Inference

6. Goldman Sachs predicts that "worldwide B2B spending will reach $4,500 billion by 2005 out of total online commerce spending of $60 trillion by that year. Furthermore, Goldman Sachs expects that 80 percent of B2B commerce worldwide will be conducted outline over the next 20 years." (p. 229)

It can be inferred from the above passage that
a. B2B commerce will collapse after 20 years.
b. only 20 percent of B2B worldwide will be conducted online after 20 years.
c. online B2B commerce will grow exponentially in the next 20 years.
d. Goldman Sachs is a B2B company.

Inference

7. Active Media Research states, "Most B-to-B websites are established for a dual purpose: to both sell products and services, either directly or indirectly (98%) and to provide information (73%)." (p. 229)

Which of the following conclusions can be drawn from the above statement?
a. Active Media Research owns many B2B Web sites.
b. Most B2B Web sites are primarily concerned with product sales.
c. Some B2B Web sites focus more on services.
d. Most B2B Web sites have two main purposes.

Main Idea

8. "B2B auctions require precision of product description and specifications. Auction sites cannot succeed unless suppliers are clear about the products or services a buyer needs and the terms under which they are to be delivered." (p. 230)

The main point of the above passage is that
a. most auction sites provide vague product description and specifications.
b. the success of many auction sites depends on unclear product description.
c. it is pivotal for the success of auction sites to provide accurate and detailed product description.
d. auction sites are not concerned about buyer needs.

Inference

9. "Although most B2B auction sites operate in narrowly defined business segments, some span several broad segments." (p. 230)

It can be concluded from the statement that
a. most B2B auction sites provide a wide array of products and services.
b. only a few auction sites operate in narrow segments.
c. most B2B auction sites are narrowly focused.
d. very few auction sites are profitable.

Supporting Details

10. According to eMarketer analyst, "less than 500 [exchanges] will remain in three years' time. Forrester Research believes that only 181 B2B exchanges will exist by 2003." (p. 231)

The Forrester Research prediction is used as an example to illustrate that
a. B2B exchange sites have robust sales.
b. most exchange sites will flourish in three years.

c. more than 50 percent of B2B exchange sites will go out of business in three years.

d. the number of B2B exchange sites will quadruple in three years.

Main Idea

11. BCG Vice President Jim Andrew predicts, "Today, there are more than 700 e-marketplaces currently in operation. Most of them face an uphill battle to survive. Ultimately, the U.S. B2B market will be characterized by a handful of e-marketplace giants that serve the overall needs of an industry, and scores of niche players serving a special segment within an industry or providing a specialized function across many industries."

Mr. Andrew's main idea in the above statement is that

a. most B2B companies will grow at least tenfold in the coming years.

b. most of the e-marketplaces will cease to exist.

c. executives of B2B companies will climb many hills.

d. these executives will fight their competitors in the battlefield.

Inference

12. What does the following passage suggest about how B2B exchanges can survive?

"BCG notes that, in order to survive among so many competitors, e-marketplaces (B2B exchanges) will need to prove to potential participants that they have staying power and offer the best opportunity to maximize competitive advantage."

a. They need to demonstrate the ability to concede to their competitors.

b. B2B exchanges must offer major discounts to the participants.

c. They must prove to the participants that they can thrive in a competitive market.

d. Most e-marketplaces do not need to worry about losing business to their competitors.

Inference

13. "What do you need to do if you intend to sell through online exchanges? Carefully review those serving your industry to be sure that the one or more that you choose will survive an exchange shakeout should that happen."

Which of the following conclusions can be drawn from the above passage?

a. Choose online exchanges that are financially unproven.

b. Select online exchanges randomly and do business with the one that has an attractive Web site.

c. Sell your products and services through the exchange that can weather an economic storm.

d. Choose a couple of exchanges that specialize in selling shakes.

Inference

14. "In general, auction sites are just what you think they are. Sellers post items to sell and buyers post bids on them. The highest bidder wins the item that is for sale, assuming the bid meets an established minimum amount. The auction sites takes a small commission from the seller's credit card account for each item sold. Buyers generally pay nothing to the auction site itself."

Based on the information presented in the above passage, which of the following CANNOT be a true statement?

© Pearson Education, Inc.

a. Sellers post items on auction sites to sell and buyers bid on them.

b. The buyer whose bid is the highest claims the item.

c. The seller pays the auction site for selling the item.

(d.) The buyer usually pays a commission to the auction site.

Supporting Details

15. "Sellers pay for listing and selling items. eBay charges an insertion fee, usually between 25 cents and $2.00, depending on the opening bid, and a fee at the end of the auction, ranging from 1.25 percent to 5 percent of the final selling price."

The example of eBay charging an insertion fee is offered to show that

(a.) eBay makes a profit from each exchange between buyer and seller.

b. eBay needs to increase its insertion fee from 5 percent to 15 percent.

c. sellers do not pay a fee after a trade is settled.

d. buyers are going to have to pay the insertion fee in the imminent future.

Daniel Wagaman

Profession: Marketing Director, Audiofy Corporation

dwagaman@audiofy.com

audiofy.com

pimsleurdirect.com

How did you choose your current profession?

I've always had an interest in the intersection of technology and how it allows greater connection between people. Marketing requires the seller to put their own views aside and really understand what someone else's needs are, and how you can best serve those needs. Using technology to connect with people and deliver something they want is very satisfying.

How did you prepare to reach your goal of becoming a professional in E-commerce/Internet Marketing?

Preparation is the most important ingredient for success. Internet marketing is a blend of business skills, statistical analysis, psychology, and Web development. Connecting these four skill sets is required for you to be truly successful in this field. Secondly, it is important to keep informed about the latest developments in the field. The Internet moves very quickly. Even as a student it pays to keep your eyes and ears open to what's happening in the marketplace.

What did you struggle with most when preparing to become an Internet Marketing expert?

Like most people I had strengths in certain areas and weaknesses in others. Most people are wired this way. Very very few people are born with natural talents in math, psychology, business and Internet technologies. Being able to work with weaknesses and play to strengths without cutting any corners was my greatest challenge.

How did you overcome/get through this struggle?

Being able to chew through huge piles of statistics to find real meaning takes a great deal of practice and discipline. It certainly did for me. Patience and discipline were the greatest skills I picked up along the way.

What do you enjoy most about your work?

I love working in a field that connects people with services and products they need in an entirely new way. E-commerce is evolving every day and for the first time in the history of advertising you can get nearly instant feedback on your work. It's an exciting field to be in and changes all the time. It's impossible to get bored, and I love it.

What advice do you have for a student considering a career in Internet Marketing?

Work hard at every class. Discipline is key to success. Embrace math and science as part of the new marketing conscience. Just writing effective copy or making a Web page isn't enough. You have to be able to process all the data that customers provide you and know why your copy or Web page was effective. Letting math and science slip while focusing on traditional marketing classes will leave you unprepared for the world of e-commerce.

In your opinion what were the three most interesting points made by the interviewee? Discuss your choices with the class.

- _____
  _____
- _____
  _____
- _____
  _____

READING

China: Online Marketing Comes of Age

As freedom to blog and chat grows on the mainland, companies are beginning to mine these online veins for information about consumers.

Pre-Reading Questions

1. Do you blog and chat on the Internet? If you do, then do you express your views more openly online than you do in person? Why? If you do not blog, then do you read blogs to see what others are saying about a topic that piques your interest?

2. Given China's secretive law enforcement, do you think blogging will become as popular and powerful a means of communication in China as it is in the United States? Explain how.

3. Many corporations read blogs and bulletin boards for research and development and for marketing purposes. Some critics believe that the government should enforce strict laws to ensure that people's right to privacy is protected. Do you agree with this position? Why, or why not?

China: Online Marketing Comes of Age

www.businessweek.com

June 12, 2007

ESL Annotation

4.11 ESL If you have students from China in your class, encourage them to give their perspectives on how the Internet has changed life in China.

1 When Time magazine issued its list of the 100 most influential people in the world last month, it included a Chinese activist little known outside of blogging circles.

"China: Online Marketing Comes of Age." Reprinted from the June 12, 2007 issue of *Business Week* by special permission, copyright © 2007 by The McGraw-Hill Companies, Inc.

© Pearson Education, Inc.

2   Zeng Jinyan, 22, detailed her experiences with China's secretive law **enforcement** after her husband Hu Jia, an AIDS and environmental activist, was detained. Zeng's postings traveled the world, **available** to those who were looking for them.

3   In China, blogs and bulletin boards have **emerged** as powerful modes of **communication** in **contrast** to the fragmented and often unreliable **traditional** media.

4   Television still reaches the single largest group of consumers, more than 700 million across the country but the Internet has become a powerful unifying force, at least in urban areas. People discuss their likes and dislikes online more freely than they may in person.

flipside
the bad effects of something that also has good effects

5   The **flipside** of this growing freedom is that brands and brand managers are now much more interested in tracking what is being said. This can provide routes to more effective marketing or early warnings of impending crises.

6   "What are they talking about? What do they say? Are they talking about safety? About cost? About customer service?" asked Sam Flemming, co-founder of CIC, a company that tracks and analyzes online chats on **specific** products.

Listening In

7   CIC has developed software that allows it to track **specific** strings of conversation. Companies like Nike, for example, use its services to find out what customers like and dislike. Automakers use CIC to find out what the buzz is on their cars and what **potential** buyers are interested in.

8   "I can tell you which models had tens of thousands of mentions in the month of August," said Flemming. "We can tell clients how much talk there is. Is the talk good or bad? Where is it happening? Are there . . . influencers?"

9   CIC first got **involved** in this business two years ago after it developed a proprietary software platform specifically to track conversations in Chinese.

10   "You listen and then, as a brand, you can figure out how to meaningfully participate in this online world where more and more consumers are spending time."

11   The **overall** reach of the Internet is still limited, but it is limited to affluent urbanites. There may be some 137 million people online—a relatively small number compared to the population of China—but these are the same people that will buy cars and expensive Nike shoes.

12   "[Some people] look at the numbers and say 'Oh, only 10% penetration.' But who sells to the other 90%?" observed Chris Reitermann, China president of advertising company OgilvyOne, which specializes in customer relationship management and interactive marketing.

13   Of these 137 million, some 50 million are regular users of bulletin board services (BBS) and 34 million blog regularly, according to the most recent official **statistics**.

14   "If you watch a news program or a talk show, the inspiration of the show comes from a BBS article, or the TV show will have a BBS where they will publish **consumer comments** about the show," Flemming said. "At one point last year, two or three of the best selling books in China were written by bloggers."

the big kid on the block
the undisputed leader

15   Television is still **the big kid on the block** when it comes to the mass market. It reaches five times more people than the Internet and it will be many years before it is challenged.

16 "TV is and will remain a very powerful **medium**," said Reitermann. "If you're a national [brand] there is no way around television. But what is happening today is that people are looking for ways to **bond** with their consumers even more. Every car brand in China advertises on television, but how do you really differentiate yourself?"

17 You can outspend your competitor, he said, or be very creative, but **ultimately** it comes down to using as many channels as possible. Television is expensive, although it can confer instant status on a brand. The Internet, meanwhile, is invaluable in generating buzz.

18 In this multichannel world, brands use every tool at their **disposal**. Television spots may therefore be **accompanied** by events, sponsorship deals, word of mouth campaigns and, increasingly, Internet word of mouth (IWOM) campaigns.

19 "The Internet is . . . becoming more important for lots of brands," said Reitermann. "Some clients of ours have spent about 30% of their **media** budget online. Those clients, maybe five years ago, spent 3–4%. You definitely see a huge **trend** towards the Internet."

20 Several companies have already enjoyed **considerable** success in China thanks to interactive and online-centric marketing campaigns.

21 Pepsi leveraged its Internet presence into **widespread** buzz last year when it challenged consumers to design ads for the company. Meanwhile, Motorola's music download **site**, motomusic.com.cn, has become the most popular in the country (among **legal** sites, anyway). It's no coincidence that handset sales have doubled in the last year. (See: Joining in: Online engagement)

22 Reitmann believes this is just the beginning. He expects even stronger growth over the coming years as China's Internet and advertising industries converge.

23 "You're basically putting the **infrastructure** in place for online advertising. The way it works now, online advertising is very **similar** to offline advertising. In the US, you buy a time slot. You pay basically for a thousand people to watch your ad, which you can't do in China yet."

24 "This stuff is coming."

Reading Comprehension Check

1. "In China, blogs and bulletin boards have emerged as powerful modes of communication in contrast to the fragmented and often unreliable traditional media."

   A conclusion that can be drawn from the above statement is that
   a. blogs are unreliable modes of communication in China.
   b. in China, bulletin boards are ineffective modes of communication.
   c. Chinese blogs and bulletin boards are more reliable than traditional Chinese media.
   d. traditional media in China is a more powerful mode of communication than blogs and bulletin boards.

© Pearson Education, Inc.

2. "Television still reaches the single largest group of consumers, more than 700 million across the country, but the Internet has become a powerful unifying force, at least in urban areas."

Which of the following conclusions can be drawn from the above statement?
a. 700 million people in China have Internet access.
b. In China, the Internet has become a powerful mode of communication in rural areas.
c. In China, the Internet is uniting people living in cities.
d. The Chinese living in rural areas have absolutely no access to the Internet.

3. What does the following statement suggest about Chinese blogs and bulleting boards?

"[In China] People discuss their likes and dislikes online more freely than they may in person."
a. The Chinese do not like to talk in public.
b. Chinese Internet users detest speaking to strangers online.
c. The Chinese do not share their likes and dislikes with others under any circumstances.
d. The Chinese feel more comfortable expressing their views online than they do in face-to-face conversations.

4. It can be inferred from paragraph 5 that companies in China are interested in monitoring what people say on blogs and bulletin boards because
a. they do not feel it is necessary to improve their marketing strategies.
b. they want to market their products more effectively.
c. they intend to deprive the Chinese people of their freedom of speech.
d. they want to compete with each other more aggressively.

5. Sam Flemming, co-founder of CIC, a company that monitors online chats in China on specific products, asked, "What are they talking about? What do they say? Are they talking about safety? About cost? About customer service?"

Which of the following conclusions can be drawn from the above statement?
a. Flemming does not seem to care about the Chinese consumers' views on certain products.
b. Flemming believes that monitoring online chats on specific products is an exercise in futility.
c. Flemming founded the company because he was intimidated by the Chinese consumers.
d. Flemming is interested in knowing about what customers like and dislike.

6. "The overall reach of the Internet is still limited, but it is limited to affluent urbanites. There may be some 137 million people online—a relatively small number compared to the population of China—but these are the same people that will buy cars and expensive Nike shoes."

What does the passage suggest about the future of Internet marketing in China?
a. In China, the number of Internet users in the coming years will most likely decrease.
b. As more and more people become rich in China, the Internet's reach will most likely expand.

c. Online marketing targets those people in China who cannot afford expensive products.

d. Online marketing has a bleak future in China.

7. "Of these 137 million, some 50 million are regular users of bulletin board services (BBS) and 34 million blog regularly, according to the most recent official statistics."

According to the passage, which of the following conclusions is logical?

a. A large percentage of Chinese Internet users shy away from blogs and bulletin boards.

b. 53 million Internet users in China never blog or post on bulletin boards.

c. Close to 50 percent of the Internet users in China write blogs and post on bulletin boards regularly.

d. Bulletin boards are less popular than blogs in China.

8. "TV is and will remain a very powerful medium," said Reitermann. "If you're a national [brand] there is no way around television. But what is happening today is that people are looking for ways to bond with their consumers even more. Every car brand in China advertises on television, but how do you really differentiate yourself?"

According to the passage, which of the following conclusions CANNOT be true?

a. Television will continue to be a powerful medium in China.

b. A Chinese company cannot do away with advertizing on television in the near future.

c. Chinese companies are exploring alternative ways to connect with their potential consumers.

d. Chinese automobile manufacturers never advertise on television.

9. "The Internet is . . . becoming more important for lots of brands," said Reitermann. "Some clients of ours have spent about 30% of their media budget online. Those clients, maybe five years ago, spent 3–4%. You definitely see a huge trend towards the Internet."

A conclusion that can be drawn from the above passage is that

a. in China, online marketing has lost its appeal to many companies.

b. some Chinese companies have increased their online media budget about 900% in the last five years.

c. online marketing in China has seen a downtrend recently.

d. Reitermann discourages his clients from advertising on the Internet because he believes that online marketing is ineffective in China.

10. Reiterman says, "You're basically putting the infrastructure in place for online advertising. The way it works now, online advertising is very similar to offline advertising. In the US, you buy a time slot. You pay basically for a thousand people to watch your ad, which you can't do in China yet."

"This stuff is coming."

It can be inferred from this passage that

a. China will never have the infrastructure for online marketing.

b. Chinese companies are under tremendous pressure to only advertise on television.

© Pearson Education, Inc.

ⓒ online marketing in China is likely to grow exponentially in the coming years.

d. online advertising is radically different from offline advertising.

Suggested Resources

Books

1. *Business at the Speed of Thought* by Bill Gates. Penguine Books Ltd. In this work, Gates argues that the capabilities of computers, software, and networks are only beginning to be harnessed.

2. *Don't Make Me Think: A Common Sense Approach to Web Usability* by Steve Krug. New Riders Press. In this book, Krug uses humor and excellent examples to prove that most Web sites are designed to reduce the user's cognitive load and make Web usability a pleasant experience.

Movies

1. *The Net.* This Hollywood thriller features Sandra Bullock playing a computer expert who is victimized by sinister hackers.

2. *Warriors of the Net* (1999). In this 1999 short film, the artist and animator Gunilla Elam shows the journey of Internet data packets. The film is made with lay audiences in mind.

Internet Sites

1. www.networksolutions.com

   This Web site provides useful tools and information on how to start a business online. If you are interested in starting your own e-commerce Web site, this is a good place for you to start.

2. http://www.commerce.gov/egov/index.htm

   This is the official Web site of the Department of Commerce, where you can find pertinent information about conducting business on the Internet. You can also apply for fishing permits and export licenses here.

Communicating with the Professor: Making an Appointment

Overview

Many students usually do not take advantage of the opportunity to meet with the professor individually. Most professors keep office hours specifically for the purpose of answering questions students may have about the course or particular assignments. In the meeting with the professor, students can ask clarification questions about their progress in the course, express concerns regarding an assignment, and even ask for help with a difficult reading selection. Students are expected to set up an appointment with the professor before showing up at her or his door.

Implications for Learning

Professors appreciate students who play a proactive role in their learning. By making an appointment with the professor to discuss class material or more general concerns, you are demonstrating to the professor that you are genuinely interested in your academic growth. Another implication is that in the real world you will be expected to make appointments with your colleagues and superiors, so setting up one-on-one conferences with your professors will give you a head start with this valuable skill.

Challenge Activity

Review some of your recent class reading assignments and consider which of the readings was the most difficult for you to fully understand. Look through the reading and highlight a few areas that are still confusing to you. Make an appointment with your professor following the guidelines laid out in your course syllabus. Bring the course reading you found challenging with you and discuss the text with your professor.

ESL Annotation

4.12 ESL Students from certain cultures might find the idea of visiting a professor alone intimidating. Be sure to explain that professors appreciate students taking the initiative to overcome barriers to learning.

© Pearson Education, Inc.

TELECOMMUNICATIONS
The Cell Phone Revolution

"In Hell all the messages you ever left on answering machines will be played back to you."

JUDY HORACEK

Objectives

IN THIS CHAPTER YOU WILL LEARN . . .

- About cell phone technology and trends
- How to recognize author's purpose
- How to understand author's tone
- Useful adjectives of tone
- How to paraphrase an original statement

Making Predictions

Consider this chapter's topic of Telecommunications. What subtopics relate to this field? (See Figure 5.1.)

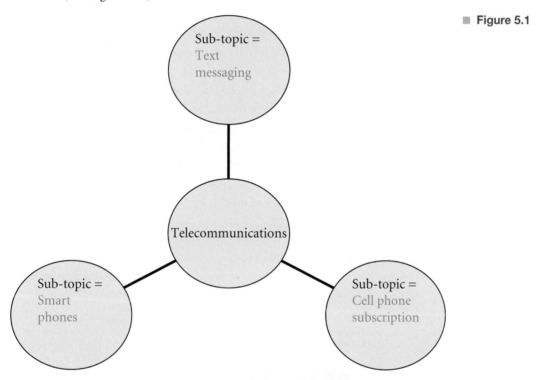

Introduction to the Discipline of Telecommunications

When you are chatting on your cell phone as you drive to work, when you page your coworker, when you are checking your voice mail, when you watch the evening news on television, or when you are surfing the Internet, you are utilizing telecommunications services.

The telegraph network was born in 1845, the telephone followed, and by 1920 the telephone and telegraph network spanned the globe. The communications revolution had begun. The evolution of telecommunications technology has transformed the way we communicate and transmit information, and this industry is one of the most rapidly growing and changing industries in the economy. This industry will continue to change, and to powerfully impact the way we conduct our lives. Faster and more accessible technologies will be invented as we move through the twenty-first century.

Students who major in telecommunications can pursue a variety of careers, including telephony, data base management, network operations, cable television, satellite communication, and Internet communication.

In this chapter you will read about how cell phone technology has changed the way we communicate. The question of whether young children should have their own cell phones and whether cell phones should be allowed to be taken into

© Pearson Education, Inc.

schools is explored. The cell phone revolution has far-reaching consequences around the globe. The effects of cell phone technology in Africa is examined in the final chapter reading.

Preview Questions

Collaboration

1. Do you own a cell phone? If you do, what prompted you to buy this particular phone?

2. What features of your cell phone do you most appreciate? What additional functions do you wish your cell phone had?

3. In your opinion, is it appropriate to use a cell phone in public places such as in a restaurant, on a bus, or just outside a college classroom? Are there contexts where cell phone use might be inappropriate?

4. Do you think the government should regulate cell phone use? If so, what types of limitations on usage would be fair?

5. Many have said that telecommunication giants—large companies that provide network services—are dominating every aspect of human communication by providing a vast array of services that were unthinkable in the past. Do you feel that these advancements in synchronizing telecommunication services have come at a cost to your freedom of choice?

Interpreting a Cartoon

■ Figure 5.2

Examine the cartoon shown here and answer the following questions in pairs.

Collaboration

1. What is amusing about this cartoon?

2. In your opinion, what message is the cartoonist trying to convey to the reader?

Discipline-specific Terminology Bank

carriers	functions	monitor	social mapping
data transmission	gadgets	multitasking	switch-hook
disables	incompatible	network	touch-tone
distinctive ringing	innovation	outdated	tracking device

Sample Paragraph

Is your cell phone **outdated** and **incompatible** with the **networks** your friends are involved in? These days telecommunication **devices** serve many **functions** and allow their users to **multitask** with a host of technological **gadgets**. Telecommunication **carriers** are in competition with one another and **monitor** consumer choices and preferences to get an edge on their rivals. One new function that some carriers are working on is a **tracking device** that can tell you exactly where other members in your cellular network are (as long as they have their mobile phones on).

EXERCISE 1

Matching Column A and Column B

Match the word in Column A with the definition in Column B. Put the letter representing the correct definition in the space preceding each term.

Column A

Word

1. _f_ incompatible
2. _g_ gadget
3. _i_ function
4. _a_ outdated
5. _h_ carriers
6. _b_ multitasking
7. _c_ network
8. _j_ tracking device
9. _d_ disables
10. _e_ monitor

Column B

Definition

a. no longer useful or modern

b. being involved with more than one activity at a time

c. a group of people, organizations, etc. that are connected or that work together

d. makes something unable to function properly

e. to carefully watch, listen to, or examine something over a period of time

f. too different to be able to work together

g. small tool or machine that makes a particular job easier

h. a business or individual that has something for people to use or buy

i. the usual purpose of a thing

j. technology that can locate and monitor

© Pearson Education, Inc.

EXERCISE 2

Fill in the Blanks

In the following sentences, fill in the blank with a word from the terminology bank that makes the sentence grammatically correct and meaningful.

carriers	disables	functions	gadgets	incompatible
monitor	multitasking	network	outdated	tracking device

1. Listening to music and watching TV while text-messaging a friend is an example of _multitasking_ .

2. You will have a problem accessing particular cell phone software if your service is _incompatible_ with the cell phone network that offers this program.

3. Modern day cell phones offer a host of advanced _functions_ that early cell phones did not include.

4. If your cell phone is not protected from external viruses, your phone is at risk of being _disabled_ .

5. Cell phone carriers _monitor_ their clients' software preferences to better understand the direction of the market.

6. Some parents install a _tracking device_ on their children's phones to monitor their phone usage.

7. The cell phone industry is volatile as multiple _carriers_ merge into larger companies, and, less commonly, larger conglomerates split into smaller ones.

8. Modern day cell phones are marketed with a host of _gadgets_ and accessories that offer consumers a wide range of services.

9. Many cell phone users belong to a cellular _network_ , which allows members extra services and privileges.

10. What is a fresh and exciting cell phone feature one year is considered _outdated_ the next.

EXERCISE 3

Collaboration

Pair Activity

Working with a partner, choose five words you have just learned, and make complete sentences with them.

1. _____

_____

2. _____

_____

3. _____

_____

4. _____

_____

5. _____

_____

Graphic Analysis

Younger people often have a different relationship with newer technologies than older generations do. The graph here shows the results of a survey that examined different age-groups' interest levels in a variety of cell phone features. Read through the survey tables and with a partner answer the questions that follow.

■ Figure 5.3

The young really are different with their cells					
Percentage of cell phone owners in each age cohort who say . . .					
	Ages 18–29	*Ages 30–49*	*Ages 50–64*	*Age 65+*	*Total*
Experiences and attitudes					
Personalized their cells by changing wallpaper or adding ring tones	85%	72%	50%	29%	65%
I have used my cell phone in an emergency and it really helped	79%	76%	70%	65%	74%
I often make cell phone calls to fill up my free time while I'm traveling or waiting for someone	61%	43%	25%	20%	41%
I have occasionally been shocked at the size of my monthly cell phone bill	47%	38%	26%	23%	36%
When I'm on my cell phone I'm not always truthful about exactly where I am	39%	23%	9%	10%	22%
Too many people try to get in touch with me because they know I have a cell phone	37%	23%	12%	5%	22%
I often feel like I have to answer my cell phone even when it interrupts a meeting or a meal	31%	26%	14%	20%	24%
Received unsolicited commercial text messages	28%	15%	15%	13%	18%
I have drawn criticism or dirty looks because of the way I used my cell in public	14%	9%	4%	3%	8%
Used cell to vote in a contest shown on TV such as "American Idol"	14%	9%	5%	1%	8%

(Continued)

© Pearson Education, Inc.

■ **Figure 5.3**   *(Continued)*

		Ages 18–29	*Ages 30–49*	*Ages 50–64*	*Age 65+*	*Total*
Features they use or want						
Use cells for text messaging		65%	37%	13%	8%	35%
	Would like this feature	14%	14%	11%	11%	13%
Use cells to take pictures		55%	27%	11%	8%	28%
	Would like this feature	16%	22%	17%	23%	19%
Use cells to play games		47%	21%	10%	3%	22%
	Would like this feature	9%	11%	12%	18%	12%
Use cells to access the internet		28%	11%	8%	8%	14%
	Would like this feature	20%	14%	16%	8%	16%
Use cells for email		17%	7%	4%	2%	8%
	Would like this feature	26%	29%	19%	13%	24%
Use cells for instant messaging		17%	6%	1%	4%	7%
	Would like this feature	19%	13%	3%	5%	11%
Use cells to search for movie listings, weather, stock prices		17%	6%	1%	3%	7%
	Would like this feature	30%	31%	15%	8%	24%
Use cells to play music		15%	6%	1%	1%	6%
	Would like this feature	27%	17%	12%	19%	19%
Use cells to record video		15%	5%	2%	1%	6%
	Would like this feature	22%	17%	13%	20%	17%
Use cells to access mobile maps and driving directions		9%	4%	1%	1%	4%
	Would like this feature	56%	51%	40%	29%	47%
Use cells for watching video or TV programs		5%	1%	1%	1%	2%
	Would like this feature	23%	15%	4%	6%	14%

Source: Pew Internet & American Life Project, Associated Press, AOL cell phone survey. March 8–28, 2006. N=1,503 (752 contacted on landlines and 751 contacted on their cell phones). In all, 1,286 cell users are in the sample. The margin of error for the cell-using population is ±3%.

From Lee Rainie and Scott Keeter, *Pew Internet Project Data Memo: Cell Phone Use.* Washington, DC: Pew Internet & American Life Project, April 2006, p. 6. Reprinted by permission of the Pew Internet & American Life Project.

1. What percentage of people in the 18–29 age group say that when they are on their cell phones, they are not always truthful about their location? What factors might motivate someone to lie about this?
   39%/Answers will vary

2. Find the Experience and Attitudes section of the chart, and look at the fourth item. Why do you think the youngest age group surveyed (the 18–29 group) is most often "shocked by the size of their monthly cell phone bill"?
   Answers will vary

3. Examine the section Features They Use or Want. What is the percentage difference in desire to conduct e-mail communication on cell phones between the oldest and youngest cell phone users?
   Approximately 13%

4. Based on your own personal experience, what could be a possible explanation for why young people use text-messaging and photo-taking features much more often than senior citizens?

These features are trendy among teenagers

READING

Reading Selection **1**

Newspaper Article

5.1 Flesch-Kincaid Grade Level 11.6

Collaboration

Four Score and . . . Mind If I Take This?

Pre-Reading Questions

Discuss the following questions before reading the article.

1. In what types of social situations would you choose NOT to answer your cell phone? Be specific.

2. Do you find it rude when a friend or family member interrupts your conversation with them to either take a call or give or receive a text message? If yes, how do you usually cope with such a situation?

3. Do you think American schools should offer techno-etiquette training? What should be included in the first lesson?

Read the article below and answer the subsequent multiple-choice questions. For the first few paragraphs, offer some questions.

Four Score and . . . Mind If I Take This?

By Ken Belson, the *New York Times*

September 30, 2007

? _____

_____

_____

_____

1   When Rudy Giuliani, **smack in the middle** of a recent speech before the National Rifle Association, stopped his talk and said that he was taking a call from his wife, Judith, it could be that he really had forgotten to shut off his handset.

smack in the middle
exactly in between

2   Or he might have orchestrated the call, as some critics are saying, to lighten his **image**. Or it might have been an attempt to lower the tension in a room where Mr. Giuliani, a Republican presidential candidate, was not universally loved, given his antigun stance while New York City's mayor.

? _____

_____

_____

_____

3   Whatever the facts, for some it was a threshold moment—not about politics, but about cell phones.

4   Are Americans so comfortable with cell phone intrusions that it is now acceptable to take a call, even in front of a hall of people? Or was the criticism that followed Mr. Giuliani's public love chat a sign that Americans **have had it** with cell phones and with the people who will take or make a call, no matter the

have had it
be in a state beyond remedy, repair, or salvage

Ken Belson, "Four Score and . . . Mind if I Take This?" From The New York Times, September 30, 2007. © 2007 The *New York Times*. All rights reserved. Used by permission and protected by the Copyright Laws of the United States. The printing, copying, redistribution, or retransmission of the Material without express written permission is prohibited. www.nytimes.com

© Pearson Education, Inc.

cross a line
to go beyond an acceptable point

?_____

_____

_____

_____

setting? "Did he **cross a line**?" asked Naomi S. Baron, a professor of linguistics at American University and **author** of the **forthcoming** book, "Always On: Language in an Online and Mobile World." "That presumes there is a line."

5   Americans have been debating techno-etiquette for at least a decade, with the cell phone a lingering issue. In New York City, the questions about cell phone manners are likely to grow more **persistent** now that the Metropolitan Transportation **Authority** has announced its intention to wire its 277 underground subway stations for calls.

6   Societies take time to adjust to **technology**, Ms. Baron said, and Americans are still struggling to define cell phone boundaries. In Europe and Asia, though, cell phones have been around longer, and many of the rules are clearer.

7   In Sweden, people think little about talking on their phones while riding a bus or train. But in Japan, phones have a "manner **mode**" button that **disables** the ringer, Ms. Baron said, and bus and train riders are encouraged to use it. (Swedes, she said, are also comfortable talking in public restrooms, but that seems to be less tolerated elsewhere.)

disables
makes unable or unfit; weaken or destroy the capability of

yak away
to keep talking without stop

8   People in Finland are not big on face-to-face chitchat, yet they freely **yak away** on their cell phones, said James Katz, the director of the Center for Mobile Communications Studies at Rutgers University.

9   In China, almost anything goes when it comes to cell phones, but in the Philippines **text** messages are the preferred means of communicating.

10   According to a **survey** of 1,503 **adults** by the Pew **Research** Center for the People and the Press, 82 **percent** of Americans say they are irritated at least occasionally by loud and annoying cell phone users who take calls in public places. An additional 8 **percent** of those surveyed said they have drawn criticism from others for using their phones in public.

11   But many people just can't stop themselves: Among adult cell phone users, 24 **percent** said they felt obliged to answer their calls even if they interrupted a meal or meeting, according to the Pew **survey**.

12   More Americans seem to be saying enough is enough. There are reminders to turn off cell phones in airplanes, churches, hospitals and theaters. More states prohibit using handsets while driving. Signs in restaurants and doctors' waiting rooms discourage phone chatter.

13   And on trains and buses there is growing pressure to keep the talk to a **minimum**—with a **network** of **shushers** willing to serve as enforcers.

network
a group

shushers
people who tell others to be quiet

14   In the workplace, too, rules are emerging. Johnson & Johnson, for example, prohibits its workers from talking on their cell phones while driving company-owned vehicles (though that is just as likely about insurance as manners). A real **estate** company fines employees $5 each time a cell phone call interrupts monthly meetings; the money is donated to charity.

15   "We've become so obsessed with being **available** that when the phone rings, we have to answer it," said Barbara Pachter, the co-**author** of "The Jerk With the Cell Phone: A Survival Guide for the Rest of Us" (Marlowe & Company, 2004). "But most things aren't necessary."

16   Yet some said they saw Mr. Giuliani's cell phone moment—contrived or not—as a sign that it is O.K. to take a call anywhere, anytime.

17   Experts on **technology** and society also wondered whether it would now become part of the shtick for other speakers, no matter how staged or derivative it may appear. Politicians might try to burnish their steelier side by

taking a call from, say, a police chief or general in the middle of a speech at a V.F.W. hall.

18   "I can easily see this in a short **period** of time becoming a **staple on the stump**," said Christine Rosen, senior editor of The New Atlantis, which focuses on **technology** and society. "We've reached a **cultural** moment where there's futile acceptance of it. It's another example of our decaying manners."

staple on the stump
something that is consistently focused on as an issue

Reading Comprehension Check

1. The example of Rudy Giuliani is given in the first few paragraphs of the article to introduce the idea that
    a. politicians like cell phone moments.
    b. people often take cell phone calls even when they are busy with another activity.
    c. cell phones are a real negative intrusion in our lives.
    d. both b and c.

2. The word *orchestrated* in the second paragraph (" . . . Or he might have orchestrated the call,") could be replaced with
    a. musical.   c. set up.
    b. delayed.   d. denied.

3. What is the main idea of paragraph 4 ("Are Americans so comfortable with cell phones . . . ")?
    a. Most Americans are tired of cell phones.
    b. Guiliani committed an error.
    c. Some people believe that taking a cell phone call in certain situations is crossing a line.
    d. A professor argues that cell phones are a public intrusion.

4. It can be implied from the paragraph comparing cell phone habits in Sweden and Japan that
    a. the Japanese as a society are stricter in their public cell phone usage.
    b. all Swedes use their cell phones in public.
    c. the Japanese live a quiet life.
    d. both cultures have similar habits in public cell phone usage.

5. The Philippines, Finland, and China are cited to make the point that
    a. all cultures use cell phones.
    b. most world cultures share similar habits regarding cell phones.
    c. different societies have different norms for cell phone interaction.
    d. the United States is far behind in cell phone technology.

6. The word *obliged* in paragraph 11 ("Among adult cell phone users, 24 percent said they felt obliged to answer their calls . . . ") could be replaced by
    a. free.   c. frustrated
    b. grateful.   d. compelled.

7. In paragraph 12, the fact that "more states now prohibit using handsets while driving" is given to support the point that
    a. handsets are not safe.
    b. public sentiment has pushed some limitations on cell phone usage.

© Pearson Education, Inc.

    c. Americans no longer believe that multitasking is always a good idea.

    d. each state has its own rules and regulations.

8. What is the topic of the article?

    a. cell phones.

    (b.) cell phone etiquette.

    c. Americans are more and more critical of public cell phone usage.

    d. comparative cell phone use around the world.

9. Read what Barbara Pachter says in paragraph 15. What is her main point?

    a. Many Americans are obsessed with being available for dates.

    b. Americans should always answer their phones, and they usually do.

    (c.) Although many people feel compelled to answer their cell phones, it often isn't that important to do so.

    d. It is not important at all to ever answer your cell phone.

10. It can be implied in the last paragraph that Christine Rosen feels that our cell phone habits

    a. say a lot about who we are as a culture.

    b. are a sign of a positive change.

    (c.) are a sign of a general decline in manners.

    d. have always been the way they are.

READING

Reading Selection **2**

Online News

5.2 Flesch-Kincaid Grade Level 10.4

Collaboration

ESL Annotation

5.3 ESL For some students schooled in other cultures, the notion of school violence may seem both foreign and shocking. The issue may warrant some background discussion before students embark upon this reading selection.

Wisconsin School Violence Leads to Cell Phone Ban: Students Have Been Using Phones to Plan Fights, Milwaukee Authorities Say

---

Pre-Reading Questions

Share your thoughts on the questions below with a classmate.

1. Do you think cell phones make school zones safer or more dangerous places? Explain.

2. Should schools confiscate cell phones from all students who have a police record? Would this be discriminatory?

Wisconsin School Violence Leads to Cell Phone Ban

MSNBC.com

January 27, 2007

1 MILWAUKEE — School brawls have gone high tech, with students using cell phones to call in reinforcements—in one case requiring police and pepper spray to break up a fight that swelled to about 20 family members on school grounds.

Associated Press, "Wis. School Violence Leads to Cell Phone Ban," MSNBC.com, January 27, 2007. Used with permission of The Associated Press. Copyright © 2007. All rights reserved.

2   The fracas earlier this month, in which six students and three **adults** were arrested, was the latest in a **surge** of cell phone–related fights and prompted Wisconsin's largest school district to ban cell phones in its 217 schools beginning Monday.

surge
a sudden increase in amount or

3   "We consider [cell phones] almost as weapons because when they call, we're the ones out in front and we don't know these people are coming," said Mike Heese, safety **security** assistant at Bradley Tech High School, where the fight happened.

4   Prosecutors are also taking a tougher stance. **Adults** who harm anyone at a school could face **felony** charges, said Milwaukee County District Attorney John Chisholm. Penalties in the past were often fines for disorderly **conduct**.

felony
committing a serious crime such as murder

Increasingly Common

5   Milwaukee joins a growing number of school districts that prohibit or limit cell phones. But many bans, including those in New York City, Los Angeles and Boston, were **imposed** because the phones cause distractions or are used to cheat.

6   Milwaukee Public Schools have had about one cell phone–augmented fight a month in the last three years, but it seems to have worsened during the last year, said Peter Pochowski, the schools' director of safety and **security**.

7   Two years ago, a fighting student used his cell phone twice in a matter of weeks to summon two carloads of family members, Pochowski said.

8   Jamilynn Brushel, 18, a senior at Bradley Tech, said she would rather see stricter **security** guards and teachers, because students who want to fight will do so even without cell phones.

9   "They won't need people coming in," Brushel said. "They'll just get people who are already here."

10   Dorcas Lopez is a mother of two, including a 12-year-old middle schooler who needs to call her when he's done with basketball. But as a social work assistant at a Milwaukee high school, she has seen kids misuse phones to get someone to lie for them to get them out of school.

11   She said she does not feel any safer with the ban. "Whatever is going to happen is going to happen," Lopez said.

Hard Line

12   The district will **expel** students who use cell phones to summon outsiders for a fight, Superintendent William Andrekopoulos said.

expel
to make a student leave a school

13   Others could be **suspended**, have their phone temporarily confiscated, or have a **conference** with the student or parents. There will be exceptions to the ban for hardship cases, he said.

14   "I think people have to rise themselves up from a level of convenience to a level of safety," Andrekopoulos said. "I think that's where we're at in this country."

Reading Comprehension Check

1. In the first sentence of the article, the word *swelled* could be replaced with
a. grew.
b. decreased.
c. remained stable.
d. cautious.

© Pearson Education, Inc.

Steven Jobs

Steven Jobs is the cofounder and CEO of Apple Inc., and is considered a leading figure in the computer industry and, with the advent of the iPhone, a trendsetter in the telecommunications industry as well. In 2007, Jobs was listed as *Fortune* magazine's Number One most powerful businessman.

Steven Paul Jobs was born on February 24, 1955, in San Francisco, California. One week after birth he was put up for adoption by his unmarried mother. After graduating high school in 1972, Jobs enrolled in Reed College in Portland, Oregon, and dropped out after only one semester. Soon after, he took a job as a technician at Atari, a manufacturer of popular video games, with the primary intent of saving money for a spiritual retreat to India. Jobs did reach his goal and backpacked around India with a Reed College friend (and, later, first Apple employee), Daniel Kottke, in search of philosophical enlightenment.

Shortly after his return, 21-year old Jobs saw an early computer that his friend Steve Wozniak had designed for his own use. Jobs persuaded Wozniak to assist him and together they founded Apple Computer Co. in April of 1976. The age of the personal computer had begun, and by December of 1980 when Apple became a publicly traded corporation, Jobs found himself in the position of industry leader and multimillionaire.

In recent years, the company has branched out beyond computers. With the introduction of the iPod portable music player, iTunes digital music software, and the iTunes Store, the company has expanded into the world of consumer electronics and music distribution.

Following the success of the iPod, Apple announced the iPhone in January 2007. The announcement was preceded by rumors and speculations that circulated for several months. The iPhone was first introduced in the United States on June 29, 2007, with much media frenzy and then with great success in France, Germany, and England in late 2007. Jobs has set his sights on the China market and the rest of the world. It was named *Time* magazine's "Invention of the Year" in 2007.

While stimulating innovation, Jobs also reminds his employees that "real artists ship," by which he means that delivering working products on time is as important as **innovation** and attractive design.

Some Questions for Group Discussion

1. Steven Jobs, perhaps one of the greatest innovators in business history, was both an adopted child and an early college dropout. Do these facts surprise you? Why or why not?

2. Jobs branched out from the personal computer industry into the world of music technology (the iPod and iTunes) and then into telecommunications (the iPhone). What do you see as the connections between these worlds? Was this a logical evolution or an accident?

3. Before Jobs figured out what he wanted to do with his life and went on to become the head of Apple Inc., he took a spiritual journey to India. In what ways can such a trip influence the course of someone's life? Do you believe that Jobs was fated to become the great innovator we all know him as regardless of such life choices, or could this trip have been a turning point? Explain.

Biographical Internet Research

Find out about another prominent figure in Telecommunications online, picking one from the list below, and share a biographical profile with your classmates:

- Thomas Edison
- Alexander Graham Bell
- Samuel Morse
- Guglielmo Marconi
- Emile Baudot

Envisioned by Steven Jobs, the iPhone is a multimedia, Internet-enabled mobile phone of slick design. The iPhone has revolutionized the industry of cell phone design and has set the course for its competitors.

2. The word *fracas* in the second paragraph could be replaced by
   a. murder.   (c.) disturbance.
   b. school party.   d. fresh.

3. What does Mike Heese, safety security assistant at Bradley Tech High School, compare cell phones to?
   a. guns.   (c.) weapons.
   b. technology.   d. safety issues.

4. It is stated in the article that other cities across the United States have banned cell phones
   a. for similar reasons.
   (b.) for different reasons.
   c. following the incidents in Milwaukee.
   d. rarely.

5. What is Bradley Tech senior Jamilynn Brushela's main point about the cell phone controversy?
   a. Banning cell phones will only make things worse.
   (b.) She thinks stricter security guards and teachers are more important.
   c. She agrees that cell phones are the chief problem.
   d. all of the above.

SKILL FOCUS
Recognizing Author's Purpose and Tone

Understanding Purpose

Examine the following four short paragraphs, all focusing on the same topic—the future of cell phones—and consider what makes each paragraph different from the others.

Passage 1

I can imagine a world where everyone is on their cell phone all the time. They will have some kind of a cellular device in each pocket. They'll be text messaging with one hand and speed dialing with the other. Isn't it time we reconsider the path we are on? The old days with less technology were simpler. Perhaps it is time we slow things down before we all end up in a cellular nightmare.

Passage 2

The future promises faster cellular connections due to higher operating speeds. Experts say that cell phones will perform more functions than they currently can. Also, it is argued that reception will be more consistent and widespread, and the price of both cellular products and services will go down.

© Pearson Education, Inc.

Passage 3

What's funny about cell phones is that only a few decades back we didn't have them, and now we can't live without them. My wife got lost in the parking lot and couldn't find me, so she called me on her cell. I asked her right then, "honey, what did we do twenty years ago when this happened?" In the future, all the information we need will always be with us in some kind of advanced device. We will be able to get lost, forget something important and make just about any kind of mistake that you can imagine, and our hand-held electronic device will save us.

Passage 4

Let me explain what you need to do to be ready for future cell phone technology. Read about all the new capacities we already have at our fingertips. There are new cellular innovations already out there that we don't even know about. The future is already here. If you are up-to-date and informed about all that is new in the world of cell phone technology, then you are the one who will have the knowledge to understand what is coming next.

Collaboration

Before we even discuss the concepts of an author's purpose and tone, let's discuss how each of these passages takes a different approach on the topic of the future of cell phones. In a small group, discuss the ways the paragraphs above are different from each other.

Recognizing an Author's Purpose

An *author's purpose* is simply his or her reason for writing a text. When we are reading, it is easy to forget that a real person, with a specific purpose in mind, at some point sat down and wrote what is now in front of us. When the author wrote the text, he or she had an *intended audience* in mind—a specific group of people that the author was writing for. For instance, an economist writing a macroeconomics textbook may assume that his or her audience will be students taking an introductory course in this discipline. A journalist for *Vogue* magazine knows his or her intended audience are people interested in the latest fashion.

An author's purpose is very much related to their intended audience and the genre, or type of writing they are doing (See Appendix II for a Guide to Genre). The author's purpose may be to inform, to entertain, or to persuade the reader, as shown below.

Purpose	*Genre*
■ To Inform	newspaper articles, textbooks, legal documents, reference materials
■ To Persuade/Convince	advertising, editorials, music/art criticism, political speeches
■ To Instruct	how-to manuals, technical guides, Math and lab-related textbooks
■ To Entertain	novels, poems, jokes, gossip columns

When trying to determine the author's purpose, read the text carefully and ask yourself, "Why did the author write this? What was he or she trying to accomplish?"

PRACTICING THE SKILL: PURPOSE

Collaboration

In the same groups as before, re-examine Passages 1 to 4 and try to determine what the author's purpose is in each reading. In your earlier discussion, you may have touched upon the different purposes of each passage.

Passage 1   *To persuade/convince*

Passage 2   *To inform*

Passage 3   *To entertain*

Passage 4   *To instruct*

Understanding Tone

┌─**ESL** Annotation

5.4 ESL The concept of "author's tone" can prove particularly difficult for many ESL students to pick up on, particularly when the clues are subtle. Extra attention should be offered to key words that signal tone.

Authors carefully choose words to convey a *tone* or feeling. An author's tone reflects his or her *attitude* toward a topic. In a conversation, you can tell if the person you are speaking with is angry, serious, sympathetic or just kidding around by the intonation, volume, and pitch of that person's voice, and by facial expression (if you can actually see him or her). In writing, however, one has to rely on the author's choice of words and style of writing to determine the tone.

If you understand the author's purpose, you are halfway there to identifying the author's tone. If the author's purpose is simply to inform, then perhaps the tone is somewhat unemotional, perhaps neutral or objective. If the author is trying to persuade the reader of something, then perhaps the tone will be critical or disapproving, or supportive and encouraging. If the writer is trying to entertain, the tone might be lighthearted, comical or sarcastic.

In mastering the reading skill of identifying author's tone, it is important that you build up a rich vocabulary of adjectives that describe tone. Otherwise, you may be faced with multiple-choice questions on a standardized test where you encounter unfamiliar words in the answer options.

Recognizing Tone Through Adjectives

Below is a list of useful words that describe tone. They are a small sampling of adjectives of tone and valuable vocabulary to have in your inventory. Many of them you may already know. They are grouped into general categories to make it easier for you to become familiar with the words. (See Appendix III for a list of more tone words.)

Objective Tones

These are often used in textbooks, newspaper and magazine articles and reference materials.

Neutral	not taking a particular side
Straightforward	simple and easy to understand
Indifferent	not having any feelings or opinions about something
Serious	earnestly stated, with a sense that what is being said is important
Instructional	to give information about a particular concept

© Pearson Education, Inc.

Emotional Tones

These are found in persuasive writings, such as editorials and political writing.

Concerned	worried about something
Sentimental	showing emotions such as love, pity or sadness too strongly
Nostalgic	longing for things or situations in the past
Remorseful	feeling sorry for something you have done
Inspirational	motivating the reader to act

Disapproving Tones

These may be found in movie/art reviews and editorials.

Critical	severely judging people or things
Pessimistic	having a negative outlook
Intolerant	not willing to accept ways of thinking that are different from your own
Gloomy	a dark, hopeless feeling
Bitter	a sour reaction

Supportive Tones

These may be found in reviews and editorials, as well as in inspirational writing.

Encouraging	showing support
Optimistic	having a bright view of the future
Sympathetic	understanding of how someone feels and supportive of their actions
Enthusiastic	showing a lot of interest and excitement about something
Convincing	trying to persuade the reader

Humorous and Sarcastic Tones

ESL Annotation

5.5 ESL Reading passages written in humorous and sarcastic tones can be particularly challenging for second language readers.

These may appear in many kinds of writing, including cartoons, literature and criticism, poetry, and newspaper columns.

Ironic	using words that are the opposite of what you really mean in order to be amusing or show that you are annoyed
Skeptical	doubting or not believing something
Cynical	unwilling to believe that someone has good or honest intentions for doing something
Mocking	laughing at something to make it seem silly
Lighthearted	cheerful, not intended to be serious
Comical	funny, especially in a strange and unexpected way
Tongue-in-cheek	said or done seriously, but meant as a joke

Collaboration

PRACTICING THE SKILL: TONE

Let's return one last time to the beginning of this section and Passages 1 to 4. From what we have just reviewed, try to determine what the author's tone is for each of the readings. Pay close attention to the language of the passages, and highlight the key words that clued you in to what the author's tone was.

	Author's Tone	*Key Clue Words*
Passage 1	serious	reconsider, nightmare
Passage 2	enthusiastic	promises, consistent, widespread
Passage 3	lighthearted	funny, get lost, mistakes, imagine
Passage 4	straightforward	read, up-to-date, informed

Flashback: Turn back to the cartoon on page 246 of this chapter with the concepts of purpose and tone in mind.

1. What is the author's purpose in creating this cartoon? ___to amuse___
2. What is the author's tone? ___ironic___

The next reading selection invites you to apply the skills you have just learned to recognize purpose and tone.

An iPhone Changed My Life (Briefly)

READING

Reading Selection **3**

Newspaper Editorial

5.6 Flesch-Kincaid Grade Level 11.5

Collaboration

Pre-Reading Questions

Consider the following questions and discuss them in a small group.

1. Do you believe a new technology can change your life? Explain.

2. How important to you is it to have a phone with all the latest technological features?

Read the personal account about iPhones below and try to determine both the author's purpose and overall tone. After you've read the whole article, fill out the chart that follows.

An iPhone Changed My Life (Briefly)

By Michelle Slatalla, the *New York Times*

July 5, 2007

1 When I took my iPhone out of the box on Friday to prove to my children that we were the first family on the block with one, I had a glimpse of what life will be like after I'm dead and they're fighting over my jewelry.

Michelle Slatalla, "An iPhone Changed My Life (Briefly)." From The *New York Times*, July 5, 2007. © 2007 The New York Times. All rights reserved. Used by permission and protected by the Copyright Laws of the United States. The printing, copying, redistribution, or retransmission of the Material without express written permission is prohibited. www.nytimes.com

© Pearson Education, Inc.

2   "Can I have it?" asked Ella, 16.

3   "I'm the oldest," said Zoe, 18.

4   "I'm the only one who doesn't already have a cellphone," said Clementine, 9.

5   "You shouldn't keep it for yourself, because you hate cellphones and don't even answer the one you have," Ella said. "You will neglect it and won't use all the **features**. Give it to someone who will appreciate it. Me."

6   "Me," Zoe said.

7   "Me," Clem said.

offspring
someone's child or children

8   I looked at my **offspring**—so eager, so easily manipulated by the hype surrounding a shiny new gadget that could perform some but not all of the same functions as the gadgets they already owned—and wondered if the situation presented an opportunity to do far more than simply lord it over the neighbors.

9   Was it too much to hope an iPhone could improve my life? After all, a nation of early adopters already had said this slim $599 lozenge with a pretty touch screen was indispensable; maybe I would, too. I imagined organizing my car pool **schedule** with a touch of the iPhone's calendar button. Then I pictured myself effortlessly e-mailing my husband from the lacrosse field, to remind him to buy beer. And I imagined him texting back as he eyed the refrigerator case: "Corona or Pacifico?" How happy we might be.

10   And why not? Although I had yet to actually activate the thing, it already had **granted** me new powers over my children.

11   "Would someone please empty the dishwasher?" I asked.

12   As all three leapt for the cutlery basket, I sauntered out of the kitchen.

13   Ella called, "Need help configuring it?"

14   "Maybe later," I said. "After you walk the dogs."

tackle
try to deal with a difficult problem

a cinch
to be almost certain to happen

15   With things going so well, I decided **to tackle** setup on my own. Thinking that it should be **a cinch**, I determined in less than 15 minutes which gadget to unplug from my **computer** to make room to plug in a new gadget, and instructed my **computer** to update the iTunes software necessary to configure the phone.

16   Then I clicked on the iTunes icon. An onscreen window delivered an ominous message: "Unable to mount disk. Broken pipe."

trolling for advice
looking for solutions

17   Broken pipe? I won't say I panicked, but when Zoe wandered in a half hour later to ask if she could touch the iPhone, I was feverishly **trolling for advice** at Macfixitforums.com.

18   I was about to erase my hard drive when she grabbed my wrist and called to her sisters, "Get Mom out of here while I set up her phone."

19   Five minutes later, everything was done except for one tiny step: activation. The AT&T system was overwhelmed, but my children already had phoned the carrier and learned that within six hours I should receive e-mail confirmation that the iPhone was working.

20   Day 2, Saturday: By the time I came downstairs for breakfast, the neighbors had gathered in the kitchen, rocking the iPhone and cooing, "Isn't it cute?"

to strike a pose
to consciously exhibit a physical expression

21   My friend Tina started snapping photos with it, prompting her 7-year-old son **to strike a pose** like the rapper Bow Wow, hunched over and making peace signs pointed toward the floor.

22   "Is there any coffee left?" I asked.

23   No one answered; they were trying to use the Google Maps feature on the iPhone to look up directions from our house to a restaurant called Toast, which is one block away and to which they walk almost every weekend.

24   By the time the neighbors had departed, my iPhone was receiving e-mail. "Subject: Feel Comfortable With Your Body Due To Penis Enlarge Patch," I read with my English muffin. I decided to take the iPhone to my tennis league playoff match to intimidate my opponents by casually pulling it out during warm-up. Unfortunately, the harsh midday sun rendered the screen unreadable and reflective, giving them the impression I was the sort of tennis player who checks lipstick in a compact mirror. They won in three sets.

25   Day 3, Sunday: The iPhone **revealed** some truths about my family that I would have preferred not knowing. After my children showed me how to copy the audio files from my **computer** to the phone, a window popped onscreen to announce that a **file** called "South Park—Cartman Farts on Kitty" would not be copied because "it cannot be played on this iPhone."

26   Who put this on my **computer**? I asked.

27   "Zoe," Ella said.

28   "Ella," Zoe said.

29   "Dad," Clementine said.

30   Later, I also learned an unpleasant truth about my chin. I realized while browsing through the photos my children copied to the iPhone that, depending on the angle, I appeared to have quite a few chins. After frantic attempts to delete the Jabba-the-Hutt shots failed, I phoned Apple customer service and learned that the only way to cleanse my iPhone was to first delete the chin shots from my computer's photo folder and then re-sync the folder's contents to the iPhone.

31   Day 4, Monday: More neighbors phoned and asked us over to play Scrabble—and to bring the iPhone if we felt like it.

32   I snapped a few photos of my friends gathered around the game board, prompting my friend Bruce's 10-year-old son to cock the bill of his baseball cap and pose like Notorious B.I.G. As Bruce agonized over his letter tiles during the third game, I pulled out the iPhone and asked, "Anybody want to hear some Neil Young?"

33   Distracted by a tinny rendition of "Helpless," Bruce failed to notice the need to protect a triple-letter-score box from my "q." I scored 31 points.

34   Later, however, the iPhone let me down. As my husband was driving home from our favorite Mexican restaurant, I wondered if Bruce would retaliate for "qi" by parking in the last empty space near our house. After using the iPhone's maps feature to zoom in on a satellite **image** of the street, I'd reported "All clear," only to remember belatedly, as we rounded the corner and saw Bruce's Saab, that Google's satellite images typically aren't updated more than once a year.

35   Day 5, Tuesday: I started to feel the cold chill of **backlash.** Tina called to say she had heard you have to send away the iPhone to replace its battery. The children left dirty dishes in the sink **despite** my attempts to play them off against one another by offering **access** to the iPhone.

backlash
a strong reaction from people against an idea or person

36   Ignoring the naysayers, I decided to use the iPhone to free me from the **drudgery** of the grocery store, or at least from the drudgery of forgetting to buy something essential. I touched the Notes button to make a shopping list,

drudgery
difficult boring work

© Pearson Education, Inc.

jotting it down
quickly taking notes

but found it difficult to use the tiny keyboard buttons to accurately type "avocado" ("scocafo") or, of all words, "apples" ("sooles"). After "2 doz eggs" came out "DOA efgs," I decided to e-mail the list to myself instead. This only took a few minutes longer than **jotting it down** on a scrap of paper.

37   Day 6, Wednesday: **Despite** the thrill of being able to browse the Web from the produce aisle to confirm that the vacuum-packed imported butter I'd found needed no refrigeration, I have started thinking seriously about returning the $599 phone, **despite** a 10 **percent** restocking fee. It hasn't really changed my life in the ways I'd hoped.

38   The return **policy** specifies that I have eight more days to decide whether to keep it. In the meantime, maybe I can figure out how to delete the South Park **file** from my **computer** without erasing my entire hard drive or breaking a pipe. None of my children has offered to help.

Title of Article:	*An iPhone Changed My Life (Briefly)*
Topic:	*iPhone*
Main idea:	*The revolutionary iPhone may complicate the lives*
	of parents with young children.
Author's Purpose:	*to entertain*
Author's Tone:	*comical*

READING

Reading Selection 4

Response Letters to Newspaper

5.7 Flesch-Kincaid Grade Level 7.8

Cell Phones for Little Kids? Can We Talk?

After reading the next Reading Selection—two letters which were written in response to a *New York Times* article entitled "Child Wants Cell Phone, Reception is Mixed" (3/29/07)—fill out the chart that follows it, to compare the two texts in terms of purpose and tone.

Cell Phones for Little Kids? Can We Talk?

Readers' Letters to the *New York Times*

April 2, 2007

LETTER 1

To the Editor:

I didn't get a cell phone until I was well out of high school, and I understood that it wasn't something that humans needed as an essence of their survival, but rather a luxury that was very convenient.

At this point, my cell phone is an 11th finger, and it is a personal travesty when I forget it at home for even a few hours.

To see these kids—barely out of diapers—romping around with cutesy cell phones makes me a little repulsed.

For one thing, no 7-year-old should be in a position not to have the supervision of an adult. And it makes me a little insecure to think that 7-year-olds have a social life **similar** to mine, in the way that they should need a cell phone, as I do.

At this rate, we're going in the direction of giving our dogs cell phones.

EMILY LOUBATON
March 29, 2007

LETTER 2

To the Editor:

As both a parent and a psychologist, I find the cell phone **debate** of great interest. My 7- and 10-year-old boys have been clamoring for cell phones, and for the moment, I have managed to hold out.

While I appreciate that parents have to make choices that best suit their families, I feel strongly that it boils down to ultimately being able to tolerate the frustration of not having what "all the kids have" (the refrain heard in my household), as well as not being in **constant** and immediate **contact** with friends and family.

Contrary to the opinion **cited** in your article, a cell phone is not a "transitional object," as the term **implies**, and giving a cell phone to a young child would seem to **hinder** the **process** of tolerating being apart from family.

hinder
block, obstruct

My children will get cell phones when they can appreciate the responsibility associated with ownership, and when they are at an age where they won't be under the **constant** supervision of an adult.

Until then, I will have to tolerate the frustration of the "but everyone has one" refrain, and my children will have to make due with all of the gadgets they just had to have, now buried in their closets.

ELLEN WESTRICH
March 29, 2007

© Pearson Education, Inc.

Letter 1

Topic: *Cell phones for kids*

Main idea: *Little kids should not be using cell phones.*

Author's Purpose: *to persuade/convince*

Author's Tone: *critical*

Letter 2

Topic: *Cell phones for kids*

Main Idea: *Children should wait until they are mature and responsible enough to use cell phones.*

Author's Purpose: *to persuade/convince*

Author's Tone: *critical*

Recommended debate topic: Should students be allowed to bring their cell phones into schools?

Brainstorm other debate topics related to Telecommunications with your peers, and present your ideas to your instructor for approval.

Your suggested debate topics:

a. _____

b. _____

c. _____

READING

Reading Selection 5

Online Forum

5.8 Flesch-Kincaid Grade Level 12.0

Should We Ban Cell Phones in School?

The following are five different perspectives on the "cell phones in school" issue. Please summarize in one sentence the views of these teachers. The first one is done for you.

Should We Ban Cell Phones in School?

From *NEA Today*

February 2004

Kenneth F. Meer, Naval Science Instructor, Easton, Maryland

1   Cell phones should be banned from classrooms but not from schools. When classes are in session, cell phones aren't.

"Should We Ban Cell Phones in School?" *NEA Today*, February 2004. Reprinted by permission of the National Education Association.

2   When a student is maneuvering around after-school activities and pick-up times, cell phones are extremely handy.

3   The school should not be held accountable if the cell phone is stolen. As with any other possession, it's the student's responsibility. If the student is too young to keep track of a cell phone, the student is too young to have one.

Summary of writer's perspective: .

Cell phones are the student's responsibility and should not be allowed on in the

classroom

Erich Ostrowski, Fourth-grade Teacher, Tucson, Arizona

4   Cell phones should absolutely be banned from school, no questions asked. My **philosophy** is that we lived a hundred years without them and we can live another hundred years without them if we chose to do so. They are nothing but a disruption to class instruction. The student (if he or she is waiting for a call) thinks about nothing but receiving that call, therefore blocking out anything that is being said, and it's simply not a necessity for being successful in school.

5   Cell phones, like many other electronic devices, can be a distraction. Students need to learn when and where a cell phone can be **appropriate**. It is rude to the presenter when some person has a cell phone ringing during his or her presentation. Students are often easily distracted as it is, and a cell phone going off in a classroom can end the learning **process** as effectively as any fire drill. This is one of those life lessons we can teach them. **Technology** is a wonderful and useful tool when used properly. I can think of **circumstances** where a student needs to be on call during school. That is where the office and secretaries come in.

Summary of writer's perspective:

Cell phones should be banned from school, chiefly because they distract

students from the learning process.

Kristopher Kaufman, Spanish Teacher, Northern Tioga School District, Pennsylvania

6   Until this year cell phones were banned from school here in Maryland. This year, cell phones are allowed for safety reasons-in case of an emergency, students can call for help (e.g., Columbine). Well, our students have now figured out that they can cheat on quizzes and tests by "texting" each other. Not only are phones distracting but now they are a cheating tool.

Summary of writer's perspective:

Allowing cell phone use in school has enabled students to

cheat on exams.

Mindy Siddell, Student in Teacher Education, Seward, Nebraska

7   Cell phones are so **ubiquitous** that it's a losing battle, especially at the high school level. They are part of the younger generation's survival kit, just as Spalding high bounce balls were to those of us from the '50s. Here's the rule in my United States history classes: The cell phone needs to be on stun **mode** (vibration). If it rings during class, the student must surrender the phone and

ubiquitous
ever present

© Pearson Education, Inc.

I get to answer it. Last year, I talked to two girlfriends, three boyfriends, and a mother. There were no repeat incidents.

Summary of writer's perspective:

While the writer believes that banning cell phones in school is an exercise in futility, she offers a solution to control student cell phone use in class.

Richard Mollette, High School History Teacher, Seattle, Washington

8   I think cell phones are okay for students to have—just not out in the classroom. Schools are very **dynamic** today and many students use their cells to **contact** parents about activities they had forgotten about.

9   Also, in my first year of teaching, I came back from a cold Thanksgiving Friday tournament to find the school locked up. No one had a cell phone, but one of my **colleagues** made his students memorize his phone number. We called him and his nice warm van, and his cell phone saved the day.

Summary of writer's perspective:

There are certain benefits to allowing cell phones in school.

Connecting Reading Skills with Standardized Testing

Recognizing the Author's Purpose and Tone

Questions focusing on author's purpose and tone typically concern the whole reading passage, not one particular section of the text. Remember that the two question types are interrelated, as an understanding of the purpose can clue you in to the tone and vice versa. If the author's purpose is to inform, then his or her tone will most likely be objective (or neutral, unbiased). If the author's purpose, however, is to persuade, then the tone might be convincing, pessimistic, or emotional. Finally, if the author's purpose is basically to entertain the reader, his or her tone will match the purpose and might be humorous, ironic, or lighthearted.

You are being asked the author's purpose if the questions are worded in any of the following ways:

- The reason the author wrote this passage is to . . .
- The primary purpose of this passage is . . .
- The author wrote this passage in order to . . .
- The main purpose of the above passage is . . .

The focus of a test question is author's tone if it is worded in one of these ways:

- The tone of this passage can be described as . . .
- What is the overall tone of the passage?
- What is the author's tone?
- The author's use of irony indicates . . .

Helpful Hints: Test Questions on Author's Purpose and Tone

Purpose

- Pay close attention to the language of the passage. Examine the author's choice of adjectives.
- Ask yourself, "Why did the author write this? Who was the intended audience? What is the genre of the reading?"
- Look for facts and opinion that may make the author's purpose clearer to you.

Tone

- Remember that insight into the author's purpose will clue you in to the tone, and vice versa.
- Think about the connotation, the emotional tone of the words.
- Most importantly, build your vocabulary by learning the meaning of many adjectives of tone.

From Reading to Writing: Paraphrasing

Overview

Restating an author or speaker's material in your own words is called **paraphrasing**. Paraphrasing the information you read is one way to address issues of comprehension. If you are able to take a section of a text and express the same ideas using different language, this tells you a lot about what you understand. In oral speech, we paraphrase all the time. Bob says to Julia, "I don't think I can work in this horrible office any more." Julia calls her friend a few minutes later and paraphrases what Bob has told her. "Bob made it clear that he is unhappy with his job and plans to move on." Notice how Julia got Bob's message across accurately without using the same words.

paraphrasing
expressing what someone has written or said in a way that is shorter or easier to understand

Paraphrasing Information

Here is an example to help you understand how paraphrasing works.

Example

Original quote: "We've become so obsessed with being available that when the phone rings, we have to answer it." (Barbara Pachter, the coauthor of *The Jerk with the Cell Phone: A Survival Guide for the Rest of Us*).

Paraphrase: According to Barbara Pachter, cell phone users feel compelled to answer their phones every time they ring due to their fear of being perceived as unavailable.

Read the following questions about the above paraphrased sentence and circle either yes or no.

1. Do you think that all of the ideas in the original quote are retained in the paraphrase? Yes   No

2. Is the language used in the paraphrase too similar to that used in the original quote? Yes   No

3. Does the paraphrased sentence mention the author of the original quote? Yes   No

© Pearson Education, Inc.

If you answered "Yes" to all of the above questions, then you understand how to paraphrase information.

Paraphrasing Quoted Speech in Text

One key to comprehending an article that you are reading is to identify and focus on examples of direct quotations in the text. Let's take an example from the fifth perspective on cell phones in schools from the article we just read on page 268.

Richard Mollette:

"I think cell phones are okay for students to have—just not out in the classroom. Schools are very dynamic today and many students use their cells to contact parents about activities they had forgotten about."

In trying to make sense of a quotation, it helps a lot to first consider the identity of the speaker. A person's perspective on an issue is very much influenced by his or her role. For example, in relation to the cell phone controversy, is this person a teacher, a student, someone in the cellular industry, etc.?

Look at the example of quoted speech again.

Who is Richard Molette? *A high school history teacher in Seattle, Washington.*
Try to paraphrase what he means from the two sentences above.

Paraphrase: *Molette believes that students should be allowed to keep their cell phones on outside of the classroom where they may need to contact their parents at some point in the day.*

Reporting Verbs

When you paraphrase, you often make use of verbs that relate to the reporting of information. Journalists make use of this category of verbs all the time in their work. You will find it much easier to master the skill of paraphrasing if you have some of the following verbs at your fingertips.

To explain	To respond	To point out
To indicate	To ask	To criticize
To argue	To make clear	To recall
To say	To state	To express
To tell	To clarify	To emphasize
To mention	To describe	To advise
To complain	To answer	

There are many paths you could have taken in your own paraphrase, above. Here are two possibilities:

Paraphrase (A)

Richard Mollette argues that there are many students who do make use of their cell phones to contact their parents and thus the phones should be permitted in the school, but just not in the classroom.

Paraphrase (B)

Richard Mollette makes the distinction between allowing students to bring cell phones into schools, which he agrees with, and permitting them to keep them on in the classroom, which he does not.

As long as you rephrase the information accurately and do not elaborate beyond what is given in the text, your paraphrase will be a successful one!

EXERCISE 4

Paraphrasing

Let's practice paraphrasing quotations within a text by revisiting Reading Selection 2 on page 254, "Wisconsin School Violence Leads to Cell Phone Ban."

In this article, there are examples of quoted speech for five people. First, turn back to the text, and highlight both the names and identities of these five speakers and their full quotations. Now do the exercise below. The first example is done for you.

Speaker #1: _Mike Heese_

Identity: _safety security assistant at Bradley Tech High School_

Paraphrase: _Heese explains that for his crew cell phones are seen as a potential threat._

Speaker #2: _Peter Pochowski_

Identity: _the school's director of safety and security_

Paraphrase: _Pochowski pointed out that cell phone related fights have increased._

Speaker #3: _Jamilynn Brushel_

Identity: _a senior at Bradley Tech_

Paraphrase: _She argued that people who want to fight can have a conflict with those who are already in the school._

Speaker #4: _Dorcas Lopez_

Identity: _Mother of two and social work assistant_

Paraphrase: _She doesn't believe a ban on cell phones in school will stop the fights._

Speaker #5: _William Andrekopoulos_

Identity: _Superintendent of the school_

Paraphrase: _He argues that now in America we have to start thinking about safety over convenience._

After doing the above exercise, you should now feel that you better understand the article that you read.

© Pearson Education, Inc.

Beware of Plagiarism: Paraphrase Instead!

verbatim
copying word for word

Presenting another's ideas **verbatim** without acknowledging the source is considered an act of plagiarism. Most educational institutions in the United States treat plagiarism as an academic crime and penalize students for stealing intellectual property. Paraphrasing is an effective way to convey another writer or speaker's idea without taking the risk of copying someone else's work. Simply put, you must acknowledge the source when you paraphrase ideas taken from a secondary source to substantiate your claim. Be sure that you mention the author's name in the paraphrased sentence. The trick to writing an effective paraphrase is to alter the language according to your writing style without changing the meaning. The purpose of paraphrasing is to make it clear to the reader that even though you composed the sentence, the ideas are not yours.

Joseph Dennis DeStefano

Interview with a Professional in the Field of Telecommunications

Profession: Director of Carrier Services (Telecom)

How did you choose your current profession?

I worked for AT&T Corporate for four years on the direct-sales side of AT&T and wanted to explore the alternate channel side of the carrier business with them. I looked at several Channel Partners that AT&T had relationships with and ultimately chose Presidio Networked Solutions. My decision was fairly simple due to Presidio's business model, which was "Focus plus commitment equals expertise."

How did you prepare to reach your goal of becoming a telecommunications director?

I have been able to achieve my short-term goals through the training that was provided to me at AT&T and by developing a solid network with industry professionals. This professional network was developed over time by being responsive and diligent with regard to my customers and other industry partners. To meet my long-term goals I will continue with my industry training to understand new technologies to better meet my customers' ever-changing environments and business needs and further expand my professional network.

What did you struggle with most when preparing for your career?

Some of the early struggles occurred when the telecom carriers changed their partner programs; they limited the types of accounts we were able to participate in and changed payment structure on us. Once this happened we needed to diversify

our carrier portfolio by partnering and developing relationships with other telecom carriers.

How did you overcome this struggle?

I addressed these problems by diversifying our carrier portfolio and getting our management team to buy into the value of the Carrier Services Program at Presidio Networked Solutions.

What do you enjoy most about your work?

What I value most is developing new relationships and maintaining them with our customers. I also enjoy the aspect of designing a customer's network that provides them greater bandwidth and allows them to roll out new applications to maximize their network and daily business operations.

What advice do you have for a student considering a career in telecommunications?

Work hard, pay attention to detail. Develop your professional network. Also manage your customer relationship by setting the proper expectation and following through on your commitments to them.

In your opinion what were the three most interesting points made by the interviewee? Discuss your choices with the class.

- _____
_____

- _____
_____

- _____
_____

EXERCISE 5

Crediting Your Sources

Working in small groups, paraphrase the following paragraphs, first by speaking them through, and then in written form. Consider your list of reporting verbs. Do not forget to give credit to the author.

1. "The usual suspects will try to copy the [iPhone] hardware, and it will take them some time, and maybe they will and maybe they won't be able to. But the software is at least five years ahead of anything we've seen out there. And it's really hard to do." Steven Jobs, 2007

   Paraphrase:

   Jobs (2007) believes that Apple's innovative iPhone will be hard to

   duplicate by its competitors in years to come.

   _____

   _____

2. "I am a believer in unconscious cerebration. The brain is working all the time, though we do not know it. At night it follows up what we think in the daytime. When I have worked a long time on one thing, I make it a point to bring all the facts regarding it together before I retire; I have often been surprised at the results. . . . We are thinking all the time; it is impossible not to think." Alexander Graham Bell, 1901

   Paraphrase:

   Alexander Graham Bell (1901) claims that the brain works non-stop, and it

   stores all the facts from our day.

   _____

   _____

Paraphrasing Checklist
Answer the questions on the checklist as you read your classmates' paraphrased sentence(s).

Writer _____

Reviewer _____

Date _____

1. Does the paraphrased sentence include the original author's name?

   _____

   _____

   (Continued)

© Pearson Education, Inc.

2. Does the paraphrase accurately restate the original idea? Are there any deviations in meaning from the original text to the paraphrase? If yes, what has changed?

_____

_____

_____

3. Does the writer use his or her own words in the paraphrased sentence? Do you see instances of plagiarism? If yes, highlight where this occurs.

_____

_____

_____

Textbook Application

The next Reading Selection allows you to apply the skills you have just learned.

Reading Selection **6**

Textbook Application

5.9 Flesch-Kincaid 7.1

Selections from *Introduction to Telecommunications* by M.A. Rosengrant, Chapter 23

Read the following selection from Chapter 23 of *Introduction to Telecommunications,* and try to correctly answer the multiple-choice questions that follow it. Once again, it may be helpful to highlight key points in the reading as you work with the passage.

■ INTRODUCTION

The advent of the cellular telephone **network** changed the landscape of communications around the world. The cellular telephone was first introduced in the early 1980s, but Bell Labs had developed cellular radio in the late 1940s. Cellular **technology** was not feasible until the advent of the transistor in the mid-1960s. Mobile telephone service was the predecessor of cellular radio service and was the first robust **method** used to provide wireless communications. The main differences between the mobile radio system and the cellular radio system are the way the networks are designed and the number of subscribers allowed in one **area**. Cellular radio is **similar** to a bee's honeycomb. Each cell within the honeycomb has a transmitter and receiver that hands off calls between cells as the user travels around the **area**.

The best way to understand cellular telephony is to equate it to all we have learned so far about the wire-line telephone **network**. Cellular telephones use DTMF dialing. Voice frequencies are the **source** of the signal. The **network** uses T1 circuits as trunks, fiber optic cable and multiplexers in their networks, and

From Martha A. Rosengrant, *Introduction to Telecommunications*, 2nd Edition, © 2005, pp. 651–652, 657–658, 663–665. Reprinted by permission of Pearson Education, Inc., Upper Saddle River, NJ.

digital switches to switch calls. The difference between the two networks is that the cellular **network** uses the airways to carry information the last mile to the customer. In addition, the customer is mobile—no longer tied to one **location**. The cellular **network** must transmit information through the airways and follow the user around the globe. Other than these two differences, the cellular **network** is very **similar** to the land-line telephone **network**.

Cellular providers are now becoming stiff competitors to land-line telephone systems as additional cellular carriers per market have helped reduce the price of a cellular call. In the beginning, the FCC allotted frequencies to two carriers per *cellular geographic serving area* (CGSA). The FCC **granted** the local telephone company one set of frequencies and gave the second set of frequencies to a new carrier who won a bid for the air space. In 1996, the FCC opened up the spectrum, allowing six additional carriers to enter each CGSA. Most areas now have more than two cellular carriers and, consequently, are converting from an analog cellular **network** to a digital cellular **network**.

cellular geographic serving area
Area that provides boundaries for cell companies' services.

Cellular Telephones

A cellular telephone is very **similar** to a standard wire-line telephone. The telephone has a touchtone pad that uses DTMF signals to transmit the telephone number to the MTSO and a switch hook used to go off-hook and on-hook as needed. In addition, a cellular telephone has several other **components** to transmit and receive signals, including a transmitter, receiver, antenna, diplexer, frequency synthesizer, and **logic** board, as shown in Figure 23–6. The transmitter and receiver are bridged to an antenna that transmits and receives signals. The diplexer separates the transmit and receive signals to **eliminate** cross over interference. The frequency synthesizer generates a reference frequency and the **logic** board tells it what frequency needs to be transmitted or received. The frequency synthesizer is responsible for converting the reference frequency to the **appropriate** frequency for that particular call. The **logic** board and the frequency synthesizer work together to make the cellular telephone a tunable **device**, unlike older mobile telephones.

The **logic** board may be viewed as the "brain" of the unit. It sends and receives messages from the BTS telling it when and how to set up a call, tear down a call, and monitor the strength of the signal during a call. The **logic** board interprets the signal level and sends messages back up to the controller at the BTS. The controller relays this message to the MTSO, which decides whether or not the call should be handed to the next cell. **Constant communication** between the MTSO, the BTS, and the cellular telephone make cellular **technology** much more sophisticated and complicated than regular land-line **technology**. The **process** is **similar** to an air traffic controller talking to the pilot of a plane. The controller and the pilot continuously exchange information about where the plane is, its **status**, and where it is going. The air traffic controller changes every time the plane enters a new air space, and the pilot exchanges messages with the new controller at the new air tower. The cell phone is **similar** to the pilot, and the cell **site** controller is **similar** to the air traffic controller. The cellular telephone must continuously exchange messages between itself and the cell **site** controller. Once the cellular user moves to a new cell, the phone starts to exchange messages with the new cell **site** controller at the new BTS.

A 32-bit **code** is also sent from the telephone to the base station. It is passed on to the MTSO where it is looked up in a database to confirm that the phone is one of the provider's subscribers. Unfortunately, people have been able to grab codes as they travel through the airways with special receiving black boxes.

© Pearson Education, Inc.

Figure 23–6
(a) A typical cell phone showing the four main **components**— antenna, receiver, touchtone pad, and transmitter. (b) A logical view of the **components** contained in a cell phone.

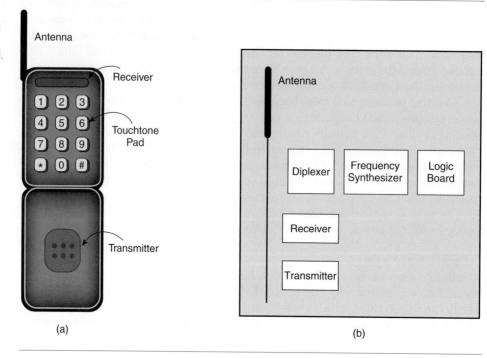

(a)

(b)

They then program stolen telephones with the new stolen codes and use the telephones to place fraudulent calls.

In the early 1990s, the power **required** to make a cellular telephone functional was fairly substantial. Small cellular phones, digital **transmission** schemes, more sophisticated microprocessors, and better cell **design** have contributed to a reduction in the power **required** by a cellular telephone. The FCC **maximum** power **output** is 7 W. A typical cellular phone requires much less. One-watt phones are now common. The battery life has also improved over the past few years. Depending upon the brand, some telephones will last hours without needing to be recharged. The prediction is that phones will continue to become more efficient and battery life will continue to improve.

Cellular phone use is being blamed for many automobile accidents. The introduction of hands-free phones has helped combat the growing concern over automobile drivers and cellular phones. Still, law **enforcement** and insurance groups are advocating bans on driving while talking on a cellular phone.

A second **phenomenon** associated with cellular **technology** is the introduction of stylish cell phones. Many colors, sizes, and carrying cases are **available** to consumers. Cellular phones, like land-line phones, are being transformed from utilitarian devices to stylish accessories.

■ 23.2 CELLULAR TELEPHONE FEATURES

Cellular telephone **features** are **similar** to land-line telephone **features**. The greatest differences are the new message-based features that are becoming very popular. Some of the most popular cellular telephone **features** are as follows.

On-hook dialing *On-hook dialing* allows the user to correct the digits of a dialed call before the call is sent. Because many users of cellular phones are

on-hook dialing
Feature that allows the user to correct the digits of a dialed call before it is sent.

moving at the same time they are dialing, the ability to correct a number before it is transmitted is not only convenient but also frugal because misdialed calls are expensive.

Signal strength indicator   A *signal strength indicator* shows how strong a signal will be or is at a particular time. In an **area** with poor cellular coverage, the signal strength indicator will show low strength, which means that the call will probably not go through or, if it does, the signal will not be good.

signal strength indicator
An indicator that shows how strong a signal is.

Call restriction   *Call restriction* is a **security** feature that reduces the chance that an unwanted call will be made by a nonallowed caller.

call restriction
A **security** feature governing users.

Alphanumeric memory   *Alphanumeric memory* is **similar** to a Rolodex. It holds names and numbers in the phone's memory.

alphanumeric memory
Memory installed that can be used to hold names and numbers of commonly called parties.

Distinctive ringing   *Distinctive ringing* allows cellular phones to be set to one of several combinations of rings, music, or other **unique** alerting **techniques**. One reason different rings are used is so the user can tell it is his or her cell phone that is ringing and not someone else's. Of course, there are a limited number of different rings.

distinctive ringing
Phones can be programmed to ring in several different ways.

Hands-free   *Hands-free* cellular telephones have become very popular due to the increased number of automobile accidents blamed on cellular use while driving. A brain cancer scare in 1999 also increased interest in hands-free phones. Though most **research** conducted so far has not linked cellular use to any type of brain cancer, the increased number of requests for a hands-free solution prompted some innovative hands-free cellular phones.

hands-free
Features that **enable** users to talk on a cellular phone without holding it.

Voice mail   *Voice mail* in the cellular world is very **similar** to voice mail offered in the wire-line world. Users enter a greeting, are given **access** to their own voice mailbox, and are allowed to **access** the mailbox from any **location**. The cellular phone displays a message saying "voice-mail message" when a call is waiting in the voice mailbox. Voice mail will continue to be one of the most popular **features** provided with cellular service. One reason cellular usage costs have dropped is the addition of value-added **features** such as voice mail that allows cellular providers to gain **income** from **items** other than minutes of use.

voice mail
Callers are able to leave voice messages for the cellular subscriber.

Call waiting   *Call waiting*, too, is similar to a call made with wire lines. Many cellular users need to be constantly connected, and call waiting provides a way to never miss a call. A call waiting beep or tone is received when the cellular user is already engaged in a conversation on the cellular telephone. The user flashes the switch hook to accept a call waiting in queue. If the user wishes to ignore the call, it may be forwarded to his or her voice mail or the caller will continue to hear ringing until he or she decides to hang up.

call waiting
Alerts cellular subscribers if a second call comes in while he/she is using the phone.

Call return   *Call return* redials the last call dialed. For **instance**, if you call 567-8899 and the line is busy, you can press *send* again after a few minutes and the phone calls the number again.

call return
Redials the last number called.

Speed dialing   *Speed dialing* is the same as the speed dial we use at home. We can program the phone with several frequently called telephone numbers and dial any of these numbers by punching in two digits instead of seven or more.

speed dialing
Allows the phone to be programmed so that a number can be dialed by dialing two numbers instead of seven or more.

© Pearson Education, Inc.

Because cellular telephone users are often on the move, they welcome such shortcuts when dialing, accepting calls, and listening for calls.

message register
Allows users to receive streams of information from the Internet.

Message register   Cellular users can now receive **data** messages on their telephone screens. A good example is that of receiving stock information, such as the price at that time. The user can also request **specific** information such as the temperature, football scores, stock prices, and so forth. The information streams in at certain intervals, and the telephone can be programmed to alert the user when a **specific** piece of information arrives.

▪ 23.3 CARRYING DATA ACROSS THE CELLULAR NETWORK

Carrying **data** over a cellular **network** is not as common as carrying **data** across a wire-line **network**, but it can be done on either the analog or the digital cellular **network**. Modems connect the PC to the cellular telephone, and special protocols have been devised to carry **data** across the radio frequencies. The most common protocols are MNP10, MNP10EC, TXCEL, and EC2. They are found in the PC card and must also exist at the far end modem owned by the ISP. Before trying to send **data** traffic using your cellular telephone, you must call your ISP to find out if it supports the correct wireless protocols. Many ISPs do not.

The highest speed you can expect to reach using your cellular telephone is 14.4 kbps. The most common speeds are 9.6 kbps or 4.8 kbps, which are very slow compared to wire-line modem speeds. Facsimiles may be transmitted by using your cellular phone at rates of 4.8 kbps or less. Transmitting large bits of **data** across the analog wireless **network** is not really possible. Most uses for cellular **data** are short **text** messages. Most cellular networks have been **converted** into digital cellular **transmission** schemes that do allow for larger bits of **data**.

The digital cellular **network** is **capable** of carrying higher **data** speeds than the analog **network**. The three digital cellular protocols handle **data transmission** differently and, as expected, are able to carry varying amounts of **data**. Entrepreneurs are working diligently on new and powerful **data transmission** standards that will allow high-speed **data** to be carried by the cellular telephone **network**. The goal of the HDR—high **data** rate—**protocol** is to allow a 2.4 Mbps standard to ride on a 1.25 MHz **channel**. Independent design companies claim they have protocols that allow **transmission** of higher bit rates than HDR. The race between the different protocols will be the **focus** for many engineers, analysts, and designers for the next few years.

▪ 23.4 SATELLITE TELEPHONE SERVICE

Satellite telephony has been one of the most-often-discussed technologies at the hundreds of telephony conferences held over the past few years. The idea of eliminating the need for extensive land-line connections intrigues the industry, and the advent of the low-orbiting satellites helped push the **concept** of satellite telephony into a reality. Three large consortiums were formed—Iridium, Globalstar, and Teledesic—with wealthy investors backing the venture.

Globalstar has **established** a worldwide telephony **network** that uses forty-eight low-orbiting satellites strategically placed around the globe. Its **network** consists of the satellites and ground stations, called gateways, that interconnect to the local telephone networks and cellular **network**. Because the satellite's orbit is low, the signal strength is greater, allowing for smaller telephones. The telephones alternate between cellular telephones and satellite phones. Globalstar can carry voice, **data**, video, fax, paging, and any other signal you can think of.

Globalstar provides service anywhere in the world except countries that have not allowed it to interconnect into local telephone networks. The local PTTs (public telephone and telegraphs) still have control over who provides telephone service in their **region**. Globalstar does offer a way to provide telephone service in remote areas of the world, though, by using the existing landline and cellular network to enhance its service and help reduce the cost of usage.

Teledesic plans to deploy low-orbiting satellites around the globe to carry all types of information—voice, **data**, and video. Teledesic does not plan to sell service directly to end users but instead is targeting service providers who are looking for **network**.

Iridium, the first to deploy satellite telephony, faced **enormous financial** trouble in the early part of the new century. Fortunately, Iridium received a large **sum** of cash that helped the company continue providing services around the world. The **technology** utilizes the Ka-band between satellites and between satellites and gateways. The L-band or low-orbiting band is used to connect to the base station telephones.

A few years ago, several large investors decided to launch a worldwide satellite telephone service. The intent was to provide dial tone anywhere in the world without the need for wires, cellular towers, or other land-oriented connections. The consortium paid billions of dollars to launch low-orbiting satellites strategically around the globe. The satellites would be used to relay calls to switching centers that would **link** into the worldwide PSTN. The object of the venture was to provide service to business travelers who often lost communications when traveling through remote parts of the world. In addition to business travelers, the consortium saw the enterprise as a way for remote villages, cities, and towns to become connected to the world **communication network**.

Iridium, however, is ahead of its time. Business people do not travel to remote places on Earth often enough to warrant the fairly high cost of a satellite phone ($3000) in addition to the cost per minute charged for each call, which is about $7. Remote villagers also are not able to pay for the high-priced telephone or the usage charges associated with each call. The only group embracing the satellite phone are the adventurous explorers who trek through the Himalayas, forge through snow to the South Pole, and navigate around the world in rowboats. Unfortunately for Iridium, there are not yet enough adventurous souls and their phone usage is not enough to repay the billions of dollars used to build the **network**.

Reading Comprehension Check

Vocabulary in Context

1. Read the Introduction section. The word *landscape* in the first sentence could be replaced with
   a. countryside.
   c. land.
   b. context/setting.
   d. speed.

© Pearson Education, Inc.

Vocabulary in Context

2. In the third sentence of the introduction ("cellular technology was not feasible until the advent of the transistor in the mid-1960s") the word *feasible* means
   a. affordable.
   b. sufficient.
   c. possible.
   d. inopportune.

Main Idea

3. The main idea of the third paragraph ("Cellular providers are now . . . ") is
   a. changes made by the FCC have made it possible for cellular providers to better compete with land-line services.
   b. frequencies are the key.
   c. land-line technology has improved significantly.
   d. new technologies have replaced old ones.

Supporting Details

4. Read the section entitled Cellular Telephones. Which is NOT listed as features shared by both cellular and standard wire-lined telephones?
   a. a touch tone pad.
   b. a switch hook.
   c. a transmitter.
   d. a logic board.

Supporting Details

5. The reference to an air traffic controller made in the second paragraph is given to illustrate the relationship between
   a. the logic board and the brain.
   b. the cell phone and the cell site controller.
   c. the receiver and the transmitter.
   d. none of the above.

Supporting Details

6. According to the reading, how are people able to make illegal calls with cell phones?
   a. by traveling through various airways.
   b. regulation has made cell phone fraudulence nearly impossible.
   c. by using black boxes to steal codes.
   d. by using special transmitters.

Supporting Details

7. What two phenomena are discussed in the final part of this section?
   a. insurance issues and cell phone accessories.
   b. the trend toward more stylish cell phone fashion and law enforcement policy.
   c. cell phone usage while driving and insurance groups.
   d. the trend toward more stylish cell phone fashion and cell phone usage while driving.

Supporting Details

8. Read the section entitled "Cellular Telephone Features." Which cell phone feature became more popular due to a concern about brain cancer?
   a. call restriction.
   b. on hook dialing.
   c. hands free.
   d. call waiting.

Supporting Details

9. According to the text, which feature is popular with cellular users who feel the need to be "constantly connected"?

a. distinctive ringing.

b. call waiting.

c. hands free.

d. both b and c.

Supporting Details

10. All of the following kinds of information are mentioned as available through "message register" EXCEPT

a. stock information.

b. the temperature.

c. sports scores.

d. movie ticket prices.

Topic

11. Read the section entitled Carrying Data Across the Cellular Network. What is the topic of the second paragraph?

a. speed of cellular phones.

b. data transmission and speed.

c. data transmission.

d. faxes.

Main Idea

12. What is the main idea of the third paragraph?

a. Entrepreneurs are competing to make faster transmissions of data with cellular telephone networks.

b. The goals of these protocols have been made clear.

c. Technology is working toward more efficient data receptors.

d. none of the above.

Supporting Details

13. Read the section Satellite Telephone Service. The objective of launching a world-wide satellite telephone service was to

a. provide better service to business travelers who travel in more remote parts of the world.

b. help remote villages to become connected to the world communication network.

c. both a and b.

d. to launch low orbiting satellites.

Author's Purpose

14. Considering the whole of the reading, what is the author's purpose in writing this text?

a. to convince readers that cell phones are the future.

b. to entertain readers with stories about cellular networks.

c. to inform readers about how cell phone systems function.

d. to compare cellular service with land-line systems.

Author's Tone

15. How would you describe the tone of this reading?

a. optimistic.

b. objective.

c. sarcastic.

d. alarmed.

© Pearson Education, Inc.

Reading Selection **7**
Additional Reading

Magazine Article

5.9 Flesch-Kincaid 7.4

Collaboration

Upwardly Mobile in Africa

Pre-Reading Questions

1. Can new technologies like cell phones change the economic level of a country? How?

2. Can you think of an example of a negative role a new technology can play in the daily life of a culture?

Upwardly Mobile in Africa

By Jack Ewing, *Business Week*

September 13, 2007

1   Precious little would seem to connect the Kenyan village of Muruguru to the 21st century. The red dirt roads become impassable in the rainy season. Only a few homes have electricity, indoor plumbing, or even a floor other than earth packed by bare feet. The villagers **survive** on corn, potatoes, and bananas

Jack Ewing, "Upwardly Mobile in Africa." Reprinted from the September 13, 2007 issue of *Business Week* by special permission, copyright © 2007 by The McGraw-Hill Companies, Inc.

they raise in hand-tilled fields, and earn a little extra cash by cultivating coffee beans that they dry outdoors on burlap sacks.

2   But a **couple** of years ago, a red and white tower appeared on a nearby hill. The **structure** is a cell-phone base station, and its arrival has changed life in Muruguru as much as any development in the past century. "I'm saving time, I'm saving money," says Grace Wachira, who runs a small business knitting cardigan sweaters in the village. Before the tower was built, she had to walk several hours to the nearest town or ride in a communal taxi to buy yarn or meet customers, and she never knew whether the person she wanted to see would be there. Now she uses her Motorola (<u>MOT</u>) handset to arrange for delivery of yarn and to communicate with buyers.

3   These days, just about every tradesman, shopkeeper, and farmer in town has a phone—or at least **access** to one. "Customers give my number to other customers. The business has grown," says Susan Wairimu, whose tailor shop sits in the row of one-story buildings that constitute the village center. And Willson Maragua's **transport** business in Muruguru, which consists of him and a used pickup truck, could hardly **function** without mobile **technology**. Local farmers, members of the Kikuyu tribe prevalent in the **area**, summon him to haul their coffee beans to a growers' **cooperative** in a nearby valley. Now Maragua, an ebullient man wearing a baseball cap that says "Bachelorette Party," lives in a home with a concrete floor and a solar **panel** on the roof to power a radio and a lightbulb—and recharge his family's two handsets. With a mobile phone, he says over a lunch of corn, potatoes, and stewed goat, "You can manage your business."

Higher Living Standards

4   Only a few years ago, places like Muruguru didn't even register in the plans of handset makers and service providers. What would a Kenyan farmer want with a mobile phone? Plenty, as it turns out. To the astonishment of the industry, people living on a few dollars a day have proven **avid** phone users, and in many parts of the world cellular airtime has become a de facto **currency**. The reason is simple: A mobile phone can dramatically improve living standards by saving wasted trips, providing information about crop prices, summoning **medical** help, and even serving as a **conduit** to banking services. "The cell phone is the single most transformative **technology** for development," says Columbia University economist and emerging markets **expert** Jeffrey Sachs.

avid
enthusiastic, dedicated

conduit
a connection that allows people to pass ideas, news, money, weapons, etc. from one place to another

5   Mobile phones are changing developing markets faster than anyone imagined. Today there are some 3 billion mobile subscriptions worldwide, and that will grow to 5 billion by 2015, when two-thirds of the people on earth will have phones, predicts Finnish handset maker Nokia Corp. (<u>NOK</u>). Nowhere is the effect more **dramatic** than in Africa, where mobile **technology** often represents the first modern **infrastructure** of any kind. The 134 million citizens of Nigeria, Africa's most populous country, had just 500,000 telephone lines in 2001 when the government began encouraging competition in telecommunications. Now Nigeria has more than 30 million cellular subscribers. Muruguru, meanwhile, had just a single pay phone before people started getting handsets a few years ago. "Communications used to be a barrier," says

© Pearson Education, Inc.

Paul Ndiritu, the former village head man. Since the advent of mobile phones, he says, "the burden has eased."

6   Yet billions of people around the world have still never used a telephone. Most of these unconnected masses live in rural areas that are much poorer and more remote than Muruguru. Now cell-phone makers and service providers understand that they can make money by bringing cell-phone service within reach of people who live on $2 a day. Users buy new phones for as little as $20—and secondhand models for far less—as well as airtime in increments of just 75 cents in Kenya, enough for nearly 10 minutes of off-peak calling.

Mobile Money Transfers

a far cry from
a great distance from the expected

7   That's **a far cry from** the European or U.S. monthly subscription model, but it works for such outfits as Millicom International Cellular (<u>MICC</u>). The Luxembourg-based company invests almost exclusively in poor countries often rocked by violence, and in the second quarter of this year saw its profits climb 65%, to $263 million. Millicom doesn't even wait for the gunfire to die down before moving into new markets, which include the Democratic Republic of Congo, Sri Lanka, and Colombia. "When you build the **network** you find really good customers," says CEO Marc J. Beuls.

8   Many economists would agree. A growing body of **evidence** suggests that **access** to communications boosts incomes and makes local economies far more efficient. Consider a group of poor fishermen in the Indian state of Kerala studied by Robert Jensen, an associate professor at Brown University. They increased their profits by an average of 8% after they began using mobile phones to find out which **coastal** marketplaces were offering the best prices for sardines. Yet **consumer** prices for fish dropped 4% because the fishermen no longer had to throw away the catch they couldn't sell when they sailed into a port after all the buyers had left. "That's what **economic** efficiencies are about—everyone is better off," says Jensen.

coastal
near a coast/beach

ingenuity
skill at inventing things, thinking of new ideas, etc.

9   With characteristic **ingenuity** and resourcefulness, villagers are proving that handsets aren't just for talking. Mobile phones, for **instance**, are becoming a way to extend **financial** services to the billions of poor people who have never seen the inside of a bank. David Omuchilili, who works as a **security** guard at a church in the town of Ngong, outside Nairobi, uses his battered, 1990s-era Ericsson (<u>ERIC</u>) to send a **portion** of his modest wages to his wife and five children in a village 180 miles away. Omuchilili pays cash to an agent for M-Pesa, a service offered by carrier Safaricom Ltd. In this case, the agent is a cell-phone dealer on a Ngong street that is crowded with stray goats and donkey carts hauling cans of water. The agent then sends a **code** number **via text** message to Omuchilili's wife, who uses the **code** to redeem cash from an M-Pesa agent close to her home.

10   Although few Kenyans have any experience with e-commerce, the M-Pesa service—pesa is Swahili for "money"—has been a runaway success since Safaricom launched it in March. Some 6,000 people a day are signing up, and Vodafone Group PLC (<u>VOD</u>)—which owns 40% of Safaricom—is thinking of extending the **concept** to India. "I used to travel home myself. This saves money," Omuchilili says after sending his wife a few dollars. "She needed money to buy food," he explains.

11   Economists are still trying to calculate the macroeconomic effect of this communications explosion, but no one doubts that it's big. Leonard Waverman,

chairman of the economics faculty at London Business School, figures that a 10% increase in a developing country's mobile-phone penetration adds 0.6 percentage points to the **economic** growth rate. Indeed, the advent of mobile communications in Africa coincides with a surge in growth. The continent's economy will expand as much as 7% this year, a 25-year high, according to the International Monetary Fund. Many other **factors** are contributing, including high **commodity** prices, fewer armed conflicts, and better government in countries such as Kenya and Tanzania. But a **fundamental principle** of economics is that markets need information to function efficiently, and cell phones are providing information to people who never had it before.

12   The telecommunications industry itself is enjoying a new level of **entrepreneurship** and job creation in the developing world. Nahashon M. Macharia, a Nairobi-based businessman, is opening new stores selling cell phones and airtime in step with the **expansion** of Safaricom's **network**. "Whenever they put up a new mast, we try to provide coverage," Macharia says above the blare of reggae music during opening celebrations for a new outlet in Othaya, a town about 50 miles from Nairobi.

entrepreneurship
making money by starting one's own business

13   There is even a whiff of startup frenzy as companies spring up to serve the mobile industry. Lagos (Nigeria)-based M-Tech Communications, **founded** in 2001, develops content—everything from ringtones to crop price information—for mobile-service providers in Kenya, Uganda, Ivory Coast, and elsewhere. "There is **significant** value in those markets, purely because of the numbers" of people, says co-founder and CEO Chika Nwobi, a graduate of East Tennessee State University. Everyone, it seems, is getting into the act. In Kenya, where Safaricom lets anyone be an airtime dealer, it's common to see vegetable stands selling bananas, tomatoes, cabbage—and scratch cards with codes that grant **access** to additional calling minutes.

14   Surprisingly, the per-minute cost of mobile service is often more expensive than in developed markets. Prepaid customers of Vodacom in the Democratic Republic of Congo, a joint venture of Vodafone and African investors, pay 26 cents per minute to make daytime calls within the **network**, compared with peak rates of roughly 10 cents a minute for U.S. cellular subscribers and 7 cents in Germany. That's because users in poor rural areas often must bear the higher cost of building out networks in areas without electricity or good highways. Safaricom, for **instance**, **wrecks** a **vehicle** a month on Kenyan roads. And theft of generators and fuel means some companies post armed guards at their cell towers.

wrecks
damages or destroys

15   To keep calling costs to a bare **minimum**, villagers keep conversations extremely short and make heavy use of **text** messaging. Flashing—calling and hanging up after the first ring—is also popular. The flash can signify, "I've arrived," "call me," or any number of other prearranged meanings. Phone sharing is also common. Some users just buy a SIM card (which is plugged into the phone to grant **access** to the **network**) for less than a dollar and borrow a phone from someone else. Many users rarely make outgoing calls, maintaining just enough prepaid **credit** to keep their accounts active and receive calls. Meshack Onsinyo Getuba, a TV and radio repairman in the Nairobi suburb of Rongai, alternates between SIM cards from two rival carriers, choosing the one that's cheapest at any given time. Mobile **technology**, he says, "has improved the lifestyle I am living," because he can call for delivery of spare parts rather than having **to fetch** them from a dealer himself.

to fetch
to buy and pick up

© Pearson Education, Inc.

proliferate
to grow in numbers rapidly

16   As mobile networks **proliferate**, they're pushing the development of other **infrastructure**. Some operators, frustrated with slow-moving power monopolies, build their own electrical lines to base stations. And mobile operators are the driving force behind new networks of fiber-optic cables. South Africa-based MTN, for **instance**, has installed its own fiber in Nigeria. That will likely lead to better broadband connections, which could **enable** English-speaking countries such as Nigeria and Kenya to become **major** outsourcing centers.

Local Operators

17   The spread of rural telephone service to the world's poor got an early boost in the villages of Bangladesh. In 1997, microlender Grameen Bank started giving advice and **credit** to local entrepreneurs, encouraging them to operate communal phone services using mobile handsets—so-called village phones. Since then the **concept** has spread around the world, and has become a profitable business for operators such as MTN. In Uganda, the carrier rolled them out in **partnership** with the Washington (D.C.)-based Grameen **Foundation** but last year took full control of the operation, which now includes 13,000 small-time entrepreneurs. "Village phones made us realize that rural areas were a market," says Francis Ssebuggwawo, a sales supervisor for MTN in Uganda.

a neck wrenching lesson
a painful, hard lesson

18   Ssebuggwawo makes that observation while steering a Ford pickup along a potholed highway that provides **a neck-wrenching lesson** in the shortcomings of **African infrastructure**. He is bound for a settlement called Wabusana, where he plans to check in with village phone operators. Wabusana is only about 50 miles north of the capital, Kampala, but the trip takes nearly three hours each way on badly paved or dirt roads marked by plots of pineapple and six-foot-high conical anthills (which provide a local specialty, sautéed ants). In a clearing, a crowd waits to receive free mosquito nets, the most affordable way to prevent malaria, **rampant** in this part of Africa.

rampant
spread across or affecting a large area, and difficult to control

19   Finally, Ssebuggwawo brakes at a collection of grim concrete and brick buildings situated at the crossing of two dirt roads. The outpost supports four village phone operators, whose stories show how the spread of telecommunications is providing a livelihood for thousands of Africans. Hasifa Nakitio, who looks to be in her early 30s, feeds 11 children—five of her own, **plus** six she takes care of for various reasons—with **income** from the village phone and by peddling cups full of *matoke*, a mashed-potato-like dish made from plantains. Nakitio says she is saving to buy a plot of land and her own house.

20   Ezeresi Serukeera, a mother of four who runs her village phone in Wabusana from a crude wooden booth, enlarged her house after she **obtained** a loan of about $385 to buy the phone gear. Serukeera, who paid back the loan in six months, even serves as a kind of local banker, a conduit for relatives in Kampala to send money home to their families. These people **transfer** airtime to Serukeera electronically, and she passes on the **equivalent** in cash minus a small **commission**, then resells the airtime minutes to other callers.

21   The operators gather with Ssebuggwawo in the dimly lit interior of one of the buildings, which quickly fills with curious children. The operators bombard him with complaints and suggestions. Why isn't MTN doing more to **promote** village phones? Why can't they sell talk time in increments of less than a minute? Why doesn't MTN's **text** message-based information service

have more news **relevant** to farmers, providing, say, the price of pineapple rather than reports on the Iraq war? As more villagers get handsets, the village phone operators point out, they will need other sources of **revenue**, such as providing information. "We have to think of ways we can add value," Ssebuggwawo agrees, taking notes.

22　　The mobile-phone industry is increasingly listening to people like these village operators, who are at the frontier of telecommunications **expansion**. Nokia's (NOK) latest phone for emerging markets, which retails for about $37 in Kenya, contains **features** such as a hookup for an **external** antenna, to better reach distant base stations, and software making it easier to track the length and cost of calls. "If we look at the next billion subscribers, the vast majority will come from emerging markets," says Kai Öistämö, Nokia's general manager for mobile phones. In India, Nokia Siemens Networks, an **equipment** joint venture with Germany's Siemens (SI), is taking the village phone **concept** a step further. The company is testing its so-called Village Connection, which allows a local entrepreneur to set up a wireless phone **network** for a few thousand dollars. Villagers can talk within the local system at a reduced rate, connecting to the more costly national **network** only for long-distance calls.

Have-Nots

23　　Of course, the spread of **technology** to places that have had none is bound to bring unforeseen **consequences**. Mobile phones can also be used to organize a guerrilla army. (The **region** around Wabusana was already the focal point of an armed **conflict** in the 1980s after the fall of Ugandan strongman Idi Amin.) And a new class of resentful have-nots could emerge among the millions of extremely poor people who still can't afford cell phones. Abraham Waigwa, a 28-year-old bricklayer who lives in Muruguru, complains he's having trouble competing with other masons whose phones allow them to be reached by **potential** employers. "I don't get jobs as often," he says. "My life is **dragging**."

dragging
moving slowly or in a difficult manner

24　　But that seems to be the minority view. "Mobile **technology** has brought many fruits, and no bad things," insists Isaac Mahenia, a schoolteacher and part-time farmer in Muruguru. Abraham Maragua, truck driver Willson Maragua's 77-year-old father, agrees that life is finally getting better in the village, and that mobile phones are part of the change. "We feel it," says Maragua, who lives in a house with a dirt floor and old newspapers covering the interior walls. As a one-time political prisoner during Kenya's **civil** strife in the 1950s, he knows what he's talking about. Says Maragua: "We didn't suffer for nothing."

Reading Comprehension Check

1. What example is NOT given to show that the Kenyan village of Muruguru is not part of the twenty-first century?
   a. impassible dirt roads.
   c. the fact that there is no library.
   b. lack of electricity.
   d. lack of plumbing.

© Pearson Education, Inc.

2. How has Grace Wachira's life changed since a cell phone station came to her village?
   a. She has a job at the cell phone base.
   b. She no longer has to travel hours to buy yarn or communicate with customers.
   c. She saves money on phone bills.
   d. none of the above.

3. In the third paragraph sentence, "Local farmers, members of the Kikuyu tribe prevalent in the area, summon him to haul their coffee beans . . . ," the word *summon* means
   a. call.
   b. stop.
   c. officially organize.
   d. sweat.

4. What reasons are given for why a Kenyan farmer would want a cell phone?
   a. A mobile phone can dramatically improve living standards by saving wasted trips.
   b. It helps to provide information about crop prices.
   c. With a cell you can summon medical help.
   d. all of the above.

5. According to the article, what service does the company M-Pesa offer?
   a. They make cell phones.
   b. They work with money transfers via cell phones.
   c. They convert currency.
   d. They build homes.

6. In the first sentence of paragraph 13, "There is even a whiff of startup frenzy as companies spring up to serve the mobile industry," the word *frenzy* could be replaced with
   a. excitement.
   b. frustration.
   c. calming.
   d. cold.

7. How do villagers keep their cell phone costs down?
   a. through text messaging instead of direct calling.
   b. They have short conversations.
   c. They use the phones in an illegal manner.
   d. both a and b.

8. What is the author's purpose?
   a. to entertain readers with a funny story.
   b. to give advice.
   c. to convince.
   d. to inform readers.

9. What is the overall tone of the article?
   a. persuasive.
   b. neutral.
   c. pessimistic.
   d. sarcastic.

10. What is the main idea of this article?
    a. The negatives of cell phone usage outweigh the pluses.
    b. Kenyans love to speak on the cell phone.
    c. The introduction of a new technology has changed many people's lives in a Kenyan village.
    d. Life doesn't really change much for most people.

Suggested Resources

Books

1. *Telecommunications Essentials, Second Edition: The Complete Global Source Guide* by Lillian Goleniewski and Kitty Wilson Jarrett. This is a telecommunications primer which can serve as a basic reference to the field.

2. *The Telephone Gambit: Chasing Alexander Graham Bell's Secret* by Seth Shulman. This book explores the theory that Bell stole the intellectual property needed to complete his masterwork, the telephone.

Movies

The Telephone (1995) This documentary examines the immeasurable impact that the telephone has had on modern life.

Internet Sites

1. http://www.telecommagazine.com

   An online magazine dedicated to the field of telecommunications.

2. http://www.antiquetelephonehistory.com

   This site explores the history of the telephone. There are some wonderful images of antique phones.

© Pearson Education, Inc.

Focusing Your Attention and Rereading

Reading comprehension suffers when the mind is distracted. It is critical that a reader works hard to focus their attention on a reading passage. Rereading gives the reader another chance to connect with the reading task at hand.

Focusing Your Attention

Overview

Does your mind ever wander while you are reading? Do you find it difficult sometimes to keep your full attention on the information in the text? Well, if you said yes to either of these questions, you are certainly not alone. There are so many potential distractions around us that can interrupt our concentration and disturb our reading process. Your cell phone might ring, someone nearby might start talking to you, or you might simply start thinking about a concern that is on your mind. You may be reading an adventure story set in India, but a voice in your head might be asking you where you want to eat lunch today. It is important to make an effort to do everything possible to keep your mind focused and "in the moment" when you are reading.

Challenge Activity

If you haven't already, read the final article of this chapter, "Upwardly Mobile in Africa," on p. 282. Try reading it from beginning to end without *any* interruptions. Set up a plan to make this work! Hide away from others, turn off your cell phone and any other electronic devices you might have.

If you can successfully do the reading without interruption, you will see how much easier it is to follow the ideas in the text and to answer the comprehension questions that follow.

Learning Implications

Concentration is a key element in comprehension. If you can develop the habit of reading without being constantly interrupted—that is, to minimize external distractions—you will see very positive results and improve your academic performance.

Rereading

Overview

It is one thing to say that you have completed a reading and another thing to say you understood what you have read. Just because your eyes have passed over a text does not guarantee that you have comprehended all of the ideas contained within it. For this reason, rereading a section of a textbook, a story, or an article can be very helpful. You might set up different goals for the first and second reading. For example, you can first do a reading straight through without stopping, and then go back and reread, but this time highlight key terms and concepts as you make your way through the text.

Challenge Activity

You have already read the final reading selection of this chapter, "Upwardly Mobile in Africa" (on p. 282). Now, try to work your way slowly through the whole article again, this time highlighting key points. When you have finished rereading the article, review your answers to the multiple-choice questions that followed that article.

Learning Implications

Rereading is not "wasting time," as some students might think. When you read a text twice, you have double the opportunity to connect with what you are reading. In some cases you may understand a reading better upon second read because your mind is more concentrated and focused. A student once said this about rereading: "The first reading serves the purpose of taking me away from the many things that are on my mind, and the second reading serves the purpose of connecting my now peaceful mind to the information in the text."

© Pearson Education, Inc.

CRIMINAL JUSTICE
Criminal Investigation

Chapter 6

"It is better that ten guilty persons escape, than that one innocent suffer."
SIR WILLIAM BLACKSTONE

Objectives   IN THIS CHAPTER YOU WILL LEARN . . .

✓ Foundation knowledge about the field of Criminal Justice

✓ How to differentiate between facts and opinions

✓ How to write persuasively

Making Predictions

Collaboration

Consider this chapter's theme of Criminal Justice. What subtopics relate to this field? (See Figure 6.1.)

■ **Figure 6.1**

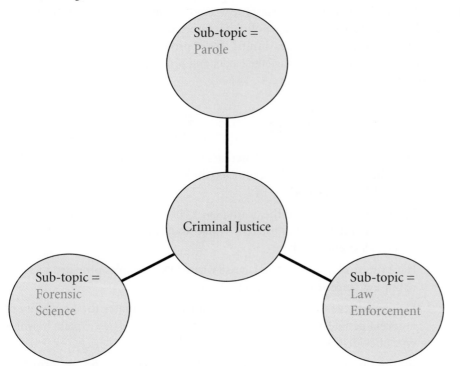

Introduction to the Field of Criminal Justice

Criminal justice professionals provide vitally important services to society. They help fellow citizens and enjoy a sense of pride as they protect them from harm and give them peace of mind. The growing emphasis on homeland security has created an unprecedented demand for criminal justice professionals. A variety of opportunities exist in:

- Prosecutors' offices and the courts
- Private investigation firms
- State, county, and city police forces
- Community and youth centers
- Correctional facilities
- Social services agencies

Criminal Justice as an academic area has evolved since its beginnings in the 1920s. Scientific research has become a major element in the increasing

© Pearson Education, Inc.

professionalization of criminal justice, and there is a strong call for the application in the justice field of evidence-based practices—that is, crime-fighting strategies that have been scientifically tested and that are based on social science research.

This chapter will primarily focus on issues related to criminal investigation. How has DNA evidence exposed some wrongful convictions? What is the role of citizen videos in uncovering police misconduct? Should juvenile offenders receive the same sentences as adults? These provocative questions, which are explored in the readings, engage the reader and provide a framework for thinking critically about criminal justice.

Preview Questions

Collaboration

1. Do you generally believe in America's criminal justice system? Do you believe the system is fair? Explain. Do you have a positive view of the police force? Why or why not?

2. In your opinion, should the death penalty be legal? If yes, for what types of crimes should it be administered? Would abolishing the death penalty make America less safe? Explain.

3. Have you read or heard about a case where DNA samples provided incriminating evidence against a suspect? Describe the case.

4. Do you believe that DNA testing completely eliminates the possibility of innocent people being wrongly convicted of a crime? If yes, explain how this type of evidence reduces the margin of error.

5. In your opinion, is it a good idea for members of a community to form their own neighborhood-watch policing units? Why or why not?

Interpreting a Cartoon

■ Figure 6.2

"For the last time! No more DNA evidence!!"

Examine the cartoon and answer the following questions in pairs.

1. What is amusing about this cartoon?
2. In your opinion, what message is the cartoonist trying to convey to the reader?

Collaboration

Discipline-specific Terminology Bank

acquittal	deterrent	interrogation	probation
alibi	evidence	misdemeanor	racial profiling
appeal	exoneration	mistrial	rehabilitation
clemency	hacker	motive	search warrant
conviction	incarceration	perjury	testimony

Sample Paragraph

Read the following paragraph, which contains some of the discipline-specific terminology you will come across in the reading selections in this chapter. Pay attention to the highlighted words, and try to figure out the meaning from the context.

> Before a suspect is **convicted** of a crime, there must be a careful review of the judicial process. Was enough **evidence** collected to make a fair judgment? Did any of the witnesses commit **perjury** on the stand while giving their **testimony** to the court? Did **racial profiling** play a role in the case? Were **interrogation** methods within the rule of law? If there is any evidence that an injustice was committed during the criminal process, the judge can declare a **mistrial** and the suspect can be **acquitted**.

EXERCISE 1

Matching Column A and Column B

Match the word in Column A with the definition in Column B. Put the letter representing the correct definition in the space preceding each term.

Column A   **Column B**

Word   **Definition**

1. <u>g</u> perjury   a. terminated trial declared invalid

2. <u>i</u> evidence   b. a reason for committing a crime

3. <u>a</u> mistrial   c. something that inhibits criminal behavior

4. <u>f</u> hacker   d. the lessening or termination of a criminal
                                sentence

© Pearson Education, Inc.

5. __d__ clemency

6. __j__ alibi

7. __b__ motive

8. __c__ deterrent

9. __h__ incarceration

10. __e__ rehabilitation

e. the attempt to reform a criminal offender

f. a computer user who illegally accesses others' computers

g. the act of making a false statement under oath

h. the act of being put in prison

i. anything useful to a judge or jury in deciding the facts of a case

j. a statement by a charged individual that he or she was nowhere near the scene of the crime

EXERCISE 2

Fill in the Blanks

In the following sentences, fill in the blank with a word from the terminology bank that makes the sentence grammatically correct and meaningful.

alibi	appeal	clemency	deterrent	evidence
hacker	motive	perjury	search warrant	testimony

1. Some politicians argue that capital punishment is a ___deterrent___ to murder.

2. His ___alibi___ was that he was out-of-state when the crime took place.

3. Criminal investigators caught a ___hacker___ breaking into government files.

4. The witness gave her ___testimony___ to the court, describing what she saw on the night of the attack.

5. The verdict was "guilty," but his lawyers said they would ___appeal___ the case.

6. The police officer flashed his ___search warrant___ before entering the suspect's apartment.

7. The case was dropped for lack of ___evidence___.

8. The convicted man was granted ___clemency___ after serving 18 years in a state penitentiary.

9. The detective force suspected that the accused kidnapper's ___motive___ was financial gain.

10. The judge ruled that the accused had contradicted himself multiple times on the stand and would face charges of ___perjury___.

Collaboration

Pair Activity

Working with a partner, choose five words you have just learned, and make complete sentences with them.

1. _____

   _____

2. _____

   _____

3. _____

   _____

4. _____

   _____

5. _____

   _____

In-class Survey: Criminal Justice Issues

Refer to the following questions to interview at least two classmates. Please take notes as they respond to your questions, and orally report your findings. Use a separate piece of paper if you need it.

Collaboration

Question	Respondent 1	Respondent 2
1. Do you think the death penalty should be legal in the United States?		
2. On a scale from 1 to 10, with 10 being the most effective, how effective a job do the police do in keeping our streets safe?		
3. Should juvenile offenders receive the same sentences for their crimes as adults do, or should they be given a second chance and given a lighter sentence? Give reasons for your position.		
4. If you had a high-level position in the field of criminal justice, what is one policy you would institute or change to make your city/town a safer place in which to live?		

© Pearson Education, Inc.

ESL Annotation

6.1 ESL Students from some cultures may not feel comfortable approaching strangers with a questionnaire. A discussion focused around this concern may be helpful.

Fieldwork Questionnaire

Please give the following survey to the people in your neighborhood, at work, or school. Tell the respondents that the survey is conducted solely for academic purposes. You can either have them write brief answers to the survey questions if they prefer, or you can write down their answers as they respond to your questions orally. Be prepared to report the results of the survey to your class later. The survey will help you learn more about societal attitudes concerning criminal justice issues. You can make two more photocopies of the survey so you will be able to question three respondents

1. Using a 5-point scale with 1 representing "very low confidence" and 5 representing "very high confidence," how much confidence do you have in the following public services in your state?

   a. The public school system _____

   b. The health care system _____

   c. The welfare system _____

   d. The criminal justice system _____

2. Use the same 5-point scale with 1 representing "very low confidence" and 5 representing "very high confidence." How much confidence do you have in the criminal justice system's response to victims of crime? _____

3. Using the same scale, how much do confidence you have in the following parts of the criminal justice system:

   a. The police _____

   b. The courts _____

   c. The corrections system _____

4. Thinking about the police in your neighborhood, using the same scale, how confident are you in the police's ability to do each of the following:

   a. Prevent crimes from happening _____

   b. Detect and arrest criminals _____

5. Thinking about the courts in your city, how confident are you in the courts' ability to do each of the following:

   a. Determine if someone is guilty _____

   b. Impose fair sentences _____

6. Thinking about the prison system in your state, how confident are you in its ability to do each of the following?

   a. Keep prisoners' from escaping _____

   b. Rehabilitate prisoners so they do not commit another offence _____

7. Using the same scale, how important do you think it is that the criminal justice system take into consideration the fact that juvenile offenders are less mature than adults? _____

8. Over the last five years, do you think that the overall crime rate in your city has gone up, stayed about the same, or decreased?
_____

9. What about property crimes such as residential break-ins and commercial theft? Do you think that over the last five years, the rate of these crimes in your city has gone up, stayed about the same, or decreased?
_____

10. When thinking about your own neighborhood compared to other neighborhoods in your city, do you think it is safer, about average, or less safe? _____

Adapted from *A Report: The 2007 National Justice Survey: Tackling Crime and Public Confidence*, Department of Justice Canada, 2007. Reproduced with the permission of the Minister of Public Works and Government Services Canada, 2009.

Graphic Analysis

Examine the graph shown here with a partner and answer the questions that follow.

Collaboration

Gender and Crime

■ Figure 6.3

	Percentage of All Arrests	
UCR Index Crime	**Males**	**Females**
Murder and nonnegligent manslaughter	89.1	10.9
Rape	98.7	1.3
Robbery	88.7	11.3
Aggravated assault	79.3	20.7
Burglary	85.5	14.5
Larceny-theft	62.3	37.7
Motor vehicle theft	82.3	17.7
Arson	83.0	17.0

Federal Bureau of Investigation, *Crime in the United States*, 2006. Washington, DC: U.S. Department of Justice, 2007.

1. According to the graph, which crime has the closest gender balance? Why do you think this is?
   Larceny/theft
   _____

© Pearson Education, Inc.

2. 89.1 percent of murders in the United States are committed by men. In your opinion, how can the fact that men kill much more frequently than women be explained? What are some factors involved?

Answers will vary.

3. Which two crime types have nearly an identical ratio in gender breakdown?

Motor vehicle theft and arson

4. Which crime has the most imbalanced gender breakdown?

Rape

5. From the information in this table, can we determine the gender of the victims of these crimes?

No. This information is not provided.

ESL Annotation

6.2 ESL It may be interesting to open up a discussion about whether this gender imbalance in criminal behavior is universal or culture-specific. ESL students can share perspectives from their native culture.

CSI: You Solve the Case!

Collaboration

We all love to play amateur detective. In this activity you and a small group of classmates will be asked to use your deductive reasoning skills in examining the "facts" of a crime scene investigation (CSI) case and making judgments about the criminal suspects. There has been a murder in Beverly Hills, California. After examining all of the presented facts, the list of leading suspects, and their stated alibis, your group's job is to decide who is most likely to be the guilty party on a scale from "most likely" to "least likely".

Facts at the Crime Scene

Fact 1: At 10:42 P.M. **Pierre Emerson III** was found dead, lying face up by the side of his outdoor swimming pool in Beverly Hills. He was found by his maid, **Ms. Johnstone,** who immediately called the Los Angeles Police Department (LAPD).

Fact 2: At 11:20 a Police Investigator determined that the cause of death was poisoning. A half-full glass of red wine with some kind of poison inside was located near a small table inches away from the victim.

Fact 3: At 11:30 P.M., the only witness, the maid, **Ms. Johnstone,** was interviewed for 40 minutes. She reported:

a. **Mr. Emerson** had seemed out of sorts all evening.

b. His lover, **Ms. Podly,** had left the premises in a limo only forty to fifty minutes before he was found dead.

c. He had received several threatening phone calls from **Mr. Samatini, Ms. Podly's** ex; two this evening and a few the night before.

d. He had also received two faxes, one last week and one yesterday from his business partner, **Mr. Lloyd,** pleading with him to agree to sign a document which would permit Mr. Lloyd to enjoy 100 percent control over business decisions regarding real estate.

e. **Mr. Emerson's** ex-wife, **Samantha,** had stopped by around 8 P.M. to pick up some items she had left behind. **Ms. Johnstone** had heard the two arguing about something to do with money, before she left around 9 P.M., slamming the door behind her.

The Five Possible Suspects

- **Miss Gwendolyn Podly**, his lover, 32, a connoisseur of fine wines. Fast-paced, eccentric, and a bit unstable, she had been secretly seeing **Mr. Emerson** for years while she was married. Her ex-husband had recently learned of this.

- **Ms. Johnstone,** his maid, 51. Reliable, yet had had a hard time adjusting to her life in the Emerson estate without **Mrs. Emerson**. She is the best friend of **Mrs. Emerson**.

- **Mr. Samatini, Ms. Podly's** ex-husband, 42. A well-built former wrestler. He had suspected his wife was seeing **Mr. Emerson**. He had recently learned that, in fact, his ex had been having an affair with **Mr. Emerson** for years.

- **Ms. Samantha Emerson**, his ex-wife, 38. A former model, she had left **Mr. Emerson** because of his infidelities. She is attached to a high-living lifestyle and felt that upon their separation she deserved more from **Mr. Emerson's** estate.

- **Mr. Jonathan Lloyd,** his business partner, 57. He had worked together in business with **Mr. Emerson** for over 15 years. While their business empire had grown, **Mr. Lloyd** was feeling more and more trapped in this partnership, unable to make any important decisions on his own. He had recently been approached secretly to work on a big real estate deal.

© Pearson Education, Inc.

Testimony Offered by the Five Leading Suspects During Police Questioning

Suspect #1: Miss Gwendolyn Podly, his lover: "Well, it all seems so foggy now. I left his place in a hurry, this is true, but that was only because I was exhausted and needed to go to my place to catch up on my sleep. I loved this man with all of my heart, and was planning to one day get married to him."

Suspect #2: Ms. Johnstone, his maid. "Like I said earlier, one minute he was reading the stock pages and the next he was face up on his back by the side of the pool. Yes, I was disappointed when things fell apart with his lovely wife, but I remained a loyal and faithful servant to him to the end."

Suspect #3: Mr. Samatini, Ms. Podly's ex-husband: "I was absolutely infuriated to learn what I had suspected all along was true, that my wife and now ex-wife was seeing him. But I am a gentle guy, you can ask anybody. I wouldn't hurt a soul. That night I was at the gym working out until way after midnight."

Suspect #4: Ms. Samantha Emerson, his ex-wife: "I stopped by and we had the same fight we always had, about money, money, money. If I had only known I would never see him again after that, I would have been nicer. He was a sweet man, but he certainly had his faults. He would never listen to my side of the story."

Suspect #5: Mr. Jonathan Lloyd, his business partner: "Yes, it is true that I was anxiously awaiting his reply to my urgent faxes, and that without his signature my deal couldn't go forward. I have already confessed that some of the information in the document was fraudulent, in that I misinformed him about the details of this big deal. But why would I kill him if I needed his signature? Anyway, as you know I was out of town on vacation in Hawaii with my kids that evening."

Verdict Time

Now that you have read the facts about the case, it is time to discuss with your group who most likely murdered Pierre Emerson III on a warm night in Beverly Hills. Discuss the case and write the names on the spectrum below.

Most likely	Possible	Least Likely

Defend Your Choices: List the factors as to why each suspect was given their "level of possible guilt" rating. Note: There is no one solution (except in the files of the LAPD). The fun is in comparing the results of your findings with another group!

_____

_____

_____

_____

_____

_____

_____

Free and Uneasy: A Long Road Back After Exoneration, and Justice Is Slow to Make Amends

Newspaper Article

6.3 Flesch-Kincaid Grade Level 11.5

Collaboration

Pre-Reading Questions

Answer the three questions below with a partner.

1. Should **exonerated** prisoners who had been kept in jail for many years receive financial compensation? What level of compensation would be fair?

2. What kinds of obstacles do ex-prisoners face getting re-established in the world outside the prison walls?

3. In your opinion, what steps can the government take to help exonerated prisoners become productive members of society?

Before reading the entire article and answering the comprehension questions that follow, ask your own questions about the first part of the article.

exonerated
officially cleared of blame and therefore not guilty

Free and Uneasy: A Long Road Back After Exoneration, and Justice Is Slow to Make Amends

By Janet Roberts and Elizabeth Stanton,
the *New York Times*

November 25, 2007

1   Christopher Ochoa graduated from law school five years out of prison and started his own practice in Madison, Wis. He has a girlfriend and is looking to buy a house.

Janet Roberts and Elizabeth Stanton, "Free and Uneasy: A Long Road Back After Exoneration, and Justice Is Slow to Make Amends." From *The New York Times*, November 25, 2007. © 2007 The New York Times. All rights reserved. Used by permission and protected by the Copyright Laws of the United States. The printing, copying, redistribution, or retransmission of the Material without express written permission is prohibited. www.nytimes.com

© Pearson Education, Inc.

?_____
_____
_____
_____
?_____
_____
_____
_____
?_____
_____
_____
_____

incarcerated
put in a prison or kept there

2 Michael Anthony Williams, who entered prison as a 16-year-old boy and left more than two years ago as a 40-year-old man, has lived in a homeless shelter and had a **series** of jobs, none lasting more than six months.

3 Gene Bibbins worked a **series** of **temporary** factory jobs, got engaged, but fell into drug addiction. Four and a half years after walking out of the Louisiana State Penitentiary at Angola, he landed in jail in East Baton Rouge, accused of cocaine possession and battery.

4 The stories are not unusual for men who have spent many years in prison. What makes these three men different is that there are serious questions about whether they should have been in prison in the first place.

5 The men are among the more than 200 prisoners exonerated since 1989 by DNA **evidence**—almost all of whom had been **incarcerated** for murder or rape. Their varied experiences are typical of what the *New York Times* found in one of the most extensive looks to date at what happens to those exonerated inmates after they leave prison.

6 The Times worked from a list of DNA-exonerated prisoners kept by the Innocence **Project**—widely regarded as the most thorough record of DNA exonerations. The Times then gathered extensive information on 137 of those whose convictions had been overturned, interviewing 115.

7 The findings show that most of them have struggled to keep jobs, pay for health care, rebuild family ties and shed the psychological effects of years of questionable or wrongful imprisonment.

8 Typically, testing of blood or semen from the crime scene **revealed** DNA pointing to another perpetrator. The authorities in some of the cases have continued to insist they convicted the right men, and have even fought efforts by some of them to sue for money.

9 About one-third of them, like Mr. Ochoa, found ways to get a stable footing in the world. But about one-sixth of them, like Mr. Bibbins, found themselves back in prison or suffering from drug or alcohol addiction.

10 About half, like Mr. Williams, had experiences somewhere between those extremes, drifting from **job** to **job** and leaning on their family, lawyers or friends for housing and other support.

to make amends
to forgive, to resolve a conflict

11 And in many cases the justice system has been slow **to make amends.**

12 The Times researched the **compensation** claims of all 206 people known by the Innocence **Project** to have been exonerated through DNA **evidence** as of August 2007. At least 79—nearly 40 **percent**—got no money for their years in prison. Half of those have **federal** lawsuits or state claims pending. More than half of those who did receive **compensation** waited two years or longer after exoneration for the first payment.

13 Few of those who were interviewed received any government services after their **release**. Indeed, **despite** being imprisoned for an average of 12 years, they typically left prison with less help—prerelease counseling, **job** training, substance-abuse treatment, housing **assistance** and other services—than some states offer to paroled prisoners.

14 "It's ridiculous," said Vincent Moto, exonerated in 1996 of a rape conviction after serving almost nine years in Pennsylvania. "They have programs for drug dealers who get out of prison. They have programs for people who really do commit crimes. People get out and go in halfway houses and have all

kinds of support. There are housing programs for them, **job** placement for them. But for the innocent, they have nothing."

15   The Times's findings are limited to those exonerated inmates the newspaper reached and do not represent the experiences of exonerated prisoners everywhere.

16   Most of the 137 exonerated inmates researched by the Times entered prison in their teens or 20s, and they stayed there while some of their peers on the outside settled on careers, married, started families, bought homes and began saving for retirement. They **emerged** many years behind, and it has been difficult **to catch up.**

17   To be sure, many in the group were already at a disadvantage when they entered prison. More than half had not finished high school. Only half could recall holding a **job** for more than a year. Some admitted to abusing drugs or alcohol or running with the wrong crowd.

18   But dozens of them had been leading lives of **stability** and accomplishment. More than 50 had held a **job** for more than two years in fields as varied as nursing, mail delivery, welding, fishing, sales and the **military**. Five had college degrees, and 20 others had completed some college or trade school.

19   Still, many of those were as unlucky as the most modestly educated when it came to finding work after their **release**. Most found that authorities were slow to wipe the convictions from their records, if they did so at all. Even newspaper articles about their exonerations seemed somehow to have had a **negative** effect in the public's mind.

20   "Any time that anyone has been in prison, even if you are exonerated, there is still a **stigma** about you, and you are **walking around with a scarlet letter**," said Ken Wyniemko, who spent more than nine years behind bars in Michigan after a rape conviction.

21   Before his conviction, he managed a bowling alley. After his **release** in 2003, he spent two fruitless years **job** hunting, and he estimates he applied for at least 100 jobs. Today, he lives off money he received in a **legal** settlement with Clinton Township in Macomb County, Mich.

22   Many of the jobs the newly released found proved short-lived, often lasting no more than a year. A few ex-prisoners like Kevin Green, who went from bingo caller to **utility** crew supervisor, changed jobs to advance their careers, but most drifted from **job** to **job** with little gain in **status** or salary.

23   Ryan Matthews, with a fiancée and 2-year-old to support, lost a **series** of jobs after he was exonerated from Louisiana's death row. He lost a shipyard **job** after his employer saw a news report about his exoneration on television.

24   Short of suing, few received substantial **compensation** from the government.

25   Given the **hodgepodge** of state **compensation** laws, an exonerated prisoner's chances of receiving any **significant sum** depend on the state where he was convicted and whether he can find a lawyer willing to **litigate** a difficult case. One man who served three years in California sued and won $7.9 million. Another, who had served 16½ years in Texas, filed a **compensation** claim and received $27,850.

26   President Bush and Congress moved in 2004 to improve the **compensation** the wrongly convicted received, adopting **legislation** that increased

to catch up
to come from behind and gain equal footing; to overtake someone or something moving

stigma
a mark of shame and disgrace

walking around with a scarlet letter
carrying around blame

hodgepodge
a lot of things put together with no order or arrangement

litigate
to engage in legal proceedings

© Pearson Education, Inc.

payments for people exonerated of **federal** crimes to $50,000 per year of imprisonment, and $100,000 per year in death penalty cases. The **legislation** included a **clause** encouraging states to follow suit, at least for wrongly convicted prisoners who had been on death row.

seized on
resorted to a method, plan, etc.,
in desperation

27   Lawyers and others **involved** with helping the exonerated have **seized on** that recommendation in pushing for improved **compensation** laws nationwide. But their efforts have gained little.

28   Only one state—Vermont—has adopted a **compensation** law since the bill passed. Twenty-one other states and the District of Columbia already had procedures for compensating the exonerated; half cap awards below $50,000 per year of incarceration.

29   Of the 124 prisoners exonerated through DNA and known to have received **compensation**, 55 got at least $50,000 for each year in prison. And most of them sued in **federal** court, claiming their **civil** rights had been violated by overzealous police officers, crime lab specialists or prosecutors. Lawyers say such cases are very difficult to win.

30   Twenty-five were convicted in states that provide no **compensation** and have collected nothing. Among them is Mr. Moto, who said he struggled this summer to raise his 10-year-old daughter on $623 a month in disability payments.

31   "You give no **compensation** to none of those guys who were wrongfully incarcerated and proved their innocence?" he said in an interview. "How can you say we believe in justice?"

Reading Comprehension Check

1. What do the three men profiled in the beginning of the article have in common?
   a. They are all prisoners.
   b. Each of them have been exonerated for a crime based on DNA evidence.
   c. They are all repeat offenders.
   d. They are still on probation.

2. The *New York Times* investigation into these cases included
   a. police detective work.
   b. research and surveying.
   c. only interviews.
   d. both research and interviews.

3. The expression "stable footing in the world" in paragraph 9 could be replaced by
   a. a desire to be mobile.
   b. balanced feet.
   c. a healthy reintegration into society.
   d. a dangerous path.

4. According to the investigation, what percentage of those who were exonerated found their way to a stable life afterward?
   a. about half.
   b. about one third.
   c. one in six.
   d. none of them.

5. What is exonerated prisoner Vincent Moto's main point in paragraph 14?
   a. The government should stop offering services to those who have actually committed crimes.

    b. Innocent prisoners should receive some special services that others do not receive.

    (c.) Truly guilty prisoners receive better services upon release than do innocent ones.

    d. none of the above.

6. What do we learn about the lives of these exonerated prisoners before they were wrongfully convicted?

    a. More than half had not finished high school.

    b. Some had issues with drug and alcohol abuse.

    c. Half had had problems holding a job.

    (d.) all of the above.

7. The case of one exonerated prisoner, Ken Wyniemko, is offered to illustrate

    a. that the road to a successful life is never far off.

    (b.) how difficult it is for many ex-prisoners to find a steady job after prison.

    c. that if you struggle hard enough you can reach your goal.

    d. the role of the government in supporting ex-prisoners.

8. According to the article, an exonerated prisoner's chances of receiving fair compensation depends on

    a. the state in which he or she was convicted.

    b. his or her legal representation.

    c. the judge.

    (d.) both a and b.

9. How much compensation did Vincent Moto receive for his wrongful conviction?

    a. $623 a month in payments.   c. His case is still pending.

    (b.) none.   d. This information is not offered.

10. What was the author's purpose in writing this article?

    a. to convince the reader that all exonerated prisoners deserve just compensation.

    b. to argue that whether or not an exonerated prisoner should receive compensation depends on the case.

    (c.) to report on the findings of a newspaper's investigation of exonerated prisoners.

    d. to entertain.

Schizophrenic Teen Looks for Justice After Murder

READING

Reading Selection **2**

Newspaper Article

6.4 Flesch-Kincaid Grade Level 8.1

Collaboration

Pre-Reading Questions

Discuss these questions in small groups.

1. If a convicted murderer's lawyer successfully makes the case that his or her client is "insane," should the killer serve time or should they be placed in a mental hospital? Explain.

© Pearson Education, Inc.

2. Do you think that claiming the "insanity defense" is taking advantage of a loophole in our criminal justice system? Are there other excuses to justify a violent crime? Explain.

3. In your view, how can law enforcement officials monitor mentally unstable members of society who could potentially pose a threat to the general public? What would be a good strategy?

Schizophrenic Teen Looks for Justice After Murder

By Pauline Arrillaga, the Associated Press

April 16, 2006

1   FLAGSTAFF, Ariz.—The phone roused Terry Clark from sleep. "Flagstaff Police Department," a voice announced, asking to speak with Mr. Clark. Terry **nudged** Dave and handed over the receiver. "My son's truck?" she heard her husband say. "Gentry?"

2   Gentry was the oldest of their three children. Had he been in a wreck? Terry crawled from bed and headed for the front door to see if her son's Toyota pickup was in the drive. She stepped out onto the porch, then stopped dead in her tracks.

3   In the dim glow of dawn, she could see that Gentry's truck was gone. Where it should have been, men in helmets stood clutching guns aimed at Terry's head. "Get against the garage!" one shouted.

4   At first, investigators told Terry only that a policeman had been shot.

5   She would hear a name, officer Jeff Moritz, and discover he was called to their neighborhood after residents reported a pickup circling, blaring loud music. The policeman had pulled the truck over and called in the license plate, then radioed dispatch once more: "999. I've been hit. 999. I've been hit."

6   The pickup—her son's pickup—sat abandoned next to the sidewalk where, Terry soon learned, the police officer had died.

7   She realized then that her son was the **prime** suspect. Not Gentry, who had been at home in bed.

8   Her middle son. Eric. The one who had been a star football player and a good student with dreams.

9   The one who just two months earlier called his own mother and father aliens.

10   The victim of the June 21, 2000, shooting was the only police officer ever killed in the line of duty in this mountain **community** north of Phoenix. He was a caring cop who cut firewood for the handicapped, a husband and father with one young son and a second on the way.

11   The accused was a 17-year-old high school senior who had a history of marijuana use and had been arrested two months earlier for drunken driving and drug possession after police found two dozen hits of LSD in his car.

12   A portrait **emerged** of a drug-crazed teen. But as the facts slowly surfaced, so did a different picture of Eric Michael Clark—that of a decent boy who had **descended** into a world of **delusion**, the terrifying existence that is **schizophrenia**.

Pauline Arrillaga, "Schizophrenic Teen Looks for Justice After Murder," April 16, 2006. Used with permission of The Associated Press. Copyright © 2006. All rights reserved.

---

nudged
to push gently to gain attention

ESL Annotation

6.5 ESL Some societies are more lenient toward juvenile offenders. This may be an interesting topic to explore with ESL students.

descended
to move from a higher to a lower place

delusion
the act of believing in something false

schizophrenia
characterized by illogical patterns of thinking

13   It took three years for Eric Clark to be found competent to stand trial and participate in his defense. When the case proceeded, his attorneys pushed for a verdict of "guilty except insane," meaning incarceration in a **psychiatric** facility. Instead, a judge found him guilty of first-degree, intentional murder and sentenced him to life in prison.

psychiatric
related to prevention of mental and emotional disorder

14   On Wednesday, the U.S. Supreme Court is to take up the case of Clark v. Arizona and the issue of just how difficult states can make it for criminal defendants to prove **insanity**.

insanity
mental illness

15   It is the first time the court has dealt with a direct **constitutional challenge** to the insanity defense since lawmakers around the country **imposed** new restrictions following John Hinckley's acquittal by reason of insanity in the 1981 shooting of President Reagan.

16   The issue is determining under what **circumstances absolution** of a criminal act is warranted.

absolution
the act of pardoning guilt or blame

17   "There are some cases," says Richard Bonnie, director of the **Institute** of Law, Psychiatry and Public **Policy** at the University of Virginia, "where a person was so mentally disturbed at the time of the offense that it would be inhumane and morally objectionable to convict and punish them."

18   Terry Clark wonders, now, when it all started.

19   Did it begin with Eric's fear of drinking tap water? It was December 1998, and a house fire forced the family to live temporarily in an apartment. Eric, then 16, worried about lead poisoning and would only drink bottled water.

20   Was that the first clue?

21   Always low-key, Eric then began to grow moody—exploding one minute, **sobbing** the next.

sobbing
to cry uncontrollably

22   Was that illness or teen angst?

23   A varsity running back at Flagstaff High, Eric dreamed of becoming a **professional** athlete. Then he lost interest in sports.

24   Terry, a school nurse, had seen her share of troubled kids. She wondered if Eric was on something, but she had had him drug-tested before and the results were **negative**. Was it **depression**? Anger management? The pieces didn't fit into one neat puzzle, and Eric's behavior grew more bizarre.

25   On June 21, 1999, Terry and Dave had their son admitted to a **mental** health center. He had abandoned his car in a road, called a police officer rude and then **reeled on** his father, using the f-word. At the center, Eric tested **positive** for marijuana. But doctors thought his behavior perhaps stemmed from pre-schizophrenia. With no **mental** illness on either side of the family, Terry pushed that idea aside.

reeled on
spoke in a loud and disrespectful manner

26   The family attended counseling sessions, and Eric seemed to improve. He promised Terry he would quit using drugs and continue seeing a therapist. She had him discharged after only three days.

27   "He's getting better," Terry **convinced** herself.

28   He got worse.

29   That fall, Eric quit school. He became obsessed with Y2K and charged $1,700 worth of survival gear on his dad's debit card. When Jan. 1, 2000, came and went, Eric was thrilled and went back to school.

30   "He's getting better," Terry thought again—until Eric started mentioning "them."

© Pearson Education, Inc.

31   "They're after me," he would tell his mother.

32   That April, in the midst of conversation, Eric referred to his mother and father as aliens.

33   "If you'd go get some tools," he told them matter-of-factly, "I'd show you."

34   Terry was relieved when, that same month, Eric was arrested on drunken driving and drug charges. She thought that would lead to help. But authorities decided to postpone **prosecution** until Eric turned 18 later in the year.

35   She and Dave searched for counselors, but Eric refused to go. Terry left messages at treatment facilities that were never returned.

36   On June 19, 2000, Eric called his mother an alien again.

37   "How would you like to be me," he said, "and never know who your real mother is?"

38   The next day, Eric seemed better, and he, Terry and Dave went to a movie together. Afterward, Eric asked if he could stay to watch another film. He hugged his folks and said goodbye.

39   Investigators **surmise** that sometime after 1:30 a.m. on June 21, 2000, Eric made his way home, sneaked into his brother Gentry's bedroom, took his keys and left in Gentry's truck.

40   What happened after that, and why, no one can know for certain. Eric's never talked about it. At the 2003 trial, prosecutors and defense attorneys presented different scenarios.

41   Both sides, and their **mental** health experts, agreed that Eric suffered from paranoid schizophrenia and was mentally ill.

42   But **legal** insanity is another matter. Arizona law spells out its qualified use as a defense.

43   "A person may be found guilty except insane if, at the time of the **commission** of the criminal act, the person was afflicted with a **mental** disease or defect of such severity that the person did not know the criminal act was wrong," the law states.

44   The prosecutor, Assistant Attorney General David Powell, argued Eric did know. One witness testified that weeks before the shooting, Eric mouthed off about his **disdain** for cops and wanting to shoot them. **Powell's** theory was Eric lured Moritz to the scene by playing loud music until residents reported him.

45   "He wanted to kill an officer that day," Powell said at trial. "And he did."

46   Defense attorneys insisted Eric's psychosis was so severe he was incapable of hatching such a plan. They noted that after the shooting, Eric called his parents from jail and explained that Flagstaff was a "platinum city" inhabited by 50,000 aliens. He told them, "The only thing that will stop aliens are bullets."

47   In his appeal to the U.S. Supreme Court, defense attorney David Goldberg asserts that Arizona law is so restrictive that it violates a mentally ill defendant's right to a fair trial. For one, he says, Arizona law **prohibited** the trial court from considering Eric's **mental** illness in weighing whether he intentionally killed a police officer.

48   Goldberg also contends that the right-wrong test is too narrow in determining **legal** insanity. Eric might have known that killing was wrong in the **abstract**, Goldberg says, but if he believed Moritz was an alien, "he didn't understand the nature of what he was doing."

---

prosecution
The act of taking legal action

surmise
conclude

disdain
to treat with contempt

prohibited
not allowed

49   The Supreme Court could establish a more **specific definition** of **legal** insanity or allow for broader **discretion** in determining when **evidence** of **mental** illness may be considered at trial.

discretion
the ability to decide responsibly

50   Its decision also could mean a retrial for Eric Clark, something the Moritz family would see as unjust.

51   "To say, gee if you're mentally ill you can be forgiven for murdering somebody, you're giving a license to kill to millions of people," says the victim's father, Dan Moritz.

52   Terry Clark says she doesn't want her son to get "off." She only wants him to get the psychiatric care he needs.

53   "Eric didn't choose to be mentally ill. It chose him," she says. "He shouldn't be punished for it."

Reading Comprehension Check

1. Why did Terry Clark stop "dead in her tracks" in paragraph 3?
   a. She was sleepy.
   b. She saw authorities pointing their guns at her.
   c. She saw her son's truck.
   d. She noticed it was dawn.

2. Which was NOT something Terry learned about the situation described in the beginning of this article?
   a. A police officer had been shot.
   b. Neighbors had reported loud music playing.
   c. The policeman had pulled her son's truck over.
   d. Her son had lots of drugs in the truck.

3. What made this case a surprising one?
   a. In this community, a police officer had never been shot and killed before.
   b. The accused did not have a criminal record.
   c. The accused was schizophrenic.
   d. both a and c.

4. What kind of verdict did Eric Clarke's lawyers' plead for?
   a. innocent.
   b. their client was guilty.
   c. their client was guilty, but insane.
   d. their client was only a juvenile.

5. The word *absolution* in the sentence "The issue is determining under what circumstances absolution of a criminal act is warranted," (paragraph 16) could be replaced by
   a. conviction.   c. resentment.
   b. forgiveness.   d. delay.

6. What position does Richard Bonnie take on the issue of the insanity defense?
   a. He is against it.   c. He supports it in some cases.
   b. He is neutral.   d. He doesn't take a position.

© Pearson Education, Inc.

Johnnie Cochran

Johnnie Cochran, one of the great criminal lawyers of his time, will be remembered for his famous line, "If the glove don't fit, you must acquit!" He led the legal defense in the legendary O. J. Simpson case in which the former football star was charged with the murder of his former wife. Cochran also represented other celebrities such as Sean Combs, Michael Jackson, and rapper Tupac Shakur. Cochran was known for his skill in the courtroom and for his advocacy of victims of alleged police abuse. Johnnie L. Cochran Jr. was born in Shreveport, Louisiana, on October 2, 1937, the great-grandson of a slave, and grew up in a prosperous family. He was raised in Los Angeles and attended UCLA, supporting himself by selling insurance policies for his father's company. He graduated in 1959 and earned his law degree from Loyola Marymount University in 1963. Cochran was inspired by the work of America's first African American Supreme Court justice, Thurgood Marshall, and decided to dedicate his life to practicing law. He felt his career was a double calling, to work for what he considered to be right and to challenge what he considered to be wrong. In his autobiography, *A Lawyer's Life*, Cochran wrote: "I read everything that I could find about Thurgood Marshall and confirmed that a single dedicated man could use the law to change society."

He passed the California bar in 1963, then took a job in Los Angeles as a deputy city attorney in the criminal division. By the late 1970s, Cochran had established his reputation in the black community. He was litigating a number of high-profile police brutality and criminal cases. In 1978 Cochran joined the Los Angeles County District Attorney's office as its first African American Assistant District Attorney.

Five years later, Cochran returned to private practice, reinventing himself as "the best in the West" by opening the Johnnie L. Cochran, Jr. law firm. Soon after, Cochran won $760,000 for the family of Ron Settles, a black college football player who, his family claimed, was murdered by the police.

He negotiated a 1993 settlement in a civil lawsuit against pop star Michael Jackson that accused him of child molestation. But it was the Simpson trial that defined him. During the five-month trial, Cochran showed off his legal skills to an audience of millions watching the case every day on their TV screens. With Cochran's defense team behind him, Simpson was acquitted of the murder of his ex-wife, Nicole.

Johnnie Cochran's excited rhetoric and flamboyance in the courtroom has been described as theatrical. His practice as a lawyer made him a wealthy man. He was said to have earned $40 million in trying cases. With his earnings, he bought and drove fancy cars and wore expensive suits.

Cochran liked to say that he worked "not only for the OJs, but also the No Js." In other words, his goal was to defend or sue in the name of those who did not have much in terms of fame or money. When Cochran died in 2005, family and friends proclaimed they "were most proud of the work he did on behalf of those in the community" rather than those with wealth and might.

Some Questions for Group Discussion

1. Cochran said that he worked "not only for the OJs, but also for the No Js." In your opinion, was this a statement confirming a worthy goal or just a smokescreen to justify Cochran's taking on America's most lucrative legal cases?

2. Do you think it is fair that wealthy clients, such as O. J. Simpson and Michael Jackson, receive more costly legal defense than the rest of us? Explain.

3. If you practiced defense law and were aware that your client had committed a serious crime, would you still agree to defend them? Explain your view.

Biographical Internet Research

Find out about another historical figure in Criminal Justice online, selecting a name from the list below, and share a biographical profile with your classmates:

- Clarence Darrow
- The Zodiac Killer
- Rodney Scott
- Janet Reno

ESL Annotation

6.6 ESL While the O. J. Simpson case reached household recognition level in the United States, many students from other cultures may be unfamiliar with this famous case. You may want to offer a brief introduction to the facts of the case to set up this biographical profile.

7. The question in paragraph 20, "Was that the first clue?" refers to
   a. evidence that Eric Clarke had major psychological problems.
   b. his mother's first signs of instability.
   c. the police investigation.
   d. none of the above.

8. The word *bizarre* in the phrase "Eric's behavior grew more **bizarre,**" (paragraph 24) means
   a. refined.   c. marketable.
   b. uncontrolled.   d. strange.

9. Which detail does NOT support the idea that Eric's condition was improving?
   a. He attended counseling sessions with his family.
   b. He promised his mother he would quit using drugs.
   c. He quit school.
   d. both b and c.

10. What is the main idea of the article?
   a. Eric Clarke's criminal behavior, which stunned his mother, was related to a schizophrenic condition.
   b. We cannot judge criminal behavior when it is connected to a mental condition.
   c. Schizophrenia is a serious mental disorder.
   d. none of the above.

SKILL FOCUS
Fact and Opinion

In many instances, the question of whether a sentence is made up of facts or opinions may seem clear-cut. Example 1 and Example 2 below are cases in point.

1. *Fact:* Criminal suspects who are found innocent are released.
2. *Opinion:* I believe that all suspects should receive a harsh interrogation.

Example 1 is a recognized truth and an observable fact. Example 2 is a judgment and a clear statement of opinion.

So why spend our valuable time on this Skill Focus area?

The answer is that the line between fact and opinion can get tricky in particular contexts, as seen in Example 3 and Example 4 below.

3. The lawyer stated that it would be in the best interests of the court to delay the trial.
4. California is a very tolerant state in the area of prisoner rights.

What may seem like an opinion (the lawyer's viewpoint) in Example 3 is actually a fact, as the sentence simply reports that the lawyer made a statement. What may seem like a fact in Example 4 (a piece of information about California) is an opinion as a judgment is made about California's prison system's level of tolerance concerning prisoner rights.

Facts

"Don't trust half of what you hear, and less of what you read."

© Pearson Education, Inc.

While this statement might seem overly skeptical, good readers think critically about what they read, and do not trust claims that are not well supported. Just because you see it in print, it doesn't mean that it is true!

A **fact** is a provable claim, that is, a statement that is verifiable.

Example
The Florida police force has doubled in the last ten years.

This is a *stated fact*. It may or may not be true, but is provable. Stated facts can go in two directions. If the above fact is shown to be true about the number of members in the Florida police force, then it is a *substantiated fact,* because it has been fact-checked and supported. If the information can be disproved, then it is a *false statement of fact* (see the diagram).

Stated Fact   →   Verifying process   →   Substantiated fact
                                                OR
                                                False statement of fact

Opinions

An *opinion* is a personal belief or judgment that is not provable.

Examples
1. The Florida police force is doing a very effective job.
2. The Florida police don't know what they are talking about.

It is important to make the distinction between *well-supported opinions* based on plausible evidence and valid reasons, and *poorly supported opinions* that seem to contradict known facts. That is to say that a *set of facts* can be used to support, or back up, an opinion.

EXERCISE 4

Finding Support

Collaboration

What types of facts might support the opinion in Example 1 above? Make a short list with a partner.

Opinion: The Florida police force is doing an effective job.

Supporting facts:

a. _____

b. _____

c. _____

EXERCISE 5

Identifying Fact and Opinion

How can you tell when you are reading a fact rather than an opinion? Consider the author's purpose in writing the piece you are reading. Is the author simply providing information about a topic, or trying to persuade the reader about a particular argument or set of arguments? Compare the two paragraphs below on random police searches.

Passage 1

Random police searches on highway checkpoints and in subway entrances have increased in the last few years. In New York City especially, the random checking of bags and other personal belongings has become commonplace. Police officials have developed a number of methods to conduct these searches working with X-ray technology and at times, police dogs.

Passage 2

Random police searches violate our privacy rights. Americans are not accustomed to this type of harassment. This really is a clear violation of police power. It is time that we speak up and put an end to this practice.

How does the author's purpose differ from Passage 1 to Passage 2? Which paragraph is more factual? Which is more opinion-based?

Of course, not all reading selections are purely fact (Passage 1) or purely opinion (Passage 2). It is often the case that an author uses a set of facts to back up an opinion. Read Passage 3, and underline any sentences that offer an opinion.

Consider the opinion put forth by the writer. What facts are used to support this viewpoint?

Passage 3

Police searches are justifiable in some cases. A few years ago, a man was searched in front of the Washington metro because he was carrying a very large bag that looked suspicious to a transit worker. It was found that the bag contained the makings of small explosives.

Signs of an Author's Point of View

There are certain words and phrases that signal that a judgment, belief or interpretation is being offered by the author.

Presentation of Opinion: Signal Phrases

In my opinion	This suggests
One possibility is	In my view
Maybe it is the case	It seems likely
I believe/I think	One idea is that

Look for descriptive adjectives that specify value judgments.

© Pearson Education, Inc.

Presentation of Opinion: Descriptive Words

effective	best
useful	worst
successful	greater
nicer	better
dishonest	wasteful
stimulating	impressive
boring	disastrous

Pay attention to key words which express uncertainty, such as the list below.

might	perhaps
seem	maybe
doubt	

Consider the Reading Type

Texts that are fact-based include:

- News reports in the form of magazine or newspaper articles are mostly factual (even though these facts are not always substantiated, and bias plays a role in which "facts" get reported).
- Textbook readings are predominantly fact-focused, as the purpose is to inform.
- Statistical data is factual (as numerical claims are verifiable).

Texts that are Opinion-based include the following:

- Newspaper or magazine editorials (editorials are, by definition, someone's opinion on an issue)
- Letters from readers to newspapers and magazines. These are usually readers' responses to articles they read.
- Internet Blogs. Members of a Web-based discussion group share their opinions.
- Quoted speech within newspaper and magazine articles often offer a diversity of perspectives on the topic featured in the article. The journalistic tone may be neutral, but interviewed sources share their viewpoints. An example of this follows:

  Steve Webb, who has been working in drug enforcement for 28 years in the Miami area, says, "We need to be stricter with drug offense sentencing if we are going to solve this problem."

Collaboration

PRACTICING THE SKILL
Practice 1

In the following short paragraphs, underline sentences that contain an opinion. Discuss with a partner what kind of factual support is offered, if any, to back up the opinion. What kind of factual evidence not given could support the view(s) of the writer?

Passage 1

One of these private groups is American Border Patrol. Its efforts have included rounding up illegal immigrants and turning them over to law enforcement. The group's director says his group has done nothing wrong. "Our borders are unprotected and the United States border patrol is derelict in his duty."

(*Excerpted from Sharon Smith, "Who's Illegal?—Shooting to Kill on the Border,"* *www.counterpunch.org, May 23, 2006*)

Factual support for offered opinion (if not given, what kind of factual details would support such a view?)

None

Evidence showing that US borders are not protected

Evidence showing that US border patrol doesn't perform effectively

Passage 2

Dear editors,

I read the article last week in your newspaper about using DNA evidence to overturn criminal sentences. I completely disagree with the writer and find this level of dependence on science to solve our criminal cases quite dangerous. Yes, it is true that DNA evidence is a useful tool in identifying criminal suspects, yet to give up on hundreds of years of time-tested crime-solving methods would be a big mistake.

Factual support for offered opinion (if not given, what kind of factual details would support such a view?)

Non-DNA based crime solving methods have been used for hundreds of years.

Evidence showing that DNA evidence has not made criminal identification more

efficient

Passage 3

Now some in law enforcement are calling for a national registry of every American's DNA profile, against which police could instantly compare crime scene specimens. Advocates say the system would dissuade many would-be criminals and help capture the rest. "This is the single best way to catch bad guys and keep them off the street," said a lawyer with a Washington firm.

(*Rick Weiss, "Push for DNA Registry Could Affect All,"* The Washington Post, *June 4, 2006*)

Factual support for offered opinion (if not given, what kind of factual details would support such a view?)

None

Evidence demonstrating that this method is the most effective

© Pearson Education, Inc.

Passage 4

Random searches in mass transit areas do not violate American's privacy rights. Extensive steps were taken to notify the public about the searches. There have been a number of efforts by terrorist groups to do damage to the U.S. infrastructure. Americans are willing to cooperate in this national effort.

Factual support for offered opinion (if not given, what kind of factual details would support such a view?)

Steps were taken to notify the public.

There have been efforts by terrorist groups to do damage to the U.S. infrastructure.

The writer could define the term "privacy rights."

Passage 5

As long as the prevalent attitude of financially irresponsible parents is that the government needs to subsidize their family dreams, reforms in our public assistance system are necessary. Reducing federal assistance will undoubtedly cause hardships for those families mired in poverty, but it would certainly rescue future children and parents from a great deal of misery and would make our streets far safer than they are.

(*Excerpted from Joe Cordill, "Parents Share Blame for Crime Stats," Letter to the Editor, July 2006*)

Factual support for offered opinion (if not given, what kind of factual details would support such a view?)

Evidence that reducing federal assistance would result in less crime

Passage 6

Many inmates are seeking changes in prison regulations or state laws in an effort to be able to use the Internet to do research or communicate with the outside world. A MYSpace spokesperson said that the site is reviewing profiles posted on behalf of inmates. The mother of a police officer killed during a robbery spoke against prisoners having MYSpace access. "This kind of thing dishonors Aubrey [her son]." "What should happen on death row is that these people should sit behind a locked door. . . ."

(*Excerpted from Kevin Johnson, "Inmates Go To Court to Seek Right to Use Internet," USA Today, November 23, 2006*)

Factual support for offered opinion (if not given, what kind of factual details would support such a view?)

This claim is an emotional response and is unverifiable.

The following Reading Selection allows you to apply the skills you have just learned.

READING

Reading Selection **3**

Newspaper Article

6.7 Flesch-Kincaid Grade Level 11.5

Collaboration

Some Say Cop Videos Misleading

Pre-Reading Questions

Work with a partner by first discussing some pre-reading questions, and then focus on applying the skill of distinguishing between fact and opinion in relation to the article.

1. How accurate do you think videotaped recordings are as criminal evidence? Are there any problems you can foresee with this type of evidence?

2. Do you think the police have the right to use force under certain circumstances? Explain.

Some Say Cop Videos Misleading

By William M. Welch, *USA TODAY*

November 30, 2006

MAR. 3 1991

William M. Welch, "Some Say Cop Videos Misleading," *USA Today,* November 30, 2006. Reprinted with permission.

© Pearson Education, Inc.

Underline all examples of stated opinions in the article. In the Opinion Box below, briefly explain each choice and draw a line connecting explanation and example. The first one is done for you.

LOS ANGELES—A **series** of recent videotaped arrests is providing an unfiltered look at often **physical**, sometimes brutal police work, due to the broadening **technology** of cell phone cameras and online video viewing.

Some law **enforcement** experts say the **technology** is shedding light on a long-standing if uncomfortable fact of life: Police frequently have to use force. And society and the law expect them to do so.

"The **core function** of police is, they're the ones who step up and use force when it is necessary," says Eugene O'Donnell, a former New York City police officer and prosecutor.

"The cops are doing our dirty work. And when someone puts it on camera and shoves it out there, we say, 'Isn't this terrible.'"

The tape of the beating of Rodney King by police in Los Angeles in 1991 had to be handed to television stations nationwide before the public saw it.

Nowadays, advances in **computer technology** and the advent of websites such as YouTube allow a person to post immediately a video online for millions of people to view.

In the latest videos:

- A man is seen being pepper-sprayed by officers in Venice Beach as he is put in a squad car. The incident happened last year but was posted online in November.

- An officer is seen punching a suspect in the face while a fellow officer tries to handcuff him during a struggle on a Hollywood street in August.

- A UCLA student is seen being shocked with a Taser stun gun by a campus police officer during a library ID check.

Some defense lawyers say the videos are giving the American public a **glimpse into** brutality they never knew existed.

Incomplete Picture?

"I can't see how anyone would think it would be OK to **mete out** punishment to someone who has been subdued and is not any threat," says John Raphling, lawyer for the man pepper-sprayed by officers.

The videos have been shocking to some Americans, a more raw real-life police drama than they may have expected after countless hours of television cop shows.

OPINION BOX

- Not everyone shares this view about the function of the police.
- Many would take offense with this claim. The negative connotation is clear.

---

glimpse into
chance to see something inside

mete out
to measure

But the videos often provide an incomplete picture of events, police and law-**enforcement** advocates say—sometimes failing to show the actions that led to the confrontation and a suspect's behavior.

And after all, some experts say, a police officer's **job** is to control violent and potentially violent people. That generally requires using a level of force just above that used by the suspect.

"Somewhere in America, cops are beating up on somebody right now. It's **legal** and justifiable, even though it may be offensive to watch," says O'Donnell, professor of law and police studies at John Jay College of Criminal Justice.

Los Angeles Police Chief William Bratton says his officers were using justifiable force in subduing suspects in the Hollywood and Venice Beach incidents, even if the video strikes viewers as disturbing.

In the Venice Beach pepper-spraying, Bratton said county prosecutors examined the video and cleared officers of wrongdoing because the video showed the man was clearly combative.

"The officers showed remarkable restraint," Bratton said. **Likewise**, the officers in the Hollywood incident were cleared after a court hearing.

Some experts say the number of videos **is bound to** increase, as will their **impact** on police work and the judicial system.

In January, video captured a San Bernardino county sheriff's deputy shooting an unarmed Air Force airman after a chase in Chino, Calif. The footage appears to show the deputy firing three times as the suspect begins to comply with orders to get up from the ground. The officer was charged with attempted **voluntary** manslaughter.

A videotape of a Westminster, Colo., police takedown of a man after a seven-hour hostage drama drew attention when it was aired on TV and the Internet in 2005. The video appeared to show officers hitting the man after he was down.

In Inglewood, Calif., a jury last year found in favor of two police officers who filed suit claiming they were unfairly disciplined after a videotaped beating of a teenager in a confrontation at a gas station in 2002.

"Because of the **technology**, everybody has a camera, and everybody's ready to use it," says Charles Whitebread, a professor of criminal **procedure** at the University of Southern California law school.

is bound to
will realistically happen

© Pearson Education, Inc.

The **impact** could be especially **significant** in Los Angeles. The city has a long and troubled history with police, use of force, and arrest videos.

Rodney King's arrest and beating after a traffic stop, videotaped by a bystander, made nationwide news. Four officers were charged with using excessive force. Their acquittal in a 1992 trial sparked riots.

The Los Angeles Police Department is still feeling the effects of a 1999 scandal involving abuses by gang-control officers in the city's Rampart Division. The city agreed to comply with a **federal** court order that **imposed** numerous requirements for managing the force and reviewing instances of **potential** abuse. It is still in effect.

"Excessive Force" Culture

Connie Rice, a **civil** rights lawyer who headed a review **panel** that investigated the scandal, credits the department with improvement in dealing with the public. "I still think LAPD has an excessive force culture," she says. "LAPD needs to tell its officers you don't get to spray people just because they **mouth off.**"

Whether the actions were justified or not, the videos have hurt the reputation of police, Whitebread says.

"It may well be that there are explanations. **At first blush**, it's pretty rough to look at," he says. "It can't do LAPD any good to have these videos disseminated."

Police are well **aware** of the power of such images. One **response** has been a move by some police forces around the country to install video cameras in police cars—allowing law **enforcement** to have its own more complete **visual** record of confrontations.

O'Donnell sees videos as possibly doing some good: They may help the public decide for itself what is reasonable force and what is not.

"People become used to the idea this is the police and what they do . . . . That may allow people to kind of clarify misconduct from things that are not misconduct.

"People see the police acting in a way that may not be pretty but may be justifiable," he said.

O'Donnell says the videos will also **demonstrate** that police are asked to bear a heavy burden in the criminal justice system, not just enforcing the law but acting as social workers with the mentally ill, the homeless and the addicted.

"It's a brutal system," says O'Donnell, "and cops **bear the brunt** of that brutality."

mouth off
to share your opinion loudly/to insult

at first blush
on first impression

bear the brunt
put up with the worst of some bad circumstance

Post-Reading Exercise

Compare with a partner what you chose to put in the Opinion Box. Discuss any differences you may have in the choices that you made.

Recommended debate topic: Should juvenile offenders receive the same prison sentences as adults?

Brainstorm other debate topics related to Criminal Justice with your peers, and present your ideas to your instructor for approval. See the next reading to help you find and develop topics.

Your suggested debate topics:

a. _____

b. _____

c. _____

The following reading will help prepare you for the debate activity by providing background information on the topic of Juvenile Crime.

Juvenile Crime

Pre-Reading Questions

6.8 Flesch Kincaid Grade Level 8.5

Before reading the text, discuss the following questions with a classmate.

1. What would motivate someone under 16 to commit a crime?
2. Should parents be held responsible for the crimes of their children? Explain.
3. What can the government do to reduce the number of juvenile crimes?

Juvenile Crime

Introduction

1   A few years ago, 13-year-old Tavaris Knight was **convicted** by a criminal court jury in Tampa, Florida, of kidnapping and raping a 43-year-old woman. Prosecutors proved that Knight, who was 12 at the time of the offense, had used a silver toy gun to force the woman away from her four young children at a playground and into the surrounding woods. Knight raped the woman twice and beat her with the gun, which he left behind. Knight's case had been transferred to adult criminal court because of the serious nature of his crimes. In closing arguments, prosecutor Michael Sinacore pointed to Knight, saying. "That young man is not a child. He stopped being a child when he forced [his victim] into the woods and

convicted
to prove someone guilty of a crime

From Frank Schmalleger, *Criminal Justice Today*, 10th ed., pp. 548–549, 562–563, © 2009. Reproduced in print and electronic formats by permission of Pearson Education, Inc., Upper Saddle River, New Jersey.

© Pearson Education, Inc.

offenders
people who break the laws

raped her." Following conviction, Knight was sentenced to 15 years in prison by Florida Circuit Judge Jack Espinosa, Jr. Knight will likely be held at a youth facility for sexual **offenders** until he is 21, at which time he could be transferred to another youth offender facility until the age of 25, followed by adult prison.

2   Crimes committed by preteens are not that unusual. In 2005, for example, a 9-year-old girl, **identified** only as Shanice K., admitted that she fatally stabbed her 11-year-old Brooklyn, New York, playmate in the heart with a steak knife during an argument over a rubber ball. The killing occurred in the midst of a Memorial Day barbecue that was being held at Shanice's home. In another example, two 12-year-old St. Lucie County, Florida, girls were charged in 2001 with trying to **drown** a classmate in a lake near her home. The victim, 12-year-old Nicole Maines, had refused to surrender her swimming mask and flippers—leading the other girls to jump into the water, grab her gear, and beat her. When the attackers shoved Maines's head underwater, a bystander, 16-year-old Hosea Rivers, jumped into the lake and pulled the girls apart. A police report noted that Maines suffered cuts and bruises all over her body.

drown
to kill by suffocating in water

3   A key finding of the Office of Juvenile Justice and Delinquency Prevention's (OJJDP's) Study Group on Serious and Violent Juvenile Offenders is that most chronic juvenile offenders begin their **delinquency** careers before age 12, and some as early as age 10. The most recent national **data** show that in 2006 police arrested about 111,600 children ages 12 and younger. These very young offenders (known as *child delinquents*) represent almost 10% of the total number of juvenile arrestees (those up to age 18).

delinquency
failure to do what law requires

4   Although states vary as to the age at which a person legally enters adulthood, **statistics** on crime make it clear that young people are disproportionately **involved** in certain offenses. A recent report, for example, found that nearly 16% of all violent crimes and 26% of all property crimes are committed by people younger than 18, though this age group makes up only 26% of the population of the United States. On average, about 17% of all arrests in any year are of juveniles, and people younger than 18 have a higher likelihood of being arrested for robbery and other property crimes than do people in any other age group. Figure 15–1 shows **Uniform** Crime Report/NIBRS **statistics** on juvenile arrests for selected offense **categories**.

5   OJJDP is a **primary source** of information on juvenile justice in the United States. A sweeping OJJDP overview of juvenile crime and the juvenile justice system in America reveals the following:

- About 1.6 million juveniles (under 18) are arrested annually in America.
- Violent crime by juveniles is decreasing.
- Younger juveniles account for a substantial **proportion** of juvenile arrests and the juvenile court caseload.
- Female delinquency has grown substantially, increasing 76% in the last ten years.
- The number of juveniles held in public facilities had increased sharply.
- Minority juveniles are greatly overrepresented in the custody population.
- Crowding is a serious problem in juvenile facilities.

One important area of juvenile rights centers on investigative procedures. In 1985, for example, the U.S. Supreme Court ruled in *New Jersey v. T.L.O.* that school children have a reasonable expectation of privacy in their personal

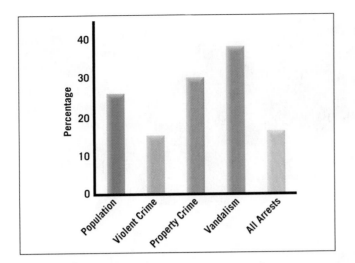

■ **Figure 15–1**

Juvenile involvement in crime versus system total 2006.

Source: Federal Bureau of Investigation, *Crime in the United States 2006* (Washington, DC: U.S. Dept. of Justice, 2007).

Note: The term *juvenile* refers to people younger than 18 years of age.

property. The case involved a 14-year old girl who was accused of violating school rules by smoking in a high school bathroom. A vice principal searched the girl's purse and found evidence of marijuana use. Juvenile officers were called, and the girl was eventually adjudicated in juvenile court and found delinquent.

6   On appeal to the New Jersey Supreme Court, the girl's lawyers were successful in having her conviction reversed on the grounds that the search of her purse, as an item of personal property, had been unreasonable. The state's appeal to the U.S. Supreme Court resulted in a ruling that **prohibited** school officials from engaging in unreasonable searches of students or their property. A reading of the Court's decision leads to the **conclusion** that a search could be considered reasonable if it (1) is based on a logical suspicion of rule-breaking actions; (2) is **required** to maintain order, discipline, and safety among students; and (3) does not **exceed** the **scope** of the original suspicion.

The Juvenile Justice Process Today

7   Juvenile court jurisdiction rests on the offender's age and **conduct**. The majority of states today define a child subject to juvenile court jurisdiction as a person who has not yet turned 18. A few states set the age at 16, and several use 17. Figure 15–3 shows the upper ages of children subject to juvenile court jurisdiction in delinquency matters, by state. When they reach their eighteenth birthday, children in most states become subject to the **jurisdiction** of adult criminal courts.

jurisdiction
the right to interpret and apply the law

8   In 2005, OJJDP reported that U.S. courts with juvenile jurisdiction annually handle slightly more than 1.6 million delinquency cases. Depending on the laws of the state and the behavior **involved**, the jurisdiction of the juvenile court may be exclusive. Exclusive jurisdiction applies when the juvenile court is the only court that has statutory authority to deal with children for **specified** infractions. For example, **status** offenses like truancy normally fall within the exclusive jurisdiction of juvenile courts. Delinquency, which involves **violation** of the criminal law, however, is often not within the juvenile court's exclusive jurisdiction. All 50 states, the District of Columbia, and the **federal** government have provisions that allow juveniles who commit serious crimes to be bound over to criminal court. Forty-six states give juvenile court

© Pearson Education, Inc.

■ **Figure 15–3**

Limit of juvenile court jurisdiction over young offenders, by state.

Source: Office of Juvenile Justice and Delinquency Prevention.

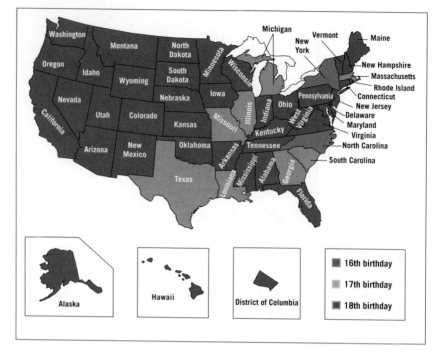

judges the power to waive jurisdiction over cases involving juveniles so that they can be transferred to criminal court. Fifteen states have "direct **file**" provisions that authorize the prosecutor to decide whether to **file** certain kinds of cases in juvenile or criminal court.

9   Juveniles who commit violent crimes or who have **prior** record are among the most likely to be transferred to adult courts. In a case that made national headlines about eight years ago, for example, Lionel Tate, who was 12 years old when he killed a 6-year-old playmate while imitating wrestling moves he had seen on TV, was tried as an adult in Fort Lauderdale, Florida: he was found guilty of first-degree murder and sentenced to life in prison without the possibility of **parole**. At the time, he was touted as the youngest person in modern American history to be sentenced to life in prison. Three years later, after intense public **debate**, Tate was released from prison and ordered to serve 11 years on **probation,** to receive counseling, and to perform 1,000 hours of **community** service. In 2005, however, 18-year-old Tate was again arrested and charged with pulling a gun on a pizza delivery man at a friend's apartment and assaulting his friend. When he was arrested, officers found a knife in his pocket. On March 1, 2006, Tate pleaded guilty to armed robbery in a plea arrangement intended to spare him a life sentence for violating probation. A few days later, however, he attempted to withdraw his plea over the objections of his attorney, who resigned. Broward County Circuit Judge Joel T. Lazarus allowed Tate to withdraw the armed robbery plea but later sentenced him to 30 years in prison for violating probation. In the courtroom, the judge told Tate, whose mother is Florida Highway Patrol trooper, that he had shown "disdain and disrespect" for the law and had "run out of second chances."

10   Where juvenile court **authority** is not exclusive, the jurisdiction of the court may be original or **concurrent**. Original jurisdiction means that a particular offense must originate, or begin, with juvenile court authorities. Juvenile courts have original jurisdiction over most delinquency petitions and

parole
the release of a prisoner based on good behavior

probation
granting a criminal freedom on the promise of good behavior

all **status** offenses. **Concurrent** jurisdiction exists where other courts have equal statutory **authority** to originate proceedings. If a juvenile has committed a **homicide,** rape, or other serious crime, for example, an arrest warrant may be issued by the adult court.

homicide
killing a person

11   Some states specify that juvenile courts have no jurisdiction over certain **excluded** offenses. Delaware, Louisiana, and Nevada, for example, allow no juvenile court jurisdiction over children charged with first-degree murder. Twenty-nine states have statutes that exclude certain serious, violent, or repeat offenders from the juvenile court's jurisdiction.

Reading Comprehension Check

1. What did the prosecuting attorney say about the 12-year-old killer, Tavaris Knight?
   a. The boy is only a boy.
   b. He should be released.
   c. The young man is not a child.
   d. both a and b.

2. "That young man is not a child" is a statement of
   a. fact.
   b. opinion.
   c. both fact and opinion.
   d. neither fact nor opinion.

3. According to the article, crimes by pre-teens are
   a. rare.
   b. happen constantly.
   c. not uncommon.
   d. all first-degree offenses.

4. What two types of crimes are committed by those under 18 disproportionate to other crime categories?
   a. violent crimes and property crimes.
   b. property crimes and kidnapping.
   c. kidnapping and drug-related offenses.
   d. larceny and arson.

5. According to a report by the OJJDP, crimes committed by _____ are increasing.
   a. male delinquents.
   b. senior citizens.
   c. drug users.
   d. female delinquents.

6. Figure 15–1 shows that juvenile crime as a percentage of total crime is highest in the category of
   a. violent crime.
   b. vandalism.
   c. theft.
   d. plagiarism.

7. In the section Juvenile Justice Process Today we read, "The majority of states today define a child subject to juvenile court jurisdiction as a person who has not yet turned eighteen." This is a statement of
   a. opinion.
   b. fact.
   c. both fact and opinion.
   d. neither fact nor opinion.

8. Figure 15–3 shows that
   a. the age for criminal suspects to be defined as "juvenile offenders" is uniform across the country.
   b. juvenile crime is increasing.

© Pearson Education, Inc.

   c. the age that criminal offenders are defined as "juvenile offenders" varies from state to state.

   d. all of the above.

9. Why was Lionel Tate's life sentence eventually reduced?

   a. because of his good conduct in prison.

   b. Juvenile court law was more lenient in Florida.

   c. He was only 12 years old when he committed the murder.

   d. New evidence came to light.

10. The states of Delaware, Nevada, and Louisiana are mentioned in the reading's final paragraph as

   a. states that have disobeyed court orders for juvenile offenders.

   b. the only states which allow juvenile court jurisdiction for first-degree murder charges.

   c. states that do not allow juvenile court jurisdiction for first-degree murder charges.

   d. states with the highest level of juvenile crime.

Connecting Reading Skills with Standardized Testing

Distinguishing Between Factual Statements and Opinions

The key to mastering fact vs. opinion–type questions is to first make an effort to fully understand what has been stated and then to ask yourself:

- Have I been given a piece of information or someone's viewpoint?
- Is what I have just read provable or not?

    Facts and opinions are often mixed together in a paragraph, with the facts offered as support for the writer's opinion or set of arguments. Pay attention to which part of the paragraph the particular exam question is focusing on and you should have no problem recognizing whether or not an opinion is present. A bell should go off in your head when key judgment words are used. Exam questions focusing on distinguishing between facts and opinion may be phrased in any of the following ways.

- Which of the following sentences from the passage represents an opinion?
- Which of the following sentences in paragraph 2 states a fact?
- In the final paragraph of the passage, which sentence expresses an opinion rather than a fact?
- In the fifth sentence of the passage, which key word signals the reader that an opinion is being expressed?
- In paragraph 3 of the passage, which sentence offers a set of facts?

Helpful Hints: Test Questions on Fact vs. Opinion

- Look for key judgment words and words that express uncertainty (see list of descriptive adjectives on p. 316).
- Consider the author's tone and purpose.

- Don't get confused between what are opinions in quotes with the fact that someone said it (for examples: "The mayor said that he hates tuna fish" is a fact because it only reports a statement).

- If a sentence is both fact and opinion, choose the answer that calls it opinion unless "both fact and opinion" is offered as an answer.

From Reading to Writing: Persuasive Writing

Whether you are writing an argumentative essay on a controversial topic, or composing a letter in response to a newspaper or magazine article that you have read, your intended goal is to persuade your audience that your opinion is credible and warrants respect.

Many of the skills used in a debate are critical to strong persuasive writing.

Keys to Writing Persuasively

- Support your arguments/opinions with relevant, detailed *facts*. Make use of readings you have worked with and any research you have done.

- Be aware of your *intended audience*. Imagine that your audience holds the opposite view. It is your job to change their mind!

- Be organized. Present your argument(s) clearly, followed by specific, supporting details.

- Use language that is forceful and convincing (do not be shy or indirect!).

> **ESL** Annotation
>
> **6.9 ESL** In many Eastern cultures directly stating your personal opinions and using persuasive power to convince others that you are right is considered impolite and immodest. In these writing cultures, opinions are expressed more indirectly.

An Example of Persuasive Writing

Context: In response to an editorial supporting random police searches

Dear editors,

I read the editorial published in last Tuesday's paper on random police searches in the subway. I absolutely disagree that police should be given the power to demand that we open up our purses and other personal belongings to them. This is America and we are not accustomed to compromising our right to privacy. I can understand the police stopping someone if they have a reasonable suspicion—for example, if someone enters a subway station with a strange-looking item or if this person is acting in a peculiar manner. But for the majority of us law-abiding citizens, it is a great insult to be stopped and forced to display our personal items. The writer makes the argument that for the purpose of national security, we have to compromise our personal freedoms. Once we begin to compromise and our freedoms are taken away, we will no longer be living in the land of the free.

With a partner, discuss whether or not the above letter is convincing (regardless of whether you agree with the writer). What techniques does the writer use to persuade his or her audience?

Collaboration

© Pearson Education, Inc.

Lawrence Kobilinsky, PhD

Profession: Professor and Chairman, Department of Sciences, John Jay College of Criminal Justice, The City University of New York

How did you choose your current profession?

After finishing my PhD in biology (studying at Mt. Sinai School of Medicine), I took a post-doctoral position at Sloan Kettering Institute. From there I got a teaching job at John Jay College of Criminal Justice in New York City, where the only science degree offered was in forensic science. I was hired as the biologist within the forensic science program. I recognized that there was much I could contribute to the field in the way of research projects. I read the leading journal in the field and decided to start several projects in forensic biology. I was fortunate in acquiring several graduate students to work with me and my research resulted in publications, thereby launching my career on the right trajectory.

How did you prepare to reach your goal of becoming a forensic scientist and DNA expert?

When I first got involved in forensic science, DNA was not a tool used for human identification and evidence analysis. In fact, most forensic practitioners knew nothing about DNA. That did not happen until the middle to late 1980s. However, once the published reports came out about the utilization of DNA in an immigration matter, I recognized the forensic significance immediately. I went to local and national meetings about forensic science, I joined several professional forensic science organizations, I continued to keep up with science and technology in the field, I published my research findings, and I taught related courses. When DNA ultimately did enter the minds of fellow criminalists, I was right on top of this new and exciting technology. I was able to purchase the first commercial DNA kit in the United States, and as a result, I got into the field early. I was soon reviewing DNA analysis records of prosecutors and advising attorneys about the strengths and weaknesses of the analyses. I lectured extensively and worked closely with the media to spread the word about the importance of this new technology. I even started to testify as an expert on DNA.

The best preparation to become a criminalist and DNA expert is to have a good general education in biology, chemistry, physics, and mathematics, and to have an open mind about a field of endeavor in which you have people's freedom and lives in your hands. Analysis of physical evidence is a great responsibility and contributes greatly to the fairness of the criminal justice system.

What did you struggle with most when preparing to build your career as an expert in criminal justice/forensic science?

Once graduating with a BS, I recognized that I required further education if I was to succeed in science. I therefore enrolled in an MS program, and when I completed that, I again realized that I needed another advanced degree to become a leader in science. I think the most difficult part of working in the forensic science field is the broad scope of the discipline and the vast amount of information that needs to be acquired to be a true expert. Hard work and discipline is essential. Even after achieving an advanced degree, you are always "going to school"—that is, reading, learning, writing articles, etc. You are always trying to keep up with new science findings and new technology. You must read the most significant journals and other science literature (books and research manuscripts) on a regular basis and at the same time, I had a high teaching load, many important consulting cases involving serious and violent crime, and in my case, a busy administrative responsibility. I have also been involved in media for the past 28 years, so there is literally very little and sometimes no time at all to relax. Going to a movie, or to the theatre is a great luxury and unfortunately this happens less often than I would like.

How did you overcome this struggle?

The answer is discipline and sacrifice. I was able to adapt to a routine where I could fit everything into my schedule. I work hard from early in the morning until the late hours of the evening. Of course, my teaching is paramount because my students come first. My administrative work comes in second but requires an extensive amount of time. I have learned to balance my career and family life. It takes a great deal of discipline and dedication to the job. My motivation and dedication remain extraordinarily high.

What do you enjoy most about your work?

I love my work and love the fact that I have the power to change my students' lives. Many of my former students have achieved great success in the field of forensic science and in other science disciplines, and this is the ultimate reward for any teacher. Some of my students are medical doctors and PhDs. Some have become laboratory directors and hold high-level positions in crime laboratories around the country. I also enjoy my media work. I am on the air on various TV programs just about every day of the workweek. I greatly enjoy talking to the public about the science utilized to solve crimes. I tell them what being a crime scene investigator is really like and try to explain that what they see on various CSI TV programs is merely entertainment. The work is far more difficult than depicted on these shows. I have also been involved in very important teaching and training on the international level. This work can change the course of criminal justice in a sovereign country. This is very exciting and important. I try to reserve the weekend for my family.

What advice do you have for a student considering a career in criminal justice?

The best advice I can give a student interested in a career in criminal justice or forensic science is to get a good basic education while in high school and in college. Students should understand that college means hard work and they should take advantage of faculty who are trying to provide them with the information that they will need to establish themselves in a good career. College is usually four years but a career in criminal justice can be ten times as long. So, it is important to understand that hard work in college will provide the tools that are needed to be successful and to enjoy a good, productive career in the future. Public service is a noble career and will provide you with a rewarding feeling of accomplishment and success.

In your opinion what were the three most interesting points made by the interviewee? Discuss your choices with the class.

- _____
  _____
- _____
  _____
- _____
  _____

Let's Back Up: Focus on Oral Argumentation

Have you ever been in a situation where you felt strongly about an idea and the person you were interacting with disagreed? We all have! How can we convince others that our way makes sense?

Practice role-playing with a partner. Alternating from 1–6, try to convince your partner of one of the following. (Try to speak without pausing for a whole minute!)

Collaboration

1. You deserve a raise at work (imagine you are speaking to your boss).
2. The speed limit should be raised by 10 mph.
3. High schools should hold regular classes in the summer.
4. College tuition should be free for all students.
5. Riding a bike to work is better than driving.
6. Women are more intelligent than men (or vice-versa).

Trying to convince others using logical argumentation can be fun! Now let's translate our oral persuasive powers into quality persuasive writing.

Practice in Persuasive Writing

Write a persuasive paragraph on this chapter's debate topic: Should juvenile offenders receive the same prison sentences as adults?

Additional Practice with Persuasive Writing

Revisit two debate topics of interest to you from previous chapters, and write a persuasive paragraph for each. You may want to first review the readings on these topics and do some additional Internet research.

Textbook Application

Read the following selection from the first chapter of a college text, *Criminal Justice Today*, and apply the skills learned in this chapter.

© Pearson Education, Inc.

READING

Reading Selection **5**

Textbook Reading

6.10 Flesch Kincaid Grade Level 12.0

From *Criminal Justice Today* by Frank Schmalleger, Chapter 1

After reading this selection, try to correctly answer the multiple-choice questions that follow. Once again, it may be helpful to highlight key points in the reading as you work with the passage.

Investigation and Arrest

If we do not maintain Justice, Justice will not maintain us.

—*Francis Bacon*

warrant

In criminal proceedings, a writ issued by a judicial officer directing a law **enforcement** officer to perform a **specified** act and affording the officer protection from damages if he or she performs it.

The modern justice **process** begins with **investigation**. After a crime has been discovered, **evidence** is gathered at the scene when possible, and a follow-up **investigation** attempts to reconstruct the **sequence** of activities. Although a few offenders are arrested at the scene of the crime, most are apprehended later. In such cases, an arrest **warrant** issued by a judge provides the **legal** basis for an apprehension by police.

An arrest, in which a person is taken into custody, limits the arrestee's freedom. Arrest is a serious step in the **process** of justice and involves a discretionary decision made by the police seeking to bring criminal sanctions to bear. Most arrests are made peacefully, but if a suspect tries to resist, a police officer may need to use force. Only about half of all people arrested are **eventually** convicted, and of those, only about a quarter are sentenced to a year or more in prison.

During arrest and before questioning, defendants are usually advised of their **constitutional** rights, as enumerated in the famous U.S. Supreme Court decision of *Miranda* v. *Arizona*. Defendants are told:

(1) "You have the right to remain silent." (2) "Anything you say can and will be used against you in court." (3) "You have the right to talk to a lawyer for advice before we ask you any questions, and to have him with you during questioning." (4) "If you cannot afford a lawyer, one will be appointed for you before any questioning if you wish." (5) "If you decide to answer questions now without a lawyer present, you will still have the right to stop answering at any time. You also have the right to stop answering at any time and may talk with a lawyer before deciding to speak again." (6) "Do you wish to talk or not?" and (7) "Do you want a lawyer?"

Although popular television programs about the criminal justice system almost always show an offender being given a rights advisement at the time of arrest, the *Miranda* decision requires only that police advise a person of his or her rights **prior** to questioning. An arrest without questioning does not require a warning. When an officer interrupts a crime in progress, public-safety considerations may make it reasonable for the officer to ask a few questions **prior** to a rights advisement. Many officers, however, feel they are on sound **legal** ground only by advising suspects of their rights immediately after arrest. **Investigation** and arrest are discussed in detail in **Chapter 7**, "Policing: **Legal Aspects**."

BOOKING

Justice cannot be for one side alone, but must be for both.

—*Eleanor Roosevelt*

booking

A law **enforcement** or correctional administrative **process** officially recording an entry into detention after arrest and identifying the person, the place, the time, the reason for the arrest, and the arresting **authority**.

Following arrest, suspects are booked. During **booking**, which is an administrative **procedure**, pictures are taken, fingerprints are made, and personal information such as address, date of birth, weight, and height is gathered. Details of the charges are recorded, and an administrative record of the arrest is created. At this time suspects are often advised of their rights again and are asked to sign a form on which each

From Frank Schmalleger, *Criminal Justice Today*, 10th ed., pp. 18–22, © 2009. Reproduced in print and electronic formats by permission of Pearson Education, Inc., Upper Saddle River, New Jersey.

right is written. The written form generally contains a statement acknowledging the advisement of rights and attesting to the fact that the suspect understands them.

Pretrial Activities

FIRST APPEARANCE

Within hours of arrest, suspects must be brought before a magistrate (a judicial officer) for an **initial** appearance. The judge will tell them of the charges against them, will again advise them of their rights, and may sometimes provide the opportunity for **bail**.

Most defendants are released on recognizance into their own care or the care of another or are given the chance to post a **bond** during their first appearance. A **bond** may take the form of a cash deposit or a property bond in which a house or other property serves as collateral against flight. Those who flee may be ordered to forfeit the posted cash or property. Suspects who are not afforded the opportunity for bail because their crimes are very serious or who do not have the needed **financial resources** are taken to jail to await the next stage in the justice **process**.

If a defendant doesn't have a lawyer, one will be appointed at the first appearance. To retain a court-appointed lawyer, the defendant may have to **demonstrate financial** hardship. The names of **assigned** lawyers are usually drawn off the roster of practicing defense attorneys in the county. Some jurisdictions use public defenders to represent indigent defendants.

All **aspects** of the first appearance, including bail bonds and possible pretrial **release**, are discussed in detail in **Chapter** 10, "Pretrial Activities and the Criminal Trial."

PRELIMINARY HEARING

The **primary** purpose of a **preliminary hearing**, also sometimes called a *preliminary examination*, is to establish whether **sufficient evidence** exists against a person to continue the justice **process**. At the **preliminary** hearing, the hearing judge will seek to determine whether there is **probable cause** to believe that (1) a crime has been committed and (2) the defendant committed it. The decision is a judicial one, but the **process** provides the prosecutor with an opportunity to test the strength of the **evidence** at his or her **disposal**.

The **preliminary** hearing also allows defense counsel the chance to assess the strength of the prosecution's case. As the prosecution presents **evidence**, the defense is said to "discover" what it is. **Hence** the **preliminary** hearing serves a discovery **function** for the defense. If the defense attorney thinks the **evidence** is strong, he or she may suggest that a plea bargain be arranged. All defendants, including those who are indigent, have a right to be represented by counsel at the **preliminary** hearing.

INFORMATION OR INDICTMENT

In some states, the prosecutor may seek to continue the case against a defendant by filing an **information** with the court. An information, which is a formal written accusation, is filed on the basis of the outcome of the **preliminary** hearing.

Other states require that an **indictment** be returned by a **grand jury** before prosecution can proceed. The grand jury hears **evidence** from the prosecutor and decides whether the case should go to trial. In effect, the grand jury is the formal indicting **authority**. It determines whether probable cause exists to charge the defendant formally with the crime. Grand juries can return an indictment on less than a unanimous vote.

The grand jury system has been criticized because it is one-sided. The defense has no opportunity to present **evidence**; the grand jury is led only by the prosecutor, often through an appeal to emotions or in ways that would not be permitted in a trial. At the same time, the grand jury is less bound by **specific** rules than a trial jury. For example, a grand jury member once told the **author** that a rape case

bail

The money or property pledged to the court or actually deposited with the court to effect the **release** of a person from **legal** custody.

preliminary hearing

A proceeding before a judicial officer in which three matters must be decided: (1) whether a crime was committed, (2) whether the crime occurred within the territorial jurisdiction of the court, and (3) whether there are reasonable grounds to believe that the defendant committed the crime.

probable cause

A set of facts and **circumstances** that would induce a reasonably intelligent and prudent person to believe that a **specified** person has committed a **specified** crime. Also, reasonable grounds to make or believe an accusation. Probable cause refers to the necessary level of belief that would allow for police seizures (arrests) of individuals and full searches of dwellings, vehicles, and possessions.

information

A formal, written accusation **submitted** to a court by a prosecutor, alleging that a **specified** person has committed a **specified** offense.

indictment

A formal, written accusation **submitted** to the court by a grand jury, alleging that a **specified** person has committed a **specified** offense, usually a felony.

grand jury

A group of jurors who have been selected according to law and have been sworn to hear the **evidence** and to determine whether there is **sufficient evidence** to bring the accused person to trial, to investigate criminal activity generally, or to investigate the **conduct** of a public agency or official.

© Pearson Education, Inc.

A criminal defendant at a **preliminary** hearing. Everyone facing criminal prosecution in the United States is guaranteed a **constitutional** right to due **process**, meaning that defendants must be afforded a fair opportunity to participate in every stage of criminal proceedings. Should due **process** rights extend to all offenders—even accused terrorists?

AP Wide World Photos

had been dismissed because the man had taken the woman to dinner first. Personal ignorance and subcultural biases are far more likely to play a **role** in grand jury hearings than in criminal trials. In defense of the grand jury system, however, defendants who are clearly innocent will likely not be indicted. A grand jury's refusal to indict can save the system **considerable** time and money by preventing cases lacking in **evidence** from further processing by the criminal justice system.

ARRAIGNMENT

arraignment

Strictly, the hearing before a court having jurisdiction in a criminal case in which the identity of the defendant is **established**, the defendant is informed of the charge and of his or her rights, and the defendant is **required** to enter a plea. Also, in some usages, any appearance in criminal court before trial.

The **arraignment** is "the first appearance of the defendant before the court that has the **authority** to **conduct** a trial." At arraignment, the accused stands before a judge and hears the information, or indictment, against him as it is read. Defendants are again notified of their rights and are asked to enter a plea. Acceptable pleas generally include (1) not guilty, (2) guilty, and (3) no contest (*nolo contendere*), which may result in conviction but can't be used later as an admission of guilt in **civil** proceedings. **Civil** proceedings, or private lawsuits, while not covered in detail in this book, provide an additional avenue of relief for victims or their survivors. Convicted offenders increasingly face suits brought against them by victims seeking to collect monetary damages.

The **Federal** Rules of **Criminal** Procedure specify that "arraignment shall be conducted in open court and shall consist of reading the indictment or information to the defendant or stating to him the substance of the charge and calling on him to plead thereto. He shall be given a copy of the indictment or information before he is called upon to plead."

Guilty pleas are not always accepted by the judge. If the judge believes a guilty plea is made under duress or is due to a lack of knowledge on the part of the defendant, the plea will be **rejected** and a plea of "not guilty" will be substituted for it. Sometimes defendants "stand mute," that is, they refuse to speak or to enter a plea of any kind. In that case, the judge will enter a plea of "not guilty" on their **behalf**.

The arraignment **process** is discussed in detail in **Chapter** 10, "Pretrial Activities and the Criminal Trial."

Everywhere across the nation, we are more concerned with ensuring that criminal activity does not repeat itself, rather than keeping criminal activity from occurring in the first place.

—Tony Fabelo, Executive Director, Texas
Criminal Justice **Policy** Council

Adjudication

Under the Sixth **Amendment** to the U.S. Constitution, every criminal defendant has a right to a **trial** by jury. The U.S. Supreme Court, however, has held that petty offenses are not covered by the Sixth **Amendment guarantee** and that the seriousness of a case is determined by the way in which "society regards the offense." For the most part, "offenses for which the **maximum period** of incarceration is six months or less are presumptively petty." In *Blanton* v. *City of North Las Vegas* (1989), the Court held that "a defendant can overcome this **presumption** and become entitled to a jury trial, only by showing that . . . additional penalties [such as fines and **community** service] viewed together with the **maximum** prison term, are so severe that the legislature clearly determined that the offense is a serious one." The *Blanton* decision was further **reinforced** in the case of *U.S.* v. *Nachtigal* (1993).

In most jurisdictions, many criminal cases never come to trial. The majority are "pleaded out," that is, they are dispensed of as the result of a bargained plea, or they are dismissed for one of a variety of reasons. Studies have found that as many as 82% of all sentences are **imposed** in criminal cases because of guilty pleas rather than trials.

In cases that do come to trial, the procedures governing the submission of **evidence** are tightly controlled by procedural law and precedent. *Procedural law* specifies the type of **evidence** that may be **submitted**, the credentials of those allowed to represent the state or the defendant, and what a jury is allowed to hear.

Precedent refers to understandings built up through common usage and also to decisions rendered by courts in **previous** cases. Precedent in the courtroom, for example, requires that lawyers request permission from the judge before approaching a witness. It also can mean that excessively gruesome **items** of **evidence** may not be used or must be altered in some way so that their factual value is not lost in the strong emotional reactions they may **create**.

Some states allow trials for less serious offenses to **occur** before a judge if defendants waive their right to a trial by jury. This is called a *bench trial*. Other states require a jury trial for all serious criminal offenses.

Trials are expensive and time-consuming. They pit defense attorneys against prosecutors. Regulated **conflict** is the rule, and jurors are **required** to decide the facts and apply the law as the judge explains it to them. In some cases, however, a jury may be unable to decide. Such a jury is said to be *deadlocked*, and the judge declares a mistrial. The defendant may be tried again when a new jury is impaneled.

The criminal trial and its participants are described fully in **Chapter** 9, "The Courts: **Structure** and Participants," and **Chapter** 10, "Pretrial Activities and the Criminal Trial."

Sentencing

Once a person has been convicted, it becomes the responsibility of the judge to impose some form of punishment. The sentence may take the form of supervised probation in the **community**, a fine, a prison term, or some combination of these. Defendants will often be ordered to pay the costs of court or of their own defense if they are able.

Prior to sentencing, a sentencing hearing may be held in which lawyers on both sides present information concerning the defendant. The judge may also ask a probation or parole officer to compile a presentence report, which contains information on the defendant's family and business situation, emotional state, social background, and criminal history. This report helps the judge make an **appropriate** sentencing decision.

Judges traditionally have had **considerable discretion** in sentencing, although new state and **federal** laws now place limits on judicial **discretion** in some cases, requiring that a sentence "presumed" by law be **imposed**. Judges still retain **enormous**

---

trial

In criminal proceedings, the examination in court of the **issues** of fact and **relevant** law in a case for the purpose of convicting or acquitting the defendant.

*While the **federal** government occasionally may make a great advance in the direction of **civil** liberties, they can also make a very disastrous reversal.*

—Supreme Court Justice Robert H. Jackson[vii]

Criminal justice cannot be achieved in the absence of social justice.

—American Friends' Service Committee[viii]

The criminal justice system is composed of a sprawling bureaucracy with many separate agencies that are largely autonomous and independent.

—Gary LaFree, Ph.D., University of New Mexico

© Pearson Education, Inc.

consecutive sentence

One of two or more sentences **imposed** at the same time, after conviction for more than one offense, and served in **sequence** with the other sentence. Also, a new sentence for a new conviction, **imposed** upon a person already under sentence for a **previous** offense, which is added to the **previous** sentence, thus increasing the **maximum** time the offender may be **confined** or under supervision.

concurrent sentence

One of two or more sentences **imposed** at the same time, after conviction for more than one offense, and served at the same time. Also, a new sentence for a new conviction, **imposed** upon a person already under sentence for a **previous** offense, served at the same time as the **previous** sentence.

LIBRARY   **WEB**
Extra   Extra

due process

A right guaranteed by the Fifth, Sixth, and Fourteenth Amendments of the U.S. Constitution and generally understood, in **legal** contexts, to mean the due course of **legal** proceedings according to the rules and forms **established** for the protection of **individual** rights. In criminal proceedings, due **process** of law is generally understood to include the following basic **elements**: a law creating and defining the offense, an impartial tribunal having jurisdictional **authority** over the case, accusation in proper form, notice and opportunity to defend, trial according to **established** **procedure**, and discharge from all **restraints** or obligations unless convicted.

discretion, however, in specifying whether sentences on multiple charges are to run consecutively or concurrently. Offenders found guilty of more than one charge may be ordered to serve one sentence after another is completed, called a **consecutive sentence**, or may be told that their sentences will run at the same time, which is called a **concurrent sentence**.

Many convictions are appealed. The appeals **process** can be **complex** and can involve both state and **federal** judiciaries. An appeal is based on the defendant's claim that rules of **procedure** were not followed properly at some earlier stage in the justice **process** or that the defendant was denied the rights guaranteed by the U.S. Constitution.

Chapter 11, "Sentencing," outlines modern sentencing practices and describes the many modern alternatives to imprisonment.

Corrections

Once an offender has been sentenced, the corrections stage begins. Some offenders are sentenced to prison, where they "do time" for their crimes. Once in the correctional system, they are classified according to local procedures and are **assigned** to confinement facilities and treatment programs. Newer prisons today bear little resemblance to the massive bastions of the past, which **isolated** offenders from society behind huge stone walls. Many modern prisons, however, still suffer from a "lock psychosis" (a preoccupation with **security**) among top- and mid-level administrators as well as a lack of **significant** rehabilitation programs.

Chapter 13, "Prisons and Jails," discusses the **philosophy** behind prisons and sketches their historical development. **Chapter 14**, "Prison Life," portrays life on the inside and delineates the social structures that develop in **response** to the pains of imprisonment.

PROBATION AND PAROLE

Not everyone who is convicted of a crime and sentenced ends up in prison. Some offenders are ordered to prison only to have their sentences **suspended** and a probationary term **imposed**. They may also be ordered to perform **community**-service activities as a condition of their probation. During the term of probation, these offenders are **required** to submit to supervision by a probation officer and to meet other conditions set by the court. Failure to do so results in revocation of probation and imposition of the original prison sentence.

Offenders who have served a **portion** of their prison sentences may be freed on parole. They are supervised by a parole officer and assisted in their readjustment to society. As in the case of probation, failure to meet the conditions of parole may result in revocation of parole and a return to prison.

Chapter 11, "Sentencing," and **Chapter 12**, "Probation, Parole, and **Community** Corrections," deal with the practice of probation and parole and with the issues surrounding it. Learn more about the criminal justice **process** at Library Extra 1–2 at cjtoday.com. For a critical look at the justice system, visit Web Extra 1–3 at cjtoday.com.

Due Process and Individual Rights

The U.S. Constitution requires that criminal justice case processing be conducted with fairness and equity; this requirement is referred to as **due process**. Simply put, *due process* means procedural fairness. It recognizes the **individual** rights of criminal defendants facing prosecution by a state or the **federal** government. Under the due **process** standard, rights violations may become the basis for the dismissal of **evidence** or of criminal charges, especially at the appellate level. Table 1–1 outlines the basic rights to which defendants in criminal proceedings are generally entitled.

TABLE 1–1 Individual Rights Guaranteed by the Bill of Rights

A right to be assumed innocent until proven guilty

A right against unreasonable searches of person and place of residence

A right against arrest without probable cause

A right against unreasonable seizure of personal property

A right against self-incrimination

A right to fair questioning by the police

A right to protection from **physical** harm throughout the justice **process**

A right to an attorney

A right to trial by jury

A right to know the charges

A right to cross-examine prosecution witnesses

A right to speak and present witnesses

A right not to be tried twice for the same crime

A right against cruel or unusual punishment

A right to due **process**

A right to a speedy trial

A right against excessive bail

A right against excessive fines

A right to be treated the same as others, regardless of race, sex, religious preference, and
other personal attributes

¹As interpreted by the U.S. Supreme Court.

Due **process** underlies the first ten amendments to the Constitution, which are collectively known as the *Bill of Rights.* It is specifically guaranteed by the Fifth, Sixth, and Fourteenth Amendments and is succinctly stated in the Fifth, which reads, "No person shall be . . . deprived of life, liberty, or property, without due **process** of law." The Fourteenth **Amendment** makes due **process** binding on the states, that is, it requires **individual** states to respect the due **process** rights of U.S. citizens who come under their jurisdiction.

The courts, and specifically the U.S. Supreme Court, have interpreted and clarified the guarantees of the Bill of Rights. The due **process** standard was set in the 1960s by the Warren Court (1953–1969), following a number of far-reaching Supreme Court decisions that affected criminal **procedure**. Led by Chief Justice Earl Warren, the Warren Court is remembered for its concern with protecting the innocent against the massive power of the state in criminal proceedings. As a result of its tireless efforts to institutionalize the Bill of Rights, the daily practice of modern American criminal justice is now set squarely upon the due **process** standard.

> *African-American men* ***comprise*** *less than 6% of the U.S. population and almost one-half of its criminal prisoners.*
>
> —Bureau of Justice **Statistics**

Reading Comprehension Check

Fact vs. Opinion

1. Examine the first sentence of this reading passage, "The modern justice process begins with investigation." This sentence

    a. expresses an opinion.   c. is a statement of fact.

    b. is false.   d. is both a fact and an opinion.

© Pearson Education, Inc.

Statistical Analysis

2. According to paragraph 2, what percentage of arrested individuals are eventually sentenced to a year or more in prison?
   a. about 25%.   c. half.
   b. about 12%.   d. none of the above.

Negative Question

3. Which is NOT listed as a defendant's constitutional right enumerated in the Supreme Court's Miranda v. Arizona decision?
   a. the right to a lawyer.
   b. the right to remain silent.
   c. the right to arms.
   d. the right to know that anything that you say can be used as evidence in a court of law.

Compare/Contrast

4. According to the article, how do arrests depicted in popular television shows differ from cases of arrest in the real world?
   a. In TV programs, offenders are read their rights at the scene of the arrest.
   b. In the real world, the Miranda decision makes it clear that offenders must be read their rights at the moment of arrest.
   c. On TV, rights advisement only need be given before questioning occurs.
   d. none of the above.

Vocabulary

5. Read the section entitled Booking. The word *attesting* in the phrase, "attesting to the fact that the suspect understands them," could be replaced by
   a. contradicting.   c. displacing.
   b. confirming.   d. meandering.

Supporting Details

6. Which is mentioned as a stage in the booking process?
   a. fingerprinting.
   b. gathering of personal information.
   c. photographs are taken.
   d. all of the above.

Supporting Details

7. Read the section Pre-trial Activities. The purpose of a bond is
   a. to protect against criminal flight.
   b. to pay off the system for one's release.
   c. to be paid in cash or property.
   d. to make sure all have the right to a lawyer.

Vocabulary

8. In the phrase "to retain a court-appointed lawyer," the word *retain* means
  a. to oversee.   c. to employ
  b. to administer.   d. to judge.

Fact vs. Opinion

9. Read the first sentence of the section Information or Indictment: "In some states, the prosecutor may seek to continue the case against a defendant by filing an information with the court."

The above is a statement of
  a. opinion.   c. both.
  b. fact.   d. neither.

Inference

10. Read the section entitled Information or Indictment. The grand jury system has been criticized because
  a. it highly favors the defendant.
  b. it forces subcultural bias to play a role.
  c. the defense does not have a voice in it.
  d. very few cases of indictment occur.

Vocabulary

11. Read the section entitled Arraignment. What does the term "stand mute" refer to?
  a. when the judge changes a "guilty" plea.
  b. when a defendant refuses to speak or enter a plea.
  c. when a defendant refuses to sit down.
  d. a location in a court of law.

Supporting Details

12. The court usually determines that a case is "petty" and is not then covered by the Sixth Amendment right to a trial if
  a. the offense carries a maximum sentence of six months or less.
  b. the offense was domestic in nature.
  c. the offense is homicide.
  d. both b and c.

Supporting Details

13. The majority of criminal cases
  a. are pleaded out.   c. last months.
  b. never come to trial.   d. both a and b.

Compare/Contrast

14. Read the section entitled Sentencing. What is the difference between a consecutive sentence and a concurrent sentence?
  a. In a consecutive sentence, two sentences run at the same time.
  b. the timing of the two sentences.
  c. In a concurrent sentence, multiple sentences run one at a time.
  d. none of the above.

© Pearson Education, Inc.

Cause and Effect

15. Read the section Probation and Parole. If someone is released on parole, they must meet certain conditions set by the court, or else

   (a.) they may be faced with a return to prison.

   b. they may have to pay a fine.

   c. the case may be retried.

   d. they will receive a threat from the judge.

READING

Reading Selection **6**

Additional Reading

Scene from a Play

6.11 Flesch-Kincaid Grade Level 3.8

Collaboration

ESL Annotation

6.12 ESL The jury system may be foreign to some of your ESL students. Be sure to offer a summary of how our jury system functions.

mandatory
required by law

Excerpt from Twelve Angry Men

Pre-Reading Questions

Discuss these questions with a classmate.

1. Do you believe the American system of trial by jury is a fair one? Explain.

2. What happens when jurors disagree on the verdict of a case?

3. Do you think race plays a role in some jurors' judgment of whether a suspect is guilty or not? Explain.

Twelve Angry Men

By Reginald Rose

**In this scene in Act I, the twelve jurors are being asked
to come to a verdict in a murder trial.**

1 Foreman: It's up to you. Just remember we've got a first-degree murder charge here. If we vote "guilty," we send the accused to the electric chair. That's **mandatory**.

2 4TH juror: I think we all know that.

3 3RD juror: Come on, let's vote.

4 10TH juror: Yeah, let's see who's where.

5 Foreman: Anybody doesn't want to vote? *[He looks around.] The others are silent.* All right. This has to be a twelve-to-nothing vote either way. That's the law. OK, are we ready? All those voting "guilty" raise your hands. *Seven or eight hands go up immediately. Several others go up more slowly. Everyone looks around the table as the* fore man *rises and begins to count hands. The* 9TH juror's *hand goes up now, and all hands are raised except the* 8TH juror's. . . .

6 Nine—ten—eleven. That's eleven for "guilty." OK. "Not guilty"? *The* 8TH juror *slowly raises his hand.* One. Right. OK, eleven to one—"guilty" Now we know where we are. *[He resumes his seat.]*

7 10TH juror: Boy-oh-boy! There's always one.

8 7TH juror [after a pause]: So, what do we do now?

9 8TH juror: Well, I guess we talk.

10 10TH juror: Boy-oh-boy!

11 3RD juror [leaning over toward the 8TH juror]: Well, look, do you really think he's innocent?

12 8TH juror: I don't know.

13 3RD juror: I mean, let's be reasonable. You sat in court and heard the same things we did. The man's a dangerous killer. You could see it.

14 8TH juror: The man! He's sixteen years old.

15 3RD juror: Well, that's old enough. He knifed his own father. Four inches into the chest.

16 6TH juror [to the 8TH juror]: It's pretty **obvious**. I mean, I was **convinced** from the first day.

17 3RD juror: Well, who wasn't? [To the 8TH juror.] I really think this is one of those open and shut things. They proved it a dozen different ways. Would you like me to list them for you?

18 8TH juror: No.

19 10TH juror: Then what do you want?

20 8TH juror: Nothing. I just want to talk.

21 7TH juror: Well, what's there to talk about? Eleven men here agree. Nobody had to think twice about it, except you.

22 10TH juror: I want to ask you something. Do you believe his story?

23 8TH juror: I don't know whether I believe it or not. Maybe I don't.

24 7TH juror: So what'd you vote "not guilty" for?

25 8TH juror: There were eleven votes for "guilty" It's not easy for me to raise my hand and send a boy off to die without talking about it first.

26 7TH juror: Who says it's easy for me?

27 8TH juror: No one.

28 7TH juror: What, just because I voted fast? I think the guy's guilty. You couldn't change my mind if you talked for a hundred years.

29 8TH juror: I'm not trying to change your mind. It's just that we're talking about somebody's life here. I mean, we can't decide in five minutes. Suppose we're wrong?

30 7TH juror: Suppose we're wrong! Suppose this whole building fell on my head. You can suppose anything.

31 8TH juror: That's right.

32 7TH juror [after a pause]: What's the difference how long it takes? We honestly think he's guilty. So suppose we finish in five minutes? So what?

33 8TH juror: Let's take an hour. The ball game doesn't start till eight o'clock.

34 7TH juror [smiling]: OK, **slugger,** be my guest. *There is a silence.*

slugger
a baseball batter who hits a lot

35 Foreman [hesitantly]: Well, who's got something to say? *He looks at the* 2ND juror. How about you?

36 2ND juror: Not me.

37 9TH juror: I'm willing to put in an hour.

38 10TH juror: Great. I heard a pretty good story last night. This woman comes running into the doctor's office, **stripped** to the waist—

stripped
to remove clothing

© Pearson Education, Inc.

39 8TH juror: That's not what we're sitting here for.

40 10TH juror: All right, then you tell me. What are we sitting here for?

41 8TH juror: Maybe for no reason. I don't know. Look, this boy's been kicked around all his life. You know—living in a **slum,** his mother dead since he was nine. He spent a year and a half in an **orphanage** while his father served a jail term for **forgery.** That's not a very good head start. He's had a pretty terrible sixteen years. I think maybe we owe him a few words. That's all.

42 10TH juror: I don't mind telling you this, mister. We don't owe him a thing. He got a fair trial, didn't he? What d'you think the trial cost? He's lucky he got it. Know what I mean? *[He rises and looks around at the others.]* Look, we're all grown-ups here. We heard the facts, didn't we? Now, you're not going to tell us that we're supposed to believe that kid, knowing what he is. Listen, I've lived among 'em all my life. You can't believe a word they say. I mean, they're born liars.

---

slum
an overcrowded area of poor housing

orphanage
a home for children without parents

forgery
the illegal production of something fake

Reading Comprehension Check

1. When the foreman says, "This has to be a twelve-to-nothing vote either way," is this a statement of fact or an opinion?
   a. an opinion.   c. both a fact and an opinion.
   b. a fact.   d. not clear.

2. The 3rd juror says, "The man's a dangerous killer. You could see it." Is this a statement of fact or an opinion?
   a. an opinion.   c. neither.
   b. a fact.   d. both a fact and an opinion.

3. The 8th juror says, "The man! He's sixteen years old." Is this a statement of fact or an opinion?
   a. an opinion.   c. neither.
   b. a fact.   d. both fact and opinion.

4. Which juror is expressing the most doubt?
   a. the 1st juror.   c. the 8th juror.
   b. the 9th juror.   d. the 10th juror.

5. When asked why he didn't vote "guilty," what reason did the 8th juror give?
   a. He was sure the boy was innocent.
   b. He didn't feel good about the case.
   c. He was sure the boy was nice.
   d. He wanted to talk first before sending the boy to die.

6. The 8th juror says, "We can't decide in five minutes." Is this a statement of fact or opinion?
   a. an opinion.   c. neither.
   b. a fact.   d. both fact and opinion.

7. What is the 8th juror referring to when he says, "That's not what we're sitting here for."?
   a. to decide the case.
   b. a dirty joke another juror was telling.
   c. the idea of rushing to a verdict.
   d. to laugh at the boy.

8. For what purpose does the 8th juror mention the boy's parents' troubled lives?
   a. to highlight the facts of the murder.
   b. to condemn the legal justice system.
   c. to build sympathy for the accused.
   d. none of the above.

9. The 10th juror says, "We don't owe him a thing." Was this a statement of fact or an opinion?
   a. an opinion.   c. neither.
   b. a fact.   d. both fact and opinion.

10. What is the main idea of this section of the play?
    a. The jury system doesn't function well.
    b. If one juror disagrees, a discussion of the case must continue.
    c. Juror #8 is causing problems.
    d. both a and c.

Suggested Resources

Books

1. *The Appeal* by John Grisham (New York: Random House, 2008). A Large company dumps chemicals in a rural community. An altruistic scrappy attorney fights back.

2. *Voices of Women from the Criminal Justice System* by Katherine Stuart Van Wormer and Clemens Bartollas. (Boston: Allyn and Bacon, 2007). This book is made up of 19 stories. Some are from female offenders, others are from female law enforcers.

3. *Careers in Criminal Justice* by W. Richard Stephens. (New York: Pearson, 2001). An array of job opportunities in the field of Criminal Justice are explored.

Movies/Plays

1. *Twelve Angry Men* (a play and a film) (1957). Directed by Sidney Lumet. An engrossing examination of a group of twelve jurors who are uncomfortably brought together to deliberate after hearing the "facts" in a seemingly open-and-closed murder trial case.

2. *The Verdict* (film) (1982). Directed by Sidney Lumet. A lawyer sees the chance to salvage his career and self-respect by taking a medical malpractice case to trial rather than settling.

© Pearson Education, Inc.

3. *Michael Clayton* (2007). Directed by Tony Gilroy. Middle-aged lawyer Michael Clayton (George Clooney) is a "fixer" who clears up complex or dirty cases on behalf of corporate clients.

Internet Sites

1. www.ncjrs.org

   The National Criminal Justice Reference Service. A very informative reference site. Explore such categories as crime prevention, corrections, the justice system, and victims.

2. www.oyez.org/tour/

   Take a virtual tour of the U.S. Supreme Court via the multimedia Oyez Project.

3. www.Courttv.com

   Court TV on the Web. Browse through some recent criminal cases displayed on the site.

Time Management

Overview

We are all very busy in our lives. Many students have work responsibilities, are involved in extracurricular activities, and have family responsibilities at home. With only 24 hours in a day, when can we find sufficient time in our schedules to sit and read assigned class readings carefully, without rushing? This is an important question to consider; the quality of reading that you do in your courses is one of the major keys to your overall success in college.

The challenge is to understand the reality of your weekly life schedule in advance, and to find pockets of time you can dedicate to working on your course readings.

Discuss these questions about reading and time management with a few of your classmates.

Collaboration

1. Take a quick glance at the final chapter reading that you just read on page 340 and the comprehension questions that follow. About how much time did it take you to do a careful reading of the article and to answer the questions? Do you think by focusing more on the reading task, you can complete a reading of this length more quickly? Or, perhaps would it help you to not rush to get a better understanding of what you are reading?

2. What time of day is the best time for you to read: early morning, in the afternoon, or late at night? Where do you like to do your reading?

3. Do you feel that "time issues" make it difficult for you to successfully complete your class readings? Explain.

Challenge Activity

Tonight, take a little time to fill out the My Week schedule on the next page, making sure to fill in all of your known daily responsibilities. Where do you have a pocket of time when you can anticipate spending time with class readings (consider where you will be at these times, and whether the environment will be conducive to focused reading)? Write "Course Reading Time" in these open slots in your schedule. When you are finished, tally up how many hours you slotted for course readings. Consider that researchers recommend that for every hour spent in the classroom, you should allot at least two hours for class reading.

© Pearson Education, Inc.

My Week							
Time	*M*	*T*	*W*	*TH*	*F*	*Sat*	*Sun*
6 AM							
7 AM							
8 AM							
9 AM							
10 AM							
11 AM							
12 PM							
1 PM							
2 PM							
3 PM							
4 PM							
5 PM							
6 PM							
7 PM							
8 PM							
9 PM							
10 PM							
11 PM							
12 AM							
1 AM							
2 AM							
3 AM							
4 AM							
5 AM							

Anticipated Hours Dedicated to Doing College Reading = _____

Learning Implications

Successful students manage their time effectively. If you build quality blocks of study/reading time into your weekly schedule, you will not find yourself rushing through course material and showing up for class unprepared. Instead, you will be well prepared for class discussions and for any pop-quizzes that your instructor may give you.

LIFE SCIENCE
Nursing

Chapter 7

"Nurses dispense comfort, compassion, and caring without even a prescription."
VAL SAINTSBURY

Objectives

IN THIS CHAPTER YOU WILL LEARN . . .

- About the field of modern day nursing and the challenges of caring for America's sick

- How to identify different patterns of text organization

- How to summarize an original text

© Pearson Education, Inc.

Making Predictions

Consider this chapter's theme of Nursing. What subtopics relate to this field? (See Figure 7.1.)

■ Figure 7.1

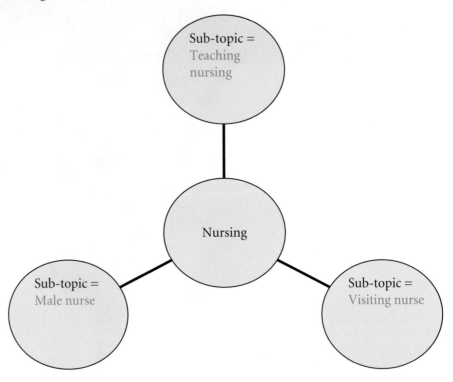

Introduction to the Discipline of Nursing

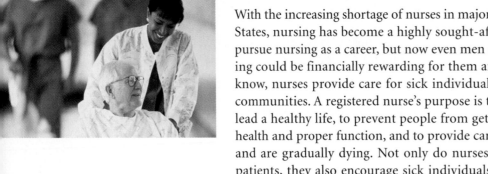

With the increasing shortage of nurses in major hospitals throughout the United States, nursing has become a highly sought-after profession. Typically women pursue nursing as a career, but now even men are gradually realizing that nursing could be financially rewarding for them and bring job satisfaction. As you know, nurses provide care for sick individuals, sometimes families, and even communities. A registered nurse's purpose is to educate individuals on how to lead a healthy life, to prevent people from getting sick, to help patients regain health and proper function, and to provide care for those who are terminally ill and are gradually dying. Not only do nurses administer medication to their patients, they also encourage sick individuals to keep a positive attitude and enhance the quality of life. Registered nurses provide care for their patients in homes, hospitals, physicians' clinics, and extended-care facilities.

While the focus of this chapter is on the discipline of Nursing, the reading selections cover several subtopics. These include junior nursing students recalling how their patients had touched their lives, recruiters looking for male nurses throughout the country, how miscommunication between physicians and nurses affect the nurses' morale, and student enrollment rising in American nursing colleges and universities as a result of an unprecedented demand for nurses. You will also read a short story about a nurse in this chapter. All of these readings will give you an appreciation for registered nurses and realization that nursing is indeed a noble profession.

Preview Questions

1. Do you have a family member who needs in-home nursing care? If yes, how do you and your family members cope with the challenge of helping to care for this individual? Be specific.

2. How long would you be willing to house and care for a relative who can no longer take care of him- or herself? How comfortable would you be allowing a professional nurse to manage critical decisions regarding your relative's lifestyle choices? What would be some of your concerns about trusting a nurse? What percentage of your monthly income would you allocate for subsidizing this relative's nursing expenses?

3. The average life expectancy of Americans has increased significantly due to the many advances in medical technology. How many years do you think the twenty-first-century American citizen can live self-sufficiently in relatively good health? At what age do you believe a senior citizen typically becomes a liability to society? Explain.

4. Senior citizens living into their eighties, nineties, and beyond pose a great challenge to the nursing profession. In what ways can the field of nursing rise to the occasion and meet the growing needs of America's aging population? Discuss the role the government can play in producing sufficient nursing graduates to deal with this demographic change.

Collaboration

Interpreting a Cartoon

■ **Figure 7.2**

"Introducing the government's new, cost-effective nursing model..."

Working in pairs, examine the cartoon shown here and answer the following questions.

© Pearson Education, Inc.

Collaboration

1. What is so amusing about this cartoon?
2. In your opinion, what is the cartoonist's intended message to the reader?

Discipline-specific Terminology Bank

anesthesiologist	cardiology	chemotherapy	clinical
coordination	critical	diabetic	diagnosis
dialysis	emergency	geriatric	humanistic
implementation	medicine	patient	peripheral
physician	preoperative	profession	recruitment

Sample Paragraph

Traditionally, women have pursued nursing as a rewarding **profession**. However, because of a shortage of nurses in the country, men are finding themselves gravitating toward nursing as a career. Nursing requires a great deal of **coordination**, **implementation**, **cooperation**, and effective **physician**-nurse **communication**, and women traditionally have proven themselves skilled at providing such care to the **patient** with affection and kindness. Nevertheless, nowadays gender roles are changing in society, making it comfortable for men to show feelings and do **humanistic** kinds of work.

EXERCISE 1

Matching Column A and Column B

Match the word in Column A with the definition in Column B. Put the letter representing the correct definition in the space preceding each term.

Column A

Word

1. __d__ critical
2. __f__ humanistic
3. __h__ coordination
4. __i__ profession
5. __g__ clinical
6. __j__ preoperative
7. __c__ chemotherapy

Column B

Definition

a. a serious situation requiring immediate action

b. a specialist who gives patients a drug to numb pain

c. the treatment of cancer with chemical substances

d. serious and dangerous

e. finding new people to join an organization

8. _a_ emergency

9. _e_ recruitment

10. _b_ anesthesiologist

f. solving human problems with kindness

g. related to the examination and treatment of patients

h. the act of a group of people working together effectively

i. a job that requires special training

j. occurring before a surgical procedure

EXERCISE 2

Fill in the Blanks

In the following sentences, fill in the blank with a word from the terminology bank below that makes the sentence grammatical and meaningful.

anesthesiologist	chemotherapy	clinical	coordination	critical
emergency	humanistic	preoperative	profession	recruitment

1. The head nurse called the _anesthesiologist_ so that he could sedate the profusely bleeding patient before the surgery.

2. The patient was brought into the hospital in such a _critical_ condition that no one thought she would survive the gunshot injury.

3. Depending on the patient's condition, sometimes _preoperative_ care is as important as the surgical procedure itself.

4. Joan has lost all of her hair as a result of _chemotherapy_ . Her doctor thinks that treating her cancer with chemical substances has been effective.

5. Sometimes, a patient's speedy recovery depends on a great deal of _coordination_ between the nurse and the physician.

6. Male nurses have proven that just like female nurses, they can have feelings for their patients and do _humanistic_ kinds of work.

7. With gender roles changing in society, the _profession_ of nursing has become attractive to men as well.

8. _Clinical_ research focuses on the examination and treatment of patients and their illnesses.

9. The _recruitment_ of registered nurses has become increasingly difficult as most universities are not producing enough graduates to keep up with the demand.

10. In an _emergency_ , sometimes the head nurse has to make crucial decisions to save the patient's life, especially if the doctor is not immediately available.

© Pearson Education, Inc.

EXERCISE **3**

Pair Activity

Pair up with a classmate and make complete sentences with five words you learned from the vocabulary exercise.

1. _____

   _____

2. _____

   _____

3. _____

   _____

4. _____

   _____

5. _____

   _____

Collaboration

Graphic Analysis

Registered nurses (RNs) in the United States are represented by several different age groups. The chart shown here represents the age distribution trend of registered nurses in the Year 1980, 2000, 2010, and 2020. As you can see, there is a highest percentage and a lowest percentage of a specific age group every year. For example, in the Year 1980 18 percent of the registered nurses were in the 25–29 age group whereas only 4 percent of the nurses were about 65 years old. Study the age distribution trend of the registered nurses in the graph with a classmate carefully and answer the questions that follow.

1. In which year(s) is the percentage of the youngest registered nurses the lowest? *2000, 2010, and 2020*

2. According to the graph, in which year is the percentage of the RNs in the 20–24 age group the highest? *1980*

3. In the Year 2010, 50–54-year-old registered nurses will comprise what percentage of the workforce? *17%*

4. As shown in the graph, the percentage of the 25–29 year old registered nurses peaked at 18 percent in the Year 1980 and then steadily declined to the 60–64 age group. Relative to the Year 1980, how is the age distribution trend different in the Years 2000, 2010, and 2020. Explain. *Answers will vary.*

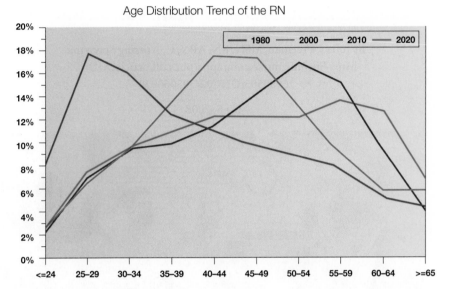

Age Distribution Trend of the RN

Source: What Is Behind HSRA'a Projected Supply, Demand, and Shortage of Registered Nurses? U.S. Department of Health and Human Services, Health Resources and Services Administration, Exhibit 4.

5. Compared to 1980, the number of the oldest registered nurses will have grown by what percentage in the Year 2020? _3%_____

6. In your opinion, why do you think there might be a higher percentage of older registered nurses in the Year 2020 compared to the Year 1980? _Answers will vary._____

Junior Nursing Students Share Patient Stories

Collaboration

Pre-Reading Questions

Before you read the following selection, get into small groups of three or four and discuss these questions based on your personal experience.

1. Have you ever encountered a nurse who treated you or your best friend or one of your family members? Discuss how this nurse took care of you or the patient. Was it an overall pleasant experience for you or the patient? Share your experience with your peers.

2. How do you think nurses make a difference in their patients' lives? Do you think that nurses are also sometimes touched by their patients? Explain how.

3. In your opinion, should junior nurses be allowed in the operating room to view an open-heart surgery? Discuss the advantages and disadvantages of sending junior nurses to the operating room.

Read the following article and answer the multiple-choice questions that follow. Write questions you may have about the text in the space provided alongside the first paragraphs.

© Pearson Education, Inc.

Junior Nursing Students Share Patient Stories

By Julia J. Freeman, MSN, RN, APN, C, *Nursing Spectrum*
http://include.nurse.com/apps/pbcs.dll/article?AID=/
20080505/ONC02/305060020

May 5, 2008

Ramapo College of New Jersey nursing students' clinical partnership with The Valley Hospital, 3W, on the students' first clinical day. Julia Freeman, RN, MSN, APN, C, clinical associate faculty, Ramapo College of New Jersey, and NP Cardiology Practice, The Valley Hospital, CCU, is third from right.

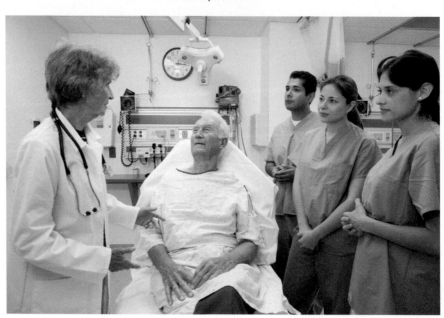

? _____
_____
_____
_____
? _____
_____
_____
_____
? _____
_____
_____

jaw dropped
to be shocked or surprised
by something

1   One of the great joys of nursing has been remembering and sharing patient care stories.

2   As a seasoned nurse and nursing instructor, it has become difficult to recall how I felt in the beginning, especially about the patients for whom I cared during my first clinical rotation.

3   The following stories were written by 21-year-olds who are junior nursing students from the Ramapo College of New Jersey in Mahwah.

4   As the students neared the end of their first clinical rotation on a cardiac telemetry unit at The Valley Hospital, Ridgewood, N.J., I wanted them to see the difference that their earnest nursing care had made in their patients' lives.

5   For their written assignment, I asked the students to think back and remember one patient whose spirit had touched their hearts over the past weeks. They had fresh, spontaneous perspectives that give anyone who reads them a feeling of **appreciation** for our future nurses.

Open Heart Surgery

6   The anesthesiologist directed me to a short stool on which I could stand. After I stepped up, the first thing that I noticed was a beating human heart right before my eyes. My **jaw dropped** so far down that I worried it might come out of the bottom of the mask.

7   The heart didn't look gross at all; in fact, it was a breathtaking sight. The lungs were **inflating** and **deflating** completely out of tune with the beating heart. The heart didn't make a sound, but **defiantly** outperformed any live concert I've seen yet. It reminded me of a level in the Nintendo game "Trauma Center," where you cut away an old aortic heart valve and **insert** a new one.

8   I was great at the game and passed that level on the first try. I had complained how simplistic the game made the **procedure**.

9   Looking back, I realize how much of an understatement that was! The most incredible part about the entire experience was in the end, when the open chest cavity was closed and the drapes were **removed**. There on the OR table I saw a patient—live and in person. It was one of the most thrilling experiences of my life.*

Ashley O'Hare

inflating
fill with air to make it swell

deflating
to collapse by releasing contained air

defiantly
resisting boldly

Pleasantly Confused

10   The patient **assigned** to me had **dementia**, something I had overlooked when doing my patient write-up the **previous** night. I have heard the phrase "pleasantly confused"; however, I couldn't say that I had ever seen or noticed anyone in that state.

11   I realized the extent of the problem after being with him for only a few moments. The patient calmly insisted that he didn't want breakfast until I returned from Boston. When I left and came back, a fellow nursing student reminded him to eat because I was back in the room.

12   He still wouldn't eat and kept offering us his breakfast. It was difficult to **decipher** his words at times. He talked about going hunting with his four sisters and how they had killed 30 or 40 deer in one day. He went on to say that he had his gun in the corner, and when I asked him why, he said, "Where else should I put it?" It was at this point that I left the room because I didn't want to laugh in his presence.

13   This patient taught me that while he may be confused, it doesn't mean that he is crazy or stupid, but rather that he is someone who is in need of help. It was nice to know that I was doing something for him just by listening and showing that I cared.

Justin Smith

dementia
loss of mental ability

decipher
understand

Cancer, Yet an Optimistic Spirit

14   A few weeks ago, I was taking care of a patient who suffered from head and lung cancer. Catherine† was an amazing woman. In addition to having cancer, she had triple **vision** in her left eye, as a result of a tumor compressing the optic nerve, and she had lost all of her hair during chemotherapy.

15   Although she was very sick, she was filled with an optimistic spirit. Catherine told me in a matter of three days, during the fall of 2005, three of the closest people in her life—her grandmother, sister, and mother—had died. At first I couldn't believe that a terrible situation like this could happen. She told

---

*It is not customary to send juniors to the operating room; however, Ashley made a passionate request to view an open-heart surgery and this wish was granted.
†The name has been changed.

© Pearson Education, Inc.

me that there is a time for everyone, and if she could handle these sad moments, she could handle her cancer.

16   She said that she had had a wonderful life and repeated many times that God had blessed her with many good things. I envisioned that cancer patients would be sad, depressed, and pessimistic. The day I met Catherine was a special day, and I will never forget her smile, optimism, and warm heart.

Katarzyna Stanczyk

The Simple Things

17 On my first day of clinical, I took care of a patient who had many problems. Laurie* had been a diabetic from the age of 22. At the age of 44, her left leg had been **amputated** below the knee and her peripheral **vision** was gone. Laurie had neuropathy in her hands and feet and had just had a fistula inserted so that she could begin dialysis in a few months.

18   I did not do anything spectacular for this patient; I assisted with AM care, which included brushing her hair. Laurie was so thankful for every little thing that I did. It really made me think; how could someone with so much going on in her life still be so thankful for something so simple? I realized that healthy people take everyday things for **granted**, like brushing our hair. When her father came in to visit, Laurie told him that, "God had sent her an angel today." I don't think that I will ever forget this person or what she has taught me.

Tanya Morris

19   I hope that these stories have helped you to think about how you felt in the beginning of your career and to remember your nursing journey and the many patients' lives that you have touched. As these students are learning, the caring nursing presence is a strong force. It touches, comforts, and brightens the moments and days of patients with limitless effects. May your success in nursing be measured by your kindness.

Julia J. Freeman, MSN, RN, APN, C, is a clinical associate faculty member at Ramapo College of New Jersey with a clinical **partnership** at The Valley Hospital. She is a nurse practitioner at The Valley Hospital CCU, Ridgewood, New Jersey. To comment on this article, e-mail editorN@nursingspectrum.com

*The name has been changed.

amputated
cut off (a part of someone's body) for medical reasons

Reading Comprehension Check

1. As used in the sentence "As a seasoned nurse and nursing instructor, it has become difficult to recall how I felt in the beginning, especially about the patients for whom I cared during my first clinical rotation," the word *seasoned* means
   a. poorly trained.
   b. inexperienced.
   c. experienced.
   d. novice.

2. In the sentence "I wanted them to see the difference that their earnest nursing care had made in their patients' lives," a synonym of *earnest* is
   a. sincere.
   b. insincere.
   c. profitable.
   d. earnings.

3. In the sentence "They had fresh, spontaneous perspectives that give anyone who reads them a feeling of appreciation for our future nurses," the word *spontaneous* could be replaced with
   a. structured.
   b. planned.
   (c.) unprompted.
   d. unnatural.

4. The main idea of this article is that
   a. junior nursing students can aggravate a patient's condition.
   b. patients are better off if they are treated by experienced registered nurses.
   c. junior nurses should not be allowed to provide patient care.
   (d.) junior nursing students make a difference in their patients' lives.

5. In giving the junior nursing students their writing assignment, Julia Freeman's main point was that
   (a.) the patient's spirit had touched their hearts.
   b. an open-heart surgery could be devastating.
   c. junior nursing students should be intimidated by the sight of a beating human heart.
   d. junior students should not pursue nursing as a career.

6. The junior nursing student's stepping up on a stool and looking at a human heart is offered as an example to support the idea that
   a. junior nurses must not be allowed to view an open-heart surgery.
   b. the presence of junior nurses in the operating room makes the surgeon nervous.
   c. watching a beating human heart can be a nightmare for junior nurses.
   (d.) junior nursing students' lives can be touched by the patients.

7. The patient with dementia is mentioned to support the point that
   a. he was simply stupid.
   b. patients with dementia avoid eating breakfast.
   (c.) the patient needed care.
   d. the patient was mentally deranged.

8. "Catherine told me how in a matter of three days, during the fall of 2005, three of the closest people in her life—her grandmother, sister, and mother—had died. At first I couldn't believe that a terrible situation like this could happen. She told me that there is a time for everyone, and if she could handle these sad moments, she could handle her cancer."

   It can be inferred from the passage that
   a. Catherine was sad and depressed about her cancer.
   b. she was pessimistic about her recovery.
   c. she had lost faith in her cancer treatment.
   (d.) Catherine was optimistic about her recovery from cancer.

9. "I did not do anything spectacular for this patient; I assisted with AM care, which included brushing her hair. Laurie was so thankful for every little thing that I did. It really made me think; how could someone with so much going on in her life still be so thankful for something so simple? I realized that healthy people take everyday things for granted, like brushing our hair. When her father came in to visit, Laurie told him that, "God had sent her an

© Pearson Education, Inc.

angel today." I don't think that I will ever forget this person or what she has taught me."

Which of the following conclusions can be drawn from the passage?

a. Junior nursing students usually do not do anything spectacular for their patients.

b. Most healthy people usually do not appreciate little things in life.

c. Laurie did not appreciate the junior nursing student brushing her hair.

d. Laurie wanted God to send her an angel.

10. The overall tone of the article is

a. humorous.

b. sarcastic.

c. inspirational.

d. shocking.

READING

Reading Selection 2

Newspaper Article

7.2 Flesch-Kincaid Grade Level 11.2

Collaboration

┌ **ESL** Annotation

7.3 ESL This topic may be of high interest to many ESL students who come from cultures where the norm is to have predominantly female nurses.

falls for

falls in love with someone, is attracted to someone

Men Are Much in the Sights of Recruiters in Nursing

Pre-Reading Questions

Discuss the following questions in small groups before reading the article.

1. When you hear the word *nurse*, what kind of image do you conjure up in your mind? Describe a nurse's physical appearance to your peers.

2. Do you truly believe that only women are capable of providing patient care as a nurse? If you do, discuss why male nurses may not be as efficient and caring as female nurses.

3. Despite a severe nursing shortage in the country, the idea that men can also pursue nursing as a rewarding career has not caught on. In your opinion, what role do you think the government and educational institutions can play in encouraging men to pursue nursing as a profession?

Men Are Much in the Sights of Recruiters in Nursing

By Eve Tahmincioglu, the *New York Times*

April 13, 2003

1   On an episode of NBC's hospital spoof "Scrubs," a female doctor **falls for** a fellow **medical** staffer but backs away when she finds out he is a male nurse—or, as she calls him, a "murse."

2   The episode, which was shown in January, prompted the president of the American Nurses Association, Barbara A. Blakeney, to write a letter to the show's producer saying it "tastelessly makes fun of men who choose to become nurses" and may "damage nurse-recruitment efforts as a result."

3   With the nursing shortage in New York and around the country reaching severe proportions, even sitcoms are not spared the wrath of the health care industry. The "Scrubs" episode and movies like "Meet the Parents"—in which a male nurse is begged by his future father-in-law, played by Robert De Niro, to become a doctor—are especially troubling to health care providers.

4   They are pinning their hopes of easing the staffing shortage on the single demographic group with the sheer numbers to make a difference: men.

5   The industry has stepped up efforts to recruit men, concentrating on those with a background in medicine, like paramedics and orderlies, but also aiming at areas like firefighting, the **military**, Wall Street and even the tattered dot-com industry.

6   Gary Liu, 31, is one of their prizes. Mr. Liu got a business degree from Baruch College and went to work for a **computer** company, but he felt unfulfilled and **fretted about** **job security**. Six months later, he left for a position as a patient **advocate** at a New York hospital. He soon decided to go into nursing for "the **financial** rewards and to help people," he said. Last summer, he was hired as a night nurse in the transplant unit of New York University Medical Center.

fretted about
felt uneasy about something

7   "I'm often asked why I didn't become a doctor," he said. "I don't have to defend myself. I'm happy with my choice."

8   The **potential** for that kind of **job** satisfaction is the message that the health care industry is trying to get across to other men. "This is not about **gender**," said Thom Schwarz, a **registered** nurse and editorial director of The American **Journal** of Nursing. "It's about caring."

9   And about money and **job stability**. At a time when most professions are stingy with both, nursing is **bucking the trend**. Nurses in the New York metropolitan **area** start at $50,000 to $70,000 a year, and in specialties like anesthesiology they make up to $100,000, according to Timothy Lehey, program director of the nurse anesthesia program at the Columbia University School of Nursing. To lure workers, some health care operations are offering signing bonuses of up to $5,000, tuition **assistance**, day care and flexible hours.

bucking the trend
going against the prevailing trend of the market

10   Nurses can pick and choose their place of employment. **Virtually** every hospital, nursing home and home-health agency in the greater New York area has a shortage, varying from 4 **percent** to 14 **percent**. Among the areas most in need of hospital nurses are the Bronx and Staten Island, and Westchester, Dutchess, Orange and Ulster Counties, according to the Greater New York Hospital Association. Specialties most in demand include critical care, preoperative care and emergency services.

11   The need for nurses is unlikely to **let up** any time soon, given the growing health care needs of aging baby boomers. By 2020, the national nursing shortage will more than triple, to 400,000 openings from 126,000 today, the Bureau of **Labor Statistics** forecasts. In New York State, the shortage is expected to reach 17,000 nurses by 2005 and double that by 2015, according to a study by the state's Education Department.

let up
cease, stop entirely

12   To help narrow the gap, the industry is going after men, who make up a mere 5.4 **percent** of the nation's 2.7 million **registered** nurses and 4 **percent** of those in the New York metropolitan **area**. In February, Johnson & Johnson, the pharmaceutical and **medical**-devices company based in New Brunswick, N.J., featured men in a $20 million public service campaign to **promote** nursing.

© Pearson Education, Inc.

13   "Nursing has slipped from the radar screen for a lot of women who are pursuing other careers, so we thought, 'Why not look at all options, including men?'" said David Swearingen, a Johnson & Johnson spokesman. "They provide a promising audience."

14   And an increasingly receptive one. "It's becoming more acceptable for men to go into nursing because society's values are changing, making it more acceptable for men to have feelings and do humanistic kinds of work," said Kathleen Ames, director of nurse recruitment for New York University **Medical** Center, where 7.4 **percent** of the nursing staff are men.

15   The pay helps. The **medical** center starts nurses at $60,000 and offers them free tuition at New York University, health benefits, 30 days of paid holidays and vacation, and a **contribution** equal to 6 **percent** of their salaries to their 403(b) plans, the nonprofit **equivalent** of a 401(k).

16   Men can be especially useful as nurses because of the **physical** strength **required** to lift patients and move **medical equipment**. Michael Cullen, a retired police officer who is a nurse with the Visiting Nurse Service of New York, is sometimes called "boostie boy" because he so often helps move heavy patients.

qualms
uneasy feelings

17   After 21 years on the Nassau County police force, Mr. Cullen, 55, had no **qualms** about going back to school and becoming a nurse. He loves the work, **despite** the occasional double take he gets. "I've had patients ask me if I'm gay," said Mr. Cullen, who is married with two grown children. "And sometimes the older men get disappointed when they see me. They say, 'I was hoping for a young, pretty girl.' But many are so sick, they couldn't care less."

18   The Visiting Nurse Service says former police officers like Mr. Cullen, as well as former soldiers and firefighters, are ideal nursing candidates not only for their strength but also for their long experience in thinking on their feet. Jobs start at $60,000 a year, compared with $45,000 five years ago, plus a signing bonus of $3,000.

19   Becoming a nurse requires a two-year associate's degree or a bachelor's degree in nursing, though some nursing schools in the New York **area** offer accelerated programs. Nursing school grants are hard to come by, but low-interest loans are readily **available**, educators say. Students can often get hospitals or other **potential** employers to pay some of the tuition in return for a pledge to work for them for a year or more after graduation.

squeamish
easily shocked or upset, or easily made to feel sick by disgusting sights

20   Of course, nursing is not for the **squeamish** or those averse to hard work. Many nurses put in 50 or even 60 hours a week, according to the American Nurse Association.

21   But Carl Ankrah, 36, of the Bronx, is ready for the **challenge**. In 2001, Mr. Ankrah got a degree in hotel management, but the industry fell on hard times after Sept. 11. The real growth industry, he decided, was health care. He is now a first-year nursing student at the College of New Rochelle's School of Nursing.

22   At times, he has wondered if he made the wrong choice—but not for long. "In a **couple** of classes where I was only one of two men, it hit me, 'What am I doing in the midst of all these ladies?'" he said. "But I said to myself, 'This is not a **gender** profession. It's a profession of people willing to sacrifice themselves and help people.'"

Reading Comprehension Check

1. As used in the sentence "On an episode of NBC's hospital spoof 'Scrubs,' a female doctor falls for a fellow medical staffer but backs away when she finds out he is a male nurse—or, as she calls him, a 'murse,'" the phrase *backs away* means
   a. to walk forward.
   (c.) to withdraw.
   b. to pursue aggressively.
   d. to consider seriously.

2. In the sentence "The episode, which was shown in January, prompted the president of the American Nurses Association, Barbara A. Blakeney, to write a letter to the show's producer saying it "tastelessly makes fun of men who choose to become nurses" and may "damage nurse-recruitment efforts as a result," the word *prompted* can be replaced with
   a. pleased.
   c. satisfied.
   (b.) provoked.
   d. delighted.

3. In the sentence "With the nursing shortage in New York and around the country reaching severe proportions, even sitcoms are not spared the wrath of the health care industry," the word *wrath* most nearly means
   (a.) anger.
   c. blessing.
   b. joy.
   d. pleasure.

4. Which of the following sentences is the best statement of the main idea of the article?
   a. Male nurses are usually not as competent as their female counterparts.
   b. Most hospitals are seriously considering hiring female nurses from overseas.
   (c.) The nursing industry is making conscious efforts to recruit men as nurses.
   d. Recruiters are not interested in hiring men for the nursing job.

5. Gary Liu's example is offered to support the idea that
   a. the nursing industry is adamant about only hiring female nurses.
   b. the nursing industry will shy away from recruiting male nurses.
   c. nursing is a losing proposition for men.
   (d.) nursing could be a financially rewarding career for men.

6. The example of nurses making $50,000 to $70,000 and, in some cases, as much as $100,000 is used to support the fact that
   a. in general, nurses are poorly compensated.
   (b.) nursing as a career can provide financial stability.
   c. there is no job stability in the nursing industry.
   d. only male nurses can make as much as $100,000 a year.

7. "To lure workers, some health care operations are offering signing bonuses of up to $5,000, tuition assistance, day care and flexible hours."

   A logical conclusion that can be drawn from the above statement is that
   a. the demand for registered nurses is dwindling.
   b. some health care operations have a huge surplus.
   (c.) nurses are in great demand.
   d. the number of registered nurses far exceeds the number of jobs available.

© Pearson Education, Inc.

Florence Nightingale (1820–1910)

Florence Nightingale's valuable contributions to nursing can be determined by the fact that her work of the Nightingale School of Nursing still continues, that one of the buildings in the School of Nursing and Midwifery at the University of Southampton is named after her, and that International Nurses Day is celebrated on her birthday every year.

Florence Nightingale was born into a rich, British family on May 12, 1820 in Florence, Grand Duchy of Tuscany. She experienced a Christian divine calling in 1837, which inspired her to become a nurse. Instead of becoming a wife and mother, which was very common in those days, she chose to become a nurse despite her parents' discouragement and devoted her entire life to caring for the poor and sick.

Her most notable contribution was caring for the injured soldiers during the Crimean War in 1854. Her tireless efforts to improve the standards of health care for the wounded earned her the title "Lady with the Lamp." She committed herself to reforming hospitals and implementing public health policies throughout England. Her famous work *Notes on Nursing: What It Is, and What It Is Not* is still used as a reference in most nursing schools throughout the world.

After her return from Crimea, she received an honorarium of £4,500 from an English public officer. She used the amount to found the Nightingale Training School for Nurses in 1860. Throughout her career, Nightingale fervidly believed that nursing schools should give students a solid background in science to understand the theoretical implications for health care. She believed that learning was perpetual, and therefore her students should never stop learning. She once wrote to her nursing students, "[Nursing] is a field of which one may safely say: there is no end in what we may be learning everyday." Graduates of the Nightingale Training School for Nurses traveled to other countries to work in hospitals and train other nurses.

Nightingale's vision of nursing, which included promoting health and wellness among the sick and preventing sickness, has become a cornerstone of most nursing schools. Although she died on August 13, 1910, in Park Lane, London, England, her legacy lives on. Three hospitals in Turkey are named after Florence Nightingale: F. N. Hastanesi in Sisli, Metropolitan F. N. Hastanesi in Gayrettepe, and Avrupa F. N. Hastanesi in Mecidiyekoy.

The Agostino Gemelli Medical Center in Rome named its wireless computer system "Bedside Florence" to honor Florence Nightingale. Many nursing foundations in the world are named after Florence Nightingale. There is Nightingale Research Foundation in Canada, which studies chronic fatigue syndrome. Last but not least, when doctors and nurses fall in love with their patients, the phenomenon is called the "Florence Nightingale Effect."

Some Questions for Group Discussion

1. Florence Nightingale was born into a wealthy British family in Italy. Although discouraged by her parents, she decided to become a nurse and remained committed to nursing until her death. Discuss what inspired her to become a nurse and care for others.

2. After caring for the wounded during the Crimean War, Florence Nightingale received a handsome honorarium. Instead of spending the honorarium on herself, she used the money to open a nursing school. Under what conditions would you be willing to use a cash prize for others? Explain.

3. Recent advancements in science and technology have made it possible for us to communicate with strangers in distant countries, find ways to prolong life, and treat people with diseases that were incurable in the past, yet we seem to be incapable of finding empathy in our hearts. In your opinion, what can be done to eradicate poverty, sickness, and hunger from the world once and for all?

Biographical Internet Research

Do research on the Internet and find humanitarians who have dedicated their lives to tending to the needs of the poor and sick. Select one from the list below and be prepared to share a biographical profile with your classmates. Discuss what inspired this person to care for others.

- Clara Barton
- Margaret Sanger
- Dorothea Lynde Dix
- Helen Fairchild
- Walt Whitman

8. "The need for nurses is unlikely to let up any time soon, given the growing health care needs of aging baby boomers. By 2020, the national nursing shortage will more than triple, to 400,000 openings from 126,000 today, the Bureau of Labor Statistics forecasts."

   It can be inferred from the passage that
   a. in 2020, the demand for registered nurses in the country will be much less than today.
   b. most of the registered nurses will retire by 2020.
   c. most nursing programs will not be able to produce enough nursing graduates in the future to meet the demand.
   d. baby boomers will not need health care by 2020.

9. Mr. Cullen, a male nurse, says, "And sometimes the older men get disappointed when they see me. They say, 'I was hoping for a young, pretty girl.' But many are so sick, they couldn't care less."

   Based on this statement, which of the following is a logical conclusion?
   a. Older men do not care about the gender of the nurse.
   b. Some older men prefer to be treated by attractive female nurses.
   c. Mr. Cullen couldn't care less about the older male patients.
   d. Only those older men who are seriously ill want to be treated by young female nurses.

10. Which of the following statements gives a clear indication that nursing is a challenging profession?
   a. Jobs start at $60,000 a year, compared with $45,000 five years ago, plus a signing bonus of $3,000.
   b. The medical center starts nurses at $60,000 and offers them free tuition at New York University, health benefits, 30 days of paid holidays and vacation, and a contribution equal to 6 percent of their salaries to their 403(b) plans, the nonprofit equivalent of a 401(k).
   c. Nursing is not for the squeamish or those averse to hard work.
   d. Nurses can pick and choose their place of employment.

SKILL FOCUS
Patterns of Organization

Most authors use different *patterns of organization* to get their meaning across to the reader. As a reader, you should familiarize yourself with how an author has structured his or her text so you can understand the author's main idea and the supporting details. Recognizing the main idea and the author's purpose can help you determine the specific pattern of organization.

Identifying the Pattern of Organization

To identify the overall pattern of organization, make sure that you:

- Recognize the topic and the main idea
- Identify the details supporting the main idea
- Know the author's purpose

ESL Annotation

7.4 ESL Students often experience difficulty identifying different patterns of organization.

© Pearson Education, Inc.

- Familiarize yourself with the transitional phrases for each pattern
- Understand how the ideas are related to each other

Although there are several different patterns of organization, this section will first introduce the six most commonly used organizational patterns in textbooks. You will have the opportunity to practice each of the patterns as we examine them. You then will be introduced to some other organizational patterns.

Six Commonly Used Organizational Patterns

1. Definition

In this type of organizational pattern, the author uses a term and provides examples to define it; sometimes more than one term is introduced. The definition organizational pattern is used in most technical textbooks such as biology, nursing, and chemistry. Authors use this pattern of organization to introduce a term and help the reader understand how this term is different from others. Consider the following passage.

Example

Segregation (physical separation of housing and services based on race) and **discrimination** (unfair and unequal treatment or access to services based on race, culture, or other bias) have permeated the global community. Although the United States has moved beyond segregation in many areas, there are still inequalities based on lack of access to equal health care. Discrimination, as it relates to health services, can involve more than just race or ethnicity. The nurse must also guard against unequal treatment related to an individual's gender, sexual orientation, or legal status. If a client feels that the nurse is being judgmental because of his or her differences, the therapeutic relationship is compromised.

(*Roberta Pavy Ramont and Dee Niedringhaus,* Fundamental Nursing Care, *2nd ed., Upper Saddle River, NJ: Pearson Prentice Hall, 2008, p. 19*)

The following table shows how the author uses the definition organizational pattern to introduce two terms in the above passage.

Term	*Definition*
segregation	Physical separation of housing and services based on race
discrimination	Unfair and unequal treatment or access to services based on race, culture, or other bias

Notice how the two terms reappear in the passage to reinforce the concepts of segregation and discrimination based on race. When you read passages that use the definition organizational pattern, ask what terms are being defined. Identifying the terms will help you understand the author's purpose as well. Now that you have seen one example of the definition organizational pattern, let's do an exercise to make sure you understand how authors use this thought pattern.

segregation
the practice of keeping people of different races or religions apart and making them live, work, or study separately

discrimination
the practice of treating one person or group of people differently from another in an unfair way

PRACTICING THE SKILL

Read the following passages, identify the term(s), and define them.

Passage 1

For more than 30 years, nursing has been concerned with the cultural differences among clients. In the early years, culture was equated with ethnicity. Ethnicity was identified by a code on the client's chart or on the addressograph plate. As the profession became aware of the need to provide for the client holistically, the words cultural awareness (knowing about the similarities and differences among cultures) crept into the professional vocabulary. The goal of cultural awareness was to end prejudice and discrimination. In fact, though, awareness often resulted in a focus on differences, without providing the nurse with the tools to meet the culturally related needs of the client.

(Fundamental Nursing Care, p. 17)

TERM: *cultural awareness*

DEFINITION: *knowing about the similarities and differences among cultures*

Passage 2

One pitfall in communicating with a person from a different culture is ethnocentrism. Ethnocentrism means interpreting the beliefs and behavior of others in terms of one's own cultural values and traditions. It assumes that one's own culture is superior. It is difficult to avoid the tendency toward ethnocentrism. Nurses, though, must be extra diligent to avoid stereotypes (oversimplified conceptions, opinions, or beliefs about some aspects of a group of people). Individuals vary greatly within any ethnic group, just as children vary within one family. The nurse must look for ways to care for each client as a unique person, regardless of category.

(Fundamental Nursing Care, p. 17)

TERM: *ethnocentrism*

DEFINITION: *interpreting the beliefs and behavior of others in terms of one's own cultural values and traditions*

TERM: *stereotypes*

DEFINITION: *oversimplified conceptions, opinions, or beliefs about some aspects of a group of people*

Passage 3

Intercultural communication occurs when members of two or more cultures exchange messages in a manner that is influenced by their different cultural perspectives (Adler et al., 1998). Communication is interrelated with all other domains. It includes verbal communication (dialects, the

© Pearson Education, Inc.

context in which language is used, etc.) and nonverbal communication. Clients may communicate quite differently with family and close friends than with unfamiliar healthcare professionals.

(Fundamental Nursing Care, p. 19)

TERM: *intercultural communication*

DEFINITION: *It occurs when members of two or more cultures exchange messages in a manner that is influenced by their different cultural perspectives.*

2. Illustration/Example

When we do not understand a complex phenomenon, an abstract concept, or a difficult term, we often ask, "Can you give me an example?" Research in Artificial Intelligence shows that we retain information rather easily when we are given appropriate examples of a key concept. Successful teachers are aware of this aspect of human nature and use the illustration/example organizational pattern to introduce the main idea or a key concept to the student. Examples are especially helpful when the subject matter is unfamiliar to the reader. Let's look at the following paragraph to understand the illustration/example pattern of organization clearly.

Example

Fidelity means to be faithful to agreements and promises. By virtue of their standing as professional caregivers, nurses have responsibilities to clients, employers, the government, and society, as well as to themselves. Nurses often make promises such as "I'll be right back with your pain medication," "You'll be all right," or "I'll find out for you." Clients take such promises seriously, and so should nurses.

(Fundamental Nursing Care, p. 39)

MAIN IDEA: Fidelity means to be faithful to agreements and promises.

EXAMPLES: Nurses making promises to their clients such as "I'll be right back with your pain medication," "You'll be all right," etc.

PRACTICING THE SKILL

Read the following passages carefully, underline the main idea, and write the examples the author provides to support the main idea.

Passage 1

Autonomy refers to the right to make one's own decisions. Nurses who follow this principle recognize that each client is unique, has the right to be what that person is, and has the right to choose personal goals.

Honoring the principles of autonomy means that the nurse respects a client's right to make decisions even when those choices seem not to be in the client's best interest. It also means treating others with consideration. In a health-care setting, this principle is violated, for example, when a nurse disregards a client's report of the severity of his or her pain.

(Fundamental Nursing Care, p. 39)

MAIN IDEA: *Autonomy refers to the right to make one's own decisions.*

EXAMPLE: *The nurse respects a client's right to make decisions even when those choices seem not to be in the client's best interest.*

Passage 2

Values are freely chosen, enduring beliefs or attitudes about the worth of a person, object, idea, or action. Values are important because they influence decisions and actions. Values are often taken for granted. In the same way that people are not aware of their breathing, they usually do not think about their values; they simply accept them and act on them. The word *values* usually brings to mind things such as honesty, fairness, friendship, safety, or family unity. Of course, not all values are moral values. For example, some people hold money, work, power, and politics as values in their lives.

(Fundamental Nursing Care, pp. 37–38)

MAIN IDEA: *Values are freely chosen, enduring beliefs or attitudes about the worth of a person, object, idea, or action.*

EXAMPLES: *honesty, fairness, friendship, safety, family unity, money, work, and power*

Passage 3

Nonmaleficence is duty to do no harm. Although this would seem to be a simple principle to follow, in reality it is complex. Harm can mean intentional harm, risk of harm, and unintentional harm. In nursing, intentional harm is never acceptable. However, the risk of harm is not always clear. A client may be at risk of harm during a nursing intervention that is intended to be helpful. For example, a client may react adversely to a medication, and caregivers may or may not always agree on the degree to which a risk is morally permissible.

(Fundamental Nursing Care, p. 39)

MAIN IDEA: *The duty to do no harm is a complex principle to follow.*

EXAMPLES:

1. *Harm can mean intentional harm, risk of harm, and unintentional harm.*

2. *A client may be at risk of harm during a nursing intervention.*

© Pearson Education, Inc.

3. Comparison and Contrast

When authors want to show how two things are similar (comparison) or different (contrast), they use the comparison and contrast organizational pattern. When comparing the two things or objects, the author focuses on their similar features. When contrasting the two objects, the author focuses on their different characteristics. Depending on the purpose, the author may focus only on the similarities between the two objects or on the differences between them, or the author may focus on both the similarities and differences between them. Let's look at an example to understand the comparison and contrast organizational pattern clearly.

Example

consumer
someone who buys or uses goods and services

The "customers" we serve in nursing today are sometimes called consumers, sometimes patients, and sometimes clients. A **consumer** is an individual, a group of people, or a community that uses a service or commodity. People who use healthcare products or services are consumers of health care. A **patient** is a person who is waiting for or undergoing medical

patient
someone who is getting medical treatment

treatment and care. The word *patient* comes from a Latin word meaning "to suffer" or "to bear." Traditionally, the person receiving health care has been called a patient. People become patients when they seek assistance because of illness. Some nurses believe that the word *patient* implies passive acceptance of the decisions and care of health professionals. Because nurses interact with family, friends, and healthy people as well as those who are ill, nurses increasingly refer to recipients of health care as clients.

client
someone who pays a person or organization for a service

A **client** is a person who engages the advice or services of someone who is qualified to provide the service. Therefore, a client is a collaborator, a person who is also responsible for his or her own health. The health status of a client is the responsibility of the individual in collaboration with health professionals.

(*Fundamental Nursing Care,* p. 9)

As the passage describes, the general category of people being served in nursing are called "customers." However, there are three types of "customers," namely "consumers," "patients," and "clients." The table below shows the similarities and differences between them.

Customers	*Similarities (comparison)*	*Differences (contrast)*
Consumers	People who are served in nursing	▪ Consumers use health care products and services.
Patients		▪ Patients receive medical treatment and care.
Clients		▪ Clients receive advice from experts and are responsible for their own health.

Now that you understand the comparison and contrast organizational pattern, do the following exercise:

PRACTICING THE SKILL

Read the following passages and point out the similarities and differences between the two things being compared and contrasted.

Passage 1

Women are not the sole providers of nursing services. The first nursing school in the world was started in India in about 250 B.C. Only men were considered to be "pure" enough to fulfill the role of nurse at that time. In Jesus's parable in the New Testament, the good Samaritan paid an innkeeper to provide care for the injured man. Paying a man to provide nursing care was fairly common. During the Crusades, several orders of knights provided nursing care to their sick and injured comrades and also built hospitals. The organization and management of their hospitals set a standard for the administration of hospitals throughout Europe at that time. St. Camillus de Lellis started out as a soldier and later turned to nursing. He started the sign of the Red Cross and developed the first ambulance service. . . .

In 1876, only three years after the first U.S. nurse received her diploma from New England Hospital for Women and Children, the Alexian brothers opened their first hospital in the United States and a school to educate men in nursing.

During the years from the Civil War to the Korean War, men were not permitted to serve as nurses in the military. Today, men have resumed their historical place in the profession. As the history of nursing continues to be written, men and women will work side by side.

(Fundamental Nursing Care, pp. 8–9)

1. What is being compared and contrasted?
   male nurses and female nurses

2. What is the similarity between male and female nurses?
   They have both provided nursing care to patients.

3. What are the differences between male and female nurses?
   Only male nurses worked at the first nursing school in the world in India.
   Several knights provided nursing care and built hospitals.
   St. Camillus de Lellis developed the first ambulance service.
   The Alexian brothers opened their first hospital in the United States to train
   male nurses.
   Only female nurses served in the military during the Civil War and the
   Korean War.

© Pearson Education, Inc.

Passage 2

One of the first questions that should be asked in any healthcare situation is "What language do you normally use to communicate?" Even though a client may understand English in a casual conversation, he or she may not be able to communicate on the technical level required during a health interview. Healthcare workers need to be aware of the dominant language of an area, as well as problems that may be caused by particular dialects. Clients from Mexico may speak 1 of more than 50 dialects. People from the Philippines may speak 1 of 87. The dialect may pose a communication barrier even if a nurse speaks the same language. Dialect differences increase the difficulty of obtaining accurate information.

Many times much more is learned from what is not said than from what is said. Nonverbal communication is vital to communicating with clients, but here cultural variations can have a big impact. For example, in Western cultures, people are expected to make eye contact during communication. In other cultures, Asian specifically, making eye contact is a demonstration of lack of respect.

Touch can convey much, but again, cultures differ on what they permit and accept. It is important for the nurse to be aware of the client's reaction to touch. During the first contact with a client, the nurse should ask permission to touch the client. When performing a procedure that involves touch, the nurse should fully explain the procedure before touching the client.

Facial expressions and hand gestures also have different meanings from one culture to another. For example, individuals of Jewish, Hispanic, and Italian heritage rarely smile because showing one's teeth can be viewed as a sign of aggression. A therapeutic relationship can be promoted or hampered by the nurse's understanding of transcultural communication.

(Fundamental Nursing Care, p. 19)

1. What is being compared and contrasted?
   verbal communication and nonverbal communication

2. What is the comparison?
   They are both ways to exchange messages.

3. What is the contrast?
   Some clients may not be able to communicate well during a health interview.
   Miscommunication may be caused by particular dialects.
   Cultural variations play a big role in nonverbal communication.
   Facial expressions and gestures have different meanings in different cultures.

Passage 3

Effective communication among healthy professionals is vital to the quality of client care. Generally, health personnel communicate through discussion, reports, and records. A *discussion* is an informal conversation between two or more healthcare personnel to identify a problem or establish strategies to resolve a problem. A report is an oral, written, or computer-based communication intended to convey information to others. For example, nurses always report on clients at the end of a work shift. A record is a written or computer-based collection of data. The process of making an entry on a client record is called *recording*, charting, or documenting. A clinical record, also called a *chart* or *client record*, is the formal, legal document that provides evidence of a client's care. Although healthcare organizations use different systems and forms for documentation, all client records contain similar information.

(Fundamental Nursing Care, p. 85)

1. What is being compared and contrasted?
   <u>a report and a record</u>

2. What is the comparison between a report and a record?
   <u>They are both ways to communicate information to others.</u>

3. What is the contrast between a report and a record?
   <u>Whereas a report can be oral, a record must be written.</u>

4. Cause and Effect

Authors use the cause and effect organizational pattern to demonstrate a causal relation between an event and its impact. Sometimes one cause can have only one effect. Other times, one cause can have several effects. Likewise, multiple causes can have only one effect, and sometimes several causes can have several effects. Look at the diagrams to understand the different types of causal relations between events and their impact.

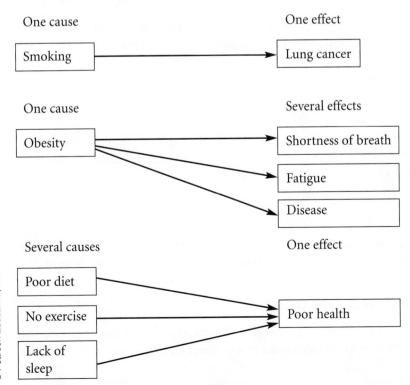

© Pearson Education, Inc.

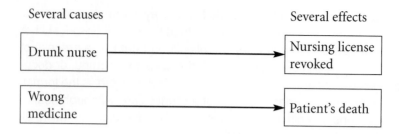

Several causes   Several effects

As you can see, the cause and effect relation is quite complex. You will need to read a passage carefully and determine exactly what is causing what effects. The following example will help you understand the cause and effect organizational pattern.

Example

The term "impaired nurse" refers to a nurse whose practice has been negatively affected because of chemical abuse, specifically the use of alcohol and drugs. Chemical dependence in healthcare workers has become a problem because of the high levels of stress involved in many healthcare settings and the easy access to addictive drugs. Substance abuse is the most common reason for actions against nurses' licenses. Between 10% and 15% of nurses are estimated to be chemically impaired. This is about the same percentage as in the general population. Employers must have sound policies and procedures for identifying situations that involve a possibly impaired nurse. Intervention in such situations is important to protect clients and to get treatment for the impaired nurse quickly.

(*Fundamental Nursing Care*, p. 37)

This passage explains the term *impaired nurse*. The cause and effect relationship established in the passage can be diagrammed as shown here.

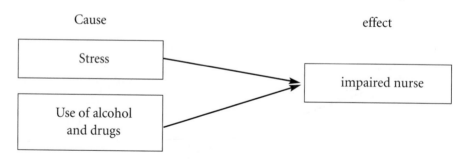

Cause   effect

By now you should have an understanding of the cause and effect organizational pattern. Let's do an exercise to further solidify what you have learned.

PRACTICING THE SKILL

Read each of the following passages carefully and answer the questions that follow to show your understanding of the cause and effect relationship.

Passage 1

Answers to essay, short-answer, and calculation questions will need to be extracted from your memory. Read the question carefully to determine what is being asked. Some students find it helpful to develop a brief outline before beginning an essay question. Check with the instructor to see if this can be written on the test paper or if you are permitted to use an additional sheet. The outline can help you organize your thoughts and can serve as a checkpoint that all important information was included. Usually, a number of key introductory words appear in essay questions. Look for these words, and do only what is required of you. Many low grades are caused by ignoring these key words.

Calculation questions are particularly troubling for many students who have convinced themselves that they cannot do math. Although math may be difficult, it is a necessary skill for a nurse. With extra practice, calculations are possible to learn. Several methods are used to do calculations.

It is important to show your work on calculations. If you are unable to arrive at the correct answer, your instructor can review your work, and will be able to tell you where you went wrong. Memorizing formulas and frequently used conversions will make calculations on tests and in the clinical area much easier.

(Fundamental Nursing Care, p. 6)

1. What are the causes of answering successfully?

   Reading the questions carefully

   Preparing a brief outline before answering questions

   Look for a number of key introductory words in essay questions

   Students can practice calculation questions.

   Memorizing formulas and frequently used conversions

2. What are the effects?

   Most of the causes mentioned above can lead to passing the tests.

Passage 2

Good communication is also important because customer service has become an important part of health care. Health care is a service industry, and clients are increasingly aware consumers. Clients frequently research their disease and the available treatments. When they come for a consultation, they expect to be given all the appropriate information. If information is not given to their satisfaction, they may look elsewhere for care. They may change doctors or refuse to allow a particular healthcare professional to administer treatment to them. Taking time to communicate

© Pearson Education, Inc.

effectively on first contact is not wasting time. In fact, it may save time, because corrections will not have to be made. Further, a well-informed client is likely to be more willing to participate in the treatment plan than one who is not well informed.

(Fundamental Nursing Care, p. 20)

Based on the information provided in this passage, make a list of the causes and their effects under each column in the table below.

Cause	*Effect*
Good communication	Satisfied customers
Unsatisfactory information	Clients go elsewhere
Taking time to communicate	Saves time making corrections later
A well-informed client	More willing to participate in the treatment plan

Passage 3

Cultural diversity affects care of the client in pain. The influx of minorities from other countries is predicted to continue, along with the growth of the proportion of minorities within the United States. This changing population means that we as healthcare providers must learn how to respond to pain in a wide range of clients. Cultural background affects pain perception. Cultural background has long been recognized as having a major influence on how one perceives and reacts to painful situations. Pain has both personal and cultural meanings. Although clients from two different cultures may experience a similar condition or surgical procedure, their pain response may differ dramatically. An understanding of pain from a cultural perspective is vital if healthcare providers are to respond to clients in a helpful manner.

(Fundamental Nursing Care, p. 23)

1. What are the causes?

   minorities from other countries immigrating to the United States

   cultural background of the patient

   clients from different cultures may experience a similar condition.

   an understanding of pain from a cultural perspective

2. What are the effects?

   Healthcare providers must learn how to respond to pain in a wide

   range of clients.

   pain perception

   Clients respond to pain differently

   Healthcare providers respond to clients in a helpful manner.

5. Classification

Authors use the classification organizational pattern to put ideas into categories according to their characteristics. These characteristics are chosen on the basis of their similarities. For example, a nursing textbook may describe the different types of drugs by their function and the reaction expected in a patient. An effective way to understand a nursing textbook that uses the classification organizational pattern is to determine how the topic is divided. If you can notice how the different characteristics are categorized, you are more likely to remember the important parts of the topic. Read the following paragraph and pay special attention to how the topic is divided into different categories.

Example

To break down the barriers among cultures, there was a movement toward cultural sensitivity (being aware of the needs and feelings of your own culture and of other cultures). Since the 1990s, a new term has been added. The profession has been talking about cultural competence—a set of practical skills, knowledge, and attitudes that must encompass the following elements:

1. Awareness and acceptance of differences
2. Awareness of one's own cultural values
3. Understanding of the dynamics of difference
4. Development of cultural knowledge
5. Ability to adapt practice skills to fit the cultural context of the client

Now it is time to take the next step past competency to culturally proficient care. For culturally proficient nurses, the five components of cultural care will be second nature. Care for clients will include consideration of their physical, psychological, emotional, spiritual, and cultural components.

(Fundamental Nursing Care, p. 17)

As you can see, the topic of the passage is cultural competence, which has five categories according to their characteristics. Notice that all of these categories are chosen on the basis of their similarities. That is, they are a set of practical skills necessary for a nurse to be culturally competent.

Now that you understand how writers use the classification organizational pattern, do the following exercise. Look for the main categories; some of these may have subtopics.

PRACTICING THE SKILL

Read the following passages carefully. Then find the topic of each passage and the different categories into which the topic is divided.

Passage 1

Nurses learn general concepts about transcultural nursing and specific facts about various cultures so that we can provide ethical and effective care to all our clients. We must understand how ideas from other cultures

© Pearson Education, Inc.

agree with or differ from our own. We must be sensitive to issues of race, gender, sexual orientation, social class, and economic situation in our everyday work. A cultural assessment has four basic elements. These data can be collected by the LPN/LVN.

1. The cultural identity of the client. How does the client identify himself or herself culturally? Does the client feel closer to the native culture or to the host culture? What is the client's language preference?

2. The cultural factors related to the client's psychosocial environment. What stressors are there in the local environment? What role does religion play in the individual's life? What kind of support system does the client have?

3. The cultural elements of the relationship between the healthcare provider and the client. What kind of experiences has the client had with healthcare providers, either now or in the past? (The nurse should also consider what differences exist between the provider's and the client's culture and social status. These differences are important in communicating and in negotiating an appropriate relationship.)

4. The cultural explanation of the client's illness. What is the client's cultural explanation of the illness? What idioms does the client use to describe it? (For example, the client may say she is suffering from ataque de nervios— an attack of the nerves. This is a syndrome in Hispanic cultures that closely resembles anxiety and depressive disorders.) Is there a name or category used by the client's family or community to identify the condition? In order for care to be client centered, no matter what culture the client is, the nurse has to elicit specific information from the client and use it to organize strategies for care.

When performing the cultural assessment, the nurse needs to consider many of the cultural domains that were mentioned earlier.

(Fundamental Nursing Care, pp. 21–22)

1. What is the topic?
    cultural assessment

2. How many categories is the topic divided into? What are they?
    Four
    1. *the cultural identity of the client*
    2. *the cultural factors related to the client's psychosocial environment*
    3. *the cultural elements of the relationship between the healthcare provider and the patient*
    4. *the cultural explanation of the client's illness*

Passage 2

Larry Purnell and B. J. Paulanka (1998) developed a model for cultural competence that describes 12 domains of culture. This assessment tool identifies ethnocultural attributes of an individual, family, or group. Box 2-2 provides a list of these domains.

> ## BOX 2-2
>
> Twelve Domains of Culture
>
> **1.** Overview, inhabited localities, and topography
>
> **2.** Communication
>
> **3.** Family roles and organization
>
> **4.** Workforce issues
>
> **5.** Biocultural ecology
>
> **6.** High-risk health behaviors
>
> **7.** Nutrition
>
> **8.** Pregnancy and childbearing practices
>
> **9.** Death rituals
>
> **10.** Spirituality
>
> **11.** Healthcare practices
>
> **12.** Healthcare practitioners

In everyday practice as a practical or vocational nurse, you will need to be aware of these domains. You will develop knowledge of different cultures, especially those in the area where you live and work. This should include becoming familiar with the part of the world where those cultures were established and the heritage of the people. It is also important for you to realize that individuals within a particular culture may have characteristics that don't "fit" their group. It is important not to generalize and stereotype a member of a group (Purnell & Paulanka, 1998).

(*Fundamental Nursing Care*, p. 18)

1. What is the topic of the passage?

    culture

2. How many parts is the topic divided into? What are they?

    12

    1. *Overview, inhabited localities, and topography*

    2. *Communication*

    3. *Family roles and organization*

    4. *Workforce issues*

    5. *Biocultural ecology*

    6. *High-risk health behaviors*

    7. *Nutrition*

    8. *Pregnancy and childbearing practices*

© Pearson Education, Inc.

9. _Death rituals_

10. _Spirituality_

11. _Healthcare practices_

12. _Healthcare practitioners_

Passage 3

Responses to pain culturally have been divided into two categories: _stoic_ and _emotive_. Stoic clients are less expressive of their pain and tend to "grin and bear it." They tend to withdraw socially. Emotive clients are more likely to verbalize their expressions of pain. They desire people around to react to their pain and assist them with their suffering. Expressive clients often come from Hispanic, Middle Eastern, and Mediterranean backgrounds. Stoic clients often come from Northern European and Asian backgrounds. However, ethnicity alone does not predict accurately how a person will respond to pain. Some individuals tolerate even the most severe pain with little more than a clenched jaw and frequently refuse pain medication.

(_Fundamental Nursing Care_, p. 23)

1. What is the topic?
   responses to pain

2. What are the categories?
   stoic and emotive

6. Chronological Order

In the chronological order organizational pattern, information is arranged in the order in which the event occurred. Chronological order is also known as time order. When you read a passage that uses the chronological order organizational pattern, pay special attention to the order in which the information is presented. Remember that the chronological pattern of organization is concerned with the sequence of events that occur over time or steps that need to be taken in sequence. Let's read the following passage to understand this type of organizational pattern.

Example

The study of transcultural nursing began in the 1950s, when Dr. Madeleine Leininger noted differences in culture among clients and nurses. As she studied cultural differences, she realized that health and illness are influenced by culture. Dr. Leininger's work encouraged a broader awareness of cultural issues (Box 2-1) and led to the study of culture within the nursing curriculum.

(_Fundamental Nursing Care_, p. 17)

You will notice that the topic of the passage is transcultural nursing, and Box 2-1 clearly shows how the study of culture within the nursing curriculum developed from 1974 to 2000. As mentioned earlier, authors use the chronological

---

BOX 2-1
Events in the History of Cultural Care

1974 Transcultural Nursing Society was established as the official organization of transcultural nursing.

1991 Dr. Leininger published theory of cultural care diversity and universality

2000 The U.S. Department of Health and Human Services (USDHHS) stated, "Healthy People 2010 is firmly dedicated to the principle that—regardless of age, gender, race or ethnicity, income, education, geographical location, disability and sexual orientation—every person in every community across the nation deserves equal access to comprehensive, culturally competent, community-based health care systems that are committed to serving the needs of the individual and promoting community health" (USDHHS, 2000)

---

order organizational pattern when they want to show the sequence of events in reference to time. It is time for you to practice recognizing the chronological order pattern of organization, and the following exercise will help you do that.

PRACTICING THE SKILL

Read the following passages, identify the topic of each of the passages, and make a list of the events described in the passage.

Passage 1

The first training for practical nurses was at the Young Women's Christian Association (YWCA) in New York City in 1892. The following year this became the Ballard School. The program of study was 3 months long, and the participants studied special techniques for caring for the sick as well as a variety of homemaking techniques. Much of the care during this time was done in the client's home, making the licensed practical nurse (LPN) as home health or visiting nurse. Eleven years later, a second school, the Thompson Practical Nursing School, was established.

In 1914, the state legislature in Mississippi passed the first laws governing the practice of practical nurses. Other states were slow to follow. By 1940, only six states had passed such laws. In 1955, the state board test pool of the NLN Education Committee established the procedures for testing graduates of approved practical/vocational education programs in all states. Graduates who passed the examination became LPNs or, in California and Texas, licensed vocational nurses (LVNs). Each state set its own passing score.

Today, a graduate of an approved LPN/LVN training program is eligible to take the National Council Licensure Examination for Practical Nursing (NCLEX-PN).

(Fundamental Nursing Care, p. 9)

1. What is the topic of the passage?
   the history of licensed practical nursing

© Pearson Education, Inc.

2. What sequence of events is presented?

1. *The first training for nurses was in New York City in 1892.*

2. *Mississippi approved the practice of practical nurses in 1914.*

3. *Six states passed similar laws to approve the practice of practical nurses in 1940.*

4. *The NLN Education Committee established a testing procedure for nursing graduates in 1955.*

5. *Today, a nursing graduate can take the NCLEX-PN exam.*

Passage 2

The procedures provided in this book give you some of the basic skills you will need to provide excellent client care. Procedures should always begin with an initial set of actions that ensure a safe, efficient, and caring environment. These actions will become second nature to you as you continue your nursing training. Icons will be used to represent this initial set of actions at the start of each procedure. In some instances, an action may be optional. However, most are not. The icons are a reminder to do these basic, important interventions in nursing care:

1. Check the physician's order.
2. Gather the necessary equipment.
3. Introduce yourself to the client.
4. Identify the client (check the client's wristband against the chart).
5. Provide privacy as needed (close the curtain).
6. Explain the procedure.
7. Wash your hands. Hand hygiene is the single most effective way to prevent disease transmission.
8. Don gloves as needed.

(Fundamental Nursing Care, p. 76)

1. What is the topic of the passage?

essential procedures in implementing care

2. How many steps need to be taken to provide good client care?

8 steps

Passage 3

Health professionals frequently report about a client by telephone. Nurses inform physicians about a change in a client's condition; a radiologist reports the results of an x-ray study; a nurse may confer with a nurse on another unit about a transferred client. The nurse receiving a telephone report should document the date and time, the name of the person giving the information, and what information was received, and should sign the notation. For example:

[date] [time] GL Messina, laboratory technician, reported by telephone that Mrs. Sara Ames's hematocrit was 39/100mL.————————
Barbara Ireland, LPN

If there is any doubt about the information given over the telephone, the person receiving the information should repeat it back to the sender to ensure accuracy.

(Fundamental Nursing Care, p. 98)

1. What is the topic of the passage?

telephone reports
_____

2. What steps are presented in the passage to receive a telephone report accurately?

Document the date and time
_____

Take the name of the person giving the information
_____

Record what information was received
_____

Sign the notation
_____

When in doubt, repeat the information back to the sender to ensure accuracy
_____

These are the six most commonly used patterns of organization you will most likely encounter in college textbooks. Identifying these patterns will help you understand the author's purpose, key concepts, and relevant bits and pieces of information.

Other Useful Patterns of Organization

In addition to those patterns just studied, there are others you may find in your reading and test-taking.

7. Process

This type of organizational pattern arranges information to describe how a process occurs. The process pattern of organization is almost the same as chronological order. The only difference is that instead of describing the order in which the *events occurred over a period of time*, the author describes the order in which *different steps occur in a process*. For example, the author may describe how to give an injection to a patient or give directions for installing medical equipment. Read the following paragraph to understand how the author uses the process pattern of organization.

Example

Injections into muscle tissue (IM injections) are absorbed more quickly than subcutaneous injections because of the greater blood supply to the body muscles. Muscles can also take a larger volume of fluid without discomfort than subcutaneous tissues can, although the amount varies somewhat, depending on muscle size, muscle condition, and the site used. An adult with well-developed muscles can usually safely tolerate up to 4 ml. of medication in the gluteus medius and gluteus maximus muscles. A major consideration in the administration of IM injections is the selection of a safe site located away from large blood vessels, nerves, and bone. Several body sites can be used for IM injections. See procedure 29-3A for administering IM injections.

© Pearson Education, Inc.

Part A: Intramuscular Injection

Interventions

1. Check the medication order for accuracy.
2. Prepare the medication from the vial or ampule.
3. Identify the client, and assist the client to a comfortable position.
4. Select, locate, and clean the site.
5. Prepare the syringe for injection.
6. Inject the medication using a Z-track technique.
7. Withdraw the needle and then release hand that has been holding skin laterally.
8. Dispose of supplies appropriately.
9. Document all relevant information.
10. Assess effectiveness of the medication at the time it is expected to act.

(Fundamental Nursing Care, p. 657)

Notice how the author describes the process of giving IM injections step by step. A registered nurse can easily follow the steps and administer IM injections to patients.

PRACTICING THE SKILL

Read the following passages carefully to understand the process pattern of organization fully and answer the questions that follow.

Passage 1

Administering Oral Medications

Tablets or Capsules

- Pour the required number into the bottle cap, and then transfer the medication to the disposable cup without touching the tablets. Usually, all tablets or capsules to be given to the client are placed in the same cup.
- Keep narcotics and medications that require specific assessments, such as pulse measurements, respiratory rate or depth, or blood pressure, separate from the others.
- Break scored tablets as needed to obtain the correct dosage. Use a file or cutting device if necessary. Discard unused tablet pieces according to agency policy.
- If the client has difficulty swallowing, crush the tablets to a fine powder with a pill crusher or between two medication cups or spoons. Mix the powder with a small amount of soft food (e.g., custard, applesauce). Note: Check with pharmacy before crushing tablets.
- Place packaged unit-dose capsules or tablets directly into the medicine cup. Do not remove the wrapper until at the bedside.

(Fundamental Nursing Care, pp. 650–651)

1. What is the topic of the passage?
   oral medications

2. What process is explained in the above passage?
   The passage explains how to administer oral medications to a patient.

3. How many steps are involved in administering oral medications to a patient?
   Five steps are involved before the patient takes the oral medication.

Passage 2

Liquid Medication

- Thoroughly mix the medication before pouring. Discard any mixed medication changed in appearance.
- Remove the cap and place it upside down on the countertop.
- Hold the bottle so the label is next to your palm, and pour the medication away from the label.
- Hold the medication cap at eye level and fill it to the desired level, using the bottom of the meniscus (crescent-shaped upper surface of a column of liquid) to align with the container scale.
- Before capping the bottle, wipe the lip with a paper towel.
- When giving small amounts of liquids (e.g., less than 5 mL), prepare the medication in a sterile syringe without the needle.
- Keep unit-dose liquids in their package and open them at the bedside.

(*Fundamental Nursing Care*, p. 651)

1. What is the topic of the passage?
   liquid medication

2. What process is explained in the above passage?
   The passage explains how to administer liquid medication to a patient.

3. How many steps are described in the above passage?
   Seven steps are described to give liquid medication to a patient.

Passage 3

Mixing Medication from Two Vials

- Withdraw a volume of air equal to the total volume of medications to be withdrawn from vials A and B.
- Inject a volume of air equal to the volume of medication to be withdrawn into vial A.
- Withdraw the needle from vial A and inject the remaining air into vial B.

  or

  Draw up the volume of air equal to the amount of solution to be drawn from vial B and inject into vial B. Leaving the needle in the vial, invert vial B and withdraw the prescribed amount of medication.

© Pearson Education, Inc.

- Withdraw the required amount of medication from vial B. The same needle is used to inject air into and withdraw medication from the second vial.

- Using a newly attached sterile needle, withdraw the required amount of medication from vial A. If using a syringe with a fused needle, withdraw the medication from vial A. The syringe now contains a mixture of medications from vials A and B.

(*Fundamental Nursing Care*, p. 656)

1. What is the topic of the passage?

administering medication from two vials

2. What process is explained in the above passage?

The above passage explains how to mix medication from two vials.

3. How many steps does a registered nurse have to go through to mix medication from two vials?

A registered nurse has to take five (5) steps to mix medication from two vials.

8. Listing (also known as Addition)

This pattern of organization arranges information in a list in no particular order. Unlike process or chronological order, there is no specific order in which information is arranged. For example, the author may show the different ways that computers are used in the field of medicine. Keep in mind that the listing pattern of organization uses transitional words such as *in addition*, *also*, and *furthermore*.

Example
Studying Effectively

It is easy to stare at a page of text and feel that you have "spent time" studying when, in fact, you may have understood very little. When you have a block of time set aside to study, make sure you use it wisely. For hints about what is most important in the text, look at the Learning Outcomes at the beginning of each chapter. . . . Another technique to employ when studying is outlining. Some students find it helpful to outline the chapter after reading it. Under the main ideas, they organize the concepts and the information that supports those ideas. . . . Study questions at the end of the chapter and/or in student workbooks are another way to help you pull out the most important information in a chapter. . . . Take advantage of all available tools. Use a computer at school or at home to access the Companion Website. . . . Studying with another person or group of three or four people can be helpful in processing information and discussing ideas.

(*Fundamental Nursing Care*, p. 3)

If you take a closer look at the passage, you will notice that the topic is how to study a textbook effectively. The authors suggest several ways to read a textbook—such as time management, preparing an outline, and studying with a partner or a small group. It should be noted that there is no particular order in which the different ways to read should occur. In other words, a good reader may prepare an outline and study with a partner and vice versa.

PRACTICING THE SKILL

Read the following passages carefully, paying attention to transition words such as *in addition, also, furthermore,* etc., and answer the questions that follow.

Passage 1

For purposes of education and research, most agencies allow student and graduate health professionals access to client records. The records are used in client conferences, clinics, rounds, and written papers or client studies. The student is bound by a strict ethical code to hold all information in confidence. It is the responsibility of the student and health professionals to protect the client's privacy by not using a name or any statements in the notations that would identify the client. Additionally, it is very important for staff and students to maintain confidentiality with work-sheets and assignment sheets. Caution must be used to ensure that papers are not left where visitors and clients may see them.

(*Fundamental Nursing Care*, p. 90)

1. What is the topic of the passage?

client records

2. What is the general idea of the passage?

It is important to keep client records confidential.

3. How is this passage an example of the listing pattern of organization?

The author uses the transition word additionally *to support the main idea,*

which is confidentiality of client records.

Passage 2

Computers make care planning and documentation relatively easy. In most facilities, nurses record nursing actions and client responses by choosing from standardized lists of care and intervention using a touch screen. The nurse can also type narrative information into the computer for further explanation or to note exceptions. Some computer programs produce a flow sheet with expected outcomes and nursing interventions. The nurse chooses the appropriate interventions for the specific client and initials them, indicating they were implemented. Others use the problem-oriented format, producing a problem list in priority order. The nurse then selects the appropriate nursing diagnoses, expected outcomes, and nursing interventions by using a light pen on the screen. The nurse uses the keyboard to type in additional information.

(*Fundamental Nursing Care*, p. 97)

1. What is the topic of the passage?

using computers for patients' records

2. What is the main idea of the passage?

Nurses use computers for care planning and documentation rather easily.

3. What transition words are used for the listing pattern of organization?

Also and then

© Pearson Education, Inc.

Passage 3

The variety of healthcare services hospitals provide usually depends on their size and location. The large urban hospitals usually have inpatient beds, emergency services, diagnostic facilities, ambulatory surgery centers, pharmacy services, intensive and coronary care services, and multiple outpatient services provided by clinics. Some large hospitals have other specialized services such as spinal cord injury and burn units, oncology services, and infusion and dialysis units. In addition, some hospitals have substance abuse treatment units and health promotion units. Small rural hospitals often are limited to inpatient beds, radiology and laboratory services, and basic emergency services. The number of services a rural hospital provides is usually directly related to its size and its distance from an urban center.

(Fundamental Nursing Care, p. 111)

1. What is the topic of the passage?
   what hospitals provide

2. What is the main idea of the passage?
   Depending on their size and location, hospitals provide a variety of healthcare services.

3. How many major details are provided to support the main idea? What are they?
   At least three major details are provided to support the main idea.
   1. *Large hospitals have inpatient beds, emergency services, and multiple outpatient services provided by clinics.*
   2. *Other large hospitals have specialized services such as spinal cord injury and burn units.*
   3. *Small rural hospitals have limited healthcare services such as inpatient beds and basic emergency services.*

9. Statement and Clarification

Using a statement and clarification pattern of organization, the author first presents a general idea and then expounds on it to help the reader understand the idea. An example of this type of pattern of organization may be a nursing text in which a statement of fact is made and discussion is provided to make that statement clear. Let's look at an example to understand the statement and clarification pattern of organization more clearly.

Example

Personal space is the distance people prefer in interactions with others. It is a natural protective instinct for people to maintain a certain amount of space immediately around them. The amount of personal space varies with individuals and cultures. When someone who wants to communicate steps too close, the receiver automatically steps back a pace or two. When providing nursing care, the nurse may need to invade a client's personal space. It is important to be aware of this and to warn the client when this will occur.

(Fundamental Nursing Care, p. 228)

Notice how the author begins the passage with a statement about people's preference for personal space. Then the statement is followed by a brief discussion of how personal space varies from culture to culture.

PRACTICING THE SKILL

Now that you understand how authors use the statement and clarification pattern of organization, read the following passages and answer the questions that follow.

Passage 1

From an early age, females and males communicate differently. Girls tend to use language to seek confirmation, minimize differences, and establish intimacy. Boys use language to establish independence and negotiate status within a group. These differences can continue into adulthood so that the same communication may be interpreted differently by a man and a woman. Many studies have found that men and women communicate differently in both content and process of communication. There is evidence to suggest that more effective communication occurs when the care provider and the client are of the same gender.

(Fundamental Nursing Care, p. 228)

1. What is the topic of the passage?
   communication

2. What general statement is made about the topic?
   Males and females communicate differently from a very young age.

3. How is this point made clear to the reader?
   The author provides a brief discussion about girls and boys using language
   for different purposes. It is further suggested that the nurse and the client
   be of the same gender.

Passage 2

The ways people walk and carry themselves are often reliable indicators of self-concept, current mood, and health. The posture of people when they are sitting or lying can also indicate feelings or mood. The nurse can validate the interpretation of the behavior by asking, for example, "You look like it really hurts you to move. I'm wondering how your pain is and if you might need something to make you more comfortable?"

No part of the body is as expressive as the face. Facial expressions can convey surprise, fear, anger, disgust, happiness, and sadness. When the message is not clear, it is important to get feedback to be sure what the person intends.

Nurses need to be aware of their own facial expressions and what they are communicating to others. Clients are quick to notice the nurse's expression, particularly when they feel unsure or uncomfortable. It is impossible to control all facial expression. However, the nurse should learn to control expressions such as fear or disgust.

(Fundamental Nursing Care, pp. 229–230)

© Pearson Education, Inc.

1. What is the topic of the passage?

   body language

2. What general statement is made about the topic?

   People's body language can convey their self-image, mood, and even health.

3. How is this point made clear to the reader?

   People's postures when they are sitting or lying can indicate their mood and

   health. Also, facial expressions can convey surprise, anger, fear, happiness,

   and sadness. Finally, nurses must be aware of their facial expressions as the

   client can easily notice if they are uncomfortable or uncertain.

Passage 3

Fear is an emotion or feeling of apprehension aroused by impending danger, pain, or other perceived threat. People may fear something that has already occurred, a current threat, or something they believe will happen. The fear may or may not be based in reality. For example, beginning nursing students may fear their first experience in a client care setting. They may be worried that clients will not want to be cared for by students or that they might inadvertently harm the clients. The nursing students' feelings of fear are real and will probably elicit a stress response. However, the instructor arranges the students' first client assignment so that the students' feared outcomes are unlikely to occur.

(*Fundamental Nursing Care*, p. 292)

1. What is the topic of the passage?

   fear

2. What general statement is made about the topic?

   Fear can be caused by perceived danger or threat.

3. How is this point made clear to the reader?

   The example of beginning nursing students is provided to clarify the general

   statement.

10. Spatial Order

Spatial order arranges details according to their location in space. An example of this pattern of organization is a layout of an operating room or an Intensive Care Unit (ICU). To help the reader visualize a person, thing, place or space, the author uses descriptive language to create a vivid image. The author may choose to describe the place or space from the north to the south, or from top to bottom, or from bottom to top, or from inside to outside. Consider the following example to understand the spatial order pattern of organization more clearly.

Example

An inclinometer (Scoliometer) measures distortions of the torso. The client is asked to bend over, with arms dangling and palms pressed together, until a curve can be observed in the thoracic area (the upper back). The Scoliometer is placed on the back and used to measure the apex (the highest point) of the curve. The client is then asked to continue bending until the curve in the lower back can be seen; the apex of this curve is then measured.

(*Fundamental Nursing Care*, p. 838)

Notice that words such as *the upper back, on the back*, and *the highest point* are used to create an image of the client's location in space. With the help of these words, the reader can almost see the client bending over and the Scoliometer placed on the back.

PRACTICING THE SKILL

Now practice reading passages that use the spatial order pattern of organization. Then answer the questions that follow each of the passages.

Passage 1

Assist the client to the examination table. Place in a comfortable position supporting injured extremity. In order for the splint to be applied properly, the client must be seated or lying down. Supporting the extremity can lessen the pain. Pad the inside of the splint and check for proper fit on the extremity. Fasten the Velcro strap, or wrap splint and extremity, evenly and snug enough to provide support but not enough to impede circulation of the limb, with an elastic bandage and fasten with clips or tape. Instruct the client to keep the extremity elevated and apply ice. Elevating the extremity above the level of the heart and applying ice aid in decreasing swelling. Apply a sling for an arm splint. The sling will help the client support the injured arm and keep it elevated.

(*Fundamental Nursing Care*, p. 856)

1. What is the topic of the passage?
   applying the splint

2. What transitional or descriptive phrases are used to signal how the client is arranged in space?
   Seated or lying down, above the level of the heart, keep it elevated

Passage 2

When the body is aligned, organs are properly supported. This allows them to function at their best, while also maintaining balance. The line of gravity is an imaginary vertical line drawn through the body's center of gravity. The center of gravity is the point at which all of the body's mass is centered and the base of support (the foundation on which the body rests) achieves balance. In humans, the usual line of gravity is drawn from the top of the head, down between the shoulders, through the trunk slightly anterior to the sacrum, and between the weight-bearing joints (hips, knees) and base of support (feet). In the upright position, the center of gravity occurs in the pelvis approximately midway between the umbilicus

© Pearson Education, Inc.

and the symphysis pubis. When standing, an adult must center body weight symmetrically along the line of gravity to maintain stability. Greater stability and balance are achieved in the sitting or supine position because a chair or bed provides a wider base of support with a lower center of gravity. When the body is well aligned, there is little strain on the joints, muscles, tendons, or ligaments.

(Fundamental Nursing Care, p. 751)

1. What is the topic of the passage?

    alignment and posture

2. Write down a few transitional or descriptive phrases that are used to signal how space is arranged.

    Through *the body's center of gravity,* from *the top of the head,* down

    between *the shoulders,* through *the trunk slightly anterior to the sacrum. . .*

Passage 3

Using Canes

Hold the cane with the hand on the stronger side of the body to provide maximum support and appropriate body alignment when walking. Position the tip of a standard cane (and the nearest tip of other canes) about 15 cm (6 in.) to the side and 15 cm (6 in.) in front of the near foot, so that the elbow is slightly flexed. Move the cane forward about 30 cm (1 ft), or a distance that is comfortable while the body weight is borne by both legs. Then move the affected (weak) leg forward to the cane while the weight is borne by the cane and stronger leg. Next, move the unaffected (stronger) leg forward ahead of the cane and weak leg while the weight is borne by the cane and weak leg. Repeat the steps. This pattern of moving provides at least two points of support on the floor at all times. Move the cane and weak leg forward at the same time, while the weight is borne by the stronger leg. Move the stronger leg forward, while the weight is borne by the cane and the weak leg.

(Fundamental Nursing Care, p. 756)

1. What is the topic of the passage?

    walking with the aid of canes

2. Write down a few transitional or descriptive phrases that are used to signal how space is arranged.

    on *the stronger side of the body, 15 cm to the side and 15 cm in front of the*

    near foot, move the cane forward about 30 cm, move the weak leg forward,

    move the unaffected leg ahead of the cane, move the stronger leg forward

Each of the organizational patterns contains transitional phrases that will help you recognize its characteristics. See a table of organizational patterns and transitional phrases in Appendix IV for further examples.

Applying the Skill

Now that you have practiced identifying different types of organizational patterns, let's practice reading full-length articles to recognize these patterns.

Learning to Work Together

Collaboration

Pre-Reading Questions

Working in small groups, discuss the following questions before you read the article.

1. What is the role of communication in providing patient care? What are the consequences of miscommunication between physicians and nurses? Who is most affected by a nurse's poor communication skills?

2. Other than communication, what are some other skills that both physicians and nurses must possess to improve patient care? Be specific.

3. There is evidence in medical literature that learning to work together is an important skill. Still, nursing graduates are not equipped with team-building skills. In your opinion, what measures must nursing programs in the United States take to teach students the value of effective team-building?

Learning to Work Together

By **Don Vaughan,** *Nursing Spectrum*
http://include.nurse.com/apps/pbcs.dll/article?AID=/20080519/PA02/105190038

May 19, 2008

1   Effective nurse-physician collaboration is rooted in **mutual** respect and **positive** dialogue. This may sound like a simple, easily achievable goal, yet dissatisfaction among nurses (and physicians) remains common.

2   In an effort to improve interdisciplinary **communication** and interaction, Thomas Jefferson University in Philadelphia recently **established** the Jefferson Center for InterProfessional Education (JCIPE), which is dedicated to improving patient care through **coordination, implementation,** and **evaluation** of a **team**-based curriculum.

3   JCIPE's centerpiece **project** is the Jefferson Health Mentors Program, which **rolled out** in September, says codirector Christine Arenson, MD, associate professor in the Department of Family and **Community** Medicine and director of the Division of Geriatric Medicine.

rolled out
introduced, began

Multidisciplinary Learning Model

4   The two-year program is **required** for all first-year health profession students, which includes those studying medicine, nursing, **physical** therapy, and

© Pearson Education, Inc.

Christine Arenson (left), MD, and Molly Rose, RN, PhD. Photo by David Debalko Photography

a chronic condition
an old, prolonged disease

occupational therapy. The students are grouped into teams of at least two medical students and one nursing student, and each **team** is partnered with a person living with **a chronic condition**, who serves as the "patient mentor."

5   Each visit with their patient mentor is focused on what the teams are studying at that time within their **individual** curriculums. Their first visit is a guided life history so they understand that "a patient with a chronic condition is a person first," Arenson explains. During their second visit, the students obtain a complete **medical** history as **required** by their **individual** disciplines. This way, Arenson says, team members learn what is common and what is unique about each discipline's **approach** to the patient.

Team-Building is Key

6   One of the **principal goals** of the Jefferson Health Mentors Program is effective **team**-building, says JCIPE codirector Molly Rose, RN, PhD, a professor in the Jefferson School of Nursing. "Just as they get to know their mentors as a person, they also get to know each other as people who are in a different discipline," she says. "Because they must work as teams, there is a lot of **communication**, which is one of the basic concepts related to collaboration and improving physician-nurse relationships."

7   "The purpose of this program is to improve patient care, safety, and **outcomes**," says Arenson. "For all of the professions to do that well, they must learn to work together. We don't want them to feel **reticent** when it comes to calling upon another discipline or asking questions related to the patients they are seeing."

reticent
not willing to talk about what you know or how you feel

8 **Medical** literature is rich with **data** demonstrating the value of effective **team**-building, Arenson and Rose conclude.

Not Always an Easy Lesson

9 "It's also clear from the business literature that people don't just **automatically** become teams," Arenson says. "They actually have to learn how to **function** in **team** roles. That's why we thought it was extremely important from the earliest stages of their education."

10 Indeed, nurses often find collaboration difficult, observes Gina Aya Nelson, RN, MSN, patient care manager at Scripps Memorial Hospital in La Jolla, Calif., and coauthor of a **research** report on nurse-physician collaboration on **medical**/surgical units **published** in the February 2008 issue of *MedSurg Nursing*.

11 The most common complaints among nurses include a **perceived** lack of respect and poor **communication** with the physicians with whom they work. Nelson says this is particularly true among relatively inexperienced graduate nurses who are still learning their way around.

12 Nelson admits to having experienced occasional conflicts with physicians over the course of her **professional** career, and as a nurse manager she also must deal with physician complaints from her staff.

13 "Sometimes the **interaction** is **negative** between nurses and physicians," she says. "But when you get both sides of the story, the common **theme** is they both want to do what's best for the patient, but they're unable to see each other's views on it."

14 Adds Arenson: "I think there continues to be less understanding than would be ideal on the part of physicians regarding the expertise and **scope** of practice of professionals outside of medicine. And there is compelling **evidence** in the safety literature about what happens when team members feel they have to defer to the physician, and they're not able to express their opinion. That's a common **source** of **medical** errors."

Proactive Approach to Conflict

15 While researching her report on nurse/physician collaboration, Nelson learned the University of Kentucky requires **medical** students to work an eight-hour **shift** with nurses so they can better understand the nurse's **role** in patient care. "The school is **unique** in that **approach**, and I think it's a good approach to improving the collaborative relationship," Nelson says.

16 It's an important issue because unresolved **conflict** can adversely **affect** a nurse's ability to do his or her **job**. It might even cause a nurse to leave the profession.

17 Experience, Nelson says, often is the best instructor.

18 "I've found that as you become more experienced, you're more **inclined to** sit down with a physician and say, "This is where I'm coming from. Let me understand where you're coming from, and let's make sure we're doing the right thing for the patient," she says. "I also think nurses tend to be more assertive as they gain experience."

inclined to
be willing to do something

Don Vaughan is a freelance healthcare writer. To comment, e-mail editorPA@nursingspectrum.com

© Pearson Education, Inc.

Reading Comprehension Check

1. The main idea of the article is that
   a. registered nurses have excellent communication skills.
   b. most physicians are generally satisfied with their interaction with nurses.
   c. it is unnecessary to improve interdisciplinary communication and interaction.
   d. effective nurse-physician collaboration requires mutual respect and good communication skills.

2. "Effective nurse-physician collaboration is rooted in mutual respect and positive dialogue. This may sound like a simple, easily achievable goal, yet dissatisfaction among nurses (and physicians) remains common."

   What is the pattern of organization shown in the above paragraph?
   a. chronological order.   c. cause and effect.
   b. classification.   d. definition.

3. "In an effort to improve interdisciplinary communication and interaction, Thomas Jefferson University in Philadelphia recently established the Jefferson Center for InterProfessional Education (JCIPE), which is dedicated to improving patient care through coordination, implementation, and evaluation of a team-based curriculum."

   The overall pattern of organization of this passage is
   a. comparison and contrast.   c. classification.
   b. cause and effect.   d. example.

4. "Each visit with their patient mentor is focused on what the teams are studying at that time within their individual curriculums. Their first visit is a guided life history so they understand that 'a patient with a chronic condition is a person first,' Arenson explains. During their second visit, the students obtain a complete medical history as required by their individual disciplines. This way, Arenson says, team members learn what is common and what is unique about each discipline's approach to the patient."

   How are the supporting details listed?
   a. cause and effect.   c. classification.
   b. comparison and contrast.   d. chronological order.

5. Dr. Molly Rose says, "Just as they get to know their mentors as a person, they also get to know each other as people who are in a different discipline . . . Because they must work as teams, there is a lot of communication, which is one of the basic concepts related to collaboration and improving physician-nurse relationships."

   The overall pattern of organization here is
   a. cause and effect.   c. classification.
   b. spatial order.   d. definition.

6. "'The purpose of this program is to improve patient care, safety, and outcomes,' says Arenson. 'For all of the professions to do that well, they must learn to work together. We don't want them to feel reticent when it comes to

calling upon another discipline or asking questions related to the patients they are seeing. '"

The above passage is organized by

a. classifying the different ways to improve patient care.

b. listing the important functions of patient care, safety, and outcomes.

c.) showing a cause/effect relationship between team-building skills and patient care, safety, and outcomes.

d. clarifying an explanation of patient care.

7. "The most common complaints among nurses include a perceived lack of respect and poor communication with the physicians with whom they work. Nelson says this is particularly true among relatively inexperienced graduate nurses who are still learning their way around."

The author's overall pattern of organization

a. contrasts the difference between male nurses and female nurses.

b. lists the changes in the nurses' perception of physicians.

c.) shows a causal relation between inexperienced graduate nurses and poor communication with the physicians.

d. summarizes the importance of effective communication skills.

8. "'Sometimes the interaction is negative between nurses and physicians,' she says. 'But when you get both sides of the story, the common theme is they both want to do what's best for the patient, but they're unable to see each other's views on it.'"

The focus on nurses and physicians shows what pattern of organization?

a.) compare and contrast.   c. chronological order.

b. listing.   d. none of the above.

9. "While researching her report on nurse/physician collaboration, Nelson learned the University of Kentucky requires medical students to work an eight-hour shift with nurses so they can better understand the nurse's role in patient care. 'The school is unique in that approach, and I think it's a good approach to improving the collaborative relationship,' Nelson says."

The pattern of organization is

a.) cause and effect.   c. chronological order.

b. spatial order.   d. definition.

10. "I've found that as you become more experienced, you're more inclined to sit down with a physician and say, 'This is where I'm coming from. Let me understand where you're coming from, and let's make sure we're doing the right thing for the patient," she says. "I also think nurses tend to be more assertive as they gain experience."

What is the overall pattern of organization of the above passage?

a. chronological order.

b.) cause and effect.

c. classification.

d. comparison and contrast.

© Pearson Education, Inc.

**DEBATABLE
TOPIC**

ESL Annotation

7.6 ESL In many cultures it is taken as a given that women are by nature pre-programmed to be more nurturing than men. It may be worth discussing that many Americans do not share such a view of gender roles.

Recommended Debate Topic: Women naturally make better nurses than men as they are genetically preprogrammed to do humanistic kinds of work.

Discuss debatable topics concerning nursing with your classmates and instructor for the debate activity.

Your suggested debate topics:

a. _____

b. _____

c. _____

READING

Reading Selection 4

Online Article

7.7 Flesch-Kincaid Grade Level 12.0

Student Enrollment Rises in U.S. Nursing Colleges and Universities for the 6th Consecutive Year

Pre-Reading Questions

With a partner, discuss the following questions before reading the article.

1. Do you know someone who is studying to be a registered nurse? What does this person say about the prospects of working as a licensed practical nurse? If you do not know anyone who is a nursing student, then what is your perception of nursing as a profession?

2. There is a shortage of registered nurses in the United States. Despite this, the nursing programs in the country have not been able to keep up with the demand for nurses. In your opinion, what do you think has caused the shortage?

3. Most of the nursing programs in the United States have not succeeded in producing enough nursing graduates to bridge the evident gap in the field. Why do you think the government has not increased federal and state funding needed to recruit new faculty and improve teaching resources despite the constantly growing need for nursing services in the United States?"

ESL Annotation

7.8 ESL This topic is of special interest to ESL students who find a career in nursing financially rewarding.

Student Enrollment Rises in U.S. Nursing Colleges and Universities for the 6th Consecutive Year

From http://www.aacn.nche.edu/Media/NewsReleases/06Survey.htm

December 5, 2006

1 WASHINGTON, D.C—The American Association of Colleges of Nursing (AACN) today released **preliminary survey data** which show that enrollment in entry-level baccalaureate nursing programs increased by 5.0 **percent** from 2005 to 2006. Though this increase is welcome, surveyed nursing colleges and universities turned away more than 32,000 qualified applicants due primarily

to a shortage of nurse educators. AACN is very concerned about the high number of qualified students being **turned away** from nursing programs each year given the national nursing shortage, which is expected to intensify through the year 2020.

turned away
refused or rejected

2   "Nursing schools nationwide are effectively answering the calls to expand student **capacity** given the growing need for nursing services in the U.S.," said AACN President Jeanette Lancaster. "With limited **resources available** to nursing schools and a dwindling population of nurse faculty, future enrollment increases may not be possible without a **significant** boost in **federal** and state funding needed to prepare new faculty, enhance teaching **resources**, and upgrade nursing school **infrastructure**."

3   In a report released in April 2006, the Health **Resources** and Services **Administration** (HRSA) projects that nursing schools must increase the number of graduates by 90 **percent** in order to adequately address the nursing shortage. With an 18.0 **percent** increase in graduations from baccalaureate nursing programs this year, schools are falling far short of meeting this **target**. By the year 2020, HRSA projects that more than one million new **Registered** Nurses (RNs) will be needed in the U.S. healthcare system to meet the demand for nursing care.

Trends in Nursing School Enrollments

4   AACN's **annual survey** is the **primary source** for actual (versus projected) **data** on enrollment and graduations reported by the nation's baccalaureate and graduate degree programs in nursing. This year's 5.0 **percent** enrollment increase is based on **data** supplied by the same 433 schools reporting in both 2005 and 2006. This is the sixth consecutive year of enrollment gains with 9.6, 14.1, 16.6, 8.1, and 3.7 **percent** increases in 2005, 2004, 2003, 2002, and 2001, respectively. **Prior** to the six-year upswing, baccalaureate nursing programs experienced six years of declining enrollments from 1995 through 2000. For a graphic depicting enrollment changes in baccalaureate nursing programs from 1994–2006, see **http://www.aacn.nche.edu/Media/ppt/94-06EnrChgs.ppt.**

5   The AACN **survey** also found that the number of graduates from entry-level baccalaureate programs increased by 18.0 **percent** from 2005 to 2006. The recent rise in graduations follows 13.4, 14, 4.3 and 3.2 **percent** increases in the number of graduates in 2005, 2004, 2003 and 2002, respectively. This upward **trend** was preceded by a six-year **period** of graduation declines from 1996 through 2001.

Qualified Students Turned Away Despite Nursing Shortage

6   Though interest in nursing careers is strong, **access** to **professional** nursing education is becoming more difficult. AACN's **preliminary** findings show that 32,323 qualified applications to entry-level baccalaureate programs were not accepted in 2006 based on responses from 449 schools. The number of qualified applications turned away each year from these programs remains high with 37,514; 29,425; 15,944; and 3,600 students turned award in 2005, 2004, 2003 and 2002, respectively. The **primary** barriers to accepting all qualified students at nursing colleges and universities continue to be insufficient faculty, clinical placement sites, and classroom space. For a graphic showing

© Pearson Education, Inc.

the number of qualified applications turned away from baccalaureate nursing programs over the past five years, see **http://www.aacn.nche.edu/Media/ppt/ 02-06TurnedAway.ppt.**

7   To help address the shortage of nursing faculty, AACN is leveraging its **resources** to secure **federal** funding for faculty development programs, collect **data** on faculty vacancy rates, identify **strategies** to address the shortage, and **focus media** attention on this important issue. This work includes:

■ Collaborating with other nursing groups to mobilize support for more **federal** funding for nursing education, including support for the Nurse Faculty Loan Program and the creation of new **legislation** such as the Nurse Faculty Education Act and the Nurse Education, **Expansion** and Development Act introduced in the 109th Congress.

■ Leading the effort to expand the Graduate **Assistance** in Areas of National Need program administered by the U.S. Department of Education to include nursing. As a result, nursing is now recognized as an **area** of national need and new funding for PhD programs in nursing is **available**.

■ Creating a new minority faculty scholarship program with The California Endowment to increase the number of nurse educators from underrepresented groups.

■ Offering a new Faculty Development **Institute** in February 2007 to help prepare and retain new nursing faculty at schools nationwide.

■ Highlighting statewide **initiatives** and other best practices related to addressing the faculty shortage via issue bulletins, white papers, **media** articles and Web **resources**.

8   For more detail on the nurse faculty shortage and AACN's **response**, see **http://www.aacn.nche.edu/Media/FactSheets/FacultyShortage.htm.**

Interest Runs High in Professional Nursing Careers

9   The **robust** interest in **professional** nursing careers can be **attributed** in part to successful outreach efforts guided by the nation's nursing schools. **Strategies** employed to increase student **capacity** this year included forming alliances with hospitals and other practice sites to address faculty and clinical space **constraints**. Some schools have expanded or opened new accelerated programs for second-degree seekers looking to **transition** into nursing while others have taken advantage of state and **federal** funding aimed at strengthening the nursing workforce. In addition to these school-based **initiatives**, both Johnson & Johnson and the Nurses for a Healthier Tomorrow coalition continued their national media campaigns to encourage careers in nursing.

10   Given the demands of today's health care system, the greatest need in the nursing workforce is for nurses prepared at the baccalaureate and higher degree levels. With the government calling for baccalaureate preparation for at least two thirds of the nursing workforce, the **evidence** clearly shows that higher levels of nursing education are linked with lower patient mortality rates, fewer errors, and greater **job** satisfaction among RNs. Last year, the American Organization of Nurse Executives (AONE), the national voice for

robust
strong

attributed
related (to), traced back to

nurse leaders in the practice arena, began calling for baccalaureate preparation for all RNs in the future. The growing complexity of patient care and the increase in patient **acuity** require that nurses have the best entry-level preparation **available**.

acuity
afflicted by a disease with a rapid onset

11   "To stabilize the nursing workforce, the **federal** government and other stakeholders must **focus** on increasing nursing school enrollments at the baccalaureate level," said Dr. Lancaster. "Besides adding to the RN workforce, graduates of baccalaureate nursing programs are much more likely to **pursue** graduate education and **achieve** the credentials needed to serve as nurse educators."

About the AACN Survey

12   Now in its 26th year, AACN's **Annual Survey** of Institutions with Baccalaureate and Higher Degree Nursing Programs is conducted each year by the association's **Data** and **Research** Center. Information from the **survey** forms the basis for the nation's premier database on trends in enrollments and graduations, student and faculty demographics, and faculty and deans' salaries. AACN **data reflects** actual counts reported in fall 2006 by nursing schools, not projections or estimates based on past reporting.

13   The **annual** AACN **survey** is a collaborative effort with **data** on nurse practitioner programs collected jointly with the National Organization of Nurse Practitioner Faculties and **data** on clinical nurse specialist programs collected with the National Association of Clinical Nurse Specialists. Complete **survey** results are **compiled** in three separate reports, which will be **available** in February 2007:

- 2006–2007 Enrollment and Graduations in Baccalaureate and Graduate Programs in Nursing
- 2006–2007 Salaries of Instructional and Administrative Nursing Faculty in Baccalaureate and Graduate Programs in Nursing
- 2006–2007 Salaries of Deans in Baccalaureate and Graduate Programs in Nursing

14   More information about the upcoming **data** reports will be posted soon on the AACN Web **site** at **http://www.aacn.nche.edu/IDS/datarep.htm.**

15   Despite this increase, more than 32,000 qualified applicants were turned away from nursing programs in 2006 due to a shortage of nurse educators (December 5, 2006).

Editor's Note: News media may obtain selected tables from these data reports by contacting Robert Rosseter at rrosseter@aacn.nche.edu or 202-463-6930, extension 231. Requests for regional data and local enrollment success stories are also welcome.

The American Association of Colleges of Nursing (AACN) is the national voice for university and four-year college education programs in nursing. Representing more than 600 member schools of nursing at public and private institutions nationwide, AACN's educational, research, governmental advocacy, data collection, publications, and other programs work to establish quality standards for bachelor's- and graduate-degree nursing education, assist deans and directors to implement those standards, influence the nursing profession to improve health care, and promote public support of baccalaureate and graduate nursing education, research, and practice. www.aacn.nche.edu

© Pearson Education, Inc.

Reading Comprehension Check

1. What is the main idea of the article?
   a. There aren't enough students interested in pursuing nursing as a professional career.
   b. Enrollment in most nursing programs has decreased by 5.0 percent from 2005 to 2006.
   c. Many qualified students are being turned away from nursing programs because there aren't enough nurse educators.
   d. There are sufficient nurse educators in the country to meet the growing demand of nursing services.

2. "The American Association of Colleges of Nursing (AACN) today released preliminary survey data which show that enrollment in entry-level baccalaureate nursing programs increased by 5.0 percent from 2005 to 2006. Though this increase is welcome, surveyed nursing colleges and universities turned away more than 32,000 qualified applicants due primarily to a shortage of nurse educators."

   What is the pattern of organization of this passage?
   a. chronological order.   c. classification.
   b. cause and effect.   d. example.

3. AACN President Jeanette Lancaster says, "With limited resources available to nursing schools and a dwindling population of nurse faculty, future enrollment increases may not be possible without a significant boost in federal and state funding needed to prepare new faculty, enhance teaching resources, and upgrade nursing school infrastructure."

   The pattern of organization of the above passage is
   a. comparison and contrast.   c. spatial order.
   b. listing.   d. cause and effect.

4. "In a report released in April 2006, the Health Resources and Services Administration (HRSA) projects that nursing schools must increase the number of graduates by 90 percent in order to adequately address the nursing shortage. With an 18.0 percent increase in graduations from baccalaureate nursing programs this year, schools are falling far short of meeting this target. By the year 2020, HRSA projects that more than one million new Registered Nurses (RNs) will be needed in the U.S. healthcare system to meet the demand for nursing care."

   What is the pattern of organization here?
   a. chronological order.   c. spatial order.
   b. comparison and contrast.   d. listing.

5. "This year's 5.0 percent enrollment increase is based on data supplied by the same 433 schools reporting in both 2005 and 2006. This is the sixth consecutive year of enrollment gains with 9.6, 14.1, 16.6, 8.1, and 3.7 percent increases in 2005, 2004, 2003, 2002, and 2001, respectively. Prior to the six-year upswing, baccalaureate nursing programs experienced six years of declining enrollments from 1995 through 2000."

The author's pattern of organization in the above is

a. comparing and contrasting data supplied by 433 schools.

b. defining the term *enrollment*.

c. showing percent enrollment increase in chronological order.

d. giving several examples of baccalaureate nursing programs.

6. "The AACN survey also found that the number of graduates from entry-level baccalaureate programs increased by 18.0 percent from 2005 to 2006. The recent rise in graduations follows 13.4, 14, 4.3 and 3.2 percent increases in the number of graduates in 2005, 2004, 2003 and 2002, respectively. This upward trend was preceded by a six-year period of graduation declines from 1996 through 2001."

What is the pattern of organization in this passage?

a. definition.   c. example.

b. classification.   d. chronological order.

7. "Though interest in nursing careers is strong, access to professional nursing education is becoming more difficult. AACN's preliminary findings show that 32,323 qualified applications to entry-level baccalaureate programs were not accepted in 2006 based on responses from 449 schools. The number of qualified applications turned away each year from these programs remains high with 37,514; 29,425; 15,944; and 3,600 students turned away in 2005, 2004, 2003 and 2002, respectively. The primary barriers to accepting all qualified students at nursing colleges and universities continue to be insufficient faculty, clinical placement sites, and classroom space."

The overall pattern of organization in the above is

a. chronological order.   c. comparison and contrast.

b. Classification.   d. Example.

8. AACN is considering steps to secure federal funding to address the nursing shortage (paragraph 7). This statement is followed by five bullets, outlining the steps AACN is planning to take. The author's overall pattern of organization in this passage is

a. listing.   c. comparison and contrast.

b. spatial order.   d. Example.

9. "The robust interest in professional nursing careers can be attributed in part to successful outreach efforts guided by the nation's nursing schools. Strategies employed to increase student capacity this year included forming alliances with hospitals and other practice sites to address faculty and clinical space constraints. Some schools have expanded or opened new accelerated programs for second-degree seekers looking to transition into nursing while others have taken advantage of state and federal funding aimed at strengthening the nursing workforce."

In this passage, the pattern of organization is

a. definition.   c. cause and effect.

b. example.   d. chronological order.

10. "Given the demands of today's health care system, the greatest need in the nursing workforce is for nurses prepared at the baccalaureate and higher

© Pearson Education, Inc.

degree levels. With the government calling for baccalaureate preparation for at least two thirds of the nursing workforce, the evidence clearly shows that higher levels of nursing education are linked with lower patient mortality rates, fewer errors, and greater job satisfaction among RNs."

What is the pattern of organization here?

a. chronological order.

c. definition.

(b.) cause and effect.

d. spatial order.

From Reading to Writing: Writing a Summary

Overview

As a college student, you may be familiar with *summary writing*. Professors often ask students to summarize a specific reading, a short story, a newspaper article, or a lecture. Depending on the purpose of the writing assignment, they may ask you to write a short summary including the main idea and a few supporting details or a long summary including the main idea, key concepts, and more details. In college, summary writing could be part of a standardized reading test, or it could be an integral part of your preparation for a final exam. It is, therefore, important for you to learn how to write a concise and accurate summary of the original text.

Three Important Characteristics of a Summary

If you have written a summary, you most probably know that it is difficult to restate the author's ideas in your own words. Remember that there are three important characteristics of a well-written, objective summary.

1. An objective summary must restate the original text accurately without altering or modifying the meaning.

2. A good summary should only include the relevant aspects of the original text. In other words, it is unnecessary to include the main point of each and every paragraph of the source in the summary.

3. The summary should be written in your own words. The trick is to change the language significantly without changing the main idea and supporting details presented in the original text. Think of yourself as an objective information processor. Your task as a summary writer is to simply present the main idea of the original source in your own language. Using your own words in writing a summary is important because you demonstrate to the reader that you have understood the original text correctly. If you copy sentences verbatim from the original text, you may be accused of plagiarism, an academic crime. (See page 404 for more information on plagiarism.)

Preparing to Write a Summary

It will be important for you to fully understand the original text so that you can write an accurate and objective summary. The following steps will help you write a good summary.

1. Read the original text carefully, paying attention to the main idea and the sections. This is particularly important if you are writing a summary of a long piece.

2. It is helpful to determine what type of text you are summarizing. For example, are you writing a summary of a research paper, a short story, or a newspaper article? The purpose of identifying the genre of the original text is twofold: you can easily identify important bits and pieces of information, and you can improve your reading skills.

3. Read the original text a second time, highlighting, underlining, circling (whatever helps you) important pieces of information.

4. In one sentence, write down the main point of each section. Be careful to use your own words, retaining the original idea.

5. Make a list of the details that support the main idea. You may not need to include minor details such as specific examples in your summary.

6. Follow steps 1 through 5 a second time, revising, adding, or deleting information as you deem necessary.

Acknowledging the Source

Most novice summary writers usually forget to mention the source of the original text, giving the reader the impression that they are presenting their own ideas in a summary. To avoid this grave error, make sure that you mention the original source and the main idea in the first sentence of your summary, making it explicit to the reader that you are simply restating someone else's ideas without expressing your opinion. Keep in mind that at no point in the summary should you use the word *I* or express your viewpoint. Let's look at a few examples of how a summary should begin. Notice how the source is followed by the main idea.

> According to Fromkin (2007), male nurses **are** as qualified (main idea) . . .
>
> In her article "Is Nursing a Noble Profession?" Smith (2006) **argues** that nursing is not necessarily (main idea) . . .
>
> Seliger and Sridhar (2008) **suggest** that registered nurses in the US (main idea) . . .
>
> Hawkins (2005) **asserts/maintains/** that nursing programs in the US are not doing (main idea) . . .

Notice the use of the simple present tense (highlighted) in each of the sentences.

Using Reporting Verbs

Good summary writers use a wide range of reporting verbs when referring to the original text. This is especially important if your summary is rather long. You need to remind the reader frequently that you are simply paraphrasing an author's ideas without expressing your opinion. Your task is to always remain objective and use reporting verbs, leaving no confusion in the reader's mind that you are stating your own ideas in the summary.

Here are some of the frequently used reporting verbs in a summary. Use them appropriately as they serve the purpose of your summary assignment.

ESL Annotation

7.9 ESL Students often do not have a strong repertoire of reporting verbs in their active vocabulary.

© Pearson Education, Inc.

Frequently Used Reporting Verbs

argue	develop	maintain	recommend
assert	discuss	note	report
claim	emphasize	observe	show
contend	examine	point out	state
demonstrate	explain	propose	study
describe	find	provide	suggest

Reminding the Reader

As mentioned previously, if your task is to write a longer summary, frequently remind the reader that, as a summary writer, you are only restating ideas presented in an original source. That is to say, your goal is to make it clear to the reader that you are not expressing your own views. You may want to remind the reader at frequent intervals that you are paraphrasing an original idea by saying:

- The author goes on to say that . . .
- The author further states that . . .
- Summer states/maintains/argues that. . .
- Smalley concludes that . . .
- Johnson believes that . . .

If you are writing a long summary, it is recommended that you mention the author's name at least three times: at the beginning, in the middle, and at the end of your summary.

Inserting Transition Words

When you provide additional information to the reader, be sure to use transition words. They serve as signposts, signaling to the reader that you are about to present another idea.

Some Transition Words

additionally	further	in addition	more importantly
also	furthermore	in fact	moreover

Avoiding Plagiarism

The term *plagiarism* is derived from the Latin word *plagiare*, which means "to kidnap." It is a writer's conscious and deliberate attempt to steal someone else's ideas and present them as her or his own. In essence, plagiarism is akin to kidnapping someone's baby and claiming that the kidnapper is the baby's biological parent. Since the baby is too young to dispute the claim, most people would usually believe that the kidnapper is indeed the mother or father of the baby.

Some cultures may be relatively tolerant of plagiarism, but plagiarism is considered to be a serious academic crime in North American educational institutions. The idea is based on the assumption that the original idea is the intellectual property of the author. It is also considered disrespectful and dishonest to borrow and use the works of distinguished authors without their consent and knowledge. A student found guilty of plagiarism can be expelled from a college or university and may find it difficult to pursue an academic career. It is, therefore, imperative that you always refer to the original source in a summary and avoid plagiarism.

Paraphrasing

When we paraphrase, we use our own words to express something that somebody has written or said. The purpose of paraphrasing is to make it easier for the reader to understand the original statement. Paraphrasing some of the sentences from the original source may be successful sometimes, but excessive paraphrasing in summary writing may give the reader the wrong impression that you do not quite understand the original work. Another reason you should avoid paraphrasing frequently in a summary is that the summary may be too close to the original text and you may be accused of plagiarism.

If you are not comfortable or confident about your ability to paraphrase, it might be worth your while to read the original source carefully, highlight the important points, and rewrite what you have understood in your own words without referring to the original. Rewriting the main points will help you write the summary accurately and in your own words.

When you write a summary of the original source, follow these steps:

1. Resist the temptation to use phrases and sentences from the original text, and always use your own words to write the summary. You may sometimes include the technical terms used in the original source.

2. Be sure to include the main idea and sufficient supporting details to make the summary clear to the reader.

3. Do not paraphrase excessively.

4. Do not lose sight of the content of the original text.

5. Use transition words to make the sentences flow smoothly. A summary without transition words can be choppy and difficult to understand.

EXERCISE 1

Read "Learning to Work Together" by Don Vaughn on page 391 carefully. Then read the four summaries below and decide which of the summaries is the most accurate and objective. For each of the summaries, write at least a couple of sentences, explaining its strengths and weaknesses.

Summaries

1. Effective nurse-physician collaboration is rooted in mutual respect and positive dialogue. This may sound like a simple, easily achievable goal, yet dissatisfaction among nurses (and physicians) remains common. The most common complaints among nurses include a perceived lack of respect and poor communication with the physicians with whom they work. It's an important issue because unresolved conflict can adversely

© Pearson Education, Inc.

affect a nurse's ability to do his or her job. It might even cause a nurse to leave the profession.

Your comments:

This summary is totally plagiarized. Every single word is taken verbatim from the original text. The summary writer has simply taken a sentence from the beginning, another sentence from the middle, and yet another sentence from the end of the original story without changing the language.

2. I really enjoyed reading Don Vaughan's article. In general, I agree with his assessment that nurse-physician collaboration can be affected by poor communication. However, I disagree with his statement that only physicians do not communicate well with the nurses. In my opinion, most registered nurses do not have the necessary skills to communicate with the physician effectively.

Your comments:

This is not a summary. This is a response to the summary. Instead of writing an objective summary, the summary writer has given a personal viewpoint, which is not allowed in this type of writing assignment.

3. In "Learning to Work Together," Vaughan states that most nurses are unhappy about their interaction with the physicians. According to the author, the nurses attribute their unsatisfactory collaboration with the physicians to poor communication and being disrespected. Vaughn mentions a two-year program instituted by Thomas Jefferson University in Philadelphia to teach both medical and nursing students team-building skills and improve their collaboration. The author concludes that if the nurse-physician collaboration issue is not resolved, then it can have a negative impact on the nurses, and some of them may even quit.

Your comments:

The summary writer has acknowledged the source in the first sentence and has refrained from expressing personal views and opinions. This is an accurate and objective summary, including the key points from the original text.

4. Physicians do not treat people outside of the field of medicine, especially registered nurses, with the respect they deserve. Nurses often complain that they are being disrespected by the physicians, and that collaborating with the physician is cumbersome, to say the least. The primary reason nurse-physician collaboration is difficult is because physicians do not communicate with the nurses effectively, making it difficult for the nurses to provide care to the patient. If this issue is not resolved, some nurses may be discouraged and leave their profession.

Your comments:

On the surface, this summary seems to be accurate. The summary writer
paraphrases some of the ideas from the original source and conveys the
main points to the reader without altering them. However, the main problem
with this summary is that the original source is not acknowledged at all. As
a result, the reader does not know if the ideas are those of the summary
writer, or if the ideas are expressed by another author, raising the issue of
authorship. For this reason, this summary falls short of being accurate and
acceptable.

Discuss the four summaries with your classmates and find out whether they
agree or disagree with your assessment.

Collaboration

Summary Writing Assignment

You have read the guidelines on writing a summary. You have seen examples
of both good and bad summaries. It is time for you now to practice writing a
summary. Read "Men Are Much in the Sights of Recruiters in Nursing" by Eve
Tahmincioglu on page 358, and write a concise and accurate summary, using
your own words. Adhere to the guidelines as you write the summary. Swap
with a classmate for feedback.

Connecting Reading Skills with Standardized Testing

Patterns of Organization

Most standardized reading exams include questions on structural skills such
as patterns of organization. These questions test your ability to identify
different patterns of organization. If you can determine the main idea of
the passage and the author's purpose, you can identify the overall pattern of
organization.

Organizational pattern-based questions usually begin as follows:

- What is the overall organizational pattern?
- The author's overall pattern of organization . . .
- The passage is organized by . . .
- How are the supporting details arranged?
- For this passage, the author uses an organizational pattern that . . .

Keep in mind that to a large extent the author's purpose determines which type
of organizational pattern is used in the passage. For example, if the author wants
to establish a causal relationship between two things, then the cause and effect
organizational pattern is appropriate for the passage.

© Pearson Education, Inc.

Gloria Tovar, RN

Profession: Registered Nurse in a Hospital

How did you choose your current profession?

It was not easy for me to choose my profession. I loved the subjects of math and science, so when I graduated from high school, I was torn between medicine and computer science. I chose medicine, but in order to enter this competitive field, I had a better chance to pursue nursing and then to switch to medicine. Then I decided to continue the nursing program, and I do not regret choosing this profession.

How did you prepare to reach your goal of becoming a registered nurse?

I attended the National University of Colombia in Bogotá, Colombia, which had the best methodology and very high standards.

What did you struggle with most when preparing to become a nurse?

I struggled with the subject of pharmacy, which usually a high percentage of students failed. The beginning of the clinical practice was not easy for me. The first day I had two patients, and I felt paralyzed in front of them. I forgot what to do. I felt pain in my hand when I gave the first injections. I cried when I saw a patient die, I fainted when a doctor was draining a leg injury, I panicked at the first emergency, and the smell of body fluids made me think, more than once, why I had chosen this career. When I rotated to the psychology in-patient clinic, I felt a lot of anxiety in the beginning. My first psychiatric patient was a female in a manic phase. I could not keep up with her energy and her lack of self-control. During the time I was her nurse, as soon as I got home, I would go to sleep because I was totally exhausted.

What did you do to overcome this struggle?

I do not exactly remember how I overcame my struggle with the clinical practice, but I believe it was seeing my patients that helped me feel better. Receiving their thanks when I gave them comfort helped me overcome those struggles that now seem insignificant to me. Since then my major wish has been to return to my hometown and serve my community.

What do you enjoy most about your work?

I have enjoyed my profession in different ways. I feel fortunate to have worked in several fields of nursing. My first job was supervising community health promoters. They needed to have a high school diploma and belong to the rural community they were going to serve. They were trained in first aid, nutrition, pregnancy wellness, family planning, immunization and disposition of garbage, and other aspects of health promotion. They are considered the first step in the health prevention pyramid. During this time I was mostly traveling to small rural towns, and I was outdoors in contact with nature and humble wonderful human beings, known as the *campesinos*. I also witnessed poverty and some less fortunate communities. This experience made me love my profession even more and be grateful for what I had, and my dream to serve my community had just begun.

My second job was in the operating room where I assisted the surgeons with the surgical instruments. Although the job was stressful, I was amazed with the wonders of the human body.

My third job was at the department of health of my state, Boyaca. I had the opportunity to participate in epidemiological studies and the implementation of health preventive programs. Also, I had the opportunity to participate in national health conventions.

At this job I met the father of my kids, and I immigrated to the USA. In the beginning I just wanted to be a housewife; however, the wish for independence gave me motivation to study for the boards leading to a career at Elmhurst Hospital.

My wish to serve my community has been fulfilled by working at the hospital. I know I cannot solve all the problems of our immigrant community, but at least I can make a difference in their health. This gives me a profound satisfaction every day. I also enjoy the diversity of my colleagues and patients, which has enhanced my tolerance and respect for the uniqueness of each individual.

What advice do you have for a student considering a career in nursing?

You need to enjoy studying and also have a sense of service, kindness, patience, and respect for the human soul. If you are a nurse who graduated from another country, learning the language is very important. Read a lot and do not be afraid to speak the language.

Nursing opens your future to a broad spectrum of fields, and if you want to climb up the ladder of the nursing profession, sky is the limit. You can count on a career in the field, which is always in high demand. Close your eyes, put your finger on a map, and you will find that they need a NURSE there.

In your opinion what were the three most interesting points made by the interviewee? Discuss your choices with the class.

- _____
  _____
- _____
  _____
- _____
  _____

Helpful Hints: Test Questions on Identifying Patterns of Organization

The following tips will help you determine the correct organizational pattern used in the passage.

- Identify the topic and main idea. Pay close attention to the topic and identify the main idea of the passage.

- Look for the supporting details. After you have identified the main idea, find the details in the passage that support it.

- Determine the author's purpose. Ask yourself why the author wrote the passage. This will help you determine the correct organizational pattern.

- Familiarize yourself with the specific transitional phrases used for each of the organizational patterns. The table in the Appendix shows the different types of transitional phrases used for each of the patterns. Learn the transitional phrases that are associated with each pattern.

Textbook Application

Read the following chapter from an introductory textbook on nursing. The purpose of this reading exercise is to give you an opportunity to practice reading authentic text. Read the chapter carefully and answer the multiple-choice questions that follow.

Succeeding as a Nursing Student

From *Fundamental Nursing Care by Roberta Pavy Ramont and Dee Niedringhaus,* Chapter 1, pp. 3–13

Welcome to a career in nursing. You have made an excellent choice for a future helping others to regain or maintain health and function. Nursing is full of rewards and challenges while you are a student and also after you graduate. This text is designed to help you recognize and overcome those challenges as well as to appreciate the rewards.

LPN/LVN training programs can be found in many different types of schools. In some states, they are part of high schools. In others, they are in community college settings, vocational training centers, or private schools.

The length of the program is dictated by the governing nursing board in each state. Some programs can be completed in about 9 months. Others take up to 2 years. Some are full-time day programs; others are part time in the evenings and/or on weekends.

People with a variety of backgrounds enter the nursing profession. Your classmates may represent a variety of life experiences, educational backgrounds, and ethnic/cultural influences. You can learn a great deal by collaborating with fellow students during your course of study. The ages of LPN/LVN students within a class may range from young adult to near retirement. Motives may also vary. Students may be realizing a lifelong dream to become a nurse or making a career change.

It may have been a long time since you studied a subject that really mattered to you, or you may have recently been in school and studied with serious commitment. In either case, here are some academic "survival skills" to help you in your vocational/practical nursing course of study.

© Pearson Education, Inc.

Reading This Textbook

Begin by reading the preface and other material in the front of the book. Become familiar with how the book is organized and any special features that will make your reading and studying easier. Review the table of contents and look over the appendices. By spending a few minutes becoming familiar with the book, you will be ready to use your book when the first reading assignment is given. The textbook is a great stand-alone reference, as well as a source for clarifying lecture material.

Read textbook assignments before the class in which the material will be covered. Reading beforehand will help you organize your thoughts, and help you spell and define words that may be used in a lecture. Although many students use highlighter pens while reading, it is much better to save the highlighter for reviewing lectures notes or marking the location of answers to the chapter's study questions (Porter, L.).

Studying Effectively

It is easy to stare at a page of text and feel that you have "spent time" studying when, in fact, you may have understood very little. When you have a block of time set aside to study, make sure you use it wisely. For hints about what is most important in the text, look at the Learning Outcomes at the beginning of each chapter. These objectives guide you in discovering the information you need to obtain from the chapter as you read and study. When an objective states "Identify three strategies to use when . . . ," go to the text, find all three strategies, and write them down. As you study, review those three strategies and when you would use them.

Another technique to employ when studying is outlining. Some students find it helpful to outline the chapter after reading it. Under the main ideas, they organize the concepts and the information that supports those ideas. You can easily do this by using the main headings in the chapter as outline headings, then listing two or three main ideas from the paragraphs beneath those headings.

Study questions at the end of the chapter and/or in student workbooks are another way to help you pull out the most important information in a chapter. First, try to answer the questions from what you have read and understood. If you are unable to answer them correctly or at all, look up the information within the chapter to find the correct answer. This will help you remember the information better than simply looking up each answer. Some students find it helpful to make up their own study questions; they anticipate what instructors might ask by using information from class notes.

Take advantage of all available tools. Use a computer at school or at home to access the Companion Website (www.prenhall.com/ramont) or the student CD for this text. These tools provide additional questions and case studies to bring the information to life and to prepare you for future practice. The website and CD also supply links to the Internet to help you with your school projects and research.

Studying with another person or group of three or four people can be helpful in processing information and discussing ideas. To be successful, the groups must be well organized. Study groups are discussed further in the next section.

Managing Time

The "average" practical/vocational nursing student is far from average. Proposing one time management template that would work for everyone is impossible. Still, being organized and having a plan will help you work within your time limits. Learning to manage your time is a skill that will benefit you during the nursing program and also in your career and in life.

Learning how to be a good student may be the most important lesson during the first few weeks of your nursing program. Study skills will support you throughout your student days and as you prepare for exams. The time taken to perfect these skills will be hours well spent. See Figure 1-1 ■ for a sample time management schedule.

The following suggestions for time management may be useful:

- Obtain a blank calendar or planner for the entire year.
- Fill in holidays, vacations, medical or dental appointments, class times, and clinical days as soon as you know them.
- Add due dates, tests, homework, and projects as they are assigned.
- Schedule study time by writing it on your calendar or planner.
- Schedule personal time for relaxation and being with other people.

Sample Time Management Schedule

	Monday	Tuesday	Wednesday	Thursday	Friday	Saturday	Sunday
0600	Sleep	Sleep	Sleep	Shower/dress	Shower/dress	Shower/dress	Sleep
0700	Shower/dress	Shower/dress	Shower/dress	Clinical	Clinical	Work	Sleep
0800	Class	Class	Class				Shower/dress
0900							Breakfast
1000							Church
1100							
1200	Lunch	Lunch	Lunch	Lunch	Lunch	Lunch	
1300	Class	Class					
1400		Library	Group project				Dinner with family
1500							
1600							
1700	Dinner	Dinner	Dinner	Dinner	Dinner	Dinner	
1800						Movie	
1900	Study group	Study	Study	Study			Laundry
2000							Study
2100			Personal time	Personal time			
2200	Personal time	Personal time	Sleep	Sleep	Personal time		Personal time
2300	Sleep	Sleep	Sleep	Sleep	Sleep		Sleep

Figure 1-1. ■ Sample time management schedule.

Group study time can be very useful when you participate regularly. Learn to plan your group study time, just as you would plan other parts of your day. Stay focused on content, and resist the urge to talk about things that are not study material. Bring four or five questions with you to discuss with the group. This can be especially helpful if you are having difficulty understanding certain concepts.

It is a good idea to break a study session down into segments. For example, a 2-hour session might include 30 minutes of lecture note review, 20 minutes of shared questions and answers, a 10-minute break, 30 minutes of quizzing, and 30 minutes of review of class objectives. This plan gives focus to the study time. The change in activities also helps to sustain people's interest and energy levels.

Taking Tests

ANSWERING MULTIPLE-CHOICE QUESTIONS

Most tests given in nursing programs will be objective, multiple-choice tests. These are the same types of questions used on the NCLEX-PN® exam. Multiple-choice questions can evaluate your knowledge of facts, as well as your ability to apply that knowledge within a client care scenario. Each question will consist of a stem and answer choices. Read each question completely in order to understand what is being asked. Then read each of the choices. Try to eliminate one or more of the choices. Examine each choice to see if anything is incorrect within the answer itself. Watch out for choices that are correct and accurate on their own, but that do not answer the question as it is written. See Box 1-1 ■ for an example.

Multiple-choice questions can test knowledge, comprehension, application, and ability to analyze. Table 1-1 ■ provides examples and comparisons of each type.

Questions that include choices such as "all of the above" or "none of the above" have been eliminated from the NCLEX-PN® examination. However, some textbooks have them as study questions, and some instructors may test with them. A choice of this type can be confirmed or eliminated easily. If you have identified one choice as being correct, then you can eliminate

© Pearson Education, Inc.

BOX 1-1

Example of a Multiple-Choice Question

Which of the following men was responsible for the reduction of maternal death related to infection transmitted by way of unwashed hands?

1. Joseph Lister
2. Louis Pasteur
3. Ignaz Semmelweis
4. Karl Crede

Although all four people were **involved** in prevention of infection and/or disease, the correct answer is 3. Ignaz Semmelweis was the person who discovered that puerperal fever was related to examination of mothers during the intra- and postpartum periods by doctors who had not washed their hands after performing autopsies.

"none of the above." If you can identify one choice that is incorrect, then "all of the above" can also be eliminated. If you can identify at least two answers as correct, then the question qualifies as an "all of the above" answer.

If you are able to narrow your choice to two options, don't spend too much time deciding between them. More likely than not, your first impression is correct. Once you have identified your choice, don't go back and change it unless you later figure out the correct response with absolute certainty.

Answering the study questions at the end of each chapter and in the student workbook will help you improve your ability to select correct answers in objective tests.

TABLE 1-1

Test Questions and Levels of Learning

LEVEL	INFORMATION REQUIRED	EXAMPLE	RATIONALE
Knowledge question	Requires recall of information. To answer a knowledge question, you need to commit facts to memory. Knowledge questions expect you to know terminology, **specific** facts, trends, sequences, classifications, **categories, criteria,** structures, principles, generalizations, and/or theories.	What does the abbreviation BRP mean? a. bathe daily b. bedrush pt c. blood pressure reading d. bathroom privileges	To answer this question correctly, you have to know the meaning of the abbreviation BRP (bathroom priviliges answer d).
Comprehension question	Requires you to understand information. To answer a comprehension question, not only must you commit facts to memory, but it is essential that you be able to translate, interpret, and determine the **implications** of the information. You **demonstrate** understanding when you translate or paraphrase information, interpret or summarize information, or determine the **implications, consequences,** corollaries, or effects of information. Comprehension questions expect you not only to know but also to understand the information being tested. You do not necessarily have to relate it to other material or see its fullest **implications**.	To evaluate the therapeutic effect of a cathartic, the nurse should assess the client for: a. increased urinary **output**. b. a decrease in anxiety. c. a bowel movement. d. pain relief.	To answer this question, you not only have to know that a cathartic is a potent laxative that stimulates the bowel, but that the increase in peristalsis will result in a bowel movement (answer c).
Application question	Requires you to utilize knowledge. To answer an application question, you must take remembered and comprehended concepts and apply them to concrete situations. The abstractions may be theories, **technical** principles, rules of procedures, generalizations, or ideas that have to be applied in a **scenario**. Application questions test your ability to use information in a new situation.	An elderly client's skin looks dry, thin, and fragile. When providing back care, the nurse should: a. apply a moisturizing body lotion. b. wash back with soap and water. c. massage back using short kneading strokes. d. leave excess lubricant on the client's skin.	To answer this question, you must know that dry, thin, fragile skin is common in the elderly and that moisturizing lotion helps the skin to retain water and become more supple. When presented with this **scenario**, you have to apply your knowledge concerning developmental changes in the elderly and the benefits of using moisturizing lotion (answer a).

TABLE 1-1			
Test Questions and Levels of Learning (*continued*)			
LEVEL	**INFORMATION REQUIRED**	**EXAMPLE**	**RATIONALE**
Analysis question	Requires you to interpret a variety of **data** and recognize the commonalities, differences, and interrelationships among present ideas. **Analysis** questions make assumptions that you know, understand, and can apply information. Now you must identify, examine, dissect, evaluate, or investigate the organization, systematic arrangement, or **structure** of the information presented in the question. This type of question tests your analytical ability.	A client who is undergoing cancer chemotherapy says to the nurse, "This is no way to live." Which of the following responses uses reflective technique? a. "Tell me more about what you are thinking." b. "You sound discouraged today." c. "Life is not worth living?" d. "What are you saying?"	To answer this question, you must understand the **communication techniques** of reflection, clarification, and paraphrasing. You must also analyze the statements and identify which **techniques** are represented. This question requires you to understand, interpret, and differentiate information to know that the correct answer is c.

Most questions on the NCLEX-PN® exam are standard multiple choice, but some new types of questions are being added. The NCLEX-PN® exam is discussed in more detail in Chapter 37 ⚭.

Several techniques are useful in calling information to mind during a test. For example, by using visualization, you may be able to picture something the instructor wrote on the board during a lecture. You may be able to "see" in your mind a poster or handout that was used during a class presentation. With some practice, you may be able to visualize a word or a passage that you read in the textbook.

ANSWERING ESSAY, SHORT-ANSWER, AND CALCULATION QUESTIONS

Answers to essay, short-answer, and calculation questions will need to be extracted from your memory. Read the question carefully to determine what is being asked. Some students find it helpful to develop a brief outline before beginning an essay question. Check with the instructor to see if this can be written on the test paper or if you are permitted to use an additional sheet. The outline can help you organize your thoughts and can serve as a checkpoint that all important information was included. Usually, a number of key introductory words appear in essay questions (Table 1-2 ■). Look for these words, and do only what is required of you. Many low grades are caused by ignoring these key words.

Calculation questions are particularly troubling for many students who have convinced themselves that

they cannot do math. Although math may be difficult, it is a necessary skill for a nurse. With extra practice, calculations are possible to learn. Several methods are used to do calculations (see Chapter 29 ⚭).

It is important to show your work on calculations. If you are unable to arrive at the correct answer, your instructor can review your work, and will be able to tell you where you went wrong. Memorizing formulas and frequently used conversions will make calculations on tests and in the clinical area much easier.

Participating in Clinical Experiences

A major part of your learning will occur during your clinical experiences. You will be assigned to assist with the care of one or more clients in a healthcare setting. This experience is extremely valuable in preparing you for the profession you have chosen. You will find that observing signs and symptoms of an illness firsthand is far more impressive than reading about them.

At first you will care for just one client, with assistance from other healthcare workers as needed. As you progress through your course of study, you will be assigned more responsibility and more clients. The clients you care for will have more complex illnesses and needs. When you study and learn about performing skills and signs to watch for, you are learning what you need to know to be a safe healthcare practitioner.

© Pearson Education, Inc.

TABLE 1-2
Key Words in Essay Exams

KEY WORD	EXPLANATION
Compare	To point out similarities and differences
Contrast	To point out differences only
Define	Several connotations: (1) to give the meaning of, (2) to explain or describe essential qualities, (3) to place it in the class to which it belongs and set it off from other **items** in the same class
Describe	Enumerate (list) the special **features** of the **topic** **Show** how the **topic** is different from **similar** or related **items** Give an account of, tell about, and give a word picture of
Discuss	Present various sides or points, talk over, consider the different sides; a discussion is usually longer than an explanation of the same subject
Explain	Make plain or clear, interpret, tell "how" to do
Identify	Show recognition
Illustrate	Describe in narrative form using "word pictures" to provide examples
Justify	Provide supporting **data** for opinions or actions
List or name	Present a group of names or **items** in a category
Outline	Give information systematically in headings and subheadings
Summarize	Present in condensed form; give main points briefly

As a student, your responsibilities in preparing for clinical experience include:

- Ensuring that you understand what you read and how to apply it to the care of real clients
- Practicing skills repeatedly so that you know exactly what to do when called on to perform those skills quickly and efficiently in the clinical setting
- Researching information about an assigned client's medical diagnosis, nursing diagnoses, problems, and needs so that you are prepared and can anticipate what could happen as you care for that client
- Asking for help when you are not sure how to proceed, but proceeding when you are sure of what you need to do
- Reporting any and all deviations from baseline that you observe while caring for clients (You may not realize the significance of your observation, especially early in the program, but other healthcare professionals will know what actions to take.)
- Taking advantage of all learning opportunities in the clinical setting. If a procedure is being done, ask if you can observe, even though the client may not be assigned to you. Spend any "downtime" during your clinical experience observing, assisting, or listening to healthcare staff.

Overview of Nursing History

To fully appreciate your position as a contemporary practical/vocational nurse, you need to understand a bit about the history of nursing. Many women and men have been influential in developing nursing into the profession it is today.

NIGHTINGALE (1820–1910)

Florence Nightingale's contributions to nursing are well documented. Her achievements in improving the standards for the care of war casualties in Crimea earned her the title "Lady with the Lamp" (Figure 1-2 ■). Her efforts in reforming hospitals and in producing and implementing public health policies also made her an

Figure 1-2. ■ Considered to be the founder of modern nursing, Florence Nightingale (1820–1910) was influential in developing nursing education, practice, and **administration**. Her 1859 **publication** *Notes on Nursing: What It Is, and What It Is Not* was intended for all women. (*Source:* © Bettmann/CORBIS. Reprinted with permission.)

accomplished political nurse. She was the first nurse to exert political pressure on government. She is also recognized as nursing's first scientist-theorist for her work *Notes on Nursing: What It Is, and What It Is Not.*

When she returned from Crimea, a grateful English public gave Nightingale an honorarium of £4,500. She used this money to establish the Nightingale Training School for Nurses in 1860. At St. Thomas Hospital in London, England, she taught her straightforward requirements.

Nightingale believed that nursing education should develop both the intellect and character of the nurse. She gave students a solid background in science to understand the theory behind their care. To develop character, by increasing their understanding of human ethics and morals, she assigned readings in the humanities. She believed that nurses should never stop learning. To her nurses she wrote, "[Nursing] is a field of which one may safely say: there is no end in what we may be learning everyday" (Schuyler, 1992). The school served as a model for other training schools. Its graduates traveled to other countries to manage hospitals and to institute training programs for nurses.

Nightingale's vision of nursing, which included public health and health promotion roles for nurses, was only partially addressed in the early days. The focus first was on developing the profession within hospitals. Although Miss Nightingale died in 1910, her influence continues in nursing today.

BARTON (1821–1912)

Clara Barton (Figure 1-3 ■) was a schoolteacher who volunteered as a nurse during the American Civil War. Her responsibility was to organize the nursing services. Barton is noted for her role in establishing the American Red Cross, which linked with the International Red Cross when the United States Congress ratified the Treaty of Geneva (Geneva Convention). In 1882, Barton persuaded Congress to ratify this treaty so that the Red Cross could perform humanitarian efforts in times of peace.

WALD (1867–1940)

Lillian Wald (Figure 1-4 ■) is considered the founder of public health nursing. Wald and Mary Brewster were the first to offer trained nursing services to the poor in the New York slums. They founded the Henry Street Settlement, and Visiting Nurse Service, which provided nursing and social services, and also organized educational and cultural activities. Soon after the founding of the

Figure 1-3. ■ Clara Barton (1821–1912) organized the American Red Cross, which linked with the International Red Cross when the U.S. Congress ratified the Geneva **Convention** in 1882. (*Source:* © Bettmann/CORBIS. Reprinted with permission.)

Henry Street Settlement, school nursing was established as an adjunct to visiting nursing.

DOCK (1858–1956)

Lavinia L. Dock (Figure 1-5 ■) was a feminist, as well as a prolific writer, political activist, suffragist, and friend of Wald. She participated in protest movements for women's rights that resulted in the 1920 passage of the 19th Amendment to the U.S. Constitution, which granted women the right to vote. In addition, Dock campaigned for legislation to allow nurses rather than physicians to control their profession. In 1893, Dock, Mary Adelaide Nutting, and Isabel

Figure 1-4. ■ Lillian Wald (1867–1940) **founded** the Henry Street Settlement and Visiting Nurse Service (circa 1893), which provided nursing and social services and organized educational and **cultural** activities. She is considered to be founder of public health nursing. (*Source:* University of Iowa, College of Nursing, Iowa City, IA.)

© Pearson Education, Inc.

Figure 1-5. ■ Nursing leader and suffragist Lavinia L. Dock (1858–1956) was active in the protest movement for women's rights that resulted in the 1920 U.S. **constitutional amendment** allowing women to vote. (*Source:* Courtesy of Millbank Memorial Library, Teachers' College, Columbia University. Reprinted with permission.)

Hampton Robb founded the American Society of Superintendents of Training Schools for Nurses of the United States and Canada. This was a precursor to the current National League for Nursing (NLN).

MALE NURSES IN HISTORY

Women were not the sole providers of nursing services. The first nursing school in the world was started in India in about 250 B.C. Only men were considered to be "pure" enough to fulfill the role of nurse at that time. In Jesus's parable in the New Testament, the good Samaritan paid an innkeeper to provide care for the injured man. Paying a man to provide nursing care was fairly common. During the Crusades, several orders of knights provided nursing care to their sick and injured comrades and also built hospitals. The organization and management of their hospitals set a standard for the administration of hospitals throughout Europe at that time. St. Camillus de Lellis started out as a soldier and later turned to nursing. He started the sign of the Red Cross and developed the first ambulance service. Friar Juan de Mena was shipwrecked off the south Texas coast in 1554. He is the first identified nurse in what would become the United States. James Derham, a black slave who worked as a nurse in New Orleans in the late 1700s, saved the money he earned to purchase his freedom. Later, he studied medicine and became a well-respected physician in Philadelphia. During the Civil War, both sides had military men who cared for the sick and wounded.

In 1876, only three years after the first U.S. nurse received her diploma from New England Hospital for Women and Children, the Alexian brothers opened their first hospital in the United States and a school to educate men in nursing.

During the years from the Civil War to the Korean War, men were not permitted to serve as nurses in the military. Today, men have resumed their historical place in the profession. As the history of nursing continues to be written, men and women will work side by side (Figure 1-6 ■).

HISTORY OF LPNS/LVNS

The first training for practical nurses was at the Young Women's Christian Association (YWCA) in New York City in 1892. The following year this became the Ballard School. The program of study was 3 months long, and the participants studied special techniques for caring for the sick as well as a variety of homemaking techniques. Much of the care during this time was done in the client's home, making the licensed practical nurse (LPN) a home health or visiting nurse. Eleven years later, a second school, the Thompson Practical Nursing School, was established.

In 1914, the state legislature in Mississippi passed the first laws governing the practice of practical nurses. Other states were slow to follow. By 1940, only six states had passed such laws. In 1955, the state board test pool of the NLN Education Committee established the procedures for testing graduates of approved practical/vocational education programs in all states. Graduates who passed the examination became

Figure 1-6. ■ Modern male nurses work side by side with their female **colleagues** to provide care to hospitalized clients.

LPNs or, in California and Texas, licensed vocational nurses (LVNs). Each state set its own passing score.

Today, a graduate of an approved LPN/LVN training program is eligible to take the National Council Licensure Examination for Practical Nursing (**NCLEX-PN**®). The examination is computerized, with a "pass" score that is standardized throughout the United States. All states have licensing laws.

Interstate endorsement (reciprocity between states) exists. This means that an LPN/LVN from one state can apply for licensure in another state without retesting. It is the responsibility of the individual nurse to contact the board of nursing in the jurisdiction where he or she wishes to work. The nurse must apply for licensure and for information regarding the scope of practice within that state. Table 1-3 ■

TABLE 1-3

Important Historical Events for LPNs/LVNs

DATE	EVENT	IMPORTANCE
1893	Ballard School at YMCA, Brooklyn, New York	First formal training for practical nurses.
1914	Mississippi legislature passed license laws for practical nurses	First laws passed to govern the practice of practical nurses.
1917	Smith-Hughes Act	Provided federal funding for vocationally oriented schools of practical nursing.
1918	Third school **established**	Even with new schools and **federal assistance**, the need for nurses could not be met because of the demand created by the war and epidemics.
1941	The Association of Practical Nurse Schools was founded; the name was changed to National Association for Practical Nurse Education (NAPNE) in 1942	Standards for practical nurse education were **established**.
1944	U.S. Department of Education commissioned an intensive study differentiating tasks of the practical nurse	The outcome of the study differentiated tasks performed by the practical nurse from those performed by the registered nurse. State boards of nursing **established** tasks that could be performed by both groups.
1945	New York **established** mandatory licensure for practical nurses	The first state to require licensure; by 1955 all other states had followed suit.
1949	The National Federation of Licensed Practical Nurses (NFLPN) was **founded** by Lillian Kuster; the name was changed to the National Association for Licensed Practical Nurse Education and Services in 1959	The discipline now had an official organization with membership limited to LPNs/LVNs.
1955	All states passed licensing laws for practical/vocational nurses	Practice of nursing by licensed practical nursing was regulated in all states.
1961	The National League of Nursing **established** a Department of Practical Nursing	Through this department, schools of practical nursing could be accredited by the NLN.
1965	American Nurses Association **published** a position paper that influenced **attitudes** about practical/vocational nursing	The paper clearly defined the two levels of nursing: **registered** nursing and **technical** nursing. The exclusion of the term *practical/vocational nurse* necessitated that the LPN/LVN prove his or her worth to provide valuable nursing interventions under the direction of a **registered** nurse.
1994	Computerized NCLEX-PN® examination **available** to graduates of practical/vocational nursing programs in all states	Allowed for more availability of test dates and interstate endorsement of licensure.

© Pearson Education, Inc.

lists important events in the history of practical/vocational nursing.

Practical/Vocational Nursing Today

OUR CUSTOMERS

The "customers" we serve in nursing today are sometimes called consumers, sometimes patients, and sometimes clients. A **consumer** is an individual, a group of people, or a community that uses a service or commodity. People who use healthcare products or services are consumers of health care. A **patient** is a person who is waiting for or undergoing medical treatment and care. The word *patient* comes from a Latin word meaning "to suffer" or "to bear." Traditionally, the person receiving health care has been called a patient. People become patients when they seek assistance because of illness. Some nurses believe that the word *patient* implies passive acceptance of the decisions and care of health professionals. Because nurses interact with family, friends, and healthy people as well as those who are ill, nurses increasingly refer to recipients of health care as *clients.*

A **client** is a person who engages the advice or services of someone who is qualified to provide the service. Therefore, a client is a collaborator, a person who is also responsible for his or her own health. The health status of a client is the responsibility of the individual in collaboration with health professionals. In this book, *client* is the preferred term, although *consumer* and *patient* may be used in some instances.

OUR PURPOSE

Nurses provide care for individuals, families, and communities. The scope of nursing practice involves four areas: promoting health and wellness, preventing illness, restoring health, and caring for the dying.

Promoting Health and Wellness

Wellness is a state of well-being. It means engaging in attitudes and behavior that enhance the quality of life and maximize personal potential. Nurses promote wellness in individuals and groups who are healthy or ill. Nurses may hold blood pressure clinics, teach about healthy lifestyles, give talks about drug and alcohol abuse, and instruct about safety in the home and workplace. Nurses who work in public health, community clinics, mental health facilities, and in occupation health settings promote health and wellness.

Preventing Illness

Illness may be defined as the highly individualized response a person has to a disease. The goal of illness prevention programs is to maintain optimal health by preventing disease. Nurses in physician's offices or health clinics administer immunizations, provide prenatal and infant care, and teach about the prevention of sexually transmitted infections.

Restoring Health

Restoring health means focusing on the ill client from early detection of disease through the recovery period. Nurses in acute care and rehabilitation facilities perform all of the following:

- Provide direct care to the ill person, such as administering medications, assisting with activities of daily living, and performing specific procedures and treatments.
- Perform diagnostic and assessment procedures, such as measuring blood pressure and examining feces for occult blood.
- Consult with other healthcare professionals about client problems.
- Teach clients about recovery activities, such as exercises that will hasten recovery after a stroke.
- Rehabilitate clients to their optimal functional level following physical or mental illness, injury, or chemical addiction.

Caring for the Dying

This area of nursing practice involves comforting and caring for people of all ages who are dying. It includes helping clients live as comfortably as possible until death and helping clients' support persons cope with death. Nurses carry out these activities in homes, hospitals, and extended care facilities. Some agencies, called hospices, are specifically designed for this purpose (see Chapter 17 ⬭).

OUR STANDARDS

Nurse practice acts, or legal acts for professional nursing practice, regulate the practice of nursing in the United States and Canada. Each state in the United States and each province in Canada has its own act.

Although practice acts may differ in various jurisdictions, they all have a common purpose: to protect the public. The title of *nurse* can legally be used *only* by an individual who is licensed as a registered nurse or a licensed practical or vocational nurse. For additional information, see Chapter 37 ⌾.

During your nursing education program, you will develop, clarify, and internalize professional values. The National Federation of Licensed Practical Nurses Inc. has identified specific standards (Box 1-2 ▪). LPNs/LVNs in all areas of practice should adhere to these standards.

OUR WORK SETTINGS
In the past, the acute care hospital was the major practice setting open to most nurses. Today the LPN/LVN works in hospitals, clients' homes, community agencies, ambulatory clinics, health maintenance organizations, and skilled nursing facilities (see Chapter 7 ⌾). See also Chapter 38 ⌾ for a description of opportunities available to the LPN/LVN.

LPNs/LVNs work under their own license under direct supervision of a physician or a registered nurse. LPNs/LVNs may be involved in clinical planning meetings because of their expertise, but they are required to do this less than other licensed healthcare providers. Their primary duty is to deliver care to the client.

Professional Organizations for LPN/LVN Students and Graduates

When a professional organization is in place to oversee the operation of a group, it becomes a **profession** rather than an occupation. Several organizations oversee the profession of practical/vocational nursing.

NATIONAL ASSOCIATION FOR PRACTICAL NURSE EDUCATION AND SERVICE
The National Association for Practical Nurse Education and Service (NAPNES) was established in 1941. This was the first national organization for the practical/vocational level of nursing. NAPNES was responsible for the accreditation of LPN/LVN education

programs from 1945 until 1984. Students can join this organization, and NAPNES publishes a journal called *The Journal of Practical Nursing.*

NATIONAL LEAGUE FOR NURSING
The National League for Nursing, formed in 1952, is an organization of both individuals and agencies. In 1961, the NLN established the Council for Practical Nursing Programs. This arm of the organization assumed responsibility for promoting the interests of LPNs/LVNs in the NLN. All of these organizations provide continuing education opportunities and publish literature of interest to the LPN/LVN.

NATIONAL FEDERATION OF LICENSED PRACTICAL NURSES
In 1949, Lillian Custer founded the National Federation of Licensed Practical Nurses (NFLPN). This organization is considered to be the official membership organization for LPNs and LVNs. Affiliate memberships are also available for those interested in the work of NFLPN but who are not LPNs/LVNs.

NFLPN welcomes LVN/LPN students as members. NFLPN provides leadership for nearly 1 million licensed practical and vocational nurses employed in the United States. It also fosters high standards of practical/vocational nursing education and practice so that the best nursing care will be available to every client.

The NFLPN serves as the central source of information on what is new and changing in practical/vocational nursing education and practice on the local, state, and national level. The organization is a three-tiered concept of local, state, and national enrollment. By participating in local, state, and national meetings and conferences, the practical/vocational nursing student can learn firsthand how a professional organization works to maintain the professional status of the membership. NFLPN also encourages continuing education and publishes a quarterly magazine, *Practical Nursing Today.* Through relationships with the National Council of State Boards of Nursing and the U.S. Congress, the NFLPN enables policy makers to better understand the role of practical/vocational nursing in the nation's healthcare delivery system (NFLPN, 2003).

© Pearson Education, Inc.

BOX 1-2

Nursing Practice Standards for the Licensed Practical/Vocational Nurse

Education

The licensed practical/vocational nurse:

1. Shall complete a formal education program in practical nursing approved by the **appropriate** nursing **authority** in a state.
2. Shall successfully pass the National Council Licensure Examination for Practical Nurses.
3. Shall participate in **initial orientation** within the employing institution.

Legal/Ethical Status

The licensed practical/vocational nurse:

1. Shall hold a current license to practice nursing as an LP/VN in accordance with the law of the state wherein employed.
2. Shall know the **scope** of nursing practice authorized by the Nursing Practice Act in the state wherein employed.
3. Shall have a personal **commitment** to fulfill the **legal** responsibilities **inherent** in good nursing practice.
4. Shall take responsible actions in situations wherein there is unprofessional **conduct** by a peer or other health care provider.
5. Shall recognize and commit to meet the **ethical** and moral obligations of the practice of nursing.
6. Shall not accept or perform **professional** responsibilities that the **individual** knows (s)he is not competent to perform.

Practice

The licensed practical/vocational nurse:

1. Shall accept **assigned** responsibilities as an accountable member of the health care **team**.
2. Shall **function** within the limits of educational preparation and experience, as related to the **assigned** duties.
3. Shall **function** with other members of the health care **team** in promoting and maintaining health, preventing disease and disability, caring for and rehabilitating individuals who are experiencing an altered health state, and contributing to the ultimate quality of life until death.
4. Shall know and utilize the nursing **process** in planning, implementing, and evaluating health services and nursing care for the **individual** patient or group.
   a. Planning: The planning of nursing includes:
      1. **Assessment** of health **status** of the **individual** patient, the family, and **community** groups
      2. **Analysis** of the information gained from **assessment**
      3. Identification of health **goals**
   b. **Implementation:** The plan for nursing care is put into practice to **achieve** the stated **goals** and includes:
      1. Observing, recording, and reporting **significant** changes that require **intervention** or different **goals**
      2. Applying nursing knowledge and skills to **promote** and maintain health, to prevent disease and disability, and to optimize functional capabilities of an **individual** patient
      3. Assisting the patient and family with activities of daily living and encouraging self-care as **appropriate**
      4. Carrying out therapeutic regimens and protocols prescribed by an RN, physician, or other persons authorized by state law
   c. **Evaluation:** The plan for nursing care and its implementations are evaluated to measure the progress toward the stated **goals** and will include **appropriate** persons and/or groups to determine:
      1. The relevancy of current **goals** in relation to the progress of the **individual** patient
      2. The involvement of the recipients of care in the **evaluation process**
      3. The quality of the nursing action in the **implementation** of the plan
      4. A reordering of priorities or new goal setting in the care plan
5. Shall participate in peer review and other **evaluation** processes.
6. Shall participate in the development of policies concerning the health and nursing needs of society and in the roles and functions of the LP/VN.

Continuing Education

The licensed practical/vocational nurse:

1. Shall be responsible for maintaining the highest possible level of **professional** competence at all times.
2. Shall periodically reassess career **goals** and **select** continuing education activities that will help to **achieve** these **goals**.
3. Shall take advantage of continuing education opportunities that will lead to personal growth and **professional** development.
4. Shall seek and participate in continuing education activities that are approved for **credit** by **appropriate** organizations, such as the NFLPN.

Specialized Nursing Practice

The licensed practical/vocational nurse:

1. Shall have had at least one year's experience in nursing at the staff level.
2. Shall present personal qualifications that are indicative of **potential** abilities for practice in the chosen specialized nursing **area**.
3. Shall present **evidence** of completion of a program or course that is approved by an **appropriate** agency to provide the knowledge and skills necessary for effective nursing services in the specialized field.
4. Shall meet all of the standards of practice as set forth in this **document**.

Source: National Federation of Licensed Practical Nurses, Inc. Copyright © 1991.

Student Organizations

HEALTH OCCUPATIONS STUDENTS OF AMERICA (HOSA)

HOSA is a nationally recognized technical career student organization, which was founded in 1976. HOSA provides a unique program of leadership and team-building development, motivation, and recognition experience. HOSA is an instructional tool integrated into the health careers classroom by the instructor. It is *intracurricular* (occurring within the framework of the school curriculum). It reinforces technical skills and supports service to the community. HOSA helps to develop the "total person." The national organization is made up of health occupations students from 42 affiliated states and Puerto Rico. HOSA's membership is made up of secondary, postsecondary, and collegiate students. Healthcare professionals, alumni, and business and industry members are welcome. There is also an associate membership category for students who are interested in health careers but who are not enrolled in a program. Through participation, the LPN/LVN student can network with other health career students. Involvement in a student organization demonstrates to students the benefits of participating in professional organizations once they have graduated.

Reading Comprehension Check

Vocabulary in Context

1. As used in the sentence "This text is designed to help you recognize and overcome those challenges as well as to appreciate the rewards," the word *overcome* means
   - a. surrender.
   - (b.) rise above.
   - c. fall down.
   - d. struggle.

Vocabulary in Context

2. "In some states, they are part of high schools. In others, they are in community college settings, vocational training centers, or private schools." (p. 409) The term *vocational* could be replaced with
   - a. fractional.
   - b. unprofessional.
   - c. congressional.
   - (d.) occupational.

Vocabulary in Context

3. In the sentence "Some students find it helpful to make up their own study questions; they anticipate what instructors might ask by using information from class notes," a synonym for the word *anticipate* is
   - a. misunderstand.
   - (b.) predict.
   - c. miscalculate.
   - d. underestimate.

Vocabulary in Context

4. As used in the sentence "It may have been a long time since you studied a subject that really mattered to you, or you may have recently been in school and studied with serious commitment," an antonym for the word *commitment* is
   - a. dedication.
   - b. obligation.
   - (c.) indifference.
   - d. promise.

Main Idea

5. The main idea of the chapter is that
   - a. pursuing nursing as a career is a poor choice.
   - (b.) aspiring nursing students should learn about the challenges of the nursing profession to overcome them and succeed.

© Pearson Education, Inc.

c. nursing is not a rewarding career because most graduates almost never find lucrative jobs.

d. only people from a certain ethnic group can succeed as nurses.

Supporting Details

6. Examples of techniques such as outlining and studying with another group are offered to support the idea that

a. nursing students are better off studying alone.

b. students can be easily distracted by others in the study group.

c. nursing students can use these techniques to study effectively.

d. outlining will make it even more difficult for students to stay focused.

Supporting Details

7. Which of the following is NOT one of the suggestions for time management on page 410?

a. Use a blank calendar or planner for the whole year.

b. Schedule study time by writing it on the calendar or planner.

c. Delete due dates, tests, homework, and projects as they are assigned.

d. Schedule personal time for relaxation and being with other people.

Inference

8. "Bring four or five questions with you to discuss with the group. This can be especially helpful if you are having difficulty understanding certain concepts." (page 411)

It can be inferred from the above passage that

a. students cannot join a study group if they bring only two questions.

b. nursing students are not allowed to ask more than five questions in one session.

c. asking questions for clarification during a group discussion can enable students to comprehend complex ideas.

d. students do not have to attend the sessions regularly.

Inference

9. "If you are able to narrow your choice to two options, don't spend too much time deciding between them. More likely than not, your first impression is correct. Once you have identified your choice, don't go back and change it unless you later figure out the correct response with absolute certainty." (page 412)

It can be concluded from the statement that

a. if students spend much time deciding between two options, they are likely to choose the correct answer.

b. it is always a good idea to go back and change the answer.

c. if students second guess themselves, they are likely to choose the incorrect answer.

d. more likely than not, the first impression is incorrect.

Author's Purpose

10. The authors' purpose in writing this chapter is to

a. deter prospective students from choosing the nursing profession.

b. convince students that it is extremely difficult to graduate from a nursing program.

c. discourage students from pursuing nursing as a career.

(d.) encourage students to the field of nursing.

Author's Tone

11. What is the overall tone of the chapter?

    a. intimidating.

    (b.) informative.

    c. sorrowful.

    d. malicious.

Fact and Opinion

12. Which of the following is NOT a fact?

    a. The first nursing school in the world was started in India in about 250 B.C.

    b. Wald and Mary Brewster founded the Henry Street Settlement, and Visiting Nurse Service, which provided nursing and social services, and also organized educational and cultural activities.

    (c.) It is a good idea to break a study session down into segments.

    d. Florence Nightingale established the Nightingale Training School for Nurses in 1860.

Fact and Opinion

13. Which of the following statement is an opinion?

    (a.) Although Nightingale died in 1910, her influence continues in nursing today.

    b. Clara Barton was a schoolteacher who volunteered as a nurse during the American Civil War.

    c. Lavinia Dock participated in protest movements for women's rights that resulted in the 1920 passage of the Nineteenth Amendment to the U.S. Constitution, which granted women the right to vote.

    d. St. Camillus de Lellis started out as a soldier and later turned to nursing.

Pattern of Organization

14. The overall pattern of organization used in Table 1-2 is

    a. comparison and contrast.

    b. chronological order.

    c. spatial order.

    (d.) definition.

Pattern of Organization

15. Which of the following patterns of organization is used in Table 1-3?

    a. comparison and contrast.

    b. definition.

    (c.) chronological order.

    d. cause and effect.

READING

Reading Selection **6**

Additional Reading

Short Story

7.11 Flesch-Kincaid Grade Level 6.3

A Nurse's Story

Pre-Reading Questions

1. In your opinion, what qualities do you think one must possess to be a good nurse? Be specific.

2. Do you think that registered nurses are well compensated for their humanistic services? What, in your opinion, is a decent salary for a full-time nurse?

Collaboration

© Pearson Education, Inc.

3. Some people believe that nurses play an even more important role than a physician in helping the patient recover. Do you agree with this position? Why, or why not?

A Nurse's Story (An Excerpt)

By Peter Baida

1   The pain in Mary McDonald's bones is not the old pain that she knows well, but a new pain. Sitting in her room in the Booth-Tiessler Geriatric Center, on the third floor, in the bulky chair by the window, Mary tries to measure this pain. She sits motionless, with a grave expression on her face, while the cheerless gray sky on the other side of the window slowly fades toward evening.

2   Mary McDonald knows what this pain comes from. It comes from a cancer that began in her colon and then spread to her liver and now has moved into her bones. Mary McDonald has been a nurse for forty years, she has **retained** the full use of her faculties, and she understands perfectly where this pain comes from and what it means.

3   "Union?" Eunice Barnacle says. "What do I want with a union?"

4   "Miss Barnacle," Mary McDonald says, looking at her from the chair by the window, "do you think you're paid what you're worth?"

5   Miss Barnacle is a lean, sharp-featured black woman in her middle twenties, with a straight nose, small teeth, wary eyes, and a **straightforward** manner, who joined the staff at Booth-Tiessler about a month ago. "This place can't afford to pay me what I'm worth," she says.

6   "That's certainly what they want you to believe, Miss Barnacle. May I ask a **nosy** question?"

7   "I suppose."

8   "What do they pay you, Miss Barnacle?"

9   "That's my business."

10   "Eight-fifty per hour. Is that about right, Miss Barnacle?"

11   Miss Barnacle, in her white **uniform**, turns pale. She has paused with her hand on the doorknob, looking over the neatly made bed to the chair where Mary McDonald is sitting. Pearl gray light falls on a walker near the chair. Mary McDonald's hands are closed in her lap, over a green-and-gold quilt. Her face is solemn.

12   "Do you think this place *knows* what you're worth, Miss Barnacle?"

13   A good death. That's what everyone wants.

14   Mary McDonald still remembers, from her first year as a nurse, well over forty years ago, a little old woman named Ida Peterson, with a tumor in her neck near the carotid artery. The call bell at the nurses' station rang, and Mary McDonald walked down the hall, opened the door, and was struck squarely in the face by something warm, wet, and red.

15   Blood from a ruptured artery gushed out of Mrs. Peterson's tracheotomy opening, out of an ulcerated site on her neck, out of her nose, out of her mouth. Mary was stunned. She saw blood on the ceiling, on the floor, on the bed, on the walls.

nosy
always trying to find out private information about someone or something

16   Mrs. Peterson had wanted to die a peaceful, dignified death, in the presence of her husband. She had wanted to die a "natural" death. Now, as the life poured out of her, she lifted her hand to wipe her nose and mouth. With wide eyes, she looked at the blood on her hand.

17   Ida Peterson had wanted a natural death, in the presence of her husband, and she was getting one, in the presence of Mary McDonald, a nurse she had known for five minutes.

18   Mrs. Peterson's blue, terrified eyes looked into Mary McDonald's eyes for the full fifteen minutes it took her to bleed to death. Her hand gripped Mary's hand. Mary did nothing. Her orders were to allow Mrs. Peterson to die a natural death.

19   Mary had never before seen an arterial bleed. She still remembers the splash of blood on her face when she stepped into Mrs. Peterson's room. She still remembers how long it took Mrs. Peterson to die. You wouldn't think that a little woman could have so much blood in her.

20   "They tell me you were some good nurse," Eunice Barnacle says, taking Mary's blood pressure.

21   "I'm still a good nurse," Mary McDonald says.

22   "They tell me you helped start the nurses' union, over at the hospital."

23   "Who tells you?"

24   "Mrs. Pierce."

25   "Ah."

26   "Mrs. Pierce says those were the days."

27   "Maybe they were."

28   Eunice loosens the blood pressure cup from Mary's arm. "Mrs. McDonald?"

29   "Yes?"

30   "That union—" Eunice hesitates, looking at the floor.

31   "What about it?" Mary says.

32   "You think it helped you?"

33   Booth's Landing is an **unpretentious** town with a population of nearly nine thousand, located among gently rolling hills on the east side of the Hudson River, fifty miles north of New York City. In every **generation**, for as long as anyone can remember, the Booths and the Tiesslers have been the town's leading families. The Booth family descends from the town's founder, Josiah Booth, a merchant of the Revolutionary War **period** whom local historians describe as a miniature **version** of John Jacob Astor. The Tiessler family descends from Klaus Tiessler, an immigrant from Heidelberg who in 1851 **founded** a factory that makes silverware.

unpretentious
simple, honest

34   "A nice town," people who live in Booth's Landing say. "A nice place to bring up a family." That's how Mary McDonald has always felt, and that's what she has always said when people ask her about the place.

35   In every **generation**, for as long as anyone can remember, one member of the Booth family has run the town's bank, and one member of the Tiessler family has run the silverware factory. The town also supports one movie theater, two sporting goods stores, two opticians, three auto repair shops, one synagogue, and nine churches. Most of the people who die in Booth's Landing were born there. Many have died with Mary McDonald holding their hands.

36   Oh, not so many, Mary thinks, pursing her lips. Not that she has kept count. Why would anyone keep count?

© Pearson Education, Inc.

philanthropic
a philanthropic person or institution gives money to people who are poor or who need money in order to do something good or useful

drifting
moving along

37   You can do worse than to live and die in a place like Booth's Landing. The air is fresh. The streets are clean and safe. The leading families have paid steady attention to their civic and **philanthropic** responsibilities. If you're sick in Booth's Landing, you go to the Booth-Tiessler **Community** Hospital. If you want to see live entertainment, you buy tickets for the latest show at the Booth-Tiessler Center for the Performing Arts. If you can no longer take care of yourself, you arrange to have yourself deposited in the Booth-Tiessler Geriatric Center.

38   At the Booth-Tiessler **Community** College, nearly fifty years ago, Mary McDonald fulfilled the requirements for her nursing degree. Now, sitting by her window on the third floor in the Geriatric Center, looking over the cherry tree in the yard below toward the river, with the odor of overcooked turnips floating up from the kitchen on the first floor, she finds her mind **drifting** over her life, back and forth, here and there, like a bird that hops from place to place on a tree with many branches.

Reading Comprehension Check

1. As used in the sentence "She sits motionless, with a grave expression on her face, while the cheerless gray sky on the other side of the window slowly fades toward evening," the word *grave* means
   a. unimportant.
   b. insignificant.
   c. serious.
   d. trivial.

2. In the sentence "Mary McDonald has been a nurse for forty years, she has retained the full use of her faculties, and she understands perfectly where this pain comes from and what it means," the word *retained* can be replaced with
   a. preserved.
   b. wasted.
   c. discarded.
   d. decimated.

3. "Miss Barnacle is a lean, sharp-featured black woman in her middle twenties, with a straight nose, small teeth, wary eyes, and a straightforward manner, who joined the staff at Booth-Tiessler about a month ago."

   The word *lean* in the above sentence means
   a. obese.
   b. overweight.
   c. thin.
   d. emaciated.

4. The overall tone of the opening paragraph is
   a. amusing.
   b. grim.
   c. cheerful.
   d. humorous.

5. "Miss Barnacle," Mary McDonald says, looking at her from the chair by the window, "do you think you're paid what you're worth?"

   Which of the following conclusions can be drawn from Mary McDonald's question?
   a. Miss Barnacle is an overpaid employee.
   b. Miss Barnacle's compensation is more than she deserves.
   c. Miss Barnacle is completely satisfied with her salary.
   d. Miss Barnacle is an underpaid employee.

6. When Mary McDonald tells Miss Barnacle that she most probably earns eight fifty an hour, Miss Barnacle turns pale. It can be inferred that.
   a. Miss Barnacle makes at least twice as much.
   b. Miss Barnacle is embarrassed that Mary McDonald knows her actual salary.
   c. Miss Barnacle is excited that Mary McDonald does not know the truth.
   d. Mary McDonald is completely mistaken about Miss Barnacle's compensation.

7. Which of the following is NOT a fact?
   a. Mrs. Ida Peterson had a tumor in her neck near the carotid artery.
   b. Mrs. Ida Peterson wanted to die a dignified death in the absence of her husband.
   c. Mrs. Ida Peterson looked into Mary McDonald's eyes for fifteen minutes before she died.
   d. Mary McDonald's orders were to allow Miss Ida Peterson to die a natural death.

8. Which of the following is an opinion?
   a. Approximately nine thousand people live in Booth's Landing.
   b. Klaus Tiessler was an immigrant from Heidelberg who founded a silverware factory in Booth's Landing in 1851.
   c. Booth's Landing is a nice place to raise children.
   d. Booth's Landing is located on the east side of the Hudson River, fifty miles north of New York City.

9. The details in paragraph 36 are offered to support the main point that
   a. it is unwise to raise children in a place like Booth's Landing.
   b. Booth's Landing is a nice place to bring up a family.
   c. senior citizens are not required to make a deposit to their checking accounts.
   d. Booth Landing is a better place for singles.

10. For the concluding paragraph, the author uses an organizational pattern that
    a. defines technical terms in the field of nursing.
    b. explains the reasons for Mary McDonald's decision to become a nurse.
    c. looks at Mary McDonald's life in chronological order.
    d. contrasts Mary McDonald and Miss Barnacle.

Suggested Resources

Books

1. *Chicken Soup for the Nurse's Soul: 101 Stories to Celebrate, Honor and Inspire the Nursing Profession* by Jack Canfield, Mark Victor Hansen, Nancy Mitchell Autio, LeAnn Thieman. HCI. This collection offers inspiring true stories of nurses making sacrifices in their everyday, life-impacting work.

2. *A Cup of Comfort for Nurses: Stories of Caring and Compassion,* Colleen Sell, Adams Media. Editor. This book brings the tales of more than fifty dedicated nurses who provide care to people selflessly but who are underappreciated.

© Pearson Education, Inc.

Movies

1. *Miss Evers' Boys* (1997). Based on a true story, this movie tells a gripping tale of medical research conducted on humans in Alabama. The protagonist, devoted Nurse Eunice Evers (played by Alfre Woodard), is faced with a dilemma when government funding is withdrawn.

2. *Nursing Diaries* (2006). In this three-episode series produced by CBS, the real life experience of nurses at Massachusetts General Hospital is followed. Each episode shows the challenges nurses face in their work.

Internet Sites

1. http://www.aacn.nche.edu/Media/NewsReleases/06Survey.htm

   This American Association of Colleges of Nursing Web site provides useful information on choosing a nursing program in the United States. If you are seriously considering pursuing a nursing career, this is a resourceful site for you.

2. http://allnurses.com/

   Nurses from all over the world find a nursing community here and learn, communicate, and network.

Patterns of Organization Across Academic Disciplines

Overview

As you take college courses, it will be important for you to understand that textbooks are organized using specific patterns of organization particular to the academic discipline. Identifying discipline-specific patterns of organization will enable you to understand the author's approach and how information is organized in each chapter. For example, if you are reading a nursing textbook, you will notice that most information is factual, and the two most common patterns of organization are cause and effect and problem-solution.

A great majority of the academic areas covered in this book fall into the categories of social science (Education, Criminal Justice, Psychology, and Political Science), life and physical science (Health, Environmental Science, and Nursing), and business (Business and Internet Marketing). The table shown here lists patterns of organization corresponding to these three academic areas.

You will notice that disciplines such as Psychology, Criminal Justice, and Political Science fall within the academic area of social science. Textbooks in each of these disciplines use listing, comparison and contrast, and cause and effect patterns of organization. In the academic area of life and physical science, disciplines such as Nursing, Environmental Science, and Health rely on process, cause and effect, and problem-solution patterns of organization. Finally, in the academic area of business, the disciplines of Business and Internet Marketing use definition and examples, problem-solution, and classification patterns of organization to impart discipline-specific knowledge to the students.

Table 1   Discipline-specific Patterns of Organization

Academic Area	*Disciplines*	*Patterns of Organization*
Social Science	Psychology Criminal Justice Political Science	Listing Comparison and Contrast Cause and Effect
Life and Physical Science	Nursing Environmental Science Health	Process Cause and Effect Problem–Solution
Business	Business E-Commerce	Definition and Examples Problem–Solution Classification

© Pearson Education, Inc.

The next table makes this point clear. It shows how each pattern of organization is used in a particular discipline. Notice that the left column shows a specific pattern of organization, and the right column lists discipline-specific examples. For example, the discipline of Political Science may use the comparison and contrast pattern of organization to describe the similarities and differences between different forms of government such as democracy and communism. Likewise, the discipline of psychology also may incorporate the comparison and contrast pattern of organization to delineate the outcome of two types of counseling. Study Table 2 to familiarize yourself with the types of patterns of organization that are typical of specific disciplines.

Table 2 Patterns of Organization and Discipline-specific Examples

Pattern of Organization	*Discipline-specific Examples*
Comparison and Contrast	1. Political Science—comparison of different forms of government 2. Criminal Justice—discussion of different types of prison system 3. Psychology—comparing the effects of two different counseling strategies
Cause and Effect	1. Environmental Science—the debilitating effects of human activity on the environment 2. Criminal Justice—a violation of law and sentencing 3. Health—consuming fast food and obesity-related illnesses 4. Nursing—treatment and the patient's health 5. Psychology—parenting and the child's behavior 6. Political Science—the presidential debate and voters choosing a candidate
Listing	1. Psychology—various signs of stress 2. Criminal Justice—using forensic science for different purposes 3. Political Science—law enforcement in different social situations
Process	1. Nursing—how to take a patient's temperature 2. Environmental Science—how a species evolves under certain conditions 3. Health—various stages of weight loss
Problem–Solution	1. Nursing—dealing with a patient who does not cooperate with the nurse 2. Environmental Science—deforestation and its effect on biodiversity 3. Health—avoiding the debilitating effects of obesity 4. Business—improving the sales of an unsuccessful product 5. E-Commerce—making consumers aware of a website to increase traffic
Definition and Examples	1. Business—different examples of entrepreneurship 2. E-Commerce—a portal and examples of its services and resources
Classification	1. Business—different categories of businesses from multinational conglomerates to small businesses 2. E-Commerce—Business Web sites and different categories such as business-to-business, business-to-consumer

Learning Implications

Familiarizing yourself with the specific patterns of organization various disciplines incorporate will help you read the textbooks with relative ease and success. You will be able to understand the author's purpose and to follow the lectures easily. Once you understand that the discipline you are studying relies on the cause-and-effect patterns of organization, you will understand that a phenomenon is caused by a single factor or several factors. Similarly, learning that studying certain disciplines such as environmental science and health require you to focus in on a problem and find a solution will enable you to complete the assignments more accurately.

© Pearson Education, Inc.

PSYCHOLOGY
Nature Versus Nurture

"Everything that irritates us about others can lead us to an understanding of ourselves."

CARL JUNG

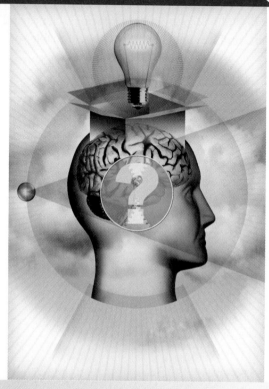

Objectives

IN THIS CHAPTER YOU WILL LEARN . . .

- Foundation knowledge about the discipline of psychology
- How to recognize and evaluate an author's argument
- How to work with a reading journal
- How to find evidence for an author's claim

Making Predictions

Consider this chapter's theme of psychology. What subtopics relate to this field?
(See Figure 8.1.)

Collaboration

■ **Figure 8.1**

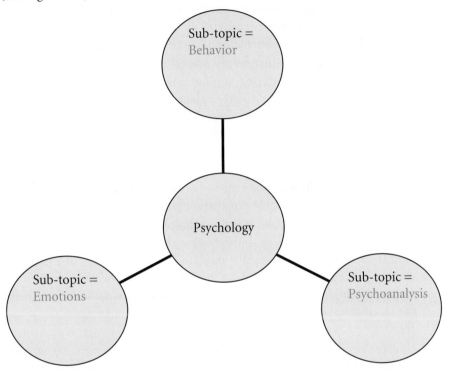

Sub-topic =
Behavior

Psychology

Sub-topic =
Emotions

Sub-topic =
Psychoanalysis

Introduction to the Field of Psychology

Psychology is formally defined as the scientific study of the behavior of individuals and their mental processes. Many psychologists seek answers to such fundamental questions as: What is human nature? And, why do we behave the way we do? Psychologists study such phenomena as cognition, perception, emotion, personality, and interpersonal relationships. Why is psychology relevant to our daily lives? Psychological research focuses on our physical and mental health, our personal growth, and our ability to understand one another.

There are many subdivisions within the field of psychology. For example, clinical psychologists focus on understanding, preventing, and relieving psychologically based distress or dysfunction; cognitive psychologists focus on cognitive processes such as language and memory; school psychologists focus on students' behavior in educational settings. Each area of psychology offers the opportunity to do both research and to apply research-based findings in a real-world setting.

This chapter focuses primarily on issues related to the "nature versus nurture" debate, which frames many research questions in the field of psychology. How similar are identical twins separated at birth? Why do people lie? How much of an effect does TV violence play on children's behavior? Are we genetically preprogrammed with a single type of intelligence, or are there multiple forms of human intelligence? These are some of the topics that will be explored in the chapter readings.

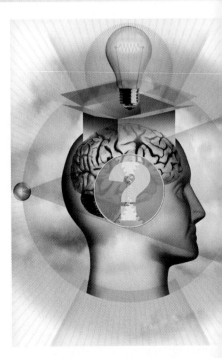

© Pearson Education, Inc.

Preview Questions

Collaboration

1. Some people believe that human behavior is largely determined by our genetic makeup while others claim that we are the products of our environment. Where do you stand on the nature vs. nurture debate? In other words, how much of human nature is genetically determined, and how much of it must be shaped by environmental factors such as parenting, education, etc.?

2. A famous psychologist once wrote a book entitled *Men Are from Mars, Women Are from Venus*. His central point is that men and women think and behave as if they were from different planets. If you think this is true, first discuss in what ways men and women behave differently. Then offer some explanations to account for these differences.

3. Many studies have focused on identical twins separated at birth and raised far away from each other by different parents. Most of these studies found remarkable similarities between the twins. Do you think this is just a coincidence, or is there a reasonable explanation for these similarities?

4. Most people believe that children learn their first language mainly through imitation. That is, they learn simply by listening and repeating. Yet, research indicates that young children all around the globe learn their first language without getting explicit instruction from their parents or teachers. How do we explain children acquiring a language so effortlessly? How do we explain the fact that adults struggle with mastering a second language while young children pick second languages up with relative ease?

5. Humans have inhabited the planet earth for thousands of years. Yet, we have not learned how to coexist in peace and harmony. Do you believe that violence is a natural part of our behavior? In other words, is conflict built into our psychological makeup?

Interpreting a Cartoon

 Figure 8.2

Reverse Psychology

Examine the cartoon shown on p. 434 and answer the following questions in pairs.

Collaboration

1. What is amusing about this cartoon?
2. In your opinion, what message is the cartoonist trying to convey to the reader?

Discipline-specific Terminology Bank

analysis	environmental	instincts	response
behavior	genetics	mental processes	self-esteem
conditioning	human nature	motivation	socialization
control group	impulses	observation	stimuli
correlation	insight	reliability	unconscious

Sample Paragraph

Read the following paragraph, which contains some of the discipline-specific terminology you will come across in the reading selections in this chapter. Pay attention to the highlighted words, and try to figure out the meaning from the context.

Those who take the behaviorist perspective seem to understand how particular **environmental stimuli** control particular kinds of **behavior**. First, behaviorists **analyze** the antecedent environmental conditions—those that precede the behavior and set the stage for an organism to make a **response** or withhold a response. Next, they look at the behavioral response, which is the main object of study—the action to be understood, predicted, and controlled. Finally they examine the **observable** consequences that follow from the response. A behaviorist, for example, might be interested in the way in which speeding tickets of varying penalties change the likelihood that motorists will drive with caution or abandon (behavioral responses). To conduct such a study, the psychologist would have to set up a **control group**, look for **correlations** between the level of penalties and motorists' driving patterns, and check for **reliability** in the study's results.

EXERCISE 1

Matching Column A and Column B

Match the word in Column A with the definition in Column B. Put the letter representing the correct definition in the space preceding each term.

Column A

Word

1. __e__ genetics
2. __j__ impulse
3. __g__ psychoanalysis

Column B

Definition

a. actions by which an organism adjusts to its environment

b. the relationship between two variables

© Pearson Education, Inc.

4. __k__ conditioning
5. __i__ reliability
6. __b__ correlation
7. __a__ behavior
8. __d__ socialization
9. __c__ motivation
10. __h__ insight

c. biological, emotional, or social impulses that activate and direct behavior

d. the lifelong process whereby an individual's behavioral patterns are shaped to conform to those regarded as desirable

e. the study of the inheritance of physical and psychological traits from ancestors

g. therapy developed by Freud, an intense prolonged technique for exploring unconscious motivations

h. the ability to see clearly and intuitively into the nature of a complex person, situation, or subject

i. the degree to which a test produces similar scores each time it is used

j. an instinctive drive or natural tendency

k. a method of controlling or influencing the way people or animals behave or think by using a gradual training process

EXERCISE 2

Fill in the Blanks

In the following sentences, fill in the blank with a word from the terminology bank that makes the sentence grammatically correct and meaningful.

behavior	conditioning	correlation	genetics	impulse
insight	motivation	psychoanalysis	reliability	socialization

1. The school psychologist realized that the failing student lacked _motivation_ to do his work.

2. The lethargic patient reacted to the _impulse_ of the shock therapy treatment.

3. The tests lacked _reliability_ as the results were radically different from one to another.

4. Recent studies have shown that _genetics_ plays a much larger role in our chances of getting certain diseases than we had previously thought.

5. Studies have shown a strong _correlation_ between smoking and lung cancer.

6. Many _socialization_ skills are learned through imitating others around you.

7. Some experts attribute differences between boys and girls to learned _behavior_.

8. Through _psychoanalysis_, the patient was able to deal with his past.

9. The dog learning the habit of responding to a bell is an example of classical __*conditioning*__.

10. The veteran psychologist shared his years of ___*insight*___ into the workings of the human mind with his young students.

EXERCISE 3

Pair Activity

Working with a partner, choose five words you have just learned, and make complete sentences with them.

1. _____

2. _____

3. _____

4. _____

5. _____

In-class Survey on Gender Roles

In order to explore stereotypes, ask two classmates, one male and one female, to complete these sentences with the first thought that comes to their mind. Please take notes as they respond to your questions. Use a separate sheet if needed. The goal is to compare the differences in the two respondents' answers. Orally report your findings to the class.

Collaboration

ESL Annotation

8.1 ESL Students with backgrounds in other cultures may hold very different stereotypes on gender roles.

Question	Respondent 1	Respondent 2
The most difficult emotion for a man to display is . . .		
The most difficult emotion for a woman to display is . . .		
Women tend to be better than men at . . .		
Men tend to be better than women at . . .		
Men get depressed about . . .		
Women get depressed about . . .		
Men are most likely to compete over . . .		
Women are most likely to compete over . . .		

© Pearson Education, Inc.

Collaboration

Graphic Analysis

Examine the figure below with a partner and answer the questions.

Five Illusions to Tease Your Brain (from *Psychology and Life,* p. 98)

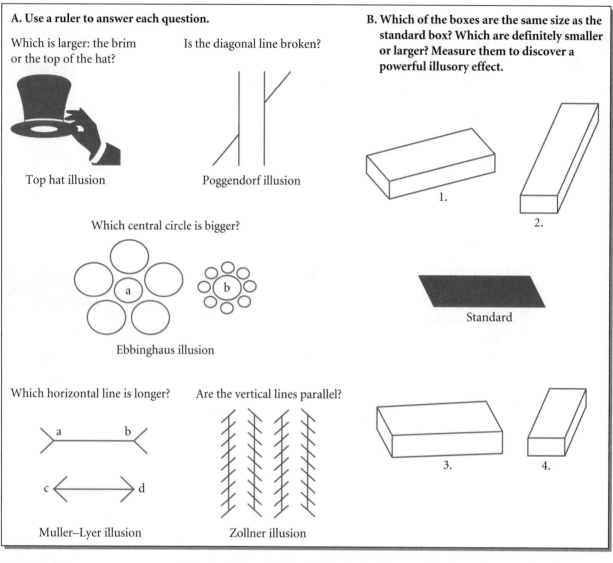

A. Use a ruler to answer each question.

Which is larger: the brim or the top of the hat?

Top hat illusion

Is the diagonal line broken?

Poggendorf illusion

Which central circle is bigger?

Ebbinghaus illusion

Which horizontal line is longer?

Muller–Lyer illusion

Are the vertical lines parallel?

Zollner illusion

B. Which of the boxes are the same size as the standard box? Which are definitely smaller or larger? Measure them to discover a powerful illusory effect.

1.

2.

Standard

3.

4.

■ **Figure 8.3**   Richard J. Gerrig and Philip G. Zimbardo, *Psychology and Life,* Discovering Psychology Edition, 18th ed., Figure 4.5 (p. 98). © 2008, 2005, 2002 Pearson Education, Inc. Reproduced by permission of Pearson Education, Inc.

READING

Reading Selection **1**

Textbook Reading

4.0 Flesch-Kincaid Grade Level

Collaboration

Why and How Do People Lie?

Pre-Reading Questions

Discuss the following questions with a partner.

1. Have you ever told a "white lie"? Under what circumstances do you think it is OK to tell a white lie?
2. Why are some people habitual liars?
3. How can you tell if someone is lying or telling you the truth?

ESL Annotation

8.2 ESL In some cultures lying is a taboo topic to focus on. Discuss this point with your class to help ESL students feel more comfortable.

Why and How Do People Lie?

By **Richard J. Gerrig and Philip G. Zimbardo,**
from *Psychology and Life* (2009)

Psychology in Your Life

1   In this **section** on language use, we have emphasized that people aspire to be **cooperative** conversationalists. For example, we suggested that people follow the **principle**, "Try to make your **contribution** one that is true." However, we know that people often fall away from this standard. When people were asked to keep diaries of the lies they told, most averaged one or two a day (DePaulo et al., 2003). But why do people lie? When the lies are relatively mild, more people lie for psychological reasons (e.g., they wish to spare themselves embarrassment) than for personal advantage (e.g., they wish to avoid an unpleasant chore). However, when lies become more serious, the motives for lying **shift** in the direction of personal advantage. In one study, participants were asked to reveal the most serious lie that they had ever told (DePaulo et al., 2004). People quite frequently committed serious lies to conceal affairs or other forbidden forms of social **contact**. People felt that they were entitled to cheat on their partners and lied in service to that sense of entitlement. Thus the lies worked for personal advantage.

2   Let's **focus** on the **mental** processes that people use to lie. Should it be easier or harder to tell a lie than to tell the truth? The answer is: It depends (DePaulo et al., 2003). Suppose you are asked, "What did you do last night?" If you choose to lie spontaneously, it might be harder for you to formulate a lie than to tell the truth. However, if you have prepared your lie in advance— because you anticipate the awkward question—you might produce your lie with great fluidity. Still, lies and truths differ from each other in some **consistent** ways. A study that reviewed the literature on the content of lies reported that liars provide fewer details in their accounts than do people who are telling the truth (DePaulo et al., 2003). In addition, liars' accounts were consistently less **plausible** and less fluent than truthful accounts.

3   These results suggest that speakers may engage different **mental** processes to produce their lies. To test this **hypothesis**, researchers have begun to analyze

plausible
believable, credible

? _____
_____
_____

? _____
_____
_____

© Pearson Education, Inc.

From Richard J. Gerrig and Philip G. Zimbardo, *Psychology and Life*, Discovering Psychology Edition, 18th ed., p. 249. © 2008, 2005, 2002 Pearson Education, Inc. Reproduced by permission of Pearson Education, Inc.

patterns of brain activity that underlie truth-telling and lying. In one study, participants were asked to lie or tell the truth about their **participation** in an incident in which a gun was fired in a hospital (Mohamed et al., 2006). To make the experience of lying as real as possible, participants in the *guilty* condition actually fired a starter pistol (loaded with blanks) in the testing room. Participants in both the *guilty* and *not-guilty* conditions answered a **series** of questions while undergoing fMRI scans. Participants in the guilty condition received **instructions** to lie about their **role** in the incident. The fMRI scans **revealed** that several areas of the brain were more active for lying than for truth-telling. For example, brain regions responsible for planning and emotion were harder at work when participants prepared their lies.

4   Another study looked into the brains of people who qualify as *pathological liars*—these are individuals who lie with **sufficient** regularity that the behavior is considered abnormal (by the types of *DSM-IV* **criteria** we describe in **Chapter 14)**. The **overall structure** of brains of the pathological liars were compared using MRI to the brains of matched controls (Yang et al., 2005). Those brain comparisons **revealed consistent** differences in the prefrontal cortex. The pathological liars, for example, had more of the type of brain tissue that allows neurons to communicate with each other. Prefrontal cortex is a **region** of the brain that plays an important **role** in planning—suggesting that the pathological liars are particularly well equipped to plan their lies. These results, however, leave open the question of cause and effect: Did pathological liars start life with brains of this type (which, perhaps, caused or allowed them to lie frequently) or did frequent lying change their brains?

Reading Comprehension Check

1. In the first sentence of the reading, the word *aspire* means
    a. sweat.   c. decline.
    (b.) aim.   d. translate.

2. What is the topic of this reading passage?
    a. people.   (c.) factors related to the act of lying.
    b. lying to your family.   d. confessions about lying.

3. What is the main idea of the second paragraph?
    a. People produce lies with great fluidity.
    b. It is always easier to lie.
    c. It is easier to tell the truth.
    (d.) It is sometimes easier to tell a lie than to tell the truth, depending on the situation.

4. A study reported that liars provide fewer details in their accounts than do people who are telling the truth. Is this a statement of fact or opinion?
    (a.) fact.   c. neither fact nor opinion.
    b. opinion.   d. none of the above.

5. Brain regions responsible for planning and emotion are mentioned as
    a. truth tellers.
    b. dormant during lying process.
    (c.) more active when people are preparing to lie.
    d. unresponsive.

6. A pathological liar is someone who
   a. lies occasionally.
   b. tells dangerous lies.
   c. lies regularly.
   d. has an occasional lapse.

7. What is the main idea of the final paragraph?
   a. The prefrontal cortex plays an important role in planning.
   b. Pathological liars' brain structures differ from the norm.
   c. pathological liars.
   d. none of the above.

8. The term *well-equipped* in the final paragraph could be replaced by
   a. ready.
   b. unprepared.
   c. distinct.
   d. irrelevant.

9. What is the author's tone in this reading passage?
   a. emotional.
   b. objective.
   c. optimistic.
   d. angry.

10. What is the author's purpose in writing this article?
    a. to entertain.
    b. to persuade.
    c. to dissuade.
    d. to inform.

READING

Reading Selection **2A**

Newspaper Article

8.3 Flesch-Kincaid Grade Level 7.8

Collaboration

The Barbers, Identical Twins, Are Not as Alike as They Look

Pre-Reading Questions

Discuss these questions in small groups. There is a second reading on identical twins that follows this one on the Barber twins. These questions apply to both reading selections.

1. Have you ever known any identical twins? If yes, did they have similar personalities?

2. In your view, how are identical twins different from the rest of us? Do identical twins have a deeper relationship than most siblings do?

3. Do you believe in the concept of the "evil twin"? Explain

The Barbers, Identical Twins, Are Not as Alike as They Look

By John Branch, the *New York Times*

October 25, 2006

1 Dawn had not arrived, but Tiki and Ronde Barber, twin stars of the N.F.L., had been at the Fox News studios in Midtown Manhattan for hours. Ronde—

John Branch, "The Barbers, Identical Twins, Are Not as Alike as They Look." From The *New York Times*, October 25, 2006. © 2006 The *New York Times*. All rights reserved. Used by permission and protected by the Copyright Laws of the United States. The printing, copying, redistribution, or re-transmission of the Material without express written permission is prohibited. www.nytimes.com.

Tiki and Ronde Barber were indistinguishable for much of their lives, and even at 31, they sometimes confuse even themselves.

the one in the crisp suit without the perfectly placed pocket square—stood outside the green room.

2   A woman approached, gave a kiss and began talking to him as if they were old friends.

3   "I'm Ronde," he said, politely interrupting. He had never seen her before.

4   "No, you're not," she said. "You're Tiki."

5   Close.

6   Tiki and Ronde. All famous pairs have an order to their names, and that is theirs, though Ronde is seven minutes older. The two were indistinguishable for much of their lives, and even at 31, they sometimes confuse even themselves.

7   On air at "Fox & Friends," Tiki halted last week as he said something about the two of them on the morning news program that he is a co-host for on Tuesdays. Ronde had joined him as a co-host that day.

8   "Did you hear that?" he asked. "I almost said, 'Tiki and I.' That is really weird."

9   They slept in the same bedroom growing up in Roanoke, Va., and again for two years at the University of Virginia. They shared an apartment after that. Rarely was one Barber without the other. Even girlfriends looked to their earrings to tell them apart: a hoop for Tiki, a round stud for Ronde.

10   But they are, by comparison, much different now, so different that they can no longer imagine living the other's life.

11   The **random** selection of the N.F.L. **draft** spun them in opposite directions in 1997: Tiki to New York City, Ronde to Tampa, Fla. They unwittingly became a social experiment about the effects of nature versus nurture.

12   In this case, nurture won.

13   "The hard thing to imagine is what if Tiki landed in Tampa and I landed in New York?" Ronde said. "We have **similar** personalities. Would I be doing

all the things he does? Would he be living a life like mine? That's what I always think about."

14   He shrugged, as if giving up on an impossible riddle.

15   "It **boggles**," he said.

boggles
is difficult to believe or very confusing

16   Tiki became a Pro Bowl running back for the Giants and leads the N.F.L. in rushing this season. He lives with his wife, Ginny, and their two young sons in an Upper East Side condominium, a home shared with Ginny's parents. Tiki is an emerging **media** personality and a friend of many New York power brokers. He plans to retire at season's end to pursue business opportunities. He is often seen at charity events or on television, wearing an Italian suit.

17   Ronde became a Pro Bowl defensive back for the Tampa Bay Buccaneers. He returned two interceptions for touchdowns on Sunday in a victory over the Philadelphia Eagles. He lives with his wife, Claudia, and their two young daughters in a 7,100-square-foot house that sits by a lake, a home shared with a room-sized golf simulator, a home theater and six cars. Ronde does some radio and television work and plans to play several more seasons. He often can be found on a golf course or on a fishing boat. For him, the first name in style is Tommy Bahama.

18   "I'm a true believer that **environment** really shapes you," Claudia said. "They came into their true and developed personalities from their **environment**, when they had to separate."

19   She called Ronde and Tampa "a perfect fit," something that is also true about Tiki and New York.

20   The Giants and Buccaneers play at Giants Stadium on Sunday—the Barbers' latest, and likely last, head-to-head meeting. In a few months, they will become even more different, no longer linked by profession.

21   Ronde Barber was in New York last week on an off day for both players. It was hardly a day off. In promoting their latest children's book, "Teammates," they **zigzagged** around Manhattan with a traveling party that included their business manager, Mark Lepselter; their editor at Simon & Schuster, Paula Wiseman; and a **couple** of large men who doubled as drivers and bodyguards.

zigzagged
moving around from point to point

22   Barber Tour 2006 took them from appearances on Fox to ABC's "Good Morning America" to ESPN's "Cold Pizza," through a slew of radio interviews, a Barnes & Noble book signing and, finally, a photo shoot for People magazine, where they are sure to be celebrated for their similarities.

23   When seen separately, the Barbers are hard to tell apart. In Manhattan, people stared at Ronde when he walked down the sidewalk. Many called him Tiki, and congratulated him for his brother's recent rushing performances. He rarely corrects the mistaken identity.

24   Tiki, 20 pounds heavier, looks like Ronde slightly inflated. Other differences require keener eyes. Ronde has a cross-stitch scar in his eyebrow from when he slipped running up carpeted stairs in bowling shoes. He has a fake front tooth, from when he was blindsided by a tree in their grandmother's yard, chasing a soccer ball that Tiki had lobbed into the air. ("I caught the tooth, though," Ronde said proudly.) He has five mostly hidden tattoos. Tiki has none.

© Pearson Education, Inc.

25   A sound man from "Good Morning America" approached to attach a microphone to Ronde's jacket.

26   "Tiki?" he guessed.

27   "Ronde," Ronde said.

28   Ronde is quite adept in front of the cameras—less polished than Tiki but an equal at improvisation and humor. When the microphones are gone, Ronde uses more colorful language. Everything about him feels just a **grade** or two more casual.

29   "He speaks his mind," said Ginny, who dated Tiki through college before they married. "Tiki is more politically correct."

30   Those close to the two joke that Ronde is the "evil twin."

31   "Ronde is the edgier **version** of the two," Lepselter said.

32   They have always been different in that way, but geography widened the divide.

33   "We were more like me before Tiki came here," Ronde said. "Tiki was always a cerebral dude, but it's been **exacerbated** with him here."

exacerbated
made a bad situation worse

fate had tossed
the situation was given/ not chosen

34   Far less certain is how things would be different if **fate had tossed** each to the other city. The Barbers wonder if Tiki would have tired of a smaller market or if he would have not known the difference, being raised in a small city. Or if Ronde would have diligently expanded his off-field public profile in New York the way Tiki has.

35   "We're ambitious in different ways," Tiki said. "And because of where he is, some of the things I do never entered his radar screen."

36   Lepselter outlined the endorsement deals of the two. Tiki's list is far longer, but Lepselter said he does not craft a deal for Tiki worried what Ronde will think.

37   "It's the same talents," Lepselter said. "It's just a different mentality."

38   Ronde, who said he would probably settle in Charlottesville, Va., when he retires, admitted that he envied some of what Tiki has.

vicariously
experienced by watching or reading about someone else doing something, rather than by doing it yourself

39   "Certainly, yeah," he said. "It's a different lifestyle, and I enjoy it when I am up here. Honestly, I don't think I could do it as much as Tiki does. I like recreation too much. But we are **somewhat** living **vicariously** through the other, especially when it comes to this king-of-**media** persona he has taken on."

40   Tiki finished a telephone interview and was asked the question in **reverse**, whether he envied what Ronde had.

41   "Not really," he said.

42   "He wishes he had a flowing, graceful golf swing like I have," Ronde said, the type of gentle jab that the two trade often, a shtick that plays well during interviews.

43   "I do wish I could play golf like he does, because everyone's always asking me to golf, and I have to **decline**," Tiki said.

44   And that neatly summed up their outlooks: One plays golf for enjoyment, the other would like to because of the networking possibilities.

45   "Where they are has partly crafted their personalities," Lepselter said. "Ronde could adapt to being a New Yorker. **Whereas**, with no disrespect to Tampa, Tiki would jump out the window if he lived there. Now, coming out of the **draft**, it would have been different. But in 2006 . . ."

46   At the book signing, the brothers engaged each autograph seeker, some obviously nervous, with smiles and banter. A woman mentioned that she ran a kiosk nearby that sold hats that can be embroidered with messages. Ronde jokingly said he could use one that read, "I'm not Tiki."

47   A few minutes later, he had one. And he wore it.

Reading Comprehension Check

1. In the first paragraph of the article on the Barber twins, the word *indistinguishable* means
  a. unique.
  b. similar.
  (c.) impossible to tell apart.
  d. wavering.

2. The twins' style of earrings are mentioned in the article as
  a. a conclusion.
  b. a personality difference.
  c. evidence of their wealth.
  (d.) a way of telling them apart.

3. The word *unwittingly*, in the sentence "They unwittingly became a social experiment about the effects of nature versus nurture." Paragraph 11 could be replaced by
  a. on purpose.
  (b.) inadvertently.
  c. smartly.
  d. rugged.

4. What is Ronde's wife Claudia's position on the nature vs. nurture debate?
  a. The article does not discuss this.
  (b.) She believes more in the nurture theory.
  c. She has a balanced viewpoint.
  d. She believes more in genetics.

5. Which is NOT mentioned as a distinguishing characteristic of the twin brothers?
  a. their difference in weight.
  b. Ronde's fake front tooth.
  (c.) their heights.
  d. Tiki's lack of tattoos.

6. What is the main idea of the article?
  a. The two twins are identical.
  (b.) Although the Barber twins are identical they have some personality differences.
  c. Both of the twins play professional football.
  d. The twins have been through a lot together.

© Pearson Education, Inc.

READING

Reading Selection **2B**

Online Article

8.4 Flesch-Kincaid Grade Level 12.0

ESLAnnotation
8.5 ESL Some ESL students may not be aware of the nature vs. nurture debate. This article may serve as a good place to discuss whether human nature is genetically determined or whether it is shaped by the environment.

inclination
a liking or preference

discrepancy
a difference between two amounts, details, etc. that should be the same

Why Are Identical Twins Different?

By **Pamela Prindle Fierro**, About.com

1   The stereotype of **identical** twins is that they are exactly alike: they look alike, they dress in matching outfits, they share the same likes and dislikes. Parents of **identical** twins know differently, however. **Despite** their shared genetic component, **identical** multiples are **unique** individuals. Though they do share similarities, they also have many differences.

2   For example, my own children have always exhibited about a twenty-five **percent** difference in their weight. When they were newborns, weighing four and five pounds, it was quite **obvious**. At other times as they've grown up, it's not noticeable. We have **confirmed** that they are indeed **identical** twins, yet people are often skeptical because they don't "look" alike.

3   They don't act alike either. One likes to dance; the other likes to play basketball. Certainly, we encourage them to **pursue** their **individual** interests, but the **initial inclination** towards these activities were all their own.

What Are Identical Twins?

4   **Identical**, or monozygotic, twins develop from a single egg/sperm combination that splits a few days after conception. Their DNA originates from a single **source**, thus their genetic makeup is the same and the characteristics that are determined by genetics will be **similar**. Monozygotic twins are always of the same **gender**, except in extremely rare cases of chromosomal defect.

5   On the other hand, fraternal, or dizygotic, multiples form when two separate eggs are fertilized by separate sperm in a single ovulation **cycle**. They are no more alike than any sibling set, sharing about 50% of their genetic markers in a **unique** combination of genes from both parents.

Environmental Differences

6   While **identical** twins form with the same set of genes, human development is not just genetic. The environment also has an **impact**. So, beginning in the early **environment** of the womb, **external** influences can change the appearance of twins. For example, some monozygotic twins share a placenta. One twin may have a more advantageous connection to the placenta, receiving the first run of nutrients. This situation can cause a size **discrepancy** between the babies, a **physical** difference that continues as they grow up. Twin-to-Twin Transfusion Syndrome (TTTS) is another condition that affects twins in the womb, and can **impact** their development.

7   While most twins grow up in the same home **environment**, there are many **circumstances** that **create** differences in the children's appearances, personalities, and interests. As the twins **approach** the teen years, they may even seek to establish dissimilar qualities in order to establish **individual** identities.

Epigenetic Differences

8   Scientists have offered a new explanation for the differences between **identical** twins. Epigenome refers to natural **chemical** modifications within a person's genome (genetic material). As an article in the *New York Times* explains, they "act on a gene like a gas pedal or a brake, marking it for higher or lower activity."

9   A study conducted by a **team** of researchers at the Spanish National Cancer Center in Madrid concluded that, while **identical** twins are born with the same epigenome, their epigentic profiles begin to diverge as they age. The differences increase as twins live longer and spend more time apart. The scientists offered two theories to explain this **phenomenon**. First, that epigentic marks are **removed** randomly as people age. Secondly, environmental influences change the pattern of epigentic marks.

10   In a *Washington Post* article Dr. Manel Esteller, lead researcher, said that "small epigenetic events before birth probably account for many of the minor distinguishing differences in the appearance, personality and general health of young twins."

11   The **research** is **significant** because changes in the epigenome may be responsible for the development of disease, like cancer. It's hoped that further study of the epigenome in **identical** twins will help researchers **pinpoint factors** that contribute to cancer.

pinpoint
to say exactly what something is, or exactly where someone or something is

Further Research: Not Actually Identical

12 A study **published** in the March 2008 issue of *The American Journal of Human Genetics* offers further explanation, even challenging the accepted **notion** that **identical** twins have **identical** genetic profiles. The **research** found changes in the DNA **sequence** between **identical** twins, reflected in Copy Number Variations (when a gene exists in multiple copies.) The **research** did not confirm whether these changes **occur** during fetal development or as twins age.

13   The **research** is **significant** because many **medical** conditions can be influenced by copy number variations, such as autism, AIDS, and lupus.

———————————

Reading Comprehension Check

1. What is the main idea of the first paragraph of the article?
  (a.) The stereotype that identical twins are exactly the same is untrue.
  b. Twins have so much in common.
  c. There is a genetic component at work with twins.
  d. both b and c.

2. What do we learn about the article's author in the second paragraph?
  a. She is an identical twin.
  b. She believes identical twins never look alike.
  (c.) She is the mother of identical twins.
  d. She is female.

© Pearson Education, Inc.

Dr. Phil

Dr. Phil McGraw has become one of the most well-known talk show hosts in the United States with his own television program, *The Dr Phil Show*. He gives advice to families and couples on a host of issues from relationship problems to health issues and legal advise. He first became known from his regular appearances on the *Oprah Winfrey Show*.

Dr. Phil was born Phillip Calvin McGraw in Vinita, Oklahoma, in 1950. He grew up with his three sisters, in the oilfields of North Texas, where his father was an equipment supplier. During McGraw's childhood, his family moved so his father could pursue a lifelong dream of becoming a psychologist. McGraw graduated from the Midwestern State University in 1975 with a BA (Bachelor of Arts) in psychology, and then went on to get a Masters in experimental psychology and a Doctorate in clinical psychology at the University of North Texas. After graduation, Phillip McGraw joined his father, Dr. Joe McGraw, in Wichita Falls, Texas, where the elder McGraw had established his private psychology practice.

In 1983, McGraw and his father joined a successful Texas businesswoman, in presenting "Pathways," a seminar to "assist people in living their lives with clarity and passion."

In 1989, McGraw was sanctioned by the Texas State Board of Examiners of Psychologists for an ethical violation involving a 19-year-old patient and employee. Because of the sanctions, McGraw was unable to practice psychology independently.

Oprah Winfrey "discovered" McGraw in 1995 when she hired his courtroom consulting firm to prepare her for a trial. Winfrey was so impressed with McGraw that she thanked him for her victory in the case, which ended in 1998. Soon after, she invited him to appear on her show. His appearance proved so successful that he began appearing weekly as a "Relationship and Life Strategy Expert" on Tuesdays starting in 1998.

In 2002, reeling from his success with Oprah, he was given his own syndicated daily TV show, *The Dr. Phil Show*. The format is an advice show, where he tackles a different topic on each show, offering advice for his guests' troubles. Some have likened him to a male Dr. Laura. McGraw has authored a number of self-help books on topics such as relationships and weight loss.

McGraw shifted focus in 2003–2004 to emphasize weight loss shows, books, and products.

In 2005, McGraw signed a five-year extension of his syndication deal, which would pay him $15 million a year and keep the show in production through the 2013–2014 television season.

McGraw attracted criticism for his unannounced visit to celebrity Britney Spears' hospital room in 2008. The visit appeared to be part of an attempt at getting Spears and her parents to take part in an "intervention" on the Dr. Phil television show. Immediately after the visit, McGraw issued public statements about Spears' situation that Spears' family spokeswoman said violated their family trust in McGraw. One professional psychologist filed a complaint with the California Board of Psychology, alleging that Dr. Phil practiced clinical psychology without a license and violated doctor-patient privilege by discussing Spears' case with the media. He also started a petition to have the Dr. Phil show removed from the air. Dr. Phil's technique, which differs considerably from traditional psychology, has been criticized by many in the profession. Dr. Phil's critics regard advice given by him to be simplistic and at times, abusive.

McGraw has said he never liked traditional counseling and was awkward in one-on-one situations.

McGraw has stated that his favorite Dr. Phil joke was told by David Letterman: "Letterman was introducing some new books coming out, and he held up one by Dr. Phil with the title *More Advice I Pulled Out of My Ass*. I thought, that's pretty funny. I liked that."

Some Questions for Group Discussion

1. Some of Dr. Phil's critics have called him an "unqualified psychologist." Do you think this is a fair label? Should Dr. Phil have the right to give advice on television?

2. Dr. Phil has been at the center of a number of high-profile controversies. Do you think TV talk-show personalities like to draw attention to themselves? What would motivate them to bring this attention on?

3. If you had the chance, would you share your personal situation live on a national TV talk show? Why or why not? What makes these kinds of talk shows so popular with the American public?

Biographical Internet Research

Find out about another historical figure in psychology online, selecting one from the following list, and share a biographical profile with your classmates:

- Dr. Laura Schlessinger
- Sigmund Freud
- Howard Gardner
- Howard Long

3. How are identical twins different from fraternal twins?
   a. Identical twins share 50 percent of genetic markers.
   b.) Identical twins develop from a single egg.
   c. Fraternal twins are always of the same gender.
   d. Identical twins share similar personalities.

4. What is the topic of this article?
   a. Identical twins are risky.
   b. Fraternal twins can be of different genders.
   c.) identical twins.
   d. twins and their parents.

SKILL FOCUS
Argument

Imagine you read the following claim in a newspaper or magazine article:

"Women live longer than men because they talk much more."

With a partner, answer the following questions about the above claim.

Collaboration

1. Would you believe the author's argument simply because you saw it in writing?

2. Would you be more likely to believe it if you learned that the person who said it was an expert? Explain.

3. What kind of proof or evidence would make such a claim more credible to you?

As we discussed in our focus on fact vs. opinion in Chapter 6, critical thinkers do not believe everything they read. Anyone can offer an argument, or a position on an issue, but a good reader, like a judge in a courtroom, will evaluate the strength of an argument based on the quality of the evidence given and on the logical reasoning used to support the claim. Note that when we discuss an author's argument, we are not referring to the more common definition of *argument* as a verbal dispute or disagreement, but as an author's opinion on an issue.

Recognizing an Author's Argument

Before you can evaluate the strength of an argument, you must first identify the issue being discussed and what the author's position is on the issue. Look at the example paragraph below.

Example
The new generation of parents are less likely to spank their kids than those of thirty or fifty years ago. Nowadays, at least in American culture, physical punishment of children is often viewed more as a sign of parental impatience than as a sign of parental attentiveness.

© Pearson Education, Inc.

What is the topic/issue being discussed? What argument is the author trying to make?

The issue under discussion is whether or not parents should spank their children. But if you said that the author's argument is that parents should not spank their children you are assuming an opinion the author clearly did not express.

The author's argument is that today's parents are less accepting of spanking kids than older generations used to be. There is no mention of this pediatrician's personal feeling about hitting kids. It may very well be the case that this pediatrician is discussing the change in societal views on spanking in order to build an argument that hitting your kids is wrong, but you would have to read more to find out if this is the direction the author is going.

It is important not to get distracted by your own personal view on an issue when trying to recognize an author's argument. A reader might feel strongly about a topic, let's say, that it is perfectly fine to spank kids, and misread the argument an author is putting forth.

Another helpful hint is to consider the identity of the author in relation to his or her position on an issue. So, for example, a corporate executive with Coca-cola might be more likely to argue in favor of maintaining soda in vending machines than a school principal would. The TV producer of a horror show is more likely make an argument in support of permitting violence on TV than would a concerned parent of three young children.

PRACTICING THE SKILL

After each of the following passages determine both the topic and the argument put forth by the writer.

Passage 1

If you've spent time with older adults, you've probably heard them make casual claims like, "My brain just doesn't work as well as it used to work." Researchers have believed for a long time that older brains function differently from younger brains. However, as brain-making techniques have become more available as research tools, an understanding of those changes has grown. Images of the brain at work reveal consistent differences in patterns of brain activity over the adult years.

(*Excerpted from the text* Psychology and Life, *Richard J. Gerrig and Philip G. Zimbardo, Discovering Psychology Edition, 18th ed. Boston: Pearson Allyn and Bacon, 2009, p. 320.*)

What is the topic?

the functioning of older brains

What is the author's argument?

There are differences in patterns of brain activity in older adults.

Passage 2

How do you decide when and what you should eat? To answer this question first think about the impact of culture. For example, people in the US typically eat three daily meals at set times; the timing of those meals relies more on social norms than on body cues. Moreover, people often choose what to eat based on social or cultural norms. Would you say "yes" if you were offered a free lobster dinner? Your answer might depend on whether you were an observant Jew (in which case you would say "no"), or a vegetarian (in which case your answer would still depend on whether you are the type of vegetarian who eats seafood).

(From *Psychology and Life*, p. 355)

What is the topic?

eating habits and culture

What is the author's argument?

Your culture has a great influence on your eating habits.

Passage 3

Why are some people happier than others? You might think this question has an easy answer: Aren't some people happier than others because better things happen to them? That's true, in part, but you might be surprised to learn that genetics has a large impact on how happy people are as they make their way through life.

(From *Psychology and Life*, p. 388)

What is the topic?

levels of happiness

What is the author's argument?

Genetics plays a role in individuals' level of happiness.

Passage 4

I'm not surprised that adults find children today to be spoiled—but I don't think this is a new phenomenon either. I think it's unfair to fault one single generation of such an old, historically common parent-child dynamic. The way I see it, in one fashion or another, we are all spoiled, but in different ways. Our society is such that everyone feels entitled, even parents.

(*from Mandela Gardner in an online blog, Seattlepi.com*)

What is the topic?

spoiled kids

What is the author's argument?

Everyone is spoiled, not just kids.

© Pearson Education, Inc.

Evaluating the Strength of an Author's Argument

Once you have identified the topic being discussed and determined the author's argument, then you may consider how credible, or believable, the author's claim is. Remember if the author's purpose is to persuade the reader of his or her general theory, opinion, or way of thinking, it is the author's responsibility to make a convincing case for the ideas put forth. It is the reader's responsibility to critically evaluate any arguments presented by the writer and to determine whether or not the author has made a strong case in support of his or her views.

Identify the Types of Support the Author Presents

Pay attention to how the author backs up his or her argument(s). The following is a short list of types of support authors make use of to back up an idea or claim.

Support for Arguments

1. **Fact-based. As discussed in Chapter 6, facts are "testable."**
   a. **Research results.** A writer might mention his or her or another researcher's study.
   b. **Statistics.** Using numerical data taken from survey work or other research models
   c. **Factual examples from the real world**. Citing reference facts (for example, "China is the most populous country in the world.")
   d. **Case studies**. Research focusing on formal observation

2. **Experiential-based**. Support coming from experience.
   a. **Logical reasoning.** An argument can grow from logical assumptions (for example, "If you take their bottles away while they are drinking, most babies will cry.")
   b. **Observations.** Many arguments are based on what we have seen and then analyzed (for example, "Once most five-year-olds realize that they are passing an ice cream shop, they are not going to let their parents go on without first demanding an ice cream.")
   c. **Expert viewpoints.** (for example, "There is a consensus among leading experts that hypnosis plays a critical role in the identification of criminal suspects.")

Consider Whether the Support Is Relevant

Sometimes an author will back up an argument with support that is not relevant to the point they are trying to make—that is, the support does not relate to their claim. Consider the following example.

Example

Clearly, the best way to deal with an alcohol problem is to see an addiction counselor.

Now, you might very well hold the same opinion as the author, but an argument should not be considered well-supported simply because you agree with it! The author might back up his or her claim by adding, "Studies have shown that the majority of addiction counselors have dealt with alcohol-related issues."

What is the connection between the fact that most addiction counselors often work with alcohol abusers AND the claim that seeing an addiction counselor is the best solution? If you can't find a connection, that's because there isn't any! Don't be fooled by weak reasoning.

Make a Final Evaluation: Is the Argument Logical and Believable?

To be believable, the author's argument must be based on logic or relevant evidence. If an author's argument seems shaky, spend a little more time with it and try to pinpoint what it is in the argument that you are skeptical about.

- Is the support not relevant to the claim?
- Is the author trying to persuade you with emotional argumentation that is not backed up by facts?
- Or does the argument go against something you already know to be true about the topic/issue?

Whatever the case, don't be shy to challenge arguments you come across in newspaper and magazine editorials and articles, textbook readings, nonfiction books, and other reading sources. Ask questions about what others say to be true, and check up on the "facts" they use to strengthen their claims.

PRACTICING THE SKILL

Read and evaluate these three passages, all on the topic of "bullies."

Passage 1

A bully can turn something like going to the bus stop or recess into a nightmare for kids. Bullying can leave deep emotional scars that last for life. And in extreme situations, it can culminate in violent threats, property damage, or someone getting seriously hurt.

If your child is being bullied, there are ways to help him or her cope with it on a day-to-day basis *and* lessen its lasting impact. And even if bullying isn't an issue right in your house right now, it's important to discuss it so your kids will be prepared if it does happen.

(*from Kids Health, http://kidshealth.org/parent/emotions/behavior/bullies.html. June 2007*)

Argument: *A bully can turn basic daily rituals into a nightmare for kids.*

Support Type for Argument: *logical reasoning, cause and effect*

Strength of Argument (your judgment from 1 to 5, with 5 being the highest): *Answers will vary.*

Justification for Your Evaluation: *Answers will vary. (Example: The argument is very logical and credible.)*

Passage 2

There are all kinds of reasons why young people bully others, either occasionally or often. Do any of these sound familiar to you?

© Pearson Education, Inc.

- Because I see others doing it
- Because it's what you do if you want to hang out with the right crowd
- Because it makes me feel, stronger, smarter, or better than the person I'm bullying
- Because it's one of the best ways to keep others from bullying me

Whatever the reason, bullying is something we all need to think about. Whether we've done it ourselves . . . or whether friends or other people we know are doing it . . . we all need to recognize that bullying has a terrible effect on the lives of young people. It may not be happening to you today, but it could tomorrow. Working together, we can make the lives of young people better.

(from "Why Do Kids Bully?" U.S. Department of Health and Human Services, Health Resources and Services Administration, http://stopbullyingnow.hrsa.gov/ kids/why-kids-bully.aspx)

Argument: *We must think more about bullying, its causes and solutions.*

Support Type for Argument: *Observation, logical reasoning, expert advice*

Strength of Argument (your judgment from 1 to 5): *Answers will vary*

Justification for Your Evaluation: *Answers will vary. (Example: The argument is very logical and credible.)*

Passage 3

Bullies are usually people who are just as uncomfortable as you are. Usually it's hard for them to make friends and the only way to get to know other people is by bullying them. Don't worry if you are being bullied, there are a lot of things you can do. You can talk to your parents and tell them what is going on. You could also go and talk to your teacher; your teacher is there to help you with your problems. You could also try to talk to the kid, maybe the bully didn't even realize that he (or she) was hurting you.

(from Danielle, a blogger on pbskids.org. © It's My Life, http://pbskids.org/ itsmylife)

Argument: *Bullies feel uncomfortable about their behavior.*

Argument: *There are a lot of things victims of bullies can do.*

Support Type for Argument: *observation, logical reasoning*

Strength of Argument (your judgment from 1 to 5): *Answers will vary.*

Justification for Your Evaluation: *Answers will vary. (Example: The argument is logical, but I would need more factual support on bullies being as uncomfortable as their victims.)*

The following Reading Selection will allow you to apply the skills learned in this chapter.

READING

Reading Selection **3**

Interview

8.6 Flesch-Kincaid Grade Level 7.4

Harvard Psychologist Howard Gardner, Interviewed on the *Pamela Wallin Show* (excerpt)

http://www.suite101.com/article.cfm/special_needs/20878/1

May 1, 1999

Howard Gardner, the Harvard psychologist who revolutionized our thinking with his **theory** of multiple intelligences in the early 80s, is now taking on the future of education.

As you read, identify all claims/arguments to the right of the **text** below, and briefly summarize what support the **author** offers to back up his claims. When you are finished compare your work with a partner.

*Can you give a shorthand **version** of your **theory** of multiple intelligences?*

1　Multiple intelligences is a psychological **theory** about the mind. It's a critique of the **notion** that there's a single **intelligence** which we're born with, which can't be changed, and which psychologists can measure. It's based on a lot of scientific **research** in fields ranging from **psychology** to anthropology to biology. It's not based on test correlations, which most other **intelligence** theories are based on.

2　The claim is that there are at least eight different human intelligences. Most **intelligence** tests look at language or **logic** or both. Those are just two of the intelligences. The other six are musical, spatial, bodily/kinestheic, interpersonal, intrapersonal, and naturalist.

3　I make two claims. The first claim is that all human beings have all of these intelligences. It's part of our species **definition**. The second claim is that, both because of our genetics and our **environment**, no two people have exactly the same profile of intelligences, not even **identical** twins, because their experiences are different.

Claim #1: *All human beings have all of these eight intelligences.*

Support for Claim: *It is part of the definition of the human species.*

4　This is where we **shift** from science to education. If we all have different kinds of minds, we have a choice. We can either ignore those differences and teach everybody the same stuff in the same way and assess everybody in the same way. Or we can say, look, people learn in different kinds of ways, and they have different intellectual strengths and weaknesses. Let's take that into account in how we teach and how we assess.

*So how should teachers who believe in your **theory** change their **approach** to teaching?*

Claim #2: *No two people have exactly the same profile of intelligences, not even identical twins.*

5　Multiple intelligences (MI) is a tool. It's not a goal. That means that you have to decide what you want to teach, and that should be based on what you think is important. Nowadays often it's other people who are telling us what to teach. That's not what I favor. But whoever makes the decisions, once those decisions are made, that's when MI can come into action.

Support for Claim: *both because of our genetics and our environment*

(Continued)

© Pearson Education, Inc.

Claim #3: *Understanding should be the goal of teaching.*

Support for Claim: *Teaching for understanding activates different intelligences.*

entails
involves, has something as a necessary part

6   In my own work, I'm a proponent of teaching for understanding, which means going deeply into topics so that students can really make use of knowledge in new situations. This is very, very different from most teaching, where people memorize material and can reproduce it on demand but can't make use of it in new situations. That's what understanding **entails.** If you favor education for understanding the way I do, then MI can be extremely helpful. Because when you are teaching a **topic,** you can **approach** the **topic** in many ways, **thereby** activating different intelligences. You can provide analogies and metaphors for different domains, invading different intelligences, and finally, you can present the key ideas in a number of different languages or symbol systems, again activating different intelligences.

7   But obviously you can't do that if you're going to spend five minutes on a **topic** and then move on to something else. Then you're almost constrained to present it one way, which is usually verbally, and to give people a short-answer test. You can see that I'm very much in opposition to the current state and national trends, which **create** more tests, often of a short-answer sort, favoring coverage or noncoverage and not probing deeply into what people really understand.

*Can standardized tests ever hope to measure children's full **intelligence?***

Claim #4: *Tests designed to measure people's intelligence are not very useful.*

Support for Claim: *What is important is the ability to demonstrate knowledge and understanding.*

jack it up
make something go higher

stacks up
compares, measures up; appears plausible or in keeping with the known facts

espoused
believed in and supported an idea, especially a political one

8   I'm not in favor of tests that are designed to measure people's **intelligence,** because frankly I don't care what **intelligence** or intelligences people have. I care whether they can do things which we value in our culture. What good is it to know if you have an IQ of 90 or 110 or even if you can **jack it up** to 120 through a lot of training if, in the end, you can't do anything.

9   I think our assessments ought to **focus** on the kinds of things we want people to understand, and they ought to give people a chance to perform their understandings. Because, at the end of the day, it doesn't matter if you have an IQ of 160 if you sit around and do nothing. What's important is whatever IQ you have or whatever profile of intelligences you have, that you can **demonstrate** knowledge and understanding of things that matter.

*How do you respond to those who say that MI **theory** is appealing, but there's no proof to back it up?*

Claim #5: *Multiple Intelligence (MI) methodology has produced better learning.*

Support for Claim: *Project Zero investigation of 42 schools using MI theory. There were better test scores and less absenteeism.*

10   There's no short answer to that question. To begin with, it's a scientific **theory,** and so it needs to be evaluated on the basis of the science on which it draws. And I think it does quite well in terms of the scientific **evidence,** even the **evidence** that's accumulated since the **theory** was first propounded 20 years ago. I have a new book coming out this fall called *Multiple Intelligences Reframed,* where in fact I discuss a few new intelligences, and also discuss the scientific **evidence** for it. So when people say it hasn't been proved, we first have to say what's the scientific evidence for and against it—and I think the scientific **evidence stacks up** pretty well.

11   Now, I've never **espoused** a particular program in schools. There are no Gardner schools, and there is no MI **approach.** So when people say it hasn't been proved, it's a senseless statement. What you have to say is, Has this particular **implementation** of MI **theory,** in this particular place, produced better student learning?

12   Mindy Kornhaber at **Project** Zero has been investigating 42 different schools which have been using MI **theory** for at least three years, and those schools report a lot of success with students, on both hard measures—how they do on tests—and on softer measures, like absenteeism and parental involvement.

13   When I was interviewed by *Time* magazine and asked about the effects of MI in schools, I was very cautious, because even if those schools are doing wonderfully, we don't know for sure whether it's because of MI. There are a hundred different things that could be going on in those schools.

14   I was criticized for being honest. The implication was that if I lied and said these schools are better and we know it's because of MI **theory**, then therefore the **theory** would have been proved correct.

15   So this question is much more detailed and **technical** than the question itself **implies**. But if you want a **flip answer**, the flip answer is, if we know the other approaches haven't worked because we wouldn't be in the situation we're in if they had, then you'd be a fool not to try something new.

flip answer
a quick reply, especially one not seriously thought out

16   But as I hope I've made clear to you, there isn't a single MI **approach**. Basically, the idea is if you value the differences among students and take them very seriously, that should have **implications** for how you present material. That's the only absolute implication from the **theory**. But whether you teach seven courses or eight courses or you teach something seven ways or eight ways, or you teach to strength or you teach to weakness, those are all decisions made by educators. They don't follow from the **theory**.

Are you working with any particular schools? Are you working with the Key School now?

17   I continue to have relationships with certain schools where I've known the people for a long time. One of them is the Key School, which is now called the Key Learning **Community**. Another is the New City School in St. Louis. I visit those schools on a regular basis. I will visit both schools this year again. But it's their school. It's not my school. And I take great pride when good things happen there, but I'm not **egocentric** enough to **assume** that it's because I make visits out there or because they've read my books. It's because they're good educators.

egocentric
caring onl about oneself, selfish

18   I think this is really important for your readers to understand, because most names they've heard of and most approaches they've heard of, somebody's got a line, so to speak, or a set of principles, so to speak, or a program or a package. I've got nothing like that. I've got a set of ideas, and I'm most interested when people use those ideas in ways that make sense to them, not when somebody else tells them you've got to teach this in seven different ways because Gardner says there's seven different intelligences.

How can people sort through all the MI stuff that's out there?

19   There's no point in doing anything with MI if you think you're doing a great **job**. You just keep doing what you're doing. It's when things aren't going as well as you want, when there are certain kids who you're not reaching, or you have kids who are excited but they're not able to

(Continued)

© Pearson Education, Inc.

demonstrate their understanding, then you've got a problem. That's when I think you should look at ideas like MI and see if they're useful.

20   I have another book coming out this year, called *The Disciplined Mind: What All Students Should Understand*. And in that book, I talk about what understanding is, and how elusive it is, and how we can **approach** deeper understanding for our kids. At the end of the book, I show how to take three topics, one from science (the **theory** of **evolution**), one from the arts (the music of Mozart), and one from history (the Holocaust), and really **engender** deep understandings by taking an MI **approach** very seriously. It's not only what I mentioned earlier the entry points, the analogies, and the model languages but also giving students lots of different ways of showing how they understand something.

21   I was once interviewed on radio about MI. I said I bet you could teach about the **Civil** War using dance, and I got lots of hate mail. I thought about it for a while, and I thought about the Spanish **Civil** War and the painting *Guernica*. And I said I bet you more people understand more about the Spanish **Civil** War from Picasso's *Guernica* than from reading the textbook on the **topic**. Almost anything can be illuminated in surprising ways if you open up your mind to the variety of intelligences.

22   Where is it said that the only way to learn about something is to read a **chapter** on it and answer a set of short-answer questions? Certainly in other countries, they don't do that. But part of our numerical, standardized test **bias** is many people think that's the only way to show something. And the greatest paradox is that people who were often the worst students when they were young are the ones who believe that the strongest, **whereas** people who were better students, who had more of a **liberal** arts education, understand that the questions we ask are more important than the answers that we come up with, and the more ways that we can think about something, the deeper our understanding is.

engender
give rise to

Claim #6: *It is possible to teach the Civil War using dance, or in a nontraditional way.*

Support for Claim: *The example of understanding the Spanish Civil War by studying Picasso's painting, Guernica*

Reading Comprehension Check

Inventory of Support/Evidence Offered: The Interview with Howard Gardner

Which of the following types of support did Dr. Gardner make use of to support his arguments? Check off the support types you saw in the article. Compare with a partner.

Types of Support for Argumentation

- [✓] **1.** Factual examples
- [✓] **2.** Statistics
- [✓] **3.** Mention of a study or a report
- [✓] **4.** Experiential examples
- [✓] **5.** Logical reasoning
- [✓] **6.** Opinion-based (emotional)

DEBATABLE TOPIC

Recommended Debate Topic: Can television be blamed for people's bad behavior?

   Brainstorm other debate topics related to psychology with your peers, and present your ideas to your instructor for approval.

Your suggested debate topics:

a. _____

b. _____

c. _____

The following articles will help prepare you for the debate as each takes a Pro or Con position on the debate topic.

No Debate: TV Violence Harms Kids

Pre-Reading Questions

Answer the following questions before exploring the text.

1. Why are violent TV shows so popular with young people?

2. Are violent youth naturally violent, or does their environment make them so? Explain.

3. If all TV violence were banned and all shows depicted only peaceful scenes, would youth violence disappear, or at least decrease dramatically?

As you read the article, consider how many arguments are offered, and the kinds of support given to back up these arguments.

READING

Reading Selection **4A**

(A Pro Argument)
Online Editorial

8.7 Flesch-Kincaid Grade Level 8.6

Collaboration

No Debate: TV Violence Harms Kids

By Linda S. Mintle, PhD,
http://DrLindaHelps.com

1 TV violence is harmful to kids. Practice these seven **strategies** to protect your kids.

2   TV violence is harmful to kids. The American Psychological Association's **Task** Force on Television and Society **published** a 1992 report stating there is a **link** between TV violence and aggression. We don't need more studies. We need **media** to pay attention to the reams of **data** we already have **available** on TV violence.

© Pearson Education, Inc.

3   Television violence has three **major** effects on children:

1. Increases in aggression. Studies of preschoolers who watched violent cartoons and other violent shows compared to children who didn't showed these differences: more arguing, disobeying of rules, uncompleted tasks and more **impulsivity**. **Furthermore**, Leonard Eron, Ph.D. from the University of Illinois, found that elementary age kids who watched lots of hours of TV were more aggressive as teenagers.

impulsivity
acting without thinking or planning

2. Kids are more fearful of the world. This is simply common sense but backed by **research**. George Gerbner, Ph.D. at the University of Pennslyvania, found that kids' TV shows contain about 20 acts of violence each hour. Watching these violent acts influence kids to view the world as a fearful place.

3. Kids are less sensitive to others. Watching violence makes you less bothered by it. And kids who watch violence are slower to get help for someone in trouble.

4   Knowing this, what can you as a parent do about TV violence?

- Be **aware** of **research** findings and make every effort to monitor your child's viewing habits.
- Limit the number of hours your child watches, i.e., limit **exposure**.
- Watch one episode of every program. This way you'll know the type and frequency of violence shown.
- Talk about what he/she sees. Ask what motivated the person to act violently and what were the effects of violent behavior on others?
- Turn off the TV or ban **specific** shows. This is not an extreme act considering what **exposure** does to kids.
- Encourage alternatives to TV viewing, preferably not violent video games or movies that have **similar negative** effects.
- Find programs that **demonstrate** healthy behavior and **positive** moral values.

5   Obviously, doing the above means you have to be **involved** in your child's life and take time to monitor and supervise **media**. Time is usually a parent's worst enemy, but the sacrifice is worth it.

6   You should also talk to other parents about what studies tell us. Many parents are simply unaware of the **negative** effects violent **media** have on their children and do not want to intentionally harm them. Point out the facts. The more we all know, the more we can do to curb violence in our society.

Reading Comprehension Check

1. What are a few arguments made by Dr. Mintle about TV and violence?
- Argument: _TV violence is harmful to kids._
- Argument: _TV violence has three major effects on children._
- Argument: _There are particular things parents can do to protect their children._

2. What types of evidence does she use to support her claims?

- Support Type: *mention of reports made by scholars*
- Support Type: *statistical*
- Support Type: *experiential, based on the author's expertise in the field*

TV Violence Doesn't Lead to Aggressive Kids, Study Says

READING

Reading Selection **4B**

(A Con Argument)
Journal Article

8.8 Flesch-Kincaid Grade Level 12.0

Collaboration

Pre-Reading Questions

With a partner, answer the theme-related questions below.

1. Do you believe it is possible that some children are born naturally aggressive? Explain.

2. What are some possible factors that might lead a child to behavioral problems in school?

3. How much do people change from childhood to adulthood? Do you believe that most aggressive children grow up to be aggressive adults? Explain.

TV Violence Doesn't Lead to Aggressive Kids, Study Says

Joan Oleck, *School Library Journal*

May 23, 2007

1 Violent television does not lead to violent children, says a new **research** paper from the **Media Institute**, countering a recent, much-heralded report from the **Federal** Communications **Commission** (FCC) stating that the opposite is true.

2 "Television Violence and Aggression: Setting the Record Straight," **refutes** an April FCC report that called for laws to curb certain television content for children.

refutes
proves that a statement or idea is not correct or fair

3 "The **debate** is not over," writes Jonathan Freedman, **author** of the paper and a professor of **psychology** at the University of Toronto, who also criticizes both the American Academy of Pediatrics and the American Psychological Association for wrongly characterizing **previous** studies of TV's effects on children. The pediatrics group in particular, he says, used "wildly inaccurate figures" in its studies.

4 "I don't think this kind of television affects children's aggression at all," Freedman, who has been studying children and television for two **decades**, told *SLJ*. "Some kids may get very excited and look like they're more aggressive because they're very excited. But if they watch some nonviolent program,

© Pearson Education, Inc.

Joan Oleck, "TV Violence Doesn't Lead to Aggressive Kids, Study Says," *School Library Journal*, May 23, 2007. Copyright © 2007 Reed Business Information, a division of Reed Elsevier Inc.

correlation
a relationship between two ideas, facts, etc., especially when one may be the cause of the other

whatever that means, **plus** some very active lively program, they'll probably behave the same way."

5   Citing the many studies examining the effect of violence on children, Freedman in his **research** paper acknowledges a kind of **correlation**: the more violence children watch, the more aggressive they become. But he emphasizes that that finding does not equate to a causal relationship.

6   "The most likely explanation of the relationship is that some children are more aggressive in general than others and that the more aggressive children prefer violent television, watch and play more aggressive games, and act more aggressively themselves," Freedman writes.

7   "The **evidence** is not overwhelming" for a causal **link**, says the paper, released by the Arlington, VA-based nonprofit **research foundation**, which specializes in **media issues**. "Instead it provides no good reason to believe that television violence causes aggression, much less serious violence."

Reading Comprehension Check

1. What argument is reported on by Joan Oleck about TV and Violence?
   - Argument: _Violent television does not lead to violent children._

2. What types of evidence does she use to support her claims?
   - Support Type: _past studies on the subject_
   - Support Type: _logical reasoning_

Connecting Reading Skills with Standardized Testing

Recognizing and Evaluating Argument

The key to recognizing author's arguments is to first understand what issue or topic is being addressed. Then to ask yourself, what position does the author take on this issue? In evaluating support for an argument, you are most likely to be asked to distinguish between fact-based and emotionally based support. You may also be tested on your ability to locate the exact type of support utilized by the author—for example, a research study, a survey, observation, logical reasoning, etc.

Exam questions focusing on argument may be phrased:

- In this reading passage, the author claims that . . .
- The author's position on this issue is . . .
- The passage suggests that the author supports the view that . . .
- Which type of support is offered for the author's claim that . . .
- Which statement offers the best support for the author's claim that . . .

Helpful Hints: Test Questions on Argument

- Make sure you first understand the literal meaning of the passage clearly. What is the topic and the main idea? What issue or issues are being discussed?
- Consider the author's purpose. Is he or she making arguments (persuasive purpose) or reporting other's claims (informing)?
- Look for opinions and ideas (these claims demand evidence!).
- Look for specific illustrations or examples of the author's claim.
- Check to make sure that the author's claim is logical and based on fact.

From Reading to Writing: Keeping Double-entry Reading Journals

The critical point has been made often in this book that the more you actively engage with a reading, the more likely you are to connect with it, to understand it fully, and to enjoy it. One way to interact with text is by keeping a "reading journal." A reading journal is basically a space to share your thoughts, ask questions and respond to ideas and points you find particularly interesting about a text you are reading. Reading journals work very well with extended reading material, such as novels and nonfiction books, and textbooks as well. In this section, we will discuss a number of ways you can work with a reading journal.

Reading Journals as a Set of Personal Reactions/Responses to Reading

When you read, it is natural to have a variety of responses to the ideas in the text. You may agree or disagree with a point made, an example mentioned may remind you of something that happened to you, or you may find a quote that you emotionally connect with.

It is useful when responding to text to keep a 'double-entry' journal. That is, to consistently use the left page of the notebook for one purpose, and the right side page for another. In the example below, the left side is used to copy a section of a text that the reader found interesting, and the right side is the personal reaction. You may remember this unit's first reading, "Why and How do People Lie."

Double-Entry Journal Example

Text	Reaction
"Let's focus on the mental processes that people use to lie." Should it be easier or harder for people to tell a lie than to tell the truth?	I think it is definitely easier to lie. Sometimes I think that telling the truth will get me into more trouble. At the same time I feel bad when I am dishonest.

(From Richard J. Gerrig and Philip G. Zimbardo, from "Why and How Do People Lie?" from Psychology and Life, *Discovering Psychology Edition, 18th ed. Boston: Pearson Allyn and Bacon, 2009, p. 249)*

© Pearson Education, Inc.

Who is the audience for your reading journal? Mainly, you are. Keeping a reading journal gives you an opportunity to have a conversation with the text. Sometimes, instructors will collect journals weekly, and may serve as another "audience" for your journal responses.

Reading Journals as a Way of Both Responding to Text and Communicating with Your Teacher about What You are Reading

In the example below, a student responds to a section of a reading (from the article you read on the Barber twins) on the right side and the teacher subsequently adds comments on the left side.

Teacher Response	Student Journal Entry
Yes, this was a nice example of how different identical twins' personalities can be. In the reading that follows this one, "Why Are Identical Twins Different," the author shows how the stereotype of identical twins being identical is far from the reality.	"Ronde could adapt to being a New Yorker. Whereas, with no disrespect to Tampa, Tiki would jump out the window if he lived there." (From *Read to Succeed*, Chap. 8, p. 444) I loved this example about different perspectives on living in a big city. It captures their personality differences. My sister and I are opposites in the same way.

Reading Journals as a Way to Ask Questions about Confusing Concepts or Difficult Terminology

Why hide from what you do not completely understand? It may be helpful to make note in your reading journal of some confusing points in the text. If your instructor will be looking at it, this gives you a chance to have some of your questions answered. You can also make use of your reading journal in class by asking about some of the points you raised while preparing the journal entry at home. See the example below from our textbook application reading (beginning on page 466). On the right is the student's response, and on the left is the instructor's response.

Teacher Response	Student Question/Concern
Good question. I think the writer is trying to make the point that it is the goal of psychologists in making professional observations to consider both their personal insight based on knowledge of the field together with what they have learned from past research. The example of the master detective is a good one.	I am not sure I understand the section (Explaining What Happens) on p. 468–469 (para. 2) about well-trained psychologists and their role in making observations. It was a little confusing.

Dr. Charlene Bang

Profession: Psychologist, James J. Peters VA Medical Center (Bronx, New York)

How did you choose your current profession?

I emigrated from Seoul, Korea, to the United States when I was 9 years old. I only knew a few words of English, "Hi," "Hello," and "Thank you." I was placed in the fourth grade in an all-white school in a small town in Pennsylvania. It was a tremendous struggle for me to adjust to this new and foreign environment due to both cultural differences and limited English proficiency. It took me at least six months for me to feel somewhat comfortable to socialize with my classmates and neighborhood kids with whom I began to play after school. In retrospect, I did the best I could to adjust and respond to the immigration and the new environment. Even at a young age, I was curious about how others responded to various new situations as I witnessed my older siblings' different and somewhat rebellious responses to the immigration. In high school, I had an opportunity to take a psychology course, during which I began to learn about human and animal responses to various environment and situations. I knew then I wanted to continue to pursue psychology to satisfy my forever increasing curiosity of human behavior.

How did you prepare to reach your goal of becoming a psychologist?

In addition to majoring in psychology and taking all required courses, I needed to overcome my fears of speaking and writing English as I quickly learned there were many presentations and writing required as a psychology major. Initially, I had many doubts about my oral presentation and writing abilities. However, I took advantage of resources (e.g., tutors, writing workshops) that were available in college. As time passed with perseverance, hard work, and improved self-confidence, I believed I would be able to overcome my fears of writing and presenting and also believed I would be able to accomplish my goal of becoming a psychologist.

What did you struggle with most when preparing to become a psychologist?

There were several challenges I needed to overcome, including low self-confidence, learning English, and completing and presenting an independent research. Completing my doctoral dissertation and oral presentation of the study were struggles. However, I knew in my mind that if I could have the strength to adjust to a new culture and learn a new language, that I could overcome challenges of completing my dissertation and oral presentation of the study.

How did you overcome/get through this struggle?

In addition to perseverance, hard work, and believing in myself, I had a great mentor who guided me each step of the way and who gave me confidence that my dissertation was possible. And of course, he encouraged me to present over and over again until I felt comfortable. I have to say having someone to guide me through the tough times was a tremendous help. In addition, I practiced, practiced, and practiced . . . oh and I practiced . . . presenting the research until I got tired of hearing my own voice.

What do you enjoy most about your work?

I currently work with veterans from various wars, many who are young, who fought and were wounded in Iraq and Afghanistan. I enjoy learning about each one of my patients' life stories as each person brings unique and special background, personality, strengths, and weaknesses. Many suffered physical and emotional traumas and teaching the veterans better coping skills and providing services that may help them to reintegrate into civilian life are extremely gratifying. Even if I can help just one veteran, I am grateful I had the opportunity to do so and all my hard work was all worthwhile.

What advice do you have for a student considering a career in psychology?

Learn to be curious about each person's life story as each person comes with different and interesting background. Learn to be nonjudgmental of each patient whom you meet and treat. Appreciate different cultural, religious, philosophical backgrounds with different beliefs and values. Think flexibly with an open mind as novel and creative approaches can serve as wonderful treatments. Have passion for the field of psychology and passion for working with special and unique individuals, as an opportunity to help each individual is a privilege every time.

In your opinion what were the three most interesting points made by the interviewee? Discuss your choices with the class.

- _____
  _____
- _____
  _____
- _____
  _____

© Pearson Education, Inc.

Practicing Reader Response

The final reading of this chapter (on p. 473) is taken from an online advice column for students. There are two advice letters and responses. Choose one of the letters, read it carefully, and write a paragraph reaction to what you have read. You can ask questions or share your personal feelings about the reading. Your instructor may ask you to write your response in a double-entry reading journal notebook.

Textbook Application

Read the following selection from the introductory chapter of the textbook, *Psychology and Life,* and try to correctly answer the multiple-choice questions which follow. Once again, it may be helpful to highlight key points in the reading as you work with the passage.

READING

Reading Selection **5**

Textbook Reading

From *Psychology and Life* (Discovering Psychology Edition, 18th ed. Boston: Pearson Allyn and Bacon, 2009, pp. 4–8) by Richard J. Gerrig and Philip G. Zimbardo

WHAT MAKES PSYCHOLOGY UNIQUE?

To appreciate the uniqueness and unity of **psychology**, you must consider the way psychologists define the field and the **goals** they bring to their **research** and applications. By the end of the book, we hope you will think like a psychologist. In this first **section**, we'll give you a strong idea of what that might mean.

DEFINITIONS

Many psychologists seek answers to this **fundamental** question: What is human nature? **Psychology** answers this question by looking at processes that **occur** within individuals as well as forces that arise within the **physical** and social **environment**. In this light, we formally define **psychology** as the scientific study of the behavior of individuals and their **mental** processes. Let's explore the critical parts of this **definition**: *scientific, behavior, individual,* and *mental.*

The scientific aspect of **psychology** requires that psychological conclusions be based on **evidence** collected according to the principles of the scientific **method**. The

scientific method consists of a set of orderly steps used to analyze and solve problems. This **method** uses objectively collected information as the factual basis for drawing conclusions. We will elaborate on the **features** of the scientific **method** more fully in **Chapter** 2, when we consider how psychologists **conduct** their **research**.

Behavior is the means by which organisms adjust to their **environment**. Behavior is action. The subject matter of **psychology** largely consists of the observable behavior of humans and other species of animals. Smiling, crying, running, hitting, talking, and touching are some **obvious** examples of behavior you can observe. Psychologists examine what the **individual** does and how the **individual** goes about doing it within a given behavioral setting and in the broader social or **cultural context**.

The subject of psychological **analysis** is most often an *individual*—a newborn infant, a teenage athlete, a college student adjusting to life in a dormitory, a man facing a midlife career change, or a woman coping with the **stress** of her husband's deterioration from Alzheimer's disease. However, the subject might also be a chimpanzee learning to use symbols to communicate, a white rat navigating a

From Richard J. Gerrig and Philip G. Zimbardo, *Psychology and Life,* Discovering **Psychology Edition,** 18th ed., pp. 4-8. © 2008, 2005, 2002 Pearson Education, Inc. Reproduced by permission of Pearson Education, Inc.

maze, or a sea slug responding to a danger signal. An **individual** might be studied in its natural habitat or in the controlled conditions of a **research** laboratory.

Many researchers in **psychology** also recognize that they cannot understand human actions without also understanding *mental processes,* the workings of the human mind. Much human activity takes place as private, **internal** events—thinking, planning, reasoning, creating, and dreaming. Many psychologists believe that **mental** processes represent the most important aspect of psychological inquiry. As you shall soon see, psychological investigators have devised ingenious **techniques** to study **mental** events and processes—to make these private experiences public.

The combination of these concerns defines **psychology** as a **unique** field. Within the *social sciences,* psychologists **focus** largely on behavior in individuals, **whereas** sociologists study the behavior of people in groups or institutions, and anthropologists **focus** on the broader **context** of behavior in different cultures. Even so, psychologists draw broadly from the **insights** of other scholars. Psychologists share many interests with researchers in *biological sciences,* especially with those who study brain processes and the biochemical bases of behavior. As part of the emerging **area** of *cognitive science,* psychologists' questions about how the human mind works are related to **research** and **theory** in **computer** science, artificial **intelligence,** and applied mathematics. As a *health science*—with links to medicine, education, law, and environmental **studies**—**psychology** seeks to improve the quality of each individual's and the collective's well-being.

Most psychological study focuses on individuals—usually human ones, but sometimes those of other species. What **aspects** of your own life would you like psychologists to study?

© Pearson Education, Inc.

Although the remarkable breadth and depth of modern **psychology** are a **source** of delight to those who become psychologists, these same attributes make the field a **challenge** to the student exploring it for the first time. There is so much more to the study of **psychology** than you might expect initially—and, because of that, there will also be much of value that you can take away from this introduction to **psychology**. The best way to learn about the field is to learn to share psychologists' **goals**. Let's consider those **goals**.

THE GOALS OF PSYCHOLOGY

The **goals** of the psychologist conducting basic **research** are to describe, explain, predict, and control behavior. These **goals** form the basis of the psychological enterprise. What is **involved** in trying to **achieve** each of them?

Describing What Happens The first **task** in psychology is to make **accurate** observations about behavior. Psychologists typically refer to such observations as their *data* (*data* is the plural, *datum* the singular). **Behavioral data** are reports of observations about the behavior of organisms and the conditions under which the behavior occurs. When researchers undertake data collection, they must choose an **appropriate** *level of analysis* and devise measures of behavior that **ensure** *objectivity*.

In order to investigate an individual's behavior, researchers may use different *levels of analysis*—from the broadest, most **global** level down to the most minute, specific level. Suppose, for example, you were trying to describe a painting you saw at a museum (see **Figure 1.1**). At a global level, you might describe it by title, *Bathers*, and by artist, Georges Seurat. At a more **specific** level, you might recount **features** of the painting: Some people are sunning themselves on a riverbank while others are enjoying the water, and so on. At a very **specific** level, you might describe the technique Seurat used—tiny points of paint—to create the scene. The description at each level would answer different questions about the painting.

Different levels of psychological description also address different questions. At the broadest level of psychological **analysis**, researchers investigate the behavior of the whole person within **complex** social and **cultural** contexts. At this level, researchers might study **cross-cultural** differences in violence, the origins of prejudice, and the **consequences** of **mental** illness. At the next level, psychologists **focus** on narrower, finer units of behavior, such as speed of **reaction** to a stop light, eye movements during reading, and grammatical errors made by children acquiring language. Researchers can study even smaller units of behavior. They might work to discover the biological bases of behavior by identifying the places in the brain where different types of memories are stored, the biochemical changes that **occur** during learning, and the sensory paths responsible for **vision** or hearing. Each level of **analysis** yields information essential to the **final** composite portrait of human nature that psychologists hope **ultimately** to develop.

However tight or broad the **focus** of the observation, psychologists strive to describe behavior *objectively*. Collecting the facts as they exist, and not as the researcher expects or hopes them to be, is of utmost importance. Because every observer brings to each observation his or her *subjective* point of view—biases, prejudices, and expectations—it is essential to prevent these personal **factors** from creeping in and distorting the **data**. As you will see in the next **chapter**, psychological researchers have developed a variety of **techniques** to maintain objectivity.

Explaining What Happens Whereas *descriptions* must stick to perceivable information, *explanations* deliberately go beyond what can be observed. In many areas of psychology, the central goal is to find regular patterns in behavioral and mental processes. Psychologists want to discover *how* behavior works. Why do you laugh at situations that differ from your expectations of what is coming next? What conditions could lead someone to attempt suicide or commit rape?

Explanations in **psychology** usually recognize that most behavior is influenced by a combination of **factors**. Some **factors** operate within the **individual**, such

FIGURE 1.1 • Levels of Analysis

Suppose you wanted a friend to meet you in front of this painting. How would you describe it? Suppose your friend wanted to make an exact copy of the painting. How would you describe it?

as genetic makeup, **motivation**, **intelligence** level, or self-esteem. These inner determinants tell something special about the organism. Other **factors**, however, operate externally. Suppose, for example, that a child tries to please a teacher in order to win a prize or that a motorist trapped in a traffic jam becomes frustrated and hostile. These behaviors are largely influenced by events outside the person. When psychologists seek to explain behavior, they almost always consider both types of explanations. Suppose, for example, psychologists want to explain why some people start smoking. Researchers might examine the possibility that some individuals are particularly prone to risk taking (an **internal** explanation) or that some individuals experience a lot of peer pressure (an **external** explanation)—or that both a disposition toward risk taking and situational peer pressure are necessary (a combined explanation).

Often a psychologist's goal is to explain a wide variety of behavior in terms of one **underlying** cause. Consider a situation in which your teacher says that to earn a good **grade**, each student must participate regularly in class discussions. Your roommate, who is always well prepared for class, never raises his hand to answer questions or volunteer information. The teacher chides him for being unmotivated and assumes he is not bright. That same roommate also goes to parties but never asks anyone to dance, doesn't openly defend his point of view when it is challenged by someone less informed, and rarely engages in small talk at the dinner table. What is your diagnosis? What **underlying** cause might account for this **range** of behavior? How about *shyness*? Like many other people who suffer from intense feelings of shyness, your roommate is unable to behave in desired ways (Zimbardo & Radl, 1999). We can use the **concept** of shyness to explain the full pattern of your roommate's behavior.

To forge such causal explanations, researchers must often engage in a creative **process** of examining a diverse collection of data. Master detective Sherlock Holmes drew shrewd conclusions from scraps of **evidence**. In a **similar** fashion, every researcher must use an informed imagination, which creatively *synthesizes* what is known and what is not yet known. A well-trained psychologist can explain observations by using her or his insight into the human experience along with the facts **previous** researchers have uncovered about the **phenomenon** in question. Much psychological **research** attempts to determine which of several explanations most accurately accounts for a given behavioral pattern.

Predicting What Will Happen   Predictions in psychology are statements about the likelihood that a certain behavior will occur or that a given relationship will be found. Often an accurate explanation of the causes underlying some form of behavior will allow a researcher to make accurate predictions about future behavior. Thus, if we believe your roommate to be shy, we could confidently predict that he would be uncomfortable when asked to have a conversation with a stranger. When different explanations are put forward to account for some behavior or relationship, they are usually judged by how well they can make accurate and comprehensive predictions. If your roommate was to blossom in contact with a stranger, we would be forced to rethink our diagnosis.

Just as observations must be made objectively, scientific predictions must be worded precisely enough to **enable** them to be tested and then **rejected** if the **evidence** does not support them. Suppose, for example, a researcher predicts that the presence of a stranger will reliably cause human and monkey babies, beyond a certain age, to respond with signs of anxiety. We might want to bring more precision to this prediction by examining the dimension of "stranger." Would fewer signs of anxiety appear in a human or a monkey baby if the stranger were also a baby rather than an adult, or if the stranger were of the same species rather than of

What causes people to smoke? Can psychologists create conditions under which people will be less likely to engage in this behavior?

© Pearson Education, Inc.

PSYCHOLOGY IN YOUR LIFE

CAN PSYCHOLOGY HELP FIND ME A CAREER?

If you've ever had a **job** you didn't like, you probably know a lot about what it means to suffer from a lack of **motivation:** You can hardly stand the idea of reporting to work; every minute seems like an hour. An important part of having a successful career is finding a work setting that provides the types of challenges and rewards that fit your motivational needs. It probably will not surprise you that researchers have studied the match between vocations and people's **individual** personalities, values, and needs.

To remain motivated for career success, you would like to have a **job** that suits your interests and serves **goals** that you consider worthwhile. A widely used test for measuring vocational interests is the *Strong Interest Inventory,* which was originated in 1927 by psychologist **Edward Strong.** To construct the test, Strong first asked groups of men in different occupations to answer **items** about activities they liked or disliked. Then the answers given by those who were successful in

particular occupations were compared with the responses of men in general to **create** a scale. Subsequent versions of the test, including a 2004 update, have added scales **relevant** to women and to newer occupations. The Strong Interest Inventory is quite successful at relating people's likes and dislikes to **appropriate** occupations (Hansen & Dik, 2005). If you take this test, a vocational counselor could tell you what types of jobs are typically held by people with interests such as yours because these are the jobs that are likely to appeal to you.

Suppose you have gotten this sort of advice about what career to **pursue.** How do you **select** a particular company to join—and how does that company **select** you? Researchers in *personnel psychology* have focused a good deal of attention on the **concept** of *person–organization fit*—the goal is to maximize the compatibility between people and the organizations that employ them (Dineen et al., 2002; Van Vianen, 2000). One research project has focused on the match

between people's personalities and the "culture" of organizations. Consider the personality factor called Agreeableness, which encodes a continuum from "sympathetic and kind" to "cold and quarrelsome" (see Chapter 13). Consider, also, a continuum of organizational cultures from those that are supportive and **team** oriented to those that are aggressive and outcome oriented. Do you see how these **dimensions** line up? **Research** suggests that job seekers who score high on Agreeableness will prefer organizations that are culturally supportive and **team** oriented (Judge & Cable, 1997). **Research** of this type suggests why it is not just your own motivational states that matter for career success: The extent to which your preferences for achieving **goals** match the organization's preferences matters as well.

So, what career path will keep you motivated for success? As with so many of life's dilemmas, psychologists have carried out **research** that can help you make this important decision.

a different one? To improve future predictions, a researcher would **create** systematic variations in environmental conditions and observe their influence on the baby's **response.**

Controlling What Happens   For many psychologists, control is the central, most powerful goal. Control means making behavior happen or not happen—starting it, maintaining it, stopping it, and influencing its form, strength, or rate of occurrence. A causal explanation of behavior is convincing if it can create conditions under which the behavior can be controlled.

A psychological prediction

Reading Comprehension Check

Supporting Detail

1. Which is NOT offered as a critical part of a definition of psychology?
   a. individual.
   b. behavior.
   c. mental.
   d. physiological.

Supporting Detail

2. Smiling, crying, running, hitting, and talking are mentioned as examples of
   a. signals.
   b. disguised behavior.
   c. observable behavior.
   d. movement.

Vocabulary

3. *Mental processes* is defined as
   a. psychological analysis.
   b. human actions.
   c. the workings of the human mind.
   d. both b and c.

Fact vs. Opinion

4. Is the following a fact or opinion? "Mental processes represent the most important aspect of psychological inquiry."
   a. an opinion.
   b. a fact.
   c. both fact and opinion.
   d. neither fact or opinion.

Inference

5. Sociology and Anthropology are mentioned
   a. as fields of social science with different foci than psychology.
   b. as similar fields.
   c. as more related to biological sciences.
   d. as examples within the field of psychology.

Vocabulary

6. The word *emerging*, in the sentence "As part of the emerging area of cognitive science," (p. 467), means
   a. deflated.
   b. rising.
   c. stagnant.
   d. neutral.

Supporting Detail

7. Which is NOT a goal of psychologists conducting research?
   a. to explain.
   b. to predict.
   c. to respond.
   d. to control behavior.

Supporting Details

8. The example of describing a painting is used to illustrate the concept of
   a. varying levels of analysis.
   b. equal analysis.
   c. individual perspective.
   d. questioning.

© Pearson Education, Inc.

Argument

9. Which of the following from the passage can be classified as an author's argument?
   a. Often a psychologist's goal is to explain a wide variety of behavior in terms of one underlying cause.
   b. Your roommate never raises his hand.
   c. Predictions are statements about the likelihood that a certain behavior will occur.
   d. all of the above.

Argument

10. What kind of support is offered for the author's claim that "scientific predictions must be worded precisely enough to enable them to be tested . . . "
    a. emotional.
    b. factual examples.
    c. both emotional and factual examples.
    d. not enough information is given to answer the question.

Patterns of Organization

11. Read the first paragraph of the section Controlling What Happens. What pattern(s) of organization is used in the first paragraph?
    a. definition and example.
    b. chronological order.
    c. compare/contrast.
    d. cause and effect.

Patterns of Organization

12. Which pattern of organization is used in the following passage, taken from the second paragraph of the section Psychology in Your Life? ". . . to construct the test, Strong **first** asked groups of men in different occupations to answer items about activities they liked and disliked. **Then** the answers given by those who were successful in particular occupations were compared with the responses of men in general to create a scale."
    a. definition and example.   c. listing.
    b. compare/contrast.   d. chronological order.

Author's Tone

13. What is the author's tone throughout this textbook chapter?
    a. optimistic.   c. sarcastic.
    b. mostly objective.   d. condescending.

Author's Purpose

14. What is the author's purpose in writing this text?
    a. to persuade.   c. to interrogate.
    b. to entertain.   d. to inform.

Main Idea

15. What is the main idea of the section Psychology in Your Life: Can Psychology
Help Find Me A Career?

   a. personality and career.
   b. There are psychological tests that can match your personality to careers
   that suit you.
   c. Edward Strong created an inventory to explore career interests.
   d. Whatever career path you choose, you will be successful.

READING

Reading Selection **6**

Additional Reading

Online Advice Column

8.9 Flesch-Kincaid Grade Level 11.5

Collaboration

Go Ask Alice! Phobias

Pre-Reading Questions

   1. Do you know of someone who is afflicted with a social phobia? Explain.

   2. Who should a new college student, living away from home, turn to if he or
   she feels emotionally troubled? What are some options open to the student?

   3. Do you believe that online advice columns, or online therapy, can be effective,
   or do you think if someone needs help it is better to talk person-to-person?
   Explain.

Go Ask Alice! Phobias

From Columbia University's Health Q & A Internet Resource

April 13, 2001

1. Dear Alice,

1   I have suffered from agoraphobia since the age of thirteen. I am now twenty.
I have tried **hypnotherapy** counseling and psychologists and herbal tablets,
but nothing seems to help me. Please, can you help a young, outgoing twenty-
year-old who wants to start living!

hypnotherapy
treatment of a health condition by
inducing prolonged sleep

Dear Reader,

2   It is understandable that you are frustrated with the **impact** that agoraphobia
has had on your life. As you have probably realized, it can take time to figure
out the best possible course of treatment. Agoraphobia is a disorder characterized by intense anxiety about having a panic episode in places or situations
from which escape could be challenging or uncomfortable. Some people

Reprinted with permission from Go Ask Alice!, Columbia University's Health Q&A Internet
Resource, at www.goaskalice.columbia.edu. Copyright © 2008 by The Trustees of Columbia
University.

© Pearson Education, Inc.

experience agoraphobia as a fear that stems from not being able to receive **assistance** during an anxiety attack. For **instance**, many people with agoraphobia fear leaving their homes alone, being in a large gathering of people, being on a bridge, or riding in various vehicles.

doom
a feeling that there is no hope for the future

3   Agoraphobia frequently is associated with other anxiety disorders, including panic disorder and **specific** phobias. Panic attacks are intense feelings of fear and often **doom**, which usually build and peak within about ten minutes of onset. Some of the most typical symptoms of a panic attack include:

- chest pain and/or heart palpitations
- trembling
- feeling faint or dizzy
- shortness of breath or difficulty catching your breath
- fear of dying
- fear of losing control
- sweating
- feeling nauseated
- strange sensations: numbness, tingling, pricking, or burning

out of the blue
an event that occurs unexpectedly

4   These attacks can be terrifying and physically overwhelming. (People experiencing panic attacks often rush to the emergency room **convinced** that they are having a heart attack.) Sometimes the attacks are prompted by a particular experience, and sometimes they seem to come **out of the blue**. Once a person has had some panic attacks, they may begin to fear having one in public and thus develop an additional panic **reaction** to these situations, and therefore, agoraphobia.

5   It's important to be as **specific** as possible when describing your experiences to your health care provider(s). This will help them to determine, with

your help, what kinds of treatment approaches might be right for you. They're likely to ask you questions such as:

- How long have you been experiencing these symptoms?
- Are there particular situations that cause you anxiety?
- How significantly do you feel your anxiety impairs your ability to **function** on a day-to-day basis?
- What are the treatments you've tried so far? What did you like about them, and what didn't seem to have an effect?

6   Also, keep in mind that although you may not have had much success with certain therapists or therapies, that doesn't mean that you couldn't find the right treatment with another therapist.

7   Some possibilities that you may want to consider with your health care provider include cognitive behavioral therapy and/or medication. **Research** has shown these treatments to be very effective in treating panic attacks and agoraphobia. Cognitive behavioral therapy is essentially just what it sounds like: an **approach** that aims to change behavior by helping a person adjust his or her way of thinking. It often includes real or imagined **exposure** (in a protected **environment**) to the situations or triggers that cause the fear. Over time, a person can learn to understand and therefore manage the fear that comes with being confronted with the traumatic object or situation and identify what **maladaptive** coping mechanisms have arisen. In doing so, that person can develop new, more reasonable ways of managing **stress**.

maladaptive
marked by faulty or inadequate adaptation

8   The National **Institute** of Mental **Health** (NIMH) reports that treatment can reduce or *completely eliminate* panic attacks in 70 to 90 **percent** of cases. (Early treatment can also help avoid the progression of panic disorder to agoraphobia.) The NIMH web **site** contains more information about treatment options and referrals to help find a therapist who specializes in treating agoraphobia. You can also **contact** the Anxiety Disorders Association of America for more information.

9   Your persistence in seeking help is commendable. With your determination to get your life back, and a good therapist who's knowledgeable about your particular concerns, there is a lot of hope.

Alice

2. Dear Alice,

January 11, 2002

10   I have social anxiety disorder and was wondering how it would be possible to see someone for help without my parents knowing about it. I know that they'd be anything but supportive. They would think I'm absolutely insane. The truth is, I've put off dealing with it, acting as if it'll just go away or that I'll outgrow it. But in reality, the older I'm getting, the worse I'm getting. I avoid as many social situations as I can. I completely panic when meeting new people. I only stay in classes that don't require any talking on my part. I've dropped so many of my classes already that I don't know what to do. It seems the only place I'm actually happy is at home or with people that I've known all my life. I want to see someone, hoping they can prescribe something for me. I'd also like to talk

© Pearson Education, Inc.

to someone and figure out where all this anxiety is coming from. Is there anyway that I can do to **achieve** this? I'm a student, currently unemployed, under my parent's insurance. . . . hope u can help!

Dear Reader,

11   About 5 million Americans have some form of social anxiety disorder, also known as social phobia. While everyone experiences nervousness or fear in social situations to a certain extent, those with social anxiety disorder are **debilitated** by their fear. They may have a **constant**, intense, and chronic fear of being watched and judged by others, or be terribly afraid of being embarrassed or humiliated by ways in which they behave. As you have described, this fear can prevent people with social anxiety disorder from doing everyday activities, such as going to school or work, and can become so much of a **focus** that they severely limit their socializing.

debilitated
made weak in body or mind

12   It's understandable that you are worried about how your parents might react to knowing what's been going on for you. Many people think that their families will blame them for how they're feeling or belittle their concerns. Being honest with your parents, however, might help you to feel more at ease; it's possible that they've noticed your behavior and wondered about it, or even struggled with **similar** feelings themselves. There's even some **evidence** that anxiety disorders may be genetic or run in families—perhaps due to environmental **factors** and patterns expressed through interpersonal interactions. Once you seek help, one of the things you can work on is deciding if you might want to discuss your social anxiety with your family, and if so, **strategies** for doing this that will be comfortable for you. Perhaps showing them this answer will help you describe your situation to them, and get any doubters to take you more seriously.

13   In the meantime, it might make sense for you to start by seeking **assistance** from people and places that will allow you to do so without your parents knowing. Depending on your age and school situation, you can explore some of the following:

- speaking with a school nurse or guidance counselor
- reaching out to a dean or another school administrator who knows you or works closely with students
- consulting with your pediatrician or another health care provider or clinic staff member who has known you for a while
- talking with a religious leader you know or a friend or mentor—even someone close to your age—to find out if s/he knows of free or low-cost services in your **area**

14   It may not feel like it, but you are by no means the only person who struggles with these **issues**. While it may feel embarrassing to ask for help, health care and school personnel are trained to help you find the support and **resources** you need, so that you can figure out what's going on and start feeling better.

15   You've also indicated that you are currently unemployed. The following may be able to provide you with services for free or for a small fee:

- Most **major** teaching hospitals have **mental** health clinics where they see people at low cost.

- There may be training institutes in your **area** for postgrads in **psychology** and social work that offer counseling at low cost, too.

- Not-for-profit organizations can assist you in finding a therapist who sees people on a sliding scale, which means that the **fees** will be adjusted based on what you can afford.

16   Looking into these options can also help you to learn as much as you can about social anxiety disorder, and the many forms of effective treatment. For example, numerous medications are now **available** through a prescription that can help **alleviate** symptoms and allow you to **focus** on figuring out what triggers anxiety for you. Many counselors also use cognitive and behavioral therapies to help manage anxiety when it crops up. Cognitive therapy is designed to help people understand how their thinking contributes to symptoms of anxiety and how to change those thought patterns and adjust their coping **strategies**. In behavioral therapy, a person learns **techniques** to decrease or overcome the behaviors associated with his or her anxiety, particularly those that cause discomfort or impair his or her ability to enjoy daily activities. When you find a counselor who's right for you, the two of you will develop a plan that meets your needs and helps you to find ways of managing your fears on a day-to-day basis.

alleviate
to make less severe

17   To get additional information about social anxiety disorder, treatment, and payment options, check out:

- National **Institute** of **Mental** Health (NIMH) web **site**
- American Psychological Association web **site**
- American Psychiatric Association web **site**
- **Mental** Help Net web site

18   Acknowledging that your anxiety is getting in your way and seeking the help you need takes courage. You deserve to get **assistance** in a way that feels safe and comfortable to you, and that allows you to get back to living a full life. Best to you,

Alice

Reading Comprehension Check

1. What is agoraphobia?
   a. an anxiety disorder.
   b. fear of spiders.
   c. a basic fear we all share.
   d. both a and b.

2. According to Alice, people with agoraphobia fear
   a. leaving their homes alone, being on a bridge.
   b. being in a large gathering of people.
   c. riding in various vehicles.
   d. all of the above.

3. All of the following are symptoms of panic attacks EXCEPT
   a. shortness of breath.
   b. fear of dying.
   c. strong appetite.
   d. sweating.

© Pearson Education, Inc.

4. What type of support is offered to back up the claim that cognitive behavioral therapy can be very effective in treating agoraphobia?
    a. the mention of research backing up the claim.
    b. emotional.
    c. personal experience.
    d. The claim is not supported in the text offered.

5. The advice columnist says that with _____ and _____, there is hope for the agoraphobic sufferer.
    a. a good therapist and heavy drugs.
    b. a calm heart and some sleep.
    c. a good therapist and determination.
    d. determination and more reading on the subject.

6. In the second letter, what reason does the student give for not going to his or her parents for support?
    a. This information is not given.
    b. The student says that they would think he or she is crazy.
    c. The student's parents are far away.
    d. The student is afraid of them.

7. What is the main idea of the second paragraph of Alice's response?
    a. Many people suffer from social anxiety.
    b. At this early stage, it is best to stay away from parents.
    c. It would be very helpful for the phobia sufferer to try to communicate with their parents.
    d. The advice is to spend more money on therapy and more time with friends.

8. What do we learn from Alice about cognitive therapy?
    a. It is designed to help people understand how their thinking contributes to symptoms of anxiety.
    b. It is not recommended for young sufferers.
    c. It teaches you how to change anxious thought patterns and adjust coping strategies.
    d. both a and c.

9. What is the final point made at the end of the letter?
    a. Social anxiety is what caused the writer to wait so long for help.
    b. Because of the writer's courage in seeking help, he or she deserves quality assistance and should seek it.
    c. The sufferer should never give up on life.
    d. none of the above.

10. What is the tone of Alice's responses?
    a. simply informational.   c. pessimistic.
    b. instructive and supportive.   d. ironic.

Suggested Resources

Books

1. *Reviving Ophelia: Saving the Selves of Adolescent Girls* by Mary Pipfer ([r.k.]: Ballantine Books, 1994). A thought-provoking collection of case studies, anecdotes, and educated commentary concerning the problems faced by today's female youth.

2. *I Know This Much Is True* by Wally Lamb ([t.k.]: Harper Collins, 1998). The book opens up about a man that has a schizophrenic twin. Lamb explores family, hardship, and what makes a person mentally ill.

3. *The Curious Incident of the Dog in the Night-time* by Mark Haddon (New York: Doubleday, 2003). The narrator of this novel is a 15-year-old autistic boy.

Movies

1. *Good Will Hunting* (1997). Directed by Gus Van Sant. Will Hunting is a boy genius who was severely abused as a child and has been in trouble with the law ever since. When Will finally agrees to get counseling to keep himself out of jail, he meets Sean, the therapist who will change his life.

2. *A Beautiful Mind* (2001). Directed by Ron Howard. A biopic of the rise of John Forbes Nash Jr., a math prodigy able to solve problems that baffled the greatest of minds. The movie explores how he overcame years of suffering through schizophrenia to win the Nobel Prize.

Internet Sites

1. Encyclopedia of Psychology

   http://www.psychology.org/

   Links to Web sites on a variety of psychology topics such as Environment, Behavior Relationships, Organizations, Publications, and more.

2. Go Ask Alice

   http://www.goaskalice.columbia.edu/index.html

   This is the health question-and-answer Internet site produced by Alice, Columbia University's Health Education Program. A site that lets you find health information via a search.

3. Mental Help Net

   http://mentalhelp.net

   Contains information on depression and personality disorders and their treatments.

© Pearson Education, Inc.

Finding Evidence in the Text

Overview

When reading, you are expected to compare the ideas discussed in a given text with your knowledge and experience of the world. One of the challenges in doing critical reading is being able to separate your own opinions, assumptions, and life experiences from those expressed by the author. So, for example, if you are evaluating an essay on the death penalty in which the author argues against it, you cannot judge the article as weakly reasoned simply because you happen to hold the opposite viewpoint. At the same time, if you agree with the author that the death penalty is wrong, in discussing the merits of the author's support for his or her arguments you can not bring in your own supporting points to back up the author's arguments. You have to find evidence for any claims made by the author in the original text itself.

In Chapter 8 we discussed the process of first recognizing what issue(s) the reading is focusing on and then identifying the author's argument(s). Evidence in support of an argument usually directly follows it. Factual evidence, or proof, comes in many forms. Some forms of evidence are statistical information, logically reasoned statements, or references to past research.

Highlighting both arguments and any evidence offered in support of them can be very helpful while reading. You can draw an arrow connecting highlighted arguments and supporting evidence, and label them accordingly. If you cannot find evidence for a claim made by the author, skim through the text again. It is easy to miss some details when you are doing a first read.

Challenge Activity

Collaboration

Read the article "Why Are Identical Twins Different" on page 446. Use a highlighter to highlight both the arguments mentioned in the text and the evidence cited in support of these claims. Using a pen, draw arrows connecting arguments and evidence, and label them. When you are finished, compare how the text now looks with that of a colleague's.

Learning Implications

The ability to find evidence in a text is a valuable skill, and not just for lawyers. Whether you are reviewing class readings for an exam, taking a multiple-choice test or doing research for an assigned paper, building a habit of physically locating evidence within a reading passage will make it much easier to follow both the major and minor ideas contained in the text.

BUSINESS
Entrepreneurship

"*A business is successful to the extent that it provides a product or service that contributes to happiness in all of its forms.*"
MIHALY CSIKSZENTMIHALYI

Objectives   IN THIS CHAPTER YOU WILL LEARN . . .

- ✅ About the fundamentals of business
- ✅ How to identify the author's bias
- ✅ How to write a business letter

© Pearson Education, Inc.

Making Predictions

Consider this chapter's theme of business. What subtopics relate to this field? (See Figure 9.1.)

■ **Figure 9.1**

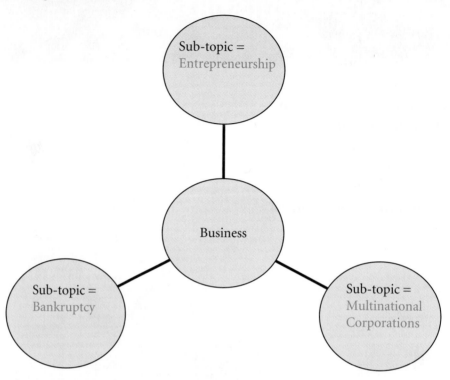

Introduction to the Discipline of Business

overhead
cost of doing business

When we come across the word *business* we think of multinational American corporations such as Exxon Mobil, Microsoft, IBM, etc. However, there are other businesses that may not be as successful as the aforementioned companies. These are relatively smaller businesses such as Kmart, Trader Joe's, and Target. There are yet other businesses that are much smaller, such as a local supermarket or a chain of restaurants. Finally, there are family-owned businesses that do not have the financial resources nor the management skills to expand nationwide. These businesses would include a local pizzeria, a small grocery store, or a florist in your neighborhood.

Regardless of their size, resources, annual revenue, or the kinds of products and services they offer, these businesses have one thing in common—they all offer either products or services to earn profits. All of these businesses try to keep their **overhead** as low as possible and maximize profits. There are inherent risks involved in running a business. For example, a company's profits may be much lower than its expenses. In this case, the company employs various strategies to stay afloat. The company may seek additional funding from venture capitalists, or it may try to find a buyer who might be interested in acquiring the company, or it may restructure the company, laying off many employees to keep the overhead low, or it may fire management and hire new people to run the company. If everything fails, then the company is forced to file for bankruptcy.

This chapter introduces the discipline of business to you. The main theme, however, is entrepreneurship, the state of being an entrepreneur. An entrepreneur is an individual who owns and manages a business and assumes the risk of making a huge profit or losing the entire investment. The articles in this chapter revolve around this theme. The reading selections address topics such as American companies hiring foreign-born chief executive officers, entrepreneurs helping multinational American companies name their products appropriately for foreign markets, choosing a career coach that is right for you, and a Russian immigrant turned entrepreneur who runs a successful business in New York City. You will also read an excerpt of a famous American play entitled *Death of a Salesman*. After you finish this chapter, you will have an understanding of how and why more and more entrepreneurs keep pursuing the American Dream of becoming financially self-sufficient.

Preview Questions

The following questions are all related to the chapter focus area of Business. Share your views in small group discussions.

Collaboration

1. Many people believe that there is "no heart in business." This brings up the debate as to whether business and ethics can coexist. Express your opinion on this topic and share some examples based on your personal experience.

2. Millions of Americans share the dream of starting a business. Do you believe that working for yourself offers a better life than working for a company or an organization? Discuss the advantages and disadvantages of entrepreneurship as opposed to simply being an employee.

3. More and more American companies are hiring employees in foreign countries to maximize profits. Critics argue that this trend, called outsourcing, hurts the local economy and deprives the American people of employment opportunities. Do you think that the government should mandate that corporations solely hire domestically, or should corporations have the freedom to act as they please?

4. Some people are concerned that the United States of America is losing its edge as a world economic leader. They worry that rising powers such as China and the European Union (EU) are a threat to America's supremacy as a leader in science and technology. Discuss what the United States must do to maintain its leadership in the world.

5. Read Csikszentmihalyi's quote at the beginning of the chapter and discuss whether the primary goal of business should be to enhance the quality of life for all. Name a few socially responsible companies that are working toward this goal. Can you think of some whose attitudes are heartless? Do you think that envisioning a world where all businesses contribute to our overall happiness is far-fetched? Explain.

© Pearson Education, Inc.

Interpreting a Cartoon

■ **Figure 9.2**

ESL Annotation

9.1 ESL This cartoon deals with the phenomenon of "outsourcing." It may be worthwhile to ask students from other countries if U.S. jobs are outsourced to their native country and what they think about this practice.

"We found someone overseas who can drink coffee and talk about sports all day for a fraction of what we're paying you."

Copyright 2005 by Randy Glasbergen. www.glasbergen.com

Collaboration

Working in pairs, examine the cartoon in Figure 9.2 and answer the following questions.

1. What is so amusing about this cartoon?
2. In your opinion, what is the cartoonist's intended message to the reader?

Discipline-specific Terminology Bank

capital	expenses	operations	reward
consume	firms	organizations	risk
corporations	incomes	production	stockholders
demand	innovations	profits	supply
employ	leadership	revenues	technology

Sample Paragraph

In a **capitalistic** system, then, businesses exist to earn **profits** for owners; an owner is likewise free to set up a new business, grow that business, sell it to other owners, or even shut it down. But **consumers** also have freedom of choice. In choosing how to pursue profits, businesses must take into account what consumers want and/or need.

> No matter how efficient a business is, it won't survive if there is no **demand** for its **goods** or **services**. Neither a snowblower shop in Florida nor a beach-umbrella store in Alaska is likely to do very well.
>
> (Ricky W. Griffin and Ronald J. Ebert, *Business*, 8th ed. Upper Saddle River, NJ: Pearson Prentice Hall, 2006, p. 4)

EXERCISE 1

Matching Column A and Column B

Match the word in Column A with the definition in Column B. Put the letter representing the correct definition in the space preceding each term.

Column A

Word

1. _f_ production
2. _e_ technology
3. _g_ innovation
4. _h_ revenues
5. _a_ corporation
6. _i_ leadership
7. _j_ employ
8. _d_ expenses
9. _b_ consumption
10. _c_ entrepreneur

Column B

Definition

a. a group of people working for business purposes
b. using goods and services
c. an individual who manages a business with risk
d. cost or charge
e. the application of science to commercial objectives
f. the process of manufacturing
g. introducing something new or different
h. the income produced by selling goods and services
i. the ability to guide and direct
j. to hire people for work

EXERCISE 2

Fill in the Blanks

In the following sentences, fill in the blank with a word from the terminology bank below that makes the sentence grammatical and meaningful.

consumption	corporation	employ	entrepreneur	expenses
innovation	leadership	production	revenues	technology

1. A _corporation_ is authorized by law to sell common shares to the public to raise capital.

2. Since Starbucks opened in major cities of China, the _consumption_ of coffee among the Chinese people has increased.

© Pearson Education, Inc.

3. ABC company's stock has suffered because of poor management and too many inexperienced people running the business. What this company needs is a real _entrepreneur_ with a vision.

4. CEOs of multinational corporations have to fly overseas quite frequently to meet with their clients and business partners, and all of their traveling _expenses_ are paid by the company.

5. Big corporations spend millions of dollars on research and development, using modern _technology_ to launch new products for commercial purposes.

6. Customers welcomed the _production_ of the much-awaited smart phone with a great deal of enthusiasm, and most stores ran out of it within a few hours.

7. Stiff competition among businesses makes technology obsolete rather quickly, and most companies are facing the pressures of constant change and _innovation_ to stay ahead of their competitors.

8. The company's strong management, cutting-edge research and development, and innovative products have resulted in increased _revenues_ quarter after quarter.

9. The multinational company was on the verge of bankruptcy, but then it prospered under the _leadership_ of the new, visionary president who turned the company around with her brilliant business ideas.

10. Customers were clamoring for the company's revolutionary product so much that it had to _employ_ many workers to keep up with the unprecedented demand.

Collaboration

EXERCISE 3

Pair Activity

Pair up with a classmate and make complete sentences with five words you learned from the vocabulary exercise.

1. _____

_____

2. _____

_____

3. _____

_____

4. _____

_____

5. _____

_____

Graphic Analysis

The Importance of Small Business in the U.S. Economy

As Figure 9.3 shows, most U.S. businesses employ fewer than 100 people, and most U.S. workers are employed by small firms. Figure 9.3(a) shows that 86.09 percent of all businesses employ 20 or fewer people and another 11 percent between 20 and 99 people. Only about one-tenth of 1 percent employ 1,000 or more. Figure 9.3(b) shows that 25.60 percent of all workers are employed by firms with fewer than 20 people; another 29.10 percent work in firms that employ between 20 and 99 people. The vast majority of these companies are owner operated. Figure 9.3(b) also shows that only 12.70 percent of workers are employed by firms with 1,000 or more employees.

(Business, p.90)

Small Businesses in the U.S. Economy

■ **Figure 9.3**

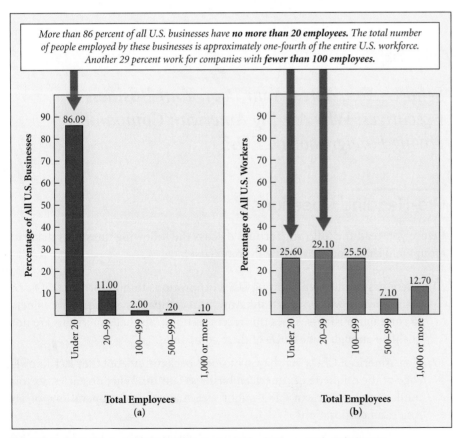

From Ricky W. Griffin and Ronald J. Ebert, *Business*, 8th ed., Figure 4.1 (p. 91), © 2006. Reproduced in print and electronic formats by permission of Pearson Education, Inc., Upper Saddle River, New Jersey.

Study the graph carefully with a classmate and answer the following questions.

1. According to Figure 9.3(a), what percentage of all U.S. businesses employ more than 20 workers? _____*13.30%*_____

© Pearson Education, Inc.

Collaboration

2. As shown in Figure 9.3(A), what is the second highest percentage of U.S. businesses that hire fewer than 100 employees? _____11%_____

3. What is the lowest percentage of U.S. businesses that employ the highest numbers of workers? _____.10%_____

4. In your opinion, why do you think that more than 86% of all U.S. businesses tend to have no more than 20 employees? __Answers will vary__

5. What percentage of all U.S. workers is employed with firms with fewer than 100 people? Examine graph 9.3(B). _____54.7%_____

6. What percentage of all U.S. workers is employed with firms with more than 100 people? Examine graph 9.3(B). _____45.2%_____

READING

Reading Selection 1

Internet Magazine Article

9.2 Flesch-Kincaid Grade Level 12.0

Collaboration

ESL Annotation

9.3 ESL This topic may be of high interest to many ESL students who come from foreign countries to pursue the American dream.

Send Us Your Tired, Your Poor, Your Business Executives: Why Are Big American Companies Hiring Foreign-born CEOs?

Pre-Reading Questions

Before you read the following article, discuss the following questions in small groups and share your answers with your classmates.

1. There has been a trend among U.S. corporations to hire foreign CEOs. In your opinion, why do you think American companies are hiring foreigners to run their business? Does this recent trend mean that Americans are not qualified enough to be CEOs of these companies?

2. Non-American CEOs may have a business background, but they lack knowledge of the etiquette of American business culture. What obstacles do you think a non-American CEO might face managing the operations of an American corporation?

3. U.S. multinational corporations do worldwide business and need CEOs who are sensitive to cross-cultural issues. In your opinion, what should U.S. business schools do to prepare American men and women to run a corporation that does business globally?

Read the following article and answer the multiple-choice questions that follow.

Send Us Your Tired, Your Poor, Your Business Executives: Why Are Big American Companies Hiring Foreign-born CEOs?

By Daniel Gross, www.slate.com

August 17, 2007

Klaus Kleinfeld, Alcoa's new president and COO

1   Earlier this week, Alcoa, the giant U.S. aluminum maker, appointed Klaus Kleinfeld, the former CEO of German industrial giant Siemens, its new president and chief operating officer—and **hence** the new CEO-heir **apparent.** Should Kleinfeld succeed current CEO Alain Belda, it would be a first: the Brazilian CEO of a Dow Jones Industrial Average component handing off stewardship of an **iconic** U.S. company—Alcoa stands for Aluminum Company of America—to another foreigner.

2   Gross's first law of journalism holds that any **phenomenon** found to **occur** three times is a **trend.** And clearly, there's a trend of Dow **components,** the iconic representation of American **corporate** achievement, appointing non-American CEOs.

3   Alcoa started the **trend** in 1999, appointing Belda, who was born in Morocco, educated in Brazil, and spent much of his career working in Alcoa's Brazilian operations, to succeed Paul O'Neill. In 2004, after several years of **lackluster** growth, Coca-Cola appointed a non-American, Neville Isdell, as CEO. Isdell's résumé reads like Graham Greene meets *Good to Great:* Born in Ireland, he went to work for Coca-Cola in 1966 in Zambia and had posts in South Africa, Australia, the Philippines, Germany, and the United Kingdom. He earned an undergraduate degree from the University of Cape Town, and it

? _____
_____
_____
_____

iconic
relating to something or someone famous

? _____
_____
_____
_____

lackluster
not very exciting or impressive

© Pearson Education, Inc.

?

saturated

unable to contain more

lip service

an expression or agreement not
followed by action

appears that his first full-time posting in Coca-Cola's Atlanta headquarters came in 2004, when he was named CEO. In March 2005, AIG, the huge insurer, became the third Dow component to appoint a foreign CEO. When legendary CEO Maurice "Hank" Greenberg stepped down, it appointed Martin Sullivan, a British man who started working for AIG in his homeland in 1971 and didn't come to New York until the mid-1990s.

4   The **trend** has continued. Not to be outdone by its rival, PepsiCo—which is not a member of the Dow Jones Industrial Average but has greater revenues than Coke—bested Coca-Cola in the **global diversity** sweepstakes. Last fall it appointed Indra Nooyi, a woman born and educated in India, as CEO. She assumed the **role** of chairman in May. Nooyi, 51, was educated at Madras Christian College and the Indian **Institute** of Management before coming to the United States to attend Yale's School of Management in 1978. An American citizen, she wears saris on occasion and retains an accent, which you can hear on [a] **conference** call.

5   In many ways, this **trend** makes complete sense. Big American businesses—like Alcoa, Pepsi, Coke, and AIG—are already **global** businesses. Based on **data** from 238 members of the Standard & Poor's 500 **Index**, S&P analyst Howard Silverblatt found that the typical member of the **index generated** 44.2 **percent** of its sales outside the United States in 2006. And the bigger the company—and the more it has **saturated** the U.S. market—the more important it is to have a CEO who is comfortable operating around the world. In the second quarter of 2007, Coca-Cola notched 66 percent of its beverage business from outside North America. Alcoa has operations in 44 countries. In its complicated earnings report, AIG doesn't explicitly say which percentage of revenues comes from outside the United States, but with each passing year, the foreign business of American International Group is less American and more international. The **notion** that American men who have spent their entire careers working in the United States—as is the case with the overwhelming majority of U.S. executives—are ideal candidates to lead such organizations seems increasingly out of date.

6   And yet, it is **somewhat** amazing that this crop of CEOs has risen to the top. For all the **lip service** paid to **diversity** and globalization, the **corporate** suites of Fortune 500 companies remain a bastion of **conformity.** (Among the Dow components, there are no women CEOs and only one African-American.) **Despite** globalization, Americans (and the world, generally) continue to believe that the United States holds something of a monopoly on the efficient management of massive **global** corporations. It's not too much of a stretch to say that Americans invented the idea (John D. Rockefeller and J. P. Morgan), institutionalized it (the MBA), and continue to make improvements on the model (Jack Welch, Jim Collins, etc.). (If you really want to feel at home when you're abroad, go into the business **section** of a bookstore—all the titles will be familiar.) The world continues to have great respect for U.S. knowledge and understanding of how to run businesses; MBAs are a **major export.** Indeed, business schools now play an extremely important **function** in America's business meritocracy, allowing foreigners and Americans without connections or **prior** experience to enter the **corporate** bloodstream.

7   But these appointments show that, to a degree, large corporations may be displacing MBA programs as the new credentialing factories. None of the

CEOs mentioned above has a graduate degree from a U.S. business school, save Nooyi of Pepsi. (Then again, the Yale School of Management regards itself as a public-**policy** school as much as a B-school.) Martin Sullivan of AIG does not appear to have attended college.

8   At one time, the immigrant's **definition** of the American dream was moving to America, working hard, learning the language, buying a home, becoming a citizen, and perhaps starting a small business. Today, that dream might also entail running one of the nation's largest businesses.

Did I miss any? Send your nominations for foreign-born CEOs of major U.S. companies to moneybox@slate.com.

Reading Comprehension Check

1. As used in the sentence "Earlier this week, Alcoa, the giant U.S. aluminum maker, appointed Klaus Kleinfeld, the former CEO of German industrial giant Siemens, its new president and chief operating officer—and hence the new CEO-heir apparent," in paragraph 1, the word *appointed* means
   a. dismissed.   (c.) selected.
   b. demoted.   d. promoted.

2. In the sentence "Should Kleinfeld succeed current CEO Alain Belda, it would be a first: the Brazilian CEO of a Dow Jones Industrial Average component handing off stewardship of an iconic U.S. company—Alcoa stands for Aluminum Company of America—to another foreigner," in paragraph 1, the word *stewardship* means
   (a.) management.   c. ownership.
   b. employees.   d. shareholders.

3. In the sentence "Gross's first law of journalism holds that any phenomenon found to occur three times is a trend," in paragraph 1, the word *trend* could be replaced with
   a. outdated.   (c.) style.
   b. obsolete.   d. unpopular.

4. The author's main idea is that
   a. American companies are leery of appointing non-American CEOs.
   b. non-American CEOs do a miserable job managing the operations of the company.
   c. non-American CEOs are absolutely not in demand in the United States of America.
   (d.) more and more American corporations are hiring non-American CEOs to run their business.

5. The example of Alcoa, the giant U.S. aluminum maker, appointing Klaus Kleinfeld its new president and CEO is offered to support the idea that
   (a.) it has become a trend among American corporations to hire foreign CEOs.
   b. most American corporations shy away from foreign-born CEOs.
   c. non-American CEOs have extremely poor English language skills.
   d. American corporations run by foreign CEOs are likely to incur huge losses.

© Pearson Education, Inc.

6. "In 2004, after several years of lackluster growth, Coca-Cola appointed a non-American, Neville Isdell, as CEO."

    It can be inferred from the above statement that
    a. before hiring Neville Isdell, Coca Cola had enjoyed several years of exponential growth.
    b. Coca Cola made a serious mistake by appointing Neville Isdell its CEO.
    c. the American CEO resigned because of medical reasons.
    d. the American CEO's performance was unsatisfactory.

7. Which of the following is a fact?
    a. Any phenomenon found to occur three times is a trend.
    b. American corporations should only hire non-American CEOs.
    c. Indra Nooyi, CEO of PepsiCo, went to Yale's School of Management in 1978.
    d. The world continues to have great respect for U.S. knowledge and understanding of how to run businesses.

8. Which of the following is an opinion?
    a. Alcoa started the trend in 1999, appointing Belda, who was born in Morocco, educated in Brazil, and spent much of his career working in Alcoa's Brazilian operations, to succeed Paul O'Neill.
    b. Nooyi, 51, was educated at Madras Christian College and the Indian Institute of Management before coming to the United States to attend Yale's School of Management in 1978.
    c. Neville Isdell went to work for Coca Cola in 1966 in Zambia.
    d. The notion that American men who have spent their entire careers working in the United States—as is the case with the overwhelming majority of U.S. executives—are ideal candidates to lead such organizations seems increasingly out of date.

9. The author's purpose in writing this article is to
    a. criticize.
    b. persuade.
    c. inform.
    d. convince.

10. "In many ways, this trend makes complete sense. Big American businesses—like Alcoa, Pepsi, Coke, and AIG—are already global businesses. Based on data from 238 members of the Standard & Poor's 500 Index, S&P analyst Howard Silverblatt found that the typical member of the index generated 44.2 percent of its sales outside the United States in 2006. And the bigger the company—and the more it has saturated the U.S. market—the more important it is to have a CEO who is comfortable operating around the world."

    The overall pattern of organization in the above passage is
    a. chronological order.
    b. spatial.
    c. cause and effect.
    d. classification.

READING

Reading Selection **2**

Online Article

Found in Translation: Avoiding Multilingual Gaffes

How a small translation company helps big brands avoid global mishaps

Pre-Reading Questions

9.4 Flesch-Kincaid Grade Level 10.5

Discuss the following questions in small groups before reading the article.

1. How important is a product name to you? In other words, what role does the name of a product play in influencing your buying decision? Explain.

2. Do you know an American product whose name means something funny or offensive in another language? Share the meaning of this product with your peers and explain to them how it may be offensive in another language.

3. Many U.S. corporations have chosen product names that are offensive in languages other than English. In your opinion, what do you think these corporations should do to save themselves from international embarrassment?

Collaboration

ESL Annotation

9.5 **ESL** Students will appreciate this article as they come from diverse linguistic backgrounds.

Found in Translation: Avoiding Multilingual Gaffes

By Malika Zouhali-Worrall, www.money.cnn.com
July 14, 2008

Vernon and Michelle Menard with one of the product names they nixed

© Pearson Education, Inc.

1   FORTUNE SMALL BUSINESS—When it comes to naming their products, many large U.S. companies have veered dangerously close to international embarrassment.

2   Take the pharmaceutical giant that wanted to call a new weight-loss pill "Tegro." It sounds harmless enough in English, but in French the word is phonetically **identical** to *t'es gros*, or "you are fat."

3   Then there was the name for a **global technology** training system that sounded exactly like the Korean for "porn movie." Not to mention the HIV medication whose German name could easily be mistaken for "foolish love."

4   Luckily for the companies **involved,** those gaffes were seen only by experts at a small U.S. company. Choice Translating, based in Charlotte, has found a profitable **niche** examining product names in multiple tongues.

niche
a special area of demand for a service

5   "It's expensive to **create** a brand identity," says Vernon Menard, who co-owns the company with his wife, Michelle. "We're cheap insurance."

6   The Menards had no intention of getting into brand **analysis** when they started out. Michelle, 37, began the translation services company in the mid-1990s while studying French and business **administration** at the University of North Carolina. Vernon, 42, bought half the business in 1999; the pair married in 2001. Since then, Choice has built a roster of about 1,000 freelance translators in more than 80 countries around the world.

7   Soon, a local branding firm came calling. To evaluate how its clients' product names would sound abroad, this company had been using bilingual students in Charlotte. "They needed more **resources,**" says Michelle, who jumped at the chance to **leverage** her **network** of translators.

leverage
use existing resources to expand further

8   By 2007, Choice Translating was making $600,000 from brand **analysis,** out of total revenues of $2 million. (Revenues in 2006 were $1.5 million.) The Menards hope that brand **analysis** will generate as much as 80% of their business within the next two years.

Translation Software Still Fails—Badly

9   Clients pay about $13,000 for an **analysis** of their brand in dozens of dialects in **target** markets. The Menards built an online **survey** form so that freelancers in the **target** market could respond quickly. The questions are simple: Does the name mean anything in the **target** market (such as an antipsychotic medication that translated to "dogs are afraid of me" in Mandarin)? Does it have any **negative** connotations (such as the pill that started with the letters "Xep," which in Russian sounds like a **slang** word for male genitalia)? How easily can it be pronounced?

slang
very informal, sometimes offensive, language that is used especially by people who belong to a particular group

10   Once the results of the online **survey** are aggregated, Choice writes a report and sends it to the client, usually within five days of the original request. Addison Whitney, another brand-consulting firm based in Charlotte, used Choice for 90 projects last year, checking its clients' product names in as many as 30 dialects.

11   "Now is a good moment to do this," says Renato Beninatto of Common Sense Advisory, a market **research** firm in Lowell, Mass., that covers the language services industry. "American companies are looking to sell more products abroad because of the cheaper dollar."

12   Even the giants of the $4.9-billion-a-year U.S. language services market have a kind word for their small rival.

13   "They've found a nice little niche there," says Kathleen Bostick, vice president of **global** business at Lionbridge Technologies, based in Waltham, Mass. Lionbridge offers brand-name **analysis** as part of a suite of "localization" services, or if the client specifically requests it.

14   Late last year Choice added a **visual-evaluation** service. The firm's **network** of native translators examine **corporate** logos for colors, shapes, and symbols that have **negative** local **connotations.** For example, white may represent purity in Western cultures, but in China it is the color of death and **mourning.** Choice has so far completed five **visual** projects for two clients.

15   Choice last year opened a **project** management office in Lima, Peru, a city Vernon knew from **previous** business ventures. Today that office houses 15 full-time Choice employees, compared with seven in Charlotte. The **network** of freelancers requires good **project** managers, and "it was hard to find talent in Charlotte," says Vernon. "We were often dealing with the leftovers after the banks had their pick. In Peru we are a top-tier employer."

16   There's no mistaking what that translates to: better talent, lower salaries, and bigger profits.

connotation
an idea or a feeling that a word makes you think of, in addition to its basic meaning

mourning
great sadness because someone has died

Reading Comprehension Check

1. As used in the sentence "When it comes to naming their products, many large U.S. companies have veered dangerously close to international embarrassment," in paragraph 1, the phrase *veered* means
   a. to move away from.
   (c.) to turn.
   b. to travel dangerously.
   d. to embarrass companies.

2. In the sentence "Luckily for the companies involved, those gaffes were seen only by experts at a small U.S. company," in paragraph 1, the word *gaffes* can be replaced with
   a. sensibility.
   c. sensitivity.
   (b.) misjudgments.
   d. wise decisions.

3. Which of the following sentences is the best statement of the main idea of the article?
   a. Most U.S. companies name their products sensitively.
   b. It is not important for U.S. multinational companies to learn what their product names mean in other languages.
   (c.) A small company helps U.S. companies avoid international embarrassment by choosing their product names carefully.
   d. Most consumers do not pay attention to the name of the product they purchase.

4. The example of the pharmaceutical giant's new weight-loss pill "Tegro" is offered to support the idea that
   a. "Tegro" means something amusing in French.
   (b.) some names that sound harmless in English may mean something offensive in another language.
   c. the new weight-loss pill "Tegro" is quite successful in France.
   d. the French people are excited about using "Tegro."

© Pearson Education, Inc.

Oprah Winfrey

Oprah Gail Winfrey, more popularly known as Oprah, is a famous American television host, business tycoon and philanthropist. She has received many honorary awards for her much-acclaimed internationally syndicated talk show, *The Oprah Winfrey Show*. In addition to being a popular talk show host, Winfrey is also a book critic, an Academy Award–nominated actress, and a magazine publisher. She has been ranked the richest African American of the twenty-first century, the only black billionaire for three consecutive years, and the most philanthropic African American who ever lived. Some people believe that she is the most influential woman in the world.

Winfrey was born on January 29, 1954, in rural Mississippi. A child born out of wedlock and raised in a Milwaukee neighborhood, she was raped at the age of 9 and gave birth to a son at the age of 14. The son died in his infancy, and she went to live with her father in Tennessee. It was there that she landed a job in radio at the age of 19. She never looked back since then, and after working as a talk show host in Chicago for a while, she finally founded her own production company and became syndicated globally.

Winfrey's meteoric rise to stardom did not happen overnight. She moved to Chicago in 1983 to host a morning talk-show *AM Chicago*. After she took over the talk show, it went from last place to the highest-rated talk show in Chicago. Such was her popularity as the talk show host that the show was renamed *The Oprah Winfrey Show*. On her twentieth anniversary show, Winfrey told her audience that the famous movie critic Roger Ebert had encouraged her sign a contact with King World. Ebert had rightly predicted that Winfrey's show would generate 40 times as much revenue as his show. According to *Time* magazine, "Few people would have bet on Oprah Winfrey's swift rise to host of the most popular talk show on TV. In a field dominated by white males, she is a black female of ample bulk. As interviewers go, she is no match for, say, Phil Donahue. . . . What she lacks in journalistic toughness, she makes up for in plainspoken curiosity, robust humor and above all, empathy. Guests with sad stories to tell are apt to rouse a tear in Oprah's eye. . . . They, in turn, often find themselves revealing things they would not imagine telling anyone, much less a national TV audience. It is the talk show as a group therapy session."

Oprah's Angel Network, founded in 1998, encourages people around the world to help the poor. The Network provides grants to nonprofit organizations and undertakes projects all over the world to alleviate poverty and improve the lives of the underprivileged. Her network has raised $51 million for the cause so far. She personally covers all costs associated with the charitable projects. She has been listed by *Business Week* as one of America's 50 most generous philanthropists. Throughout her illustrious career, she has donated an estimated $303 million. She donated $10 million to support the Hurricane Katrina victims in New Orleans. Winfrey has helped 250 African American men get a college education. She received the first Bob Hope Humanitarian Award at the 2002 Emmy Awards for her services to television and film.

Some Questions for Group Discussion

1. Oprah Winfrey had an extremely difficult childhood and grew up in abject poverty. Still she persevered in her professional goals and became a talk show host at the age of 19. Discuss what inspired her to become a businesswoman and philanthropist.

2. As an African American woman, Winfrey had to work hard to climb up the ladder of success. Nevertheless, she overcame all the barriers with diligence and persistence and became extremely rich. Discuss the reasons for her phenomenal success.

3. There are more than 200 billionaires in the United States of America. Yet, not all of them are philanthropists. Winfrey is one of few billionaires who donate generously. Discuss why most of the billionaires keep their enormous wealth to themselves and do not share it with the poor and hungry.

Biographical Internet Research

Do research on the Internet and select a successful entrepreneur from the list below of individuals who have amassed wealth and have donated substantial amounts of money for a noble cause. Be prepared to share their biographical profiles with your classmates.

- Bill Gates
- Chris Gardner
- John D. Rockefeller
- George Soros
- Warren Buffet

5. A small U.S. company, Choice Translating, is mentioned to support the fact that
   a. the company has not made any profits since it was founded.
   (b.) examining product names can be a profitable business.
   c. most U.S. companies do not need help from experts to name their products.
   d. only those companies who hire Choice Translating can do business internationally.

6. "'It's expensive to create a brand identity,' says Vernon Menard in paragraph 5, who co-owns the company with his wife, Michelle. 'We're cheap insurance.'"

   A logical conclusion that can be drawn from the above statement is that
   a. Vernon Menard charges an exorbitant amount of money to examine product names.
   b. the company offers free brand analysis to many U.S. companies.
   (c.) the Menards charge U.S. companies a reasonable amount for brand analysis.
   d. it is very expensive to analyze product names.

7. All of the following statements are facts EXCEPT
   a. Choice Translating generated total revenues of $2 million in 2007.
   b. Vernon Menard and Michelle Menard are co-owners of Choice Translating.
   (c.) Brand analysis will generate 80 percent of Choice Translating's revenue in the next two years.
   d. Choice Translating's revenue was $1.5 million in 2006.

8. The author's primary purpose is to
   a. entertain.   c. persuade.
   (b.) inform.   d. convince.

9. The overall tone of the article is
   a. detached.   c. concerned.
   (b.) objective.   d. reverent.

10. Throughout the article, which type of support is offered for the author's claim that brand analysis could be a profitable business for translation companies?
    a. emotional   c. irrelevant
    (b.) objective   d. sentimental

SKILL FOCUS
The Author's Bias

You can tell an author's attitude toward the chosen subject matter by paying attention to his or her word choice. The author may have a bias for or against the subject. This opinionated view of the subject may be positive or negative. By recognizing the author's positive or negative attitude toward the subject, you can determine whether the author has a bias for or against the topic.

Sometimes the author does *not* have a positive or a negative attitude toward the topic. In this case, the writing is considered unbiased, without being subjective at all. An unbiased author simply presents opposing viewpoints without challenging or defending a particular view. In unbiased writing, the tone is usually neutral, objective, and straightforward.

ESL Annotation

9.6 ESL It is difficult for ESL students to determine the author's bias because of their limited English language proficiency. Make sure to go over this skill in detail.

© Pearson Education, Inc.

To determine the author's bias accurately, pay attention to the following details:

- Does the author use mostly positive language to discuss the subject?
- Does the author use mostly negative language to discuss the subject?
- Does the author simply present both positive and negative aspects of the topic?
- Does the author present facts or opinions?

In addition, do the following to get a clue to the author's bias:

- Find the author's topic and main idea.
- See if the author's attitude toward the subject is positive or negative.
- Consider if the author has taken a subjective, one-sided approach.
- Find opinions expressed in biased writing.
- If you are unable to find either a positive or negative attitude toward the subject, then you can safely conclude that the writing is unbiased.

Let's examine two examples to understand how to determine if the author has a bias—and, if so, what it is.

Example 1

The production of tangible goods once dominated most economic systems, but today information resources play a major role. Businesses rely on market forecasts, on the specialized knowledge of people, and on economic data for much of their work. After AOL acquired Time Warner, the new business was initially called AOL Time Warner. But marketing research information suggested that people saw the new name as being confusing and **unwieldy.** Hence, the firm's name was eventually shortened back to simply Time Warner.

Further, much of what the firm does results either in the creation of new information or the repackaging of existing information for new users. Time Warner produces few tangible products. Instead, America Online provides online services for millions of subscribers who pay monthly access fees. Time Warner Entertainment produces movies and television programming. Turner Broadcasting System, a subsidiary, gathers information about world events and then transmits it to consumers over its Cable News Network (CNN). Essentially, then, Time Warner is in the information business.

(*Ricky W. Griffin and Ronald J. Ebert,* Business, *8th ed. Upper Saddle River, NJ: Pearson Prentice Hall, 2006,* p. 10)

Let's start with the topic and main idea.

Topic: Information resources

Main idea: Information resources play a major role in most economic systems nowadays.

Now let's see if the author sounds positive or negative toward the subject. You will notice that the author refrains from giving an opinion and chooses to remain objective. The above passage, therefore, is an example of unbiased language.

---

unwieldy
bulky, unmanageable

Example 2

McDonald's has become an international icon of the fast-food industry. With 30,000 restaurants in 121 countries, the Golden Arches have become as recognizable to foreign consumers as the shape of a Coca-Cola bottle. Yet in recent years, McDonald's seems to have lost its competitive edge both at home and abroad. In the United States, for example, the company's menu is seen as unhealthy, its stores are outdated, and its customer service skills seem to be slipping. McDonald's no longer leads in technology, with rivals inventing new processing and cooking technologies. The firm's traditional markets, children and young men, are spending less on food while markets McDonald's does not target, notably women and older consumers, spend more. Profits have dropped and Starbucks has replaced McDonald's as the food industry success story.

(Business, *p. 31*)

Topic: McDonald's

Main idea: McDonald's is losing its competitive edge both at home and abroad.

If you read the passage carefully, you will notice that the author uses negative adjectives such as *outdated* and *unhealthy* to describe McDonald's. It is reasonable to conclude that the author is biased against McDonald's.

PRACTICING THE SKILL

Now that you have looked at one example of unbiased writing and another of the author's bias, read the following passages carefully and answer the questions that follow.

Passage 1

Inflation occurs when widespread price increases occur throughout an economic system. How does it threaten stability? Inflation occurs when the amount of money injected into an economy outstrips the increase in actual output. When this happens, people will have more money to spend, but there will still be the same quantity of products available for them to buy. As they compete with one another to buy available products, prices go up. Before long, high prices will erase the increase in the amount of money injected into the economy. Purchasing power, therefore, declines.

(Business, *p. 35*)

1. What is the topic?
   Inflation.

2. What is the main idea?
   Inflation occurs when people have more money to spend but the products
   available for purchase are limited.

3. What is the author's attitude toward the topic?
   The author is unbiased against the topic.

© Pearson Education, Inc.

Passage 2

When Starbucks opens new stores in small towns, it threatens locally-owned cafes and contributes to the loss of the local flavor of Main Streets across America. Big chains like Starbucks homogenize our lives and leave us wondering what makes my town look any different from other towns. The time is now to support our local businesses and to protest big chain takeovers of our communities.

1. What is the topic?

Big chains in small towns.

2. What is the main idea?

Big retail chains are threatening the existence of locally owned businesses.

3. What is the author's attitude toward the topic?

The author expresses a bias against retail chains, such as Starbucks.

Passage 3

Two of Enron's notorious plans were code-named Death Star and Ricochet. With Death Star, Enron took advantage of the payouts through which the state managed its power grid. Essentially, California paid as much as $750 per megawatt hour to persuade providers not to ship power on over-burdened power lines, especially those running north to south. To create the illusion of congestion on these lines, Enron began overbooking ship-ments and scheduling power transmissions that it had no intention of making. In each case, it then collected money from the state for changing plans that it never meant to carry out.

(*Business, p. 11*)

1. What is the topic?

Enron.

2. What is the main idea?

Enron took advantage of the payouts it received from the State of California.

3. What is the author's attitude toward the topic?

The author is reporting information. There is no clear bias.

Passage 4

Outsourcing does not threaten American jobs whatsoever. On the con-trary, outsourcing leads to the creation of more high-quality jobs in the United States. This is because the great majority of jobs that are out-sourced have been relatively low-skill in nature. Athletic shoes are pro-duced in factories in Southeast Asia, while the shoe companies' corporate jobs remain in the US. With higher production abroad, more corporate managers and supervisors are needed at home.

1. What is the topic?

   Outsourcing.

2. What is the main idea?

   Outsourcing is a benefit, not a threat, to American labor.

3. What is the author's attitude toward the topic?

   The author shows a bias in favor of the practice of outsourcing.

Passage 5

More and more, credit card companies are taking advantage of their clients by adding additional small fees to monthly credit card bills. For example, many clients unknowingly sign on for such services as 'credit protector' or 'travel advantages' programs, and then see these fees add up over time. When clients realize that they are paying for these unwanted services and try to cancel them, the companies make the cancellation process multi-stepped and tedious to discourage clients from discontinuing these high profit add-ons.

1. What is the topic?

   The practices of credit card companies.

2. What is the main idea?

   Credit card companies act dishonorably in pushing their clients to sign up for

   additional small fee services.

3. What is the author's attitude toward the topic?

   The author is clearly biased against credit card companies and

   their business practices.

Now that you have practiced identifying the author's bias, let's practice reading full-length articles to recognize the author's attitude toward the subject.

How to Find the Right Career Coach

Pre-Reading Questions

In a small group of classmates, discuss the following questions.

1. Have you ever spoken to someone for career advice? Why did you choose this person to discuss your career choice, and how much did you value her or his advice? Was this person a qualified career counselor, a best friend, or a family member?

READING

Reading Selection **3**

Online Article

9.7 Flesch-Kincaid Grade Level 7.4

Collaboration

© Pearson Education, Inc.

2. Other than communication, what specific skills must a good career counselor have to help people choose a rewarding career? Be specific.

3. Some people believe that it is important to speak to a qualified career coach before choosing a career path. Others think that choosing a career is a personal matter, and that people should rely on themselves to make a decision about their career. What is your opinion?

How to Find the Right Career Coach

By Anne Fisher, senior writer, www.money.cnn.com
August 4, 2008

Plenty of people claim to be qualified to help you make your next career move. To make sure they can deliver the goods, heed these 9 tips.

FORTUNE

got laid off
lost a job, became unemployed

1   **Dear Annie:** I've had a 14-year career in **financial** services, but I just **got laid off** and I don't think it makes sense to look for another **job** like my old one. (They're disappearing rapidly.) I'd like to get some solid advice and coaching as I think about my next move—including which other industry I might be able to **transfer** my skills to—so I've been thinking about hiring a coach. But an Internet search turns up a bewildering variety of choices. How do I pick the right one?

GOODBYE TO BANKING

2   **Dear G.B.:** Alas, anyone can call himself or herself a career coach (or a life coach), and many thousands of people do. So, as you've noticed, finding someone who can help you reposition yourself and move your career forward takes some diligence.

3   "Even many legitimate career coaches impart advice from a theoretical **perspective**, since they have little or no field experience in the areas where they're presuming to counsel you," says John McKee (www.johnmmckee .com), himself an executive coach with 30 years' experience. To increase your chances of identifying a good coach, McKee offers this checklist on what to look—and look out—for:

1. Work experience. Does the coach have real-world work experience that is comparable to yours? McKee notes that about 80% of self-designated career coaches have actually been trained in life coaching, and may have few practical suggestions on how to help you **achieve** your work-related **goals.**

"If you needed surgery, would you rather have it done by someone who has performed the operation before, or by someone who has only studied it?" asks McKee.

2. Credentials. Choose a coach who belongs to trade organizations like the International Coach Federation (ICF) and the Worldwide Association of Business Coaches (WABC). These designations are a sign of some formal training, and of adherence to general standards of professionalism.

3. Credibility. "Your coach should be active and **visible** in the industry," says McKee. Has he or she written any books? **Published** articles in, or been interviewed by, **major media**? Been asked to speak at **professional** conferences?

"Substantiating the person's reputation is **crucial**," says McKee. "You want a coach for whom coaching was a first career choice, not a default choice that he or she may not be 100% committed to."

4. Testimonials. Will the coach provide you with references from past clients? If not, or if you're offered just one or two, beware: There may be less there than meets the eye.

5. Methods. Some coaches insist that you come to their offices in person; others will meet with you at the local coffee shop if you like, or work with you by phone or e-mail. If you would prefer a particular **approach** to meeting, make sure the coach you're considering offers it. McKee has doubts about the value of group sessions, by the way: "To get the most **bang for your buck**, it's generally better to **conduct** your sessions one-on-one."

bang for your buck
more buying power for your money

6. Goals. "A good coach should be able to help you determine your **overall goals**," says McKee. "Even before that, you should establish **specific** milestones: When can you expect to see results, and what might those results look like?" Otherwise, he says, you're just driving without directions.

7. Consultation. Your first encounter is critical in establishing the chemistry—or lack thereof—with a coach, who after all will be sharing intimate details of your life. "Take full advantage of the **initial consultation**," says McKee. But keep in mind, that first meeting should be free. "Anyone who charges for a first meeting **raises a red flag**," he says.

raises a red flag
creates an alarming situation that requires immediate attention

8. Guarantee. Say that, **despite** all your **research,** your work with the career coach you **select** doesn't lead anywhere. In that case, what recourse will you have? Will he or she refund your money, extend the term of service, or what?

"Try to find out in advance how often the person has had to give someone a refund, and for what reason," urges McKee. "Many good coaches have been obliged to do this, and those with **integrity** will be willing to explain those situations without hesitation."

9. Fees. McKee points out that rates vary wildly, with coaches who **target** middle managers charging anywhere from $75 to $500 for sessions that may last an hour or a whole day. Some coaches want to meet with you just once or twice, to help you figure out some first steps in a new direction, while others work longer-term, on a weekly or monthly basis.

© Pearson Education, Inc.

penny-wise and pound-foolish
stingy about small expenses and
extravagant about large ones

Some provide you with books or other materials to supplement your coaching sessions; others don't. Make sure you understand up front how much you will be paying and for what. "It's okay to be cost-conscious," says McKee, "but avoid being **penny-wise and pound-foolish.**" Don't just hire the least costly coach, in other words—especially if the intended goal of the coaching, or one of them anyway, is to help you make more money.

4   Readers, what do you say? Have you ever hired a career coach? How did it work out? Any advice for others who might be considering a coach? Post your thoughts on the Ask Annie blog.

Reading Comprehension Check

1. The main idea of the article is that
   a. before making a final decision, people should speak to a qualified career coach at least nine times.
   b. people should blindly believe those who claim to be qualified career coaches.
   c. most career coaches are delivery boys.
   d. people should be extremely careful in choosing the right career coach.

2. "'If you needed surgery, would you rather have it done by someone who has performed the operation before, or by someone who has only studied it?' asks McKee."

   In this passage, McKee is
   a. biased against experienced career coaches.
   b. biased in favor of inexperienced career coaches.
   c. biased against inexperienced career coaches.
   d. completely unbiased.

3. "Choose a coach who belongs to trade organizations like the International Coach Federation (ICF) and the Worldwide Association of Business Coaches (WABC). These designations are a sign of some formal training, and of adherence to general standards of professionalism."

   In this passage, the author is
   a. biased in favor of coaches who have good credentials.
   b. biased against coaches who belong to trade organizations.
   c. not in favor of coaches with poor credentials.
   d. not biased against coaches in general.

4. "'Your coach should be active and visible in the industry,' says McKee. 'Has he or she written any books? Published articles in, or been interviewed by, major media? Been asked to speak at professional conferences?'"

   In this passage, McKee
   a. is unbiased.
   b. is biased in favor of less prominent coaches.

c. is biased against active and visible coaches.

d. is biased against less active and visible coaches.

5. "Will the coach provide you with references from past clients? If not, or if you're offered just one or two, beware: There may be less there than meets the eye."

In the passage above, the author

a. is biased against coaches with few or no references.

b. is unbiased.

c. is biased in favor of coaches with weak credibility.

d. is biased against coaches with strong credibility.

6. "Some coaches insist that you come to their offices in person; others will meet with you at the local coffee shop if you like, or work with you by phone or e-mail. If you would prefer a particular approach to meeting, make sure the coach you're considering offers it. McKee has doubts about the value of group sessions, by the way: 'To get the most bang for your buck, it's generally better to conduct your sessions one-on-one.'"

In the passage above, the author

a. is unbiased.

b. is biased in favor of coaches who hold group sessions with their clients.

c. is biased in favor of coaches who meet with their clients individually.

d. favors coaches who meet with their clients only once.

7. "'A good coach should be able to help you determine your overall goals,' says McKee. 'Even before that, you should establish specific milestones: When can you expect to see results, and what might those results look like?' Otherwise, he says, you're just driving without directions."

In this passage, McKee expresses a bias in favor of

a. coaches who help their clients establish long-term goals.

b. career coaches who help their clients carry a millstone around their neck.

c. people who drive without directions.

d. coaches who teach their clients how to drive.

8. "Your first encounter is critical in establishing the chemistry—or lack thereof—with a coach, who after all will be sharing intimate details of your life. 'Take full advantage of the initial consultation,' says McKee. But keep in mind, that first meeting should be free. 'Anyone who charges for a first meeting raises a red flag,' he says."

In the passage above, McKee is biased against

a. coaches who do not charge for initial consultation.

b. coaches who provide free service to their clients.

c. people who do not wish to pay for a first meeting with a coach.

d. coaches who charge their clients for initial consultation.

9. "Say that, despite all your research, your work with the career coach you select doesn't lead anywhere. In that case, what recourse will you have? Will he or she refund your money, extend the term of service, or what? 'Try to find out in advance how often the person has had to give someone a refund, and

© Pearson Education, Inc.

for what reason,' urges McKee. 'Many good coaches have been obliged to do this, and those with integrity will be willing to explain those situations without hesitation.'"

In this passage, the author expresses a bias in favor of
a. those coaches who give a refund if their clients do not land a job.
b. those clients who refuse to ask for a refund.
c. those coaches who are unwilling to tell how often they had to give a refund.
d. those coaches who are reluctant to explain why they had to give a refund.

10. "'It's okay to be cost-conscious,' says McKee, 'but avoid being penny-wise and pound-foolish.' Don't just hire the least costly coach, in other words—especially if the intended goal of the coaching, or one of them anyway, is to help you make more money."

In the passage above, the author expresses a bias against
a. clients who are not penny-wise and pound-foolish.
b. the most expensive coaches.
c. clients who are penny-wise and pound-foolish.
d. those coaches who provide free service to their clients.

DEBATABLE TOPIC

Recommended Debate Topic: Outsourcing takes jobs away from the American people and hurts the U.S. economy.

Discuss debatable topics related to business with your classmates and instructor for the debate activity.

Your suggested debate topics:

a. _____

b. _____

c. _____

READING

Reading Selection 4

Online Article

9.8 Flesch-Kincaid Grade Level 6.7

Collaboration

How She Does It—Anya Ponorovskaya

Pre-Reading Questions

Discuss the following questions with a small group of your classmates.

1. Do you know someone who came to the United States as an immigrant and made the American dream come true? Tell what this person did to become successful.

2. Most immigrants come to the United States with extremely limited financial resources. Yet, some of them manage to pursue their dreams despite the adverse circumstances. Discuss the driving force behind these people that helps them persevere in their goals.

3. Some people believe that it is better to have a stable job with benefits. Others think that the rewards of entrepreneurship are worth taking the risk of starting one's own business. In your opinion, what are the advantages and disadvantages of working for an employer compared to starting a business? Would you rather work for an employer, or be an entrepreneur? Give specific reasons for your choice.

How She Does It— Anya Ponorovskaya

By Michele Zipp, www.workingmother.com

1   She's a single mom who arrived in America a Russian refugee. She vacations with her ex and his girlfriend. And her preferred **method** of transportation is her bicycle. Who is this **eclectic** woman? Anya Ponorovskaya, a one-woman entrepreneurial powerhouse!

2   Anya's mom was just twenty-four years old when she left Leningrad with her two young kids. "I cannot imagine having the life she'd had and always be so **positive** the way she is." Anya shares. "She survived living in a communist country with two kids . . . and all the while maintained a **positive** outlook on life. She had no mother to help her the way I have her—no **assistance** at all. She arrived in a totally new world . . . so brave."

3   **Eventually,** Anya put herself through **design** school at FIT by bartending and running a start-up real **estate** company (which to this day still exists). In a record month, she was able to put away $30,000 from these two jobs! We're doing the math and are seriously impressed. Her love of fashion took her to Florence, Italy's Poly Moda **design** school where she completed her studies and began to embark on the greatest "**job**" of her life—being a mom. Dimitri Maxim-Ilya Joseph Williot was born to her and her then boyfriend. Anya couldn't decide on one name so gave him four, though she often calls her now-nine-and-a-half-year-old Dima.

4   When she returned to NY in 2003, she joined some partners and signed the lease on a small, **dilapidated** storefront in New York's NoLita neighborhood to open a women's boutique, selling clothes and accessories that look great on women for work and play. It would be called GirlCat. Having very little money left, she **rolled up her sleeves** and did all renovations herself. She even **hauled** sheetrock across town—scavenged from a lumber yard around the corner from her son's school. Neighbors were so impressed they hired her to renovate their lofts in the neighboring SoHo neighborhood. More work meant more **income** which provided her with capital to complete the store and buy out her partners. "Opening a store and believing in its success with a three-and-a-half-year-old son was terrifying. Deciding not to buy a cup of coffee in the morning so that Dima could have a slice of pizza for dinner was my reality at the time of the opening of my first store," she confesses.

eclectic
including a mixture of many different things or people

ESL Annotation

9.9 ESL This story may be of high interest to immigrant students as it details a success story of a political refugee.

dilapidated
old, broken, and in very bad condition

rolled up her sleeves
got ready for a challenging task

hauled
carried or pulled something heavy

© Pearson Education, Inc.

5   (She and Dima's father were no longer together.) Those were difficult times, but Anya knew she couldn't work for anyone else. "I needed my own hours. I felt I had no choice—I couldn't do 9 to 5."

6   "I was cutting wood to make shelves, and Dima knows mommy is going to get a store! He said, 'Mommy is that where the bread and cheese will go?' For him, a store meant one thing only—food." Food it did bring them, but in a different way than Dima expected. The store took off, and a second **location** with the same intent was opened in a substantially larger space, yet it was equally in need of repair. Once again Anya got to work. And in her free time, she worked on designing her line of women's wear, which she debuted in her third boutique that opened in 2007—this time in Brooklyn's Boerum Hill neighborhood.

7   "A single mother will always succeed because she really has no choice," Anya said. Her son is the reason she takes risks because without them, there is often no pay-off. But she admits that taking on all their responsibilities as a single mom wasn't without some fear. She says that she had to grow up fast and **assume** responsibility not just for Dima, but her employees. "Every action I take reflects on another human," she tells us.

8   "I feel a huge responsibility to protect my son," she says. Being a working mom helps her **achieve** that, and she relishes in the fact that her business not only helps her provide for her own family, but for her employees. "It fills me with an **enormous** sense of satisfaction that there are 10 people paying rent, paying taxes, and living based on something I created. I feel like I am positively impacting my immediate **community**—decreasing unemployment. It feels great that I **built something from the ground up** that provides for people with a **job** they like."

9   "My goal is to keep my family happy so I must keep myself happy. Don't go against your own grain or punish yourself. It is so easy to feel a tremendous amount of guilt as a mother, but the only thing you can really do is make sure that you are happy and following your heart.

10   In return your children will feel the rewards of that. As a mother you never feel like you can do enough, but you must accept yourself so that your children can."

11   Dima's dad is a part of his life—both their lives. "I have a great relationship with his father and his father's girlfriend. We have keys to each other's places, we eat together, we vacation together. Dima feels like he has a complete family. All it takes is to let go of anger. This is the hardest thing to do but also the most rewarding. Dima feels like he has a really big family. He has asked me, 'why do people need to get married?'"

12   Anya's life/work balance is **intertwined**. When she's not bicycling around town with him (an accessory Anya is rarely without), Dima's at school weekdays and at grandma's house two days a week—she's teaching him Russian. And he's with his dad on weekends. He also spends time at GirlCat. "I try to **create** something fun for him while I am working—choosing fabrics for my designs, painting prints and patterns for my customized linings. It goes like this: 'Honey, I want a cherry blossom print. Can you incorporate these colors?'"

13   As far as her designs, the female body is what inspires her. Her clothes are **impeccably** tailored and incredibly flattering for all body types. "I love

built something from ground up
started something challenging from the beginning, with little resources

intertwined
twisted together or closely related

impeccably
completely perfect and impossible to criticize

love love love when my customers are thankful for the pieces I **create**," she tells us. "When I hear 'for my body it's very hard to find a good fit' and they walk away thrilled with my clothes there is nothing better. I work tirelessly to **create** proper patterns, proper fittings just so I can feel good about the product I put out. My repeat customers are my best indication of success. There was a woman who posted a testimonial on yelp.com and I have never met her but her words have been so **significant** in making me believe in myself. She probably still has no idea how grateful I am for her words."

14　　　Anya is working to expand her eponymous line to include handbags and footwear to **create** a **core** collection that is "season-less, age-less, and flattering to a **range** of body types."

15　　　But it's Dima who inspires her and advises her. "Recently he said 'I don't like that on you. Actually, I don't like the last four dresses you made. I like simple shapes, no prints.' It's funny because it was a total affirmation on my instincts. He keeps me on my toes. If I tell him I need something, he makes sure I find it. He contributes to everything I do. If I need a skirt, he goes with me and hunts one down. He doesn't let me get **sidetracked**! He's always been that way."

sidetracked
forced to stop doing or saying something by being made interested in something else

16　　　"One day, I was talking about increasing sales to my salesgirls and all the things we should do. Dima was there and all of a sudden he jumped up and said 'I have an idea!' He ran into the street and yelled 'Who wants to buy my mommy's dresses? At the best prices ever?' I told him, 'Dima this isn't a flea-market!'" But it made her and her salesgirls think: maybe a flea market isn't such a bad idea.

17　　　Dima's future certainly seems headed for work in a creative field. Anya tells us that he wants to be an inventor. And it's his mom who he looks up to. "I inspire him because he sees I don't give up and he knows that I'm a tough mommy. When he had a hard time recently and overcame it, he was very proud of himself. He told me, 'You teach me not to give up.'"

Check out Anya's designs and learn more about her boutiques at www.anyaponorovskaya.com.

Reading Comprehension Check

1. It can be implied from paragraph 2 of the reading that
   a. Anya's mom has lots of friends.
   b. Anya doesn't get along with her mom.
   (c.) Anya's mom struggled before coming to the U.S.
   d. Having two children is perfect all families.

2. Anya moved to Italy . . .
   a. as a political refugee.
   b. to get out of New York.
   c. because her mom was there.
   (d.) to attend a design school.

© Pearson Education, Inc.

3. The word scavenged, in paragraph 4 "She even hauled sheetrock across town-scavenged from a lumber yard . . ." means _____.
   a. to search through discarded material.
   b. stolen.
   c. borrowed.
   d. disintegrated.

4. In paragraph 4, the detail of Anya sacrificing her morning cup of coffee in order to buy her son a slice of pizza for dinner is offered to make the point that . . .
   a. Anya would give up eating for her son.
   b. starting your own business as a single mom involves struggle.
   c. saving money is the key to small business.
   d. Anya's son was pressuring her.

5. If Anya shows a bias in her view of business models, it is
   a. in favor of innovative small businesses.
   b. in favor of large scale homogenous businesses.
   c. against creative enterprises.
   d. against American-owned companies.

6. Anya states, "Every action I take reflects on another human," (para. 7). She makes this point in discussing . . .
   a. her relationship with her son.
   b. Her relationship with her employees.
   c. Both a and b.
   d. Her relationship with her boss.

7. "Being a working mom helps her achieve that, and she relishes in the fact that her business not only helps her provide for her own family, but for her employees." (para. 8). In this sentence, the word relishes could be replaced by _____.
   a. to feel disgusted by.   c. feel great pleasure.
   b. to keep calm.   d. to lose control.

8. The example of the woman who posted a testimonial on yelp.com (para. 13) is offered to show . . .
   a. how satisfied customers help Anya believe in herself and her work.
   b. the unpredictable nature of business.
   c. that success is not all that it seems.
   d. you can never trust your own judgment.

9. The author's tone in this article is
   a. deflated.   c. mysterious.
   b. deeply emotional.   d. optimistic.

10. The main idea of the reading is that . . .
   a. With inspiration and determination, Anja was able to find success as a businesswoman in America.
   b. Anja's son inspires her.
   c. Political refugees all have the motivation to succeed in their new lives.
   d. One should try to maintain contacts with their ex-husbands and ex-wives.

From Reading to Writing: Writing a Business Letter

Overview

In your academic and professional career, you may be required to write many different types of letters. For example, you may need to write an inquiry letter, a response to a request made by your coworker or client, a complaint letter, a sales letter, or a letter of resignation. In this section, you will learn how to write a formal letter to your business professor in response to her request for information. Read Professor Profit's letter carefully and see what specific information she is asking you to provide in your written response. Use Professor Profit's letter as a model, as you write your response.

> Demand and Supply University
> Dollarville, Cash 11032
> USA

November 15, 2008
Business Students
P.O. Box 112
Global Learning, Reading Town

Dear Student:

Thank you for actively participating in the Business course. I hope you have learned the fundamental principles of U.S. business in this course. In order to make the learning atmosphere more conducive, I am asking you to write a letter responding to two questions:

1. What has been the most intellectually stimulating and interesting subject matter you have learned in this course? Why was it interesting?

2. What key concepts or lessons have you found particularly difficult to understand and why? Be specific.

It is required that your letter be no longer than one page. The purpose of this limit is to give you an opportunity to be precise and clear. Write clear answers to the aforementioned questions and get to the point quickly. I suggest that you be as specific as you can in response to the second question so that we can solve your confusions expediently.

The letter is due next week. Begin to write the preliminary draft of your letter today. In the next lesson, you will be asked to share your letter with your peers for feedback on form, content, and organization. You will rewrite your letter incorporating your peers' suggestions and submit the revised draft to me next week.

The purpose of writing this letter is twofold. First, we will discuss your confusions and/or questions in class. Second, we can use your valuable input to enhance the Business course.

© Pearson Education, Inc.

I am looking forward to reading your response letter. If you have any questions about the assignment, please do not hesitate to ask.

Sincerely,

Nickel Profit

Professor Nickel Profit, MBA

As you write your response to Professor Profit's request, keep in mind the following key criteria for this writing assignment:

1. Type of Letter: Response to Professor Profit's request
2. Audience: Professor Profit
3. Purpose: Respond to the two questions raised in the letter written by Professor Profit.
4. Tone: Polite but not excessively formal. Be careful not to use ornamental language to impress the reader. Keep the language simple, precise, and clear.
5. Length: No longer than 1 page
6. Vocabulary: Remember to incorporate new words you are learning from this chapter.
7. Feedback: Use the following form to provide constructive criticism to your peer's response letter.

Feedback Form

When you finish writing your response to Professor Profit's letter, ask your peer to read it and answer the questions on this form. You will also read your peer's response letter and evaluate it. By reviewing your peer's writing, you will learn to read with a critical eye and provide constructive feedback. Your valuable suggestions will enable your peer to make the necessary revisions to get the message across to the intended reader in a precise and clear manner. While it is important that you provide critical comments on your peer's writing, it is also useful to give feedback in a constructive way. Avoid being overly critical and suggest ways to make the letter more effective. Read the following questions carefully before you read your peer's letter in response to Professor Profit's request.

Writer's _____

Reviewer's _____

Date _____

1. Does the letter address Professor Profit appropriately? How does the letter begin?

   _____

   _____

   _____

2. What is the approximate length of the letter? Do you think the letter's length is sufficient?

_____

_____

_____

3. Is the writer's language appropriate for a business letter? What business terms are used in the letter?

_____

_____

_____

4. Does the writer provide clear answers to the questions raised by Professor Profit? Do you think Professor Profit will find your peer's answers acceptable? Why, or why not?

_____

_____

_____

5. Does the writer use polite language? Is the letter too formal, informal, or casual?

_____

_____

_____

6. Is the language used in the letter lucid and straight to the point?

_____

_____

_____

7. Does the writer give clear examples and appropriate reasons to answer Professor Profit's questions?

_____

_____

_____

8. Do you think Professor Profit will understand, after reading the response letter, why your peer has difficulty understanding certain key concepts?

_____

_____

_____

© Pearson Education, Inc.

Connecting Reading Skills with Standardized Testing

The Author's Bias

A standardized reading exam may ask you to recognize the author's bias for or against the topic. These questions test your ability to identify the author's attitude toward the subject, which may be positive or negative. Sometimes the author may be totally objective toward the topic, in which case the writing is considered to be unbiased. By paying attention to the language authors use, you can determine whether they are biased or unbiased.

Questions that test your ability to recognize the author's bias usually begin as follows:

- In the passage above, the author's attitude toward the topic is . . .
- In this passage, the author expresses a bias in favor of . . .
- In this passage, the author has a bias in favor of . . .
- In this passage, the author is biased against . . .
- In the passage above, the author's attitude toward the topic is . . .

Remember that if the author is subjective, then the point of view may be negative or positive, and the writing is considered biased. However, if the author is objective, then the tone is neutral, straightforward, or matter-of-fact, and the writing is considered unbiased.

Helpful Hints: Test Questions on Recognizing the Author's Bias

The following tips are meant to help you recognize the author's bias for or against the topic:

- Identify the topic and main idea. These will give you a clue to the author's bias toward the topic.
- Look for positive or negative language. Pay attention to biased language, which may have positive or negative connotations.
- How does the author sound? Ask yourself whether the author sounds positive or negative toward the topic.
- Look for a subjective viewpoint. As you read, see if the author has a one-sided viewpoint. Keep in mind that some authors afford the convenience of not acknowledging the counterargument.
- Find opinions in the writing. Most pieces of biased writing often contain opinions. Taking a close look at the opinions will help you recognize the author's bias.
- Does the author have an attitude? Sometimes the author may not have a positive or negative attitude toward the subject. In this case, the writing is considered objective or unbiased.

Mary Anne Poatsy

Interview with a Professional in the Field of Business

Current profession: College professor in Business/Computer Science and author.

Former job/profession: Vice President, Shearson Lehman Brothers, Municipal Bond Department (I worked with municipalities and toll road and sewer authorities to help structure municipal bond issues that were used to finance the expansion or creation of these municipal projects).

How did you choose your current profession?

I had studied in college to become an elementary teacher—but was always good in math. When I graduated from college, it was very difficult to find a good teaching job, so I applied for a job as a Trust Administrative Assistant at State Street Bank in Boston. I really liked what I did, and felt that I would rather pursue a career in banking instead of teaching. I was advised to get my Masters in Business Administration (MBA), which I did from Northwestern University. While at Northwestern, I realized that the best jobs for finance were on Wall Street—so I interviewed with many Wall Street Investment Banking firms and eventually chose the position in the Municipal Bond Department at Shearson Lehman Hutton. In essence, the profession chose me. I did not really have it as a life goal to become an investment banker.

How did you prepare to reach your goal of becoming a businesswoman and a professor?

The one bit of advice that I tell many young people is to get a good education. I think being well-rounded is better than studying one particular field—unless you have a particular passion or gift in that one field. I did not have a passion for any particular career, I just knew what I was good at—which is that I work well with people and I have a good ability to explain difficult concepts to people. That is why I initially chose teaching. Both of those abilities have served me well in my career on Wall Street, in a subsequent career as a Certified Financial Planner, and now as a college instructor, but my general knowledge and ability to learn and work hard has also enabled me to succeed.

What did you struggle with most when preparing to become a Business professor?

Time investment is huge in anything you want to do well. My struggle has been balancing the time I put into my careers and the time I should spend with my family, my friends, and myself.

How did you get through this struggle?

Good things don't come by just sitting around. I know that effort generally equals reward, so I look upon hard work and the sacrifices it calls for as worth it in the end. So far, I have been right. I just grin and bear it—as I know I can do almost anything difficult for a specific period. Having said that, though, it's important while working hard to take some periodic breaks so that you don't become completely burned out and end up resenting what you do.

What do you enjoy most about your work?

As an investment banker, I loved working on a wide variety of projects, traveling around the country, and working with and meeting many smart, interesting people. As a professor, I love the challenge of explaining difficult (and easy) concepts to students and watching as they "get it." I also love the fact that every 14 weeks many aspects of my job changes. As an author, I love working with a group of people who are constantly thinking of ways to improve the task of delivering instructional material to students.

What advice do you have for a student considering a career in business?

For any career, you need to work hard, keep an open mind, and challenge yourself constantly to be better than you were yesterday. It's best when you choose a career that you are interested in, regardless of the money. Making money is drudgery if you don't like what you do. You have a long life ahead of yourself. Find out what you're really best in and choose careers that fit you, rather than trying to fit yourself into a career that might not be right for you and your abilities.

In your opinion what were the three most interesting points made by the interviewee? Discuss your choices with the class!

- _____
  _____

- _____
  _____

- _____
  _____

© Pearson Education, Inc.

Textbook Application

Read the following chapter from an introductory textbook on business. As you know, this reading exercise gives you an opportunity to practice reading authentic text. Read the chapter carefully and answer the multiple-choice questions that follow.

READING

Reading Selection **5**

Textbook Reading

Understanding the U.S. Business System

What Goes Up Continues to Go Up

The sign in front of a Florida Shell gasoline station summed it up nicely: The "prices" for the three grades of gasoline sold at the station were listed as "An arm," "A leg," and "Your firstborn." While the sign no doubt led to a few smiles from motorists, its sentiments were far from a laughing matter. Indeed, in mid-2004 retail gasoline prices in the United States were at an all-time high, exceeding $2 per gallon in most places. But while gasoline prices have often fluctuated up and down, the upward price spiral in 2004 left consumers, government officials, and business leaders struggling to find answers.

What made this gas crisis unusual was that it was the result of an unusual confluence of supply, demand, and **global** forces. In the past, for **instance,** gas prices generally increased only when the supply was reduced. For example, an Arab embargo on petroleum exports to the United States

"Higher energy costs flow into every nook and cranny of the economy."
~Daniel Yergin,
Chairman, Cambridge Energy Research Associates

From Ricky W. Griffin and Ronald J. Ebert, *Business*, 8th ed., pp. 3-8, © 2006. Reproduced in print and electronic formats by permission of Pearson Education, Inc., Upper Saddle River, New Jersey.

in 1971 led to **major** price jumps. But these higher prices spurred new exploration, and as new oil fields came online, prices **eventually** dropped again. **Subsequent** supply disruptions due to political problems in Venezuela, Nigeria, and Iraq have also contributed to reduced supplies and **hence** higher prices at different times.

But the **circumstances underlying** the 2004 increases were much more **complex**. First of all, the supply of domestically produced gasoline in the United States has dropped steadily since 1972. This has been due to the facts that **domestic** oil fields have been nearly exhausted at the same time that new sources were being **identified** in many other parts of the world. **Hence, global** supplies have been increasing at a rate that has more than **offset** the declines in **domestic** production. As a result, the United States has been relying more and more on foreign producers.

Second, demand for gasoline in the United States has continued to rise. A growing population, the increased popularity of gas-guzzling SUVs and other big vehicles, and strong demand for other products (plastics, for **instance**) that require petroleum as a raw material have all contributed to increased demand. For example, in 2002 the United States consumed 7,191 million barrels of oil. This total was greater than the combined consumption of Germany, Russia, China, and Japan. As prices escalated, fears grew that there could be **major economic** damage. In the words of one **expert**, "Higher **energy** costs flow into every nook and cranny of the economy."

The **final** piece of the puzzle, surprisingly enough, was a surging **global** economy. As nation after nation started to recover from the **global** downturn that had slowed **economic** growth, the demand for oil and gasoline also surged. More people were buying cars, and petroleum refiners worked around the clock to help meet the unprecedented demand for gasoline. China, in particular, has become a **major consumer** of petroleum.

So, rather than weak supplies, it was strong **global** demand that was propelling the price increases that swept the country. And these price increases were leading to a wide array of **consequences.** For one thing, automobile manufacturers stepped up their **commitment** to making more fuel-efficient cars. Refiners posted record profits. And even local police officers were kept busy combating a surge in gasoline theft.

The Meaning of "Business"

1 Define the nature of U.S. *business* and identify its main goals and functions.

business

Organization that provides goods or services to earn profits

profits

Difference between a business's revenues and its expenses

What do you think of when you hear the word *"business"*? Does it conjure images of successful corporations such as Shell Oil and IBM? Or of less successful companies like Enron and Kmart? Are you reminded of smaller firms, such as your local supermarket or favorite restaurant? Or do you think of even smaller family-owned operations, such as the car-repair shop around the corner, your neighborhood pizzeria, or the florist down the street?

All these organizations are **businesses**—organizations that provide goods or services that are then sold to earn profits. Indeed, the **prospect** of earning **profits**—the difference between a business's revenues and expenses—is what encourages people to open and expand businesses. After all, profits reward owners for risking their money and time. The legitimate right to **pursue** profits distinguishes a business from those organizations,

© Pearson Education, Inc.

such as most universities, hospitals, and government agencies, which run in much the same way but which generally don't seek profits.[1]

Consumer Choice and Consumer Demand   In a capitalistic system, then, businesses exist to earn profits for owners; an owner is **likewise** free to set up a new business, grow that business, sell it to other owners, or even shut it down. But consumers also have freedom of choice. In choosing how to **pursue** profits, businesses must take into account what consumers want and/or need. No matter how efficient a business is, it won't **survive** if there is no demand for its goods or services. Neither a snowblower shop in Florida nor a beach-umbrella store in Alaska is likely to do very well.

Opportunity and Enterprise   But if enterprising businesspeople can identify either unmet **consumer** needs or better ways of satisfying **consumer** needs, they can be successful. In other words, someone who can spot a promising opportunity and then develop a good plan for capitalizing on it can succeed. The opportunity always involves goods or services that consumers need and/or want—especially if no one else is supplying them or if existing businesses are doing so inefficiently or incompletely.

Quality of Life   Businesses produce most of the goods and services we consume, and they employ most working people. They **create** most new innovations and provide a vast **range** of opportunities for new businesses, which serve as their suppliers. A healthy business climate also contributes directly to the quality of life and standard of living of people in a society. New forms of **technology**, service businesses, and international opportunities promise to keep production, consumption, and employment growing indefinitely. Business profits enhance the personal incomes of millions of owners and stockholders, and business taxes help to support governments at all levels. Many businesses support charities and provide **community** leadership. Of course, some businesses also

"Your Honor, my client pleads guilty to an overzealous but well-intentioned pursuit of the profit motive."

harm the **environment**, and their decision makers sometimes resort to unacceptable practices for their own personal **benefit**.

In this **chapter**, we first **trace** the history of U.S. business. We then examine **economic** systems around the world. Once you understand the differences among them, you will better appreciate the workings of the U.S. system. We also investigate the concepts of demand and supply and their **role** in private enterprise.

The Evolution of Business in the United States

The landscape of U.S. business has evolved dramatically since the nation's founding. A look at the history of U.S. business shows an **evolution** from small sole proprietorships to today's intricate **corporate** structures and an evolving **perspective** on business accountability. It also sets the stage for better understanding how our business system works.

The Factory System and the Industrial Revolution

With the coming of the Industrial Revolution in the middle of the eighteenth century, manufacturing was changed dramatically by advances in **technology** and by the development of the factory system. Replacing hundreds of cottage workers who had turned out one item at a time, the factory system brought together in one place the materials and workers **required** to produce **items** in large quantities and the new machines needed for mass production.

The factory system also reduced duplication of **equipment** and allowed firms to buy raw materials at better prices by buying in large lots. Even more important, it encouraged specialization of **labor**. Mass production replaced a system of highly skilled craftspeople who performed all the different tasks **required** to make a single item. Instead, a **series** of semiskilled workers, each trained to perform only one **task** and aided by specialized **equipment**, greatly increased **output**.

Laissez-Faire and the Entrepreneurial Era

Despite problems during the nineteenth century, the U.S. banking system began freeing businesses from European capital markets. In addition, improvements in transportation—steamboat navigation on **major** rivers and the development of railroads—soon made it economical to move products to distant markets.

Another key feature of the times was the rise on a grand scale of the entrepreneur. Like businesses in many other nations, U.S. business embraced the **philosophy** of *laissez-faire*—the idea that the government should not interfere in the economy. Rather, it should let business run without regulation and according to its own "natural" laws.

Risk taking and entrepreneurship became hallmarks of aggressive practices that created some of the biggest companies in the country and, **ultimately**, the world. During the last half of the 1800s, for **instance**, Andrew Carnegie **founded** U.S. Steel and Andrew Mellon created the Aluminum Company of America (Alcoa). J. P. Morgan's Morgan **Guarantee** and Trust came to dominate the U.S. **financial** system, and John D. Rockefeller's

2 **Trace** the history of business in the United States and the changing view of business accountability.

Industrial Revolution

Major mid-eighteenth-century change in production characterized by a **shift** to the factory system, mass production, and the specialization of **labor**

© Pearson Education, Inc.

Standard Oil controlled—in fact, monopolized—the petroleum industry. But these entrepreneurs all too often saw themselves as being accountable to no one.

The growth of these businesses increased the national standard of living and made the United States a world power. But the **economic** power of such firms made it difficult, if not impossible, for competitors to enter their markets. Complete market control became a watchword in many industries, with **major** corporations opting to collude rather than compete. Price fixing and other forms of market **manipulation** became business as usual, with captains of industry often behaving as robber barons. Reacting against unethical practices and the unregulated struggle for dominance, critics called for corrective action and, **ultimately**, for antitrust laws and the breakup of monopolies. Specifically, society began to demand greater accountability from big businesses—accountability to **function** in ways that did not trample on the rights of others.

Among other important laws, the Sherman Antitrust Act of 1890 and the Clayton Act of 1914 were passed specifically to limit the control that a single business could gain over a market. Other laws **sought** to regulate a variety of employment and advertising practices, and still others regulated the ways in which businesses could handle their **financial** affairs. This antitrust **legislation** was the basis for the U.S. government's recent lawsuit against Microsoft Corporation. (**Appendix I** gives more information about the **legal environment** of U.S. business, much of which is rooted in this era.)

The Production Era

The concepts of specialization and mass production were further refined in the early twentieth century, when many experts **sought** to **focus** management's attention on the production **process**. Relying on the advice of efficiency experts, managers began to further boost **output** by scientifically studying jobs and defining the "one best way" to perform those jobs. Dubbed *scientific management* by its advocates in the early 1900s, this model of management paved the way for a new era of business.

production era

Period during the early twentieth century in which U.S. business focused primarily on improving productivity and manufacturing efficiency

This new **production era** began to emerge in 1913 when Henry Ford introduced the moving **assembly** line. Ford's **focus** was on manufacturing efficiency: By adopting fixed workstations, increasing **task** specialization, using the concepts of scientific management, and moving the work to the worker, Ford dramatically increased productivity and lowered prices. And in so doing, he made the automobile affordable for the average person.

Unfortunately, both the growth of corporations and improved **assembly**-line **output** came at the expense of worker freedom. The dominance of big firms made it harder for individuals to go into business for themselves, and in some cases employer-run company towns gave people little freedom of choice, either in selecting an employer or in choosing what products to buy. Business accountability was again called into question, and new pressures **emerged** for balance.

This need for accountability and balance led to changes in how both the government and workers related to business. For **instance**, the production era witnessed the rise of **labor** unions and the advent of collective bargaining (see **Chapter** 8). In addition, the Great **Depression** of the 1930s and World War II prompted the government to intervene in the **economic** system on an unprecedented scale. Today, economists and politicians often refer to business, government, and **labor** as the three countervailing powers in U.S. society. Although all are big and all are strong, each is limited by the power of the other two.

The Marketing Era

After World War II, the demand for **consumer** goods that had been frustrated by wartime shortages fueled new **economic** growth in the United States. **Despite brief** recessions, the 1950s and 1960s were prosperous. Production continued to increase, **technology** to advance, and the standard of living to rise. During this era, a new **philosophy** of business came of age: the marketing **concept**. Previously, businesses had been production and sales oriented. They tended to produce what other businesses produced, what they thought customers wanted, or simply what owners wanted to produce. Henry Ford, for example, supposedly said that his customers could buy his cars in whatever color they wanted—as long as it was black!

According to the marketing concept, however, business starts with the customer. Producers start by determining what customers want and then provide it. Successful **practitioners** of the marketing **concept** include such companies as Procter & Gamble (P&G) and Anheuser-Busch. Such firms let consumers choose what best suits their needs by offering an array of products within a given market (toothpaste or beer, for example). Moreover, they also rely heavily on marketing and advertising to help shape **consumer** awareness, preferences, and tastes. Perspectives on business accountability also changed with the advent of the marketing **concept**, with central **issues** being truth-in-advertising, advertising directed at children, and so forth.

marketing concept

Idea that a business must focus on identifying and satisfying consumer wants in order to be profitable

The Global Era

The 1980s saw the continuation of technological advances in production, **computer technology**, information systems, and communications capabilities. They also witnessed the emergence of a truly **global** economy. U.S. consumers now drive cars made in Japan, wear sweaters made in Italy, and listen to CD players made in South Korea. Elsewhere around the world, people drive Fords, drink Pepsi, wear Levi's, use Dell computers, and watch Disney movies and television shows.

As we will see in **Chapter** 5, globalization is a fact of life for most businesses today. Improved **communication** and transportation, in addition to more efficient international methods for financing, producing, distributing, and marketing products and services, have combined to open distant marketplaces to businesses as never before.

Admittedly, many U.S. businesses have been hurt by foreign competition. Many others, however, have profited from new foreign markets. International competition has also forced many U.S. businesses to work harder to cut costs, increase efficiency, and improve quality. From an accountability **perspective**, key **issues** associated with globalization include worker rights in offshore production facilities and balancing the costs and benefits of outsourcing. We explore a variety of important trends, opportunities, and challenges in the new **global** era throughout this book.

The Information Era

The turn of the century has been **accompanied** by what might be called the *information era*, fueled largely by the Internet. Internet usage in North America grew from about 100 users per 1,000 people in 1995 to

© Pearson Education, Inc.

China opened its economy to foreign investors in the 1980s and joined the World Trade Organization in 2001. Now the Chinese buy as many cars as the Germans and more photographic film than the Japanese. They also buy more cell phones than anyone anywhere, and the opening of the Chinese market has created a windfall for makers of wireless handsets, including Motorola (U.S.), Siemens (Germany), Samsung (South Korea), and Nokia (Finland).

more than 750 users per 1,000 by 2005. The growth rate in Western Europe, however, has been even faster and is becoming increasingly **significant** in the Asia Pacific **region** as well. How has the growth of the Internet affected business? For one thing, it has given a **dramatic** boost to trade in all sectors of the economy, especially services. If the Internet makes it easier for all trade to grow, this is particularly true for trade in services on an international scale.

The Internet has also helped to level the playing field, at least to some extent, between larger and smaller enterprises, regardless of their products. In the past, a substantial **investment** was needed to enter some industries and to expand into foreign markets. Now, however, a small business in central Missouri, southern Italy, eastern Malaysia, or northern Brazil can set up a Web **site** and compete with much larger businesses located around the world. And finally, the Internet holds **considerable potential** as an effective and efficient networking **mechanism**. So-called business-to-business networks, for **instance**, can **link** firms with suppliers, customers, and strategic partners in ways that make it faster and easier for everyone to do business. The emergence of the information era also continues to define such accountability **issues** as rights to privacy.

*Most of these software developers are among the 65,000 engineers that the Indian state of Andhra Pradesh graduates every year—up from 7,500 just 10 years ago. Microsoft operates an R&D center in the capital city of Hyderabad, where Oracle, **Computer** Associates, and IBM also have facilities. The city is prospering as a hub not only for software programming, but for telephone call centers and pharmaceuticals as well.*

Reading Comprehension Check

Vocabulary in Context

1. As used in the sentence "What made this gas crisis unusual was that it was the result of an unusual confluence of supply, demand, and global forces," (p. 516) the word *confluence* means
   a. divergence.
   (b.) collection.
   c. branching out.
   d. separate forces.

Vocabulary in Context

2. "Subsequent supply disruptions due to political problems in Venezuela, Nigeria, and Iraq have also contributed to reduced supplies and hence higher prices at different times." (p. 517)

The term *disruptions* could be replaced with

a. improvements.

b. refinements.

c. continuity.

d. interruptions. ✏

Vocabulary in Context

3. In the sentence "This has been due to the facts that domestic oil fields have been nearly exhausted at the same time that new sources were being identified in many other parts of the world," (p. 517) a synonym for the word *exhausted* is

a. replenished completely.

b. used up completely. ✏

c. replaced completely.

d. improved completely.

Main Idea

4. The main idea of the chapter is that

a. different types of global economic systems affect the landscape of U.S. business.

b. U.S. businesses have evolved dramatically since the nation was founded. ✏

c. competition plays little or no role in the U.S. economic system.

d. demand and supply do not affect resource distribution in the United States.

Supporting Details

5. Examples of different eras in U.S. business such as the Industrial Revolution, the Entrepreneurial Era, the Production Era, the Marketing Era, etc. are offered to support the idea that

a. the nature of U.S. business has not changed significantly since the country was founded.

b. the Industrial Revolution was a consequence of the Marketing Era.

c. the landscape of U.S. business has changed significantly since the nation's founding. ✏

d. The Entrepreneurial Era and the Marketing Era happened simultaneously.

Supporting Details

6. Which of the following is NOT mentioned as an era in the evolution of business in the United States?

a. the Global Era.

b. the Information Era.

c. the Demand and Supply Era. ✏

d. the Entrepreneurial Era.

Inference

7. "After World War II, the demand for consumer goods that had been frustrated by wartime shortages fueled new economic growth in the United States." (p. 521)

It can be inferred from the above passage that

a. after World War II, the economy was extremely sluggish in the United States.

b. in the aftermath of World War II, U.S. economy plummeted.

c. there was little or no economic growth in the United States during World War II. ✏

d. the demand for consumer goods faded after World War II.

Inference

8. "How has the growth of the Internet affected business? For one thing, it has given a dramatic boost to trade in all sectors of the economy, especially

© Pearson Education, Inc.

services. If the Internet makes it easier for all trade to grow, this is particularly true for trade in services on an international scale." (p. 522)

A logical conclusion that can be drawn from the above statement is that
a. the growth of the Internet has given a boost to trade in services only in the United States.
b. the growth of the Internet has negatively impacted trade in services.
c. since the advent of the Internet, trade in products has not been as robust as trade in services.
d. trade in products has far surpassed trade in services.

Author's Purpose

9. The authors' primary purpose in this chapter is to
a. persuade the reader to found a small business in the United States.
b. convince students that they should conduct business with businesses in Europe and Asia.
c. deter the reader from pursuing a career in business.
d. educate the reader on the evolution of business in the United States.

Author's Tone

10. The overall tone of the chapter is
a. intimidating.
b. objective.
c. sorrowful.
d. concerned.

Fact and Opinion

11. Which of the following is NOT a fact?
a. In mid-2004 gasoline prices were at an all-time high in the United States.
b. In 2002 the American people consumed 7,191 million barrels of oil.
c. Most universities, hospitals, and government agencies do not seek profits.
d. The supply of domestically produced gasoline has dropped steadily in the United States since 1972.

Fact and Opinion

12. Which of the following is NOT an opinion?
a. Most U.S. corporations did business unethically during the Entrepreneurial Era.
b. Henry Ford introduced the moving assembly line in 1913.
c. Andrew Carnegie, J. P. Morgan, and John Rockefeller were immoral businessmen.
d. Technological advances in production and computer technology have made a negative impact on globalization.

Pattern of Organization

13. The overall pattern of organization of the section entitled What Goes Up Continues to Go Up (p. 516) is
a. listing.
b. classification.
c. cause and effect.
d. comparison and contrast.

Argument

14. Which statement does NOT offer support for the author's claim that "As nation after nation started to recover from the global downturn that had slowed economic growth, the demand for oil and gasoline also surged"?

a. China became a major consumer of petroleum.

b. More people were buying cars all over the world.

c.) Weak supplies propelled the price increases in the United States.

d. Petroleum refiners worked long hours to meet the demand for gasoline.

Author's Bias

15. "Admittedly, many U.S. businesses have been hurt by foreign competition. Many others, however, have profited from new foreign markets. International competition has also forced many U.S. businesses to work harder to cut costs, increase efficiency, and improve quality. From an accountability perspective, key issues associated with globalization include worker rights in offshore production facilities and balancing the costs and benefits of outsourcing."

In this passage, the author expresses a bias in favor of

a. emerging foreign markets.

b.) U.S. businesses.

c. international competition.

d. globalization.

Death of a Salesman

Pre-Reading Questions

1. In your opinion, how does a person choose a career, and what role do parents play in influencing their children's career choice?

2. What is your definition of success? In other words, how is a person's success measured? Be specific.

3. Some people believe that one succeeds in a professional career by getting ahead of one's colleagues. Others think that the key to success is in cooperating with one's peers. What is your opinion? Do you think that people are better off competing with their coworkers, or do you believe that people can get ahead by cooperating with their colleagues?

Collaboration

Death of a Salesman

By Arthur Miller

An excerpt from Act One; two men are in an upstairs bedroom.

1 BIFF: Why does Dad mock me all the time?

HAPPY: He's not mocking you, he—

BIFF: Everything I say there's a twist of mockery on his face. I can't get near him.

© Pearson Education, Inc.

HAPPY: He just wants you to make good, that's all. I wanted to talk to you about Dad for a long time, Biff. Something's—happening to him. He—talks to himself.

BIFF: I noticed that this morning. But he always mumbled.

HAPPY: But not so noticeable. It got so embarrassing I sent him to Florida. And you know something? Most of the time he's talking to you.

BIFF: Wha"s he say about me?

HAPPY: I can't make it out.

BIFF: What's he say about me?

HAPPY: I think the fact that you're not settled, that you're still kind of up in the air . . .

BIFF: There's one or two other things depressing him, Happy.

HAPPY: What do you mean?

BIFF: Never mind. Just don't lay it all to me.

HAPPY: But I think if you just got started—I mean—is there any future for you out there?

BIFF: I tell ya, Hap, I don't know what the future is. I don't know—what I'm supposed to want.

HAPPY: What do you mean?

BIFF: Well, I spent six or seven years after high school trying to work myself up. Shipping clerk, salesman, business of one kind or another. And it's a **measly** manner of existence. To get on that subway on the hot mornings in summer. To devote your whole life to keeping stock, or making phone calls, or selling or buying. To suffer fifty weeks of the year for the sake of a two-week vacation, when all you really desire is to be outdoors, with your shirt off. And always to have to get ahead of the next fella. And still—that's how you build a future.

HAPPY: Well, you really enjoy it on a farm? Are you content out there?

BIFF (*with rising agitation*): Hap, I've had twenty or thirty different kinds of jobs since I left home before the war, and it always turns out the same. I just realized it lately. In Nebraska when I herded cattle, and the Dakotas, and Arizona, and now in Texas. It's why I came home now, I guess, because I realized it. This farm I work on, it's spring there now, see? And they've got about fifteen new colts. There's nothing more inspiring or—beautiful than the sight of a mare and a new colt. And it's cool there now, see? Texas is cool now, and it's spring. And whenever spring comes to where I am, I suddenly get the feeling, my God, I'm not gettin' any-where! What the hell am I doing, playing around with horses, twenty-eight dollars a week! I'm thirty-four years old, I oughta be makin' my future. That's when I come running home. And now, I get here, and I don't know what to do with myself. (*After a pause*) I've always made a point of not wasting my life, and everytime I come back here I know that all I've done is to waste my life.

HAPPY: You're a poet, you know that, Biff? You're a—you're an idealist!

BIFF: No, I'm **mixed up** very bad. Maybe I oughta get married. Maybe I oughta get stuck into something. Maybe thats my trouble. I'm like a boy. I'm not married, I'm not in business, I just—I'm like a boy. Are you content, Hap? You're a success, aren't you? Are you content?

measly
very small and disappointing in size, quantity, or value

mixed up
confused, uncertain

HAPPY: Hell, no!

BIFF: Why? You're making money, aren't you?

HAPPY (*moving about with energy, expressiveness*): All I can do now is wait for the merchandise manager to die. And suppose I get to be merchandise manager? He's a good friend of mine, and he just built a terrific **estate** on Long Island. And he lived there about two months and sold it, and now he's building another one. He can't enjoy it once it's finished. And I know that's just what I would do. I don't know what the hellm workin' for. Sometimes I sit in my apartment—all alone. And I think of the rent I'm paying. And it's crazy. But then, it's what I always wanted. My own apartment, a car, and plenty of women. And still, goddammit, I'm lonely.

BIFF (*with enthusiasm*): Listen, why don't you come out West with me?

HAPPY: You and I, heh?

BIFF: Sure, maybe we could buy a ranch. Raise cattle, use our muscles. Men built like we are should be working out in the open.

HAPPY (*avidly*): The Loman Brothers, heh?

BIFF (*with vast affection*): Sure, we'd be known all over the counties!

HAPPY (*enthralled*): That's what I dream about, Biff. Sometimes I want to just rip my clothes off in the middle of the store and outbox that goddam merchandise manager. I mean I can outbox, outrun, and outlift anybody in that store, and I have to take orders from those common, petty sons-of-bitches till I can't stand it any more.

BIFF: I'm tellin' you, kid, if you were with me I'd be happy out there.

HAPPY (*enthused*): See, Biff, everybody around me is so false that I'm constantly lowering my ideals . . .

BIFF: Baby, together we'd **stand up for** one another, we'd have someone to trust.

stand up for
support or defend someone

HAPPY: If I were around you—

BIFF: Hap, the trouble is we weren't brought up to grub for money. I don't know how to do it.

HAPPY: Neither can I!

BIFF: Then let's go!

HAPPY: The only thing is—what can you make out there?

BIFF: But look at your friend. Builds an **estate** and then hasn't the peace of mind to live in it.

HAPPY: Yeah, but when he walks into the store the waves part in front of him. That's fifty-two thousand dollars a year coming through the revolving door, and I got more in my pinky finger than he's got in his head.

BIFF: Yeah, but you just said—

HAPPY: I gotta show some of those **pompous**, self-important executives over there that Hap Loman can make the **grade**. I want to walk into the store the way he walks in. Then I'll go with you, Biff. We'll be together yet, I swear. But take those two we had tonight. Now weren't they gorgeous creatures?

pompous
characterized by an overblown display of importance

BIFF: Yeah, yeah, most gorgeous I've had in years.

HAPPY: I get that any time I want, Biff. Whenever I feel disgusted. The only trouble is, it gets like bowling or something. I just keep knockin' them over and it doesn't mean anything. You still run around a lot?

BIFF: Naa. I'd like to find a girl—steady, somebody with substance.

HAPPY: That's what I long for.

BIFF: Go on! You'd never come home.

© Pearson Education, Inc.

HAPPY: I would! Somebody with character, with resistance! Like Mom, y'know? You're gonna call me a bastard when I tell you this. That girl Charlotte I was with tonight is engaged to be married in five weeks. (*He tries on his new hat.*)

BIFF: No kiddin'!

HAPPY: Sure, the guy's in line for the vice-presidency of the store. I don't know what gets into me, maybe I just have an overdeveloped sense of competition or something, but I went and ruined her, and **furthermore** I can't get rid of her. And he's the third executive I've done that to. Isn't that a crummy characteristic? And to top it all, I go to their weddings! (*Indignantly, but laughing*) Like I'm not supposed to take bribes. Manufacturers offer me a hundred-dollar bill now and then to throw an order their way. You know how honest I am, but it's like this girl, see. I hate myself for it. Because I don't want the girl, and, still, I take it and—I love it!

BIFF: Let's go to sleep.

HAPPY: I guess we didn't settle anything, heh?

BIFF: I just got one idea that I think I'm going to try.

HAPPY: What's that?

BIFF: Remember Bill Oliver?

HAPPY: Sure, Oliver is very big now. You want to work for him again?

BIFF: No, but when I quit he said something to me. He put his arm on my shoulder, and he said, "Biff, if you ever need anything, come to me."

HAPPY: I remember that. That sounds good.

BIFF: I think I'll go to see him. If I could get ten thousand or even seven or eight thousand dollars I could buy a beautiful ranch.

HAPPY: I bet he'd back you. 'Cause he thought highly of you, Biff. I mean, they all do. You're well liked, Biff. That's why I say to come back here, and we both have the apartment. And I'm tellin' you, Biff, any babe you want . . .

BIFF: No, with a ranch I could do the work I like and still be something. I just wonder though. I wonder if Oliver still thinks I stole that carton of basketballs.

HAPPY: Oh, he probably forgot that long ago. It's almost ten years. You're too sensitive. Anyway, he didn't really fire you.

BIFF: Well, I think he was going to. I think that's why I quit. I was never sure whether he knew or not. I know he thought the world of me, though. I was the only one he'd let lock up the place.

WILLY (*below*): You gonna wash the engine, Biff?

HAPPY: Shh!

(*Biff looks at Happy, who is gazing down, listening. Willy is mumbling in the parlor.*)

HAPPY: You hear that?

(*They listen. Willy laughs warmly.*)

BIFF: (growing angry): Doesn't he know Mom can hear that?

WILLY: Don't get your sweater dirty, Biff!

(*A look of pain crosses Biff's face.*)

HAPPY: Isn't that terrible? Don't leave again, will you? You'll find a **job** here. You gotta stick around. I don't know what to do about him, it's getting embarrassing.

WILLY: What a simonizing **job**!

  BIFF: Mom's hearing that!

WILLY: No kiddin', Biff, you got a date? Wonderful!

HAPPY: Go on to sleep. But talk to him in the morning, will you?

  BIFF (*reluctantly getting into bed*): With her in the house. Brother!

HAPPY (*getting into bed*): I wish you'd have a good talk with him.

(*The light on their room begins to fade.*)

  BIFF (*to himself in bed*): That selfish, stupid . . .

HAPPY: Sh . . . Sleep, Biff.

(*Their light is out. Well before they have finished speaking, Willy's form is dimly seen below in the darkened kitchen. He opens the refrigerator, searches in there, and takes out a bottle of milk. The apartment houses are fading out, and the entire house and surroundings become covered with leaves. Music **insinuates** itself as the leaves appear.*)

insinuates
–here, introduces itself very quietly, gently; can also mean to say something unpleasant without saying it directly

Reading Comprehension Check

1. The word *mock* in the first sentence of the excerpt could be replaced by
   a. create.
   b. make fun of.
   c. compliment.
   d. placate.

2. What is Happy and Biff's relationship?
   a. father and son.
   b. two friends.
   c. brothers.
   d. neighbors.

3. What is Biff's tone in the first part of the reading?
   a. optimistic.
   b. depressed.
   c. objective.
   d. amused.

4. A farm with horses is mentioned as
   a. a place of great beauty.
   b. a place where Biff is wasting his time.
   c. a big opportunity.
   d. both a and b.

5. It can be inferred that Happy views the world of the wealthy as
   a. an ideal.
   b. empty and lonely.
   c. impossible to get to.
   d. his brother's world.

6. When Happy says, "I mean I can outbox, outrun, and outlift anybody in that store," is this a statement of fact or an opinion?
   a. a fact.
   b. an opinion.
   c. both a fact and an opinion.
   d. neither.

7. When Happy says, "I gotta show some of those pompous, self-important executives over there that Hap Loman can make the grade," he is showing bias
   a. against high-level businesspeople.
   b. in favor of poor people.
   c. in favor of corporate executives.
   d. against farmers.

© Pearson Education, Inc.

8. How does Happy support the argument that he has an "overdeveloped sense of competition"?
   a. He explains his jealousy toward his brother.
   b. He always wants to switch jobs.
   c. He tells how he stole some girlfriends away from successful businessmen.
   d. He is never satisfied with his current girlfriend.

9. What is the tone at the end of the scene?
   a. curious.
   b. anxious and agitated.
   c. nostalgic.
   d. spirited.

10. What is the main idea of this scene from *Death of a Salesman?*
    a. Two sons worry about their father.
    b. Happy is successful, but unhappy.
    c. Two brothers are desperate to escape their unsatisfactory lives.
    d. Their mother wants them to be quiet and go to sleep.

Suggested Resources

Books

1. *The Tipping Point* by Malcolm Gladwell. Back Bay Books. Citing many successful examples from the business world, Gladwell argues in his popular book that little changes can have big effects on human behavior.

2. *Business @ the Speed of Thought: Succeeding in the Digital Economy* by Bill Gates. Business Plus. In this book, Gates provides a 12-step program for companies that want to do business in the next millennium. He claims that how companies gather and disseminate information will determine their success or failure.

Movies

1. *Wall Street* (1987). Directed by Oliver Stone. In this movie based on the stock market in the United States, Michael Douglas plays a Wall Street trader who is driven by greed. The movie looks at big businesses in the 1980s, questioning a corrupt system that values profit at the cost of humanity.

2. *The Pursuit of Happyness* (2006). Directed by Gabriele Muccino. Inspired by the true story of Chris Gardner, a successful and wealthy Chicago businessman and philanthropist, this heartwarming movie shows how diligent, hard-working people can make their dreams come true.

Internet Sites

1. http://www.executivelibrary.com/

   Executives from U.S. corporations such as Boeing, Intel, Microsoft, and the New York Stock Exchange (NYSE) visit this Web site for the best business information sources. It has a public library that contains most of the visible and useful business sites.

2. http://www.investors.com

This Website is the online edition of the *Investor's Business Daily*, founded by the American entrepreneur Bill O'Neil. Here you can read business news, and analyst reports and learn about promising U.S. and foreign businesses.

Discipline Focus: Negotiating with International Business Partners

American businesses import products from many countries and export products and services all over the world. Signing a contract to finalize a deal with an international business partner requires negotiation skills. Keep in mind that negotiation is a complex process, which involves a gamut of factors that are culturally determined. What is appropriate and inappropriate in a business meeting depends on where the business meeting is taking place. Being aware of the contrasting cultural values of the country where you are negotiating a business deal can help you avoid confrontation and succeed in getting a signed contract. The following table shows how negotiation is viewed in the North American culture and in other cultures.

ESL Annotation

9.10 ESL This section will not only be useful for both American students who may one day be involved with international business, but also for ESL students to compare business etiquette practices in their global region to that of North American norms.

Contrasting Cultural Values

	North America	*Latin America*	*Middle East*	*Asia*
Time	Time is money. Meetings must start and end on time.	Meetings may not start on time. It is considered normal if a business meeting does not start promptly.	It is important to establish friendship before a business meeting begins.	People and relationships are more important than time.
Decision	The individual makes her/his own decision and is responsible for it.	The individual makes her/his own decision and is usually responsible for it.	The individual makes a decision after consulting with friends and coworkers.	The individual makes a decision only after the group or her/his supervisor agrees with it.
Promise	Not delivering on a promise can be serious.	Making a promise and not keeping it can be excused.	Making a promise is equated with delivering on the promise and is understood that way.	Making a promise is often considered politeness and is not to be taken seriously.
Task	Only one task is to be performed in a linear manner.	Several things can happen at the same time during a business meeting.	Several tasks can be accomplished simultaneously.	Frequent interruptions during a business meeting are normal.
Truth	Always tell the truth no matter what.	Truth depends on time and situation.	Graciousness is more important than being truthful.	It is more important to save face than to tell the truth.

(Continued)

© Pearson Education, Inc.

Contrasting Cultural Values

	North America	*Latin America*	*Middle East*	*Asia*
Discussion	Discussions are necessary to clarify things.	Discussions are good and necessary.	Discussions tend to be long and intense.	Discussions are brief. Speaking too much can be viewed as a sign of arrogance. Thus, the Persian saying, "God gave us two ears, but only one mouth."
Conflicts	It is important to resolve a conflict in a face-to-face conversation.	Conflicts are handled indirectly first.	A mediator is usually involved to resolve a conflict.	Harmony is of utmost importance when resolving a conflict. A mediator is involved in conflict and resolution.
Physical Distance	Two people talking stand at least 2½ feet apart from each other.	Two people conversing with each other stand 2 feet apart from each other.	Two people of the same gender talking stand 18 inches apart from each other.	Two people talking stand at least 3–4 feet apart from each other.
Eye Contact	It is important to make direct eye contact with the listener.	It is important to make direct eye contact with the listener.	Eyes are lowered or averted to show respect.	Eyes are lowered as a sign of respect.
Contract	Signing a contract is closing a business deal.	A contract is a means of closing a deal.	A contract is seen as an agreement, which can be changed if the situation changes.	A contract is a means of establishing a relationship. The contract can be revised if the situation changes in the future.
Introduction	The two parties shake hands and introduce themselves verbally.	The two parties may shake hands and introduce themselves verbally.	The two parties may embrace and kiss each other on the cheek, especially if they have met before.	Instead of introducing themselves verbally, it is common for the two parties to first exchange business cards, especially Japan.
Communication	Communication is direct. It is important to state exactly what one means and a direct response is expected.	Communication may be indirect. The meaning is expressed more through emotion than words.	Saying "yes" means that the message is understood, not that the speaker agrees with the business counterpart.	Saying "maybe" is a polite way to say "no."

Learning Styles

Overview

Your academic success will largely depend on how you learn new bits and pieces of information. Keep in mind that learning styles differ from individual to individual. Those who are auditorily dependent must hear information in the form of a lecture, for example, to learn the content. In contrast, others who are visually dependent need to see information on the blackboard, or on posters, or projection screens, or in the textbook. Social learners like to interact with their peers, raising and responding to pertinent questions. On the other hand, independent learners would rather study alone. They set their academic goals and are self-motivated. Spatial learners have the ability to visualize how things are situated in space. Verbal learners, however, lack this ability and rely on verbal skills to learn a new subject matter.

Those who prefer to deal with tangible objects are called *applied learners,* and those who prefer to work with concepts and ideas are called *conceptual learners.* In addition, *creative learners* are not afraid to make mistakes and take risks. They are imaginative and learn through investigation and discovery. Last but not least, *pragmatic learner* are conformists. They find it easy to learn when things are logical and systematic. Some students are good at answering multiple-choice questions, but they have difficulty writing in prose form. Others find it relatively easy to write an academic essay, but they dread the idea of taking a test consisting of multiple-choice questions. It will be important for you to discover how you learn best so that you can optimize learning.

Students often complain that their professors never explain to them how to learn discipline-specific material. However, professors are aware of the fact that different students have different learning styles. For this reason, they do not explain how to learn the material best. If you take into account that students have different learning styles, you will realize that it is impossible for the professor to recommend one learning technique that works for all students. Depending on your learning style, your approach to learning new information should be based on how you learn well.

You may have more than one learning style, but you will need to determine what you do really well. Do you find it cumbersome to listen to a lecture and take notes at the same time? Or do you feel at ease simply copying information down from the blackboard and then revisiting your notes at home for further reflection and analysis? Do you read maps easily or with great difficulty? Do you find performing certain academic tasks more easily than others?

Perhaps you can make a list of the academic tasks that you have no difficulty performing and those you find troublesome.

Implications for Your Learning

The sooner you determine what your learning style is, the better off you will be succeeding in college. It should be noted, though, that just as people change over time, your learning style might also change. It is also possible that you have more

© Pearson Education, Inc.

than one learning style. Knowing how you learn best will help you understand why you find certain aspects of a course troublesome or easy. Once you know your weaknesses and strengths in learning, you can adapt to different teaching styles. Finally, it is always a good idea to speak to the professor about the course requirements, your learning styles, and your professor's expectations so that you can get the most out of the course and perform well.

Challenge Activity

Some people learn by visualizing the concept. That is, they are visually dependent. Others learn by listening to lectures or audiotapes, meaning they are auditorily dependent. Yet others learn by making a list of new ideas or by taking notes. Depending on people's learning styles, they learn differently. If you want to know how you learn best, go to the following Web site and complete the questionnaire: http://www.vark-learn.com/english/page.asp?p=questionnaire

POLITICAL SCIENCE
American Government

"It is rather for us to be here dedicated to the great task remaining before us . . . and that government of the people, by the people, for the people, shall not perish from the earth."

ABRAHAM LINCOLN

Objectives

IN THIS CHAPTER YOU WILL LEARN . . .

- About the U.S. political system
- How to navigate a text bringing together combined skills
- How to write to a political representative about a community concern

© Pearson Education, Inc.

Making Predictions

Consider this chapter's theme of political science. What subtopics relate to this field? (See Figure 10.1.)

■ **Figure 10.1**

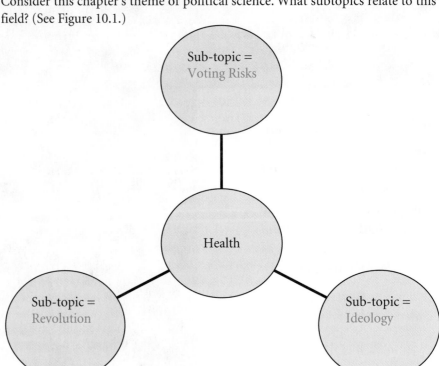

Introduction to the Discipline of Political Science

The United States has witnessed changing perceptions of political science in the twenty-first century as a result of recent wars and terrorist attacks. In the past, people used to think that politics was exclusively for the politicians, and that political science as a discipline had little or no bearing on people's lives. However, terrorist threats to America's national security, U.S. relations with oil-producing countries, and violent crimes committed in countries around the world have caused students, activists, and intellectuals to take politics seriously. Many people who took no interest in political involvement, thinking it was for the government to deal with political matters, are now playing an active role in the governmental process. It may be the case that the American people are dissatisfied with America's foreign policy, or that they are concerned about their beloved country's image in the world, or that they are afraid of another terrorist attack. Perhaps they are following politics more closely because of anger, fear, insecurity, and controversial issues that concern them. Whatever the reason, political scientists are obviously pleased with the resurgence of interest in politics among the American people and claim that politics determine and influence economics and education. Some even argue that politics plays an important role in every facet of human life.

In this chapter, you will become familiar with political science as a discipline. The articles included in this chapter relate to issues of immigration, racial discrimination, democracy, and other aspects of government. As you read the articles carefully, you will understand how politics is intricately woven into the fabric of society.

Preview Questions

With a small group of your classmates, discuss the following questions.

1. In his famous Gettysburg Address, U.S. President Abraham Lincoln said, "It is rather for us to be here dedicated to the great task remaining before us . . . and that government of the people, by the people, for the people, shall not perish from the earth." Do you believe that this is true of America today? Do you believe that every citizen in the country has political power? Explain. Can you think of another country in the world where Lincoln's vision of democracy is more or less realized?

2. Many people seem to have little or no interest in political involvement, arguing that it is for the government to worry about political matters. Others believe that a true democracy can only thrive when its citizens play an active role in the governmental process. Where do you stand on the issue of political involvement? Do you keep yourself abreast of local and national politics?

3. Despite the fact that U.S. citizens over the age of 18 are eligible to vote, the reality is that only 52 percent of eligible voters actually exercise their right to vote. Discuss what factors might keep the rest of the voters from participating in the electoral process. Given these factors, what would motivate non-voters to turn out at the polls?

4. According to the law, only U.S.-born citizens have the right to run for the presidency, and naturalized citizens are excluded from this privilege. In your opinion, should immigrant political figures such as Arnold Schwarzenegger be allowed to become the president of the United States of America?

5. In the United States, we often speak of the virtues of a democratic form of government—that is, a system where political representatives are chosen by citizens of the country. Is democracy always the best system of governance? Are there any shortcomings to the concept of democracy? Can you think of other forms of government that may be superior to democracy?

Interpreting a Cartoon

■ Figure 10.2

"You can't take the Ethics course-you're a Political Science major."

© Pearson Education, Inc.

Collaboration

Working in pairs, examine the cartoon in Figure 10.2 and answer the following questions.

1. What is humorous about this cartoon?
2. In your opinion, what is the cartoonist's intended message for the reader?

Discipline-specific Terminology Bank

activist	constitutional	legislation	propaganda
apathy	dictatorship	lobbying	referendum
authority	diplomacy	platform	representation
campaign	ideology	pluralism	sovereignty
candidate	incumbent	primaries	stability

Sample Paragraph

In an American presidential election, it is often the case that an **incumbent** runs against a **candidate** from the opposing political party. The incumbent usually has the advantage of not being as heavily challenged in the **primaries**, and often has a more defined **platform** after having served in the Oval Office for four years. The incumbent also has the **authority** to use his/her presidential power during the political **campaign** to win the attention of the American public.

EXERCISE 1

Matching Column A and Column B

Match the word in Column A with the definition in Column B. Put the letter representing the correct definition in the space preceding each term.

Column A

Word

1. _h_ ideology
2. _i_ constitutional
3. _g_ referendum
4. _f_ incumbent
5. _a_ dictatorship
6. _e_ sovereignty
7. _c_ activist
8. _j_ pluralism
9. _b_ legislation
10. _d_ lobbying

Column B

Definition

a. a system of absolute political control given to one person
b. a piece of law
c. someone who takes direct action to achieve a political goal
d. the act of representing political interest
e. the independent status of a state
f. currently in office
g. the submission of a law to a direct vote by the people

      h. the political doctrine, or belief system of
         an individual

      i. in accordance with the constitution
        of a government

      j. condition in which many cultures
       coexist within a society and maintain
       their cultural differences

EXERCISE 2

Fill in the Blanks

In the following sentences, fill in the blank with a word from the terminology bank below that makes the sentence grammatical and meaningful.

activist	constitutional	dictatorship	ideology	incumbent
legislation	lobbying	pluralism	referendum	sovereignty

1. The accused used his _constitutional_ right to not speak to anyone but his attorney.

2. In Cuba's _dictatorship_ the people have little voice in political matters.

3. An environmental _activist_ tied himself to a tree to protest the logging industry's deforestation.

4. His _ideology_, or belief system, was considered radical during the time he ruled the country.

5. There was strong _lobbying_ in the nation's capital for a change in the government's gun-control policy.

6. California held a _referendum_ on whether or not the state wanted to set term limits on the governorship.

7. The senate passed new job-training _legislation_ after a sustained fight on the Senate floor.

8. The North East region of an Eastern European country declared independence and then asked the rest of the world to recognize their _sovereignty_.

9. The _incumbent_ mayor dropped out in the middle of a hard-fought political race and decided not to run again.

10. In the United States we can see _pluralism_ at work with people from many religious and cultural backgrounds sharing in the political process.

EXERCISE 3

Collaboration

Pair Activity

Pair up with a classmate and form complete sentences with five words you learned from the vocabulary exercise.

© Pearson Education, Inc.

1. _____

_____

2. _____

_____

3. _____

_____

4. _____

_____

5. _____

_____

Collaboration

Create Your Own Survey with a Political Focus

Throughout the text, you have been asked a number of times to conduct an in-class or field survey, working with questions related to the academic focus of the chapter. In Chapter 2 on nutrition, you asked respondents about their dietary habits. In Chapter 3, the survey was on personal connections to environmental issues. Chapter 6 offered a survey on attitudes on issues related to crime. Finally, Chapter 8 on psychology included a survey exploring stereotypes on gender roles.

As this is the final chapter and you now have had some experience with surveying, this time it is your turn to organize an interesting survey with a political focus, and then to administer your survey to at least two respondents.

Some Tips

- Focus your survey around a particular issue. Some examples are immigrant rights, women in politics, support for a particular candidate, gun control, etc.

- Try to steer away from issues that will make respondents feel uncomfortable. Some topics—abortion for example—are very controversial and may result in some respondents not wanting to take part in your survey.

- Do not ask for respondents' names, and make sure that you let respondents know that the survey is anonymous and that the results will in no way be connected to personal identities.

- You may need to make use of a separate piece of paper to organize your survey.

Survey Worksheet

Question	Respondent 1	Respondent 2
1.		
2.		

3.		
4.		

ESL Annotation

10.1 ESL In many world cultures it is considered taboo to survey strangers about their political beliefs. It may be useful to introduce ESL students to our cultural tradition of political surveying.

Post-Survey Discussion: Share the results and analysis of your survey work with the class!

Graphic Analysis

Voting Choices in the 2004 U.S. Presidential Election by Personal Characteristic

Total	Percent of All	Bush (15%)	Kerry (48%)	Total	Percent of All	Bush (15%)	Kerry (48%)
Gender				*Education*			
Male	49	53	46	High School Diploma or less	48	54	45
Female	51	49	50	Some college	26	45	51
Gender and Marriage				College degree or more	52	49	50
Married men	31	59	40	*Religion*			
Single men	16	40	58	Protestant	51	61	38
Married women	30	57	42	Roman Catholic	25	55	44
Single women	19	35	64	Jewish	4	26	74
Ethnicity				*Annual Family Income*			
African American	10	14	86	$20,000–$39,999	20	47	52
Asian American	3	34	64	$40,000–$59,999	20	51	48
Caucasian	79	57	42	$60,000–$74,999	15	53	46
Chicano/Latino	5	45	54	$75,000 and over	35	54	45
Age							
18–29	20	43	55				
30–44	32	52	47				
45–64	36	54	45				
65 and older	12	55	45				

■ **Figure 10.3**

Los Angeles Times national exit poll results, 2004 U.S. Presidential Election. Copyright © 2004 by The *Los Angeles Times*. Reprinted with permission. All rights reserved.

The graph in Figure 10.3 represents how demographic characteristics play a significant role in determining which candidate a citizen will vote for. In this case, we have the example of the 2004 U.S. presidential election where George Bush

© Pearson Education, Inc.

ran for the Republican Party against John Kerry of the Democratic Party. After studying it, answer the following questions.

1. In which two categories can we see the widest disparity in voting choice?

   African Americans voted for Kerry by 86% to Bush's 14%; Jewish voters chose Kerry over Bush by 74% to 26%.

2. Can you think of any explanations for the great disparity outlined in question 1?

   Answers will vary.

3. What was the relationship between education level and voting choice in the 2004 presidential election?

   The majority of those with some college experience voted for Kerry. The majority of voters with a high school diploma or less voted for Bush.

4. What correlation can we make between the age of voters and their choice for president?

   The majority of younger voters (18–29) chose Kerry. Older voters were more likely to choose Bush.

READING

Reading Selection **1**

Government Document

10.2 Flesch-Kincaid Grade Level 12.0

Collaboration

The Declaration of Independence: The Want, Will, and Hopes of the People

---

Pre-Reading Questions

With a classmate answer these questions before reading the selection.

1. One of the oft-quoted claims of the Declaration of Independence, a political document written by America's founders, is that "all men are created equal." Do you believe this claim to be true? Do you think that in most countries government policy is guided by this principle?

2. According to the Declaration of Independence, all people have the "unalienable rights" to life, liberty, and happiness. However, there are certain groups of people who firmly believe that these virtues should pertain to a privileged few. If you were to speak to one of these groups, how would you convince them that liberty and happiness are for all?

3. At the time the Declaration of Independence was written, most of the nation's founders themselves owned slaves, not practicing what they preached. Knowing this fact about the writers, how much faith can we put into the authenticity of their egalitarian principles? Might slave owning be justified given the historical context of the times? (Slave ownership was a common practice among the wealthy in the late eighteenth century.)

The Declaration of Independence: The Want, Will, and Hopes of the People

In Congress, July 4, 1776
The Unanimous Declaration of the Thirteen United States of America

1 When in the Course of human events it becomes necessary for one people to dissolve the political bands which have connected them with another and to **assume** among the powers of the earth, the separate and equal station to which the Laws of Nature and of Nature's God entitle them, a decent respect to the opinions of mankind requires that they should declare the causes which impel them to the separation.

2 We hold these truths to be **self-evident**, that all men are created equal, that they are endowed by their Creator with certain unalienable Rights, that among these are Life, Liberty and the pursuit of Happiness. — That to secure these rights, Governments are instituted among Men, deriving their just powers from the **consent** of the governed, — That whenever any Form of Government becomes destructive of these ends, it is the Right of the People to alter or to abolish it, and to **institute** new Government, laying its **foundation** on such principles and organizing its powers in such form, as to them shall seem most likely to effect their Safety and Happiness. Prudence, indeed, will dictate that Governments long **established** should not be changed for light and transient causes; and accordingly all experience hath shewn that mankind are more disposed to suffer, while evils are sufferable than to right themselves by abolishing the forms to which they are accustomed. But when a long train of abuses and usurpations, pursuing invariably the same Object evinces a **design** to reduce them under absolute Despotism, it is their right, it is their duty, to throw off such Government, and to provide new Guards for their future **security**. — Such has been the patient sufferance of these Colonies; and such is now the necessity which constrains them to **alter** their former Systems of Government. The history of the present King of Great Britain is a history of repeated injuries and **usurpations**, all having in direct object the establishment of an absolute Tyranny over these States. To prove this, let Facts be **submitted** to a candid world.

3 He has refused his Assent to Laws, the most wholesome and necessary for the public good.

4 He has forbidden his Governors to pass Laws of immediate and pressing importance, unless **suspended** in their operation till his Assent should be **obtained**; and when so **suspended**, he has utterly neglected to attend to them.

5 He has refused to pass other Laws for the **accommodation** of large districts of people, unless those people would **relinquish** the right of Representation in the Legislature, a right inestimable to them and formidable to tyrants only.

6 He has called together legislative bodies at places unusual, uncomfortable, and distant from the depository of their Public Records, for the sole purpose of fatiguing them into compliance with his measures.

7 He has dissolved Representative Houses repeatedly, for opposing with manly firmness his invasions on the rights of the people.

8 He has refused for a long time, after such dissolutions, to cause others to be elected, **whereby** the Legislative Powers, incapable of Annihilation, have returned

---

ESL Annotation

10.3 ESL Many ESL students have the goal of passing the citizenship exam. Knowledge of The Declaration of Independence is very helpful in this regard.

self-evident
clearly true and needing no proof

usurpations
wrongful seizure or exercise of authority

relinquish
give up your position, power, rights, etc.

© Pearson Education, Inc.

to the People at large for their exercise; the State remaining in the mean time exposed to all the dangers of invasion from without, and convulsions within.

9   He has endeavoured to prevent the population of these States; for that purpose obstructing the Laws for Naturalization of Foreigners; refusing to pass others to encourage their migrations hither, and raising the conditions of new Appropriations of Lands.

10   He has obstructed the **Administration** of Justice by refusing his Assent to Laws for establishing Judiciary Powers.

11   He has made Judges dependent on his Will alone for the tenure of their offices, and the amount and payment of their salaries.

12   He has erected a multitude of New Offices, and sent hither swarms of Officers to harass our people and eat out their substance.

13   He has kept among us, in times of peace, Standing Armies without the **Consent** of our legislatures.

14   He has affected to render the **Military** independent of and superior to the **Civil** Power.

15   He has combined with others to subject us to a jurisdiction foreign to our constitution, and unacknowledged by our laws; giving his Assent to their Acts of pretended **Legislation**:

16   For quartering large bodies of armed troops among us:

17   For protecting them, by a mock Trial from punishment for any Murders which they should commit on the Inhabitants of these States:

18   For cutting off our Trade with all parts of the world:

19   For imposing Taxes on us without our **Consent**:

20   For depriving us in many cases, of the **benefit** of Trial by Jury:

21   For transporting us beyond Seas to be tried for pretended offences:

22   For **abolishing** the free System of English Laws in a neighbouring Province, establishing therein an **Arbitrary** government, and enlarging its Boundaries so as to render it at once an example and fit instrument for introducing the same absolute rule into these Colonies.

23   For taking away our Charters, abolishing our most valuable Laws and altering fundamentally the Forms of our Governments:

24   For suspending our own Legislatures, and declaring themselves invested with power to legislate for us in all cases whatsoever.

25   He has **abdicated** Government here, by declaring us out of his Protection and waging War against us.

26   He has **plundered** our seas, ravaged our coasts, burnt our towns, and destroyed the lives of our people.

27   He is at this time transporting large Armies of foreign Mercenaries to compleat the works of death, desolation, and tyranny, already begun with **circumstances** of Cruelty & Perfidy scarcely paralleled in the most barbarous ages, and totally unworthy the Head of a civilized nation.

28   He has constrained our fellow Citizens taken Captive on the high Seas to bear Arms against their Country, to become the executioners of their friends and Brethren, or to fall themselves by their Hands.

29   He has excited **domestic** insurrections amongst us, and has endeavoured to bring on the inhabitants of our frontiers, the merciless Indian Savages whose known rule of warfare, is an undistinguished destruction of all ages, sexes and conditions.

abolishing
officially ending a law, system, etc.

abdicated
refused to continue being responsible for something

plundered
stole money or property from a place while fighting in a war

30   In every stage of these Oppressions We have Petitioned for **Redress** in the most humble terms: Our repeated Petitions have been answered only by repeated **injury**. A Prince, whose character is thus marked by every act which may define a Tyrant, is unfit to be the ruler of a free people.

redress
correction or reformation

31   Nor have We been wanting in attentions to our British brethren. We have warned them from time to time of attempts by their legislature to extend an unwarrantable jurisdiction over us. We have reminded them of the **circumstances** of our emigration and settlement here. We have appealed to their native justice and **magnanimity**, and we have conjured them by the ties of our common kindred to disavow these usurpations, which would **inevitably** interrupt our connections and correspondence. They too have been deaf to the voice of justice and of **consanguinity**. We must, therefore, acquiesce in the necessity, which denounces our Separation, and hold them, as we hold the rest of mankind, Enemies in War, in Peace Friends.

magnanimity
the quality of being forgiving

consanguinity
relationship by blodd

32   We, therefore, the Representatives of the United States of America, in General Congress, Assembled, appealing to the Supreme Judge of the world for the rectitude of our intentions, do, in the Name, and by **Authority** of the good People of these Colonies, solemnly publish and declare, That these united Colonies are, and of Right ought to be Free and Independent States, that they are Absolved from all Allegiance to the British Crown, and that all political connection between them and the State of Great Britain, is and ought to be totally dissolved; and that as Free and Independent States, they have full Power to levy War, conclude Peace, **contract** Alliances, establish Commerce, and to do all other Acts and Things which Independent States may of right do. — And for the support of this Declaration, with a firm **reliance** on the protection of Divine Providence, we mutually pledge to each other our Lives, our Fortunes, and our sacred Honor.

Reading Comprehension Check

1. "When in the Course of human events it becomes necessary for one people to dissolve the political bands which have connected them with another and to assume among the powers of the earth, the separate and equal station to which the Laws of Nature and of Nature's God entitle them, a decent respect to the opinions of mankind requires that they should declare the causes which impel them to the separation."

In the above sentence, the word *impel* means
a. cause to move away from.   (c.) cause to move forward.
b. cause to move backward.   d. cause to move downward.

2. The main idea of the Declaration of Independence is that
a. every person's right to life, freedom, and happiness is alienable.
b. it is morally right to deprive some people of liberty and happiness.
c. only a special group of people have the right to liberty and happiness.
(d.) the right to life, liberty, and happiness is unalienable.

3. The facts related to the King of Great Britain are presented to prove the main point that
a. he was a generous and just king.   c. he was a kind king.
(b.) he was a tyrant.   d. he was a lenient king.

© Pearson Education, Inc.

4. "But when a long train of abuses and usurpations, pursuing invariably the same Object evinces a design to reduce them under absolute Despotism, it is their right, it is their duty, to throw off such Government, and to provide new Guards for their future security."

   It can be inferred from the above statement that
   (a.) people have the right to fight the government to defend their country.
   b. people should unquestionably surrender to despotism.
   c. citizens of a country must not rise against the government.
   d. people ought to accept abuses without ever complaining.

5. The primary purpose of the Declaration of Independence is
   a. to criticize the king of Great Britain.
   (b.) to persuade the readers to declare freedom from the despotic king of Great Britain.
   c. to describe the king of Great Britain in detail.
   d. to define the meaning of despotism.

6. The overall tone of the Declaration of Independence is
   a. humorous.   c. neutral.
   b. reverent.   (d.) inspirational.

7. The overall pattern of organization of the Declaration of Independence is
   a. classification.   c. generalization and example.
   (b.) cause and effect.   d. spatial order.

8. Which of the following sentences is a statement of fact?
   a. "We hold these truths to be self-evident, that all men are created equal."
   b. "... men are endowed by their Creator with certain unalienable Rights."
   (c.) "He has kept among us, in times of peace, Standing Armies without the Consent of our legislatures."
   d. "... among these rights are Life, Liberty and the pursuit of Happiness."

9. Which sentence is a statement of opinion?
   a. "He has plundered our seas, ravaged our coasts, burnt our towns, and destroyed the lives of our people."
   b. "He has dissolved Representative Houses repeatedly, for opposing with manly firmness his invasions on the rights of the people."
   c. "He has refused to pass other Laws for the accommodation of large districts of people, unless those people would relinquish the right of Representation in the Legislature, a right inestimable to them and formidable to tyrants only."
   (d.) "In every stage of these Oppressions We have Petitioned for Redress in the most humble terms."

10. "We, therefore, the Representatives of the United States of America, in General Congress, Assembled, appealing to the Supreme Judge of the world for the rectitude of our intentions, do, in the Name, and by Authority of the good People of these Colonies, solemnly publish and declare, That these united Colonies are, and of Right ought to be Free and Independent States, that they are Absolved from all Allegiance to the British Crown, and that all political connection between them and the State of Great Britain, is and ought to be totally dissolved; and that as Free and Independent States, they have full Power to levy War, conclude Peace, contract Alliances, establish

Commerce, and to do all other Acts and Things which Independent States may of right do."

In this passage, the author is in favor of

a. immediately submitting to all allegiance to the British Crown.
(b.) declaring independence from the State of Great Britain.
c. obeying the king of Great Britain unconditionally.
d. developing strategies to cooperate with the King of Great Britain.

READING

Reading Selection **2**

Newspaper Article

10.4 Flesch-Kincaid Grade Level 12.0

Collaboration

Immigrants Raise Call For Right to Be Voters

Pre-Reading Questions

ESL Annotation

10.5 ESL This topic is particularly relevant to those immigrant students who want to participate in the electoral process but can't.

Discuss the following questions in small groups before reading the article.

1. U.S. law stipulates that one must be a citizen in order to be eligible to vote. In your opinion, why do you think the U.S. government has excluded lawful immigrants from this privilege?

2. Permanent U.S. residents argue that they are no different from U.S. citizens in that they work hard, contribute to society, and pay state and federal taxes. They believe that they are being treated like second-class citizens in their lack of political representation. Do you think that these legal immigrants have a valid concern? Why, or why not?

3. Some argue that a true democracy is only conceivable when no one is excluded from the electoral process. Yet, in the United States, certain people such as convicted felons, prisoners, illegal immigrants, permanent residents, and citizens without proper documentation are denied the right to vote. Can a true democracy exist when a country's citizens and noncitizens are discriminated against in this manner? Explain.

Immigrants Raise Call For Right to Be Voters

By Rachel L. Swarns, the *New York Times*

August 9, 2004

1   For months, the would-be revolutionaries plotted strategy and lobbied local politicians here with the age-old plea, "No taxation without representation!" Last month, some of the unlikely insurgents—Ethiopian-born restaurateurs, travel agents and real **estate** developers in sober business suits—declared that victory finally seemed within reach.

From Rachel L. Swarns, "Immigrants Raise Call For Right to Be Voters." From The *New York Times*, August 9, 2004. © 2004 The *New York Times*. All rights reserved. Used by permission and protected by the Copyright Laws of the United States. The printing, copying, redistribution, or retransmission of the Material without express written permission is prohibited. www.nytimes.com

© Pearson Education, Inc.

2   Five city council members announced their support for a bill that would allow thousands of immigrants to vote in local elections here, placing the nation's capital among a handful of cities across the country in the forefront of efforts to offer voting rights to noncitizens.

3   "It will happen," said Tamrat Medhin, a civic activist from Ethiopia who lives here. "Don't you believe that if people are working in the **community** and paying taxes, don't you agree that they deserve the opportunity to vote?"

4   Calling for "democracy for all," immigrants are increasingly pressing for the right to vote in municipal elections. In Washington, the proposed bill, introduced in July, would allow permanent residents to vote for the mayor and members of the school board and city council.

franchise
the right to vote

5   In San Francisco, voters will decide in November whether to allow noncitizens—including illegal immigrants—to vote in school board elections. Efforts to expand the **franchise** to noncitizens are also bubbling up in New York, Connecticut and elsewhere. Several cities, including Chicago, and towns like Takoma Park, Md., already allow noncitizens to vote in municipal or school elections.

6   But in most cities, voting remains a right reserved for citizens, and the prospects for the **initiatives** in Washington and San Francisco remain uncertain. The proposals have inspired fierce opposition from critics who say the laws would undermine the value of American citizenship and raise **security** concerns in the aftermath of the Sept. 11 terrorist attacks. Washington's mayor, Anthony Williams, has expressed his support for extending voting rights to permanent residents, but has yet to garner a majority of supporters on the 13-member city council. In San Francisco, critics have questioned whether the law would violate the state's Constitution.

akin to
similar to something

7   In this city, where Ethiopian restaurants and El Salvadoran travel agents dot many urban streets, advocates argue that permanent residents are paying taxes and fighting and dying for the United States as soldiers in Iraq while lacking a voice in local government. They describe the ban on immigrant voting as **akin to** the kind of taxation without representation that was a **major** cause of the American **Revolution**.

8   They also note that the United States has a long history of allowing noncitizens to vote. Twenty-two states and **federal** territories at various times allowed noncitizens to vote—even as blacks and women were barred from the ballot box—in the 1800s and 1900s.

9   Concerns about the radicalism of immigrants arriving from southern and Eastern Europe in the late 19th and early 20th centuries led states to restrict such voting rights. By 1928, voting at every level had been **restricted** to United States citizens. Today, some argue, those rights should be restored to noncitizens.

10   "They're paying taxes, they're working, they're contributing to our prosperity," said Jim Graham, the councilman who introduced the bill here. "And yet they're not able to exercise the franchise.

11   "This is part of our history. A lot of people don't know what the history of this nation is in terms of immigrant voting; they don't understand even that localities can determine this issue. It's a very healthy discussion."

12   Critics counter that the proposed laws would make citizenship irrelevant and pledges of allegiance to the United States meaningless. It is a touchy political issue, particularly in an election year when many politicians across

party lines are lobbying for support from Hispanic voters, and many politicians have tried to sidestep it altogether.

13   Democrats have most often sponsored the **initiatives**, but some also oppose
them. In Washington, where Congress has the right to override city laws, some
Republicans said they would try to overturn the immigrant voting bill if it passed.

Reading Comprehension Check

1. Who is referred to as "unlikely insurgents" in the first paragraph of the article?
   a. revolutionaries.   c. city council members.
   b. Ethiopian-born professionals. d. illegal immigrants.

2. Why were these men in suits calling for "no taxation without representation"?
   a. They are tax-payers who cannot vote.
   b. They do not pay taxes.
   c. They are voters who cannot pay taxes.
   d. none of the above.

3. In the second paragraph, in ". . . placing the nation's capital among a handful of cities across the country in the forefront of efforts to offer voting
   rights to noncitizens," the word *forefront* means
   a. position.   b. back.   c. head.   d. middle.

4. What is the connection between Washington D.C. and San Francisco in this
   article?
   a. Both are vacation destinations.
   b. Both are famous cities.
   c. Both had noncitizens' right to vote on the political agenda.
   d. Each has a strong anti-immigrant movement.

5. Those who oppose permitting noncitizens to vote argue that giving them
   this right will
   a. bring more illegal immigrants into the country.
   b. hurt the economy.
   c. incite terrorism and destroy our constitution.
   d. undermine the value of American citizenship and raise security concerns.

6. What is Washington D.C. Councilman Jim Graham's main point concerning
   this issue?
   a. Immigrants contribute, but they cause security concerns.
   b. Immigrants help make America prosperous, but they cannot exercise
      their vote.
   c. Some immigrants help America, and others hurt it.
   d. History is not on the side of immigrants.

7. The word *touchy* in paragraph 12 ("It is a touchy political issue, particularly in
   an election year") could be replaced with
   a. soft.   b. feel.   c. sensitive.   d. unfair.

8. What is the author's purpose in writing this article?
   a. to entertain.
   b. to inform readers about a political issue.
   c. to persuade readers to support his ideas.
   d. to inform readers about the history of immigrant voting.

© Pearson Education, Inc.

9. What is the author's tone?
   a. frustrated.
   b. optimistic.
   (c.) mostly objective.
   d. humorous.

10. What evidence do we have that the author is somewhat biased in favor of giving noncitizens the right to vote?
   (a.) He only offers quotes from those on the side of noncitizen voting rights.
   b. He offers a balanced analysis of both sides of the issue.
   c. He does not mention why anyone would be against permitting noncitizens to vote.
   d. He interviews people from only wealthy backgrounds.

READING

Reading Selection **3A**

Internet Blog

10.6 Flesch-Kincaid Grade Level 9.8

Collaboration

Leaders, Scholars Analyze Youth Apathy

Pre-Reading Questions

In small groups, consider the following questions before focusing on the following two articles (please note that Reading Selection 3B is on page 553).

1. Why do you think so many young people show little interest in politics? What factors play a role in youth apathy?

2. What can be done to encourage more young people to participate in the electoral process?

3. In the United States, a citizen must be 18 or older to be eligible to vote. Is this a fair minimum age? Should the voting requirement be lowered, or should it be made higher? Explain.

Leaders, Scholars Analyze Youth Apathy

By Erika Ray, independentcollegian.com

April 1, 2004

1   Young **adults** often exercise apathy on the subjects of voting, politics and other **aspects** of civic life, and Monday night was no exception.

2   At the Society of **Professional** Journalists' eighth-**annual** First **Amendment** Freedom Forum, a **panel** of four addressed the **topic** of "Willful Ignorance: Why Young People Seem Tuned Out" to an audience of about 30 students, faculty, staff and **community** members in the Law Center Auditorium.

3   "We just need to look around the room to address student apathy," said Peter Ujvagi, one of the speakers who is also an Ohio state representative for Toledo and a ranking minority member of the Higher Education Subcommittee.

4   "It's not only the college-aged students who have tuned out; it's the 20-somethings and the 30-somethings," added David Mindich, chairman of the journalism and mass **communication** department at Saint Michael's College in Vermont and the keynote speaker at the forum.

5   "We're not reading the newspaper as a **generation**," he added.

6   Mindich said in 1972, 46 **percent** of college-aged students and two-thirds of people in their 30s read the newspaper every day, compared to the 20 **percent** of both college-aged students and people in their 30s who now do.

7   If newspapers aren't where students are getting the news, Mindich proposed they were getting it from television. However, he quickly **debunked** that **theory** when he said the median age of TV news viewers was 60 years old, according to recent **data**.

debunked
showed that an idea or belief is false

8   "For every viewer over the age of 60, there is a viewer under the age of 60 watching the news," he said.

9   After ruling out newspapers and TV as the sources for news for young people, Mindich mentioned the Internet. However, he said e-mail was the No. 1 reason young people log on to the Internet, with America Online Instant Messenger and schoolwork ranking above the 11 **percent** of people who said the Internet is their **major source** of news.

10   "How are they getting informed?" Mindich asked. "In many cases, they are not. There were times where young people were nearly as tuned in as their elders were. This has changed."

11   Mindich then addressed the power and value of entertainment.

12   "The lure of entertainment has always been stronger than politics," he said, citing the fact that 17 **percent** of young **adults** could name three Supreme Court justices compared to the 72 **percent** who could name at least three Stooges.

13   He added that the entertainment industry is huge, with news encompassing a tiny sliver of it, as seen with Victoria Sinclair on the Naked News.

14   "In chasing young viewers, we should not be like Victoria Sinclair," he said, adding that the news industry simply cannot compete with the entertainment value of sitcoms like "Friends."

15   He said a **major** problem is people, especially young people, not having time to follow the news.

16   "We gotta demand that young people follow it," he said. "Journalists should make it easier for people to follow the news. I don't think it would hurt journalists to add some road signs. It's extremely troubling that not enough people read the newspaper or an online **equivalent**. If a citizen abandons knowledge, he **relinquishes** power as well."

relinquishes
to give up

17   Fritz Wenzel, a political writer from The Blade who has nine years of experience covering politics, understands having to add explanatory information to his articles for those not following the news.

18   "It's frustrating that everything I am writing is not being grasped by the reader," he said. "I have to go back to the beginning every time because I know every day new people are coming into it."

19   At the forum, Wenzel focused on this year's presidential election, and the candidates' **strategies** toward campaigning.

© Pearson Education, Inc.

20   He said former presidential hopeful Howard Dean's campaign failed, although it seemed to have momentum from August to October 2003, because it focused on getting the votes of young **adults**. Wenzel said people campaigning for Dean would **focus** on getting e-mail addresses from voters.

21   "That's how they could get a hold of you because you can get your e-mail anywhere," Wenzel said. "It obviously didn't work, but I'm **reluctant** to blame the youth entirely. Think of young people today and all the things they have to do. They've actually got to live their lives and there's not a lot of time for students to stop."

22   He said candidates instead **focus** on senior citizens—who tend to vote in large numbers—on **issues** that **affect** them, such as prescription drugs and Medicare; **issues** he said people in college don't have to deal with.

23   "They tune out because these candidates are not talking to them," Wenzel said.

attest
show or prove that something is true

24   One speaker who can **attest** to that fact is 27-year-old Ellen Grachek, a Toledo councilwoman for the fifth district, an attorney for Allotta and Farley and a former UT Student Government vice president.

25   "If young people are not a force to be reckoned with, politicians are more easily able to write them off," said Grachek, who was appointed to city council at 25, becoming the youngest woman to serve that post in Toledo.

26   "The truth is, we don't vote," she added. "We view voting as a choice, not an obligation. Young people don't realize, understand or appreciate the power of their vote. I'm here to tell you it matters. I care about what young people say, but young people need to vote." She said students should get involved with issues that affect them.

apathy
lack of interest or concern

27   "**Apathy** is not a **function** of youth," Grachek said. "It's hard to comment on apathy because I myself am not apathetic. I take initiative when others don't and I give a damn about what's happening around me."

28   Ujvagi echoed Grachek's **comments** on voting when he said young people don't vote because they don't comprehend that voting could **affect** something important to them.

29   "This year as we see difficulties, [hopefully] young people will see some of that and vote," Ujvagi said.

30   He also focused on the **debate** that young people could be drafted into the Army, but weren't able to vote. He said Ohio was the state that helped lower the voting age to 18 with the 26th **Amendment**, but there was still the issue of becoming **registered** to vote.

31   "It was a real challenge because there was only one place to register," Ujvagi said, speaking of the Lucas County Board of Elections. "It has become easy to get registered to vote. You can do it in three minutes; five minutes."

32   "If young folks don't vote," Grachek added, "they don't voice their opinions."

33   The forum was co-sponsored by The Alliance of **Construction** Professionals, the IBEW Local 8 and the UT communication department.

Reading Comprehension Check

1. The word *aspect* in the first sentence of the article could be replaced with
   a. color.
   (c.) features.
   b. needs.
   d. responsibilities.

2. What can we infer from the quotation by Peter Ujvagi, a speaker at the meeting of the Society of Professional Journalists: "We just need to look around the room to address student apathy"?
   (a.) There were few students in attendance.
   b. Everyone there was uninterested.
   c. Only students were in the audience.
   d. We can not make an inference based on the given information.

3. What do we learn about college student newspaper readership?
   (a.) It has gone down significantly since 1972.
   b. It has gone down modestly.
   c. It has increased.
   d. It has remained steady.

4. After ruling out newspapers, television, and the Internet, where does David Mindich, chairman of the Journalism and Mass Communication department at Saint Michael's College, say young people are getting the news?
   a. on the street.
   (b.) He argues that young people are not informed.
   c. from various sources.
   d. from their peers.

5. Twenty-seven-year-old Ellen Grachek, a Toledo councilwoman, is quoted in the article as saying, "It's hard to comment on apathy because I myself am not apathetic. I take initiative when others don't and I give a damn about what's happening around me." Is Grachek's comment a statement of fact or an opinion?
   a. a statement of fact.
   b. both a fact and an opinion.
   (c.) an opinion.
   d. the reader needs more information to make this determination.

READING

Reading Selection **3B**

Internet Magazine Article

10.7 Flesch-Kincaid Grade Level 9.8

Collaboration

Should the Voting Age Be Lowered?

Timothy Noah, www.slate.com

November 7, 2000

1   Today, as voters flocked to the polls, one group was staging demonstrations around the country to protest its exclusion from the electoral **process**. That group was children. You probably think Chatterbox is kidding. He isn't. "Lower the Vote" protests were planned for Election Day in 14 states,

© Pearson Education, Inc.

ESL Annotation

10.8 ESL The age of voting eligibility varies across the globe. It may be interesting to ask students from other countries about the voting age and other voter registration requirements in their native culture.

unanimity
everyone being of one mind

deference
respect

including California, Texas, Florida, and Massachusetts. According to its Web page,

> Lower the Vote is a **partnership** of various youth rights organizations and independent organizers all committed to lowering the voting age in the United States of America. We believe that the current voting age denies millions of deserving U.S. citizens the **fundamental** right to vote and should be lowered.
>
>   Young people are tired of being treated like second-class citizens in America. They are tired of facing oppression at the hand [of] adult American society. They are tired of unconstitutional age restrictions. They are tired of being stereotyped by the **media** as violent, lazy, stupid and apathetic. Above all else, young people want to be a partner in the political **process**. They want the right to vote, to have a voice in the American democratic **process**.

2   Obviously, the first question you want answered is, "How far do they want to lower it?" Apparently there isn't much **unanimity** about this within the youth rights movement (whose constituent groups include the National Youth Rights Association; the Youth Rights Action League; Americans for a Society Free From Age Restrictions, or ASFAR; the Association for Children's Suffrage; and YouthSpeak). John Anderson, the 1980 independent presidential candidate, who is currently teaching **constitutional** law at Nova Southeastern University in Fort Lauderdale, Fla., has been pushing to lower the voting age for several years. Reached today by phone, he told Chatterbox:

> Given the abilities of young people I think to get a driver's license and to operate motor vehicles and otherwise begin to **assume** some of the responsibilities that you normally put in the category of being **adults**, I think that it's not unreasonable to contemplate that we would lower it to 16.

3   The Cambridge, Mass., City Council plans to hold a hearing on Nov. 16 in which it will consider lowering the voting age to 16 for city council and school committee races; if the measure clears the city council, it will be forwarded to the Statehouse as a home-rule petition. But others in the movement consider enfranchisement at 16 to be too restrictive. Vita Wallace, then aged 16, advocated eliminating the age limit *entirely* in a 1991 article for *The Nation*:

> What I suggest is that children be allowed to grow into their own right to vote at whatever rate suits them individually. . . . As for the ability to read and write, that should never be used as a criterion for eligibility, since we have already learned from painful past experience that literacy tests can be manipulated to insure **discrimination**. In any case, very few illiterates vote, and probably very few children would want to vote as long as they couldn't read or write. . . . I think I would not have voted until I was 8 or 9, but perhaps if I had known I could vote I would have taken an interest sooner.

4   This sentiment was echoed in a 1997 *Brown Daily Herald* interview with Anthony Fotenos, founder of the Association for Children's Suffrage. Fotenos said that although the ideal constituency would be 10 to 18, toddlers should be eligible, too.

5   Among the many reasons Chatterbox can think of *against* lowering the voting age even to 16 is that voters at the low end of the youth spectrum rarely exercise their rights now. In 1971, out of **deference** to the powerful argument that 18-year-olds were old enough to die in Vietnam, the 26th **Amendment**

lowered the voting age from 21. (Ironically, the **author** of that **amendment**, Sen. Jennings Randolph of West Virginia, lived to the ripe old age of 96.) What did America's youth do with this newfound right? As little as possible! The failure of young folks to vote has **spawned** a small nonprofit industry aimed at getting them interested, and the embarrassing quadrennial ritual of having presidential candidates answer inappropriate or irrelevant "youth-oriented" questions on MTV. At the risk of sounding peevish, Chatterbox thinks that if young people want more of the vote, they will first have to finish what's on their plate.

spawned
made something happen or start to exist

6   Alex Koroknay-Palicz, president of the National Youth Rights Association, disagrees. Chatterbox caught up with Koroknay-Palicz, a fuzzy-bearded 19-year-old who attends American University, early this evening in D.C.'s Franklin Park. He and five other protesters were standing at the foot of a statue of Cmdr. John Barry, father of the American Navy, and waving magic-markered posterboard signs that said things like "Lower the Voting Age" and "Democracy = Voting." Korknay-Palicz argued to Chatterbox that lowering the voting age would stimulate greater **participation** among those over 18. "The fact that people have been denied the right to vote for the first 18 years of their lives has given them a sense of powerlessness when it comes to voting and civic **participation**," he said. If the voting age were lowered, it would help them establish "good voting habits for the rest of their lives."

7   But the makeup of Korknay-Palicz's ragtag group of protesters called into serious question whether the under-18 set even *wanted* the vote. There were only six of them. (They said there had been about a dozen before I got there. According to Korknay-Palicz, the National Youth Rights Association has about 400 members nationwide.) Of the six, five were already 18, **hence** able to vote *now*. (All five did so today.) The sixth was a stocky and **somewhat** charismatic fellow in a black T-shirt named Jason Gerber. "I operate a small business. Why am I not allowed to vote?" he bellowed into a megaphone as rush-hour commuters sped by. But even Jason (who attends Montgomery College and, had he been enfranchised today, would have voted for Libertarian candidate Harry Browne) really doesn't have much to complain about. He's 17. He'll be able to vote within a year!

8   Anyway, to establish the sort of lifelong habit that Korknay-Palicz is talking about, you'd have to start voting a lot earlier than 16. In order to assess the fitness of the under-16 crowd to make decisions that would **affect** the broad polity, Chatterbox **posed** a few questions to his 7-year-old son, Willie:

> *Do you think you should be able to vote?*
> Yes.
> *Do you think you should be able to go to bed whenever you want?*
> No.
> *If you could choose dinner every night, what would it be?*
> Pasta.
> *Do you think you should be able to drive a car?*
> No.

What can Chatterbox say? He's a very levelheaded child. But he still shouldn't be allowed to vote.

© Pearson Education, Inc.

Barack Hussein Obama

Barack Obama made history in 2008 when he became the first African American elected to the presidency. Barack Hussein Obama was born on August 4, 1961, in Honolulu, Hawaii, to Barack Obama Sr., a Kenyan, and Ann Dunham, a white American from Kansas. His parents met at the University of Hawaii where his father was a foreign student. They separated when Obama was just 2 and later divorced. Obama's father returned to Kenya and saw his son only once more before dying in a car accident in 1982.

Obama was always a very strong student, graduating from Columbia University with a degree in political science, and later going on to receive a law degree from Harvard University. While at Harvard, Obama served as the first black president of the Harvard Law Review.

Between his time at Columbia and Harvard, Obama moved to Chicago and worked as a community organizer for three years, from 1985 to 1988. He worked for a community organization called the Developing Communities Project. Some of his accomplishments with the DCP included helping to set up a job training program, a college preparatory tutoring program, and a tenants' rights organization.

After receiving his law degree, Obama taught constitutional law at the University of Chicago Law School from 1992 until 2004. In 1993 he joined Davis, Miner, Barnhill & Galland, a 12-attorney law firm specializing in civil rights **litigation** and neighborhood economic development.

Obama's political rise began when he was elected to the Illinois Senate in 1996. Once elected, Obama gained bipartisan support for legislation involving health care law, tax credits for low-income workers, and **subsidies** for childcare. Obama won re-election to the Illinois Senate in 1998 and again in 2002. In 2000, however, he lost a Democratic primary run for the U.S. House of Representatives.

A great moment in Obama's political career was when he was asked to write and deliver the keynote address for the 2004 Democratic National Convention in Boston, Massachusetts. Drawing examples from U.S. history, Obama criticized partisan politics and asked Americans to find unity in diversity. "There is not a liberal America and a conservative America; there's the United States of America."

Six months later he was sworn in as a U.S. senator on January 4, 2005. He served proudly in his role as Illinois senator for two years, and in February 2007 he announced his candidacy for President of the United States. Throughout the campaign, Obama identified his top three priorities as ending the war in Iraq, increasing energy independence, and working toward providing health care for all Americans. In what would become one of the most dramatic presidential primary races in U.S. history, Obama battled Senator Hillary Clinton for the Democratic ticket; he emerged victorious in the end. He then battled Senator John McCain for the presidency and was elected President on November 4, 2008.

Obama met his wife Michelle, a fellow lawyer, in 1989 when he was employed as a summer associate at a Chicago law firm. They married in 1992 and have two daughters.

Some Questions for Group Discussion

1. Many people believe that to be a candidate for President of the United States you have to be born into a rich family. Yet, Obama came from a humble background, raised mostly by his mother and grandmother. What made the difference in Obama's rise to the top?

2. The media uses the label African American when discussing Barack Obama. Yet, his mother was a white American. Why do you think the media focuses more on Obama's black ancestry? Do you think this is fair and accurate? Explain.

3. At the 2004 Democratic National Convention in Boston, Obama urged the American people to reconcile their political differences and unite. Discuss what forces unite and divide citizens of a country.

Biographical Internet Research

Do research on the Internet and find out about another historical figure in political science, chosen from the list below. Share a biographical profile with your classmates.

- Niccolò Machiavelli
- Thomas Jefferson
- Mao Zedong
- Arnold Schwarzenegger
- John F. Kennedy

Reading Comprehension Check

1. The word *flocked*, in the first sentence of the reading, means
   a. denied.
   b. ran away from.
   (c.) went to a place in large numbers.
   d. panicked.

2. What is the tone in the first few paragraphs of the reading, where the voice of the Lower the Vote organization is heard?
   a. humorous.   c. contented.
   b. objective.   (d.) angry and determined.

3. According to John Anderson, the 1980 independent presidential candidate, to what age should the voting age be lowered?
   (a.) 16.   c. 18.
   b. 17.   d. 9.

4. What argument is offered in opposition to lowering the voting age?
   a. Young people cannot drive.
   (b.) Young people who are currently eligible to vote often do not do so.
   c. Young people are enthusiastic about politics.
   d. none of the above.

5. What is the message behind Chatterbox interviewing his 7-year-old son at the end of the Internet piece?
   a. There is no message.
   b. Even little kids should have this right.
   (c.) The thought of allowing young, immature kids to vote is ridiculous.
   d. Young people have sophisticated knowledge of the political world.

SKILL FOCUS
Combined Skills

So far you have focused on one reading skill in each chapter. By now you have learned reading skills such as vocabulary in context, main idea, supporting details, making inferences, purpose and tone, fact and opinion, argument, patterns of organization, and author's bias. You have also practiced answering multiple-choice questions after each of the reading selections. You may have noticed that some Reading Comprehension questions refer to a "particular point" in the article, and that others are related to the "overall meaning" of the article. Particular-point questions test reading skills such as vocabulary in context, supporting details, fact and opinion and making inferences. On the other hand, overall-meaning questions focus on the entire article instead of referring to just a specific part of the text. Overall-meaning questions focus on the main idea, author's purpose, and tone.

It is important to note that while you have focused on only one skill in each chapter, most standardized reading tests require you to read a full-length article and answer multiple-choice questions including *both* particular-point and overall-meaning questions. It is, therefore, necessary for you to master combined skills so that you can readily identify whether you need to focus on a particular point of the text, or whether you should look at the overall meaning of the text.

© Pearson Education, Inc.

When we read, we usually do so holistically—that is, we take the whole of the reading into consideration and do not consider just one aspect of the passage. It may be useful for the purposes of skill review, however, to map out key aspects of a reading as a way of entering and connecting to a text.

Read the following section of an article about the American identity, and review the reading selection map that follows.

Example

Melting Pot or Salad Bowl?

harnessed
directed or captured the force of something

The American self-image has always **harnessed** a creative tension between pluralism and assimilation. On the one hand, immigrants traditionally have been expected to immerse themselves in the American "melting pot," a metaphor popularized by the playwright Israel Zangwill's 1908 drama *The Melting Pot*, in which one character declares:

> Understand that America is God's Crucible, the great Melting-Pot where all the races of Europe are melting and reforming! A fig for your feuds and vendettas! Germans and Frenchmen, Irishmen and Englishmen, Jews and Russians—into the Crucible with you all! God is making the American.

Nor were Zangwill's sentiments new ones. As far back as 1782, J. Hector St. John de Crèvecoeur, a French immigrant and keen observer of American life, described his new compatriots as:

> . . . a mixture of English, Scotch, Irish, French, Dutch, Germans, and Swedes. . . . What, then, is the American, this new man? He is neither an European nor the descendant of an European; hence that strange mixture of blood, which you will find in no other country. I could point out to you a family whose grandfather was an Englishman, whose wife was Dutch, whose son married a French woman, and whose present four sons have now four wives of different nations. He is an American . . . leaving behind him all his ancient prejudices and manners. . . .

The melting pot, however, has always existed alongside a competing model, in which each successive immigrant group retains a measure of its distinctiveness and enriches the American whole. In 1918 the public intellectual Randolph Bourne called for a "trans-national America." The original English colonists, Bourne argued, "did not come to be assimilated in an American melting pot. . . . They came to get freedom to live as they wanted to . . . to make their fortune in a new land." Later immigrants, he continued, had not been melted down into some kind of "tasteless, colorless" **homogeneous** Americanism but rather added their distinct contributions to the greater whole.

homogeneous
consisting of parts or members that are all the same

The balance between the melting pot and transnational ideals varies with time and circumstance, with neither model achieving complete dominance. Unquestionably, though, Americans have internalized a self-portrait that spans a spectrum of races, creeds, and colors. Consider the popular motion pictures depicting American troops in action during the Second World War. It became a Hollywood cliché that every platoon included a farm boy from Iowa, a Brooklyn Jew, a Polish millworker from Chicago, an Appalachian woodsman, and other diverse examples of mid-20th century American manhood. They strain at first to overcome their differences, but by film's end all have bonded—as Americans.

Real life could be more complicated, and not least because the African-American soldier would have served in a segregated unit. Regardless, these films depict an American identity that Americans believed in—or wanted to.

(*from "American Identity: Ideas, Not Ethnicity," by Michael J. Friedman, http://www.america.gov/st/diversity-english/2008/February/ 20080307154033ebyessedo0.5349237.html, February 13, 2008*)

Reading Selection Map

Main Idea	The American identity has always been defined by a compromise between assimilation and pluralism.
An Argument	"The balance between the melting pot and transnational ideals varies with time and circumstance."
Supporting Detail (for argument)	The popular movies of World War II always contained a diverse group of American soldiers.
A Fact	In 1918 the public intellectual Randolph Bourne called for a "trans-national America."
An Opinion	"Understand that America is God's Crucible, the great Melting-Pot where all the races of Europe are melting and reforming."
Author's Tone	Straightforward and unemotional
Author's Purpose	To inform
(An example of) a Pattern of Organization	Cause and effect Cause: Hollywood wanted to portray an image of a united America. Effect: By the end of most WWII war films, all the different types of Americans were bonded.
An Inference	We can infer that life for African American soldiers in WWII was a great struggle, beyond the given fact that they were segregated.

Now that you have had a chance to see a reading passage mapped out, read another section from the same article and practice mapping by skill area.

PRACTICING THE SKILL

Passage

Individualism and Tolerance

If American identity embraces all kinds of people, it also affords them a vast menu of opportunities to make and remake themselves. Americans historically have scorned efforts to trade on "accidents of birth," such as great inherited wealth or social status. Article I of the U.S. Constitution bars the government from granting any title of nobility, and those who cultivate an air of superiority toward their fellow Americans are commonly disparaged for **"putting on airs,"** or worse.

putting on airs
acting superior or snobbish

Americans instead respect the "self-made" man or woman, especially where he or she has overcome great obstacles to success. The late 19th-century American writer Horatio Alger, deemed by the *Encyclopedia Britannica* perhaps the most socially influential American writer of his

© Pearson Education, Inc.

ethos
moral element

generation, captured this **ethos** in his many rags-to-riches stories, in which poor shoeshine boys or other street urchins would rise, by dint of their ambition, talent, and fortitude, to wealth and fame.

In the United States, individuals craft their own definitions of success. It might be financial wealth—and many are the college dropouts working in their parents' garage in hopes of creating the next Google, Microsoft, or Apple Computer. Others might prize the joys of the sporting arena, of creating fine music or art, or of raising a loving family at home. Because Americans spurn limits, their national identity is not—cannot be—bounded by the color of one's skin, by one's parentage, by which house of worship one attends.

Americans hold differing political beliefs, embrace (often wildly) divergent lifestyles, and insist upon broad individual freedoms, but they do so with a remarkable degree of mutual tolerance. One key is their representative form of government: No citizen agrees with every U.S. government decision; all know they can reverse those policies by persuading their fellow citizens to vote for change at the next election.

Another key is the powerful guarantees that protect the rights of all Americans from government overreaching. No sooner was the U.S. Constitution ratified than Americans demanded and received the Bill of Rights: 10 constitutional amendments that safeguard basic rights.

There simply is no one picture of a "typical" American. From the powdered-wigged Founding Fathers to the multiracial golf champion Tiger Woods, Americans share a common identity grounded in the freedom—consistent always with respecting the freedom of others—to live as they choose. The results can bemuse, intrigue, and inspire. Cambodia's biggest hip-hop star, born on a Cambodian farm, lives in southern California. (He goes by the name "praCh.") Walt Whitman, the closest Americans have produced to a national poet, would not have been surprised. "I am large," Whitman wrote of his nation, "I contain **multitudes**."

multitudes
a great number

Reading Selection Map

Main Idea	*In the U.S. - individuals craft their own definitions of success.*
An Argument	*There is simply no one picture of an American.*
Supporting Detail (for argument)	*Multi-racial golf champion Tiger Woods.*
A Fact	*Articles of the U.S. Constitution bars the government from granting any title of nobility.*
An Opinion	*Americans respect the "self-made" man.*
Author's Tone	*Confident, Positive.*
Author's Purpose	*To persuade.*
(An example of) **a Pattern of Organization**	*"Self-made" man - Horatio Alger.*
An Inference	*Walt Whitman would have been amused by PraCh.*

Now that you have reviewed and practiced the combined skills, read the following full-length article and answer the multiple-choice questions that follow.

READING

Reading Selection **4**

Newspaper Article

10.9 Flesch-Kincaid Grade Level 12.0

Collaboration

A Portrait of a Young Man as a Beijing Student Leader

Pre-Reading Questions

Discuss the following questions with a small group of your classmates.

1. Countries in the world are led by different forms of government. There are democratic countries, there are countries led by a communist government, there are monarchies, and there are dictatorships. In your opinion, what is the best form of government? Give specific reasons to support your answer.

2. In a democratic country, citizens have freedom of speech. In other words, they can speak against the government without apprehension if they believe it has violated the constitution or if it has done injustice to its citizens. However, in a communist country, citizens are usually afraid of speaking against the government in public. Why do you think a communist country suppresses freedom of speech?

3. Groups of students, activists, and intellectuals gathered in Tiananmen Square in Beijing, China, on June 4, 1989, to protest against the authoritarian and autocratic policies of the ruling Chinese Communist Party. The protesters asked for democratic reform within the structure of the government. Instead of agreeing to the protesters' demands, the Chinese Communist Party ordered the military to shoot them. The military followed their orders and shot the protestors indiscriminately, leaving approximately two to three thousand civilians dead. In your opinion, why do you think the Chinese government responded so violently to the protesters?

A Portrait of a Young Man as a Beijing Student Leader

By Sheryl Wudunn, The *New York Times*

June 3, 1989

1 The following is a profile of one of the student protesters written a day before the massacre.

2   Four months ago a scrawny, scraggly-haired student gave speeches about human rights that baffled his classmates, who wondered how anyone could **harbor** such a passion for what was then a remote **concept** like democracy.

harbor
to keep or maintain

3   Now, Wang Dan, a 20-year-old history student at Beijing University, is a national figure. He carries a beeper and is **accompanied** by two bodyguards, signs of his new **status** as perhaps the single most prominent leader of the student democracy movement that has thrust the Government into a political crisis.

4   He is rather embarrassed to talk about how his personal life has changed. But when his mail is given to him, he lets on that he has already received a dozen

Sheryl Wudunn, "A Portrait of a Young Man as a Beijing Student Leader." From The *New York Times*, June 3, 1989. © 1989 The *New York Times*. All rights reserved. Used by permission and protected by the Copyright Laws of the United States. The printing, copying, redistribution, or retransmission of the Material without express written permission is prohibited. www.nytimes.com

© Pearson Education, Inc.

love letters. Certainly he has been the subject of some wild rumors. Some people say he has taken part in Politburo meetings, while others say he has been martyred in various grim ways.

5   Two students from the eastern city of Suzhou, who arrived in Beijing the other day, were surprised to learn that Mr. Wang was still alive. They said they had held a ceremony in Suzhou to mourn his passing.

"I'm Not Afraid"

6   What emerges from the last seven weeks is a picture of a survivor: an intellectual lacking charisma or oratorical skill, but bold enough and determined enough to remain a student leader **despite** factional **bickering** and Government criticisms.

bickering
arguing, disputing

7   While other student leaders **focus** on tactics and mundane matters like where to obtain megaphones, Mr. Wang stands out as the leader who dares to articulate a world very unlike China today.

8   "I'm not afraid," Mr. Wang said. "I've nothing to be afraid of. I don't think they will be able to imprison me for as long as Wei Jingsheng." Mr. Wei is a dissident who was sentenced a decade ago to 15 years in prison.

9   There are other prominent student leaders, like Wuer Kaixi and Chai Ling from Beijing Normal University, but it is Mr. Wang who seems to have had the greatest influence. Mr. Wuer's popularity tumbled 10 days ago when he proposed leaving the square, and Miss Chai's **role** seems limited to the students now occupying the square.

10   Mr. Wang refuses to evaluate his own **role** as a leader, but admits there have been mistakes and lessons.

11   "I have one regret," Mr. Wang said. "I failed to persuade the elite intellectuals to give us direct support." Intellectuals should have been more **involved** in helping to lead the movement, he says.

Need for Coherent Goals

12   Mr. Wang believes that the intellectuals joined too late, and he suggests that one of the results of this is that the students did not have **coherent** goals.

coherent
logically connected, consistent

13   "I think that the student movements in the future should be firmly based on something solid, such as the democratization of campus life or the realization of **civil** rights according to the Constitution," Mr. Wang said. "Otherwise, the result is chaos."

14   Although many of the students' demands—press freedom, direct talks with the Government and the uprooting of corruption among officials—were more practical than in past demonstrations, they had no **framework**.

15   While certain themes, like opposition to official corruption, gained the support of workers, Mr. Wang says he believes the movement is not ready for worker **participation** because the principles of democracy must first be absorbed by students and intellectuals before they can be spread to others.

The Limits of Democracy

16   The recent student movement went way beyond just ideas, and Mr. Wang has learned that there are limits to how one can apply those ideas, especially the **concept** of democracy.

17   When students went on their hunger strike, any **policy** decision that was made had to be voted in unanimously by all the fasting students, whose numbers grew from 1,000 to 3,000.

18   Another difficulty was the election of a student leadership.

19   "You can't have direct democracy where everyone is electing leaders and trying to get **involved** because it only results in frequent changes of leaders and causes disorder," Mr. Wang said.

20   Another problem that **hampered** the student movement was the bickering among leaders. Most recently, a **debate** centered on whether to stay at or leave Tiananmen Square, which students invaded more than two weeks ago.

hampered
made someone have difficulty moving, or doing or achieving something

21   Mr. Wang and his fellow students from Beijing University and other colleges in the capital have essentially retreated from the square, which has lately been occupied mainly by students from outside Beijing.

Popular Throughout

22 Through all this, Mr. Wang has remained a leader, partly because he is from Beijing University, the nation's most prestigious school, and partly because he has become a nationwide figure who has been **involved** all along, from the hunger strike to the talks with the Government.

23   In part Mr. Wang seems to have held on to his constituency because he has learned to sense how far his supporters are willing to go.

24   Other times, he displayed **a knack** for public relations. Mr. Wang says he did not **spearhead** the hunger strike, but when the idea became popular and a list of participants was posted, his name was the first on the list.

knack
a natural ability to do something well

spearhead
lead an attack or an organized action

25   "The hunger strike was **significant**," Mr. Wang said, "because it brought out the ordinary people's enthusiasm."

Reading Comprehension Check

After answering each question, identify the specific reading skill.

1. "Four months ago a scrawny, scraggly-haired student gave speeches about human rights that baffled his classmates, who wondered how anyone could harbor such a passion for what was then a remote concept like democracy."

    In the sentence above, the word *baffled* means
    a. amused.   c. appeased.
    b. entertained.   (d.) perplexed.

    Identify the reading skill *Vocabulary in context*

2. Which of the following sentences is the best statement of the main idea in the entire article?
    a. Intellectuals generally do not support students' fight for justice in China.
    b. The Chinese Communist Party was pleased with the Tiananmen Square protests.
    (c.) Wan Dang is a prominent student leader of the student democracy movement against the government of China.
    d. The student movement brought about economic reforms in China.

    Identify the reading skill *Main idea*

© Pearson Education, Inc.

3. According to Wang Dan, one of the reasons the student movement failed was that
   a. he was only 20 years old.
   b. it was extremely difficult to elect a student leadership.
   c. his peers were confused by his speeches about human rights.
   d. other student leaders such as Wuer Kaixi and Chai Ling were not influential at all.

   Identify the reading skill *Supporting Details*

4. "Four months ago a scrawny, scraggly-haired student gave speeches about human rights that baffled his classmates, who wondered how anyone could harbor such a passion for what was then a remote concept like democracy."

   A logical conclusion that can be drawn from the above statement is that
   a. most students were unfamiliar with the concept of democracy.
   b. most students were cognizant of the concept of democracy.
   c. most students despised the scrawny, scraggly-haired student.
   d. most students lacked passion.

   Identify the reading skill *Inference*

5. The main purpose of the article is to
   a. convince the reader that they should support Wang Dan.
   b. educate the reader on the student movement against the authoritarian Chinese Communist Party.
   c. contrast the activities of the different student leaders.
   d. explain the relationship between students and intellectuals in Beijing.

   Identify the reading skill *Purpose*

6. The overall tone of the article is
   a. instructional.   c. nostalgic.
   b. humorous.   d. clinical.

   Identify the reading skill *Tone*

7. Which of the following is a statement of fact?
   a. Wang Dan does not get along with Wuer Kaixi and Chai Ling.
   b. Wang Dan studies economics at Beijing University.
   c. Wang Dan is a 20-year-old student from Beijing University.
   d. Wang Dan was killed during the Tiananmen protests.

   Identify the reading skill *Fact vs. Opinion*

8. Which of the following is a statement of opinion?
   a. Wang Dan is a 20-year-old history student at Beijing University.
   b. Wang Dan carries a beeper and is accompanied by two bodyguards.
   c. Two students from Souzhou were surprised to learn that Wang Dan was still alive.
   d. Wang Dan should have worked more closely with Wuer Kaixi and Chai Ling.

   Identify the reading skill *Fact vs. Opinion*

9. "There are other prominent student leaders, like Wuer Kaixi and Chai Ling from Beijing Normal University, but it is Mr. Wang who seems to have had the greatest influence. Mr. Wuer's popularity tumbled 10 days ago when he proposed leaving the square, and Miss Chai's role seems limited to the students now occupying the square."

For this passage, the author uses the overall organizational pattern that
a. argues that Chai Ling is a more efficient student leader than Wang Dan is.
b. contrasts the influence of Wang Dan and Wuer Kaizi and Chai Long.
c. discusses the negative effects of influential student leaders.
d. illustrates conversational behaviors of Wuer Kaixi and Chai Ling.

Identify the reading skill *Patterns of Organization*

10. "Through all this, Mr. Wang has remained a leader, partly because he is from Beijing University, the nation's most prestigious school, and partly because he has become a nationwide figure who has been involved all along, from the hunger strike to the talks with the Government."

In this passage, the author expresses
a. a bias in favor of dismissing Mr. Wang as a student leader.
b. a bias in favor of fighting with the Government through violent means.
c. no bias in profiling Mr. Wang as a student leader.
d. a bias against restricting Beijing University from participating in protests.

Identify the reading skill *Author's bias*

Recommended Debate Topic: Should U.S. Permanent Residents be allowed to vote?
    Discuss controversial topics related to political science with your classmates and instructor for the debate activity.

DEBATABLE TOPIC

Your suggested debate topics:

a. _____

b. _____

c. _____

ESL Annotation

10.10 ESL While non-U.S. citizens will most likely understand the term "U.S. Permanent Residents" (also labeled "green-card holders"), many U.S.-born citizens may need some explanation.

READING

Reading Selection **5**

Political Speech

10.11 Flesch-Kincaid Grade Level 8.3

Barack Obama's Inaugural Address

Pre-Reading Questions

Before you read President Obama's inaugural speech, discuss these questions in small groups.

Collaboration

1. A newly-elected U.S. president's inaugural speech always gets much media attention. How much importance do you give to the promises of a new president? Do you believe that a new president can play an instrumental role in transforming American society? Explain.

2. In his inaugural speech, President Obama proclaimed, "we gather because we have chosen hope over fear, unity of purpose over conflict and discord." Discuss which fears, conflicts, and discords in twenty-first century America, according to the president, were weakening the fabrics of the country.

© Pearson Education, Inc.

3. President Obama's father was a black Kenyan, his mother was a white American, and he was born in Hawaii. What, in your opinion, is President Obama's identity? Do you consider him to be black, white, both, neither, or something else? In dealing with America's complex racial issues, how do you think his own racial background will influence his decision-making ability in this area?

Barack Obama's Inaugural Address

Published: January 20, 2009

1   My fellow citizens: I stand here today humbled by the **task** before us, grateful for the trust you have bestowed, mindful of the sacrifices borne by our ancestors.

2   I thank President Bush for his service to our nation . . . as well as the generosity and cooperation he has shown throughout this **transition**.

3   Forty-four Americans have now taken the presidential oath.

4   The words have been spoken during rising tides of prosperity and the still waters of peace. Yet, every so often the oath is taken amidst gathering clouds and raging storms. At these moments, America has carried on not simply because of the skill or **vision** of those in high office, but because We the People have remained faithful to the ideals of our **forebears**, and true to our founding documents.

forbears
ancestors

5   So it has been. So it must be with this **generation** of Americans.

6   That we are in the midst of crisis is now well understood. Our nation is at war against a far-reaching **network** of violence and hatred. Our economy is badly weakened, a consequence of greed and irresponsibility on the part of some but also our collective failure to make hard choices and prepare the nation for a new age.

7   Homes have been lost, jobs shed, businesses shuttered. Our health care is too costly, our schools fail too many, and each day brings further **evidence** that the ways we use **energy** strengthen our adversaries and threaten our planet.

8   These are the indicators of crisis, subject to **data** and **statistics**. Less measurable, but no less profound, is a sapping of confidence across our land; a nagging fear that America's **decline** is inevitable, that the next **generation** must lower its sights.

9   Today I say to you that the challenges we face are real, they are serious and they are many. They will not be met easily or in a short span of time. But know this America: They will be met.

10 On this day, we gather because we have chosen hope over fear, unity of purpose over **conflict** and discord.

11 On this day, we come to proclaim an end to the petty grievances and false promises, the recriminations and worn-out **dogmas** that for far too long have strangled our politics.

dogmas
prescribed doctrine

12 We remain a young nation, but in the words of Scripture, the time has come to set aside childish things. The time has come to reaffirm our enduring spirit; to choose our better history; to carry forward that precious gift, that noble idea, passed on from **generation** to **generation**: the God-given promise that all are equal, all are free, and all deserve a chance to **pursue** their full measure of happiness.

13　　In reaffirming the greatness of our nation, we understand that greatness is never a given. It must be earned. Our journey has never been one of short-cuts or settling for less.

14　　It has not been the path for the faint-hearted, for those who prefer leisure over work, or seek only the pleasures of riches and fame.

15　　Rather, it has been the risk-takers, the doers, the makers of things—some celebrated, but more often men and women obscure in their **labor**—who have carried us up the long, rugged path towards prosperity and freedom.

16　　For us, they packed up their few worldly possessions and traveled across oceans in search of a new life. For us, they **toiled** in sweatshops and settled the West, endured the lash of the whip and plowed the hard earth.

toiled
to engage in hard and continuous work

17　　For us, they fought and died in places like Concord and Gettysburg; Normandy and Khe Sanh.

18　　Time and again these men and women struggled and sacrificed and worked till their hands were raw so that we might live a better life. They saw America as bigger than the **sum** of our **individual** ambitions; greater than all the differences of birth or wealth or faction.

19　　This is the journey we continue today. We remain the most prosper-ous, powerful nation on Earth. Our workers are no less productive than when this crisis began. Our minds are no less inventive, our goods and services no less needed than they were last week or last month or last year. Our **capacity** remains undiminished. But our time of standing pat, of pro-tecting narrow interests and putting off unpleasant decisions—that time has surely passed.

20　　Starting today, we must pick ourselves up, dust ourselves off, and begin again the work of remaking America.

21　　For everywhere we look, there is work to be done.

22　　The state of our economy calls for action: bold and swift. And we will act not only to create new jobs but to lay a new **foundation** for growth.

23　　We will build the roads and bridges, the electric grids and digital lines that feed our commerce and bind us together.

24　　We will **restore** science to its rightful place and **wield** technology's won-ders to raise health care's quality . . . and lower its costs.

wield
to use effectively

25　　We will harness the sun and the winds and the soil to fuel our cars and run our factories. And we will transform our schools and colleges and univer-sities to meet the demands of a new age.

26　　All this we can do. All this we will do.

27　　Now, there are some who question the scale of our ambitions, who sug-gest that our system cannot tolerate too many big plans. Their memories are short, for they have forgotten what this country has already done, what free men and women can **achieve** when imagination is joined to common purpose and necessity to courage.

28　　What the cynics fail to understand is that the ground has shifted be-neath them, that the stale political arguments that have consumed us for so long, no longer apply.

29　　The question we ask today is not whether our government is too big or too small, but whether it works, whether it helps families find jobs at a decent wage, care they can afford, a retirement that is dignified.

© Pearson Education, Inc.

30   Where the answer is yes, we intend to move forward. Where the answer is no, programs will end.

31   And those of us who manage the public's dollars will be held to account, to spend wisely, reform bad habits, and do our business in the light of day, because only then can we **restore** the vital trust between a people and their government.

32   Nor is the question before us whether the market is a force for good or ill. Its power to generate wealth and expand freedom is unmatched.

33   But this crisis has reminded us that without a watchful eye, the market can spin out of control. The nation cannot prosper long when it favors only the prosperous.

34   The success of our economy has always depended not just on the size of our gross **domestic** product, but on the reach of our prosperity; on the ability to extend opportunity to every willing heart—not out of charity, but because it is the surest **route** to our common good.

35   As for our common defense, we reject as false the choice between our safety and our ideals.

36   Our founding fathers faced with perils that we can scarcely imagine, drafted a charter to assure the rule of law and the rights of man, a charter expanded by the blood of generations.

37   Those ideals still light the world, and we will not give them up for expedience's sake.

38   And so, to all other peoples and governments who are watching today, from the grandest capitals to the small village where my father was born: know that America is a friend of each nation and every man, woman and child who seeks a future of peace and dignity, and we are ready to lead once more.

39   Recall that earlier generations faced down fascism and communism not just with missiles and tanks, but with the sturdy alliances and enduring convictions.

emanates
to flow out, issue

40   They understood that our power alone cannot protect us, nor does it entitle us to do as we please. Instead, they knew that our power grows through its use. Our **security emanates** from the justness of our cause; the force of our example; the tempering qualities of humility and restraint.

41   We are the keepers of this legacy, guided by these principles once more, we can meet those new threats that demand even greater effort, even greater cooperation and understanding between nations. We'll begin to responsibly leave Iraq to its people and forge a hard-earned peace in Afghanistan.

specter
source of terror

42   With old friends and former foes, we'll work tirelessly to lessen the **nuclear** threat and roll back the **specter** of a warming planet.

43   We will not apologize for our way of life nor will we waver in its defense.

44   And for those who seek to advance their aims by inducing terror and slaughtering innocents, we say to you now that, "Our spirit is stronger and cannot be broken. You cannot outlast us, and we will defeat you."

45   For we know that our patchwork heritage is a strength, not a weakness.

46   We are a nation of Christians and Muslims, Jews and Hindus, and non-believers. We are shaped by every language and culture, drawn from every end of this Earth.

47   And because we have tasted the bitter swill of **civil** war and segregation and **emerged** from that dark **chapter** stronger and more united, we cannot

help but believe that the old hatreds shall someday pass; that the lines of tribe shall soon dissolve; that as the world grows smaller, our common humanity shall reveal itself; and that America must play its **role** in **ushering in** a new era of peace.

ushering in
the introduction of something new

48　　To the Muslim world, we seek a new way forward, based on **mutual** interest and **mutual** respect.

49　　To those leaders around the globe who seek to sow **conflict** or blame their society's ills on the West, know that your people will judge you on what you can build, not what you destroy.

50　　To those who cling to power through corruption and deceit and the silencing of dissent, know that you are on the wrong side of history, but that we will extend a hand if you are willing to unclench your fist.

51　　To the people of poor nations, we pledge to work alongside you to make your farms flourish and let clean waters flow; to nourish starved bodies and feed hungry minds.

52　　And to those nations like ours that enjoy relative plenty, we say we can no longer afford **indifference** to the suffering outside our borders, nor can we consume the world's **resources** without regard to effect. For the world has changed, and we must change with it.

indifference
lack of interest or concern

53　　As we consider the road that unfolds before us, we remember with humble gratitude those brave Americans who, at this very hour, patrol far-off deserts and distant mountains. They have something to tell us, just as the fallen heroes who lie in Arlington whisper through the ages.

54　　We honor them not only because they are guardians of our liberty, but because they embody the spirit of service: a willingness to find meaning in something greater than themselves.

55　　And yet, at this moment, a moment that will define a **generation**, it is precisely this spirit that must inhabit us all.

56　　For as much as government can do and must do, it is **ultimately** the faith and determination of the American people upon which this nation relies.

57　　It is the kindness to take in a stranger when the levees break; the selflessness of workers who would rather cut their hours than see a friend lose their **job** which sees us through our darkest hours.

58　　It is the firefighter's courage to storm a stairway filled with smoke, but also a parent's willingness to nurture a child, that finally decides our fate.

59　　Our challenges may be new, the instruments with which we meet them may be new, but those values upon which our success depends, honesty and hard work, courage and fair play, tolerance and curiosity, loyalty and patriotism—these things are old.

60　　These things are true. They have been the quiet force of progress throughout our history.

61　　What is demanded then is a return to these truths. What is **required** of us now is a new era of responsibility—a recognition, on the part of every American, that we have duties to ourselves, our nation and the world, duties that we do not grudgingly accept but rather seize gladly, firm in the knowledge that there is nothing so satisfying to the spirit, so defining of our character than giving our all to a difficult **task**.

62　　This is the price and the promise of citizenship.

© Pearson Education, Inc.

creed
belief system

63   This is the **source** of our confidence: the knowledge that God calls on us to shape an uncertain destiny.

64   This is the meaning of our liberty and our **creed**, why men and women and children of every race and every faith can join in celebration across this magnificent mall. And why a man whose father less than 60 years ago might not have been served at a local restaurant can now stand before you to take a most sacred oath.

65   So let us mark this day in remembrance of who we are and how far we have traveled.

66   In the year of America's birth, in the coldest of months, a small band of patriots huddled by dying campfires on the shores of an icy river.

67   The capital was abandoned. The enemy was advancing. The snow was stained with blood.

68   At a moment when the outcome of our **revolution** was most in doubt, the father of our nation ordered these words be read to the people:

69   "Let it be told to the future world that in the depth of winter, when nothing but hope and virtue could **survive**, that the city and the country, alarmed at one common danger, came forth to meet it."

70   America, in the face of our common dangers, in this winter of our hardship, let us remember these timeless words; with hope and virtue, let us brave once more the icy currents, and endure what storms may come; let it be said by our children's children that when we were tested we refused to let this journey end, that we did not turn back nor did we falter; and with eyes fixed on the horizon and God's grace upon us, we carried forth that great gift of freedom and delivered it safely to future generations.

71   Thank you. God bless you.

72   And God bless the United States of America.

Reading Comprehension Check

After answering each question below, identify the reading skill and write it in the blank space.

1. "My fellow citizens: I stand here today humbled by the task before us, grateful for the trust you have bestowed, mindful of the sacrifices borne by our ancestors."

   In the above sentence, the word *humbled* means
   a. arrogant.   (c.) made meek.
   b. proud.   d. stumbled.

   Identify the reading skill *Vocabulary in context*

2. "The words have been spoken during rising tides of prosperity and the still waters of peace. Yet, every so often the oath is taken amidst gathering clouds and raging storms. At these moments, America has carried on not simply because of the skill or vision of those in high office, but because We the People have remained faithful to the ideals of our forebears, and true to our founding documents."

Which of the following sentences is the best statement of the main idea in the entire passage?

a. A great flood has destroyed America's prosperity.

b. America cannot possibly overcome the obstacles facing the nation.

c. Only skilled and visionary people can read and understand our founding fathers' documents.

d. America has weathered many storms because of its ideals and its people's faith in the Constitution.

Identify the reading skill _Main idea_

3. "We remain a young nation, but in the words of Scripture, the time has come to set aside childish things. The time has come to reaffirm our enduring spirit; to choose our better history; to carry forward that precious gift, that noble idea, passed on from generation to generation: the God-given promise that all are equal, all are free, and all deserve a chance to pursue their full measure of happiness."

Which of the following is NOT mentioned in the above paragraph?

a. God.

b. a reference to the American spirit.

c. a select group of people have the right to happiness.

d. the time has come to act as mature adults.

Identify the reading skill _Supporting details_

4. President Obama states, "On this day, we come to proclaim an end to the petty grievances and false promises, the recriminations and worn-out dogmas that for far too long have strangled our politics."

A logical conclusion that can be drawn from the above passage is that

a. the American people must make false promises.

b. the American people have to rethink our political outlook.

c. the American people must stand firm and hold on to our age-old beliefs.

d. the American people should strangle their corrupt politicians.

Identify the reading skill _Inference_

5. In giving his inaugural speech, President Obama's primary purpose is to

a. to give people hope in light of difficult times.

b. remind Americans of the Constitution.

c. threaten the enemies of America.

d. fix America's troubled economy.

Identify the reading skill _Purpose_

6. What is the overall tone of this speech?

a. dark.　　c. sarcastic.

b. optimistic.　　d. sardonic.

Identify the reading skill _Tone_

7. Which of the following is a statement of fact?

a. We are a nation of Christians and Muslims, Jews and Hindus, and nonbelievers.

b. Starting today, we must pick ourselves up, dust ourselves off, and begin again the work of remaking America.

© Pearson Education, Inc.

   c. This is the meaning of our liberty and our creed, why men and women and children of every race and every faith can join in celebration across this magnificent mall.

   d. What is demanded then is a return to these truths.

Identify the reading skill *Fact vs. Opinion*

8. Which of the following is a statement of opinion?

   a. Our founding fathers . . . drafted a charter to assure the rule of law and the rights of man.

   b. Forty-four Americans have now taken the presidential oath.

   c. And because we have tasted the bitter swill of civil war and segregation and emerged from that dark chapter stronger and more united, we cannot help but believe that the old hatreds shall someday pass.

   d. Homes have been lost, jobs shed, businesses shuttered.

Identify the reading skill *Fact vs. Opinion*

9. "And because we have tasted the bitter swill of civil war and segregation and emerged from that dark chapter stronger and more united, we cannot help but believe that the old hatreds shall someday pass; that the lines of tribe shall soon dissolve; that as the world grows smaller, our common humanity shall reveal itself; and that America must play its role in ushering in a new era of peace."

The overall pattern of organization of this passage is

   a. classification.   c. comparison and contrast.

   b. chronological order.   d. cause and effect.

Identify the reading skill *Patterns of Organization*

10. "To the Muslim world, we seek a new way forward, based on mutual interest and mutual respect."

In this passage, the author

   a. approves of better relations with the Muslim world.

   b. supports non-Muslims in the United States.

   c. is biased against the Muslim world.

   d. implies that all men are created equal.

Identify the reading skill *Inference*

From Reading to Writing: Writing to a Political Representative

Overview

In representative democracies, the voters elect representatives to act as legislators, and, as such to voice and protect their general interest. When a member of a community has a concern they would like to raise, they have the right to contact their local representative, whether it be a city council member, state senator, mayor, or house representative. Voters, of course, can also contact politicians in higher offices, such as their governor or the president, but local representatives are more likely to respond to community concerns.

   There are a few important points to keep in mind when writing a political representative, whether it be by e-mail or standard post.

- Try to write your letter in a formal voice.

  Begin your letter respectfully with "Dear Councilwoman Green," or "Dear Mayor Jones." Choose more formal vocabulary in the body of your letter. Avoid colloquial usage terms such as "gonna" or "wanna," etc. So, for example "I'm gonna explain what I wanna do for our community" becomes "I am going to explain what I want to do for our community." Choice of language goes a long way in getting political representatives to pay attention to the concerns you are expressing.

- In the first sentence, offer some context by making clear what your connection is to the issue you are addressing.

  Introduce your identity in relation to the issue at hand. If you are a college student writing about the lack of financial aid funding coming from the state, begin your letter by saying, "I am a junior at Smith and Smith college and. . . ." If you are a teacher and want to voice your opinion on how overcrowded your classrooms have become, you might begin your letter with "I am a fifth-grade teacher at Central Elementary and . . . "

- Get to the point. Be clear and straightforward.

  Politicians and their staff are busy people with many community members competing for their attention. Keep your letter short and focused. Introduce your relation to the issue, briefly describe the problem or community concern, and clearly express what actions you think your representative should take to improve the situation. Do not digress from the issue at hand by discussing your life story or by sharing your feelings about the particular politician's political problems. This would only serve to distract your reader from the real concerns you would like to see addressed.

An Example Letter to a Representative

Dear Councilwoman Rogers,

   I am a freshman at Dandelion Community College and I am writing to you about the strict parking rules in the residential area just outside the campus. I have gotten two tickets already for parking on nearby residential streets around 5:40 PM, where the parking signs state that you can only park after 6:00 PM. I know there are many other students like me who drive to college after working all day and need to park before 6:00 in order to make to it class on time.

   The problem is that there is nowhere else around to park. The campus parking lot is always full that late in the day and there are no public parking lots in the area. I have already addressed this issue to my campus dean, but I think there is a lot you can do to alleviate the situation. First, you should consider changing the parking rules within three blocks of the campus, so that students can park legally on the street at any hour of the day. Another possible solution would be to build a modest-sized public parking lot somewhere within walking distance of the campus.

   Thank you, Councilwoman Rogers, for considering my concerns. I look forward to hearing from you soon about this matter.

                                                          Sincerely,
                                                          Jane Doe

© Pearson Education, Inc.

Collaboration

Writing a Letter to Send to a Local Representative

Before doing any writing for a letter you can later send, spend a few minutes with a classmate, making a list of complaints/concerns you have about your community.

Choose one community concern to be the focus of your letter. Consider to whom you would like to address this concern—a community board member, a state representative, the mayor, etc. Make sure you know the name of the political representative to whom you are writing.

Concern/Issue:

Name and title of political representative:

Write a letter addressing a community concern and send it via e-mail or post. You should be able to locate political representatives' e-mail and office addresses easily through an Internet search. We hope you will receive a prompt response to your letter. Good luck!

ESL Annotation

10.12 ESL In many cultures, it is not typical to communicate with local representatives, beyond an urgent family emergency. It would be worthwhile to foster a discussion about the American tradition of writing letters voicing community concerns.

Connecting Reading Skills with Standardized Testing

Combined Skills

When you take a standardized, multiple-choice reading exam, it is critical that you pay close attention to exactly what is being asked in each question. Now that you have reviewed the different skill areas that are tested on such exams, you are better prepared to accurately identify the question types you are offered.

One way to categorize question types is to distinguish between *particular-point* questions and *overall-meaning* questions.

Particular-point questions focus on a particular expression, sentence or paragraph within a reading. Vocabulary, supporting details, fact and opinion, and some inference questions fit this description.

Overall-meaning type questions, however, focus on the passage as a whole, and not on just one part of the text. Questions then that focus on the reading's main idea, author's purpose, and tone can be categorized this way.

When you first glance at a question on a standardized reading exam, try to identify the question type before answering the question. You can practice below by writing the question type to the right of each question:

Question	*Question Type*
A. We can infer from sentence three that the author's political views are . . .	Particular point
B. The main point of the passage is that . . .	Overall meaning
C. Which sentence in the last paragraph is an opinion?	Particular point
D. The author wrote this passage with the intention of . . .	Overall meaning
E. What did the author do to hide his political identity?	Particular point
F. The word *closeted* in paragraph 4 means . . .	Particular point

Bryan Pu-Folkes

Profession: Immigration Attorney/Community Activist

How did you choose your current profession?

I am not certain how I or one would characterize my current profession. At this precise moment in time I am an immigration attorney and I run and manage the Community Journal, a new community development nonprofit organization that I founded a little over a year ago. I chose each of these jobs, duties, or professions, if you will, for different but connected reasons.

I began a law practice for three fundamental reasons: (1) to generate sustainable revenue in order to economically secure myself and my family; (2) to help individuals and families in need in an area that I have experience and ability; and (3) to help shape public policy in areas that I am passionate about, namely human rights, the United States economy, and foreign trade.

I founded the Community Journal to help develop a mechanism for neighborhood multiethnic civic engagement, to strengthen the local economy, and to further support efforts to build bridges among diverse communities in my neighborhood.

How did you prepare to reach your goal of becoming a community activist/immigration lawyer?

I never planned to be a "community activist" and therefore never made a proactive decision to formally prepare for this role. However, in retrospect, I do believe that I was preparing for such a leadership position from a very young age. As the youngest of four boys I often found myself in a position where I had to speak up if I wanted to be heard. As the product of an interracial and bicultural marriage, I grew up seeing and understanding that the commonality of humankind far eclipses any personal differences. As the son of immigrant parents who faced discrimination as well as linguistic, economic, and cultural challenges, I learned early on of the need to exercise creativity and ingenuity in order to overcome problems and to access resources. As a child growing up in a large family, three older brothers, a younger sister, and several first cousins, I learned of the value of strategic partnerships—where each individual in a community can be better off than if they were outside of that partnership and that the benefits of that partnership are only sustainable when there is transparency, equity, and fairness.

I also never planned to be an immigration attorney. Sure, I went to law school but I didn't practice immigration law until twelve years after graduation. My decision to practice immigration law was more pragmatic than anything else. I founded a nonprofit immigration advocacy and service organization in 1999, which gave me a lot of knowledge and contacts in the area of immigration. Since I had a law degree, it made sense to open an immigration practice.

What did you struggle with most when preparing to build your career as a community activist/immigration attorney?

Two of the largest challenges in building my career were (1) feeling good and certain about my decisions and (2) being effective at accomplishing the goals set out for myself.

One of the difficulties of being known as a "community activist" is that it is mostly an amorphous term that can mean different things to different people. Feelings of respect, dignity, and pride often don't flow from that vagueness. When I first graduated from law school I worked as a corporate attorney in two very large and prestigious Wall Street firms. Few people may have understood the details of my work but while I worked there I instantly won praise and respect from those who asked me about my profession. The work that I do now is often looked upon as a personal sacrifice. Something that is admirable and possibly necessary, but something few would choose to do for themselves.

The second challenge of community organizing and activism is the difficulty of accomplishing goals when I believe that the process of how that accomplishment is achieved is just as important as the goal itself. This challenge behind process is even more difficult when you are working with a wide range of stakeholders, personalities, and competing interests, as well as with cultural, linguistic, and religious differences.

The challenge of opening a law practice is multifold and similar to the challenge of beginning any small enterprise.

How did you overcome this struggle?

I am very introspective, which helps me to focus on the work that I do. I am able to achieve the clarity I need for my work by constantly asking myself why it is that I do what I do. I am also an optimist and believe that I can have an appreciable impact on the world around me. I believe that given the right circumstances people will sacrifice a little at times, and a lot at times, to help another person and to improve the world around them. I believe strategic partnerships are the key to

(Continued)

© Pearson Education, Inc.

success in the home, at work, and in the community. I believe it is tough, but definitely possible to find where an individual's personal interest aligns with the community's public interest and then to make great things happen.

What do you enjoy most about your work?

The common thread in my work is that I love being a builder and an entrepreneur. I find that my passion is sharing a vision with others and then working toward the sustainable realization of that vision.

What advice do you have for a student considering a career related to political science?

My advice to students considering any career is to think intensely about what makes you tick. Be introspective and think about why it is that you are interested in political science or a particular person, job, group, or agency. Research groups, organizations, agencies, and individuals that excite, interest, or intrigue you. Apply for jobs or internships and ask for informational interviews with these organizations and individuals. Ask a lot of questions and listen carefully. Keep an open mind and learn from how different people approach tasks and initiatives. Constantly challenge yourself and don't be afraid to try and to fail and to try again.

After reading the interview, in your opinion what were the three most interesting points made by the interviewee? Discuss your choices with the class.

- _____

  _____

- _____

  _____

- _____

  _____

Helpful Hints

- Take the time to read each question twice. Make sure you understand what each question is asking you.

- Pay attention to "negative questions" such as, "Which political party did NOT endorse this candidate?" or "All of the following are examples of political ideologies EXCEPT . . ." Often the negative term in a negative question is capitalized to highlight it.

- Be aware of whether a question is of the "overall meaning" type or "particular point" type. Understand that to answer some "particular point" questions you will have to re-read the sentences, which precede and follow the sentence the question pertains to.

Textbook Application

Read the following chapter from an introductory book on political science. As you know, this reading exercise will give you an opportunity to practice reading and answering multiple-choice questions based on authentic text. You are likely to come across this type of text when you take mainstream courses in college.

A Science of Politics

READING

Reading Selection **6**

Textbook Reading

10.13 Flesch-Kincaid Grade Level 8.2

1 A SCIENCE OF POLITICS?

War and terrorism have revived interest in politics in the United States. Students and attentive citizens who a few years ago turned away from politics are paying attention again. U.S. electoral turnout, with voters angered by the war in Iraq and spurred by controversies over candidates and their policies, is up from lows of 50 **percent** in presidential elections. For political scientists, the uptick in interest is welcome, but many still worry that Americans (and many other nationalities) are becoming depoliticized. Why has declining interest in politics been the **trend** for many years? Is it disgust at politicians and their **constant**, empty struggle for partisan advantage? Is it a feeling of helplessness, a sense that **individual** citizens do not matter? Is it the perception that Washington is the playground of rich and powerful interest groups who simply buy whatever they want, including politicians? Or is it a healthy sign that in relatively good times people naturally turn to other concerns? If the economy is not bad and world problems seem distant, why follow politics? Perhaps anger and **controversy** are needed to renew interest in politics.

It is the **thesis** of this book that politics matters. If you do not take an interest and participate, someone else will, and they will influence the decisions that govern your lives. Will they take us to war in a foreign land? Who might have to fight in that war? You. Will they **alter** the tax **code** to favor certain citizens and corporations? Who will have to pay in taxes what others avoid paying? You. Will they set up government

QUESTIONS TO CONSIDER

- Why did politics fall out of favor? Is it now back in favor?
- What does it mean to "never get angry at a fact"?
- Why did Aristotle call politics "the master science"?
- What did Machiavelli bring to the study of politics?
- How are legitimacy, sovereignty, and **authority** different but **similar**?
- Is the Iraqi government now legitimate? How can you tell?
- Is politics largely biological, psychological, **cultural**, **rational**, or irrational?
- How can something as messy as politics be a science?

From Michael G. Roskin, *Political Science: An Introduction*, pp. 1–5, 8–12. Copyright © 2008 by Pearson Education, Inc. Reprinted by permission.

© Pearson Education, Inc.

programs whose costs escalate far beyond what anyone had foreseen? Who then will have to pay these costs? You. One of the tasks of this book is to make you **aware** of what politics is and how it works so that you can look after yourself and prevent others from using you. The ignorant are manipulated.

Many find politics distasteful, and perhaps they are right. Politics may be inherently immoral or, at any rate, amoral. Misuse of power, influence peddling, and outright corruption are prominent **features** of politics. But you need not like the thing you study. Biologists may behold a disease-causing bacterium under a microscope. They do not "like" the bacterium but are interested in how it grows, how it does its damage, and how it may be eradicated. Neither do they get angry at the bacterium and smash the glass slide with a hammer. Biologists first understand the forces of nature and then work with them to improve humankind's existence. Political scientists try to do the same with politics.

■ THE MASTER SCIENCE

Aristotle, the founder of the **discipline**, called politics "the master science." He meant that almost everything happens in a political **context**, that the decisions of the *polis* (the Greek city-state) governed most other things. Politics, in the words of Yale's Harold Lasswell, is the study of "who gets what." But, some object, the **economic** system determines who gets what in countries with free markets. True, but who determines if we shall have a free-market system? Who tells Bill Gates that he must split up his giant Microsoft, a decision worth billions of dollars? Politics is intimately connected to economics.

Suppose something utterly natural strikes, like a hurricane. It is the political system that decides whether and where to build dikes and whether and which of the victims to **aid**. The disaster is natural, but its **impact** on society is controlled in large part by politics. How about science, our bacteriologists squinting through microscopes? That is not political. But who **funds** the scientists' education and their **research** institutes? It could be private charity (the donors of which get tax breaks), but chances are the government plays a **major role**. When the U.S. government decided that AIDS **research** deserved top **priority**, funding for other programs was cut. Bacteria and viruses may be natural, but studying them is often quite political. In this case, it pitted gays against women concerned with breast cancer. Who gets what: funding to find a cure for AIDS or for breast cancer? The choice is political.

Because almost everything is political, studying politics means studying nearly everything. Some students **select** "interdisciplinary majors." Political science already is one, borrowing from and overlapping with all of the other social sciences. At times, it is hard to tell where history, human geography, economics, sociology, anthropology, and **psychology** leave off and political science begins. Here, briefly, is how political science relates to the other social sciences.

HISTORY

History is one of the chief sources of **data** for political scientists. When we discuss the politics of the Third French Republic (1871–1940), the growth of presidential power under Franklin Roosevelt (1933–1945), and even something as recent as the Cold War (1947–1989), we are studying history. But historians

---

discipline   A field of study, often represented by an **academic** department or **major**.

KEY CONCEPTS

"NEVER GET ANGRY AT A FACT"

This basic point of all serious study sounds commonsensical but is often **ignored**, even in college courses. It actually traces back to the extremely **complex** thought of the German philosopher Hegel, who argued that things happen not by caprice or accident but for good and **sufficient** reasons: "Whatever is real is **rational**." That means that nothing is completely accidental and that if we apply reason we will understand why something happens. We study politics in a "naturalistic" **mode**, not getting angry at what we see but trying to understand how it came to be.

For example, we hear of a politician who took money from a lobbyist. As political scientists, we push our anger to the side and ask questions like: Do most politicians in that country take money? Is it an old tradition and does the culture of this country accept it? Do the people even expect politicians to take money? How big are campaign expenses? Can the politician possibly run for office without taking money? In short, we see if extralegal exchanges of cash are part and parcel of the political system. If they are, it makes no sense to get angry at an **individual** politician. If we dislike it, we may then consider how the system might be reformed to discourage the taking of money on the side. And reforms may not work. Japan reformed its electoral laws in an attempt to stamp out its **traditional** "money politics," but little changed. Like bacteria, some things in politics have lives of their own.

and political scientists look for different things and handle **data** differently. Typically, historians study one episode in detail, digging up documents, archives, and news accounts on the **topic**. They have masses of **data** focused on one point but venture few or no generalizations. Political scientists, on the other hand, begin by looking for generalizations. We may take the findings of historians and compare and **contrast** them. A historian might do a detailed study of Weimar Germany (1919–1933); a political scientist might put that study alongside studies of France, Italy, and Russia of the same **period** to see what similarities and dissimilarities can be found. To be sure, some historians do comparative studies; they become de facto political scientists.

HUMAN GEOGRAPHY

Human geography (as distinct from **physical** geography) has in recent **decades** been neglected by political scientists, although it influences politics more than many realize. The territorial component of human behavior—borders, **ethnic** areas, trade flows, centralization of power, and regions—have great political ramifications. Strife in Afghanistan, Chechnya, and Iraq are heavily geographical problems, as is Canada's unsettled federalism, from which some Quebecers wish to depart. French political scientist André Siegfried pioneered the use of maps to explain regional political variations, a technique of today's electoral studies. The "red" and "blue" states in U.S. presidential elections show the relevance of political geography.

ECONOMICS

Economics, proclaim some economists, is the subject matter of politics. (Political scientists are apt to claim the opposite.) True, many political quarrels are **economic**: Who gets what? **Sufficient economic** development may be the basis

© Pearson Education, Inc.

for democracy; few poor countries are democratic. A declining economy may doom democracy, as was the fate of the Weimar Republic and recently of Russia. What policies **promote economic** development? How big a **role** should government have? Is the *euro* **currency** making Europe more united? When economists get into questions of **policy**, they become "political economists." A relatively new school of political science, "**rational**-choice **theory**," shares the **economic perspective** that humans generally **pursue** their self-interests.

SOCIOLOGY

Parts of sociology and political science merge. Sociologist Seymour Martin Lipset is equally renowned as a political scientist. He was among the first to **demonstrate** the close connection between democracy and level of wealth. As we shall consider in the next **chapter**, political science conventionally starts by looking at society to see "who thinks what" about politics. In demonstrating how political views vary among social classes, regions, religions, genders, and age groups, sociology gives an **empirical** basis to political culture, public opinion, and electoral studies.

ANTHROPOLOGY

Anthropology, which traditionally focused on nonliterate societies, may seem of little relevance to political science. But the descriptive and interviewing **techniques** of anthropology have been heavily adopted by political scientists. The subfield of political culture could be viewed as a branch of anthropology. Japanese deference patterns, which we still see today, were laid down more than a millennium ago. Some current political systems still reserve political power for traditionally influential families or clans. In Central Asia the families of *emirs* who ruled under the Persians did so under the Russian tsars, the Communists, and now the newly independent states. In Africa, voting and violence follow tribal lines.

PSYCHOLOGY

Psychology, particularly social **psychology**, contributes much to political science's understanding of which personalities are attracted to politics, why and under what **circumstances** people obey **authority** figures, and how people form national, group, and voting attachments. Studies of Hitler, Stalin, and Mao Zedong are often based on psychological theories. Psychologists are especially good with **methodology**; they devise ways to study things objectively and teach us to doubt claims that have holes in them. Asking questions in a "blind" manner and "controlling" for certain **factors** are **techniques** developed from **psychology**.

■ POLITICAL POWER

Political science often uses the findings of other social sciences, but one feature distinguishes it from the others—its **focus** on power. Our second founding father (after Aristotle) is the Renaissance Florentine philosopher Niccolò Machiavelli, who emphasized the **role** of power in politics. You can take all the **factors** and approaches mentioned previously, but if you are not using them to study power—which is a very broad subject—you are probably not doing political science.

---

methodology   The **techniques** for studying questions objectively.

Some people dislike the **concept** of **political power**. It smacks of coercion, inequality, occasionally of brutality. Some speakers denounce "power politics," suggesting governance without power, a happy band of brothers and sisters regulating themselves on the basis of love and sharing. Communities formed on such a basis do not last; or if they do last it is only by transforming themselves into conventional structures of leaders and led, buttressed by obedience patterns that look suspiciously like nasty old power. Political power seems to be built into the human condition. But why do some people hold political power over others? There is no definitive explanation of political power. Biological, psychological, **cultural**, **rational**, and irrational explanations have been put forward.

BIOLOGICAL

Aristotle said it first and perhaps best: "Man is by nature a political animal." (Aristotle's words were *zoon politikon*, which can be translated as either "political animal" or "social animal." The Greeks lived in city-states in which the *polis* was the same as society.) Aristotle meant that humans live naturally in herds, like elephants or deer. Biologically, they need each other for sustenance and survival. It is also natural that they array themselves into ranks of leaders and led, like all herd animals. Taking a cue from Aristotle, a modern biological explanation would say that forming a political system and obeying its leaders is innate human behavior, passed on to future generations with one's genes. Some thinkers argue that human politics shows the same "dominance hierarchies" that other mammals set up.

The advantage of the biological **approach** is its simplicity, but it raises a number of questions. If we grant that humans are naturally political, how do we explain the instances when political groups fall apart and people disobey **authority**? Perhaps we should modify the **theory**: Humans are imperfectly political (or social) animals. Most of the time people form groups and obey **authority**, but sometimes, under certain **circumstances**, they do not. This begs the question of which **circumstances promote** or undermine the formation of political groups.

PSYCHOLOGICAL

Psychological explanations of politics and obedience are closely allied with biological theories. Both posit needs **derived** from centuries of **evolution** in the formation of political groups. The psychologists have refined their views with **empirical research**. One is the famous Milgram study, in which unwitting subjects were instructed by a professor to administer progressively larger electric shocks to a victim. The "victim," strapped in a chair, was actually an actor who only pretended to suffer. Most of the subjects were willing to administer potentially lethal doses of electricity simply because the "professor"—an **authority** figure in a white lab smock—told them to. Most of the subjects disliked hurting the victim, but they rationalized that they were just following orders and that any harm done to the victim was really the professor's responsibility. They surrendered their actions to an **authority** figure.

Psychological studies also show that most people are naturally conformist. Most members of a group see things the group's way. Psychologist Irving Janis found many foreign **policy** mistakes were made in a climate of "groupthink," in which a leadership **team** tells itself that all is well and that

---

© Pearson Education, Inc.

political power   Ability of one person to get another to do something.

the present policy is working. Groups tend to ignore doubters who tell them, for **instance**, that the Japanese will attack Pearl Harbor in 1941 or that the 1961 Bay of Pigs landing of Cuban exiles will fail. Obedience to **authority** and groupthink suggest that humans have deep-seated needs—possibly innate—to fit into groups and to go along with their **norms**. Perhaps this is what makes human society possible, but it also makes possible horrors such as the Nazi Holocaust and the more recent Iraqi massacres.

CULTURAL

How much of human behavior is learned as opposed to biologically inherited? This is the very old "nurture versus nature" **debate**. For much of the twentieth century, the *cultural theorists*—those who believe behavior is learned—dominated. Anthropologists concluded that all differences in behavior were **cultural**. **Cooperative** and peaceful societies raise their children that way, they argued. Political communities are formed and hold together on the basis of **cultural** values transmitted by parents, schools, churches, and the mass **media**. Political science developed an interesting subfield called *political culture*, whose researchers found that a country's political culture was formed by many long-term **factors**: religion, child rearing, land tenure, and **economic** development.

Cultural theorists see trouble when the political system gets out of touch with the **cultural** system, as when the shah of Iran attempted to modernize an Islamic society that did not like Western values and lifestyles. The Iranians threw the shah out and celebrated the return of a medieval-style religious leader, who voiced the values favored by **traditional** Iranians. **Cultural** theories can also be applied to U.S. politics. Republicans often win elections by articulating the values of religion, family, and self-**reliance**, which are deeply ingrained into American culture. Many thinkers believe **economic** and political development depend heavily on **culture**.

The **cultural approach** to political life holds some optimism. If all human behavior is learned, bad behavior can be unlearned and society improved. Educating young people to be tolerant, **cooperative**, and just will gradually change a society's culture for the better, according to this view. Changing culture, however, is extremely difficult, as the American occupiers of Iraq discovered.

The Declaration of Independence, here signed in large bold letters by John Hancock, embodied a rational view of politics. (Library of Congress)

culture   Human behavior that is learned as opposed to inherited.

Culture contributes a lot to political behavior, but the **theory** has some difficulties. First, where does culture come from? History? Economics? Religion? Second, if all behavior is **cultural**, various political systems should be as different from each other as their cultures. But, especially in the realm of politics, we see **similar** political **attitudes** and patterns in lands with very different cultures. Politicians everywhere tend to become corrupt, regardless of culture.

RATIONAL

Another school of thought approaches politics as a **rational** thing; that is, people know what they want most of the time, and they have good reasons for doing what they do. Classic political theorists, such as Hobbes and Locke, as we shall see in the next **chapter**, held that humans form "**civil** society" because their powers of reason tell them that it is much better than anarchy. To safeguard life and property, people form governments. If those governments become abusive, the people have the right to dissolve them and start anew. This Lockean **notion** greatly influenced the U.S. Founding Fathers.

The biological, psychological, and **cultural** schools downplay human reason, claiming that people are either born or conditioned to certain behavior, and individuals seldom think rationally. But how can we then explain cases in which people break away from group **conformity** and argue independently? How can we explain a change of mind? "I was for Jones until he came out with his terrible **economic policy**, so now I'm voting for Smith." People make **rational** judgments like that all the time. A political system based on the **presumption** of human reason stands a better chance of governing justly and humanely. If leaders believe that people obey out of biological inheritance or **cultural** conditioning, they will think they can get away with all manner of corruption and misrule. If, on the other hand, rulers fear that people are **rational**, they will respect the public's ability to discern wrongdoing. Accordingly, even if people are not completely **rational**, it is good that rulers think they are.

IRRATIONAL

Late in the nineteenth century, a group of thinkers expounded the view that people are basically **irrational**, especially when it comes to political power. They are emotional, dominated by myths and stereotypes, and politics is really the **manipulation** of symbols. A crowd is like a wild beast that can be whipped up by charismatic leaders to do their bidding. What people regard as **rational** is really myth; just keep feeding them myths to control them. The first practitioner of this school was Mussolini, founder of fascism in Italy, followed by Hitler in Germany. A soft-spoken Muslim fundamentalist, Osama bin Laden, got an irrational hold on thousands of fanatical followers. Believing the myth that America was the enemy of Islam, some willingly ended their lives in terrorist acts.

There may be a good deal of truth to the irrational view of human political behavior, but it has catastrophic **consequences**. Leaders who use irrationalist **techniques** start believing their own propaganda and lead their nations to war, **economic** ruin, or tyranny. Some detect irrationalism even

---

rational Based on the ability to reason.

irrational Based on the power of fears and myth to cloud reason.

© Pearson Education, Inc.

in the most advanced societies, where much of politics consists of screaming crowds and leaders striking heroic poses.

POWER AS A COMPOSITE

There are **elements** of truth in all these explanations of political power. At different times in different situations, any one of them can explain power. Tom Paine's pamphlet *Common Sense* rationally explained why America should separate from Britain. The drafters of both the U.S. Declaration of Independence and the Constitution were imbued with the rationalism of their age. Following the philosophers then popular, they framed their arguments as if human political activity were as logical as Newtonian physics. Historian Henry Steele Commager referred to the Constitution as "the crown jewel of the enlightenment," the culmination of an age of reason.

But how truly **rational** were they? By the late eighteenth century, the thirteen American colonies had grown culturally separate from Britain. People thought of themselves as Americans rather than as English colonists. They increasingly read American newspapers and communicated among themselves rather than with Britain. Perhaps the separation was more **cultural** than **rational**.

Nor can we forget the psychological and irrational **factors**. Samuel Adams was a gifted firebrand, Thomas Jefferson a powerful writer, and George Washington a charismatic general. The American break with Britain and the founding of a new order was a **complex** mixture of all these **factors**. The same **complex** mixture of **factors** goes into any political system you can mention.

KEY CONCEPTS

THE SUBFIELDS OF POLITICAL SCIENCE

Most political science departments divide the discipline into several subfields. The bigger the department, the more subfields it will likely have. We will get a least a **brief** introduction to all of them in this book.

U.S. Politics focuses on institutions and processes, mostly at the **federal** level but some at state and local levels. It includes parties, elections, public opinion, and executive and legislative behavior.

Comparative Politics examines politics within other nations, trying to establish generalizations and theories of democracy, **stability**, and **policy**. It may be focused on various regions, as in "Latin American politics" or "East Asian politics."

International Relations studies politics among nations, including **conflict**, diplomacy, international law and organizations, and international political economy. U.S. foreign **policy** has one foot in U.S. politics and one in international relations.

Political Theory, both classic and modern, attempts to define the good polity, often focused on **major** thinkers.

Public Administration studies how bureaucracies work and how they can be improved.

Constitutional Law studies the applications and **evolution** of the Constitution within the U.S. **legal** system.

Public Policy studies the interface of politics and economics with an eye to developing effective programs.

To be sure, at times one factor seems more important than others, but we cannot exactly determine the weight to give any one factor. And notice how the various **factors** blend into one another. The biological **factors** lead to the psychological, which in turn lead to the **cultural**, the **rational**, and the irrational, forming a seamless web.

One common mistake made about political power is viewing it as a **finite**, measurable quantity. Power is a connection among people, the ability of one person to get others to do his or her bidding. Political power does not come in jars or megawatts. Revolutionaries in some lands speak of "seizing power," as if power were kept in the national treasury and they could sneak in and grab it at night. The Afghan Taliban "seized power" in 1995–1996, but they were a minority of the Afghan population. Many Afghans hated them, and some fought them. Revolutionaries think that they **automatically** get legitimacy and **authority** when they "seize power"; they do not. Power is earned, not seized.

Is power **identical** to politics? Some power-mad people (including more than a few politicians) see the two as the same, but this is an oversimplification. We might see politics as a combination of goals or policies and the power necessary to **achieve** them. Power, in this view, is a **prime** *ingredient* of politics. It would be difficult to imagine a political system without political power. Even a religious figure who ruled on the basis of love would be exercising power over followers. It might be "nice power," but it would still be power. Power, then, is a sort of *enabling device* to carry out or implement policies and decisions. You can have praiseworthy **goals**, but unless you have the power to implement them, they remain wishful thoughts.

Others see the essence of politics as a *struggle for power*, a sort of gigantic game in which power is the goal. What, for example, are elections all about? The getting of power. There is a danger here, however. If power becomes the goal of politics, devoid of other purposes, it becomes cynical, brutal, and self-destructive. The Hitler **regime** destroyed itself in the worship of power. Obsessed with retaining presidential power, President Nixon ruined his own **administration**. As nineteenth-century British historian and philosopher Lord Acton put it, "Power tends to corrupt; absolute power corrupts absolutely."

■ IS POLITICS A SCIENCE?

If we cannot pinpoint which **factors** contribute what weight to politics, how can politics be a science? Part of the problem here is the **definition** of *science*. The original meaning of science, from the French, is simply "knowledge." Later, the natural sciences, which rely on measurement and calculation, took over the term. Now most people think of science as **precise** and factual, supported by experiments and **data**. Some political scientists (as we will consider later) have attempted to become like natural scientists; they **quantify data** and manipulate them statistically to validate **hypotheses**. The quantifiers make some good contributions, but usually they **focus** on small questions of detail rather than on large questions of meaning. This is because they generally have to stick to areas that can be quantified: public opinion, election returns, and congressional voting.

quantify To measure with numbers.
hypothesis An **initial theory** a researcher starts with, to be proved by **evidence**.

© Pearson Education, Inc.

Reading Comprehension Check

Vocabulary in Context

1. As used in the sentence "War and terrorism have revived interest in politics in the United States," the word *revived* means
   a. degenerated.
   (c.) restored.
   b. disqualified.
   d. terrorized.

Vocabulary in Context

2. "Will they set up government programs whose costs escalate far beyond what anyone had foreseen? Who then will have to pay these costs? You." (pp. 577–578)

   The word *escalate* could be replaced with
   (a.) increase.
   c. plummet.
   b. decrease.
   d. decelerate.

Vocabulary in Context

3. In the sentence "They do not 'like' the bacterium but are interested in how it grows, how it does its damage, and how it may be eradicated," a synonym for the word *eradicated* is
   a. fortified.
   c. strengthened.
   (b.) obliterated.
   d. emboldened.

Main Idea

4. The main idea of the chapter is that
   a. people should not concern themselves with political issues.
   b. only political leaders need to understand how politics works.
   c. politics is only for the politicians.
   (d.) it is in the interest of people to keep themselves abreast of politics.

Supporting Details

5. The examples of Bill Gates splitting up his giant Microsoft, a hurricane striking an area, and bacteriologists squinting through microscopes are offered on page 578 to support the idea that
   a. political science has little or no bearing on economics.
   (b.) almost everything is influenced by politics.
   c. studying political science does not teach us anything about the other sciences.
   d. political science is not related to the other social sciences.

Supporting Details

6. The main point that "History is one of the chief sources of data for political scientists," (p. 578) is supported by which of the following examples?
   a. Historians and political scientists analyze data differently.
   b. Historians and political scientists look for different things.
   (c.) When we discuss the Cold War (1947–1989), we are studying history.
   d. Political scientists look for generalizations.

Making Inferences

7. "Aristotle, the founder of the discipline, called politics 'the master science.' He meant that almost everything happens in a political context, that the decision

of the *polis* (the Greek city-state) governed most other things. Politics, in the words of Yale's Harold Lasswell, is the study of 'who gets what.' But, some object, the economic system determines who gets what in countries with free markets. True, but who determines if we shall have a free-market system? Who tells Bill Gates that he must split up his giant Microsoft, a decision worth billions of dollars?" (p. 578)

Which of the following conclusions can be drawn from the above statement?

a. There is no relation between politics and economics.
b. The economic systems determine politics.
c. Aristotle was the founder of economics.
d. Politics is intimately connected to economics.

Author's Purpose

8. The author's primary purpose in writing this chapter is to
   a. persuade the reader not to be concerned with political issues.
   b. inform the reader that only political scientists should be concerned with political science.
   c. convince the reader that politics matters.
   d. explain to the reader that politics is not intimately connected to economics.

Author's Tone

9. The overall tone of the chapter is
   a. humorous.   c. convincing.
   b. nostalgic.   d. excited.

Patterns of Organization

10. "Typically, historians study one episode in detail, digging up documents, archives, and news accounts on the topic. They have masses of data focused on one point but venture few or no generalizations. Political scientists, on the other hand, begin by looking for generalizations. We may take the findings of historians and compare and contrast them. A historian might do a detailed study of Weimar Germany (1919–1933); a political scientist might put that study alongside studies of France, Italy, and Russia of the same period to see what similarities and dissimilarities can be found. To be sure, some historians do comparative studies; they become de facto political scientists." (p. 579)

    The author's overall pattern of organization
    a. lists the changes in the discipline of political science.
    b. is to compare and contrast historians and political scientists.
    c. summarizes the changes in the discipline of history.
    d. shows the effects of economics on political science.

Fact and Opinion

11. Which of the following is a statement of fact?
    a. Because almost everything is political, studying politics means studying nearly everything.
    b. Although they ended centuries of monarchy in 1975, in 2002 the Laotian Communist Regime kneeled before a new bronze statue of the king who founded Laos's monarchy 650 years earlier.

© Pearson Education, Inc.

c. Arguably, the Council was the best government Iraq will ever have, but few valued it.

d. New governments, on the other hand, have shaky legitimacy; their citizens have little or no respect for them.

Fact and Opinion

12. Which of the following is a statement of opinion?
    a. Classic political theorists, such as Hobbes and Locke, held that humans form "civil society" because their powers of reason tell them that it is much better than anarchy.
    b. The Iranians threw the Shah out and celebrated the return of a medieval-style religious leader, who voiced the valued favored by traditional Iranians.
    c. Many thinkers believe economic and political development depend heavily on culture.
    d. One is the famous Milgram study, in which unwitting subjects were instructed by a professor to administer progressively larger electric shocks to a victim.

Argument

13. "Psychological studies also show that most people are naturally conformist. Most members of a group see things the group's way. Psychologist Irving Janis found many foreign policy mistakes were made in a climate of 'groupthink,' in which a leadership team tells itself that all is well and that the present policy is working. Groups tend to ignore doubters who tell them, for instance, that the Japanese will attack Pearl Harbor in 1941 or that the 1961 Bay of Pigs landing of Cuban exiles will fail. Obedience to authority and groupthink suggest that humans have deep-seated needs—possibly innate—to fit into groups and to go along with their norms. Perhaps this is what makes human society possible, but it also makes possible horrors such as the Nazi Holocaust and the more recent Iraqi massacres." (pp. 581–582)

    The author's claim that "most people are naturally conformist" is
    a. inadequately supported based upon opinion.
    b. adequately supported based upon facts.
    c. adequately supported based upon opinion.
    d. inadequately supported based upon facts.

Author's Bias

14. "One common mistake made about political power is viewing it as a finite, measurable quantity. Power is a connection among people, the ability of one person to get others to do his or her bidding. Political power does not come in jars or megawatts. Revolutionaries in some lands speak of 'seizing power,' as if power were kept in the national treasury and they could sneak in and grab it at night. The Afghan Taliban 'seized power' in 1995–1996, but they were a minority of the Afghan population. Many Afghans hated them, and some fought them. Revolutionaries think that they automatically get legitimacy and authority when they 'seize power'; they do not. Power is earned, not seized." (p. 585)

In this passage, the author
a. is biased in favor of seizing power.
b. is biased against earning power.
c. is biased against political power.
(d.) is biased in favor of earning power.

Making Inferences

15. "Is power identical to politics? Some power-mad people (including more than a few politicians) see the two as the same, but this is an oversimplification. We might see politics as a combination of goals or policies and the power necessary to achieve them. Power, in this view, is a prime ingredient of politics. It would be difficult to imagine a political system without political power. Even a religious figure who ruled on the basis of love would be exercising power over followers. It might be 'nice power,' but it would still be power. Power, then, is a sort of enabling device to carry out or implement policies and decisions. You can have praiseworthy goals, but unless you have the power to implement them, they remain wishful thoughts." (p. 585)

    In the passage above, the author implies that
    (a.) power is necessary to achieve political goals.
    b. power corrupts.
    c. power is an overrated factor.
    d. only a few politicians really have any power.

READING

Reading Selection **7**

Additional Reading

Novel (Satire)

10.14 Flesch-Kincaid Grade Level 7.0

Collaboration

Animal Farm

Pre-Reading Questions

Animal Farm is considered to be one of the greatest political novels of the twentieth century. In this scene at the beginning of the novel, Major, a 12-year-old pig and animal leader makes a speech in the barn to the other animals of an English farm. Before reading the excerpt, discuss the following questions with a group of your classmates.

1. When politicians speak passionately about their ideals, do you usually believe them? Why or why not?

2. What is the difference between patriotism and jingoism? In your view, what is a true patriot?

3. In your opinion, if a group of people is being exploited and generally treated unfairly by the government do you think they have the right to protest and plan a revolution? Explain.

© Pearson Education, Inc.

Animal Farm (An excerpt)

By George Orwell

1946

1   All the animals were now present except Moses, the tame raven, who slept on a perch behind the back door. When Major saw that they had all made themselves comfortable and were waiting attentively, he cleared his throat and began:

2   "Comrades, you have heard already about the strange dream that I had last night. But I will come to the dream later. I have something else to say first. I do not think, comrades, that I shall be with you for many months longer, and before I die, I feel it my duty to pass on to you such wisdom as I have acquired. I have had a long life, I have had much time for thought as I lay alone in my stall, and I think I may say that I understand the nature of life on this earth as well as any animal now living. It is about this that I wish to speak to you.

3   "Now, comrades, what is the nature of this life of ours? Let us face it: our lives are miserable, laborious, and short. We are born, we are given just so much food as will keep the breath in our bodies, and those of us who are **capable** of it are forced to work to the last atom of our strength; and the very instant that our usefulness has come to an end we are slaughtered with hideous cruelty. No animal in England knows the meaning of happiness or leisure after he is a year old. No animal in England is free. The life of an animal is misery and slavery: that is the plain truth.

4   "But is this simply part of the order of nature? Is it because this land of ours is so poor that it cannot afford a decent life to those who dwell upon it? No, comrades, a thousand times no! The soil of England is fertile, its climate is good, it is **capable** of affording food in abundance to an enormously greater number of animals than now inhabit it. This single farm of ours would support a dozen horses, twenty cows, hundreds of sheep—and all of them living in a comfort and a dignity that are now almost beyond our imagining. Why then do we continue in this miserable condition? Because nearly the whole of the produce of our labour is stolen from us by human beings. There, comrades, is the answer to all our problems. It is summed up in a single word—Man. Man is the only real enemy we have. Remove Man from the scene, and the root cause of hunger and overwork is abolished for ever.

5   "Man is the only creature that consumes without producing. He does not give milk, he does not lay eggs, he is too weak to pull the plough, he cannot run fast enough to catch rabbits. Yet he is lord of all the animals. He sets them to work, he gives back to them the bare **minimum** that will prevent them from starving, and the rest he keeps for himself. Our labour tills the soil, our dung fertilises it, and yet there is not one of us that owns more than his bare skin. You cows that I see before me, how many thousands of gallons of milk have you given during this last year? And what has happened to that milk which should have been breeding up sturdy calves? Every drop of it has gone down the throats of our enemies. And you hens, how many eggs have you laid in this last year, and how many of those eggs ever hatched into chickens? The rest have all gone to market to bring in money for Jones and his men. And you, Clover, where are those four foals you bore, who should have been the support and

pleasure of your old age? Each was sold at a year old—you will never see one of them again. In return for your four confinements and all your labour in the fields, what have you ever had except your bare rations and a stall?

6 "And even the miserable lives we lead are not allowed to reach their natural span. For myself I do not grumble, for I am one of the lucky ones. I am twelve years old and have had over four hundred children. Such is the natural life of a pig. But no animal escapes the cruel knife in the end. You young porkers who are sitting in front of me, every one of you will scream your lives out at the block within a year. To that horror we all must come—cows, pigs, hens, sheep, everyone. Even the horses and the dogs have no better fate. You, Boxer, the very day that those great muscles of yours lose their power, Jones will sell you to the **knacker** who will cut your throat and boil you down for the fox they grow old and toothless, Jones ties a brick round their necks and drowns them in the nearest pond.

knacker
a person who buys animal carcasses for slaughter.

7 "It is not crystal clear, then, comrades that all the evils of this life of ours spring from the tyranny of human beings: Only get rid of Man, and the produce of our **labor** would be our own. Almost overnight we could become rich and free. What then must we do? Why, work night and day, body and soul, for the overthrow of the human race! That is my message to you comrades. Rebellion! I do not know when that Rebellion will come. It might be in a week or in a hundred years, but I know, as sure as my feet, that sooner or later justice will be done. Fix your eyes on that, comrades, throughout the short remainder of your lives! And above all, pass on this message of mine to those who come after you, so that future generations shall carry on the struggle until it is victorious.

8 "And remember, comrades, your **resolution** should never **falter**. No argument must lead you astray. Never listen when they tell you that Man and the animals have a common interest, that the prosperity of the one is the prosperity of the others. It is all lies. Man serves the interests of no creature except himself. And among us animals let there be perfect unity, perfect comradeship in the struggle. All men are enemies. All animals are comrades."

falter
to hesitate or waver in action

9 At this moment there was a tremendous uproar. While Major was speaking four large rats had crept out of their holes and were sitting on their hindquarters, listening to him. The dogs had suddenly caught sight of them, and it was only by a swift dash for their holes that the rats saved their lives. **Major** raised his trotter for silence.

10 "Comrades" he said, "Here is a point that must be settled. The wild creatures, such as rats and rabbits—are they our friends or our enemies? Let us put it to the vote. I propose this question to the meeting: Are rats comrades?"

11 The vote was taken at once, and it was agreed by an overwhelming majority that rats were comrades. There were only four dissentients, the three dogs and the cat, who was afterwards discovered to have voted on both sides. Major continued:

12 "I have little more to say. I merely repeat, remember always your duty of enmity towards Man and all his ways. Whatever goes upon two legs is an enemy. Whatever goes upon four legs, or has wings, is a friend. And remember also that in fighting against Man, we must not come to resemble him. Even when you have conquered him, do not adopt his vices. No animal must ever

© Pearson Education, Inc.

live in a house, or sleep in a bed, or wear clothes, or drink alcohol, or smoke tobacco, or touch money, or engage in trade. All the habits of Man are evil. And, above all, no animal must ever tyrannize over his own kind. Weak or strong, clever or simple, we are all brothers. No animal must ever kill any other animal. All animals are equal."

Reading Comprehension Check

1. In the introduction to his speech, what does Major say he is going to speak about first?
  a. his dream.
  b. his old age.
  (c.) the nature of life.
  d. the barn story.

2. What does Major say about the life of an animal?
  a. It is mostly happy.
  (b.) It is miserable.
  c. It is life where enough good food is offered.
  d. both a and c.

3. When Major says, "no animal is free in England," we can infer that the author's intention was to
  a. send a critical message on the cruelty of zoos.
  b. slaughter the pigs.
  (c.) focus the reader's attention on the issue of human slavery.
  d. compare the lives of pigs, horses, and other animals.

4. What does Major mean when he says, "Man is the only animal that consumes without producing"?
  (a.) Man takes without making an effort.
  b. Man only knows how to work.
  c. Man is lazy and therefore has no power.
  d. Animals are to blame.

5. What is Major's ultimate purpose in making this speech?
  a. debate.
  (b.) rebellion.
  c. escape.
  d. compromise.

6. When Major asks, "Are rats comrades?", we can infer that Orwell, the writer, is asking which of these political questions?
  a. Does power bring some groups to exclude other groups?
  b. Are humans better than animals?
  c. Are all men created equal?
  (d.) both a and c.

7. To whom is Major referring when he says, "Even when you have conquered him, do not adopt his vices"?
  (a.) humans.
  b. pigs.
  c. power.
  d. animals.

8. Which "evil of man" is NOT mentioned in Major's speech?
  a. drinking alcohol.
  b. wearing clothes.
  (c.) listening to music.
  d. smoking tobacco.

9. In the last line of this excerpt, Major says, "All Animals are equal." Considering what we know about power relations between groups of people, what can we expect will happen to this animal ideal?
   a. It will prosper and a truly egalitarian society will result.
   b. The animals will learn how to accept each other.
   c. It will fall apart as some animals will want to dominate other animals.
   d. none of the above.

10. What is the tone of this excerpt?
    a. pessimistic.
    b. angry, yet inspired.
    c. objective.
    d. nostalgic.

Suggested Resources

Books

1. *Long Walk to Freedom: The Autobiography of Nelson Mandela* (Holt McDougal, 2000). In this autobiography, secretly written in prison on Robben Island over a period of 27 years, the South African President Nelson Mandela describes his struggle for freedom from the apartheid regime. He discusses how he persevered under trying circumstances with his indomitable spirit.

2. *Animal Farm* by George Orwell (1st World Library–Literary Society, 1946). A classic political allegory by George Orwell. Orwell uses animal characters in order to draw the reader away from the world of current events into a fantasy space where the reader can grasp ideas and principles more clearly. At the same time, Orwell personifies the animals so that they symbolize real historical figures. An eye-opening, humorous, somewhat dark view of what power does to people.

Movies

1. *The Candidate* (1972). Directed by Michael Ritchie. Californian lawyer Bill McKay (played by Robert Redford) fights for the little man. His charisma and integrity get him noticed and he is persuaded to run for the Senate against an incumbent he is expected to lose to. It's agreed he can handle the campaign his own way, on his own terms. But once he's in the race and his prospects begin to improve, the deal begins to change.

2. *The Contender* (2000). Directed by Rod Lurie. The vice president has died while in office. The president wants to leave a legacy of having put a woman in the office of vice president. Senator Laine Hanson gets his nomination, but information and disinformation about her past surfaces that threatens to throw off her confirmation.

Internet Sites

1. http://www.uscis.gov/portal/site/uscis

   This is the U.S. Citizenship and Immigration Services Web site where you can find information about visiting the United States either temporarily or

© Pearson Education, Inc.

permanently, passing the new naturalization exam, filling out immigration forms, and applying for Permanent Residence.

2. http://www.un.org/

The United Nations' official Web site. Learn about UN issues around the globe. Find statistical information about all the countries of the world. Read in detail about how this world governing body functions.

3. http://www.independent.co.uk/news/world/politics/

The Independent is a British publication, which is trusted for its breaking news on world politics. Here you can read stories of a host of political issues affecting the world.

Improving Reading Fluency

Overview

To improve reading fluency, it is important for you to know what fluent readers do. Fluent readers read rapidly for comprehension, recognize words rapidly and automatically, draw on a very large vocabulary, integrate text information with their own knowledge base, recognize the purpose for reading, comprehend the text as necessary, shift purpose to read strategically, constantly monitor their own comprehension of the text, recognize and repair misunderstanding, and read critically to evaluate information. They employ a wide range of strategies such as skimming and scanning (see Chapter 2 for details), annotations, highlighting the text, etc.

If your goal is to become a fluent reader, then you will need to build a large vocabulary that is readily accessible, have a range of reading strategies at your disposal for successful comprehension, become a strategic reader by framing questions as you read, and avail yourself of every opportunity to read so that you can develop fluency and automaticity. Diversify your reading experiences by exposing yourself to different genres of reading such as short stories, magazine articles, novels, poems, editorials, etc.

It is recommended that before you read the text, explore key vocabulary, answer any pre-reading questions, and reflect on previous texts in connection with the new text. While you read, you can make an outline or write a summary of the original text. You can also examine the author's attitude toward the topic, determine sources of difficulty so that you can ask your professor or peers for clarification, and make predictions as to what will happen next. After you finish reading, you can complete a graphic organizer—a diagram, a picture, or a graph that enables you to organize information in a way that is easy to see and remember—based on text information, answer comprehension questions, and connect the content to your personal experiences.

Keep in mind that fluent readers preview a text, make predications as to what will happen next in the text, summarize, learn new words from context and through the analysis of word formation, use context throughout to maintain understanding, recognize how the text is organized, formulate appropriate questions about the text, and repair miscomprehension.

Remember that reading fluency development involves rapid and automatic word recognition, the ability to recognize basic grammatical information, and the combination of word meanings and structural information.

Implications for Your Reading

© Pearson Education, Inc.

Developing fluency has several implications for your reading. By improving your reading fluency, you will be able to search for information, comprehend a text rather quickly, learn new information, and synthesize and evaluate information. Since you will be taking many courses in college and will have several reading assignments to complete, it is imperative that you develop reading fluency by employing effective reading strategies.

Most Frequent Words of the Academic Word List by Sublist

The Academic Word List (AWL) consists of high frequency English words that university students are supposed to have incorporated into their speech and writing. The AWL includes ten sublists that range from the most frequently occurring words in academic contexts (Sublist 1) to the comparatively less frequently occurring words (Sublist 10). Your primary goal is to master these words and build them into your active vocabulary.

Sublist 1 of the Academic Word List—Most Frequent Words in Families

This sublist contains the most frequent words of the Academic Word List in the Academic Corpus.

analysis
approach
area
assessment
assume
authority
available
benefit
concept
consistent
constitutional
context
contract
create
data
definition
derived
distribution
economic
environment
established
estimate
evidence
export
factors
financial
formula
function
identified
income
indicate
individual
interpretation
involved
issues
labor
legal
legislation
major
method
occur
percent
period
policy
principle
procedure
process
required
research
response
role
section
sector
significant
similar
source
specific
structure
theory
variables

Sublist 2 of Academic Word List—Most Frequent Words in Families

This sublist contains the second most frequent words in the Academic Word List from the Academic Corpus.

achieve
acquisition
administration
affect
appropriate
aspects
assistance
categories
chapter
commission
community
complex
computer
conclusion
conduct
consequences
construction
consumer
credit
cultural
design
distinction
elements
equation
evaluation
features
final
focus
impact
injury
institute
investment
items
journal
maintenance
normal
obtained
participation
perceived
positive
potential
previous
primary

Averil Coxhead, The Academic Word List. Reprinted by permission of Averil Coxhead. http://www.victoria.ac.nz/lals/resources/academicwordlist/information.aspx

purchase
range
region
regulations
relevant
resident
resources
restricted
security
sought
select
site
strategies
survey
text
traditional
transfer

Sublist 3 of Academic Word List—Most Frequent Words in Families

This sublist contains the third most frequent words of the Academic Word List in the Academic Corpus.

alternative
circumstances
comments
compensation
components
consent
considerable
constant
constraints
contribution
convention
coordination
core
corporate
corresponding
criteria
deduction
demonstrate
document
dominant
emphasis
ensure
excluded
framework
funds

illustrated
immigration
implies
initial
instance
interaction
justification
layer
link
location
maximum
minorities
negative
outcomes
partnership
philosophy
physical
proportion
published
reaction
registered
reliance
removed
scheme
sequence
sex
shift
specified
sufficient
task
technical
techniques
technology
validity
volume

Sublist 4 of Academic Word List—Most Frequent Words in Families

This sublist contains the fourth most frequent words of the Academic Word List in the Academic Corpus.

access
adequate
annual
apparent
approximated
attitudes
attributed
civil

code
commitment
communication
concentration
conference
contrast
cycle
debate
despite
dimensions
domestic
emerged
error
ethnic
goals
granted
hence
hypothesis
implementation
implications
imposed
integration
internal
investigation
job
label
mechanism
obvious
occupational
option
output
overall
parallel
parameters
phase
predicted
principal
prior
professional
project
promote
regime
resolution
retained
series
statistics
status
stress
subsequent
sum
summary
undertaken

© Pearson Education, Inc.

Sublist 5 of Academic Word List—Most Frequent Words in Families

academic
adjustment
alter
amendment
aware
capacity
challenge
clause
compounds
conflict
consultation
contact
decline
discretion
draft
enable
energy
enforcement
entities
equivalent
evolution
expansion
exposure
external
facilitate
fundamental
generated
generation
image
liberal
licence
logic
marginal
medical
mental
modified
monitoring
network
notion
objective
orientation
perspective
precise
prime
psychology
pursue
ratio
rejected

revenue
stability
styles
substitution
sustainable
symbolic
target
transition
trend
version
welfare
whereas

Sublist 6 of Academic Word List—Most Frequent Words in Families

abstract
accurate
acknowledged
aggregate
allocation
assigned
attached
author
bond
brief
capable
cited
cooperative
discrimination
display
diversity
domain
edition
enhanced
estate
exceed
expert
explicit
federal
fees
flexibility
furthermore
gender
ignored
incentive
incidence
incorporated
index
inhibition
initiatives

input
instructions
intelligence
interval
lecture
migration
minimum
ministry
motivation
neutral
nevertheless
overseas
preceding
presumption
rational
recovery
revealed
scope
subsidiary
tapes
trace
transformation
transport
underlying
utility

Sublist 7 of Academic Word List—Most Frequent Words in Families

adaptation
adults
advocate
aid
channel
chemical
classical
comprehensive
comprise
confirmed
contrary
converted
couple
decades
definite
deny
differentiation
disposal
dynamic
eliminate
empirical
equipment

extract
file
finite
foundation
global
grade
guarantee
hierarchical
identical
ideology
inferred
innovation
insert
intervention
isolated
media
mode
paradigm
phenomenon
priority
prohibited
publication
quotation
release
reverse
simulation
solely
somewhat
submitted
successive
survive
thesis
topic
transmission
ultimately
unique
visible
voluntary

Sublist 8 of Academic Word List—Most Frequent Words in Families

abandon
accompanied
accumulation
ambiguous
appendix
appreciation
arbitrary
automatically

bias
chart
clarity
conformity
commodity
complement
contemporary
contradiction
crucial
currency
denote
detected
deviation
displacement
dramatic
eventually
exhibit
exploitation
fluctuations
guidelines
highlighted
implicit
induced
inevitably
infrastructure
inspection
intensity
manipulation
minimised
nuclear
offset
paragraph
plus
practitioners
predominantly
prospect
radical
random
reinforced
restore
revision
schedule
tension
termination
theme
thereby
uniform
vehicle
via
virtually
widespread
visual

Sublist 9 of Academic Word List—Most Frequent Words in Families

accommodation
analogous
anticipated
assurance
attained
behalf
bulk
ceases
coherence
coincide
commenced
incompatible
concurrent
confined
controversy
conversely
device
devoted
diminished
distorted/distortion—*equal figures*
duration
erosion
ethical
format
founded
inherent
insights
integral
intermediate
manual
mature
mediation
medium
military
minimal
mutual
norms
overlap
passive
portion
preliminary
protocol
qualitative
refine
relaxed
restraints
revolution
rigid

© Pearson Education, Inc.

route
scenario
sphere
subordinate
supplementary
suspended
team
temporary
trigger
unified
violation
vision

Sublist 10 of the Academic Word List—Most Frequent Words in Families

This sublist contains the least frequent words of the Academic Word List in the Academic Corpus.

adjacent
albeit
assembly
collapse
colleagues
compiled
conceived
convinced
depression
encountered
enormous
forthcoming
inclination
integrity
intrinsic
invoked
levy
likewise
nonetheless

notwithstanding
odd
ongoing
panel
persistent
posed
reluctant
so-called
straightforward
undergo
whereby

Guide to Genre

Read to Succeed exposes its readers to a diversity of text genres. The word *genre* is borrowed from French, meaning type or sort. Each Reading Selection has an indication of its genre. It is critical before beginning to read a text that readers are aware of both the source and genre of the text they are about to read. Embarking on a given text without knowing its genre is like turning the ignition of a transportation vehicle with no knowledge of whether you are driving a plane, a boat, or a bus! The genre of a text offers a clear context for the reader, often determines the author's purpose for writing, and keys the reader in to such elements as the author's tone and bias and, perhaps more fundamentally, the kind of vocabulary that one could expect within a given genre. For example, if you are reading an *editorial* about the situation in the Middle East you can predict that the author's goal is to persuade the reader to share his or her opinion. Thus, the author of an editorial will try to use persuasive language to achieve a certain goal. However, if you are reading a *newspaper article* on the situation in the Middle East, the author's primary purpose will usually be to report information on the topic and to expose the reader to a number of different perspectives on the issues being reported on. That is not to say that newspaper articles are neutral and show no bias. This is clearly not the case. What is true is that editorials, by definition, are written with the primary purpose of expressing a viewpoint. This distinction between one genre (editorial) and another (newspaper article) is critical, and successful readers understand this. A list of all of the genres offered in *Read To Succeed* follow, with a short description of each genre type and some strategies on how best to approach these as readers.

Genres in *Read to Succeed* Reading Selections

Newspaper/magazine/online article—This genre reports on a topic or an event and is mostly informational. Readers first must understand the general theme, context, and topic area of a news article before trying to make sense of the details. Consider how the choice of subtopics and examples given key you into the author's bias.

Newspaper editorial—These are opinion columns written with the goal of persuading the reader. Readers should first try to understand the author's general position on the topic being discussed, and then try to analyze how the author goes about proving his or her argument(s).

Textbook reading—This type of genre involves discipline-specific academic content. Textbook chapters are usually assigned for given college courses. The content of a text chapter often reinforces material discussed in class, so the more active of a learner you are during your course lectures, the easier it will be to

© Pearson Education, Inc.

work with the textbook readings. Good highlighting skills are essential in pulling out key terms and concepts.

Memoir—A memoir is a type of autobiographical writing. It is important for readers to understand the general context when reading a memoir. Is this a famous person you are interested in learning about, or someone who has had a life experience that you would like to know more about? Pay close attention to the memoirist's life perspectives and to key turning points in the memoirist's life experience and the lessons that can be learned from them.

Interview—An interview consists of a question and answer session. Often famous people or experts in a particular field are interviewed in magazines and newspapers. In *Read to Succeed*, there are question/answer interviews with professionals who work in the academic majors covered in this text. As in reading a memoir, the key is to try to understand the interviewed person's perspective and some of the main points they are trying to make. If you have some background knowledge on this person, it will make it much easier to connect with what they have to say.

Poetry—This particular genre is literary work often in metrical form. The key is to pay close attention to symbolic meaning and to the author's choice of words. Remember that the meaning of a poem is open to subjective interpretation.

Newspaper/magazine letters to the editor—This type of reading contains letters from newspaper readers in response to an editorial. First, make sure you have a grasp of the topic that these readers are responding to. Consider individual perspectives and how readers' viewpoints vary.

Online forum—In this genre, Internet readers share their opinion on a topic. Again, as is the case with letters to the editor, some knowledge of the topic/policy/article that is being discussed goes a long way. Remember also that Internet audiences are global.

Scene from a play—This genre presents the reader with an excerpt from a theater script. Remember, you are reading direct speech in this genre. Pay attention to conversational style as it often keys readers in to the characters' emotional state and how they interrelate with other characters. Notice deviations from standard language (regional dialects/slang/ idiomatic expressions).

Online advice column—These are reading selections where experts offer their advice to Internet readers' questions. The advice columnist's language is usually coaxing and reassuring as it is their goal to guide readers through difficult situations. Focus mostly on the main points of advice offered.

Novel—These are works of fiction, extensive in length. In first entering a novel, consider the setting (time and location), and the voice of the narrator. Robert Scholes's words about reading novels are instructive:

> In considering the voices within our text, students will be encouraged to . . . ask who speaks it, where they come from, and what values that they share are embodied in their speech . . . who is speaking to us? What kind of voice is that? Does it present itself as reliable, trustworthy? How does it establish

its authority? How does that voice compare to the voices of characters as they are represented? Is the narrator a character? Is the narrator the author? Do characters speak always in one voice, or in more than one? How do different characters speak to one another? The length of a novel requires prolonged engagement. One needs time to read it, time to discuss it, and time to write responses to it.

Official government document—These are often replete with legalese (legal terms) and the tone is usually authoritative. You may have to read these line by line, very carefully as the texts are written in a formal, somewhat inaccessible manner.

Internet blog—This is a Web site designed by an individual with or without qualifications, with the goal of moderating an Internet chat forum. A good reader using critical thinking skills can distinguish between an incoherent piece of writing (often with basic grammar and spelling errors) and a well-written opinion. Just because a piece of writing appears online does not mean that a reader should accept it as an expert opinion. This does not mean that readers should devalue amateur writing. On the contrary, the beauty of most blogs is that it offers readers the opportunity to share perspectives with one another in an informal forum.

© Pearson Education, Inc.

Additional Adjectives of Tone

The skill focus for Chapter Five is 'Author's Purpose and Tone'. In that chapter, there is a list of adjectives of tone divided by categories (disapproving tone, humorous tones, supportive tones, etc . . . see Chapter Five).

As students find these vocabulary words particularly useful and a key to understanding what they are reading, an additional set of adjectives of tone are provided below:

Words that Describe Tone with Positive Connotations

admiring	affectionate	calming
excited	forgiving	respectful
grateful	loving	playful
warm	reverent	compassionate

Words that Describe Tone with Negative Connotations

ashamed	conceited	cruel
defensive	insulting	threatening
arrogant	indignant	superior
revengeful	scornful	self-pitying

Patterns of Organization and Transition Words

Patterns of Organization	Transition Words
1. To add or show sequence	again, also, and, and then, besides, equally important, finally, first, further, furthermore, in addition, in the first place, last, moreover, next, second, still, too
2. Comparison	also, in the same way, likewise, similarly, in comparison, as compared to
3. Contrast	although, and yet, but, but at the same time, despite (this/that), even so, even though, for all that, however, in contrast, in spite of, nevertheless, notwithstanding, instead, rather, conversely, in comparison, on the contrary, on the other hand, regardless, still, though, yet
4. Exemplification	after all, an illustration of, for example, for instance, indeed, in fact, it is true, of course, specifically, that is, to illustrate, truly, namely
5. Spatial Order	above, adjacent to, below, elsewhere, farther on, here, near, nearby, on the other side, opposite to, there, to the east, to the left
6. Chronological Order	after a while, afterward, as long as, as soon as, at last, at length, at that time, before, earlier, formerly, immediately, in the meantime, in the past, lately, later, meanwhile, now, presently, shortly, simultaneously, since, so far, soon, subsequently, then, thereafter, until, until now, when, currently
7. Summarize or Conclude	all in all, altogether, as has been said, in brief, in conclusion, in other words, in particular, in short, in simpler terms, in summary, on the whole, that is, therefore, to put it differently, to summarize
8. Cause and Effect	accordingly, as a result, because, consequently, for this purpose, hence, otherwise, since, then, therefore, thereupon, thus, to this end, with this object, so
9. Process	First, second, third, next, then, finally
10. Emphasis	Even, indeed, in fact, as a matter of fact, of course, truly

© Pearson Education, Inc.

Text Credits

Chapter 1

Boyd, Hannah, "The Lowdown on Single-Sex Education." Article reprinted with permission from Education.com, a website with thousands of articles for parents of preschool through grade 12 children, www.education.com

Caldaro, John-Michael, "Letter to the Editor Re: 'How to Educate Young Scientists (editorial July 3, 2006)'," *The New York Times*, July 9, 2006. Reprinted by permission of John-Michael Caldaro.

Desjardins, Gabriel, "Letter to the Editor Re: 'How to Educate Young Scientists (editorial July 3, 2006)'," *The New York Times*, July 9, 2006. Reprinted by permission of Gabriel Desjardins.

Dreifus, Claudia, "A Conversation with Eric Mazur: Using the 'Beauties of Physics' to Conquer Science Illiteracy." From *The New York Times*, July 17, 2007. © 2007 The New York Times. All rights reserved. Used by permission and protected by the Copyright Laws of the United States. The printing, copying, redistribution, or retransmission of the Material without express written permission is prohibited. www.nytimes.com

Editorial, "How to Educate Young Scientists." From *The New York Times*, July 3, 2006. © 2006 The New York Times. All rights reserved. Used by permission and protected by the Copyright Laws of the United States. The printing, copying, redistribution, or retransmission of the Material without express written permission is prohibited. www.nytimes.com

Fisk, Peg, "Letter to the Editor Re: 'How to Educate Young Scientists (editorial July 3, 2006)'," *The New York Times*, July 9, 2006. Reprinted by permission of Peg Fisk.

From Neha Singh and Khin Mai Aung, "A Free Ride for Bullies." From *The New York Times*, September 23, 2007. © 2007 The New York Times. All rights reserved. Used by permission and protected by the Copyright Laws of the United States. The printing, copying, redistribution, or retransmission of the Material without exermission is prohibited. www.nytimes.com

Gallup Poll, July 2002. Reprinted by permission of The Gallup Organization.

Gootman, Elissa, From "Undercount of Violence in Schools." From *The New York Times*, September 20, 2007. © 2007 The New York Times. All rights reserved. Used by permission and protected by the Copyright Laws of the United States. The printing, copying, redistribution, or retransmission of the Material without express written permission is prohibited. www.nytimes.com

Hill, Caitlin E., "Letter to the Editor Re: 'How to Educate Young Scientists (editorial July 3, 2006)'," *The New York Times*, July 9, 2006. Reprinted by permission of Caitlin E. Hill.

Johnson, James A. et al., From *Foundations of American Education*, 14th ed., pp. 4–15. Published by Allyn and Bacon/Merrill Education, Boston, MA. Copyright © 2008 by Pearson Education. Reprinted by permission of the publisher.

Johnson, James, et al. *Foundations of American Education*, 14th ed., pp. 38, 49, 120, 143, 164. Published by Allyn and Bacon/Merrill Education, Boston, MA. Copyright © 2008 by Pearson Education. Reprinted by permission of the publisher.

Langdon, Carol A. and Vesper, Nick, Adapted from "The Sixth Phi Delta Kappa Poll of Teachers' Attitudes toward the Public Schools," *Phi Delta Kappan*, *81*(8) (April 2000), pp. 607–611. Reprinted by permission of Phi Delta Kappan.

Lefort, Michelle, "Learning and Teaching a Two-Way Calle in Boston," *USA Today*, December 20, 2005. Reprinted with permission.

Medina, Jennifer, From "Recruitment by Military in Schools Is Criticized." From *The New York Times*, September 7, 2007. © 2007 The New York Times. All rights reserved. Used by permission and protected by the Copyright Laws of the United States. The printing, copying, redistribution, or retransmission of the Material without express written permission is prohibited. www.nytimes.com

Nelson, Virginia, "Letter to the Editor Re: 'How to Educate Young Scientists (editorial July 3, 2006)'," *The New York Times*, July 9, 2006. Reprinted by permission of Virginia Nelson.

Ottino, Julio M.,. "Letter to the Editor Re: 'How to Educate Young Scientists (editorial July 3, 2006)'," *The New York Times*, July 9, 2006. Reprinted by permission of Julio M. Ottino.

Reprinted with the permission of Scribner, a Division of Simon & Schuster, Inc., from *Teacher Man: A Memoir* by Frank McCourt. Copyright © 2005 by Green Peril Corp. All rights reserved.

"Should We Reward Good Grades with Money and Prizes?" *NEA Today*, May 2004, p. 39. Reprinted by permission of the National Education Association.

States, Rebecca A., "Letter to the Editor Re: 'How to Educate Young Scientists (editorial July 3, 2006)'," *The New York Times*, July 9, 2006. Reprinted by permission of Rebecca A. States.

Vacca, Richard T., Interview reprinted by permission of Richard T. Vacca.

Chapter 2

Associated Press, "Study: Ban on Fast-Food TV Ads May Cut Obesity," *USA Today*, November 20, 2008. Used with permission of The Associated Press. Copyright © 2008. All rights reserved.

Bazelon, Emily, "Fat Chance." From *The New York Times*, May 6, 2007. © 2007 The New York Times. All rights reserved. Used by permission and protected by the Copyright Laws of the United States. The printing, copying, redistribution, or retransmission of the Material without express written permission is prohibited. www.nytimes.com

Burros, Marian, From "Eating Well: Is Organic Food Provably Better?" From *The New York Times*, July 16, 2003. © 2003 The New York Times. All rights reserved. Used by permission and protected by the Copyright Laws of the United States. The printing, copying, redistribution, or retransmission of the Material without express written permission is prohibited. www.nytimes.com

Burros, Marian and Warner, Melanie, "Bottlers Agree to a School Ban on Sweet Drinks." From *The New York Times*, May 4, 2006. © 2006 The New York Times. All rights reserved. Used by permission and protected by the Copyright Laws of the United States. The printing, copying, redistribution, or retransmission of the Material without express written permission is prohibited. www.nytimes.com

Elliot, Stuart, From "Telling Dieters a Pill Works Only if They Work, Too." From *The New York Times*, May 9, 2007. © 2007 The New York Times. All rights reserved. Used by permission and protected by the Copyright Laws of the United States. The printing, copying, redistribution, or retransmission of the Material without express written permission is prohibited. www.nytimes.com

From "Fresh Produce, the Downside." From *The New York Times*, December 1, 2003. © 2003 The New York Times. All rights reserved. Used by permission and protected by the Copyright Laws of the United States. The printing, copying, redistribution, or retransmission of the Material without express written permission is prohibited. www.nytimes.com

Manore, Melinda and Thompson, Janice, Excerpts pp. 132, 216, 302, 372, 395, 548, and 582 from *Nutrition: An Applied Approach* by Janice Thompson and Melinda Manore. Copyright © 2006 by Pearson Education, Inc. Reprinted by permission.

Manore, Melinda, and Thompson, Janice, *Nutrition: An Applied Approach*, pp. 1–13. Copyright © 2009 by Pearson Education, Inc. Reprinted by permission.

O'Neil, John, From "Vital Signs: Mental Health; Mothers' Minds and Babies' Bellies." From *The New York Times*, April 8, 2003. © 2003 The New York Times. All rights reserved. Used by permission and protected by the Copyright Laws of the United States. The printing, copying, redistribution, or retransmission of the Material without express written permission is prohibited. www.nytimes.com

Panter, Jonathan. Letter to the Editor, "My Soda, My Choice," *The New York Times*, May 15, 2006. Reprinted by permission of Jonathan Panter.

Pressner, Amanda, "The 9 Most Common Kitchen Mistakes Even Healthy Women Make … and why they're robbing your food of nutrients," Shape.com. © Weider Publications, LLC, a subsidiary of American Media, Inc. Reprinted with permission.

Shute, Nancy, From "Over the Limit? Americans young and old crave high-octane fuel, and doctors are jittery," *U.S. News & World Report*, April 15, 2007. Copyright 2007 U.S. News & World Report, L.P. Reprinted with permission.

The Food Guide Pyramid. Washington, DC: U.S. Department of Agriculture, August 1992.

Thompson, Janice, Interview reprinted by permission of Janice Thompson.

Chapter 3

Audesirk, Gerald, Audesirk, Teresa, and Byers, Bruce E., Figs. 28–11 (p. 570), 28–15 (p. 573), 28–16 (p. 574), and 28–17 (p. 574). Excerpts, pp. 114, 130, 291, 358, 498, 570–577, 589–590, and 598 from *Biology: Life on Earth* 8th ed. by Teresa Audesirk, Gerald Audesirk and Bruce E. Byers. Copyright © 2008 by Pearson Education, Inc. Reprinted by permission. Users may not print out or reproduce copies of the material without permission of Pearson Education, Inc.

Audesirk, Teresa, Audesirk, Gerald and Byers, Bruce E., pp. 570–577 from *Biology: Life on Earth* 8th ed. Copyright © 2008 by Pearson Education, Inc. Reprinted by permission.

Burwell, Jill E., From "*New York Times* Readers Respond to 'The Evidence for Global Warming'," July 8, 2006. Reprinted by permission of Jill E. Burwell.

Butt, Maggie, "Meltwater." Copyright © 2008 by Maggie Butt. Reprinted by permission of Maggie Butt. From *Feeling the Pressure: Poetry and science of climate change*, ed. Paul Munden. Berne, Switzerland: British Council, 2008.

Christy, John R., "My Nobel Moment." Reprinted from The Wall Street Journal, November 1, 2007. © 2007 Dow Jones & Company. All rights reserved.

Deeds, Ralph, From "*New York Times* Readers Respond to 'The Evidence for Global Warming'," July 8, 2006. Reprinted by permission of Ralph Deeds.

Gordon, Eugene I., From "*New York Times* Readers Respond to 'The Evidence for Global Warming'," July 8, 2006. Reprinted by permission of Eugene I. Gordon.

Hoag, Hannah, "Global Warming Already Causing Extinctions, Scientists Say," *National Geographic News*, November 28, 2006. Reprinted by permission of National Geographic Society.

Howard, Brian, "The World's Water Crisis," E/The Environmental Magazine, September-October 2003. Reprinted by permission of Featurewell.com, Inc.

Hughes, Kathleen A., "To Fight Global Warming, Some Hang a Clothesline." From *The New York Times*, April 12, 2007. © 2007 The New York Times. All rights reserved. Used by permission and protected by the Copyright Laws of the United States. The printing, copying, redistribution, or retransmission of the Material without express written permission is prohibited. www.nytimes.com

Hurld, Kathy, and Zobrist, Marcus, Interview reprinted by permission of Marcus Zobrist and Kathy Hurld.

McGough, Roger, "Give and Take" by Roger McGough from *Good Enough to Eat* (© Roger McGough 2002) is reproduced by permission of PFD (www.pfd.co.uk) on behalf of Roger McGough.

Nelson, Bryn, "Going Green On Top," MSNBC, April 16, 2008. Copyright 2008 by MSNBC Interactive News, LLC. Reproduced with permission of MSNBC Interactive News, LLC in the format Textbook via Copyright Clearance Center.

Pape, Eric, From "The Costa del Norte." From *Newsweek*, April 16, 2007. © 2007 Newsweek, Inc. All rights reserved. Used by permission and protected by the Copyright Laws of the United States. The printing, copying, redistribution, or retransmission of the Material without express written permission is prohibited. www.newsweek.com

Shipman, Rebecca, From "*New York Times* Readers Respond to 'The Evidence for Global Warming'," July 8, 2006. Reprinted by permission of Rebecca Shipman.

Silver, Jacob, From "*New York Times* Readers Respond to 'The Evidence for Global Warming'," July 8, 2006. Reprinted by permission of Jacob Silver.

Theil, Stefan, From "Conservation: Coming Back from the Brink," *Newsweek*, –October 16, 2006. Reprinted by permission of the author.

Wheeler, Dennis, From "*New York Times* Readers Respond to 'The Evidence for Global Warming'," July 8, 2006. Reprinted by permission of Dennis Wheeler.

Chapter 4

"China: Online Marketing Comes of Age." Reprinted from the June 12, 2007 issue of *Business Week* by special permission, copyright © 2007 by The McGraw-Hill Companies, Inc.

Cox, Barbara G. and Koelzer, William, *Internet Marketing* (NetEffect Series), 1st ed., pp. 5, 6, 8, © 2004. Reproduced in print and electronic formats by permission of Pearson Education, Inc., Upper Saddle River, New Jersey.

Cox, Barbara G. and Koelzer, William, From *Internet Marketing* (NetEffect Series), 1st ed., pp. 10–15, © 2004. Reproduced in print and electronic formats by permission of Pearson Education, Inc., Upper Saddle River, New Jersey.

Glasner, Joanna, "Internet's Gender Gap Narrows." http://www.wired.com/techbiz/startups/news/2006/03/70441. Copyright © 2008 Condé Nast Publications. All rights reserved. Originally published in Wired.com. Reprinted by permission.

Graham, Jefferson, "Got a Search Engine Question? Ask Mr. Sullivan," *USA Today*, August 1, 2006. Reprinted with permission.

MarketingCharts. Reprinted by permission of MarketingCharts.

Mintz, Harold K., "How to Write Better Memos," *Chemical Engineering*, January 26, 1970, pp. 136–139. Copyright 1970 by Chemical Week Associates. Reproduced with permission of Chemical Week Associates in the format Textbook via Copyright Clearance Center.

Pfanner, Eric, "Web Sites Go Fishing in TV's Advertising Revenue Stream." From *The New York Times*, November 19, 2007. © 2007 The New York Times. All rights reserved. Used by permission and protected by the Copyright Laws of the United States. The printing, copying, redistribution, or retransmission of the Material without express written permission is prohibited. www.nytimes.com

Rosenbloom, Stephanie, "www.FriesWithThat?.com." From *The New York Times*, August 5, 2007. © 2007 The New York Times. All rights reserved. Used by permission and protected by the Copyright Laws of the United States. The printing, copying, redistribution, or retransmission of the Material without express written permission is prohibited. www.nytimes.com

Wagaman, Daniel, Interview reprinted by permission of Daniel Wagaman.

Chapter 5

Associated Press, "Wis. School Violence Leads to Cell Phone Ban," MSNBC.com, January 27, 2007. Used with permission of The Associated Press. Copyright © 2007. All rights reserved.

DeStefano, Joseph Dennis, Interview reprinted by permission of Joseph Dennis DeStefano.

Ewing, Jack, "Upwardly Mobile in Africa." Reprinted from the September 13, 2007 issue of *Business Week* by special permission, copyright © 2007 by The McGraw-Hill Companies, Inc.

Keeter, Scott, and Rainie, Lee, *Pew Internet Project Data Memo: Cell Phone Use.* Washington, DC: Pew Internet & American Life Project, April 2006, p. 6. Reprinted by permission of the Pew Internet & American Life Project. Ken Belson, "Four Score and ... Mind if I Take This?" From *The New York Times*, September 30, 2007. © 2007 The New York Times. All rights reserved. Used by permission and protected by the Copyright Laws of the United States. The printing, copying, redistribution, or retransmission of the Material without express written permission is prohibited. www.nytimes.com

Loubaton, Emily, "Letter to the Editor Re: 'Child Wants Cellphone; Reception Is Mixed'," *The New York Times*, April 2, 2007. Reprinted by permission of Emily Loubaton.

Rosengrant, Martha A., From *Introduction to Telecommunications*, 2nd Edition, © 2005, pp. 651–652, 657–658, 663–665. Reprinted by permission of Pearson Education, Inc., Upper Saddle River, NJ.

"Should We Ban Cell Phones in School?" *NEA Today*, February 2004. Reprinted by permission of the National Education Association.

Slatalla, Michelle, "An iPhone Changed My Life (Briefly)." From *The New York Times*, July 5, 2007. © 2007 The New York Times. All rights reserved. Used by permission and protected by the Copyright Laws of the United States. The printing, copying, redistribution, or retransmission of the Material without express written permission is prohibited. www.nytimes.com

Westrich, Ellen, "Letter to the Editor Re: 'Child Wants Cellphone; Reception Is Mixed'," *The New York Times*, April 2, 2007. Reprinted by permission of Ellen Westrich.

Chapter 6

Adapted from *A Report: The 2007 National Justice Survey: Tackling Crime and Public Confidence*, Department of Justice Canada, 2007. Reproduced with the permission of the Minister of Public Works and Government Services Canada, 2009.

Arrillaga, Pauline, "Schizophrenic Teen Looks for Justice After Murder," April 16, 2006. Used with permission of The Associated Press. Copyright © 2006. All rights reserved.

Cordill, Joe, From "Parents Share Blame for Crime Stats," Letter to the Editor, July 2006. http://blogs.usatoday.com/oped/2006/07/parents_share_b.html. Reprinted by permission of Joe Cordill.

Federal Bureau of Investigation, *Crime in the United States, 2006*. Washington, DC: U.S. Department of Justice, 2007.

Kobilinsky, Lawrence, Interview reprinted by permission of Lawrence Kobilinsky.

Roberts, Janet, and Stanton, Elizabeth, "Free and Uneasy: A Long Road Back After Exoneration, and Justice Is Slow to Make Amends." From *The New York Times*, November 25, 2007. © 2007 The New York Times. All rights reserved. Used by permission and protected by the Copyright Laws of the United States. The printing, copying, redistribution, or retransmission of the Material without express written permission is prohibited. www.nytimes.com

Rose, Reginald, From *Twelve Angry Men* by Reginald Rose, copyright © 1955, 1997 by Reginald Rose. Used by permission of Penguin, a division of Penguin Group (USA) Inc.

Schmalleger, Frank, From *Criminal Justice Today*, 10th ed., pp. 18–22, © 2009. Reproduced in print and electronic formats by permission of Pearson Education, Inc., Upper Saddle River, New Jersey.

© Pearson Education, Inc.

Schmalleger, Frank, From *Criminal Justice Today*, 10th ed., pp. 548–549, 562–563, © 2009. Reproduced in print and electronic formats by permission of Pearson Education, Inc., Upper Saddle River, New Jersey.

Welch, William M., "Some Say Cop Videos Misleading," *USA Today*, November 30, 2006. Reprinted with permission.

Chapter 7

Baida, Peter, From *A Nurse's Story* by Peter Baida. Reprinted by permission of International Creative Management, Inc. Copyright © 2001 by Peter Baida for *The Gettysburg Review*.

Freeman, Julia J., "Junior Nursing Students Share Patient Stories," *Nursing Spectrum*, May 5, 2008, Vol. 20, No. 9, New York/New Jersey edition. Copyright 2008. Nursing Spectrum. All rights reserved. Used with permission.

Niedringhaus Dee, and Pavy, Ramont Roberta, From *Fundamental Nursing Care*, 2nd ed., pp. 3–13, © 2008. Reproduced in print and electronic formats by permission of Pearson Education, Inc., Upper Saddle River, New Jersey.

Niedringhaus Dee, and Pavy, Ramont Roberta, Excerpts from *Fundamental Nursing Care*, 2nd ed., © 2008. Reproduced in print and electronic formats by permission of Pearson Education, Inc., Upper Saddle River, New Jersey.

Press Release, *Student Enrollment Rises in U.S. Nursing Colleges and Universities for the 6th Consecutive Year*. Washington, DC: American Association of Colleges of Nursing, December 5, 2006. Reprinted with permission of the American Association of Colleges of Nursing.

Tahmincioglu, Eve, "Men Are Much in the Sights of Recruiters in Nursing." From *The New York Times*, April 13, 2003. © 2003 The New York Times. All rights reserved. Used by permission and protected by the Copyright Laws of the United States. The printing, copying, redistribution, or retransmission of the Material without express written permission is prohibited. www.nytimes.com

Tovar, Gloria, Interview reprinted by permission of Gloria Tovar.

Vaughan, Don, "Learning to Work Together," *Nursing Spectrum*, May 19, 2008, Vol. 17, No. 10, Philadelphia Tri-State edition. Copyright 2008. Nursing Spectrum. All rights reserved. Used with permission.

Chapter 8

Bang, Charlene, Interview reprinted by permission of Charlene Bang.

Branch, John, "The Barbers, Identical Twins, Are Not as Alike as They Look." From *The New York Times*, October 25, 2006. © 2006 The New York Times. All rights reserved. Used by permission and protected by the Copyright Laws of the United States. The printing, copying, redistribution, or retransmission of the Material without express written permission is prohibited. www.nytimes.com

From Danielle, a blogger on pbskids.org. © It's My Life, http://pbskids.org/itsmylife

Gardner, Howard, Excerpts from an interview from the Pamela Wallin Show, June 1, 1999. Reprinted by permission of Howard Gardner.

Gardner, Mandela, From an online blog, http://seattlepi.nwsource.com/health/252423_condor19.html. Reprinted by permission of Mandela Gardner.

Gerrig, Richard J., and Zimbardo, Philip G., *Psychology and Life*, Discovering Psychology Edition, 18th ed., Figure 4.5 (p. 98). © 2008, 2005, 2002 Pearson Education, Inc. Reproduced by permission of Pearson Education, Inc.

Gerrig, Richard J., and Zimbardo, Philip G., *Psychology and Life*, Discovering Psychology Edition, 18th ed., pp. 4–8. © 2008, 2005, 2002 Pearson Education, Inc. Reproduced by permission of Pearson Education, Inc.

Gerrig, Richard J., and Zimbardo, Philip G., *Psychology and Life*, Discovering Psychology Edition, 18th ed., p. 249. © 2008, 2005, 2002 Pearson Education, Inc. Reproduced by permission of Pearson Education, Inc.

Gerrig, Richard J., and Zimbardo, Philip G., *Psychology and Life*, Discovering Psychology Edition, 18th ed., pp. 320, 355, 388. © 2008, 2005, 2002 Pearson Education, Inc. Reproduced by permission of Pearson Education, Inc.

KidsHealth. From http://kidshealth.org/parent/emotions/behavior/bullies.html. This information was provided by KidsHealth, one of the largest resources online for medically reviewed health information written by parents, kids, and teens. For more articles like this one, visit KidsHealth.org or TeensHealth.org. © 1995 – 2009 The Nemours Foundation. All rights reserved.

Mintle, Linda S., "No Debate: TV Violence Harms Kids," www.drlindahelps.com. Reprinted by permission of Linda S. Mintle. Dr Linda Helps © 2009.

Oleck, Joan, "TV Violence Doesn't Lead to Aggressive Kids, Study Says," *School Library Journal*, May 23, 2007. Copyright © 2007 Reed Business Information, a division of Reed Elsevier Inc.

Prindle Fierro, Pamela. "Why Are Identical Twins Different? Studies Explain the Differences in Individuals with Supposedly Matching Genes." © 2009 by Pamela Prindle Fierro (http://multiples.about.com/od/funfacts/a/differenttwins.htm). Used with permission of About, Inc. which can be found online at www.about.com. All rights reserved.

Reprinted with permission from *Go Ask Alice!*, Columbia University's Health Q & A Internet Resource, at www.goaskalice.columbia.edu. Copyright © 2008 by The Trustees of Columbia University.

Chapter 9

Ebert, Ronald J., and Griffin, Ricky W., From *Business*, 8th ed., pp. 3–8, © 2006. Reproduced in print and electronic formats by permission of Pearson Education, Inc., Upper Saddle River, New Jersey.

Ebert, Ronald J., and Griffin, Ricky W., From *Business*, 8th ed., pp. 4, 10, 11, 31, 35, © 2006. Reproduced in print and electronic formats by permission of Pearson Education, Inc., Upper Saddle River, New Jersey.

Ebert, Ronald J., and Griffin, Ricky W., From *Business*, 8th ed., Figure 4.1 (p. 91), © 2006. Reproduced in print and electronic formats by permission of Pearson Education, Inc., Upper Saddle River, New Jersey.

Fisher, Anne, "How to Find the Right Career Coach," *Fortune*, August 5, 2008 posted, CNNMoney.com (*Fortune*). © 2008 Time Inc. All rights reserved.

Gross, Daniel, "Send Us Your Tired, Your Poor, Your Business Executives: Why Are Big American Companies Hiring Foreign-Born CEOs?" *Slate Magazine*, www.Slate.com, August 17, 2007. Copyright 2007 Washingtonpost.Newsweek Interactive, LLC and Slate.

Miller, Arthur. From *Death of a Salesman* by Arthur Miller, copyright 1949, renewed © 1977 by Arthur Miller. Used by permission of Viking Penguin, a division of Penguin Group (USA) Inc.

Poatsy, Mary Anne. Interview reprinted by permission of Mary Anne Poatsy.

Zipp, Michele, "How She Does It – Anya Ponorovskaya," www.workingmother.com. Reprinted by permission of Working Mother Media.

Zouhali-Worrall, Malika, "Found in Translation: Avoiding Multilingual Gaffes," July 14, 2008, CNNMoney.com (*Fortune Small Business*). © 2008 Time Inc. All rights reserved.

Chapter 10

Coxhead, Averil, The Academic Word List. Reprinted by permission of Averil Coxhead. http://www.victoria.ac.nz/lals/staff/Averil-Coxhead/awl/

Los Angeles Times national exit poll results, 2004 U.S. Presidential Election. Copyright © 2004 by The Los Angeles Times. Reprinted with permission. All rights reserved.

Noah, Timothy, "Should the Voting Age Be Lowered?" *Slate Magazine*, www.Slate.com, November 7, 2007. Copyright 2007 Washingtonpost.Newsweek Interactive, LLC and Slate.

Orwell, George, Excerpt from *Animal Farm* by George Orwell, copyright 1946 by Harcourt, Inc. and renewed 1974 by Sonia Orwell, reprinted by permission of the publisher, and Copyright © George Orwell, 1945 by permission of Bill Hamilton as the Literary Executor of the Estate of the Late Sonia Brownell Orwell and Secker & Warburg Ltd.

Pu-Folkes, Bryan, Interview reprinted by permission of Bryan Pu-Folkes.

Ray, Erika, "Leaders, Scholars Analyze Youth Apathy," *The Independent Collegian*, April 1, 2004. Reprinted by permission of The Independent Collegian.

Roskin, Michael G., From *Political Science: An Introduction*, pp. 1–5, 8–12. Copyright © 2008 by Pearson Education, Inc. Reprinted by permission.

Swarns, Rachel L., "Immigrants Raise Call For Right to Be Voters." From *The New York Times*, August 9, 2004. © 2004 The New York Times. All rights reserved. Used by permission and protected by the Copyright Laws of the United States. The printing, copying, redistribution, or retransmission of the Material without express written permission is prohibited. www.nytimes.com

Wudunn, Sheryl, "A Portrait of a Young Man as a Beijing Student Leader." From *The New York Times*, June 3, 1989. © 1989 The New York Times. All rights reserved. Used by permission and protected by the Copyright Laws of the United States. The printing, copying, redistribution, or retransmission of the Material without express written permission is prohibited. www.nytimes.com

© Pearson Education, Inc.

© Pearson Education, Inc.